Handbook on Animal-Assisted Therapy

Second Edition

Handbook on Animal-Assisted Therapy

THEORETICAL FOUNDATIONS AND GUIDELINES FOR PRACTICE

Second Edition

Edited by

Aubrey H. Fine

California State Polytechnic University
Professor–Graduate Pedagogical Studies
College of Education and Integrative Studies

Amsterdam • Boston • Heidelberg • London
New York • Oxford • Paris • San Diego
San Francisco • Singapore • Sydney • Tokyo

Academic Press is an imprint of Elsevier

Academic Press is an imprint of Elsevier
525 B Street, Suite 1900, San Diego, California 92101-4495, USA
84 Theobald's Road, London WC1X 8RR, UK

This book is printed on acid-free paper. 

Library of Congress Cataloging-in-Publication Data

Handbook on animal-assisted therapy : theoretical foundations and guidelines for practice / edited by Aubrey H. Fine–2nd ed.
p. cm.
Includes index.
ISBN-13: 978-0-12-369484-3 ISBN-10: 0-12-369484-1 (hard cover : alk. paper)
1. Animals–Therapeutic use–Handbooks, manuals, etc. 2. Pets–Therapeutic use–Handbooks, manuals, etc. 3. Human-animal relationships–Handbooks, manuals, etc. I. Fine, Aubrey H.

RM931.A65H36 2006
615.8'515–dc22 *2006007816*

For information on all Academic Press publications visit our Web site at www.books.elsevier.com

ISBN-13: 978-0-12-369484-3
ISBN-10: 0-12-369484-1

PRINTED IN THE UNITED STATES OF AMERICA
08 09 9 8 7 6 5 4 3 2

ABOUT THE EDITOR

Dr. Fine has been a faculty member at California State Polytechnic University for 24 years. Recipient of many awards, he earned the California State University system's Wang Award in 2001 for exceptional commitment, dedication, and exemplary contributions within the areas of education and applied sciences, and Educator of the Year in 1990, by the Learning Disability Association of California. Animals have been an integral part of Dr. Fine's clinical practice for over three decades. His clinical practice primarily focuses on the treatment of children with attention, behavioral, adjustment, and developmental disorders. His practice includes four therapy dogs and birds. In addition to his expertise in the area of AAT, Dr. Fine has published several academic books, numerous articles, and video documentaries on parent/child relationships, therapeutic recreation, sports psychology, and learning and attention disorders.

To all my therapy animals over the past three decades (Sasha, Puppy, P.J., Hart, Shrimp, Magic, Snowflake, Starlight, Tikvah, Coshe, Spikey, Tilly, Boomer, and Houdini) who have been inspirational in extending my abilities to work with and support others.

This book is especially dedicated to my dear Shrimp. You have been a dedicated and loving companion for so many years. You are fondly treasured by all for your gentleness and warmth.

Finally, to my wife, Nya, and sons Sean and Corey, our love and work with animals have strengthened our relationship and our family. I am blessed to have you all in my life. You are all the spark in my heart.

CONTENTS

SECTION II
Animal-Assisted Therapy: Conceptual Model and Guidelines for Quality Assurance

SECTION III
Best Practices in Animal-Assisted Therapy: Guidelines for Use of Animal-Assisted Therapy with Special Populations

FOREWORD

The mid-twentieth century proved to be an unsettled time for human relationships with animals. Perhaps most significantly, agriculture was transformed from a symbiotic, ancient contract with animals, wherein both humans and animals benefited from the relationship, into an exploitative, industrialized pursuit of efficiency, profit, and productivity. The traditional notion of husbandry-based animal care—elevated in the 23rd Psalm into a powerful metaphor for God's ideal relationship to humans—was debased by the "application of industrial methods to the production of animals," as one textbook of animal science puts it. Equally significant, in barely 100 years, the number of people engaged in an agricultural way of life went from half the population to well under 2%. The close connection between shepherd and flock, herdsman and cattle, was lost in the rush to modernize. At roughly the same historical moment, the use of animals in biomedical research and toxicology proliferated, thereby further eroding the close and mythic connection more "primitive" societies enjoyed with animals, and again degrading animals to disposable utilitarian objects, with no telos or awareness.

In the face of these cataclysms, one could reasonably fear for the loss of the mystical significance of animals for the human psyche, the numinous view so beautifully expressed in the ancient cave paintings of Lascaux or in American Indian fetishes, beadings, and rituals. The dominance of urban life, far removed from nature and animals, and the ascendance of a mechanistic Weltanschauung and its handmaiden technology seemed to threaten our intimate connection to animals and its archetypal place in our consciousness.

Fortunately, archetypes are not abandoned so easily. The place for animals in human consciousness was not lost, but merely transformed. The integral role of animals in everyday life was, to be sure, transmuted by the process of modernism, but was by no means eliminated; instead it assumed new forms more suited to urban life in a highly industrialized society.

In the first place, the new and patently exploitative uses of animals we have delineated did not remain unchallenged for long. Natural reverence for animals, once integral and essential to the categoreal apparatus through which we understand the world, evolved into moral concern for animals, and their treatment has emerged as a major social–ethical movement demanding checks against the relentless commodification of animals. The robust rise of animal and environmental ethical thinking clearly attests to human unwillingness to relinquish our connection to animals and nature.

Second, the alienation and loneliness engendered by urbanization, erosion of the nuclear and extended family, proliferation of divorce, the phenomenon of latch-key children, our greatly extended life span, and the general tendencies of cities to create Gesellschaft rather than Gemeinschaft, coupled with the ubiquitous human need to love and be loved and be needed, ushered in a new function for companion animals as filling that void. The vast majority of pet owners today claim that their animals are "members of the family."

It was thus not surprising that animals would emerge as powerful allies in the therapeutic and psychotherapeutic enterprise. As nonjudgmental, inexhaustible, fountains of love and loyalty, animals were natural vehicles for penetrating the shell surrounding the disturbed, the isolated, and the mentally or physically disabled, just as they alleviate urban loneliness and facilitate human interactions (cf. the culture of "dog people" in large cities). What has now become a systematic field of study was intuitively obvious to many of us, as when I "treated" my brother's acute loneliness at being away from home for the first time by providing him with a kitten or put a child unable to walk due to cerebral palsy on my horse's back, while he "walked on eggs" and she radiated a smile I will never forget. Anyone who has known a blind person with a service dog can confirm that degree to which a service animal provides wings to such a person. But we are incalculably better off having the knowledge base recounted in this excellent book.

This volume is a treasure trove for anyone interested in human–animal relationships and a necessity for those professionally involved with clinical psychology, animal-assisted therapy, service animals, animal ethics, or what today is called "the human–animal bond." Herein, one can find erudite discussions on the cultural significance of animals, various forms of animal-assisted therapy, the psychology of animal cruelty, and even a discussion of the welfare of therapy animals, a much needed area unfortunately passed over in the earlier years of the field. I know of no better collection in this area, and it provides an excellent foundation for future scholars and practitioners in this inevitably burgeoning area, as well as an excellent ingression into what, paraphrasing Jon Katz, we may call "the new work of companion animals."

Dr. Bernard E. Rollin
University Distinguished Professor
Department of Philosophy
Colorado State University

PREFACE

It has been over 6 years since our first edition of this handbook was published. Since that time, animal-assisted interventions (AAI—a broad term that includes what we have traditionally called either "animal-assisted therapy" or "animal-assisted activities," as well as other terms) have continued to generate tremendous interest in the general sector, perhaps because of people's curiosity about the human–animal bond. Additionally, even within this short period of time, there have been some changes in the area that could benefit from clarification and documentation. We believe that this volume will be an important contribution to the literature on animal-assisted interventions in promoting a clearer understanding of the scope of practice. The contributors to the book continue to take a critical analysis of what are best practices in AAI and provide the readers with a glimpse to what is needed in the future to develop more evidence-based practices.

Animals have been an integral part of my clinical practice for over three decades. My initial experiences were discovered serendipitously, but ever since my work with a tiny gerbil and children with learning disabilities, I have become fascinated with the genuine power of the human–animal bond. When I first accepted the editorship of this handbook, I was excited about the opportunity because of my genuine enthusiasm about AAI; I was also compelled to put together a book that helped clarify some of the misconceptions about the topic. Furthermore, I wanted to develop a book that not only imparted a strong theoretical overview but also provided clinicians, as well as those interested in AAI, with a clearer understanding of the value of the human–animal bond as well as potential methods for application.

There have been many changes in this new addition, including several new chapters on topics such as animals as social supports and the clinical role of animals in therapeutic interventions with children, adolescents, and their caregivers, as well as the importance of involving veterinarians with a family practice perspective in supporting AAI.

The chapters in this book are divided into four major sections. The strength of each section relates to how the chapters are closely interrelated. It will become apparent to the reader that the therapeutic use of animals is an emerging approach that is built on a long history of our association with and curiosity about other living beings. Qualitatively, AAI demonstrate a significant contribution to the overall quality of life. Nevertheless, there is a strong need for more evidence-based research that quantifies the value of these approaches.

It is important to point out that the scientific and clinical community investigating these interventions is built on interdisciplinary professions that bridge the worlds of mental and physical health professionals, with their counterparts in ethology, animal behavior, and animal welfare. As noted previously, one of the major weaknesses of animal AAI is the limited scientific evidence demonstrating its efficacy. It is also hoped that the contents of this book will act as an impetus for further empirical investigations into the therapeutic use of animals in clinical practices.

Section I consists of six chapters that focus on the conceptualization of the human–animal bond and incorporate chapters addressing numerous topics. The book begins with a chapter by Serpell that provides a historical exploration of the value of human–animal relationships. The chapter is followed by one written by Kruger and Serpell, which provides an excellent overview of the various definitions of AAI and the various theoretical models that have been used to explain how AAI may work. The reader will find this introductory chapter extremely helpful in conceptualizing the broad scope of AAI. The chapter is followed by one prepared by Katcher and Beck who provide an overview of where AAI has come from and the difficult road it continues to battle to justify its efficacy.

The section culminates with three other chapters. The chapters address the comprehensive review of the research explaining the psychosocial benefits of animals, as well as an explanation of the value of animals as social supports. The final chapter provides a comprehensive explanation of the physiological benefits found as a consequence of the human–animal bond.

Section II focuses on the conceptual models of AAI and contains two descriptive chapters providing an overview of designing and implementing AAI services. This information is invaluable in understanding how to develop institutionally based treatment programs. In the chapter by Fredrickson-MacNamara and Butler, the readers will become more acquainted with models and standards to consider in selecting certain species of animals with various populations. The chapter also focuses on the factors that affect the performance of various animal species. For those readers interested in designing and implementing AAI programs in health and mental health organizations, Mallon and colleagues have updated their previous chapter to provide the reader with a series of concerns that must be addressed for effective program intervention. The writers incorporate within their discussion various organizational, staff, and client issues that must be considered.

Section III documents the therapeutic efficacy of the human–animal relationship with specific populations. Chapters discuss using animals with specific populations, including children, persons with chronic disorders and AIDS, and the elderly, as well as the application of AAI in specialized settings. A couple of other chapters have also been incorporated that clarify how animals can be naturally included in psychotherapy and techniques on how to incorporate animals in working with and understanding families. Readers will also find a chapter by Ascione and colleagues on animal abuse, as well as research on the relationship between animal abuse and interpersonal violence.

Section IV, the final section of the book, consists of six chapters that are more general in nature. A chapter by Anderson highlights a few instruments that can be utilized to assess the efficacy of AAI. The readers will find these instruments useful in assessing the impact of their work. Wood developed a chapter that provides readers with some insight on how to search the AAT literature. The readers should find this chapter useful in staying more updated with current trends. A passionate chapter in this section has also been written by Arkow describing some new strategies and alternatives for humane education.

The last three chapters within this section address several current and important subjects. Serpell, Coppinger, and Fine address the importance of safeguarding the animal's welfare and discuss the ethical concerns that must be taken into consideration while engaging in AAI. The chapter promotes a better understanding by clinicians while working alongside therapy animals. Timmins and Fine prepared a chapter discussing the importance of developing healthy relationships with family practice veterinarians and what their contribution to AAI can be. In the final chapter, Turner, Wilson, and finally Fine and Mio, present various points of views on the future direction of AAI. Each of the sections provides a glimpse to future directions in the field. Within the Turner, Wilson, and Fine and Mio sections, arguments are made for the need for more scientific scrutiny of AAI. All sections offer some suggestions of what needs to occur.

It is hoped that this book will become an impetus for further study and investigation. No one can forecast with accuracy the future, but I believe that after more applicable research is documented, the findings will help AAI become more commonly practiced and respected.

ACKNOWLEDGMENTS

This book could have not been written without the support of all the contributing authors. Their insight into the field of animal-assisted therapy and the human–animal bond has made this a meaningful project to steward and edit. I would like to thank Nikki Levy and Barbara Makinster from Elsevier who were very supportive throughout this project. A special thank-you is also given to Melinda Ritchie at Elsevier for her leadership, guidance, and editorial support.

I would also like to thank Rudy Gomez, Cynthia Eisen, and Dr. Ron Kotkin who took their time to review several chapters in the book and provide some input. Their comments and feedback were very important to the formation of the final text.

Finally, I want to thank my wife Nya who has been very supportive during this entire process. Her encouragement and shared love of animals also has made this project more meaningful.

Aubrey H. Fine
December 2005

SECTION I

Conceptualization of the Animal–Human Bond

FOUNDATION FOR UNDERSTANDING ANIMAL-ASSISTED THERAPY

CHAPTER 1

Animal-Assisted Interventions in Historical Perspective

JAMES A. SERPELL

Center for the Interaction of Animals and Society, Department of Clinical Studies, School of Veterinary Medicine, University of Pennsylvania, Philadelphia, Pennsylvania 19104

I. INTRODUCTION

Although every topic has its own unique history that can be explored, analyzed, and interpreted, the limits of historical inquiry are inevitably bound by the quantity and quality of surviving documents and artifacts. Unfortunately, surviving historical accounts of humans' relationships with animals are both unusual and sketchy, and the little documentary evidence that exists tends to refer to the lives of the rich and famous. Our knowledge of how ordinary people in the past related to animals, or made use of their companionship, remains indistinct and largely speculative. Even where the historical evidence is relatively complete, there is a danger of overinterpreting it—of attributing values, attitudes, and sentiments that make sense to us from a modern perspective, but which would not necessarily have possessed any meaning for our historical predecessors. All of this demands that we treat historical evidence with an appropriate degree of caution.

With this proviso in mind, this chapter attempts to provide a brief historical account of the various ways in which animals in general, and companion animals in particular, have been perceived as contributing to human mental

Handbook on Animal-Assisted Therapy: Theoretical Foundations and Guidelines for Practice, 2e

and physical health. While attempting to set this work in historical context, the chapter will not attempt a detailed review of recent studies of animal–human therapeutic interactions, as this material has already been adequately covered elsewhere (see Serpell, 1996; Wilson and Turner, 1998; Kruger *et al.*, 2005).

II. ANIMAL SOULS AND SPIRITUAL HEALING

In the history of human ideas concerning the origins and treatment of illness and disease, nonhuman animals play a variety of important roles. The precise characteristics of these roles depend, however, not only on the prevailing view of animals but also on the particular supernatural or "scientific" belief systems in which they are imbedded.

Probably the most archaic of these belief systems, usually referred to as "animism," involves the concept that all living creatures, as well as other natural objects and phenomena, are imbued with an invisible soul, spirit, or "essence" that animates the conscious body, but that is able to move about and act independently of the body when the bearer is either dreaming or otherwise unconscious. According to the typical animist worldview, all manifestations of sickness or misfortune are the direct result of assaults against a person's soul or "essence" by other angry or malevolent spirits encountered during these periods of unconsciousness. In some cases, these spiritual assaults are thought to be retaliatory, the result of some deliberate or inadvertent moral transgression on the part of the person. Alternatively, the person may be the innocent victim of an attack by spirits acting on behalf of a malevolent shaman or witch. Clues to the origins of spiritual assaults are often provided by the content of the dreams or visions that immediately preceded a particular bout of illness, injury, or misfortune (Benedict, 1929; Campbell, 1984; Eliade, 1964; Hallowell, 1926; Martin, 1978; Nelson, 1986; Serpell, 2005; Speck, 1977; Wenzel, 1991).

Animist belief systems are characteristic of all hunting and foraging societies, and among these societies, offended animal spirits are often viewed as the most common source of malign spiritual influences. Many Inuit peoples believe, for example, that the spirits of hunted animals, like the ghosts of murdered humans, are capable of seeking vengeance. To avoid this happening, all animals, whether dead or alive, are treated with great respect. Otherwise, the hunter or his family can expect to suffer some misfortune: the animals will no longer allow themselves to be killed or they may take their revenge by afflicting someone with disease, physical handicap, or even death (Wenzel, 1991). As an Inuit informant once eloquently expressed it:

> The greatest peril in life lies in the fact that human food consists entirely of souls. All the creatures that we have to kill and eat, all those that we have to strike

> down and destroy to make clothes for ourselves, have souls, like we have, souls that do not perish with the body, and which must therefore be propitiated lest they should avenge themselves on us for taking away their bodies. (Rasmussen, 1929:56)

In other hunting and foraging cultures, more specialized sets of moral relations existed between people and the animals they hunted for food. For instance, many Native American and Eurasian peoples believed in the concept of personal "guardian spirits" (Benedict, 1929; Hultzkrantz, 1987). Among the Ojibwa (Chippewa) and their Algonkian neighbors, these spirits were known as *manito* and were commonly represented as the spiritual prototypes or ancestor figures of wild animals. All of these *manito* were thought of in highly anthropomorphic terms. They were easily offended, capricious, and often bad-tempered, but they could also be appeased and, to some extent, cajoled by ritual means. Living animals were regarded as "honored servants" of their respective *manito*, and one such spirit apparently presided over and represented all of the earthly members of its species. At the same time, animals were also viewed as temporary incarnations of each *manito* who sent them out periodically to be killed by favored hunters or fishermen. For this reason, hunters invariably performed deferential rituals upon killing an animal so that its "essence" would return to the *manito* with a favorable account of how it was treated.

According to the Ojibwa worldview, the activities of *manito* explained nearly all the circumstances of everyday life. Every natural object, whether animate or inanimate, was charged with spiritual power, and no misfortune, whether illness, injury, death, or failure in hunting or fishing, was considered accidental or free from the personalized intent of one *manito* or another (Landes, 1968). Animal guardian spirits were also believed to vary in terms of power. Some species, especially small and relatively insignificant ones, such as the majority of insects and such things as mice, rats, or squirrels, were believed to possess correspondingly limited spiritual influence and rarely furnished people with useful guardian spirits. In contrast, more physically impressive species, such as bears, bison, wolves, or eagles, were deemed to possess extraordinary spiritual power and were therefore eagerly sought after as patrons (Benedict, 1929; Landes, 1968).

The methods used to obtain the patronage of these kinds of guardian spirits varied from culture to culture, but they almost invariably involved some form of physical ordeal (Benedict, 1929). Among the Ojibwa, young men at puberty were expected to isolate themselves in the forest and endure long periods of fasting, sleeplessness, and eventual delirium in an effort to obtain visions. Those who were successful experienced vivid hallucinations in which their "souls" entered the spirit world and encountered one or more *manito* who offered their future help and protection in return for a variety of ritual obligations. *Manito* advice or assistance could sometimes be discerned through natural portents and coincidences, but more often, guidance came indirectly through the medium of subsequent dreams and visions. At such times the person's "soul" was believed to reenter the supernatural dimension and confer with its spiritual guardian. The content of dreams was therefore considered of primary importance as a guide to action in daily life (Landes, 1968).

In some societies, it was considered virtually suicidal to injure, kill, or eat any member of the same species as one's guardian spirit. Like the ancient mariner's albatross, it could result in the withdrawal of spiritual patronage and cause general misfortune, illness, and death. However, and in an equally large number of cultures, the guardian spirit specifically awarded its protégé the authority to kill members of its own species (Benedict, 1929; Hallowell, 1926).

As in most fields of individual achievement, not all men and women were equally good at obtaining the support of animal guardian spirits. Some never obtain visions and were regarded as "empty, fearful, and cowardly" for the rest of their lives. A small minority, however, displayed extraordinary visionary talents and were henceforth regarded as medicine men, sorcerers, or shamans (Landes, 1968).

III. ANIMAL POWERS AND SHAMANISM

Mircea Eliade (1964) refers to shamanism as an "archaic technique of ecstasy" derived from guardian spirit belief. Both represent quests for magico-religious powers, and shamans differ from everyone else only in "their capacity for ecstatic experience, which, for the most part, is equivalent to a vocation" (Eliade, 1964: 107). Although shamanic power was derived from the assistance of one or more guardian spirits, the relationship between the shaman and his spiritual "helpers" or "familiars" was both more intimate and more intense than that attained by ordinary persons. In most cases, the shaman not only earned the patronage of guardian spirits but also developed the capacity to control them.

Shamans, typically, could achieve this power at will by entering a state of trance or ecstasy, usually induced by monotonous chanting, drumming, and dancing, and commonly assisted by the consumption of psycho-active drugs. Such states were considered to be analogous to death—the only other time when a person's "essence" becomes truly detached from the body and capable of independent actions in time and space. According to Eliade, this ecstatic "out-of-body" experience enables the shaman to divest himself of human form and recover the situation that existed at the beginning of time when no clear distinctions separated humans from animals. As a result, he is able to reestablish friendship with animals, acquire knowledge of their language, and have the ability to transform himself into an animal as and when occasion demands.

The result is a kind of symbiosis in which the person and the guardian spirit fuse to become two aspects of the same individual (Eliade, 1964).

Although they occasionally take human form, the vast majority of shamanic "familiars" are animals of one kind or another. Once he has adopted this disguise, the shaman is able to move about freely, gather information, and perform magical acts at a distance from his body. It is unclear from the various anthropological accounts, however, whether the animal spirit had its own independent existence when not in the shaman's service or whether it was simply a material form assumed by the shaman when engaging in the practice of magic. Stories and legends concerning shamans provide conflicting evidence in this respect. In some, shamans are said to be able to disappear when attacked or pursued, whereupon all that will be seen is some swift-footed animal or bird departing from the scene. If this animal is injured or killed, the shaman will experience an identical mishap wherever his or her body happens to be. However, shamans never killed or consumed the flesh of animals belonging to their familiar's species, implying that these spirits existed separately and could easily be mistaken for ordinary animals (Speck, 1918).

Depending on their particular talents, shamans are believed to be able to foretell the future, advise on the whereabouts of game animals, or predict impending catastrophes. Their ability to control the forces of nature can also be employed to manipulate the weather, subdue animals, or bring them close to the hunter. Above all, because all manifestations of ill health are thought to be caused by angry or malignant spirits, shamans possess a virtual monopoly on the treatment of sickness. Because the shaman is generally the only individual capable of visiting the spirit world at will through the agency of his animal "familiars," he provides the only reliable method of discovering and counteracting the spiritual origins of physical and mental illness (Eliade, 1964; Speck, 1918).

IV. ANIMISM IN CLASSICAL AND MEDIEVAL TIMES

Although animist belief systems are particularly characteristic of hunting and foraging peoples, they have also persisted in a variety of forms in many pastoral nomadic and agricultural societies where they often coexist, through a process of synchretic fusion, with more recently imposed religious creeds and practices. An interesting contemporary example still flourishes among Central American indigenous peoples such as the Maya. Although Christianized and agricultural, the Mayan inhabitants of Chamula in the Mexican province of Chiapas believe in the existence of individual "soul animals," or *chanul*, that are assigned to each person at birth by the celestial powers, and which share reciprocally every stroke of fortune that their human counterparts experience.

All *chanul* are nondomesticated mammals with five digits and are physically indistinguishable from actual wild animals. Indeed, a person may only discover the identity of his soul animal through its recurrent appearance in dreams or with the help of a shaman (Gossen, 1996).

The Maya believe that most illness is the result of an injury inflicted upon a person's *chanul*. These injuries may be inflicted deliberately via witchcraft, by another person mistaking one's *chanul* for an ordinary animal and hurting or killing it, or it may be "self-inflicted" in the sense that the person may allow himself or herself to experience overly intense emotions, such as intense fear, rage, excitement, or sexual pleasure, that can frighten or upset the *chanul*. The people of Chamula are also extremely reluctant to kill any wild mammal with five digits, as by doing so they believe they might inadvertently kill themselves or a friend or relative.

As far as curative measures are concerned, the only traditional remedy for an illness resulting from damage to one's soul animal is to employ the services of a shaman who will use various rituals and the influence of his own, more powerful soul animals to discover the source of the affliction and counteract it. According to Mayan folklore, shamans and witches also possess the ability to adopt the material form of their *chanul* in order to gain access to the supernatural realm (Gossen, 1996).

The purpose of dwelling on this particular example of contemporary Amerindian belief in soul animals is that it illustrates, according to Gossen (1996), the remarkable tenacity of animistic–shamanistic ideas and practices in Central America, despite the coercive influence of nearly five centuries of imported Roman Catholicism. Similarly, in Europe and around the Mediterranean basin, it appears that vestiges of comparable belief systems survived in a number of local and regional healing cults, at least until the early modern period.

In the preclassical period the connection with animism was particularly obvious. In ancient Egypt, for example, the entire pantheon was dominated by distinctly shamanic images of animal-headed gods and goddesses, including the dog-headed Anubis who guided the souls of the dead on their journey through the underworld and whose other roles included physician and apothecary to the gods and guardian of the mysteries of mummification and reincarnation. Dogs and snakes were also the sacred emblems of the Sumerian goddess, Gula the "great physician," and of the Babylonian and Chaldean deity, Marduk, another god of healing and reincarnation (Dale-Green, 1966; Swabe, 1994).

In the classical period the animist associations are somewhat less prominent but still readily discernible. Within the Greek pantheon, the gods were less often represented as animals, but they retained the shamanic ability to transform themselves into animals in order to disguise their true identities.

Dogs and serpents also played a central role in the cult of Asklepios (Aesculapius), the son of Apollo, who was known as the god of medicine and the divine physician. Asklepios's shrine in the sacred grove at Epidaurus functioned as a kind of ancient health resort. Like modern-day Lourdes, it attracted crowds of suppliants seeking relief from a great variety of maladies. As part of the "cure," it provided an early instance of institutional, animal-assisted therapy. Treatment involved various rites of purification and sacrifice followed by periods of (drug-induced?) sleep within the main body of the shrine. During their slumbers the god visited each of his "patients," sometimes in human form but more often in the guise of a snake or a dog that licked them on the relevant injured or ailing portions of their anatomy. It appears that the dogs that lived around the shrine may have been specially trained to lick people. It was believed that these animals actually represented the god and had the power to cure illness with their tongues (Dale-Green, 1966; Toynbee, 1973). Inscribed tablets found within the precincts of the temple at Epidaurus testify to the miraculous powers of the local dogs:

> Thuson of Hermione, a blind boy, had his eyes licked in the daytime by one of the dogs about the temple, and departed cured. A dog cured a boy from Aigina. He had a growth on his neck. When he had come to the god, one of the sacred dogs healed him while he was awake with his tongue and made him well.

Although evidently material in form, the healing dogs and snakes at Epidaurus clearly fulfilled much the same function as shamanic spirit helpers. Through their ability to renew themselves periodically by shedding their skins, not to mention their potentially venomous qualities, snakes have always possessed strong associations with healing, death, and reincarnation (Morris and Morris, 1968). Likewise, in mythology, the dog is commonly represented as an intermediary between this world and the next. Some authors have attributed this to the dog's carrion-eating propensities, whereas others ascribe it to the dog's proverbial watchfulness and alertness to unseen "spiritual' threats," as well as its liminal, ambiguous status as a voluntary occupant of the boundary zone separating human and animal, culture and nature (Serpell, 1995; White, 1991).

During the early centuries of Christianity, traces of ancient shamanic ideas and practices were still prevalent throughout much of Europe. In addition to being healers, most of the early Celtic saints and holy men of Britain and Ireland were distinguished by their special rapport with animals, and many, according to legend, experienced bodily transformations into animal form (Armstrong, 1973; Matthews, 1991). St. Francis of Assisi, who appears to have been influenced by Irish monastic traditions, has also been described as a "nature mystic." Among other feats, he preached sermons to rapt audiences of birds and was able to pacify rabid wolves (Armstrong, 1973). One of his followers, St. Anthony of Padua (1195–1231), preached so eloquently to the fishes in the sea that they all lined up along the shoreline to listen to his words of wisdom (Spencer, 1993).

The particular notion that dogs could heal injuries or sores by touching or licking them also persisted well into the Christian era. St. Roch, who, like Asklepios, was generally depicted in the company of a dog, seems to have been cured of plague sores by the licking of his canine companion. St. Christopher, St. Bernard, and a number of other saints were also associated with dogs, and many of them had reputations as healers.

A faint ghost of older, shamanistic traditions can also be detected in the curious medieval cult of the greyhound saint, St. Guinefort. Guinefort, or so the legend goes, was unjustly slaughtered by his noble master who mistakenly believed that the dog had killed and devoured his child. Soon afterward, however, the babe was found sleeping peacefully beside the remains of a huge, predatory serpent that Guinefort had fought and killed. Overcome with remorse, the knight threw the dog's carcass into a well, covered it with a great pile of stones, and planted a grove of trees around it to commemorate the event. During the 13th century, this grove, about 40 km north of the city of Lyons, became the center of a pagan-healing cult. Peasants from miles around brought their sick and ailing children to the shrine where miraculous cures were apparently performed (Schmitt, 1983).

Centuries later, the close companionship of a "spaniel gentle or comforter"—a sort of nondescript, hairy lap dog—was still being recommended to the ladies of Elizabethan England as a remedy for a variety of ills. William Harrison, in his *Description of England* (1577), admitted to some skepticism on the subject: "It is thought by some that it is verie wholesome for a weake stomach to beare such a dog in the bosome, as it is for him that hath the palsie to feele the dailie smell and savour of a fox. But how truelie this is affirmed let the learned judge." The learned Dr. Caius, author of *De Canibus Britannicus* (1570), was less inclined to doubt: "though some suppose that such dogges are fyt for no service, I dare say, by their leaves, they be in a wrong boxe." He was of the opinion that a dog carried on the bosom of a diseased person absorbed the disease (Jesse, 1866).

Thus, over historical time, a kind of progression occurs from a strong, archaic belief in the supernatural healing power of certain animals, such as dogs, to increasingly vague and superstitious folk practices in which the special "spiritual" qualities of the animal can no longer be discerned, and all that remains is a sort of "quack" remedy of dubious therapeutic value. In medieval Europe, this trend was associated with the church's vigorous suppression of pre-Christian and unorthodox religious beliefs and practices. In the year 1231 AD, in an effort to halt the spread of religious dissent in Europe, the office of the papal inquisition was created in order to provide the church with an instrument for identifying and combating heresy. Prior to this time, religious and secular authorities had adopted a relatively lenient attitude to the variety of pagan customs and beliefs that abounded locally throughout Europe. The inquisition systematically rooted them out and obliterated them. Ancient nature cults and rituals connected with pre-Christian deities or sacred groves, trees, streams, and wells were ruthlessly extirpated. Even the harmless cult of St. Guinefort was the object of persecution. A Dominican friar, Stephen of Bourbon, had the dead dog disinterred and the sacred grove cut down and burnt, along with the remains of the faithful greyhound. An edict was also passed making it a crime for anyone to visit the place in the future (Schmitt, 1983).

Although the picture is greatly distorted by the inquisition's peculiar methods of obtaining and recording evidence, it appears that the so-called witch craze that swept through Europe between the 15th and the 17th centuries originated as an attack on local folk healers or cunning folk, the last degenerate practitioners of archaic shamanism (Briggs, 1996; Serpell, 2002). According to the establishment view, not only did these medieval witches consort with the devil in animal form, they also possessed the definitively shamanic ability to transform both themselves and others into animals (Cohn, 1975). In Britain and Scandinavia, witches were also believed to possess supernatural "imps" or "familiars," most of which appeared in animal form. In fact, judging from the evidence presented in contemporary pamphlets and trial records, the majority of these "familiars" belonged to species we nowadays keep as pets: dogs, cats, cage birds, mice, rats, ferrets, and so on (Ewen, 1933; Serpell, 2002; Thomas, 1971). In other words, close association or affinity with animals, once a sign of shamanic power or budding sainthood, became instead a symptom of diabolism. Animal companions still retained a certain "otherworldly" quality in the popular imagination of the Middle Ages and the Renaissance, but mainly as potential instruments of *maleficium*, the power to harm others by supernatural means.

All of these trends also reflected the marked medieval tendency to impose rigid separation between human and nonhuman animals, a tendency that was reinforced by ideals of human conduct that emphasized self-control, civility, and chastity, while at the same time rejected what were then viewed as animal-like attributes, such as impulsiveness, coarseness, and licentiousness (Elias, 1978; Salisbury, 1995; Serpell, 2005).

V. ANIMALS AS AGENTS OF SOCIALIZATION

The close of the 17th century, and the dawn of the so-called age of enlightenment, brought with them certain changes in the public perception of animals that have been thoroughly documented by historians of the early modern period (e.g., Maehle, 1994; Thomas, 1983). These changes included a gradual increase in sympathetic attitudes to animals and nature and a gradual decline in the anthropocentric attitudes that so characterized the medieval and Renaissance periods (Salisbury, 1994). The perception of wild animals and wilderness as threatening to human survival also decreased in prevalence, while the practice of pet keeping expanded out of the aristocracy and into the newly emergent, urban middle classes. This change in animal-related attitudes and behavior can be plausibly attributed, at least in part, to the steady migration of Europeans out of rural areas and into towns and cities at this time. This rural exodus helped to distance growing sectors of the population from any direct involvement in the consumptive exploitation of animals and removed the need for value systems designed to legitimize or reinforce such practices (Serpell, 1996; Serpell and Paul, 1994; Thomas, 1983).

The notion that nurturing relationships with animals could serve a socializing function, especially for children, also surfaced at about this time. Writing in 1699, John Locke advocated giving children "dogs, squirrels, birds or any such things" to look after as a means of encouraging them to develop tender feelings and a sense of responsibility for others (Locke, 1699:154). Deriving their authority from the works of John Calvin and Thomas Hobbes, many 18th-century reformers believed that children could learn to reflect on, and control, their own innately beast-like characteristics through the act of caring for and controlling real animals (Myers, 1998). Compassion and concern for animal welfare also became one of the favorite didactic themes of children's literature during the 18th and 19th centuries, where its clear purpose was to inculcate an ethic of kindness and gentility, particularly in male children (Grier, 1999; Ritvo, 1987; Turner, 1980).

In the late 18th century, theories concerning the socializing influence of animal companionship also began to be applied to the treatment of the mentally ill. The earliest well-documented experiment in this area took place in England at The York Retreat, the brainchild of a progressive Quaker called William Tuke. The York Retreat employed treatment methods that were exceptionally enlightened when compared with those that existed in other mental institutions of the day. Inmates were permitted to wear their own clothing, and they were encouraged to engage in handicrafts, to write, and to read books. They were also allowed to wander freely around the retreat's courtyards and gardens that were stocked with various small domestic animals. In his *Description of the Retreat* (1813:96), Samuel Tuke, the founder's grandson, described how the internal courtyards of the retreat were supplied "with a number of animals; such as rabbits, sea-gulls, hawks, and poultry. These creatures are generally very familiar with the patients: and it is believed they are not only the means of innocent pleasure; but that the intercourse with them, sometimes tends to awaken the social and benevolent feelings."

During the 19th century, pet animals became increasingly common features of mental institutions in England and elsewhere. For example, in a highly critical report on the appalling conditions endured by the inmates of Bethlem Hospital during the 1830s, the British Charity Commissioners suggested that the grounds of lunatic asylums "should be stocked with sheep, hares, a monkey, or some other domestic or social animals" to create a more pleasing and less prison-like atmosphere. Such recommendations were evidently taken seriously. According to an article published in the *Illustrated London News* of 1860, the women's ward at the Bethlem Hospital was by that time "cheerfully lighted, and enlivened with prints and busts, with aviaries and pet animals," whereas in the men's ward the same fondness was manifested "for pet birds and animals, cats, canaries, squirrels, greyhounds &c. . . . . [some patients] pace the long gallery incessantly, pouring out their woes to those who listen to them, or, if there be none to listen, to the dogs and cats" (cited in Allderidge, 1991).

The beneficial effects of animal companionship also appear to have been recognized as serving a therapeutic role in the treatment of physical ailments during this period. In her *Notes on Nursing* (1880), for instance, Florence Nightingale observed that a small pet "is often an excellent companion for the sick, for long chronic cases especially."

VI. ANIMALS AND PSYCHOTHERAPY

Despite the apparent success of 19th-century experiments in animal-assisted institutional care, the advent of scientific medicine largely eliminated animals from hospital settings by the early decades of the 20th century (Allderidge, 1991). For the following 50 years, virtually the only medical contexts in which animals are mentioned are those concerned with zoonotic disease and public health or as symbolic referents in psychoanalytic theories concerning the origins of mental illness.

Sigmund Freud's ideas concerning the origins of neurosis tended to reiterate the Hobbesian idea of mankind's inherently beast-like nature (Myers, 1998). According to Freud, infants and young children are essentially similar to animals, insofar as they are ruled by instinctive cravings or impulses organized around basic biological functions such as eating, excreting, sexuality, and self-preservation. Freud referred to this basic animal aspect of human nature as the "id." As children mature, their adult care-givers "tame," or socialize, them by instilling fear or guilt whenever the child acts too impulsively in response to these inner drives. Children, in turn, respond to this external pressure to conform by repressing these urges from consciousness. Mental illness results, or so Freud maintained, when these bottled-up animal drives find no healthy or creative outlet in later life and erupt uncontrollably into consciousness (Shafton, 1995).

Freud interpreted the recurrent animal images that surfaced in his patients' dreams and "free associations" as metaphorical devices by means of which people disguise unacceptable thoughts or feelings. "Wild beasts," he argued, "represent passionate impulses of which the dreamer is afraid, whether they are his own or those of other people" (Freud, 1959:410). Because these beastly thoughts and impulses are profoundly threatening to the "ego," they are locked away in dark corners of the subconscious where they can be safely ignored, at least during a person's waking hours. To Freud and his followers, the aim of psychoanalysis was to unmask these frightening denizens of the unconscious mind, reveal their true natures, and, thus, effectively, to neutralize them (Serpell, 2000).

Freud's concept of the "id" as a sort of basic animal "essence" in human nature bears more than a superficial resemblance to animistic and shamanistic ideas concerning animal souls and guardian spirits and the "inner" or spiritual origins of ill health (Serpell, 2000). In the works of Carl Jung, particularly his discussions of mythological archetypes in dreams and visions and his concept of the "collective unconscious," this resemblance becomes more or less explicit (Cook, 1987). It is also echoed in the writings of Boris Levinson, the founder of "pet-facilitated therapy." In his book *Pets and Human Development* Levinson states that

> One of the chief reasons for man's present difficulties is his inability to come to terms with his inner self and to harmonize his culture with his membership in the world of nature. Rational man has become alienated from himself by refusing to face his irrational self, his own past as personified by animals. (Levinson, 1972:6)

The solution to this growing sense of alienation was, according to Levinson, to restore a healing connection with our own unconscious animal natures by establishing positive relationships with real animals, such as dogs, cats, and other pets. He argued that pets represent "a half-way station on the road back to emotional well-being" (Levinson, 1969:xiv) and that "we need animals as allies to reinforce our inner selves" (Levinson, 1972:28). Levinson went beyond the Freudian idea that animals were essentially a symbolic disguise for things we are afraid to confront in the flesh to arguing that relations with animals played such a prominent role in human evolution that they have now become integral to our psychological well-being (Levinson, 1972:15).

VII. ANIMALS, RELAXATION, AND SOCIAL SUPPORT

Since the mid-1980s, and at least partly in response to the skepticism of the medical establishment, the theoretical emphasis has shifted away from these relatively metaphysical ideas about animals as psychospiritual mediators toward more prosaic, scientifically "respectable" explanations for the apparent therapeutic benefits of animal companionship (Serpell, 2000). The primary catalyst for this change of emphasis was a single ground-breaking study of 92 outpatients from a cardiac care unit who, statistically speaking, were found to live longer if they were pet owners (Friedman *et al.*, 1980). This finding prompted a whole series of other health-related studies (see Garrity and Stallones, 1998; Friedmann *et al.*, 2000), as well as stimulated a lot of discussion concerning the possible mechanism(s) responsible for the apparent salutary effects of pet ownership. Of these, at least two have stood the test of time. According to the first, animals are able to induce an immediate physiologically dearousing state of relaxation simply by attracting and holding our attention (Katcher *et al.*, 1983). According to the second, companion animals are capable of providing people with a form of stress-reducing or stress-buffering social support (McNicholas and Collis, 1995; Serpell, 1996; Siegel, 1990).

Although the dearousing effects of animal contact have been demonstrated by a considerable number of recent studies, little evidence exists at present that these effects are responsible for more than transient or short-term improvements in physiological parameters, such as heart rate and blood pressure (Friedman, 1995). In contrast, the concept of pets serving as sources of social support seems to offer a relatively convincing explanation for the more long-term benefits of animal companionship.

Cobb (1976) defined social support as "information leading the subject to believe that he is cared for and loved, esteemed, and a member of a network of mutual obligations." More recent authors, however, have tended to distinguish between "perceived social support" and "social network" characteristics. The former represents a largely qualitative description of a person's level of satisfaction with the support he or she receives from particular social relationships, whereas the latter is a more quantitative measure incorporating the number, frequency, and type of a person's overall social interactions (Erikson, 1994). However we choose to define it, the importance of social support to human well-being has been acknowledged implicitly throughout history. Loneliness—the absence of social support—has always been viewed as such a painful and unpleasant sensation that, since time immemorial, societies have used solitary confinement, exile, and social ostracism as methods of punishment. The autobiographical accounts of religious hermits, castaways, and prisoners of war provide a clear picture of the psychological effects of social isolation. Most describe feelings equivalent to physical torture, which increase gradually to a peak before declining, often quite sharply. This decrease in pain is generally associated with the onset of a state of apathy and despair, sometimes so severe that it involves complete catatonic withdrawal (Serpell, 1996).

Since the early 1990s, an extensive medical literature has emerged confirming a strong, positive link between social support and improved human health and survival (see Eriksen, 1994; Esterling *et al.*, 1994; House *et al.*, 1988; Sherbourne *et al.*, 1992; Vilhjalmsson, 1993). The precise mechanisms underlying these life-saving effects of social support are still the subject of some debate, but most authorities appear now to agree that the principal benefits arise from the capacity of supportive social relationships to buffer or ameliorate the deleterious health effects of prolonged or chronic life stress (Ader *et al.*, 1995). In theory, this salutary effect of social support should apply to any positive social relationship; any relationship in which a person feels *cared for*, *loved*, or *esteemed*. As far as the vast majority of medical researchers and practitioners are concerned, however, the only relationships that are assumed to matter are those that exist between closely affiliated persons—friends, marital partners, immediate family members, and so on. Despite the growing evidence of recent anthrozoological research, the notion that animal companions might also contribute socially to human health has still received very limited medical recognition (Serpell, 1996).

VIII. CONCLUSIONS

For most of human history, animals have occupied a central position in theories concerning the ontology and treatment of sickness and disease. Offended animal spirits were often believed to be the source of illness, injury, or misfortune, but, at the same time, the assistance of animal guardian spirits—either one's own or those belonging to a "medicine man" or shaman—could also be called upon to mediate in the process of healing such afflictions.

Although such ideas survived here and there into the modern era, the spread of anthropocentric and monotheistic belief systems during the last 1000 to 2000 years virtually annihilated animist belief in the supernatural power of animals and animal spirits throughout much of the world. In Europe during the Middle Ages, the Christian church actively persecuted animist believers, branding them as witches and heretics and identifying their "familiar spirits" with the devil and his minions in animal form.

During the period of the "enlightenment," the idea that pet animals could serve a socializing function for children and the mentally ill became popular, and by the 19th century the introduction of animals to institutional care facilities was widespread. However, these early and preliminary experiments in animal-assisted therapy were soon displaced by the rise of scientific medicine during the early part of the 20th century. Animals continued to play a somewhat negative symbolic role in the development of psychoanalytic theories concerning the origins of mental illness, but no further medical discussion of their value as therapeutic adjuncts occurred until the late 1960s and 1970s when such ideas resurfaced in the writings of the influential child psychotherapist Boris Levinson.

Recent interest in the potential medical value of animal companionship was largely initiated by a single study that appeared to demonstrate life-prolonging effects of pet ownership among heart attack sufferers. This study has since prompted many others, most of which have demonstrated either short-term relaxing effects of animal contact or long-term health improvements consistent with a view of companion animals as sources of social support. Despite these findings, the positive therapeutic value of animal companionship continues to receive little recognition in mainstream medical literature and, as a field of research, it is grossly undersupported by government funding agencies.

Considered in retrospect, it is difficult to escape the conclusion that the current inability or unwillingness of the medical establishment to address this topic seriously is a legacy of the same anthropocentrism that has dominated European and Western thinking since the Middle Ages (Serpell, 2005). With the gradual demise of this old-fashioned and prejudiced mindset, it is hoped that we can return to a more holistic and open-minded view of the potential contribution of animals to human well-being.

REFERENCES

Ader, R. L., Cohen, N., and Felten, D. (1995). Psychoneuroimmunology: Interactions between the nervous system and the immune system. *Lancet* **345**, 99–103.

Allderidge, P. H. (1991). A cat, surpassing in beauty, and other therapeutic animals. *Psychiatr. Bull.* **15**, 759–762.

Anderson, W. P., Reid, C. M., and Jennings, G. L. (1992). Pet ownership and risk factors for cardiovascular disease. *Med. J. Austr.* **157**, 298–301.

Armstrong, E. A. (1973). "Saint Francis: Nature Mystic." University of California Press, Berkeley.

Benedict, R. F. (1929). The concept of the guardian spirit in North America. *Mem. Am. Anthropol. Assoc.* **29**, 3–93.

Briggs, R. (1996). "Witches and Neighbours." Vicking, London.

Campbell, J. (1984). "The Way of the Animal Powers." Times Books, London.

Cobb, S. (1976). Social support as a moderator of life stress. *Psychosom. Med.* **38**, 300–314.

Cohn, N. (1975). "Europe's Inner Demons." Basic Books, New York.

Cook, D. A. G. (1987). Jung, Carl Gustav (1875–1961). *In* "The Oxford Companion to the Mind" (R. Gregory, ed.), pp. 403–405. Oxford University Press, Oxford.

Dale-Green, P. (1966). "Dog." Rupert Hart-Davis, London.

Eliade, M. (1964). "Shamanism: Archaic Techniques of Ecstacy" (trans. W. R. Trask). Routledge, New York.

Elias, N. (1978). "The Civilizing Process," (trans. E. Jephcott) Basil Blackwell, Oxford.

Eriksen, W. (1994). The role of social support in the pathogenesis of coronary heart disease: A literature review. *Family Pract.* **11**, 201–209.

Esterling, B. A., Kiecolt-Glaser, J., Bodnar, J. C., and Glaser, R. (1994). Chronic stress, social support, and persistent alterations in the natural killer cell response to cytokines in older adults. *Health Psychol.* **13**, 291–328.

Ewen, C. L'E. (1933). "Witchcraft and Demonianism." Heath Cranton, London.

Friedman, E. (1995). The role of pets in enhancing human well-being: Physiological effects. *In* "The Waltham Book of Human-Animal Interaction: Benefits and Responsibilities of Pet-Ownership" (I. Robinson, ed.), pp. 33–53. Pergamon, Oxford.

Friedmann, E., Katcher, A. H., Lynch, J. J., and Thomas, S. A. (1980). Animal companions and one-year survival of patients after discharge from a coronary care unit. *Public Health Rep.* **95**, 307–312.

Friedmann, E., and Thomas, S. A. (1995). Pet ownership, social support, and one-year survival after acute myocardial infarction in the Cardiac Arrhythmia Suppression Trial (CAST). *Am. J. Cardiol.* **76**, 1213–1217.

Friedmann, E., Thomas, S. A., and Eddy, T. J. (2000). Companion animals and human health: Physical and cardiovascular influences. *In* "Companion Animals and Us" (A. L. Podberscek, E. S. Paul, and J. A. Serpell, eds.), pp. 125–142. Cambridge University Press, Cambridge.

Freud, S. (1959). "The Interpretation of Dreams" (trans. J. Strachey). Basic Books, New York.

Garrity, T. F., and Stallones, L. (1998). Effects of pet contact on human well-being: Review of recent research. *In* "Companion Animals in Human Health" (C. C. Wilson and D. C. Turner, eds.), pp. 3–22. Sage, Thousand Oaks, CA.

Gossen, G. H. (1996). Animal souls, co-essences, and human destiny in Mesoamerica. *In* "Monsters, Tricksters, and Sacred Cows: Animal Tales and American Identities" (A. J. Arnold, ed.), pp. 80–107. University Press of Virginia, Charlottesville, VA.

Grier, K. C. (1999). Childhood socialization and companion animals: United States, 1820–1870. *Soc. Anim.* **7**, 95–120.

Hallowell, A. I. (1926). Bear ceremonialism in the Northern Hemisphere. *Am. Anthropol.* **28**, 1–175.

House, J. S., Landis, K. R., and Umberson, D. (1988). Social relationships and health. *Science* **241**, 540–545.

Hultzkrantz, A. (1987). On beliefs in non-shamanic guardian spirits among the Saamis. *In* "Saami Religion" (T. Ahlbäck, ed.), pp. 110–123. Donner Institute for Research in Religious and Cultural History, Åbo, Finland.

Jesse, G. R. (1866). "Researches into the History of the British Dog," Vols. 1 and 2. Robert Hardwicke, London.

Katcher, A. H., Friedmann, E., Beck, A. M., and Lynch, J. J. (1983). Looking, talking and blood pressure: The physiological consequences of interaction with the living environment. *In* "New Perspectives on Our Lives with Companion Animals" (A. H. Katcher and A. M. Beck, eds.), pp. 351–359. University of Pennsylvania Press, Philadelphia, PA.

Kruger, K., Trachtenburg, S., and Serpell, J. A. (2004). Can animals help humans heal? "Animal-Assisted Interventions in Adolescent Mental Health." Center for the Interaction of Animals & Society, Philadelpia, PA (http://www2.vet.upenn.edu/research/centers/cias/publications.html).

Landes, R. (1968). "Ojibwa Religion and the Midéwiwin." University of Wisconsin Press, Madison, WI.

Levinson, B. (1969). "Pet-Oriented Child Psychotherapy." Charles C Thomas, Springfield, IL.

Levinson, B. (1972). "Pets and Human Development." Charles C Thomas, Springfield, IL.

Locke, J. (1699). "Some Thoughts Concerning Education." Reprinted with an introduction by F. W. Garforth (1964). Heinemann, London.

Maehle, A.-H. (1994). Cruelty and kindness to the "brute creation": Stability and change in the ethics of the man-animal relationship, 1600–1850. *In* "Animals and Human Society: Changing Perspectives" (A. Manning and J. A. Serpell, eds.), pp. 81–105. Routledge, London.

Martin, C. (1978). "The Keepers of the Game." University of California Press, Berkeley.
McNicholas, J., and Collis, G. M. (1995). The end of a relationship: Coping with pet loss. *In* "The Waltham Book of Human-Animal Interaction: Benefits and Responsibilities of Pet-Ownership" (I. Robinson, ed.), pp. 127–143. Pergamon, Oxford.
Morris, R., and Morris, D. (1968). "Men and Snakes." Sphere Books, London.
Myers, O. E. (1998). "Children and Animals." Westview Press, Boulder, CO.
Nelson, R. K. (1986). A conservation ethic and environment: The Koyukon of Alaska. *In* "Resource Managers: North American and Australian Hunter-Gatherers" (N. M. Williams and E. S. Hunn, eds.), pp. 211–228. Institute of Aboriginal Studies, Canberra.
Rasmussen, K. (1929). Intellectual life of the Iglulik Eskimos. *In* "Report of the Fifth Thule Expedition," Vol. 7(1), p. 56.
Ritvo, H. (1987). "The Animal Estate: The English and Other Creatures in the Victorian Age." Harvard University Press, Cambridge, MA.
Salisbury, J. (1994). "The Beast Within: Animals in the Middle Ages." Routledge, London.
Schmitt, J.-C. (1983). "The Holy Greyhound: Guinefort, Healer of Children since the 13th Century" (trans. M. Thom). Cambridge University Press, Cambridge.
Serpell, J. A. (1995). From paragon to pariah: Some reflections on human attitudes to dogs. *In* "The Domestic Dog: Its Evolution, Behaviour and Interactions with People" (J. A. Serpell, ed.), pp. 245–256. Cambridge University Press, Cambridge.
Serpell, J. A. (1996). "In the Company of Animals," 2nd Ed. Cambridge University Press, Cambridge.
Serpell, J. A. (2000). Creatures of the unconscious: Companion animals as mediators. *In* "Companion Animals and Us" (A. L. Podberscek, E. S. Paul, and J. A. Serpell, eds.), pp. 108–121. Cambridge University Press, Cambridge.
Serpell, J. A. (2002). Guardian spirits or demonic pets: The concept of the witch's familiar in early modern England, 1530–1712. *In* "The Animal/Human Boundary" (A. N. H. Creager and W. C. Jordan, eds.), pp. 157–190. University of Rochester Press, Rochester.
Serpell, J. A. (2005). Animals and religion: Towards a unifying theory. *In* "The Human-Animal Relationship" (F. de Jonge and R. van den Bos, eds.), pp. 9–22. Royal Van Gorcum, Assen.
Serpell, J. A., and Paul, E. S. (1994). Pets and the development of positive attitudes to animals. *In* "Animals and Human Society: Changing Perspectives" (A. Manning and J. A. Serpell, eds.), pp. 127–144. Routledge, London.
Shafton, A. (1995). "Dream Reader: Contemporary Approaches to the Understanding of Dreams." SUNY Press, Albany, NY.
Sherbourne, C. D., Meredith, L. S., Rogers, W., and Ware, J. E. (1992). Social support and stressful life events: Age differences in their effects on health-related quality of life among the chronically ill. *Qual. Life Res.* **1**, 235–246.
Siegel, J. M. (1980). Stressful life events and use of physician services among the elderly: The moderating role of pet ownership. *J. Personal. Soc. Psychol.* **58**, 1081–1086.
Speck, F. G. (1918). Penobscot shamanism. *Mem. Am. Anthropol. Assoc.* **6**, 238–288.
Speck, F. G. (1977). "Naskapi," 3rd Ed. University of Oklahoma Press, Norman, OK.
Spencer, C. (1993). "The Heretic's Feast." 4th Estate, London.
Swabe, C. W. (1994). Animals in the ancient world. *In* "Animals and Human Society: Changing Perspectives" (A. Manning and J. A. Serpell, eds.), pp. 36–58. Routledge, London.
Thomas, K. (1971). "Religion and the Decline of Magic." Penguin Books, Harmondsworth.
Thomas, K. (1983). "Man and the Natural World: Changing Attitudes in England, 1500–1800." Allen Lane, London.
Toynbee, J. M. C. (1973). "Animals in Roman Life and Art." Thames & Hudson, London.
Tuke, S. (1813). "Description of the Retreat." Reprinted with an introduction by R. Hunter and I. Macalpine (1964). Dawsons, London.

Turner, J. (1980). "Reckoning with the Beast: Animals, Pain, and Humanity in the Victorian Mind." Johns Hopkins University Press, Baltimore.

Vilhjalmson, R. (1993). Life stress, social support and clinical depression: A reanalysis of the literature. *Soc. Sci. Med.* 37, 331–342.

Wenzel, G. (1991). "Animal Rights, Human Rights: Ecology, Economy and Ideology in the Canadian Arctic." Belhaven Press, London.

White, D. G. (1991). "Myths of the Dog-man." Chicago University Press, Chicago.

Wilson, C. C., and Turner, D. C. (eds.) (1998). "Companion Animals in Human Health." Sage, Thousand Oaks, CA.

CHAPTER 2

Animal-Assisted Interventions in Mental Health: Definitions and Theoretical Foundations

KATHERINE A. KRUGER AND JAMES A. SERPELL

Center for the Interaction of Animals and Society, Department of Clinical Studies, School of Veterinary Medicine, University of Pennsylvania, Philadelphia, Pennsylvania 19104

I. INTRODUCTION

As described in Chapter 1, the advent of scientific medicine toward the end of the 19th century had the effect of displacing companion animals from therapeutic settings until the 1960s, when the concept was revived in the writings of Boris M. Levinson. In his book *Pet-Oriented Child Psychotherapy*, Levinson described the benefits that his dog brought to his counseling sessions with children and youth and provided numerous examples of ways in which animals could enhance therapy (Levinson, 1969). Levinson intended for this material based largely on case studies and anecdotes to inform and encourage future research into the various beneficial effects that he observed. While this has occurred to some degree, more often Levinson's writings have been used to justify the implementation of animal-assisted interventions (AAIs) in the absence of valid efficacy studies.

Despite their long history and the unequivocally positive media attention they typically receive, animal-assisted interventions are currently best described as a category of promising complementary practices that are still struggling to demonstrate their efficacy and validity. Some attempts have been

Handbook on Animal-Assisted Therapy: Theoretical Foundations and Guidelines for Practice, 2e

made to standardize terminology and procedures, and various certificate programs are now being offered in association with colleges and universities. However, if the field is to move beyond its fringe status, it must begin to follow the path taken by other alternative and complementary therapies (e.g., acupuncture, chiropractic) that have established their credibility by means of carefully controlled clinical trials and valid efficacy studies. With that objective in mind, the goals of this chapter are to clarify the distinction between therapy and other assistive or recreational uses of animals and then to explore some of the theories that underlie the incorporation of animals into therapeutic contexts.

II. DEFINING ANIMAL-ASSISTED INTERVENTIONS

In their critical review of the literature on animal-assisted interventions, Beck and Katcher (1984) aptly state that "a clear distinction should be made between emotional response to animals, that is, their recreational use, and therapy. It should not be concluded that any event that is enjoyed by the patients is a kind of therapy." Although this statement was made more than 20 years ago, the term *animal-assisted therapy* continues to be applied to an array of programs that would not qualify as therapy in any scientific/medical sense of the word. The *Oxford English Dictionary* (1997) defines *therapy* as "the medical treatment of disease; curative medical or psychiatric treatment." In contrast, *recreation* is defined as a "pleasant occupation, pastime or amusement; a pleasurable exercise or employment." Despite the obvious distinction, there is a tendency in certain quasi-medical fields to weaken or confuse the meaning of the word *therapy* by linking it to experiences that may provide transient relief or pleasure but whose practitioners cannot ethically or credibly claim to diagnose or change the course of human disease (e.g., aromatherapy, massage therapy, crystal/gemstone therapy). Regrettably, this is also the case with many programs that are promoted as animal-assisted therapy. Just as we would not refer to a clown's visit to a pediatric hospital as clown-assisted therapy, the urge to call animal recreation and visitation programs therapy should be resisted.

In her review of the literature, LaJoie (2003) reported finding 20 different definitions of animal-assisted therapy (AAT) and 12 different terms for the same phenomenon (e.g., pet therapy, pet psychotherapy, pet-facilitated therapy, pet-facilitated psychotherapy, four-footed therapy, animal-assisted therapy, animal-facilitated counseling, pet-mediated therapy, pet-oriented psychotherapy, companion-animal therapy, and co–therapy with an animal). This multiplicity of terms and definitions creates confusion both within the field and without. In an attempt to promote the standardization of terminology, the Delta Society (n.d.), one of the largest organizations responsible for the certification of therapy animals in the United States, has published the following widely cited definitions of animal-assisted therapy and animal-assisted activity.

- Animal-assisted therapy: AAT is a goal-directed intervention in which an animal that meets specific criteria is an integral part of the treatment process. AAT is directed and/or delivered by a health/human service professional with specialized expertise and within the scope of practice of his/her profession. Key features include specified goals and objectives for each individual and measured progress.
- Animal-assisted activity: AAA provides opportunities for motivational, educational, recreational, and/or therapeutic benefits to enhance quality of life. AAAs are delivered in a variety of environments by specially trained professionals, paraprofessionals, and/or volunteers in association with animals that meet specific criteria. Key features include absence of specific treatment goals; volunteers and treatment providers are not required to take detailed notes; visit content is spontaneous.

Although the Delta Society lists horses as being animals eligible for certification through their PetPartners program, interventions involving the use of horses typically fall under the jurisdiction of a separate group of agencies. Prominent among these is the North American Riding for the Handicapped Association (NARHA), its subsection the Equine Facilitated Mental Health Association (EFMHA), and its affiliate partner the American Hippotherapy Association (AHA), which provide separate definitions for the terms *equine-facilitated psychotherapy* (EFP) and *hippotherapy*.

- EFP is an experiential psychotherapy that includes equine(s). It may include, but is not limited to, a number of mutually respectful equine activities, such as handling, grooming, longeing (or lunging), riding, driving, and vaulting. EFP is facilitated by a licensed, credentialed mental health professional working with an appropriately credentialed equine professional. EFP may be facilitated by a mental health professional that is dually credentialed as an equine professional (EFMHA, 2003). EFP denotes an ongoing therapeutic relationship with clearly established treatment goals and objectives developed by the therapist in conjunction with the client. The therapist must be an appropriately credentialed mental health professional to legally practice psychotherapy and EFP (EFMHA, 2005).
- Hippotherapy is done by an occupational, physical, and speech therapist who has been specially trained to use the movement of the horse to facilitate improvements in their client/patient. It does not teach the client how to ride the horse. Therapists use traditional techniques such as

neurodevelopmental treatment and sensory integration along with the movement of the horse as part of their treatment strategy. Goals include improving balance, coordination, posture, fine motor control, improving articulation, and increasing cognitive skills (AHA, 2005).

While we include specific definitions of EFP and hippotherapy for the sake of comparison and completeness, the Delta Society definition of AAT is general enough to include these sorts of interventions. What should be emphasized is that these definitions of animal-assisted therapy, equine-facilitated psychotherapy, and hippotherapy all share the following attributes.

1. The intervention involves the use of an animal or animals.
2. The intervention must be delivered by or under the oversight of a health/human service professional who is practicing within the scope of his/her professional expertise.

It should be noted that the Delta Society definitions include statements about the need for participating animals to "meet specific criteria," whereas those utilized by the EFMHA and AHA do not. Ensuring the suitability of an animal for any type of work is of paramount importance for both the animals and the humans involved, and many facilities do require a formal behavioral evaluation prior to allowing animals to interact with clients or patients. However, the criteria by which animals are determined to be suitable for this work are highly variable and often subjective, and what particular interventions require from animals may be diverse and changeable (e.g., some practitioners see a benefit to using skittish or behaviorally challenging animals with particular clients). It is also worth mentioning that formalized behavioral screenings and certifications are not available for all species being used as therapeutic adjuncts, so while these assurances are desirable when available, their absence does not necessarily disqualify a program from being considered therapy. Questions regarding an animal's suitability for therapy work arise primarily from risk management considerations (e.g., patient safety; liability issues) and concerns about animal welfare. However, these considerations are extraneous to a general definition of therapy. Certainly, such issues should be given top priority when developing and implementing AAIs, but they do not help us define therapy, as an intervention can still achieve therapeutic goals without formal criteria being met by the participating animal(s) (see, e.g., Wells and colleagues [1997] on the use of feral cats in psychotherapy).

While it would be preferable for this chapter to include only information from studies and programs that adhere strictly to the definition of AAT outlined earlier—specifically those that are facilitated by health/human service professionals within the scope of their professional expertise and that have clear treatment goals—too few studies and programs fulfill all the necessary criteria. Therefore, for the purposes of this chapter, animal-assisted therapy, animal-assisted activities, and various equine-facilitated programs are grouped together under the more general term *animal-assisted interventions*—defined here as "any intervention that intentionally includes or incorporates animals as part of a therapeutic or ameliorative process or milieu." The *Oxford English Dictionary* (1997) defines *intervention* as "the action of intervening, 'stepping in', or interfering in any affair, so as to affect its course or issue." This definition provides the flexibility needed to discuss programs that can fit within a medical model and those of a more quasi-medical nature but which still seek to "affect the course" of people's lives in a positive direction.

Guide, assistance, and service animals are purposefully excluded from the aforementioned definition of AAIs. The Americans with Disabilities Act of 1990 (ADA) defines a *service animal* as "any guide dog, signal dog, or other animal individually trained to provide assistance to an individual with a disability" (United States Department of Justice [USDOJ], 1996). The role of the service animal, as defined by the ADA, is to perform some of the functions and tasks that the individual cannot perform as a result of their disability (USDOJ, 1996). While the use of a service animal may provide some psychological benefits to its handler (e.g., decreased feelings of loneliness and isolation, or increased socialization), and not withstanding the nascent use of psychiatric service dogs (Psychiatric Service Dog Society, 2003), service animals are typically viewed as tools rather than treatments and thus do not constitute an animal-assisted intervention as we define the term.[1,2]

III. THEORETICAL FRAMEWORKS

The field of animal-assisted interventions currently lacks a unified, widely accepted, or empirically supported theoretical framework for explaining how

[1] It should be noted that because service animals are not legally considered pets, the ADA includes special provisions that allow for service animals to accompany their handlers into businesses and public places where pets are typically prohibited; the same is not true of therapy animals. While obtaining the status of "therapy animal" may provide a pet with limited entrée into places where animals are typically prohibited (e.g., hospitals, nursing homes, psychiatric facilities), therapy animals and their handlers are not granted any rights or protections under the ADA.

[2] An emerging issue in this field is the growing use of emotional support animals (ESA). The role these animals play has blurred the boundaries among pet ownership, mental health treatment, and the use of service animals. Unlike guide and service animals, ESAs do not necessarily receive special training, perform specific tasks, or accompany their handlers outside the home. Although very little authoritative information has been written on the topic, it appears that in order for an animal to qualify as an ESA, a healthcare provider must simply prescribe the animal for a patient with an emotional disability. In many cases, this prescription is all that differentiates ESAs from pets. As of this writing, ESAs are a controversial issue, with some suggesting that ESAs are an abuse and misinterpretation of the intent of the ADA (Grubb, 2002), whereas others seek to characterize ESAs as bona fide service animals (Bazelon Center for Mental Health Law, n.d.).

and why relationships between humans and animals are potentially therapeutic. A considerable variety of possible mechanisms of action have been proposed or alluded to in the literature, most of which focus on the supposedly unique intrinsic attributes of animals that appear to contribute to therapy. Others emphasize the value of animals as living instruments that can be used to affect positive changes in patients' self-concept and behavior through the patients' acquisition of various skills and acceptance of personal agency and responsibility. This section presents an overview of the theories found most commonly in the literature and, in some cases, those that seem to offer the best frameworks for future study.[3]

A. Intrinsic Attributes of Animals as Contributors to Therapy

The notion that animals possess certain inherent qualities that may facilitate therapy is widespread in the AAI literature. According to this view, the mere presence of the animal, its spontaneous behaviors, and its availability for interaction may provide opportunities and confer benefits that would be impossible, or much harder, to obtain in its absence.

1. Reduction of Anxiety and Arousal

The idea that the presence of, or interactions with, animals can produce calming effects in humans is commonly cited in the AAI literature. One popular explanation for this phenomenon is derived from E. O. Wilson's (1984) so-called *biophilia hypothesis*. This theory asserts that humans possess a genetically based propensity to attend to, and be attracted by, other living organisms (Kahn, 1997) or, as Wilson put it, an "innate tendency to focus on life and lifelike processes" (as cited in Gullone, 2000). The foundation of biophilia is that from an evolutionary standpoint, humans increased their chances of survival through their attention to, and knowledge of, environmental cues. Clinically speaking, it is hard to imagine a better pairing of attributes—a tool that can simultaneously engage and relax the patient. To quote Melson (2001):

[3] At this point we need to acknowledge a personal bias. Animal-assisted interventions are practiced with individuals at virtually every stage of life and with a vast array of mental and physical diagnoses. Our previous work in this area focused largely on animal-assisted interventions in adolescent mental health (Kruger *et al.*, 2004), and consequently, much of what appears in this chapter is a reflection of that narrow exploration of this broad and highly diverse field. We have tried nevertheless to ensure that the information included here is relevant to interventions practiced with individuals of all ages and with a wide variety of mental health diagnoses.

> [Watching] animals at peace may create a coupling of decreased arousal with sustained attention and alertness, opening the troubled child to new possibilities of learning and growth. The child can then experience unconditional love and models of good nurturing, practice caring sensitively for another, and assume mastery tempered with respect.

Although there are abundant references in the literature that suggest the presence of animals can sometimes exert calming or dearousing effects on people (Bardill and Hutchinson, 1997; Brickel, 1982; Friedmann *et al.*, 1983; Mallon, 1994a,b; Mason and Hagan, 1999; Reichert, 1998; Reimer, 1999), there are no convincing data demonstrating that these effects are due to any innate attraction to animals. Additionally, Serpell (1996) points out that "it has been known since the 1950s that any stimulus which is attractive or which concentrates the attention has a calming effect on the body," suggesting that animals may be just one means to this end. Moreover, even proponents of biophilia acknowledge that individual experience and culture play important roles in determining people's responses to animals (Kahn, 1997; Serpell, 2004).

Brickel (1985) offers learning theory as another explanation for the potential anti–anxiolytic benefits of animals in therapeutic contexts. According to learning theory, an activity that is pleasurable will be self-reinforcing and will be more likely to occur in the future. Unpleasant or anxiety-provoking activities, e.g., enduring painful or embarrassing visits to a therapist, may result in avoidance or withdrawal behavior. Just as enjoyable activities are self-reinforcing, avoidance of pain and discomfort provides a negative reinforcement by assuring minimal exposure to the painful stimulus. Brickel (1982) suggests that animals introduced in a therapeutic context may serve as a buffer and divert attention from an anxiety-generating stimulus that the patient faces. This interference allows for self-monitored control over exposure to the stimulus instead of withdrawal and avoidance (e.g., a child may choose to reveal sexual abuse first to the therapy animal rather than revealing it directly to the therapist). If the theory holds, repeated exposure through the animal's diverting properties, together with nonaversive consequences, should result in the reduction or extinction of anxiety. Brickel does not offer an explanation for why animals, in particular, are apparently so diverting, and it is presumably necessary to resort to other theories to account for this.

While evolutionary and learning theories have not adequately explained why some humans report feeling calmer when an animal is present, numerous researchers have attempted to examine and measure various human physiologic responses to interaction with animals. Studies that have focused on the anti–anxiolytic effects of an animal presence have typically measured heart rate and blood pressure as indicators of arousal (DeMello, 1999; Friedmann *et al.*, 1980, 1983; Katcher *et al.*, 1983), although a subset of studies have collected information on additional variables such as skin temperature, behavioral manifestations of stress, state/trait anxiety, and levels of cholesterol, triglycerides, and phenylethylamine in the plasma (Anderson *et al.*, 1992; Freidmann *et al.*, 2000; Hansen *et al.*, 1999; Nagengast *et al.*, 1997; Odendaal and Lehmann, 2000; Wilson, 1991). As with much of the literature on AAIs, findings in this area are conflicting and, regrettably, fundamental methodological differences between the studies make it impossible to draw any firm conclusions about the impact that animals may have on human arousal, as both positive and negative effects have been reported.

Based on all of the available research, the most credible conclusion that one can draw at this stage is that the presence of certain animals can produce calming effects for some people in some contexts, but Wilson's (1991) finding that interacting with an animal was more stressful than reading quietly does highlight the need for studies that compare animal-assisted interventions with activities with similar aims but that do not incorporate animals. In other words, a finding that the presence of an animal decreases arousal does not rule out the possibility that other interventions or activities that do not include animals may be as, or more, effective.

2. Social Mediation

The observation that animals can serve as catalysts or mediators of human social interactions and may expedite the rapport-building process between patient and therapist is often noted in the AAI literature. AAI practitioners and theorists have suggested that animals stimulate conversation by their presence and unscripted behavior and by providing a neutral, external subject on which to focus (Fine, 2000; Levinson, 1969). Studies that have attempted to look at the social-facilitation effects of animals have produced similarly positive results across a range of populations (e.g., children with physical disabilities; the elderly; college students; typical dog owners; and adult and adolescent psychiatric inpatients). Also, drawing from psychoanalytic theory, there are ample references in the AAI literature to patients being able to reveal or discuss difficult thoughts, feelings, motivations, conflicts, or events by projecting them onto a real or fictional animal (Mason and Hagan, 1999; Reichert, 1998; Reimer, 1999; Wells *et al.*, 1997; Serpell, 2000). Reichert (1998) provides this example from her clinical experience with a sexually abused child:

> I told one child that Buster [a dog] had a nightmare. I then asked the child, "What do you think Buster's nightmare was about?" The child said, "The nightmare was about being afraid of getting hurt again by someone mean."

In support of the notion of expedited rapport building, several studies conducted with college students produced evidence that people are perceived as happier, friendlier, wealthier, less threatening, and more relaxed when they appear in a picture with a friendly animal versus how they are perceived when the same picture is shown with the animal omitted (Lockwood, 1983; Rossbach and Wilson, 1992; Wells and Perrine, 2001). In three studies that examined a small number of subjects walking with and without their dogs in familiar and unfamiliar areas, all found significant increases in positive social interactions with strangers when the dogs were present (Eddy *et al.*, 2001; Mader *et al.*, 1989; Messent, 1983). Finally, in a seminal pilot study, Corson and colleagues (1977) investigated the impact of a dog-walking program on a small number of adult and adolescent psychiatric inpatients ($n = 50$, with only five subjects being studied in-depth) who were considered to be socially withdrawn and unresponsive to other forms of treatment. The quantitative findings of this study included decreases in the response time to questions posed by the therapist, exponential increases in the number of words used in responses, and increases in the percentage of questions answered.

Studies of the ability of animals to alter perceptions of social desirability and to increase positive social interactions between strangers have been uniformly positive. When considered alongside the large numbers of anecdotal statements attesting to the power of animals to hasten the building of rapport between patient and therapist, as well as to facilitate meaningful interaction between the two, these findings have important healthcare implications. If the presence of an animal can make the therapist appear happier, friendlier, less threatening, and more relaxed, it seems reasonable to believe that some patients would achieve a greater sense of comfort more quickly. In addition to enhancing the patient's perception of the healthcare provider, the presence of an animal provides a benign, external topic of conversation on which to focus, which may further hasten and enhance the development of a working alliance. Given that compliance and retention in treatment, as well as treatment outcomes, may be strongly related to the quality of the therapeutic relationship, this particular aspect of animal-assisted interventions merits urgent investigation.

3. Attachment Theory, Transitional Objects, and Social Needs

The AAI literature abounds with anecdotal statements concerning the loving bonds that are forged between humans and animals (Bardill and Hutchinson, 1997; Harbolt and Ward, 2001; Kale, 1992; Mallon, 1994b), with the implication that these attachments are part of what helps clients achieve therapeutic gains. With regard to attachment, Triebenbacher (1998) writes,

> Humans have an innate, biologically-based need for social interaction, and this interaction becomes increasingly focused toward specific figures. Behaviors such as following, smiling toward, holding, and touching are evident in the reciprocal relationship between child and attachment figure. . . . These behaviors can be exhibited

> not only toward primary attachment figures but substitutes or supplemental figures as well.

Certainly, the behaviors that Triebenbacher describes can be observed in human interactions with animals, and there is no question that people form attachments with animals, but correlations between attachment and positive therapeutic outcomes have yet to be convincingly established in relation to AAIs. Theories related to attachment and social needs are, nonetheless, conceptually helpful in developing an understanding of the potential value of incorporating animals into therapeutic contexts.

Encompassed within the broad concept of attachment is the phenomenon of the "transitional object." While transitional objects are primarily considered the purview of very young children, the existence of a transitional effect in AAIs is alluded to sufficiently often in the literature (Katcher, 2000; Levinson, 1970, 1978, 1984; Mallon, 1994b; Reichert, 1998; Triebenbacher, 1998) to warrant further attention. The transitional object, as defined by Winnicott (1951), is an item or object, such as a blanket or soft toy, that serves a comforting function for a child and helps alleviate the normal developmental stress of separation from the primary caregiver (Cwik, 1991). In therapeutic contexts, animals are often described as alleviating the stress of the initial phases of therapy by serving a comforting, diverting role until the therapist and patient have developed a sound rapport.

While animals may serve as both attachment figures and transitional objects, it is important to note that the roles of attachment figure and transitional object are, by definition, mutually exclusive. "Attachment" implies a long-lasting emotional bond, whereas "transitional" implies a passage from one condition to another and the absence of a lasting bond. To quote Cwik (1991), "The fate of the [transitional] object is that it slowly loses meaning as transitional phenomena spread out over the child's whole cultural field." In the context of animal-assisted interventions, the role of the animal as a transitional object would appear to be more therapeutically desirable than that of an attachment figure. The purpose of a transitional object is to act as a bridge to a higher or more socially acceptable level of functioning, not to serve as a substitute for failed or inadequate human relationships. This is not to say that forming emotional bonds with animals should be entirely discouraged but that the fostering of strong attachments in the course of brief treatments may be ethically and therapeutically unsound.

Attachment is also one component of Robert Weiss' (1974) theory of "social provisions," a needs-based theory in some ways akin to Maslow's "hierarchy of needs" (1970), which assumes that some aspects of a person's psychological well-being can only be met through the medium of social relationships. In addition to attachment, Weiss (1974) included the need for social integration, reassurance of worth, reliable alliance, guidance, and opportunities for nurturance among these necessary social provisions. Weiss's ideas permeate the AAI and "human–animal bond" literature, particularly in relation to the putative role of animals as outlets for nurturing behavior (Beck and Katcher, 1996; Enders-Slegers, 2000; Lapp and Scruby, 1982; Mallon, 1994a).

Finally, some mention should be made of the influence of Carl Rogers' (cited in Allen, 2000) ideas concerning "nonevaluative empathy" and "unconditional positive regard" in studies of both pet ownership and AAIs (see, e.g., Katcher, 1983). The twin notions that companion animals are "empathic," i.e., able to "sense" and respond to people's feelings and emotions, and unconditionally loving are cited so often in the AAI literature that they have acquired the status of clichés. Nevertheless, arguing from a Rogerian perspective, the potential value of animals as nonjudgmental confidantes and sources of unconditional positive regard might repay more detailed empirical investigation.

B. Animals as Instruments of Cognitive and Behavioral Change

A final set of theories relevant to this discussion concern the use of animals as living, interactive tools that can be used to help people see both themselves and the world in new ways and add new skills and responses to their behavioral repertoires. Although there is some overlap between these theories and those described in the previous section, what sets them apart is their emphasis on the formation of a working relationship between the patient and the animal. Most programs that incorporate equines draw heavily from these theories, as do programs that incorporate animal training and caretaking into their protocols.

1. Cognitive and Social Cognitive Theories

Cognitive and social cognitive theories are founded on the belief that there is a continuous reciprocal relationship among a person's cognitions, behavior, and environment (e.g., if I think I'm a bad person, I will behave like a bad person, and will therefore be treated like a bad person by those around me). The goal of therapy is to bring about positive changes in a person's self-perceptions—and hence their behavior—via improvements in, for example, self-esteem, self-efficacy, internalized locus of control, and so on. Learning and change take place through observation, imitation, direct instruction, and/or association (Allen, 2000; LaJoie, 2003).

The notion of wanting clients to learn appropriate behaviors through observation is common in the literature on animal-assisted interventions (Fine,

2000; Rice *et al.*, 1973; Taylor, 2001; Vidrine *et al.*, 2002) and is sometimes referred to as "modeling," a term first coined by Bandura and colleagues (1961). Another benefit often ascribed to AAIs is the ability of animals to help people learn about appropriate social interactions and the cause and effect of their behavior (Brooks, 2001; Nebbe, 1991). Animals are thought to be uniquely helpful in providing feedback on social behavior due to their unambiguous, "honest," and immediate responses to both pleasurable and aversive stimuli. Bardill and Hutchinson (1997) provide a clear example of this phenomenon:

> Graham [a cocker spaniel that lives in a closed adolescent psychiatric unit] responds positively and affectionately to acts of kindness many times during the day. Negative behaviors toward Graham, such as teasing or rough play, are responded to by Graham's avoidance of the perpetrator and peer pressure [from the other adolescents on the unit].

Three additional and interrelated aspects of social cognitive theory appear relevant to the use of animals in therapeutic roles: "self-efficacy," "performance accomplishment," and "personal agency." Self-efficacy is a belief in one's ability to perform behaviors that will create an expected and desirable outcome, and performance accomplishment involves the successful performance of a behavior that was once feared (Allen, 2000). These two concepts are related in that Bandura (cited in Allen, 2000) theorized that performance accomplishment was the single most efficient method for increasing feelings of self-efficacy. Also related is the notion of "personal agency," a condition in which people come to believe that they can make things happen that will be of benefit to themselves and others (Allen, 2000). Animal-assisted interventions are often structured around creating enhancement in these three realms.

Cognitive theories also offer us a reason to be circumspect in our enthusiasm about the benefits of animal-assisted interventions that aim to ameliorate feelings of helplessness or inferiority. As Newman and Newman (1995) remind us, the social environment does not reward all skills and achievements equally. It is extremely difficult for a person who does not excel in culturally valued skills to compensate through the mastery of others. Thus, if an intervention aims to provide long-term and generalized increases in feelings of self-efficacy, it needs to offer the acquisition of skills that are high in social desirability, offer a convenient means for continued learning (and thus continued positive feedback) after the end of the intervention, and offer a high likelihood of successful mastery. To date, there have been no long-term follow-up studies of the impact or efficacy of animal-assisted interventions. Although some have attempted to determine if changes in behavior could be observed beyond the context of the intervention (generally school and home) (Katcher and Wilkins, 1998; Kogan *et al.*, 1999), the results are conflicting, and as yet no evidence exists that long-standing benefits are derived from participation in these programs.

2. Role Theory

Role theory is similar to social cognitive theory in that its emphasis is on the way the social environment shapes the developmental process. In this theoretical framework, a role is defined as any set of behaviors that has a socially agreed-upon function and an accepted code of norms (Biddle, Biddle, and Thomas as cited in Newman and Newman, 1995). The theory holds that as people enter new roles, they modify their behavior to conform to these role expectations (Newman and Newman, 1995). Obviously, whether these changes in behavior are positive or negative depend on the role that is assumed and the context in which it is assumed.

Interventions that aim to modify behavior sometimes do so by asking clients to assume a new role that may offer opportunities for learning and positive change. This differs from role playing in that rather than simply acting out a role, individuals actually assume a new role (Siegel *et al.*, n.d.). The rationale against using simple role play is that clients may see themselves as merely performing a part, and when they step outside the role, they may also stop the behaviors associated with it. Proponents of a role assumption approach believe that it offers a greater chance for the successful assimilation of new behaviors into a patient's repertoire (Siegel *et al.*, n.d.).

Numerous animal-assisted intervention models appear to fit within this theoretical framework, and to some extent, any program that provides individuals with an opportunity to train or care for animals allows the person to assume the role of teacher or caretaker (Brickel, 1985). Despite the compelling nature of the anecdotes that exist in the literature (Corson *et al.*, 1975; Rochberg-Halton, 1985), no evidence has been offered to suggest that the effects of role assumption are superior to role play, that benefits are long lasting, or that behavioral changes persist beyond the context of the intervention.

IV. SUMMARY AND CONCLUSIONS

Based on what we have presented, it is clear that despite the longevity of the practice of including animals in therapeutic contexts and the unvaryingly positive media attention that animal-assisted interventions receive, the field is still struggling to define itself and gain credibility as a form of complementary medicine. Recent attempts have been made to standardize terminology, but there has, as yet, been no formalized field-wide consensus on a particular set of terms, definitions, and practices. There is, however, some agreement that therapy is distinct from other types of animal-centric activities and is set apart by the involvement of appropriately credentialed health/human services professionals and by the need for formalized treatment plans and goals.

As demonstrated, animal-assisted interventions draw from an impressive variety of disciplines and perspectives (e.g., genetics, biology, developmental psychology, psychoanalytic theory, behaviorism). Theories regarding the mechanisms responsible for therapeutic benefits tend to center on either the notion that animals possess unique attributes that can facilitate and contribute to therapy or the idea that developing a working relationship with an animal can lead to positive changes in cognition and behavior through the acquisition of novel skills and the acceptance of personal agency and responsibility. While impressive in their variety and scope, not a single theory that appears in this chapter has been adequately tested empirically, and most studies have returned equivocal or conflicting results when the necessary testing has been attempted.

To move the field of AAIs forward, studies must begin to focus on and answer some of the most basic research questions. With very few exceptions, the research that has been conducted to date has not been designed or controlled in ways that bring AAIs closer to becoming empirically supported treatments. Study samples have tended to be small, unrepresentative and heterogeneous, and without adequate control groups. In going forward, of utmost importance is the careful definition of the population under examination and what is to be measured, as well as a need for controlled designs and stated outcomes that are relatively impervious to expectancy and demand effects, and to self-report or personal interest biases (for information on developing controlled clinical trials, see the National Center for Complementary and Alternative Medicine, 2004). Additionally, most studies that have examined AAIs have reported on the positive benefits that are observed while in the context of the therapeutic milieu but have not examined whether these effects carry over into other contexts or if they are retained over time. Rigorous efficacy and effectiveness research conducted by individuals trained in clinical research and program evaluation is needed. In the absence of such research, and despite the many potential benefits that have been advanced in the AAI literature, the scientific and medical communities will continue to assume little or no long-term beneficial impact of these interventions.

REFERENCES

Allen, B. P. (2000). "Personality Theories: Development, Growth, and Diversity" (3rd Ed.). Allyn and Bacon, Boston, MA.

American Hippotherapy Association (2005). Frequently asked questions about hippotherapy. Available at http://www.narha.org/PDFFiles/FAQ_Hippotherapy.pdf.

Americans with Disabilities Act of 1990 (1990). Pub. L. No. 101–336, § 2, 104 Stat. 327.

Anderson, W. P., Reid, C. M., and Jennings, G. L. (1992). Pet ownership and risk factors for cardiovascular disease. *Med. J. Aust.* **157**, 298–301.

Bandura, A., Ross, D., and Ross, S. A. (1961). Transmission of aggression through imitation of aggressive models. *J. Abnorm. Soc. Psychol.* **63**, 575–582.

Bardill, N., and Hutchinson, S. (1997). Animal-assisted therapy with hospitalized adolescents. *J. Child. Adolesc. Psychiatr. Nurs.* **10**(1), 17–24.

Bazelon Center for Mental Health Law (n.d.). Fair housing information sheet # 6: Right to emotional support animals in "no pet" housing. Available at http://www.bazelon.org/issues/housing/infosheets/fhinfosheet6.html.

Beck, A. M., and Katcher, A. H. (1984). A new look at pet-facilitated therapy. *J. Am. Vet. Med. Assoc.* **184**(4), 414–421.

Beck, A. M., and Katcher, A. H. (1996). "Between Pets and People: The Importance of Animal Companionship." Purdue University Press, West Lafayette, IN.

Brickel, C. M. (1982). Pet-facilitated psychotherapy: A theoretical explanation via attention shifts. *Psychol. Rep.* **50**, 71–74.

Brickel, C. M. (1985). Initiation and maintenance of the human-animal bond: Familial roles from a learning perspective. *Marriage Family Rev.* **8**(3/4), 31–48.

Brooks, S. (2001). Working with animals in a healing context. *Reaching Today's Youth*, **Winter**, 19–22.

Corson, S. A., Corson, E. O'L., and Gwynne, P. H. (1975). Pet-facilitated psychotherapy. *In* "Pet Animals and Society" (R. S. Anderson, ed.), pp. 19–36. Williams and Wilkins, Baltimore, MD.

Corson, S. A., Corson, E. O'L., Gwynne, P. H., and Arnold, L. E. (1977). Pet dogs as nonverbal communication links in hospital psychiatry. *Comprehen. Psychiat.* **18**(1), 61–72.

Cwik, A. J. (1991). Active imagination as imaginal play-space. *In* "Liminality and Transitional Phenomena" (M. Schwartz-Salant and M. Stein, eds.), pp. 99–114. Chiron, Wilmette, IL.

Delta Society. (n.d.). About animal-assisted activities & animal-assisted therapy. Available at http://www.deltasociety.org/aboutaaat.htm.

DeMello, L. R. (1999). The effect of the presence of a companion-animal on the physiological changes following the termination of cognitive stressors. *Psychol. Health* **14**, 859–868.

EFMHA (2005). EFP efficacy. Available at http://www.narha.org/SecEFMHA/Efficacy.asp

Eddy, J., Hart, L. A., and Boltz, R. P. (2001). The effects of service dogs on social acknowledgments of people in wheelchairs. *J. Psychol.* **122**(1), 39–45.

Enders-Slegers, M.-J. (2000). The meaning of companion animals: Qualitative analysis of the life histories of elderly cat and dog owners. *In* "Companion Animals and Us: Exploring the Relationships between People and Pets" (A. L. Podberscek, E. S. Paul, and J. A. Serpell, eds.), pp. 237–256. Cambridge University Press, Cambridge.

Equine Facilitated Mental Health Association (EFMHA). (2003). What is equine facilitated psychotherapy (EFP)? Available at http://www.narha.org/sec_efmha/default.asp.

Fine, A. H. (2000). Animals and therapists: Incorporating animals in outpatient psychotherapy. *In* "Handbook on Animal-Assisted Therapy: Theoretical Foundations and Guidelines for Practice" (A. H. Fine, ed.), pp. 179–211. Academic Press, New York.

Friedmann, E., Katcher, A. H., Lynch, J. J., and Thomas, S. A. (1980). Animal companions and one-year survival of patients after discharge from a coronary care unit. *Public Health Rep.* **95**, 307–312.

Friedmann, E., Katcher, A. H., Thomas, S. A., Lynch, J. J., and Messent, P. R. (1983). Social interaction and blood pressure. *J. Nerv. Mental Dis.* **171**(8), 461–465.

Freidmann, E., Thomas, S. A., and Eddy, T. J. (2000). Companion animals and human health: Physical and cardiovascular influences. *In* "Companion Animals and Us: Exploring the

Relationships between People and Pets" (A. L. Podberscek, E. S. Paul, and J. A. Serpell, eds.), pp. 125–142. Cambridge University Press, Cambridge.

Grubb, D. (2002). CODA, Coalition of Assistance Dog Partners. Available at http://www.gdui.org/cado.html.

Gullone, E. (2000). The biophilia hypothesis and life in the 21st century: Increasing mental health or increasing pathology? *J. Happ. Stud.* **1**, 293–321.

Hansen, K. M., Messinger, C. J., Baun, M. M., and Megel, M. (1999). Companion animals alleviating distress in children. *Anthrozoös* **12**(3), 142–148.

Harbolt, T., and Ward, T. H. (2001). Teaming incarcerated youth with shelter dogs for a second chance. *Soc. Anim.* **9**(2), 177–182.

Kahn, P. H. (1997). Developmental psychology and the biophilia hypothesis: Children's affiliation with nature. *Dev. Rev.* **17**, 1–61.

Kale, M. (1992). At risk: Working with animals to create a new self-image. *InterActions* **10**(4), 6–9.

Katcher, A. H. (1983). Man and the living environment: An excursion into cyclical time. *In* "New Perspectives on Our Lives with Companion Animals" (A. H. Katcher and A. M. Beck, eds.), pp. 519–531. University of Pennsylvania Press, Philadelphia, PA.

Katcher, A. H., Friedmann, E., Beck, A. M., and Lynch, J. J. (1983). Looking, talking and blood pressure: The physiological consequences of interaction with the living environment. *In* "New Perspectives on Our Lives with Companion Animals" (A. H. Katcher and A. M. Beck, eds.), pp. 351–359. University of Pennsylvania Press, Philadelphia, PA.

Katcher, A. H. (2000). The future of education and research on the animal-human bond and animal-assisted therapy. Part B: Animal-assisted therapy and the study of human–animal relationships: Discipline or bondage? Context or transitional object? *In* "Handbook on Animal-Assisted Therapy: Theoretical Foundations and Guidelines for Practice" (A. H. Fine, ed.), pp. 461–473. Academic Press, New York.

Katcher, A., and Wilkins, G. G. (1998). Animal-assisted therapy in the treatment of disruptive behavior disorders in children. *In* "The Environment and Mental Health" (A. Lundberg, ed.), pp. 193–204. Lawrence Erlbaum, Mahwah, NJ.

Kogan, L. R., Granger, B. P., Fitchett, J. A., Helmer, K. A., and Young, K. J. (1999). The human-animal team approach for children with emotional disorders: Two case studies. *Child Youth Care Forum* **28**(2), 105–121.

Kruger, K., Trachtenberg, S., and Serpell, J. A. (2004). Can animals help humans heal? Animal-assisted interventions in adolescent mental health. Available at http://www2.vet.upenn.edu/research/centers/cias/pdf/CIAS_AAI_white_paper.pdf.

LaJoie, K. R. (2003). "An Evaluation of the Effectiveness of Using Animals in Therapy." Unpublished doctoral dissertation, Spalding University, Louisville, KY.

Lapp, S. A., and Scruby, L. (1982). Responsible pet relationships: A mental health perspective. *Health Values: Achieving High Level Wellness* **6**(1), July–August, 20–25.

Levinson, B. (1970). Pets, child development, and mental illness. *J. Am. Vet. Med. Assoc.* **157**(11), 1759–1766.

Levinson, B. M. (1969). "Pet-Oriented Child Psychotherapy." Charles C Thomas, Springfield, IL.

Levinson, B. M. (1978). Pets and personality development. *Psychol. Rep.* **42**, 1031–1038.

Levinson, B. M. (1984). Human/companion animal therapy. *J. Contemp. Psychother.* **14**, 131–144.

Lockwood, R. (1983). The influence of animals on social perception. *In* "New Perspectives on Our Lives with Companion Animals" (A. H. Katcher and A. M. Beck, eds.), pp. 64–71. University of Pennsylvania Press, Philadelphia, PA.

Mader, B., Hart, L. A., and Bergin, B. (1989). Social acknowledgments for children with disabilities: Effects of service dogs. *Child Dev.* **60**, 1529–1534.

Mallon, G. P. (1994a). Cow as co-therapist: Utilization of farm animals as therapeutic aides with children in residential treatment. *Child Adolesc. Soc. Work J.*, **11**(6), 455–474.

Mallon, G. P. (1994b). Some of our best therapists are dogs. *Child Youth Care Forum* **23**(2), 89–101.

Maslow, A. H. (1970). "Motivation and Personality," 2nd Ed. Harper Row, New York.

Mason, M. S., and Hagan, C. B. (1999). Pet-assisted psychotherapy. *Psychol. Rep.* **84**, 1235–1245.

Melson, G. F. (2001). "Why the Wild Things Are: Animals in the Lives of Children." Harvard University Press, Cambridge, MA.

Messent, P. R. (1983). Social facilitation of contact with other people by pet dogs. *In* "New Perspectives on Our Lives with Companion Animals" (A. H. Katcher and A. M. Beck, eds.), pp. 37–46. University of Pennsylvania Press, Philadelphia, PA.

Nagengast, S. L., Baun, M. M., Megel, M., and Leibowitz, J. M. (1997). The effects of the presence of a companion animal on physiological arousal and behavioral distress in children during a physical examination. *J. Pediatr. Nurs.* **12**(6), 323–330.

National Center for Complementary and Alternative Medicine (NCCAM). (2004). Applying for NCCAM Clinical Trials Grants: Points to Consider. Available at http://nccam.nih.gov/research/instructions/poc.htm.

Nebbe, L. L. (1991). The human-animal bond and the elementary school counselor. *School Counsel.* **38**(5), 362–371.

Newman, B. M., and Newman, P. R. (1995). "Development Through Life: A Psychosocial Approach," 6th Ed. Brooks/Cole, New York.

Odendaal, J. S. J., and Lehmann, S. M. C. (2000). The role of phenylethylamine during positive human-dog interaction. *Acta Vet. Brno.* **69**, 183–188.

"Oxford English Dictionary" (2nd Ed.) (1997). Oxford University Press.

Psychiatric Service Dog Society, (2003). Psychiatric Service Dog Tasks. Available at http://www.psychdog.org/tasks.html.

Reichert, E. (1998). Individual counseling for sexually abused children: A role for animals and storytelling. *Child Adolesc. Soc. Work J.* **15**(3), 177–185.

Reimer, D. F. (1999). "Pet-Facilitated Therapy: An Initial Exploration of the Thinking and Theory behind an Innovative Intervention for Children in Psychotherapy." Unpublished doctoral dissertation, Massachusetts School of Professional Psychology, Boston, MA.

Rice, S. S., Brown, L. T., and Caldwell, H. S. (1973). Animals and psychotherapy: A survey. *J. Commun. Psychol.* **1**, 323–326.

Rochberg-Halton, E. (1985). Life in the Treehouse: Pet therapy as family metaphor and self-dialogue. *Marriage Family Rev.* **8**(3–4), 175–189.

Rossbach, K. A., and Wilson, J. P. (1992). Does a dog's presence make a person appear more likable? Two studies. *Anthrozoös* **5**(1), 40–51.

Serpell, J. A. (1996). "In the Company of Animals: A Study of Human-Animal Relationships" (Canto, ed.). Cambridge University Press, Cambridge.

Serpell, J. A. (2000). Creatures of the unconscious: Companion animals as mediators. *In* "Companion Animals and Us: Exploring the Relationships between People and Pets" (A. L. Podberscek, E. S. Paul, and J. A. Serpell, eds.), pp. 108–121. Cambridge University Press, Cambridge.

Serpell, J. A. (2004). Factors influencing human attitudes to animals and their welfare. *Anim. Welf.* **13**(Suppl.), 145–152.

Siegel, W. L., Murdock, J. Y., and Colley, A. D. (n.d.). "Learning to Train Dogs Reduces Noncompliant/Aggressive Classroom Behaviors of Students with Behavior Disorders." Unpublished manuscript.

Taylor, S. M. (2001). "Equine Facilitated Psychotherapy: An Emerging Field." Unpublished master's thesis, Saint Michael's College, Colchester, VT.

Triebenbacher, S. L. (1998). Pets as transitional objects: Their role in children's emotional development. *Psychol. Rep.* **82**, 191–200.

United States Department of Justice (1996). Commonly asked questions about service animals in places of business. Available at http://www.usdoj.gov/crt/ada/qasrvc.htm.

Vidrine, M., Owen-Smith, P., & Faulkner, P. (2002). Equine-facilitated group psychotherapy: Applications for therapeutic vaulting. *Issues Ment. Health Nurs.* **23**, 587–603.

Weiss, R. S. (1974). The provision of social relationships. *In* "Doing unto Others" (Z. Rubin, ed.), pp. 17–26. Prentice Hall, Engelwood Cliffs, NJ.

Wells, E. S., Rosen, L. W., and Walshaw, S. (1997). Use of feral cats in psychotherapy. *Anthrozoös* **10**(2/3), 125–130.

Wells, M., and Perrine, R. (2001). Pets go to college: The influence of pets on students' perceptions of faculty and their offices. *Anthrozoös* **14**(3), 161–167.

Wilson, C. C. (1991). The pet as anxiolytic intervention. *J. Nerv. Ment. Dis.* **179**(8), 482–489.

Wilson, E. O. (1984). "Biophilia." Harvard University Press. Cambridge, MA.

Winnicott, D. W. (1951). Transitional objects and transitional phenomena. *In* "Playing and Reality" (D. W. Winnicott, ed.), pp. 1–25. Basic Books, New York.

CHAPTER 3

New and Old Perspectives on the Therapeutic Effects of Animals and Nature

AARON H. KATCHER AND ALAN M. BECK
Animal Therapy Association and the Center for the Human–Animal Bond, Purdue University, West Lafayette, Indiana 47907

Before the 20th century, human medicine treated diseases with a pharmacopoeia pieced together from personal experience, professionally accumulated lore, and custom. A physician's actions were based on whim, intuition, received wisdom, or personal experience, not governed by professional or scientific consensus. Now the medical profession is heading toward evidence-based medicine (Daly, 2005; Eddy, 2005), which is dependent on the explicit and judicious use of current best evidence in making decisions about patient care; i.e., the application of the scientific method to medical practice based on a foundation of critical studies testing the efficacy of individual treatments and combinations of treatments. Psychiatry, with some resistance from the pharmaceutical industry, is also moving in the same direction (Jensen *et al.*, 2005; March *et al.*, 2005). Animal-assisted therapy (AAT) is a volunteer activity that has marginal acceptance based on the almost universal fondness for cute animals and a general belief that animals and nature are among life's good things. If AAT is to gain acceptance as a legitimate treatment modality, much more information will have to be forthcoming. The purpose of this chapter is to outline strategies for acquiring the information necessary to ground AAT in reliable evidence so that it might have a place in clinical medicine. The authors decided to adopt this approach because there has not been any critical evidence published that would necessitate a revision of the conclusions of other articles on the subject (Beck, 2000; Beck and Katcher, 1984, 2003) or those of other researchers (Wilson and Barker, 2003).

The first requirement for establishing AAT as an evidence-based therapeutic modality is having the evidence. Unfortunately, the field from its inception has relied on individual case reports, poorly designed studies, "pilot" investigations, studies published in books and proceedings volumes, and even self-published studies in book form (Beck and Katcher, 1984). This kind of publication protects papers from the stringent review afforded by refereed journals. Two of the most famous papers in the field are the budgie study (Mugford and M'Comisky, 1975), in which the number of subjects was too small to permit statistical analysis, and the original self-published evidence in support of the "Eden alternative" (Thomas, 1994), in which the evidence consisted of four graphs with no indication of the number of subjects and no statistical analysis. There is a general impression that "Edenizing" a nursing home lessens medication usage, and most observers believe it is a better alternative to the general nursing home facility (Thomas, 1996). In the years since Levinson's (1969) initial review of the state of the field, two specialty journals have appeared to give authors a venue for publication, but the preponderance of citations in AAT papers from these two journals, *Anthrozoös* and *Society and Animals,* still speaks to the failure of authors to find a home for their studies in the journals that influence clinicians in the fields of psychology, psychiatry, nursing, social work, and education. Most articles about human–animal interactions published in more traditional medical journals have been, by and large, studies of the relationship between pet ownership and human health or review articles (e.g., Friedmann *et al.*, 2003; Ulrich, 1984; Walter-Toews, 1993).

Evidence-based medicine rests on firm pillars of epidemiological evidence and controlled studies testing the interventions suggested by the epidemiological investigations. We would not be advocating lowering of blood lipids, cessation of cigarette smoking, exercise regimens, or the Mediterranean diet if there were not unequivocal longitudinal and cross-sectional (synchronic) studies suggesting a strong relationship among cholesterol, cigarette smoking, exercise, and diet and coronary artery disease. Equally strong studies suggest that lowering cholesterol, exercising, and smoking cessation reduce risk from that disease. Epidemiological evidence for a relationship between pet ownership and overall health, or specific disease incidence, is at best inconsistent (Friedmann, 2000). The literature on pets and health contrasts with the much larger body of evidence that relates social support to health (Ross, 2005; Subramanian *et al.*, 2005; Wilkinson and Marmot, 2003). In fact, one may conclude that cat ownership does not improve health and may even be detrimental (Friedmann, 2000; Friedmann and Thomas, 1995; Rajack, 1997).

What is needed at this juncture, even before contemplating the difficulty of clinical trials in this area, is a firm foundation for predicting positive health benefits from pet ownership. Published results are generally positive, but often only one kind of human–animal relationship is considered. At the present level of our knowledge, we have to entertain the notion that some kinds of pets, cats, for example, may be significantly less beneficial than dogs (Headey, 1999; Siegel, 1990) or even have detrimental effects. In many cases, dogs alone may be important to the intervention by stimulating walking (Bauman *et al.*, 2001; Messent, 1983) or improved social interaction with others (McNicholas and Collis, 2000; Wells, 2004). The impact of animal contact can be different for male and female owners (Miller *et al.*, 1992) or be especially important for a specific age group, as dog and cat contact early in one's life protects a person from allergy in the future (Ownby *et al.*, 2002). Indeed, it may be useful to distinguish the value of animal contact apart from the benefits of human–human contact, which has pronounced and well documented effects. (Lynch, 2000; Schone and Weinick, 1998). Once such epidemiological evidence is at hand, it would be possible to make specific recommendations for the therapeutic placement of pets. However, there is a peculiar problem with framing therapeutic interventions with pets that should be recognized.

Evidence-based medicine is absolutely dependent on random assignment therapeutic trials for its factual base. The trials need not be double blind; obviously a study of diet or exercise cannot be a double-blind trial. Animal contact, as an experimental variable, can be compared to a comparable control variable, such as music (Voith *et al.*, 1984). However, there are some circumstances in which random assignment intervention trials present real difficulty. It is universally recognized that church attendance, even when other variables are controlled for, is positively associated with better health (Ferraro and Albrecht-Jensen, 1991). The effect is not trivial and is much more consistent than the evidence for the relationship between pet ownership and health. However, having that information, it is difficult to frame a recommendation for a therapeutic study. Do you assign people to attend church and compare them with people who read the *New York Times* on a Sunday morning? Is it possible to assign people to attend church and expect the same effects as you have in people who attend by conviction (or their spouse's conviction)? Attempts to randomize prayer could not find any impact on health, although other neotic (intuitively useful but not easily assessable) therapies such as music, imagery, and touch did have some effects (Krucoff *et al.*, 2005). Problems arise when a therapeutic effect is potentially dependent on a social relationship. For someone attending church, a social relationship exists between a person and *both* God and the congregation. For the pet owner, a social relationship exists between the owner and the pet and also the people who relate to the owner through the pet. Can such social links be created by assignment?

Moreover, studies of pet ownership and health introduce an added moral complexity to therapeutic trials. What kind of responsibility does the experimenter have to the animal used in study? At the very least the experimental team must monitor the health and well-being of the animal and the tensions, if any, the animal creates in the host family for the duration of the study. The team should also consider if it is incumbent upon them to remove the pet from the adoptive home if its welfare is in danger. Unfortunately, that places the investigators in an ethical dilemma. They are interested in completing the study, and ending the participation of a study member by removing the pet threatens the integrity of the study. Without some neutral arbiter, the pet's welfare cannot be assured.

Although dogs are a major focus of people in the field—perhaps because of their own attachments (see later) or because support for studies often comes from the pet industry and dogs contribute disproportionately to that industry's income—consideration should be given to other, less demanding animals in the absence of clear indications of a clear therapeutic advantage of dogs. In studies with children, fish, amphibians, reptiles, and small mammals elicited positive emotional responses and active caregiving responses and signs of bonding from children and adolescents (Katcher and Teumer, 2006; Katcher and Wilkins, 2000). Many of these animals are contained in cages and make less social demands on their caregivers than animals such as dogs and horses.

In other studies, having animals as a focus of interest can improve family dynamics. Parents who were given a bird feeder and an initial supply of birdseed identified family involvement as a particularly beneficial aspect of the program, and 90% of contacted families were still feeding birds 1 year after program termination (Beck *et al.*, 2001). In general, children frequently turn to their pets as a way of mitigating life's stress, such as starting school for the first time (Melson *et al.*, 1997). Alzheimer's disease patients who are often too agitated to eat properly are less agitated in a room with a fish tank, gain more weight, and even express fewer disruptive behaviors when fish tanks are placed in the dining area (Edwards and Beck, 2002).

There is even reason to propose the use of robotic animals, either as a control experience or as the experimental intervention (Kimura *et al.*, 2005; Melson *et al.*, 2005; Yokoyama, 2005). There are none of the moral concerns attendant to placement of a live animal. Problems introduced by virtue of personality differences between breeds of dogs do not arise, and the robotic animal does not place any demands on family resources (i.e., cost of food, time needed to exercise pet, trouble in cleaning up, and effects of noise). The use of such robotic animals will be dependent on obtaining data about the duration of interest shown by owners, frequency of interaction, and measures of interaction that go beyond the subject's recollected account (i.e., electronic modification of the robot to determine the frequency and duration of use). Robotic animals would also be useful in determining the limits of the human tendency to project individuality, personality, and emotional attachment onto animals (Shioya *et al.*, 2005).

The second large area of activity that is subsumed under AAT is the direct use of an animal as a therapeutic tool in a patient encounter. These interactions are relatively brief in duration, they are guided by the therapist, and the client does not take permanent possession or responsibility for the animal. AAT as practiced now is not conceptualized as primary therapy (Beck and Katcher, 1996). There are no studies in which all medications are stopped and the patient is treated only with AAT and the control group given a placebo. AAT is by nature a kind of auxiliary therapy akin to art, horticultural, dance, and occupational therapies. However, AAT is a bit more peculiar than art or dance therapy. No one would teach only pottery in occupational therapy or Balinese shadow dancing in dance therapy. Yet it is the convention of AAT therapists to work only with the animals to which they are strongly bonded. Most therapists work only with their own animals. This bonding between therapists and their pets (Katcher, 2000) creates problems not only because of the issue of bias but also because choosing the best animal for a patient involves changing therapists, and there is no body of professionals who can speak to the relative merits of different kinds of animals or (see earlier discussion) animal surrogates.

Sometimes intellectual clarity can be obtained by a kind of a thought experiment. We would like to have the reader imagine two pentagonal buildings a hundred yards away from each other. One has a series of rooms built about a central court with outward facing windows that overlook an encircling ring of trees, shrubs, and lawn, as well as windows looking into the central court, which is illuminated by a skylight and has a fountain with a pool inhabited by brightly colored koi (*Cyprinus carpio*). Each of the rooms is equipped to have a different kind of experience with animals. One is a large space that can be used for agility trials in dogs or even exotic beasts such as llamas. Another contains a collection of smaller animals in cages that can be tended, played with, and used as a stimulus for learning. A third might be a large aviary with provision for tending plants as well. Other rooms are smaller and can be used for intense work with a single animal or play with a robotic animal of some sort.

The other building has no outer windows, but where the windows would be, large liquid crystal screens display continually changing images of colorful geometrical shapes. There are windows that face onto the central court, but the court, brightly illuminated as well, contains a number of sculptures of intricate inorganic shapes. Within the rooms there would be activities such as are usually part of occupational therapy: painting and working with other media, music, and dance.

With those two facilities at the disposal of a research group, it would be possible to randomly assign children to a type of conventional auxiliary therapy such as occupational therapy, art, dance, or music as the control experience, and some form of AAT as the experimental therapy. The experimental therapy could be chosen by the diagnostic team and would not be a therapist specializing in whatever animal that claims his/her affections. Observers could be chosen who are not recruited from the ranks of animal enthusiasts and hence do not have an obvious bias.

Obviously, this perfect design is not possible, but it is good to have an idea of what would be ideal. Now the challenge is to design studies that more closely approximate the ideal than what we do now. Knowing what the perfect study could contain helps identify the failings and possible confounders, which then can be somewhat mitigated with a variety of design tools, such as controls, stratification, pilot studies, and sample size.

The focus of this volume and most of the writings in the field on animals and nature as therapy misses the most salient questions at this time in our history, culture, and social organization. Those questions revolve around what the effects are of subtracting nature and contact with animals from our experience as children and adults in industrialized societies. Indeed, the same questions could be asked about the huge increase in urban growth in the nonindustrialized world as well. As late as 1910, more than half the population of the United States was found in farms. With the advent of the automobile and the decline in the family farm in favor of industrial farming, as well as the progressive usurpation of farm land by suburban growth, animals and uncultivated open spaces moved farther and farther from our daily lives. As late as 50 years ago, live animals were found in butcher shops and fish markets displayed whole fish. Now children never see an intact animal displayed in shops either dead or alive.

There is a long history documenting the importance of contact with nature for all (Ulrich, 1993) and the special roles of nature for children (Kahn, 1999; Kahn and Kellert, 2002; Melson, 2001; Rud and Beck, 2003). However, with the advent of television and then video games and the increasing anxiety about dangers to children if their play is unsupervised, fewer and fewer children are spending time out of doors, exploring nature, and placing themselves in a position to see wild animals firsthand (Louv, 2005). Organized sports are just that, "organized," and the children are ferried to play on sterile greens where vigorous mowing and poisoning hold nature back. This secular trend toward decreasing experience with nature, and decreasing time spent out of doors, has gone along with increasing rates of ADHD (Kuo and Taylor, 2004), juvenile obesity, and childhood type 2 diabetes (Haslam and James, 2005) as more and more children spend less and less time out of doors. In a more metaphorical sense, both children and adults have developed a decreasing capacity to pay attention to what is out there in the real world and are increasingly locked into a virtual world of television, computers, computer games, ipods, and cellular telephones that draws the person away from direct interaction with their world.

We desperately need to know what the effects of the subtraction of nature and nature-directed activity have been in the lives of our children. If there is any general conclusion that we can carry away from what we know about AAT and the effects of animals on health and mental state, it is that these effects may be large, especially in people who are vulnerable by virtue of a predisposing genetic or environmentally acquired constitution. The importance of knowing the harm this great subtraction has accomplished outweighs the understanding of artificial contact such as occurs between patient and therapist or volunteer in AAT and the clinical significance of any limited contact between patients and AAT practitioners.

What follows is a list of questions that have considerable value in setting an agenda for human–animal relationship research.

- How much of the rapid growth of children diagnosed with ADHD and children in special education has to do with the increasing lack of experience with animals and nature as well as decreased opportunity for physical activity?
- How much of the increasing difficulty that boys experience in completing high school and college stems from unmet needs for activity and contact with animals and nature?
- How could contact with nature and animals be used to reform our present method of schooling in which learning and physical inactivity are so strongly linked?
- How does the lack of experience with animals and nature affect our capacity for language, narration, and metaphor?
- How do human and animal companionship interrelate: Are they additive, competitive, or both? When can one substitute for the other, and when can it not?
- What changes in our social structure can bring about a greater interaction between people and nature if it is found that lack of such interaction has detrimental effects?

These are just some of the questions that can be asked, but they all focus on the larger problem: the decreasing level of contact with nature and animals in our society. They are also aimed at what mechanisms can be instated to create a sustained relationship between animals and people, not a temporary clinical relationship based on a perhaps misapplied medical model for what is really a societal problem.

REFERENCES

Bauman, A. E., Russell, S. J., Furber, S. E., and Dobson, A. J. (2001). The epidemiology of dog walking: An unmet need for human and canine health. *Med. J. Aust.* **175**(11–12), 632–634.

Beck, A. M. (2000). The use of animals to benefit humans, animal-assisted therapy. *In* "Handbook on Animal-Assisted Therapy: Theoretical Foundations and Guidelines for Practice" (A. H. Fine, ed.), pp. 21–40. Academic Press, New York.

Beck, A. M., and Katcher, A. H. (1984). A new look at pet-facilitated therapy. *J. Am. Vet. Med. Assoc.* **184**, 414–421.

Beck, A. M., and Katcher, A. H. (1996). "Between Pets and People: The Importance of Animal Companionship." Purdue University Press, West Lafayette, IN.

Beck, A. M., and Katcher, A. H. (2003). Future directions in human-animal bond research. *Am. Behav. Sci.* **47**(1), 79–93.

Beck, A. M., Melson, G. F., da Costa, P. L., and Liu, T. (2001). The educational benefits of a ten-week home-based wild bird feeding program for children. *Anthrozoös* **14**, 19–28.

Daly, J. (2005). "Evidence-Based Medicine and the Search for a Science of Clinical Care." California, Milbank Books on Health and the Public.

Eddy, D. M. (2005). Evidence-based medicine: A unified approach. *Health Affairs* **24**, 9–17.

Edwards, N. E., and Beck, A. M. (2002). Animal-assisted therapy and nutrition in Alzheimer's disease. *West. J. Nurs. Res.* **24**, 697–712.

Ferraro, K. F., and Albrecht-Jensen, C. M. (1991). Does religion influence adult health? *J. Sci. Study Religion* **30**(2), 193–202.

Friedmann, E. (2000). The animal–human bond: Health and wellness. *In* "Handbook on Animal-Assisted Therapy: Theoretical Foundations and Guidelines for Practice" (A. H. Fine, ed.), pp. 41–58. Academic Press, New York.

Friedmann, E., and Thomas, S. A. (1995). Pet ownership, social support, and one-year survival after acute myocardial infarction in the Cardiac Arrhythmia Suppression Trial (CAST). *Am. J. Cardiol.* **76**, 1213–1217.

Friedmann, E., Thomas, S. A., Stein, P. K., and Kleiger, R. E. (2003). Relation between pet ownership and heart rate variability in patients with healed myocardial infarcts, *Am. J. Cardiol.* **91**, 718–721.

Giles, L. C., Glanek, G. F. W., Luszcz, M. A., and Andrews, G. R. (2005). Effect of social networks on 10 year survival in very old Australians: The Australian longitudinal study of aging. *J. Epidemiol. Commun. Health* **59**, 574–579.

Haslam, D. W., and James, W. P. T. (2005). Obesity. *Lancet* **366**, 1197–1206.

Headey, B. (1999). Health benefits and health costs savings due to pets: Preliminary estimates from an Australian national survey. *Soc. Indicat. Res.* **47**, 233–243.

Jensen, P. S., Garcia, J. A., Glied, S., Crowe, M., Foster, M., Schlander, M., Hinshaw, S., Vitiello, B., Arnold, L. E., Elliott, G., Hechtman, L., Newcorn, J. H., Pelham, W. E., Swanson, J., and Wells, K. (2005). Cost-effectiveness of ADHD treatments: Findings from the multimodal treatment study of children with ADHD. *Am. J. Psychiatr.* **162**, 1628–1636.

Kahn, P. H., Jr. (1999). "The Human Relationship with Nature: Development qnd Culture." MIT Press, Cambridge, MA.

Kahn, P. H., Jr., and Kellert, S. (2002). "Children and Nature: Psychological, Sociocultural and Evolutionary Investigation." MIT Press, Cambridge, MA.

Katcher, A. H., and Teumer, S. P. (2006). A 4-year trial of animal-assisted therapy with public school special education students. *In* "Handbook on Animal-Assisted Therapy: Theoretical Foundations and Guidelines for Practice" (A. H. Fine, ed.). Elsevier (this volume).

Katcher, A. H., and Teumer, S. P. (2006). Conducting an AAT program for children and adolescents in special education in public schools: Reality and expectancy. Manuscript in preparation.

Katcher, A. H., and Wilkins, G. G. (2000). The Centaur's lessons: Therapeutic education through care of animals and nature study. *In* "Handbook on Animal-Assisted Therapy: Theoretical Foundations and Guidelines for Practice" (A. H. Fine, ed.), pp. 153–177. Academic Press, New York.

Katcher, A. H., Friedmann, E, Beck, A. M., and Lynch, J. J. (1983). Looking, talking and blood pressure: the physiological consequences of interaction with the living environment. *In* "New Perspectives on Our Lives with Companion Animals" (A. H. Katcher and A. M. Beck, eds.), pp. 351–359. University of Pennsylvania Press, Philadelphia, PA.

Kimura, R., Sugiyama, Y., Ohkubo, E., Naganuma, M., Hiruma, K., Horiguchi, A., Abe, N., Hatano, E., Suzuki, K., Sekine, K., Akiko Hiranuma, A., and Yamanouchi, K. (2005). Child and pet-robot interaction in children's hospital (1) theoretical issues and procedure. SICE Annual Conference. Okayama, August 8–10, 2005 Okayama University, Japan.

Krucoff, M. W., Crater, S. W., Gallup, D., Blankenship, J. C., Cuffe, M., Guarneri, M., Krieger, R. A., Kshettry, V. R., Morris, K. Oz, M., Pichard, A., Sketch, Jr., M. H., Koenig, H. G., Mark, D., and Lee, K. L. (2005). Music, imagery, touch, and prayer as adjuncts to interventional cardiac care: the monitoring and actualization of neotic trainings (MANTRA) II randomized study. *Lancet* **366**, 211–217.

Kuo, F. E., and Taylor, A. F. (2004). A potential natural treatment for attention-deficit/hyperactivity disorder: Evidence from a national study. *Am. J. Public Health* **94**, 1581–1586.

Levinson, B. M. (1969). "Pet-Oriented Child Psychotherapy." Charles C Thomas, Springfield, IL.

Louv, R. (2005). "Last Child in the Woods: Saving Our Children from Nature—Deficit Disorder." Algonguin Books, Chapel Hill, NC.

Lynch, J. J. (2000). "A Cry Unheard: New Insights into the Medical Consequences of Loneliness." Bancroft Press, Baltimore, MD.

March, J. S., Silva, S. G., Compton, S., Shapiro, M., Califf, R., and Krishnan, R. (2005). The case for practical clinical trials in psychiatry. *Am. J. Psychiatr.* **162**, 836–846.

McNicholas, J., and Collis, G. M. (2000). Dogs as catalysts for social interactions: Robustness of the effect. *Br. J. Psychol.* **91**, 61–70.

Melson, G. F. (2001). "Why the Wild Things Are: Animals in the Lives of Children." Harvard University Press, Cambridge, MA.

Melson, G. F., Kahn, P. H., Jr., Beck, A. M., Friedman, B., Roberts, T., and Garrett, E. (2005). Robots as dogs? Children's interactions with the robotic dog AIBO and a live Australian Shepherd. *In* "Extended Abstracts of CHI 2005." ACM Press, New York.

Melson, G. F., Schwarz, R. L., and Beck, A. M. (1997). Importance of companion animals in children's lives: Implications for veterinary practice. *JAVMA* **211**, 1512–1518.

Messent, P. R. (1983). Social facilitation of contact with other people by pet dogs. *In* "New Perspectives on Our Lives with Companion Animals" (A. H. Katcher and A. M. Beck, eds.), pp. 37–46. University of Pennsylvania Press, Philadelphia.

Miller, D., Staats, S., and Partlo, C. (1992). Discriminating positive and negative aspects of pet interaction: Sex differences in the older population. *Soc. Indicat. Res.* **27**, 363–374.

Mugford, R. A., and M'Comisky, J. G. (1975). Some recent work on the psychotherapeutic value of cage birds with old people. *In* "Pet Animals and Society" (R. S. Anderson, ed.), pp. 54–65. Baillière Tindall, London.

Ownby, D. R., Johnson, C. C., and Peterson, E. L. (2002). Exposure to dogs and cats during the first year of life and the risk of allergic sensitivity at six to seven years of age. *J. Am. Med. Assoc.* **288**, 963–972.

Rajack, L. S. (1997). "Pets and Human Health: The Influence of Pets on Cardiovascular and Other Aspects of Owners' Health." Doctoral dissertation, University of Cambridge.

Ross, N. (2005). Health, happiness, and higher levels of social organization. *J. Epidemiol. Commun. Health* **59**, 614.

Rud, A. G., Jr., and Beck. A. M. (2003). Companion animals in Indiana elementary schools. *Anthrozoös* **16**, 241–251.

Schone, B. S., and Weinick, R. M. (1998). Health-related behaviors and the benefits of marriage for elderly persons. *Gerontologist* **38**, 618–627.

Shioya, M., Ohkubo, E., Sasaki, T., Kimura, R., and Naganuma, M. (2005). Evaluation of temporal change of patient concentration during robot assisted activity by means of eye contact analysis. SICE Annual Conference. Okayama, August 8–10, 2005. Okayama University, Japan.

Siegel, J. M. (1990). Stressful life events and use of physician services among the elderly: The moderating role of per ownership. *J. Personal. Soc. Psychol.* **58**, 1081–1086.

Subramanian, S. V., Kim, D., and Kawachi, I. (2005). Covariation in the socioeconomic determinants of self rated health and happiness: A multivariate multilevel analysis of individuals and communities in the USA. *J. Epidemial. Commun. Health* **59**, 664–669.

Thomas, W. H. (1994). "The Eden Alternative: Nature, Hope and Nursing Homes." Eden Alternative Foundation, Sherburne, NY.

Thomas, W. H. (1996). "Life Worth Living: The Eden Alternative in Action." VanderWyk & Burnham, Acton, MA.

Ulrich, R. S. (1984). View through a window may influence recovery from surgery. *Science* **224**, 420–421.

Ulrich, R. S. (1993). Biophilia, biophobia, and natural landscapes. *In* "The Biophilia Hypothesis" (S. R. Kellert and E. O. Wilson, eds.), pp. 73–137. Island Press, Washington, DC.

Voith, V. L., Glickman, L. T., Smith, S., Hamilton, G., Ryer, E., Shofer, F., Lung, N., and Griffith, L. (1984). "Comparison of the Effects of Companion Animals and Music on Nursing Home Residents: A Controlled Intervention Study." American Veterinary Medical Association, Schaumburg, IL.

Walter-Toews, D. (1993). Zoonotic disease concerns in animal assisted therapy and animal visitation programs. *Can. Vet. J.* **34**, 549–551.

Wells, D. L. (2004). The facilitation of social interactions by domestic dogs. *Anthrozoös* **17**, 340–352.

Wilkinson, R., and Marnot, M. (2003). "Social Determinants of Health: The Solid Facts," 2nd Ed. WHO Publications, Copenhagen.

Wilson, C., and Barker, S. (2003). Challenges in designing human-animal interaction research. *Am. Behav. Sci.* 47(1), 16–28.

Yokoyama, A. (2005). The trial of RAA/RAT in the clean room at the pediatrics ward. SICE Annual Conference. Okayama, August 8–10, 2005 Okayama University, Japan.

CHAPTER 4

Animals as Social Supports: Insights for Understanding Animal-Assisted Therapy

JUNE MCNICHOLAS
Croit Cullach, 4 Durnamuck, Dundonell, Ross-shire, IV23 2QZ, Scotland, United Kingdom

GLYN M. COLLIS
Hawthorn Park, Rothesay, Isle of Bute, PA20 0BA, United Kingdom

Research into the benefits of "animal-assisted therapy" has seen considerable growth over recent years and has gained interest and recognition among many health professionals. However, much less research has centered on examining the mechanisms underlying why or how animal-assisted therapy may be effective. This chapter examines the concept of *social support* as a major factor in successful programs of animal-assisted therapy. Empirical evidence for the presence of supportive functions derived from pet animals is presented.

I. WHAT IS SOCIAL SUPPORT?

Social support is a generic term covering a variety of positive acts, interpersonal transactions, and social provisions that arise from social relationships and which are widely accepted to enhance human health and well-being.

House and colleagues (1988) distinguished between aspects of relationships at the structural and functional levels using the following scheme.

a. The existence of an identifiable social network that may be made up of a variety of relationship types but which gives a sense of embeddedness in

Handbook on Animal-Assisted Therapy: Theoretical Foundations and Guidelines for Practice, 2e

a community or network and acts against feelings of loneliness and isolation.

b. The nature of the composition of a social network—how it is made up of family members, friends, and acquaintances, and the duration of these relationships—influences people's self-identity and roles played within a network and expectations of others' behavior toward them.

c. The functional content of relationships and how relationships may provide costs and/or benefits. Functional content may be characterized by provisions of help, intimacy, social support, companionship, or conflict and demands placed by particular relationships.

Whereas the first two aspects of relationships are primarily structural and the third functional, each of these has attracted research into how relationships may influence health. At the level of the existence of a social network, absence of an adequate identifiable network is equated with loneliness and isolation. Loneliness is associated with higher risk of physical and psychological morbidity. Vaux (1988) distinguishes between social and emotional loneliness. Social loneliness refers to an impoverished or absent social network, whereas emotional loneliness refers to the absence of particular types of close relationship in a network such as friends or family members who can provide a sense of emotional security. Samter (1994) also takes up this theme in her examination of lonely people. She reports that many lonely people do not have impoverished social networks; rather, they lack specific close relationships. This may arise through absent family connections or through inadequate social skills to form close relationships. Shyness, low self-esteem, poor communication skills, and inability to perceive potentially developing relationships hinder the formation of close relationships and leave social networks predominantly characterized by an absence of close relationships, even though these networks may, numerically, appear adequate.

The importance of the presence of close relationships has been researched extensively by Derlega and co-workers (1993) and Henderson (1992), both of whom report a higher incidence of depression, anxiety, and physical illness in people lacking close relationships. It would appear that even for people with relatively sparse networks, in numerical terms, it is the perception of lacking specific relationships that is most linked with adverse health outcomes.

The link between absence of close relationships and risk to physical and psychological health may be explained through the functions that these particular relationships afford. For Derlega *et al.* (1993) and Henderson (1992), a critical element is the availability of a confidant, a trusted relationship in which to confide problems and to offer help or comfort. Weiss (1974) points to the "need to be needed." Other researchers (e.g., Taylor and Altman, 1987) emphasize the reciprocity of relationships and their associated relational obligations. However, these functions can be seen to be encompassed by a much wider concept, that of *social support*. Although often loosely used as a term to describe a variety of rather general feelings arising from relationships, the concept has a history of research that focused specifically on how relationship functions can impact health.

II. ORIGINS OF SOCIAL SUPPORT RESEARCH

The origins of research into social support can be traced to two separate seminal papers. Taking as their starting points a question of why some people appear to suffer adverse responses (such as anxiety and physical illness) to stress while other people do not, the major focus centered on social relationships. For Cassell (1976), the important element was "meaningful social contact" and the presence or absence of social relationships. His emphasis on social contact can be seen to be the foundation of later research into size, composition, and frequency of contact of social networks and their impact on well-being. Cobb (1976) focused on the "meaningful" element of this proposal and examined the functions provided from social relationships, defining social support as the process whereby interpersonal transactions afford "information leading the subject to believe he is cared for and loved, esteemed, and a member of a network of mutual obligations." Thus social support was seen as the provision of goods, services, and emotional resources at times of need and is regarded as an important coping resource that can alleviate the adverse effects of stressful events.

Cobb proposed four components of social support.

1. Emotional support: the expression of caring and concern for a person, giving provision of comfort, reassurance, and a sense of belongingness.
2. Esteem support: the expression of positive regard to the person, reaffirming self-worth, confidence, and competence in the face of a threat to self-esteem.
3. Tangible/instrumental/practical support: the direct assistance to cope with a problem or task.
4. Informational support: advice, feedback, and information to help in the person's assessment of appropriate action.

Cobb suggested that social support derived from social relationships can provide protection from anxiety and depression and related illnesses and could accelerate recovery from illness through fostering positive regard and practical help. This belief has been supported by later research into the mortality and morbidity associated with coronary heart disease (Eriksen, 1994), recovery from surgical procedures (Kulik and Mahler, 1989), incidence of depression (Henderson, 1992), and maintenance of more general psychological well-being under stress (Winefield *et al.*, 1992).

The components of social support, as described by Cobb, highlight the potential roles that different relationships play in physical and psychological health. Whereas emotional support may be associated primarily with close relationships that offer availability of a confidant, other, less intimate relationships may provide esteem support or practical or informational support.

Research into the value of supportive relationships to physical and psychological health has experienced huge growth in the last three decades since the work of Cobb (1976). It is now well established that the support provided from social relationships can exert a powerful beneficial effect on both physical and psychological well-being. Numerous review articles and meta-analyses (Sarason *et al.*, 1997; Schwarzer and Leppin, 1992) attest to the importance of social relationships and the functions they serve in the adjustment to major stresses, such as bereavement (Littlewood, 1992), recovery from illness (Glass, 1993), coping with the physical and psychological effects of surgery (Kulik and Mahler, 1989), and the maintenance of psychological well-being and freedom from anxiety (DeMakis and McAdams, 1994).

In what remains perhaps the most highly influential paper in the area, Cohen and Wills (1985) outlined the mechanisms underlying the beneficial effects of social support. They put forward two possible mechanisms whereby social support derived from relationships may reduce the severity of responses to a stressful event and the associated risks to health and well-being. This is illustrated schematically in Fig. 1.

The first of these mechanisms lies in the perception of the availability of an existing supportive network. The knowledge that helps and supports (see the types defined by Cobb (1976)) can be mobilized if the need arises is

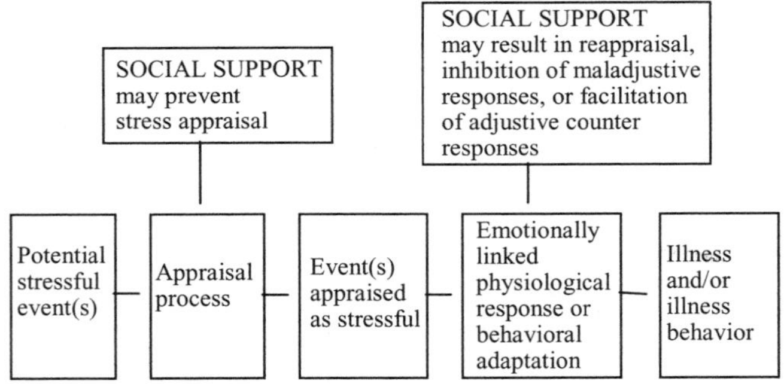

FIGURE 1 Points at which social support may interfere with the hypothesized causal link between stressful events and illness (from Cohen and Wills, 1985).

believed to exert an influence on the perception of the severity of a stressor. A stressor for which help or solution is immediately recognized as available is unlikely to produce responses severe or prolonged enough to have an impact on health. This mechanism is referred to as the *main effect hypothesis*, where social support, just by the knowledge of its existence, reduces stress responses to some events. The second mechanism, and perhaps the most widely endorsed, is that of the *buffering hypothesis*. This hypothesis proposes that the supportive functions provided from social relationships (emotional support, esteem support, instrumental support, and informational support) intervene *after* the perception of an event as stressful and exert their effect by reducing the severity and chronicity of the stress responses, thus avoiding or moderating risks to health.

Some researchers have further explored the nature of the types of support provided by relationships. Cutrona and Russell (1990) proposed that support provided should match the need demanded by the nature of the stressor. For example, an event that is perceived to threaten self-esteem should be "matched" by support of the type that reaffirms worth and competence. Although not universally endorsed, this notion of matching does appear to have some foundation, especially where stressors are long term and the demands for coping change over time. Littlewood (1992) suggests that the adjustment to bereavement is assisted in the earlier stages by emotional support when the impact of bereavement is primarily emotional shock and numbness and the need to express emotional distress. Later in the process, a need for support of a practical and informational nature is called for as the bereaved person adjusts to the need to construct a new way of life.

This pattern of a need for emotional support in initial stages of a stressor is repeated across a number of situations, such as adjustment to loss of functionality (Glass *et al*., 1993), diagnosis of a life-threatening illness such as cancer (Wortman, 1984), or coronary heart disease (Berkman and Syme, 1979). It would appear that the provision of emotional support is central to successfully coping with a number of major and lesser stressful events, so the question of who and what sort of relationships can provide this as a potential buffer to stress responses and/or illness becomes vital. Furthermore, is emotional support solely derived from human relationships?

III. CAN RELATIONSHIPS WITH PET ANIMALS PROVIDE SOCIAL SUPPORT?

For many people the relationship with their pets is very important. It may be central to their day-to-day routines; their pet may be more consistent than human relationships. But can pet relationships afford social support?

At one level, presence/ownership of a pet animal can be seen to enhance provisions of social support in that pets act as powerful social catalysts to facilitate interactions between people. It is now firmly established that being accompanied by a pet animal, especially a dog, increases the number of positive social interactions between owner/handler and other people dramatically (Messent, 1982; McNicholas and Collis, 2000). Recent unpublished research also suggests that cat owners experience similar increases in social contact through being seen with their cats in gardens, shopping for cat food, and casual talk with neighbors. Thus pets may be seen as *indirect* providers of social support, as they act as catalysts for human–human interactions in that they are able to provide access to a structural social network and in that relationships formed may lead to human relationships that may provide one or more elements of social support. Empirical evidence is presented later in this chapter.

However, are relationships with pets like relationships with people? Can they provide similar relationship provisions to those derived from human relationships? Does it *matter* that a pet is not human? Dr. Glyn Collis, coauthor of this chapter, offers the following view:

What goes on between people and companion animals is most often described, almost without a second thought, in terms of social interactions and social relationships. These social interactions and relationships may not necessarily be seen as the same in all respects as social interactions and relationships with people, but it seems intuitively obvious that they are nonetheless comparable. If this were not the case, it is unlikely that a concept such as social support would be so readily used in connection with the some of the effects that companion animals have on people.

Observing people interacting with pets gives the impression that one is observing a social interaction. Pets are spoken to as one speaks to a person, though more as to a young child than an adult (Hirsch-Pasek and Trieman, 1982; Mitchell, 2001). Pets themselves show volition in bidding for social engagement with the person, and sometimes avoiding it. Both individuals show clear indications of emotion directed toward or about the other.

People use the language of relationships to describe their perceptions of pet ownership: a good friend, company, just like a member of the family, stops me feeling lonely, he loves me, someone to talk to, and so on. Numerous scales have been constructed to measure the qualities of the person–pet relationship but, perhaps more persuasively, pet owners will readily complete questionnaires designed to tap person–person relationships such as Furman's network of relationships inventory (Bonas *et al.*, 2000), and the data are consistent with a relationship interpretation. Children too will report that their pets are suitable for some kinds of social support roles but not for others (McNicholas and

Collis, 2001). Thus, it seems that a relationship model has a lot to commend it.

However, there is one potentially troubling issue that should be faced before we accept that companion animals may have therapeutic effects and other positive influences on people's well-being because we engage in social interactions and/or social relationships with them. It is generally understood by pet owners that dogs and cats and other pet species are not humans and that the difference is non-trivial: "It's just like he understands everything I say and do, but I know he doesn't really." So, how can it be that people simultaneously know that pets are not people while in a great many respects interacting and relating to them as though they were?

One rather mechanistic answer might be along the following lines. Humans habitually categorize things, but how might pets be categorized? Pets are not really like people, but they are not much like anything else either. They sit around the house, but they are not like pieces of furniture. They are entertaining, but they are not like a television, an audio system, or a computer. Dogs in particular are a source of exercise outdoors, but they are not like bicycles or skateboards. Perhaps pets are not really similar to people but simply have more similarity to people than to any other class of thing that comes to mind, presumably because they are animate. This might conceivably explain why many people are willing to agree to a statement of categorization such as "a pet is just like a member of the family" (Cain, 1985), although it is notable that agreement with this kind of statement is far more likely when respondents are prompted to consider a pet in such a role (Hodkin *et al.*, 1998). However, the categorization approach seems much less plausible as an explanation of why people habitually interact with and relate to pets as though they were people.

The answer to this puzzle lies in the description quoted above: "It's just like he understands everything I say and do, but I know he doesn't really." This reveals a readiness to behave as though one condition were true (". . . he understands everything I say and do . . .") while also accepting an alternative reality ("I know he doesn't really"). At first sight this appears to be self-deception on the part of the pet owner, a rather pejorative description. However, the ability and indeed readiness to engage in "as if" states like this is an important characteristic of human cognition, shared with very few other species. Children develop the capacity for pretence typically just prior to two years (Bretherton, 1984). When a child holds a banana with one end next to his ear and the other end by his mouth and speaks in the manner he has heard adults use when they engage in a telephone conversation, we don't really doubt that he understands the difference between a banana and a telephone handset. It seems the most natural thing in the world to accept that the child is involved in pretend play, and is cognitively able to cope with the two realities—the object being held is a telephone, but it's really a banana. An ability to simultaneously engage with alternative realities is pervasive in the lives of adults too, and not just in light-hearted activities such as being absorbed with the plot and characters in a work of fiction. Counterfactual reasoning is a powerful process of reasoning about events in the real world by considering possibilities that are believed to be untrue. It is thus a very reasonable human thing to interact and relate to companion animals as if they were more human than they actually are.

Reassuringly, perhaps, it is not necessary that we are sure precisely what our companion animals are truly capable of, how near or far from humanity they are; all we need to do is to set aside the belief that they are precisely the same as people. Of course, if we were to believe that they were precisely the same as people, we would have no need to set anything aside, so we can be relaxed about the different views people have about the intelligence of their pets.

Any doubts about the reality of acting in an "as if" mode in interactions with animals should be dispelled by recent analyses of how adult humans involve animals in discourse with other people by "speaking for" the pet in order to accomplish a communicational goal with another person. For example, Tannen (2004) describes the mother of four-year-old Jason speaking for her two small dogs: "We're naughty, but we're not as naughty as Jason, he's the naughtiest." This utterance was marked as though it came from the dogs by a high-pitched register as in baby talk and followed immediately, in her normal tone, by: "Okay, careful there, Jason, remember." The interpretation was that Clara moderated a potentially confrontational message using humor introduced by speaking as if she were the pet.

Thus far, we have used the two terms *social relationship* and *social interaction* without drawing a clear distinction between the two concepts. While social interactions are basic processes in the construction of social relationships, the nature and properties of relationships are quite different from the nature and properties of social interactions (Hinde, 1997). Social interactions take place in the "here and now." They are primarily behavioral in nature and mostly observable (if not understood) by external observers. In contrast, relationships are primarily representational in nature, and as such they persist in the absence of the other individual. Typically, relationships have a history that is meaningful to the individuals. The content of the talk an owner directs toward a pet often reveals an awareness of a history of interactions with that animal. For example, there may be reference to past episodes of interaction in a manner that indicates that the experience of those past interactions affects the present; the person remembers, and expects the animal to remember too. Clearly, the relationship has a history represented in the mind of the owner, and presumably at some level in the pet too.

Our internal representations of a relationship are much more than just memories of episodes of interaction. Rather, they seem to function as a mental model, allowing us to make sense of what has happened in the past and providing a set of expectations of what is likely to happen in the future. We can predict with reasonable confidence how someone we know well will react to particular things we might say and do, and we probably know of circumstances when their reactions are unpredictable. The nature of an animal's cognition is much less clear, but anticipations of the owner's likely behavior are clearly present in typical pet species such as dogs and cats, and those anticipations are far more appropriately described as understanding rather than in terms of a collection of stimulus–response links.

Because social relationships are representational in nature, they cannot be observed directly. Inferences about relationships may be drawn from observing certain kinds of consistency in social interactions over time (Hinde, 1997), but often the talk of one or both participants is a more valuable source of information. In the case of human–animal relationships, the nature of an owner's talk to and about a pet often reveals that the owner has constructed an identity for the animal and amended his/her self-identity to incorporate the role of the pet (Sanders, 2003).

It is not uncommon for pet owners to state that they believe their pet understands their moods and perceives when they are feeling sad or distressed, and that they (the owners) frequently turn to their pets for emotional comfort, sometimes in preference to human relationships. In other words, they *believe* that the pet is communicating an ability to offer social/emotional support. This, coupled with the ability of pets to act as a "social ice breaker," facilitating interactions between people, points to two ways in which pet animals can provide access to social support: (a) *directly* through the close relationship between pet and owner and (b) *indirectly* through providing a means of facilitating interactions with other people, leading to a sense of belonging and social integration, and as a platform for forming deeper, more permanent relationships.

IV. TESTS OF THE SOCIAL SUPPORT MODEL

A. Direct Support via the Relationship between Owner and Pet

Research by the authors and their team at the University of Warwick sought to test the hypothesis that pets can provide valuable social support functions to their owners. Previously unpublished studies examining the role of pets as *direct* providers of emotional/psychological support are presented here. The first study looks at the role of pets in the adjustment to and recovery from breast cancer; the second study examines the supportive role of pets in early stage spousal bereavement.

B. Why Could Support from Pets Help in Such Circumstances? Where Would Pets Fit in a Support Network?

For most problems, human support should be regarded as the best form of support. However, for some people, support from human relationships may be absent simply because they lack sufficient human relationships. In other circumstances, accessing human support may be difficult because it is hard to ask for or people who are expected to give support fail to do so for a variety of reasons.

When one considers the initial effects of bereavement or diagnosis of serious illness, the following aspects are prominent.

- The feelings or fears are too intense and too painful to express easily.
- Expressing intense emotions can make the sufferer feel socially uncomfortable.
- The expression of intense emotions may be uncomfortable for others to deal with.

The result can be that people do not seek help or support or that other people do not know how to offer it. Social support from pets may operate in the following ways.

- Provision of additional support that could "top up" existing human social support.
- As a replacement for lacked human support.
- As a "cushion" against fluctuations in human support or inappropriate (i.e., "mismatched") support.
- Pets may help reorganize and reestablish routines and initiate social contacts in a particularly "normalizing" way.
- There is no feeling of awkwardness in seeking support.
- Pets may provide a "refuge" from the strains of human interactions, a release from relational obligations, and breathing space and an opportunity for free expression.

These propositions were examined in two studies. The first examined the role of pets for women adjusting to the diagnosis and treatment of breast cancer.

C. Support from Pets: Effects on Recovery and Adjustment to Diagnosis and Treatment of Breast Cancer

Paradoxically, better survival rates and physical treatments can result in more psychological concerns for cancer patients. In particular many patients report the following difficulties.

- Withdrawal of initial support, e.g., after the diagnosis and treatment phases.
- Difficulty in self-adjustment to the identity of a person who has had cancer.
- Some symptoms may remain.
- Stigma/fears of recurrence.

In addition, frequent relationship difficulties may arise. This may be due to disfigurement from surgery or treatments, which cause the cancer patient to withdraw into herself due to feelings that she is physically altered (e.g., through mastectomy or lumpectomy) and therefore less desirable or loved. Seeking support from partners and family may be avoided through these feelings. A diagnosis of cancer not only affects the patient, it has a major impact on all her family. Many cancer patients report that they felt the need to "be brave" for the sake of their families, thus denying themselves opportunities to seek support. It is in such circumstances that it may be hypothesized that non-human relationships (i.e., pet animals) could exert special benefits within a support network.

To examine the role of pets in the adjustment and recovery from cancer treatment, the team at Warwick recruited 68 female patients from five breast cancer support groups in the English Midlands. The mean age range of subjects was 51 years to 60 years. Just over half (51.4%) of the subjects owned pets (18 dogs, 15 cats, and 3 other pets), whereas the remainder did not own any pets of any kind.

Subjects were asked to complete questionnaires to determine age, occupation, and household composition (in particular whether they lived alone or with a partner and/or family); the social support questionnaire (Sarason *et al.*, 1983), which was adapted to permit pet relationships to be nominated; self-perceived health and number of doctor visits; and attribution and control of the illness plus coping and adjustment scales derived from the functional living index—cancer (Schipper *et al.*, 1984), the European organization for research and treatment of cancer quality of life questionnaire (Aaronson *et al.*, 1993), and the Nottingham health profile (Hunt *et al.*, 1981).

Results indicate that support from pets was valued by subjects. Of the 27 items contained in the social support questionnaire (Sarason *et al.*, 1983) relating to perceived support,

- 87.8% of subjects who had pets said their pets fulfilled at least one important type of support
- 43.3% fulfilled at least 10 support functions
- 4.2% fulfilled more than 20 functions

Notably, these are provisions such as comfort (especially tactile comfort), a sense of being cared for, trust, and disclosing emotions and feelings that subjects felt unready or uneasy in disclosing to their human sources of support.

There were no significant differences between the lengths of time a pet had been owned, but there were indications that the type of pet may be important. Dog owners reported greater support from their pets than cat owners or owners of other types of pets. This may be due to the particular routines associated with dog ownership, such as dog walking. Some subjects reported that the casual, regular meetings with known dog walkers was particularly "normalizing," as they retained a daily routine and many of the people met were not aware of the subject's illness or treatment and thus no change in social interactions was experienced.

Unlike many previous studies, this research did not indicate that pet ownership significantly enhanced perceptions of self-reported health. In fact, somewhat surprisingly, it was found that pet owners made *more* visits to their doctor than nonowners. Subsequent analyses indicated that pet ownership was significantly related to better feelings of control over the disease and treatment and that this, in turn, was related to more use of doctor services as a mechanism for positive coping.

Findings from this research indicate that pets do indeed constitute beneficial sources of social support to breast cancer patients. Subjects particularly valued tactile comfort from pets, especially for those receiving invasive surgery, which altered their own perceptions of self and self-esteem. Also the fact that pets and their routines of care were relatively unaffected by the subject's diagnosis and treatment allowed subjects to retain a degree of normality at a time when all other routines were disrupted.

This study indicates important findings on the benefits of pet–person relationships. Many treatments for cancer, e.g., chemotherapy, result in reduced immune functioning in patients during treatment phases, and pet ownership is frequently discouraged as being a potential health risk for zoonoses in immunocompromised people, ignoring the benefits that may be derived from the person–pet relationship. Subjects in this study endorsed many of the proposed ways in which pets could provide valuable social support. Pets were regarded as providing additional sources of emotional support that could either help replace a lack of human support at crucial times or could act as "cushions" when suitable human support fluctuated in availability. Support seeking from pets did not require any disclosure of fears or distress that might otherwise impose strains on human relationships. Similarly, the relationship with a pet remains unchanged despite the illness and can constitute a valuable sense of normality at a time when most other aspects of life are abnormal.

A second test of the support model was conducted with a sample of subjects adjusting to spousal bereavement.

D. Pets as Providers of Social Support: Evidence from a Longitudinal Study of Spousal Bereavement

Loss of a close human relationship through bereavement is a major stressful life event, involving not only a loss of emotional bonds but also a major disruption to most aspects of daily life. Provision of social support is considered crucial in adjusting to these major life changes, particularly in the early stages of adjustment. Most research has focused on the benefits of support from human relationships at this time. Few investigations included the potential contribution of nonhuman, i.e., pet, relationships.

The research team at the University of Warwick sought to examine the role of person–pet relationships in the adjustment to the first year following spousal bereavement. Subjects were 167 recently widowed people aged 40–75 years. Of these, 115 were female and 52 were male. Permission was granted to access current death records at the office of registration of births, deaths, and marriages in Coventry, United Kingdom. Potential subjects were contacted by researchers by letter, which also included literature on coping with bereavement and a list of support organizations in their area. Over 52% of people contacted volunteered to take part in the study.

Interviews were arranged to take place at 3, 6, and 11 months after bereavement. (This latter interview was timed to avoid the occurrence of particularly painful feelings that may arise at the time of the first anniversary of the loss.) In the course of the interviews, information as to the cause of death and various demographic details were gathered. Instruments derived from the influence of relationships (Berscheid *et al.*, 1989) and the impact of event scale (Horowitz *et al.*, 1979) were administered to control for intensity/dependency of the relationship with the deceased and the nature of the death, e.g., sudden/unexpected vs after a prolonged illness. In addition, subjects completed items relating to the cooccurrence of other stressful life events; ability to drive/be mobile together with the social support questionnaire (Sarason *et al.*, 1983); a social support seeking from pets questionnaire; and two symptom checklists examining the frequency of minor physical and psychological indictors of distress, such as disturbances to sleep and appetite, physical ailments, cognitive disturbances, intrusive thoughts, and concentration difficulties.

Subjects were divided into five groups: non–pet owners ($N = 106$), owners of both cats and dogs ($N = 9$), dog owners ($N = 30$), cat owners ($N = 18$), and owners of other species such as birds or fish ($N = 4$). Analyses of variance were carried out on scores from symptom checklists. Factors were gender, ability to drive, cooccurrence of other life events, and pet ownership. Covariates were age, influence of the relationship with the deceased, impact of bereavement, and social support from human relationships.

Results indicated that at 3 months after bereavement, owners of cats and/or dogs reported significantly fewer physical symptoms of distress than non-owners or owners of other pet species. This is illustrated in Fig. 2. There were no significant group differences in incidence of psychological symptoms of distress.

Although symptoms of distress decreased for all groups by 6 months after bereavement, there was a continued main effect of pet ownership on incidence of physical symptoms as shown in Fig. 3.

Once again there was no significant effect of group on psychological symptomatology. However, turning to pets as sources of support predicted lower levels of both physical symptoms and psychological symptoms as illustrated in Fig. 4.

Dog owners reported the most support from their pets, perhaps because of greater involvement in daily routines, e.g., dog walking. However, support received by cat owners and dog owners from their pets did not differ significantly.

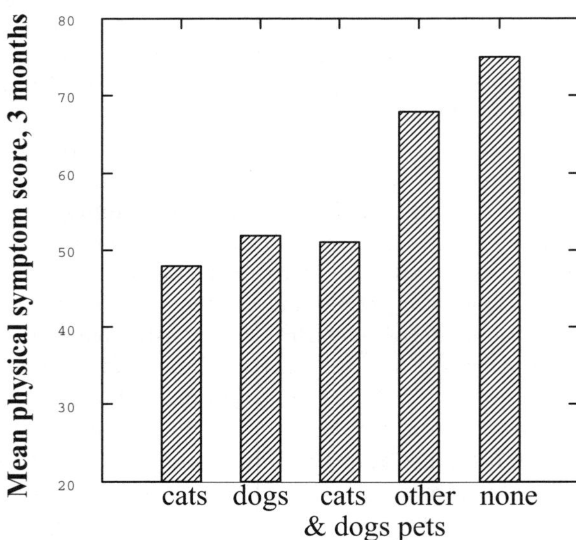

FIGURE 2 Owners of cats and/or dogs reported significantly fewer physical symptoms [$F(4,135) = 3.8$, $p = 0.006$] at 3 months after bereavement than nonowners or owners of other species of pets.

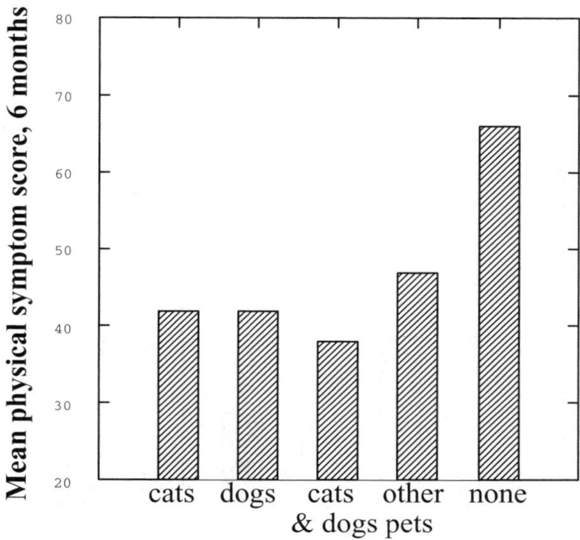

FIGURE 3 Continued main effect of pet ownership on physical symptoms [$F(4,131) = 2.93$, $p = 0.023$] at 6 months after bereavement.

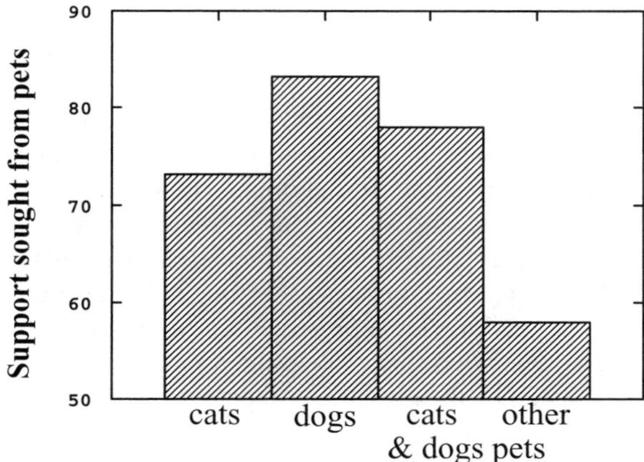

FIGURE 4 Support seeking from pets predicted lower levels of physical symptoms ($r = 0.31$, $p = 0.021$) and psychological symptoms ($r = 0.35$, $p = 0.009$). Support seeking from pets differed among groups.

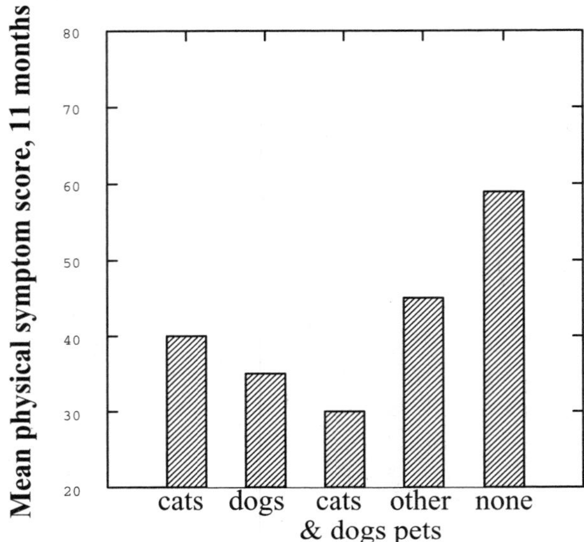

FIGURE 5 By 11 months after bereavement the main effect of group on physical symptoms disappeared [$F(4,125) = 0.402$, n.s.].

At 11 months after bereavement, the main effect of pet ownership on incidence of physical symptoms was not significant, although nonowners continued to report a greater incidence of symptoms of distress as shown in Fig. 5.

The study indicates pet ownership and the support derived from pets can be valuable in the early stages of bereavement and that pet support appears to be additional to, and independent from, human support. Subjects reported that pets provided vital stability to daily routines, giving "a reason to get up each morning," as well as alleviating a sense of "aloneness." This should not be interpreted as alleviating the loneliness that inevitably accompanies spousal bereavement; rather, pets provide a presence that reduces the feeling of isolation. Many subjects described this as helping combat the "entering an empty house syndrome," whereby the presence of a pet was especially comforting and reduced renewed sense of loss and isolation when entering a home formerly occupied by the subject and his/her deceased spouse.

Dog-owning subjects reported that the daily routine of dog walking provided not only a sense of routine but also a sense of normality in casual contact with other dog walkers, many of whom would not be aware of the recent bereavement. This contrasted with feelings of social awkwardness or even avoidance that frequently occurred in interactions with people to whom the deceased was known.

Pets also provided an outlet for emotions that could not be expressed easily. The pain of bereavement can be so severe that few bereaved people can verbally express it. Fear of "breaking down" and causing embarrassment to self or others can also lead to an unwillingness to attempt to disclose emotions. Numerous subjects reported crying while holding or in the company of their pets, which helped release some of the painful emotions. As one subject expressed, "If I can talk about it, I talk to my daughter; if I can't, I cry with my dog."

Studies into the role of pets in the social networks of people coping with major stressful events, such as breast cancer and spousal bereavement, help identify how pets may provide valuable support through the nature of the close relationship between owner and pet. This is regarded as being a direct source of support. However, pets have been shown to act as "social catalysts," facilitating interactions between people and thus providing a sense of "embeddedness," as described by House *et al.* (1988). This increased social facilitation constitutes support via indirect means in that the beneficial effects are derived from human contact that is, in itself, a consequence arising from pet ownership.

V. PETS AS FACILITATORS OF SOCIAL CONTACT

Numerous studies have established that pets can act as powerful "social ice breakers," facilitating social interactions between people. Messent (1982) reported that users of a park experienced significantly higher numbers of chance conversations with other park users when accompanied by a dog than when alone or accompanied by a child in a stroller.

McNicholas and Collis (2000) demonstrated that the catalytic effect of dogs remains robust outside parks or traditional dog-walking areas even when the dog is specifically trained not to solicit attention from passersby and irrespective of whether dog and/or handler is "smart" or "scruffy" in appearance. Cats, too, appear to act as social catalysts. Anecdotal evidence from surveys into benefits of pet ownership have frequently cited cats as facilitating human interactions through being present with their owners while gardening or awaiting their owners by the front gate, or even by owners striking up conversation in supermarkets while shopping for cat food! Indeed, it is likely that any pet that accompanies a person outside the home will attract social interaction from passersby.

Although pet owners report that these encounters are positive and enjoyable, perhaps giving a sense of "embeddedness," as described by House *et al.* (1988), few studies have examined whether they positively influence health and well-being for ordinary pet owners. However, several studies suggest that the social facilitation afforded by pets is valued greatly by people who may be at risk of greater social isolation through age or disability.

Rogers and colleagues (1993) reported that elderly people who owned dogs took twice as many daily walks as peers who did not own dogs and that they engaged in conversations about their dogs with passersby. Dog owners reported significantly less dissatisfaction with their social, physical, and emotional states than nonowners as measured by the older Americans resource survey. Studies into the social facilitation of service dogs for people with disabilities also highlight the significant increases in acknowledgements, conversations, and friendly interactions when handlers were accompanied by their dogs (Eddy *et al.*, 1988).

In a United Kingdom study of recipients of Dogs for the Disabled, Lane and co-workers (1998) examined the benefits that could arise from having a service dog. These included (a) a social facilitator, enabling contact with other people; (b) an affectionate companionable relationship, extending beyond a working relationship; (c) a relationship offering emotional and esteem support (e.g., as a source of comfort, empathy, and the sense of being competent and valued); and (d) an influence on self-perceived physical health.

The study also examined the association between any increased provision of social integration and social support and the nature of the relationship between dog and recipient on self-reported health and well-being.

Of the 57 recipients of Dogs for the Disabled, 92% reported frequent conversations with passersby when out with their dogs, and 75% reported they had made new friends through their dog, indicating that the dogs were facilitating social interactions. Seventy two percent of recipients said that their dog was one of their most valued relationships, with 70% reporting that their dog was as important "as a friend," as a working dog. A further 70% of recipients stated that they turned to their dog for comfort if they felt sad or anxious, and 59% shared most of their feelings with their dog.

Although all recipients of Dogs for the Disabled suffered permanent, often degenerative, health conditions, over half (51%) reported fewer worries about their health and a surprising 47% believed their physical and psychological health had improved since having a dog. This enhanced sense of physical and psychological well-being appears to be associated with the roles of the dog as a social facilitator, a close affectionate companion, and a source of esteem and support. Figure 6 illustrates correlations between questionnaire items measuring each of these.

VI. CAN SUPPORT MODELS BE EXTENDED TO EXPLAIN THE SUCCESS OF ANIMAL-ASSISTED THERAPY PROGRAMS?

The support model discussed has been derived from studies of beneficial effects of pet ownership. The question arises of whether the same, or similar, bene-

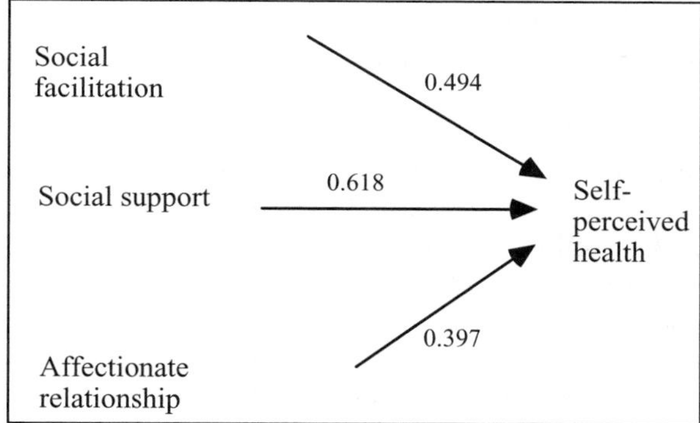

FIGURE 6 Correlations among questionnaire items measuring social facilitation, affectionate relationship, social support, and recipients' self-perceived health. Correlations are significant at $p < 0.05$.

fits may be derived when an animal is part of a visiting/therapy program and not owned by the participant in the program.

A. Benefits from Relationships with Therapy Animals

Several studies suggest that forming a relationship with an animal in the course of an animal-assisted therapy program can indeed lead to many of the benefits associated with receiving of social support. Burgon (2003) examined the psychotherapeutic effects of a horse riding program in six adult females suffering a range of mental health problems. In addition to riding, the program was composed of sessions on caring for the horse, stable management, and the building of a relationship between horse and rider. Subjects reported increased confidence and self-esteem and stated that these were transferred to other areas of the riders' lives. A similar study by Bizub and colleagues (2003) examined the outcome of a 10-week riding program for adults with psychiatric disabilities. The program again involved the opportunity to form bonds with the horses as well as riding activities. Results indicated that the participants in the program benefited from an increased sense of self-efficacy and self-esteem from both the relationship and the riding activities.

Contact with a therapy animal has also been demonstrated to reduce loneliness in elderly residents of long-term care facilities (Banks and Banks, 2002) and to reduce anxiety in hospitalized psychiatric patients (Barker and Dawson, 1998). Such studies suggest that many of the beneficial relationship provisions available to pet owners are also available from relationships formed with animals encountered in therapy programs.

B. Therapy Animals as Providers of Indirect Support/Social Facilitation

The role of an animal in facilitating social interactions between people and the benefits this may bring to any treatment program is widely supported by research. Wood and co-workers (2005) refer to this as "social capital" in that pets provide valued opportunities for people to make social contact with others. In treatment settings the increased social interaction and communication/desire to communicate stimulated by the presence of an animal has been found to benefit elderly schizophrenic patients over a 1-year controlled trial (Barak *et al.*, 2001) and to lead to improvements on the activities of the daily living scale, including independent self-care and personal hygiene through use of therapy animals as "modeling companions."

Visiting animal programs have also been found to stimulate greater initiation of social interactions among residents of long-term care facilities (Berstein *et al.*, 2000) and to improve social integration in socially withdrawn children during classroom visits by a dog (Kotrschal and Ortbauer, 2003). Kotrschal and Ortbauer (2003) also found that the class became socially homogeneous due to a decrease in aggressive and hyperactive behaviors; although the children spent considerable time watching and interacting with the dog, more attention was paid to the teacher than previously.

C. Other Mechanisms Underlying Benefits of Animal-Assisted Therapy

The provision of social support from animals, whether direct or indirect, is not the only potential explanation underlying successes of animal-assisted therapy programs. Some studies suggest that physiological benefits arising from interaction with a visiting animal may not be confined to participants in a program but may also occur in staff. Barker and colleagues (2005) measured serum cortisol, epinephrine, norepinephrine, salivary cortisol, salivary IgA, and blood for lymphocyte counts in 20 health care workers before and after interacting with a therapy dog. Although the main aim of the study was to determine optimal times for measuring stress and immune function (found to be 45 min. postcondition), it was also discovered that stress reduction may occur after as little as 5 minutes of interaction with a therapy dog.

Interestingly, another study examined levels of salivary cortisol in therapy dogs undergoing a 5-day training course in order to investigate whether they experience feelings of stress during the performance of therapy-related tasks. No significant increases in salivary cortisol were apparent in the dogs, indicating that training for therapy work is not stressful for the dogs (Haubenhofer *et al.*, 2005). This finding is particularly important as it addresses a necessary question of the effect of therapy programs on the animals themselves. Any benefits to people that derive from animal contact require constant vigilance for the animals' well-being.

Contact with animals may benefit particular populations who have deficits in their abilities to initiate social interactions with other people. Social signals from animals are less complex than from humans, and the reduced processing load may permit a greater degree of social understanding and social interaction than would be otherwise possible. A current project in the southwest of England is investigating the effects of "teaching" children with autism how to initiate social interactions with a friendly dog that attends the children's class each day. Preliminary findings indicate that such "taught" interactions improve communication skills in some autistic children both with the dog and with the teaching staff.

In summary, animal-assisted therapy can be demonstrated to be effective for many clinical and nonclinical populations. However, any benefits arising from contact with animals, whether personal pets or visiting animals, are probably highly dependent on an individual's liking for animals, former or current pet ownership, and level of ease felt in the company of animals. Animal-assisted therapy may not, therefore, be suitable in all instances. Now that they have achieved considerable recognition among health professionals, the goal for investigations into the effectiveness of animal-assisted therapy programs is to identify for whom the programs would be successful and the mechanisms that underlie successful implementation.

REFERENCES

Aaronson, N. K., Ahmedzai, S., Bergman, B., *et al.* (1993). The European Organisation for Research and Treatment of Cancer QLQ-C30: A quality-of-life instrument for use in international clinical trial in oncology. *J. Natl. Cancer Inst.* **85**, 365–376.

Banks, M. R., and Banks, W. A. (2002). The effects of animal-assisted therapy on loneliness in an elderly population in long-term care facilities. *J. Gerontol. Ser. A Biol. Sci. Med. Sci.* **57**, 428–432.

Barak, Y., Savorai, O., Mavashev, S., and Beni, A. (2001). Animal-assisted therapy for elderly schizophrenic patients: A one-year controlled trial. *Am. J. Geriatr. Psychiatr.* **9**, 439–442.

Barker, S. B., and Dawson, K. S. (1998). The effects of animal-assisted therapy on anxiety ratings of hospitalized psychiatric patients. *Psychiatr. Serv.* **49**, 797–801.

Barker, S. B., Kniseley, J. S., McCain, N. L., and Best, A. M. (2005). Measuring stress and immune response in healthcare professionals following interaction with a therapy dog: A pilot study. *Psychol. Rep.* **96**, 713–729.

Berkman, L., and Syme, S. L. (1979). Social networks, resistance and mortality: A nine-year follow-up study of Alameda County residents. *Am. J. Epidemiol.* **115**, 684–694.

Bernstein, P. L., Friedmann, E., and Malaspina, A. (2000). Animal-assisted therapy enhances resident social interaction and initiation in long-term care facilities. *Anthrozoos* **13**, 213–224.

Berscheid, E., Snyder, M., and Omoto, A. M. (1989) The Relationship Closeness Inventory. *J. Personal. Soc. Psychol.* **57**, 792–807.

Bizub, A. L., Joy, A., and Davidson, L. (2003). "It's like being in another world": Demonstrating the benefits of therapeutic horseback riding for individuals with psychiatric disability. *Psychiatr. Rehab. J.* **26**, 377–384.

Bonas, S., McNicholas, J., and Collis, G. M. (2000). Pets in the network of family relationships. *In* "Companion Animals and Us" (A. L. Podbercek, E. S. Paul, and J. A. Serpell, eds.). Cambridge University Press, Cambridge UK.

Bretherton, I. (1984). "Symbolic Play." Academic Press, New York.

Burgon, H. (2003). Case studies of adults receiving horse-riding therapy. *Anthrozoos* **16**, 229–240.

Cain, A. O. (1985). Pets as family members. *Marriage Family Rev.* **8**, 5–10.

Cassel, J. (1976). The contribution of the social environment to host resistance. *Am. J. Epidemiol.* **104**, 107–123.

Cobb, S. (1976). Social support as a moderator of life stress. *Psychosom. Med.* **38**, 300–314.

Cohen, S., and Wills, T. A. (1985). Stress, social support, and the buffering hypothesis. *Psychol. Bull.* **98**, 310–357.

Cutrona, C. E., and Russell, D. W. (1990). Type of social support and specific stress: Toward a theory of optimal matching. *In* "Social Support: An Interactionist View" (B. R. Sarason, I. G. Sarason, and G. R. Pierce, eds.). Wiley. New York.

De Makis, G. J., and McAdams, D. P. (1994). Personality, social support and well-being among first year college students. *College Stud. J.* **28**, 235–243.

Derlega, V. J., Metts, S., Petronio, S., and Margulis, S. T. (1993). "Self Disclosure." Sage, Newbury Park, CA.

Eddy, J., Hart, L. A., and Boltz, R. P. (1988). The effects of service dogs on social acknowledgement of people in wheelchairs. *J. Psychol.* **122**, 39–45.

Eriksen, W. (1994). The role of social support in the pathogenesis of coronary heart disease: A literature review. *Family Pract.* **11**, 201–209.

Furman, W. (1989). The development of children's social networks. *In* "Children's Social Networks and Social Support" (D. Belle, ed.). Wiley, New York.

Glass, T. A., Matchar, D. B., Belyea, M., and Feussner, J. R. (1993). Impact of social support on outcome in first stroke. *Stroke* **24**, 64–70.

Haubenhofer, D., Mostl, E., and Kirchengast (2005). Cortisol concentrations in saliva of humans and their dogs during intensive training courses in animal assisted therapy. *Wiener Tierarztliche Monatsschrift* **92**, 66–73.

Henderson, A. S. (1992). Social support and depression. *In* "The Meaning and Measurement of Social Support" (H. O. F. Veiel and U. Bauman, eds.). Hemisphere, New York.

Hinde, R. A. (1997). "Relationships: A Dialectical Perspective." Psychology Press, Hove, UK.

Hirsch-Pasek, K., and Trieman, R. (1982). Doggerel: Motherese in a new context. *J. Child Language* **9**, 229–237.

Hodkin, B., Vacheresse, A., and Buffett, S. (1996). Concept of family: Methodological issues in assessing perceived family membership. *In* "Research on Family Resources and Needs Across the World" (M. Cusinato, ed.). Milan: Edizioni Universitaire di Lettere Economia Diritto.

Horowitz, M., Wilner, N., and Alvarez, W. (1979). Impact of event scale: A measure of subjective stress. *Psychosom. Med.* **41**, 209–218.

House, J. S., Landis, K. R., and Umberson, D. (1988). Social relationships and health. *Science* **241**, 540–544.

Hunt, S. M., McKenna, S. P., McEwan, J., *et al.* (1981). The Nottingham Health Profile: Subjective health status and medical consultations. *Soc. Sci. Med.* **15**, 221–229.

Kotrschal, K., and Ortbauer, B. (2003). Behavioural effects of the presence of a dog in a classroom. *Anthrozoos* **16**, 147–159.

Kulik, J. A., and Mahler, H. I. M. (1989). Social support and recovery from surgery. *Health Psychol.* **8**, 221–238.

Lane, D. R., McNicholas, J., and Collis, G. M. (1998). Dogs for the disabled: Benefits to recipients and welfare of the dog. *Appl. Anim. Behav. Sci.* **59**, 49–60.

Littlewood, J. (1992). "Aspects of Grief: Bereavement in Adult Life." Routledge, London.

McNicholas, J., and Collis, G. M. (2000). Dogs as catalysts for social interactions: Robustness of the effect. *Br. J. Psychol.* **91**, 61–70.

McNicholas, J., and Collis, G. M. (2001). Children's representations of pets in their social networks. *Child Care Health Dev.* **27**(3), 279–294.

Messent, P. R. (1983). Social facilitation of contact with other people by pet dogs. *In* "New Perspectives in Our Lives with Companion Animals" (A. H. Katcher and A. M. Beck, eds.). University of Philadelphia Press, Philadelphia, PA.

Mitchell, R. W. (2001). Americans' talk to dogs: Similarities and differences with talk to infants. *Research on Language and Social Interaction* **34**, 183–210.

Rogers, J., Hart, L. A., and Boltz, R. P. (1993). The role of pet dogs in casual conversations of elderly adults. *J. Soc. Psychol.* **133**, 265–277.

Samter, W. (1994). Unsupportive relationships: Deficiencies in the support-giving skills of the lonely person's friends. *In* "Communication of Social Support" (B. R. Burleson, T. L. Albrecht, and I. G. Sarason, eds.). Sage, Thousand Oaks, CA.

Sanders, C. R. (2003). Actions speak louder than words: Close relationships between human and nonhuman animals. *Symb. Interact.* **26**, 405–426.

Sarason, B. R., Sarason, I. G., and Garung, R. A. R. (1997). Close personal relationships and health outcomes. *In* "Handbook of Personal Relationships: Theory, Research and Interventions" (S. Duck, ed.). Wiley, New York.

Sarason, I. G., Levine, H. M., Basham, R. B., and Sarason, B. R. (1983). Assessing social support: The Social Support Questionnaire. *J. Personal. Soc. Psychol.* **44**(1), 127–139.

Schipper, H., Clinch, J., McMurray, A., *et al.* (1984). Measuring the quality of life of cancer patients: The Functional Living Index. *J. Clin. Oncol.* **2**, 472–483.

Schwarzer, R., and Leppin, A. (1992). Social support and mental health: A conceptual and empirical overview. *In* "Life Crises and Experiences of Loss in Childhood" (L. Montada, S.-H. Filipp, and M. J. Lerner, eds.). Erlbaum, Hillsdale, NJ.

Tannen, D. (2004). Talking the dog: Framing pets as interactional resources in family discourse. *Res. Lang. Soc. Interact.* **37**, 399–420.

Taylor, D. A., and Altman, I. (1987). Communication in interpersonal relationships: Social penetration processes. *J. Soc. Psychol.* **75**, 79–90.

Vaux, A. (1988). "Social Support: Theory, Research and Intervention." Praeger, New York.

Weiss, R. (1974). "Loneliness: The Experience of Emotional and Social Isolation." MIT Press, Cambridge, MA.

Winefield, H. R., Winefield, A. H., and Tiggemann, M. (1992). Social support and psychological well-being in younger adults: The multi-dimensional support scale. *J. Personal. Assess.* **58**, 198–210.

Wood, L., Giles-Corti, B., and Bulsara, M. (2005). The pet connection: Pets as a conduit for social capital? *Soc. Sci. Med.* **61**, 1159–1173.

Wortman, C. B. (1984). Social support and the cancer patient: Conceptual and methodological issues. *Cancer* **53**, 2339–2360.

CHAPTER 5

Community Context and Psychosocial Benefits of Animal Companionship

LYNETTE A. HART

Department of Population Health and Reproduction, School of Veterinary Medicine, University of California, Davis, California 95616

I. COMMUNITY CONTEXT AFFECTING THE HUMAN–ANIMAL RELATIONSHIP

Animal-assisted activities (AAAs) and animal-assisted therapy (AAT) are typically considered in settings where the contact with the animal is scheduled, often for a person in a residential facility. This chapter asserts that a full-time relationship with an animal offers greater potential to enhance the person's life and that most compatible relationships with animals afford benefits to the person and animal. Thus, the entire range of companionship with animals, from ordinary pet through assistance animal, can be examined in a therapeutic context. The assistance dog performs many special tasks, and at the same time is a companion dog (Hart, 2003). The number of types of assistance that dogs can provide continues to broaden, and methods for training assistance dogs also are more varied than in the past, but still without standardized certification criteria.

In a climate of expanding successes in uses of animals as human companions, and dogs particularly as service providers, it is important to emphasize that potential benefits of the companionship rest on a beneficial relationship

Handbook on Animal-Assisted Therapy: Theoretical Foundations and Guidelines for Practice, 2e

with compatibility. Epidemiological studies of pet keeping, which are community based, have produced useful results showing that geographic context is important.

Instead of using epidemiological methods and considering who benefits from pets and who does not, most published studies have focused on documenting the health benefits of pets and developing standardized techniques for offering people contact with companion animals. The role of pets is often examined among individuals who are self-selected as enthusiastic companions of pets, such as middle-class women, or perhaps populations of vulnerable individuals, such as those with disabilities, Alzheimer's disease or AIDS, or the elderly. Profiling pets as consistent as aspirin in their effects is not useful when attempting to assess and even predict which individuals would be likely to benefit from periodic or sustained contact with companion animals. To be able to effectively "prescribe" pets, we will need to become knowledgeable about those cases where pets are not associated with health benefits or may even add to the burden of individuals. We may need to admit that pets could be harmful in some circumstances.

We can consider a representative range of individuals with their varied responses to companion animals by using epidemiological methods and assessing entire communities to identify subcultures where there are certain individual circumstances, neighborhoods, geographical features, or special situations in which pets are associated with beneficial health parameters, as well as those where pets may be correlated with adverse impacts. Using these methods, classic studies in the 1980s revealed positive correlates of pet ownership for certain individuals, whereas correlates were neutral or negative for others. Ory and Goldberg (1984) reported that pets were associated with negative indicators for elderly women living in rural settings, but with positive indicators for women in suburban and urban settings, as shown in Fig. 1. More work would be needed to clarify the source of this difference, but it seems likely that the role of pets in small towns and rural areas may have differed from that in urban and suburban areas. The combination of higher socioeconomic status and pet ownership was associated with more positive indicators of happiness for women (Fig. 2; Ory and Goldberg, 1983). Pet ownership was more commonplace among less affluent women than among affluent women, as represented in Fig. 3. Being weakly attached to a pet was associated with having a spouse that was not a confidant when compared with nonowners and attached owners (Fig. 4) and was also associated with unhappiness (Fig. 5).

Garrity and colleagues (1989) reported no significant health correlates for pet ownership overall in the elderly people studied, but then found highly significant benefits for individuals who were especially vulnerable due to bereavement during the previous year with loss of a spouse. Among the grieving individuals in this group who had few confidants, pet ownership and attach-

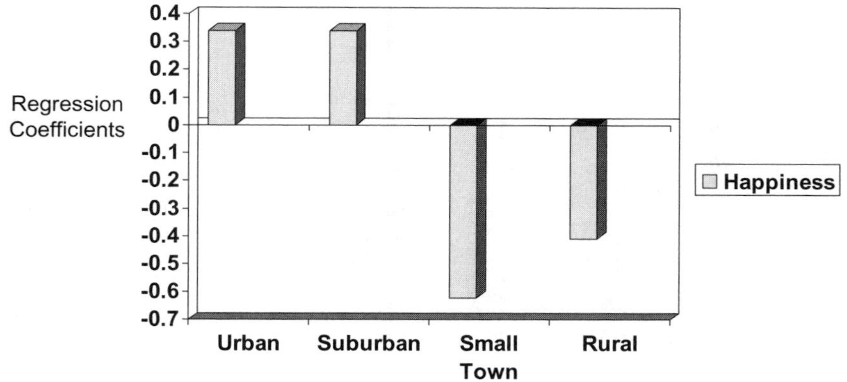

FIGURE 1 Happiness and likelihood of pet ownership by geographic residence ($P < 0.05$; Ory and Goldberg, 1984).

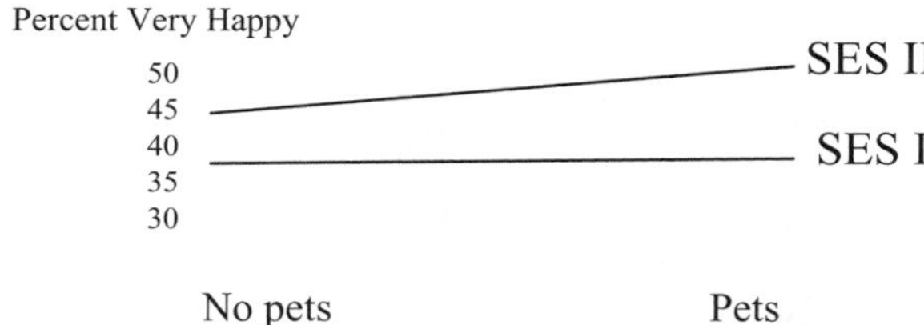

FIGURE 2 Happiness of women as related to pet ownership, controlling for socioeconomic status ($P < 0.05$; Ory and Goldberg, 1983).

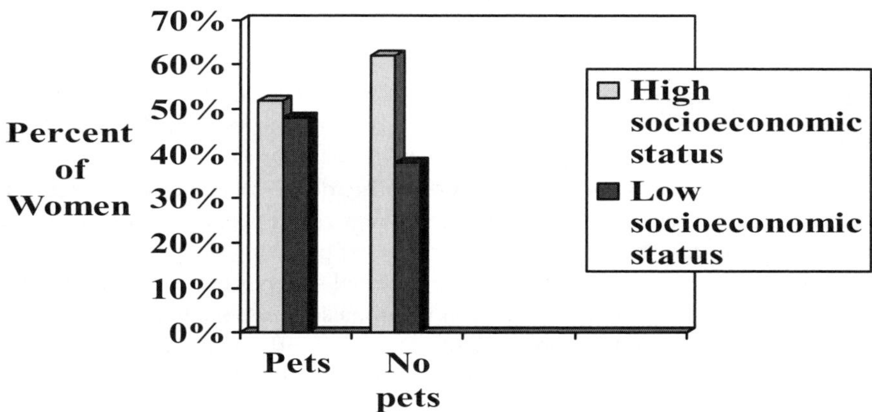

FIGURE 3 Pet ownership of women as related to affluence ($P = 0.002$; Ory and Goldberg, 1983).

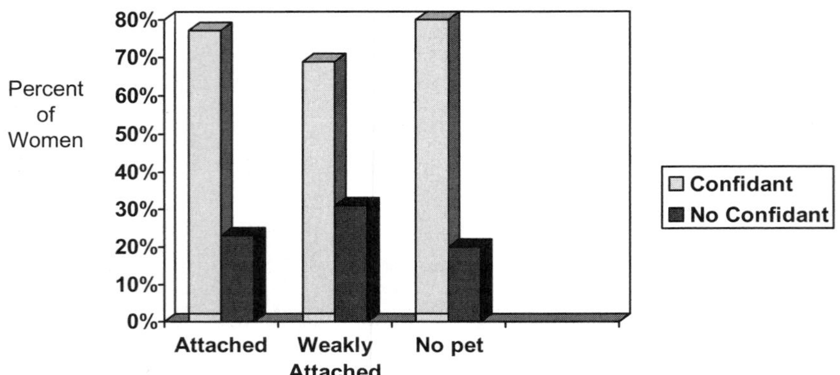

FIGURE 4 Pet attachment of women as related to spouse as confidant (P = 0.03; Ory and Goldberg, 1983).

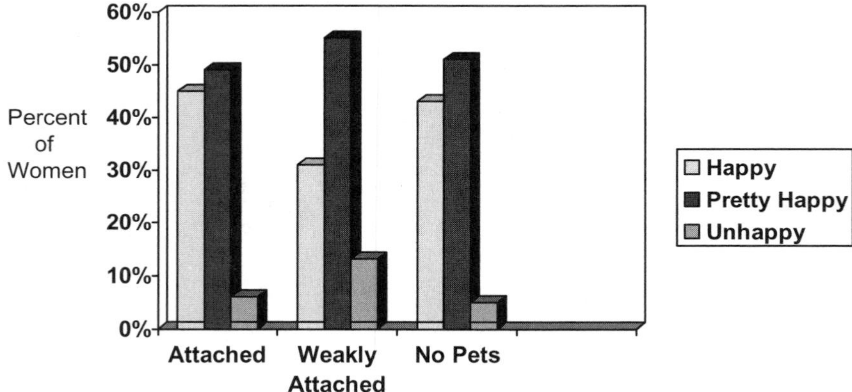

FIGURE 5 Pet attachment as related to happiness of women (P = 0.01; Ory and Goldberg, 1983).

ment to the pet were associated with a lower incidence of depression. Bereaved individuals who had few confidants and were without pets or those with little attachment to their pets were more likely to report being depressed.

A more recent community-based, longitudinal study examined over a 1-year period whether attachment to companion animals was associated with changes in health among older people (Raina *et al.*, 1999). Although nonowners showed greater deterioration in their activities of daily living than pet owners, the pet owners were younger, married or living with someone, and more physically active. Pet ownership significantly modified the relationship between social support and the change in psychological well-being of participants over the 1-year period.

When people are burdened in their personal circumstances or health status, they still may benefit from pets (despite the care required), especially if they select a lower effort animal, such as a cat rather than a dog. Benefits were associated with pet companionship for men with AIDS (Castelli *et al.*, 2001) and middle-aged women giving care to family members with Alzheimer's disease (Fritz *et al.*, 1996), especially when they selected a lower effort pet, a cat, thus attending to their level of energy and other responsibilities when selecting the type of pet and its associated requirements for care.

The term *pet* covers a wide range of animals and relationships, as families acquire pets to fill different roles and the pets are treated differently depending on the families' traditions and expectations. Pet-keeping practices vary with neighborhood and community. A study of residents in Salt Lake County (Zasloff and Hart, unpublished result) revealed that residents' zip code areas were highly predictive of the sources of pets residents used in acquiring their pets. Certain zip code areas showed high levels of pet adoptions from shelters, whereas other neighborhoods favored purebred animals, and feral cats were adopted in other areas. Whether animals carried any identification reflected the sources where they were obtained, once again revealing subcultures of pet-keeping practices within Salt Lake County.

Various positive and negative correlates of pet ownership have been reported in certain contexts, but more work will be needed to determine when and whether pets play a causal role or are simply correlates of other underlying causes. Epidemiological studies provide a first approach that reveals differences among subgroups, which can then be studied in more detail. Pet ownership can be better understood by employing epidemiological methods that include statistical representation of the entire community of interest. The entire context, including the community affluence, the geography, and age, gender, and ethnicity of participants, should be studied. By specifically examining microneighborhoods and subcultures, we can more accurately profile and understand the range of styles of pet ownership characteristic in our diverse societies.

II. PETS ENHANCING THE QUALITY OF LIFE

Companion animals offer one of the most accessible enhancements to a person's quality of life. They are themselves an unconditional support system that can be drawn on at any time of day or night, when family members or friends may be busy with other things or unreachable. Having warm and accepting companionship near at hand provides essential comfort, relaxation, and entertainment—available whenever it is especially needed. The animal's demands are simple and uncomplicated and, because the animal does not talk, the conflicts are few as long as the person avoids most behavior problems with the animal through careful selection and management. Human relationships, or the lack of them, play a central role in being either stress producing or health promoting. In a classic study of 9-year mortality data, increased mortality rates were associated with each decrease in social connection (Berkman and Breslow, 1983). Adding supportive groups to assist grieving spouses was found in one study to be effective only with those individuals who had inadequate emotional support because some had already reestablished sufficient emotionally supportive relationships (Barrett, 1978). Everyone's life brings with it periods of challenge and heartbreak when reliance on friends and family can make a substantial difference in morale and the ability to regain an optimistic view. Despite the array of family, friends, and support services that are available, at times people who are at their greatest vulnerability will be without the social relationships they need for a reasonable quality of life.

People who may be at particular risk include those persons who are facing hearing, visual, or mobility disabilities, living alone in later years, or experiencing the onset of serious medical problems. While some crises are temporary, their initial impact may be almost paralyzing. Modern living requires coping with rapid changes and complexity and often brings social isolation that leaves people without the social or family support they need during unexpected crises. Anyone living alone who is socially isolated and possibly experiencing heightened medical problems may begin to feel profoundly alone and lack the will and the ability to move forward. Geographic mobility commonly forces people to relegate their extended family connections to telephone or e-mail connections rather than interacting in person. The high costs of loneliness and a lack of social support to human health are well documented (House *et al.*, 1988). Loneliness and depression have been linked with a wide array of diseases, including cancer and cardiovascular disease (Lynch, 1977), leading to the suggestion that depression is a central etiologic factor of these diseases (Chrousos and Gold, 1992).

Discussions within the research literature refer to assistance dogs and companion dogs, often as though they are discrete categories, while actually, an assistance dog at the same time fulfills the role of a close companion dog. This is a gray area, as therapy animals are also conventional family pets, even as they fully play a therapeutic role. Conversely, companion animals can provide therapeutic aspects much as would a specifically designated therapeutic dog (Hart, 2003). In this chapter, the author assumes that compatible companion animals often play meaningful therapeutic roles, being more full-time than some AAAs and AAT.

Most AAAs and AAT are directed at individuals who are institutionalized rather than at precarious individuals who still live at home but are in jeopardy nonetheless. However, for those who are struggling to continue living independently, it is reasonable to believe that companion animals can make a difference and perhaps prolong their period of independent living, lessening or delaying their requirements for institutional living or even in-home nursing care. Such a trial has not been conducted. One community program placed animals with elderly individuals, provided some support for their care, and arranged for a longitudinal assessment (Lago *et al.*, 1989); however, participants, most of whom had been given dogs, were challenged with their own health problems. Animals requiring lower effort than dogs, such as cats, may have been more appropriate companions for these elderly persons. The effects of cat ownership have not been studied extensively in this context, but one correlational study in Australia found better scores on psychological health among cat owners than nonowners (Straede and Gates, 1993). A study by Karsh and Turner (1988) reported that long-term cat owners were less lonely, anxious, and depressed than nonowners, and owners also reported some improvements in blood pressure. Moving into a state of permanent institutional living involves crossing a great divide that sharply curtails the person's quality of life, reduces contact with the world at large, and increases the cost of living. If companion animals can provide psychosocial health benefits, an investment in providing animal companionship for such individuals could make a significant difference in the person's health, perhaps extending by many months or even a few years the period of carrying on a normal lifestyle.

Companion animals provide a readily available source of warm support that can be compensatory for human companionship. Dogs provide exuberant attention to their human companions, and cat-owning women rank their cats higher than their husbands in providing affection and unconditional love (Zasloff and Kidd, 1994a). Although animals in positive relationships enhance the quality of life for people in many situations, the beneficial psychosocial effects of companion animals are measured most easily with individuals who are psychologically vulnerable; the psychosocial effects are not as obvious in more average situations. As people age, their former social networks generally shrink as they leave the workplace, move into smaller homes, lose friends and family members who have moved away or died, or experience chronic health problems. For such individuals, having companion animals living with them offers a source of reliable and accessible companionship. In one study of elderly dog owners, a majority said their dog was their only friend and believed their relationship with their dog was as strong as with humans (Peretti, 1990).

Individuals with severe physical disabilities who use wheelchairs can be motivated by a service dog to perform physical tasks for the dog, while also benefiting socially themselves, even while, as a working partner, the dog provides assistance with physical tasks. Children with mental or other disabilities can benefit from the extraordinary experience of therapeutic horseback riding, an occasion affording joyous human social support as well as the unique sensation and physical challenge of riding the horse (Hart, 1992). Empirical research has identified four areas of psychosocial benefits of companion animals that arise in normal family settings as well as in more challenging circumstances; these effects are reviewed in this section.

A. Companion Animals for Loneliness and Depression

What people value most in their relationships with dogs and cats is the companionship they offer. Animal companionship, although commonplace, offers a psychosocial benefit that can provide a meaningful and substantial comfort. Loneliness, lack of companionship, depression, and lack of social support are major risk factors that can impede a person's well-being and even increase the likelihood of suicide or other maladaptive behaviors. Individuals who are experiencing periods of adversity or its onset are at a heightened vulnerability, feeling more needy and subject to feelings of loneliness and depression. As a key benefit, companionship with animals can be associated with people suffering less depression and loneliness. The animals deeply comfort their human companions and apparently serve as a buffer of protection against adversity (Siegel, 1993). The concept of social support creating both main and buffering effects against stress is well known in discussions of human social support (Thoits, 1982); Siegel (1993) extended the buffering effects to include the support companion animals provide.

Various methods have been used to assess the effects of contact with companion animals on human well-being. Descriptive, correlational, experimental, and epidemiological research designs are used to test the possibility that animals provide social support. Correlational studies often are hypothesis based, whether cross-sectional or longitudinal. Studies based on a structural approach to social support assess simply whether or not a pet is present. The more complex buffering perspective evaluates whether an animal was intervening to soften the impact of stressful life events. Psychological, social, behavioral, and physical types of well-being were examined in a review of relevant studies (Garrity and Stallones, 1998). After expressing some cautions, the authors concluded that the benefits from contacts with pets seem consistent with the benefits supported by studies of human social support. The benefits appeared to occur on psychological, physical, social, and behavioral levels but were apparent only in certain situations. Pet association frequently appeared beneficial both directly and as a buffering factor during stressful life circumstances, but this did not occur for everyone. Among elderly women, the strength of the relationship with their pets was unrelated to levels of depression (Miller and Lago, 1990). Similarly, an initial study of war veterans found pet ownership associated with improved morale and health (Robb, 1983), but later, no differences were observed in an analysis of the full sample (Robb and Stegman, 1983).

1. Elderly People

Among elderly people in one study who were grieving the loss of their spouses within the previous year and who lacked close friends, a high proportion of individuals without pets described themselves as depressed, whereas low levels of depression were reported by those with pets, even though no differences in health status were found between those with and without pets among elderly people in general (Garrity *et al.*, 1989). Similarly, no differences in health status were found among people 21 to 64 years of age with and without pets (Stallones *et al.*, 1990). Although pets were associated with less depression among these deeply bereaved elderly individuals, a similar effect was not found for the general population.

It is essential to bring up a caveat, however: People who seek out animal companionship may be more skilled in making choices that maintain their own well-being. The traits of dependability, intellectual involvement, and self-confidence (comprising the skills of planful competence) are strong characteristics that continue throughout life, and individuals who as young people express planful competence seem able to absorb adverse life events in stride and take effective actions to keep their lives on track (Clausen, 1993). A decision to live with an animal could be one aspect of taking effective action in one's life. Individuals keeping pets may also have had different social skills and abilities that were reflected in the decision to have a pet. However, it may be tempting to ascribe the difference found in this study to the interactions with the pet, reflecting the laughter that a pet invariably brings, the responsibility to nurture another individual, and the loving devotion of a pet.

Living alone, although common in the United States, may itself be inherently stressful. Loneliness occurs often in elderly people and is associated with various diseases. In another correlational study, elderly women living alone were found to be in better psychological health if they resided with an animal. They were less lonely, more optimistic, more interested in planning for the future, and less agitated than those women who lived without a pet (Goldmeier, 1986). Those women with pets who were living with other relatives did not show a measurable psychological boost. A similar protective effect of companion animals was found among women graduate students who lived alone: Those living with a companion animal, a person, or both rated themselves as less lonely than those living entirely alone (Zasloff and Kidd, 1994b).

2. People with Mental Illnesses

It is commonplace to hear that even service dogs that provide instrumental assistance are valued primarily for the companionship they offer. The significant role of companionship, contact comfort, and affection from a dog is formalized in the case of psychiatric service dogs, where a primary task is this comforting, playing a role in helping stabilize the mental health of someone who is mentally ill; the warmth and acceptance offered in specific tasks such as providing tactile contact can calm a person who is manic or lighten someone's depression (Psychiatric Service Dog Society, 2005). Psychiatric service dogs are at the forefront of extending the service dog concept to a wider clientele, as persons work with trainers and peers in training their own dogs; the dog is one aspect of their treatment, along with human health professionals, veterinary professionals, pharmaceuticals, and dog trainers.

In a study of depressed community-dwelling elderly, participants were less negative psychologically after prolonged exposure to pet birds (Mugford and M'Comisky, 1975). A better-controlled study examined the depression in elderly men who were exposed to an aviary at an adult day health care program (Holcomb *et al.*, 1997). No difference occurred in depression levels of the men overall with the presence of the aviary; however, a greater reduction in depression was associated with greater utilization of the aviary. The men who sought out the aviary also apparently experienced increased social interaction with family and staff members, whereas the men who ignored the aviary did not. Animal-assisted therapy also has been used as an experimental intervention for depression in college students. The group given AAT subsequently was found to have lower scores on the Beck depression inventory than the control group (Folse *et al.*, 1994). Surprisingly, the AAT in conjunction with group psychotherapy was no more effective than the control, whereas the AAT alone was associated with a reduction in depression.

3. People with a Disability or Requiring Clinical Care

Providing an assistance dog to someone with a disability is a major intervention with psychosocial effects. Loss of hearing is an invisible disability that limits communication and predisposes people to feeling isolated and lonely, but a dog serves as a full-time companion. Although animals cannot participate in a complex conversational interchange, they are conversational partners that respond behaviorally to the statements and moods of their human companions. They also facilitate socializing within the neighborhood more than is anticipated prior to having a hearing dog (Hart *et al.*, 1996). People with impaired hearing who had a hearing dog rated themselves as less lonely after receiving their dogs and also were less lonely than those who were slated to receive a hearing dog in the near future.

In a study of elderly people in a skilled rehabilitation unit, some participants were given a budgerigar in a cage for a period of 10 days and others were not. At the pretest, all participants were lonely. Loneliness and morale did not change with the treatment, but depression decreased significantly (Jessen *et al.*, 1996). A study of AAT provided once or three times a week to elderly people in long-term facilities found a significant reduction of loneliness that was not manifest in the control group (Banks and Banks, 2002).

4. Conclusions

Animals alleviate loneliness for women living alone but not those living with others, and they seem to offer some psychological protection to people who are deeply grieving and isolated. These findings are consistent with a view that animals may compensate and provide people with basic, daily, essential psychosocial requirements that are lacking. If basic requirements are met by family or friends, however, it seems that a ceiling is reached such that significant positive effects are difficult to measure. People differ in the extent to which they draw on the animal companionship that could offer them some comfort.

B. Socializing Effects of Animals

Empirical data point toward the strong socializing impact of animals. Considering institutional environments, visits offering AAAs improved social interactions among residents and staff in a psychiatric facility for elderly women (Haughie *et al.*, 1992) and in a residential home (Francis *et al.*, 1985). In two other studies, visits with animals to nursing homes for patients with Alzheimer's disease improved their social interactions (Kongable *et al.*, 1989; Beyersdorfer and Birkenhauer, 1990).

The absence of a supportive network of social companionship leads to depression, stress, suppression of the immune system, and various disease states (Serpell, 1986/1996). Social companionship buffers and reduces the impact of such stress and anxiety. Viewed in this context, animal companionship offers an accessible compensatory alternative. Animals are consistently available companions—appreciated by people who have spent much of their lives living with animals. While they do not respond verbally to conversation, they convincingly convey their love and affection to their human companions, responding enough that people almost inevitably speak to their animals. Dogs are avid companions, staying with a person more than cats and provoking social interactions (Miller and Lago, 1990). Dogs are more interactive when living with a solitary person than with a family, essentially providing compensatory social contact for those who live alone (Smith, 1983).

Animals, especially a soft and furry one such as a rabbit, but even a turtle, stimulate people to socialize with other people, often with the animal as a topic of conversation (Hunt *et al.*, 1992). People may start conversations, laugh, and exchange stories more when a dog is present than when they are alone (Messent, 1984), an effect evident to anyone who takes a friendly animal walking in a neighborhood. The powerful socializing effect is a primary benefit for people using wheelchairs who have a service dog (Eddy *et al.*, 1988). The dog serves to normalize the social environment for the person with a disability who might otherwise be ignored or treated awkwardly. For those with a hearing loss, a hearing dog provides unexpected social benefits, increasing social interactions for the person within the neighborhood and community (Hart *et al.*, 1996).

As full-time companions, dogs and cats themselves are conversational partners, even though they do not respond with verbal conversation. Almost everyone talks to their own bird (Beck and Katcher, 1989), dog (Rogers *et al.*, 1993), or cat. In addition, the animals provoke people to speak to others. Animals stimulate friendly conversations, even with strangers. The animals provide a comfortable topic of conversation. People who walk their dogs regularly talk about their dogs whether or not the dogs are present at the time (Rogers *et al.*, 1993). A study of people using assistance dogs reported that social facilitation, social support, and an affectionate relationship were all correlated with the person's self-perceived health (Lane *et al.*, 1998). Participants described how the dog created social opportunities with people while also serving as an essential family member and friend.

C. Motivating Effects of Animals

Animals inspire and motivate people to engage in constructive activities. People may spontaneously decide to arrange to bring an animal into a nursing home, school, or hospital on a regular basis. As individuals or small groups adopted this practice, it came to be known as offering AAAs or, if integrated into an overall treatment plan for the patient, AAT. Volunteers find it rewarding to share their animals with others who enjoy them, such that many make commitments to visit facilities routinely. Such remarkable motivation probably would not occur if the person were visiting the nursing home alone. The animal partner is the essential participant that makes the effort of the volunteer worthwhile. The main contribution of the animal to AAAs may be in inspiring the volunteer, because human visitors alone were found in one study to be as effective as pets alone or human visitors with pets in eliciting smiling and alertness from nine male and four female patients (Hendy, 1987). However, a more recent, quasi-experimental repeated measures design involving five

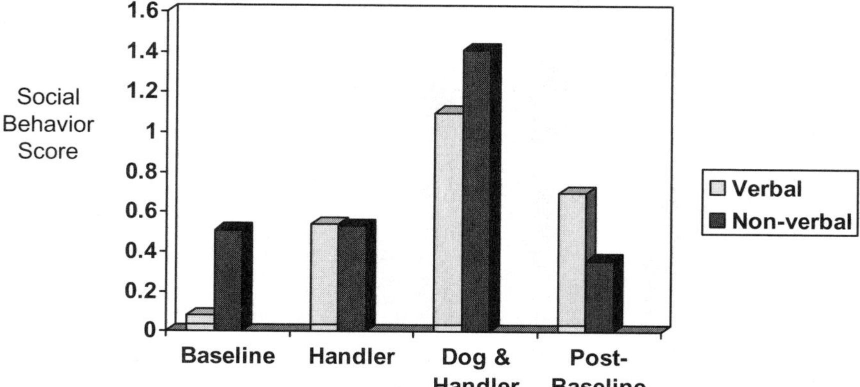

FIGURE 6 Social behavior of men in long-stay psychiatry with therapy dogs (significance not reported; Hall and Malpus, 2000).

elderly male patients in a psychiatric facility showed an increase, although not reported as significant, in verbal and nonverbal interaction that was numerically greater when the dog was present than if only the handler was present (Hall and Malpus, 2000), as shown in Fig. 6.

As anyone with an active dog knows, dogs motivate people to take walks, an effect documented among people before and after adopting a dog (Serpell, 1991). After adopting a dog, people increased their daily walking sharply. Similarly, elderly people in southern California who kept dogs reported spending 1.4 hours per day outdoors with the animal (Siegel, 1990).

In a challenged group of 10 noninstitutionalized children with pervasive developmental disorders, the children were more focused (especially on the dog), more aware of their social environments, and more playful with exposure to a dog (Martin and Farnum, 2002). The dog appeared to play a motivational role in focusing the children's attention so that they were less attentive to distractions.

Studying a clinical population of elderly schizophrenic patients in a 1-year blinded trial, exposure to AAT was associated with a significant improvement in socialization, as shown in Fig. 7, as well as some enhancement of activities of daily living and general well-being (Barak *et al.*, 2001).

D. Calming Effects of Animals

Looking at fish in an aquarium relaxes and relieves anxiety for patients in a dental waiting room (Katcher *et al.*, 1984). This calming and comforting effect

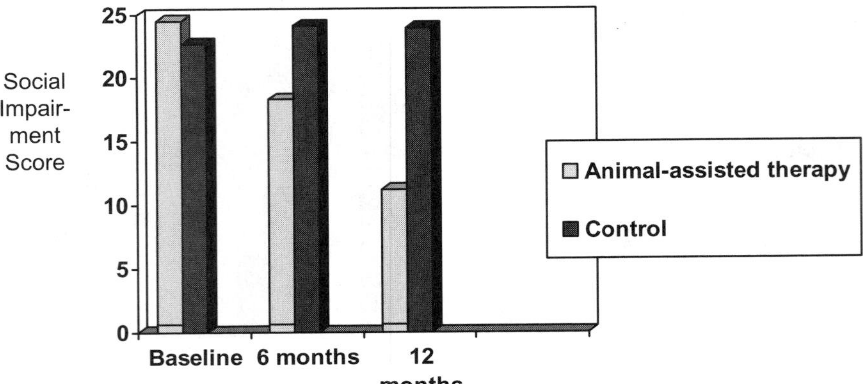

FIGURE 7 Social impairment in elderly schizophrenic patients ($P < 0.01$; Barak *et al.*, 2001).

from animals applies to individuals with Alzheimer's disease (Fritz *et al.*, 1995). Those patients still living at home had fewer aggressive and anxious outbursts if they had regular exposure to a companion animal as compared with patients lacking an animal. The calmer behavior is undoubtedly less distressing and exhausting to the caregiver, who invariably is at risk for burnout in this challenging situation. Similar calming effects have been reported in therapeutic settings. During group therapy with dissociative patients, a therapy dog offered a calming influence and also alerted the therapist to distressed patients (Arnold, 1995). A therapy dog's visits to a psychiatric ward have also been associated with a substantial reduction in noise levels (Walsh *et al.*, 1995).

The calming effects of animals are especially valuable with children exhibiting attention deficit/hyperactivity disorder and conduct disorders. Therapeutic interventions in a learning setting have shown that animals capture and hold children's attention and direct their attention outward (Katcher and Wilkins, 1997). Calming the children is a first essential step. With their attention mobilized and directed outward, agitation and aggression diminish, creating a better teaching environment. Behavioral improvements generalized somewhat but did not carry over to all contexts. In a classroom study of children with Down's syndrome, a real dog provided a more sustained focus than an imitation dog for positive and cooperative interactions with the dog and the adult (Limond *et al.*, 1997).

The most dramatic recent evidence for animals calming people has been in studies of dogs assisting people who have frequent seizures. Particular anxiety arises for such people, who never know exactly when a seizure will occur.

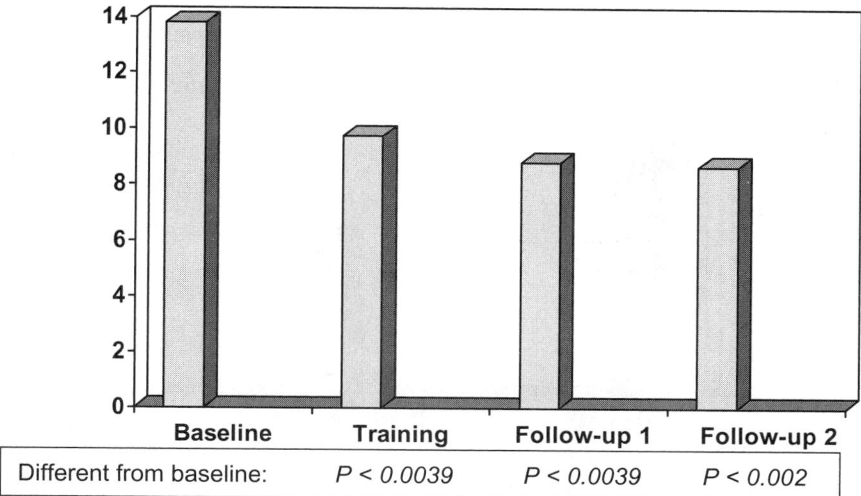

FIGURE 8 Number of seizures before and after acquiring trained seizure-alert dog (Strong *et al.*, 2002).

Training service dogs to assist persons who have seizures then led to the discovery that the dog often was alerting prior to the seizure, giving the person some advance notice to prepare for the seizure (Strong *et al.*, 1999). It was found that having some warning by specially trained seizure-alert dogs of oncoming tonic–clonic seizures led to a reduction in the frequency of seizures (Brown and Strong, 2001; Strong *et al.*, 2002), presumably reflecting the person being more relaxed and less anxious. This considerable reduction was found for 9 of the 10 participants in the study, as shown in Fig. 8. Pet dogs also are known to sometimes spontaneously react to epileptic seizures in their human owners, as was reported for 40% of dogs living with epileptic children; of these, 40% showed anticipatory ability (Kirton *et al.*, 2004). Similarly, 31% of pet dogs were reported by epilepsy patients to respond to seizures; of these, 33% alerted to seizure onset (Dalziel *et al.*, 2003). However, fear, aggression, and avoidance responses in pet dogs responding to seizures can be detrimental to the dogs if they are not specially trained (Strong and Brown, 2000).

In a clinical population of hospitalized psychiatric patients, exposure to AAT was associated with reduced state anxiety levels for patients with a variety of psychiatric diagnoses, especially patients with psychotic disorders, shown in Fig. 9, but also for those with mood and other disorders; this was in contrast with a recreation session that was associated with reduced anxiety only for patients with mood disorders (Barker and Dawson, 1998).

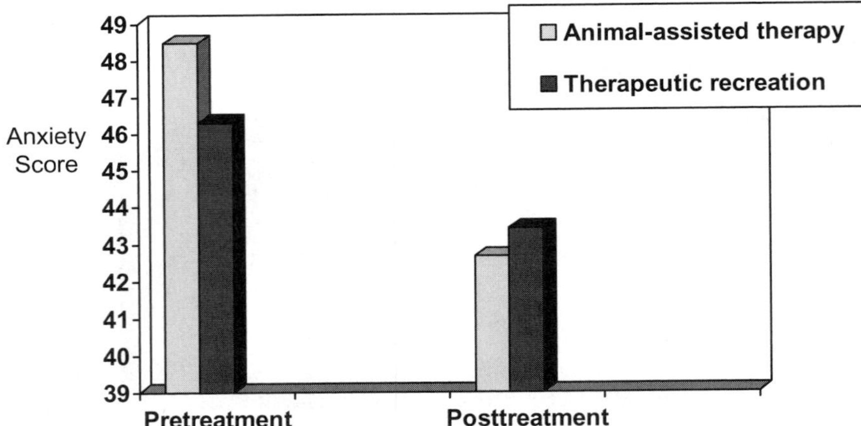

FIGURE 9 State-trait anxiety inventory scores of patients with psychotic disorders ($P < 0.006$; Barker and Dawson, 1998).

III. NORMALIZING EFFECTS OF ANIMALS

Most AAT has been directed toward vulnerable people with little prospect of a full recovery of function and health. Yet, all people are likely to experience periods in their lives of heightened vulnerability. Everyone at some time experiences severe illness or disability, suffers through the illness or death of family members, and, if they live long enough, sustains the adverse consequences of aging. These experiences can create a precarious vulnerable state, particularly if the person lacks a strong network of social support. Whether this precipitating problem represents a new entrenched or a temporary vulnerability, companion animals can normalize a stressful circumstance. They offer engaging and accepting interactions without reflecting back the discomfort, concern, and agitation of the difficult situation. An animal communicates a message such as "It's not as bad as it seems; everything is fine" and thus helps put people more at ease.

A. Facilitating Normality for Children

Dogs normalize the social environment, as illustrated in a study of schoolchildren who used wheelchairs in classes comprised primarily of able-bodied children. The children using wheelchairs who had service dogs consistently were approached more often on the playground than those without service dogs (Mader *et al.*, 1989). The dogs overrode the able-bodied children's discomfort with a child's disability and thus promoted a more normal psychosocial environment for the child. The presence of the dog ensured a more welcoming and warm reception so that the child with the disability who had a dog was treated more as though able-bodied. A variant of this effect relates to the fact that older siblings nurture and care for younger siblings. However, the youngest siblings or only children normalize their environment by giving heightened attention to their animals, thus providing themselves with nurturing opportunities they otherwise would miss (Melson, 1988).

B. Ameliorating Mental and Emotional Crises

Companion animals normalizing a social environment were also shown in a study of patients with Alzheimer's disease who were still living at home with family caregivers. Aggressive outbursts and episodes of anxiety were less common among patients who had regular contact with companion animals (Fritz *et al.*, 1995). For the caregiver, this calming influence of the animal on the patient reduces the stress of coping with this difficult disease in a family member, perhaps delaying the time when the patient has to be placed in an institutional facility. Siegel (1993) has proposed that animals play the role of a stress buffer that softens the impact of stressful events, a suggestion she made after finding that elderly people with companion animals, especially dogs, did not increase their medical visits during times of stressful life events. Elderly people lacking animals characteristically increased their medical visits following stressful life events. It is common for people with a service dog or a police dog to value the dog's psychosocial contributions above the instrumental assistance; in addition to extraordinary companionship, the dog facilitates social interactions (P. Knott, personal communication).

IV. INDIVIDUALITY IN HUMAN RESPONSES TO ANIMALS

The psychosocial effects described here are not evidence for prescribing companion animals generally to individuals who are lonely or depressed. The effects of a particular animal can be positive or negative, varying with the person and the context. Responses to animals are a highly individual matter, depending on the person's previous life experience with animals, the person's current health and responsibilities, and the species and breeds of animals. Someone who had dogs or cats in early childhood would be more likely to respond to animals in later life than someone with little animal experience. In middle and older age, people are generally drawn to the species and perhaps even breeds they had enjoyed previously (Kidd and Kidd, 1989). However, medical, economic, and housing situations may limit the practicality of acquiring the most favored species and breed.

A. Role of Personal Experience with Animals

Small children are strongly attracted to their companion dogs and cats (Kidd and Kidd, 1987), as well as to other, less familiar, small animals, such as a rabbit or turtle (Hunt *et al.*, 1992). The attitudes toward dogs and cats and pet keeping of parents and grandparents strongly influence children (Kidd and Kidd, 1997). As adults, people have a wealth of memories of experiences with animals, including positive and negative occasions that may enhance or attenuate their responses to particular animals. There are no naive adult subjects. Efforts to offer AAA/T or to provide enhanced contact with animals generally offer a particular type of experience, one that is not tailored to the specific preexisting attachments that each individual person has had with animals. Many strongly prefer a particular breed. A woman who has always kept a German Shepherd is likely to retain that strong preference, even in her eighties when she weighs less than the dog. Offering her a bird or a cat, although safer, may not be helpful. One size does not fit all. Paradoxically, old age is the period when people are most strongly and deeply attached to their animals, yet this also is the age where the fewest people keep animals. The people most likely to benefit from companion animal ownership are the least likely to have companionship with animals (Poresky and Daniels, 1998).

B. Attachment and Compatibility with an Animal

The psychosocial benefits of companion animals are strongest when the person is strongly attached to the animal (Garrity *et al.*, 1989). It has been found that people who were relatively more compatible with their pets reported better mental health overall and fewer physical symptoms; the fit between the animal and the owner on physical, behavioral, and psychological dimensions, as measured by compatibility, is key to enjoying the benefits (Budge *et al.*, 1998). Optimal attachment and compatibility are more likely when the animal is of the person's preferred species and breed. Some results suggested that dogs were more salient for participants than cats in maintaining morale in the family (Albert and Anderson, 1997). Other work has suggested that cats may elicit attachment as strongly as dogs (Zasloff and Kidd, 1994a). These studies indicate that psychosocial benefits of pets relate to the companionship they offer, not usually to the instrumental or physical assistance they provide.

V. CONCLUSIONS

This chapter emphasizes the role that companion animals play in people's quality of life. These contributions can enhance anyone's life, but they are crucial for persons whose network of social support is limited. Research literature on human social support documents the essential role of relationships for avoiding early mortality and morbidity. By offering meaningful love and comfort, animals provide support that somewhat substitutes when human companionship is lacking. Animals can play a major positive role in people's lives, particularly if the animal is well suited to the person's living situation, the person is able to easily manage caring for the animal, and behavior problems are avoided. Health professionals have an opportunity to provide leadership in assisting in individualized pet placements with follow-ups to increase the rate of success and anticipate problems before they become serious. Many volunteers who currently bring animal-assisted activities to individuals residing in institutions could with guidance assist precarious individuals still living within the community. Such leadership is also needed to develop new creative solutions for offering more flexible means of having continued contact with animals in later life, but associated with less demanding responsibilities. Community-based councils that include the various constituencies concerned with human and animal health would be well positioned to begin tackling these challenges.

REFERENCES

Albert, A., and Anderson, M. (1997). Dogs, cats, and morale maintenance: Some preliminary data. *Anthrozoos* **10**, 121–124.

Arnold, J. C. (1995). Therapy dogs and the dissociative patient: Preliminary observations. *Dissociat. Progr. Dissociat. Disord.* **8**, 247–252.

Banks, M. R., and Banks, W. A. (2002). The effects of animal-assisted therapy on loneliness in an elderly population in long-term care facilities. *J. Med. Sci. Gerontol.* **57A**, M428–M432.

Barak, Y., Savorai, O., Mavashev, S., and Beni, A. (2001). Animal-assisted therapy for elderly schizophrenic patients: A one-year controlled trial. *Am. J. Geriatr. Psychiatr.* **9**, 439–442.

Barker, S. B., and Dawson, K. S. (1998). The effects of animal-assisted therapy on anxiety ratings of hospitalized psychiatric patients. *Psychiatr. Serv.* **49**, 797–801.

Barrett, C. (1978). Effectiveness of widows' groups in facilitating change. *J. Consult. Counsel. Psychol.* **46**, 20–31.

Beck, A. M., and Katcher, A. H. (1989). Bird-human interaction. *J. Assoc. Avian Vet.* **3**, 152–153.

Berkman, L., and Breslow, L. (1983). "Health and Ways of Living: Findings from the Alameda County Study." Oxford University Press, New York.

Beyersdorfer, P. S., and Birkenhauer, D. M. (1990). The therapeutic use of pets on an Alzheimer's unit. *Am. J. Alzheimer's Care Relat. Disord. Res.* **5**, 13–17.

Brown, S. W., and Strong, V. (2001). The use of seizure-alert dogs. *Seizure* **10**, 39–41.

Budge, R. C., Spicer, J., Jones, B., and St. George, R. (1998). Health correlates of compatibility and attachment in human-companion animal relationships. *Soc. Anim.* **6**, 219–234.

Castelli, P., Hart, L. A., and Zasloff, R. L. (2001). Companion cats and the social support systems of men with AIDS. *Psychol. Rep.* **89**, 177–187.

Chrousos, G. P., and Gold, P. W. (1992). The concepts of stress and stress disorders: Overview of physical and behavioral homeostasis. *J. Am. Med. Assoc.* **267**, 1244–1252.

Clausen, J. A. (1993). "American Lives: Looking Back at the Children of the Great Depression." Free Press, New York.

Dalziel, D. J., Uthman, B. M., McGorray, S. P., and Reep, R. L. (2003). Seizure-alert dogs: A review and preliminary study. *Seizure* **12**, 115–120.

Eddy, J., Hart, L. A., and Boltz, R. P. (1988). The effects of service dogs on social acknowledgements of people in wheelchairs. *J. Psychol.* **122**, 39–45.

Folse, E. B., Minder, C. C., Aycock, M. J., and Santana, R. T. (1994). Animal-assisted therapy and depression in adult college students. *Anthrozoos* 7, 188–194.

Francis, G., Turner, J. T., and Johnson, S. B. (1985). Domestic animal visitation as therapy with adult home residents. *Int. J. Nurs. Stud.* **22**, 201–206.

Fritz, C. L., Farver, T. B., Hart, L. A., and Kass, P. H. (1996). Companion animals and the psychological health of Alzheimer's patients' caregivers. *Psychol. Rep.* 78, 467–481.

Fritz, C. L., Farver, T. B., Kass, P. H., and Hart, L. A. (1995). Association with companion animals and the expression of noncognitive symptoms in Alzheimer's patients. *J. Nerv. Ment. Dis.* **183**(8), 359–363.

Garrity, T. F., and Stallones, L. (1998). Effects of pet contact on human well-being. *In* "Companion Animals in Human Health" (C. C. Wilson and D. C. Turner, eds.), pp. 3–22. Sage, Thousand Oaks, CA.

Garrity, T. F., Stallones, L., Marx, M. B., and Johnson, T. P. (1989). Pet ownership and attachment as supportive factors in the health of the elderly. *Anthrozoos* **3**, 35–44.

Goldmeier, J. (1986). Pets or people: Another research note. *Gerontologist* **26**, 203–206.

Hall, P. L., and Malpus, Z. (2000). Pets as therapy: Effects on social interaction in long-stay psychiatry. *Br. J. Nurs.* **9**, 2220–2225.

Hart, L. A. (1992). Therapeutic riding: Assessing human versus horse effects. *Anthrozoos* **5**, 138–139.

Hart, L. A. (2003). Pets along a continuum: Response to "What is a pet?" *Anthrozoos* **16**, 118–122.

Hart, L. A., Zasloff, R. L., and Benfatto, A. M. (1996). The socializing role of hearing dogs. *Appl. Anim. Behav. Sci.* **47**, 7–15.

Haughie, E., Milne, D., and Elliott, V. (1992). An evaluation of companion pets with elderly psychiatric patients. *Behav. Psychother.* **20**, 367–372.

Hendy, H. M. (1987). Effects of pet and/or people visits on nursing home residents. *Int. J. Aging Hum. Dev.* **25**, 279–291.

Holcomb, R., Jendro, C., Weber, B., and Nahan, U. (1997). Use of an aviary to relieve depression in elderly males. *Anthrozoology* **10**, 32–36.

House, J. S., Landis, K. R., and Umberson, D. (1988). Social relationships and health. *Science* **241**, 540–545.

Hunt, S. J., Hart, L. A., and Gomulkiewicz, R. (1992). Role of small animals in social interaction between strangers. *J. Soc. Psychol.* **133**, 245–256.

Jessen, J., Cardiello, F., and Baun, M. M. (1996). Avian companionship in alleviation of depression, loneliness, and low morale of older adults in skilled rehabilitation units. *Psychol. Rep.* **78**, 339–348.

Karsh, E. B., and Turner, D. C. (1988). The human-cat relationship. *In* "The Domestic Cat: The Biology of Its Behaviour" (D. C. Turner and P. Bateson, eds.). Cambridge University Press, Cambridge.

Katcher, A., and Wilkins, G. G. (1997). Animal-assisted therapy in the treatment of disruptive behavior disorders in children. *In* "The Environment and Mental Health: A Guide for Clinicians" (A. Lundberg, ed.), pp. 193–204. Lawrence Erlbaum Associates, Mahwah, NJ.

Katcher, A., Segal, H., and Beck, A. (1984). Comparison of contemplation and hypnosis for the reduction of anxiety and discomfort during dental surgery. *Am. J. Clin. Hypnosis* **27**, 14–21.

Kidd, A. H., and Kidd, R. M. (1987). Reactions of infants and toddlers to live and toy animals. *Psychol. Rep.* **61**, 455–464.

Kidd, A. H., and Kidd, R. M. (1989). Factors in adults' attitudes toward pets. *Psychol. Rep.* **65**, 903–910.

Kidd, A. H., and Kidd, R. M. (1997). Changes in the behavior of pet owners across generations. *Psychol. Rep.* **80**, 195–202.

Kirton, A., Wirrell, E., Zhang, J., and Hamiwka, L. (2004). Seizure-alerting and -response behaviors in dogs living with epileptic children. *Neurology* **62**, 2302–2305.

Kongable, L. G., Buckwalter, K. C., and Stolley, J. (1989). The effects of pet therapy on the social behavior of institutionalized Alzheimer's clients. *Arch. Psychiatr. Nurs.* **3**, 191–198.

Lago, D., Delaney, M., Miller, M., and Grill, C. (1989). Companion animals, attitudes toward pets, and health outcomes among the elderly: A long-term follow-up. *Anthrozoos* **3**, 25–34.

Lane, D. R., McNicholas, J., and Collis, G. M. (1998). Dogs for the disabled: Benefits to recipients and welfare of the dog. *Appl. Anim. Behav. Sci.* **59**, 49–60.

Limond, J. A., Bradshaw, J. W. S., and Corrnack, K. F. M. (1997). Behavior of children with learning disabilities interacting with a therapy dog. *Anthrozoos* **10**, 84–89.

Lynch, J. J. (1977). "The Broken Heart: The Medical Consequences of Loneliness." Basic Books, New York.

Mader, B., Hart, L. A., and Bergin, B. (1989). Social acknowledgements for children with disabilities: Effects of service dogs. *Child Dev.* **60**, 1528–1534.

Martin, F., and Farnum, J. (2002). Animal-assisted therapy for children with pervasive developmental disorders. *West. J. Nurs. Res.* **24**, 657–670.

Melson, G. F. (1988). Availability of and involvement with pets by children: Determinants and correlates. *Anthrozoos* **2**, 45–52.

Messent, P. R. (1984). Correlates and effects of pet ownership. *In* "The Pet Connection: Its Influence on Our Health and Quality of Life" (R. K. Anderson, B. L. Hart, and L. A. Hart, eds.), pp. 331–340. University of Minnesota, Minneapolis, MN.

Miller, M., and Lago, D. (1990). The well-being of older women: The importance of pet and human relations. *Anthrozoos* **3**, 245–251.

Mugford, R., and M'Comisky, J. (1975). Some recent work on the psychotherapeutic value of cage birds with old people. *In* "Pet Animals and Society, a BSAVA Symposium" (R. S. Anderson, ed.), pp. 54–65. Bailliere Tindall, London.

Ory, M. B., and Goldberg, E. L. (1983). Pet possession and life satisfaction in elderly women. *In* "New Perspectives on Our Lives with Companion Animals" (A. H. Katcher and A. M. Beck, eds.), pp. 303–317. University of Pennsylvania Press, Philadelphia, PA.

Ory, M. B., and Goldberg, E. L. (1984). An epidemiological study of pet ownership in the community. *In* "The Pet Connection: Its Influence on Our Health and Quality of Life" (R. K. Anderson, B. L. Hart, and L. A. Hart, eds.), pp. 320–330. University of Minnesota, Minneapolis, MN.

Peretti, P. O. (1990). Elderly-animal friendship bonds. *Soc. Behav. Personal.* **18**, 151–156.

Poresky, R. H., and Daniels, A. M. (1998). Demographics of pet presence and attachment. *Anthrozoos* **11**, 236–241.

Psychiatric Service Dog Society. http://www.psychdog.org. Accessed 09/02/05.

Raina, P., Waltner-Toews, D., Bonnett, B., Woodward, C., and Abernathy, T. (1999). Influence of companion animals on the physical and psychological health of older people: An analysis of a one-year longitudinal study. *J. Am. Geriatr. Soc.* **47**, 323–329.

Robb, S. S. (1983). Health status correlates of pet-human association in a health impaired population. *In* "New Perspectives on Our Lives with Companion Animals" (A. H. Katcher and A. M. Beck, eds.), pp. 318–327. University of Pennsylvania Press, Philadelphia, PA.

Robb, S. S., and Stegman, C. E. (1983). Companion animals and elderly people: A challenge for evaluators of social support. *Gerontologist* **23**, 277–282.

Rogers, J., Hart, L. A., and Boltz, R. P. (1993). The role of pet dogs in casual conversations of elderly adults. *J. Soc. Psychol.* **133**, 265–277.

Serpell, J. (1986/1996). Health and friendship. *In* "In the Company of Animals: A Study of Human-Animal Relationships," pp. 108–126. Cambridge University Press, Cambridge UK.

Serpell, J. (1991). Beneficial effects of pet ownership on some aspects of human health and behavior. *J. R. Soc. Med.* **84**, 717–720.

Siegel, J. (1990). Stressful life events and use of physician services among the elderly: The moderating role of pet ownership. *J. Personal. Soc. Psychol.* **58**, 1081–1086.

Siegel, J. M. (1993). Companion animals: In sickness and in health. *J. Soc. Issues* **49**, 157–167.

Smith, S. L. (1983). Interactions between pet dog and family members: An ethological study. *In* "New Perspectives on Our Lives with Companion Animals" (A. H. Katcher and A. M. Beck, eds.), pp. 29–36. University of Pennsylvania Press, Philadelphia, PA.

Stallones, L., Marx, M. B., Garrity, T. F., and Johnson, T. P. (1990). Pet ownership and attachment in relation to the health of U.S. adults, 21 to 64 years of age. *Anthrozoos* **4**, 100–112.

Straede, C. M., and Gates, G. R. (1993). Psychological health in a population of Australian cat owners. *Anthrozoos* **6**, 30–42.

Strong, V., and Brown, S. W. (2000). Should people with epilepsy have untrained dogs as pets? *Seizure* **9**, 427–430.

Strong, V., Brown, S., Huyton, M., and Coyle, H. (2002). Effect of trained seizure alert dogs on frequency of tonic-clonic seizures. *Seizure* **11**, 402–405.

Strong, V., Brown, S. W., and Walker, R. (1999). Seizure-alert dogs: Fact or fiction? *Seizure* **8**, 62–65.

Thoits, P. (1982). Conceptual, methodological, and theoretical problems in studying social supports as a buffer against life stress. *J. Health Soc. Behav.* **23**, 145–159.

Walsh, P. G., Mertin, P. G., Verlander, D. F., and Pollard, C. F. (1995). The effects of a "pets as therapy" dog on persons with dementia in a psychiatric ward. *Aust. Occup. Ther. J.* **42**(4), 161–166.

Zasloff, R. L., and Kidd, A. H. (1994a). Attachment to feline companions. *Psychol. Rep.* **74**, 747–752.

Zasloff, R. L., and Kidd, A. H. (1994b). Loneliness and pet ownership among single women. *Psychol. Rep.* **75**, 747–752.

CHAPTER 6

The Animal–Human Bond: Health and Wellness

ERIKA FRIEDMANN AND CHIA-CHUN TSAI
University of Maryland School of Nursing, Baltimore, Maryland 21201

Health comprises the integration of psychological, physical, social, environmental, and spiritual aspects of an individual into a functional whole (Audy, 1971; Sterling, 2003; Thomas *et al.*, 2002; Thomas *et al.*, 2003). Maximal health and wellness is life lived to its fullest. Individuals achieve optimal functioning along their personal continuums from minimal to optimal individual capacity. Individuals with personal, environmental, or physical limitations can achieve a high degree of health and wellness by living to their maximal capacities in a combination of these spheres (Audy, 1971). Healthy individuals live in harmony with themselves, others, and their environments.

Animal-assisted therapy (AAT) is one of several ways that animals can enhance or compromise individuals' health. While this chapter focuses on physical indicators of health, it is important to remember the interconnections among the physical, social, and psychological components of health. Thus the psychological and social impact of friendly animals reported in Chapter 5 will also impact the physical aspects discussed here. Psychosocial factors either promote health by moderating or promote disease by enhancing pathological processes (Audy, 1971). Psychosocial as well as physiological challenges play important roles in the pathogenesis of chronic disease (Thomas *et al.*, 1997).

Handbook on Animal-Assisted Therapy: Theoretical Foundations and Guidelines for Practice, 2e

AAT refers to a general category of interventions without a common protocol. In general, AAT involves introduction of a companion animal to an individual who does not own that animal with the expectation that the introduced animal will provide short-term benefits to the individual at least while the animal is present. The impact of an animal on any one aspect of health will have effects on and affect other aspects.

AAT varies tremendously among implementations. It can involve the introduction of one or more animals of the same or different species to an individual in a private or group setting. The introduced animal(s) is accompanied by an individual responsible for the safe introduction and interaction of the pair.

The focus of most research addressing benefits of pet ownership or interaction with friendly animals stems from their potential to decrease loneliness and depression, reduce stress and anxiety, and provide a stimulus for exercise (Friedmann and Thomas, 1985). Stress, anxiety, and depression are associated with the hyperactivity of the sympatho–adrenal–medulla (SAM) system, the hypothalamic–pituitary–adrenal axis (HPA), and abnormal platelet reactivity (Musselman *et al.*, 1998; Rozanski *et al.*, 1999). Chronic stimulation of these responses increases the likelihood of chronic disease morbidity and mortality (McEwen, 1998). SAM hyperactivity results in increased catecholamine release (Louis *et al.*, 1975; Veith *et al.*, 1994; Wyatt *et al.*, 1971), reduced heart rate (HR) variability/increased sympathetic tone (Musselman *et al.*, 1998), decreased myocardial perfusion, and ventricular instability (Corbalan *et al.*, 1974; DeSilva *et al.*, 1978; Julius and Nesbitt, 1996; Skinner, 1981, 1985). In response to stress and depression, the HPA system initiates a series of neurohormonal responses and releases corticosteroids into the bloodstream (Arato *et al.*, 1986; Banki *et al.*, 1992; Nemeroff *et al.*, 1984; Pasic *et al.*, 2003; Rozanski *et al.*, 1999). The combination of stress and anxiety and/or depression and the physiological components of these responses enhances the risk of cardiac mortality (Lampert *et al.*, 2000; Rozanski *et al.*, 1999). Excessive stress and psychological distress contribute to diseases of the skin and respiratory tract, as well as disruption in immune function and cardiovascular disease.

The presence of or interacting with friendly animals is conceptualized as a means of alleviating distress caused by loneliness and depression as well as decreasing physiological stress responses. The physiological outcomes studied as indicators of distress/stress include elevated blood pressure (BP), heart rate, peripheral skin temperature, and cortisol (Baun *et al.*, 1991), in addition to risk factors for and mortality among patients with coronary heart disease.

AAT is designed to benefit individuals by reducing stress and loneliness and inducing attention to and interaction with the outside world. For the purpose of this chapter, AAT is defined as interactions including the introduction of a friendly animal owned by another person into a naturally occurring situation or the simulation of a naturally occurring situation for the purpose of affecting the individual's health or well-being.

I. HEALTH BENEFITS FROM ANIMAL-ASSISTED THERAPY

Several studies completed since the mid-1990s directly address the impact of AAT on physiological indicators of health or stress/distress. The mixed results of the studies highlight the importance of considering the method of introduction of the animal and the way the AAT is conducted in developing interventions to meet specific goals.

A. Individual Animal-Assisted Therapy

Evidence for the success of an individual AAT in decreasing physiological indicators of stress is largely derived from studies using dogs with children, although individual AAT was effective at reducing stress among adults. In these studies, one animal interacts with each person in an individually oriented session.

The presence of a friendly dog was effective at reducing BP and HR of 2- to 6-year-old children undergoing simulations of routine physical examinations compared with the same children without a dog (Nagengast *et al.*, 1997). Although the presence of a friendly dog was effective at reducing behavioral signs of distress in 2- to 6-year-old children undergoing actual physical examinations when compared with other children without a dog present, the physiological antiarousal effects of the AAT were not replicated (Hansen *et al.*, 1999).

Asking children to interact with a dog during a stressful activity was somewhat successful at reducing stress indicators. Havener (2001) used AAT to reduce anxiety in 20 children 7 to 11 years old who were undergoing a dental surgical procedure. The children were encouraged to touch, pet, and talk to a dog that was lying beside them. There were no differences in peripheral skin temperature responses to the dental procedure between children with and those without a dog present during the procedure. Physiological indicators of stress while children who were distressed were waiting for the dentist were lower among those waiting with the dog present.

Individual AAT in the form of an aquarium also has been successful at improving some measures of stress in adults. In a study of individual AAT that relied on paper-and-pencil tests to measure physiological status, having aquariums in their hospital rooms reduced "stress levels" of adults awaiting heart transplants (Cole and Gawlinski, 2000).

Attitudes toward an AAT animal influence its effectiveness. Playing with a friendly dog appeared to mute physiological arousal during play activities of pediatric cardiology inpatients who developed rapport with the dog during individual AAT. Heart rate, BP, oxygen saturation, and respiratory rate were recorded before, during, and after 10–20 minutes of interacting with dogs by the patients and at least one parent. The increase in the child's respiratory rate was negatively correlated with rapport with the dog. The better the rapport, the smaller the increase during interaction. Decreases in respiratory rate were most frequent during physical contact between the dog and the patient (Wu *et al.*, 2002). Including the child's physical exertion level in the analysis would strengthen the evidence.

Healthcare professionals also can benefit from AAT. Interacting with a therapy dog for 5 minutes led to decreased stress as assessed with serum and salivary cortisol. The magnitude of the decreases in cortisol during 5 minutes of AAT was similar to decreases during 20 minutes of rest or 20 minutes of AAT (Barker *et al.*, 2005).

B. Group Animal-Assisted Therapy

The physiological effects of an AAT group and a child-life therapy group were similar for 70 children (mean age 9.9 years) hospitalized for an extended time, mostly for chronic diseases (Kaminski *et al.*, 2002). In both groups children were able to move around freely and choose activities of their choice with parents and/or staff and volunteers. Salivary cortisol, HR, and BP did not change significantly from before to after AAT or group child-life therapy or differ between the participants in the two therapies, despite observations of a more happy affect after AAT.

An aquarium in the dining room provided group AAT in a unique study of food intake among nursing home residents with dementia. The weight loss typically experienced in this population is due to failure to eat rather than changes in metabolic state. Introduction of an aquarium to the group dining room led to increased nutritional intake and weight gain. The aquarium held residents' attention and encouraged them to spend more time eating (Edwards and Beck, 2002).

Individual AAT in which a friendly dog was present during a stressful activity was beneficial for reducing physiological indicators of distress in children and adults. The benefits of individual AAT were documented for the time the animals were present, but extension of the effects beyond the time of interaction was not documented. Group AAT did not improve physiological indicators of distress but did encourage nursing home residents with dementia to remain in the dining room and eat.

AAT was demonstrated to be effective for reducing stress indicators in situations where the individual's response with and without the animal present were compared, but not when different individuals participated and did not participate in AAT. Inconsistencies in the results of investigations of the effectiveness of AAT highlight the importance of methodological design in evaluating its effectiveness. It is important to consider the appropriateness of the specific implementation of AAT to obtain the desired outcome. Schwartz and Patronek (2002) provide excellent insight into many of the methodological issues to be considered in design and interpretation of studies assessing the anxiety-reducing effects of AAT.

A larger and ever-increasing body of research provides a theoretical basis for the positive impact of AAT on human health. Some of the research relies on epidemiological research methods that study groups of people in their natural environments, whereas other research relies on data from experimental studies over short durations in laboratory or home conditions. Two intervention studies examined the physiological impact of giving people pets.

II. EPIDEMIOLOGICAL EVIDENCE FOR HEALTH BENEFITS

Epidemiological methods allow nonmanipulative investigation of the association between specific characteristics or exposures and health outcomes by examining large groups of subjects in their natural settings. Single epidemiological studies provide evidence of association but are not conclusive with respect to causation. The combined evidence from several epidemiological studies provides strong support for causation of health outcomes, usually mortality or morbidity.

The integrative aspect of the various components of health is demonstrated by the combined contributions of social, psychological, environmental, and physical factors to chronic diseases. Coronary heart disease was among the first chronic diseases for which the contribution of social and psychological factors was demonstrated (Jenkins, 1976a,b). Pets were conceptualized as a contributor to the social aspect of health. The cardiovascular system was a logical starting point for evaluating the possible effects of owning pets on human health (Friedmann *et al.*, 1980).

Several case control studies demonstrate the association of owning a pet with cardiovascular health. In the first study of this type, pet ownership was associated with survival among patients who were hospitalized for heart attacks, myocardial infarctions, or severe chest pain, angina pectoris (Friedmann *et al.*, 1980). Only 5.7% of the 53 pet owners compared with 28.2% of the 39 patients who did not own pets died within 1 year of discharge from a coronary care unit. The relationship of pet ownership to improved survival was independent of the severity of the cardiovascular disease. That is, among people with equally severe disease, pet owners were less likely to die than nonowners. Owning a pet did not appear to substitute for other forms of social support, such as being married or living with others. This study was replicated and extended to a larger number of subjects with improved measures of cardiovascular physiology and psychosocial status (Friedmann and Thomas, 1995). Among 369 patients who had experienced myocardial infarctions and had ventricular arrhythmias, life-threatening irregular heartbeats, after them, both owning pets and having more support from other people tended to predict 1-year survival. As in the previous study the association of pet ownership with survival could not be explained by differences in the severity of the illness, psychological or social status, or demographic characteristics between those patients who owned pets and those who did not.

The possibility that some species of animals might provide distinct benefits to their owners while others might not gained limited support from epidemiological evidence. In Friedmann and Thomas' (1995) study, dog owners were approximately 8.6 times as likely to be alive in 1 year as those who did not own dogs. The effect of dog ownership on survival did not depend on the amount of social support or the severity of the cardiovascular disease. In contrast, cat owners were more likely to die than people who did not own cats. The relationship of cat ownership to survival was confounded by the effect of social support, which was low among cat owners and among those who died, and by the overrepresentation among cat owners of women, who were almost two times as likely to die as men. A subsequent study of 6-month survival among 454 patients who were admitted to a hospital for myocardial infarction also suggested that cat ownership might have a different health impact than dog ownership (Rajack, 1997). Cat owners were more likely to be readmitted for further cardiac problems or angina than people who did not own pets. However, in contrast to the previous studies, pet ownership was not related to 6-month survival or to other indicators of health. The one difference between dog and cat owners' cardiovascular health must be interpreted cautiously; one significant difference among many comparisons raises the possibility of a chance effect.

Pet ownership may protect people from developing coronary heart disease or slow its progression in addition to influencing the survival of individuals who have experienced myocardial infarctions. Several cross-sectional studies and one longitudinal descriptive epidemiological study addressed the differences between pet owners and nonowners in health indicators. Among 5741 people attending a screening clinic in Melbourne, Australia, risk factors for coronary heart disease were significantly greater among the 4957 pet nonowners than among the 784 pet owners. For men, plasma levels of cholesterol and triglycerides and systolic BP were higher among pet nonowners than pet owners. For women, differences in risk factors between pet owners and nonowners occurred only for those women who are most susceptible to coronary heart disease, women in the menopausal and postmenopausal age groups (Anderson *et al.*, 1992). A study of senior citizens ($n = 127$) also indicated that pet owners have lower serum triglyceride levels than nonowners (Dembicki and Anderson, 1996). Both studies indicated that dog owners exercised more than other study participants. While dog owners were more likely to exercise than owners of other pets, there were no systematic differences in other health-related behaviors between pet owners and nonowners or between dog and cat owners. In contrast, a random sample of 5079 adults from Canberra and Queanbeyan, New South Wales, Australia, interviewed in 2000 and 2001, approximately 57% of whom were pet owners, revealed no significant reduction in cardiovascular risk factors or in use of health services for pet owners (Parslow and Jorm, 2003; Jorm *et al.*, 1997). In fact, pet owners had higher diastolic BP after controlling for age, sex, and education than those without pets (Parslow *et al.*, 2003). When the older group—those 60 to 64 years old—was examined separately, there was no evidence for a health benefit (Parslow *et al.*, 2005). Differences in patterns of pet ownership may be responsible for the apparent discrepancies. Pet ownership was considerably more common in the New South Wales survey than in Melbourne. Types of pets were not evaluated in the New South Wales survey.

In several surveys, owning a pet was related to proxies for physiological health such as medical visits, number of health problems, or functional status. In large representative sample surveys of the populations of Germany and Australia, after taking into account demographic predictors of health status, people who owned pets made fewer medical visits than those who did not (Headey *et al.*, 2002). In the United States, pet owners ($n = 345$) among the 938 Medicare enrollees in an HMO reported fewer medical visits, including both fewer total doctor contacts and fewer respondent-initiated medical contacts, over a 1-year period than nonowners (Siegel, 1990). Further analyses of data indicated that pet ownership was a significant moderator of the impact of psychological distress on doctor contacts, independent of the effects of health status, depressed mood, and other demographic factors. For individuals who did not own pets, psychosocial distress, as assessed by stressful life events, was directly correlated with doctor contacts; the higher the stress level, the more contacts. However, for pet owners, increased stress levels did not predict more physician contacts. There was also evidence for differences in the effects of dogs and other pets on health as assessed by health behavior. For individuals who did not own dogs, doctor contacts increased as life events increased. In contrast, among dog owners, life events were unrelated to respondent-initiated doctor contacts.

A Canadian longitudinal telephone survey of adults 65 years and older also supported a positive impact of pet ownership on respondents' ($n = 995$) ability to complete activities of daily living at study entry and 1 year later. After controlling for physical activity, age, and living situation, the ability to complete activities of daily living decreased more in 1 year for people who did not own pets than for people who kept them (Raina *et al.*, 1999).

One of the major questions arising in studies finding an association of pet ownership with health status is whether data are due to people with better health status choosing to own or interact with pets. If so, the better health could predate the pet exposure. Thus the causal relationship would begin with better health status and end with pet ownership. The question of which came first, pet ownership or better health, was addressed in a novel longitudinal study. A cohort of 343 people who entered into a population study in 1921 were asked in 1977 about their history of playing with pets and then were followed for 15 years. There was no relationship of pet-related behavior in 1977 to long-term survival. This was true even when looking separately at individuals with low social support (Tucker *et al.*, 1995). These data do not support the supposition that better health predates or causes more interaction with pets.

Introduction of an animal into a living situation can lead to improved health status. Adopting a pet was associated with improved health status for the adopters (Serpell, 1991). People who adopted dogs or cats from an animal shelter ($n = 71$) experienced significant reductions in minor health problems, including headaches, hay fever, and painful joints, 1 month after adopting the pet. Dog adopters ($n = 47$) maintained the decrease in minor health problems over the 10-month duration of the study, whereas cat owners did not. In this study, dog owners both appeared to walk slightly more at baseline and reported increased frequency and duration of walking at 10 months. This suggests the possibility that adoption of a cat could have encouraged the owner to spend additional time at home and thus forego walks. The physiological benefits associated with acquiring a dog could have been the result of increased physical activity engendered in walking the animal. In fact, the absence of long-term benefits for cat owners supports this possibility. However, those who adopted dogs already tended to walk more at baseline than those who adopted other animals and the control group. The differences in walking may have been a reflection of other differences in lifestyle and availability of time for walking and caring for a dog. Differences in the health experience of those who adopted dogs versus cats also may be confounded by differences in stressful life events (Serpell and Jackson, 1994). Introducing pets and plants into nursing homes similarly was associated with an improvement in minor health problems, as evidenced by reduction in amount spent on medications (Montague, 1995).

Dog and cat ownership might have different associations with health status as evidenced by two case control studies (Friedmann *et al.*, 1995; Rajack, 1997) and two longitudinal studies (Serpell, 1991; Siegel, 1990). Too few pet owners own only other species in these studies to begin to explore differences in health among them. The mechanisms for differences in health status of dog and cat owners as well as which aspects of health might be differentially affected by these animals remain to be evaluated. It does appear that owning a dog encourages people to exercise more. The likelihood that there are differences in the contribution of dogs and cats to their respective owners' health also raises questions about differences between people who choose to own dogs and those who choose to own cats. Differences are generally limited to the amount of exercise the individuals take (Anderson *et al.*, 1992; Dembicki *et al.*, 1996). However, Serpell's (1991) study demonstrates that these differences may be determinants of which pet people choose to keep rather than the result of acquiring a dog.

III. EXPERIMENTAL OR QUASI-EXPERIMENTAL RESEARCH

In an attempt to understand how, from a physiological perspective, pets provide the benefits detailed earlier, a number of researchers have investigated the short-term effects of companion animals on people. These short-term effects, measured on the timescale of minutes rather than months or years, may be the bases for the long-term effects demonstrated in epidemiological studies as well as for other, more subtle effects of pet ownership.

The vast majority of the studies of the effect of animals on human physiology utilize experimental techniques in which the physiological effect of an image of an animal or an animal stimulus is measured. Although the epidemiological studies cited earlier include pets of all types, a majority of the studies of the short-term impact of animals on human physiology are limited to the effects of dogs. This is largely a matter of convenience because dogs are kept as pets so frequently and they are easy to handle. In research investigating the short-term stress-reducing effects of animals, two types of potential health benefits were investigated: direct effects on physiological indicators of stress and stress moderating or buffering effects. The experimental and quasi-experimental studies investigate whether explicitly and/or implicitly observing animals is associated with direct effects on people's physiology or associated with moderating people's stress responses. Researchers have evaluated people's responses to three different exposures to animals: (1) people explicitly looking at or observing animals or pictures of animals, (2) people implicitly observing or being in the presence of animals, and (3) people touching or interacting with animals.

A. Effects of Explicitly Looking at or Observing Animals or Pictures of Animals

Studies of the impact of looking at or observing animals document the direct impact of animals on people's responses to scenes and the people in them (Lockwood, 1983; Rossbach and Wilson, 1992) and examine the physiological indicators of parasympathetic nervous system arousal while and/or immediately after watching animals (i.e., Eddy, 1995, 1996; Globisch *et al.*, 1999; Katcher *et al.*, 1983). Only one research group (Katcher *et al.*, 1983) addressed the effect of explicitly looking at or observing animals on people's responses to stressors.

Friendly domestic animals have been used effectively in the advertising and publicity industries to impute safety, believability, and trustworthiness to people who accompany them (Lockwood, 1983). Research supports the positive influence of looking at animals on some of people's moods and perceptions. Young adults rated scenes and the people depicted in pictorial scenes were rated as significantly more friendly (Lockwood, 1983), less threatening (Lockwood, 1983), happier (Lockwood, 1983; Rossbach *et al.*, 1992), and more relaxed (Rossbach *et al.*, 1992). In contrast, pictures of animals culturally associated with fear elicited negative feelings and physiological arousal (Globisch *et al.*, 1999).

Physiological indicators of parasympathetic nervous system arousal also indicate that looking at or observing domestic animals is associated with relaxation. Blood pressures of normotensive and hypertensive adults decreased progressively while watching fish swim in an aquarium (Katcher *et al.*, 1983). The duration of the decreases was greater when observing an aquarium with fish than when looking at an aquarium with plants and moving water but without fish and than when looking at a wall.

Looking at familiar nondomestic animals can lead to decreases in physiological arousal. The BP and HR of a chimpanzee's caretaker and research assistants who assisted with the chimpanzee ($n = 9$) tended to be lower while watching the chimp than during a relaxation period (Eddy, 1995). In a single case report, the BP and HR of a 26-year-old male snake owner was lower during a 6-minute period of watching his pet than during the preceding 6 minutes when he sat alone and relaxed (Eddy, 1996).

The potential stress response–moderating effects of watching animals first was in a study of the physiological impact of watching fish swim in an aquarium (Katcher *et al.*, 1983). Blood pressure increases in response to reading aloud were less pronounced after watching fish than after watching other stimuli.

Studies of people observing fish and chimpanzees indicate that observing animals from a safe position often encourages people to relax. The constant motion of the animals studied in this context characteristically attracts the observer's attention. Evidence presented through the comparison of the fish in the aquarium with the fishless aquarium and the wall supports the contention that this attraction might be a prerequisite for continued relaxation over a longer time span (Katcher, 1981). Katcher suggested the biophilia hypothesis as one reason for people's extended attention to the fish swimming in the tank compared with other stimuli. Data obtained during observation of loud, rambunctious chimpanzees suggest that profound tranquility and serenity might not be prerequisites for the decreased parasympathetic nervous system arousal while watching animals (Friedmann, Thomas, and Eddy, 2000).

B. Effects of Implicitly Observing or Being in the Presence of an Animal

Observing or being in the presence of animals without being instructed to attend to them both impacts indicators of physiological arousal (Friedmann *et al.*, 1983) and moderates stress responses. This situation contrasts with the previous group of studies where individuals were directed explicitly to focus on the animals.

The presence of a dog accompanying a researcher had a direct impact on cardiovascular and psychological indicators of arousal. In a study of BP in the home setting, children's (n = 38) BP during the entire experiment was lower among those who had the dog present for the first half of the experiment than those who had the dog present for the second half of the experiment (Friedmann *et al.*, 1983).

The effect of presence of a friendly dog on the stress response to several stressors has been evaluated. The presence of a friendly dog attenuated the cardiovascular stress responses of thirty-eight 9- to 15-year-old children to reading aloud (Friedmann *et al.*, 1983). In a similar study conducted among college students (n = 193), the presence of a dog caused significant moderation of HR, but not BP, responses (Locker, 1985). In a group of 25 community-living older adults with slightly elevated BP, mean arterial pressure (MAP) and diastolic BP (DBP) responses to a social stressor were lower with a companion animal present than without a companion animal present (Friedmann *et al.*, 2005).

The presence of a dog moderated responses to cognitive stressors in some situations but not others. Neither BP nor HR responses to two cognitive stressors, mental arithmetic and oral interpretation of drawings, differed between dog-owning college students accompanied by their dogs and those who were not accompanied by their dogs (Grossberg *et al.*, 1988). In contrast, in a study of women's (n = 45, mean age of 39 years) cardiovascular stress responses, the presence of a dog led to reduced cardiovascular reactivity compared with the presence of another person, even when the person was chosen by the subject to provide support (Allen *et al.*, 1991). Extending this study, the cardiovascular reactivity of married couples (n = 240) to stressors while one member of the couple was alone, with a pet or friend, with their spouse, or with their spouse and their pet was examined. People who owned pets had lower resting BPs and experienced less of an increase in BP during cold pressor tests and mental arithmetic than nonowners. Among pet owners, their smallest responses to stressful tasks were when the pet was present (Allen *et al.*, 2002). The authors concluded that the nonjudgmental aspect of the support afforded by the pet was responsible for decreasing the stress response. This is consistent with other research indicating greater stress responses in the presence of more judgmental or authoritative individuals (Long *et al.*, 1982).

A more recent study of the effects of the presence of an animal on women's cardiovascular responses to a number of everyday stressors in the normal home environment led to different results (Rajack, 1997). There were no differences in the cardiovascular responses of dog owners with their dogs present (n = 30) and nonowners (n = 30) to running up and down the stairs and reading aloud. Dog owners tended to have greater HR responses to hearing the alarm clock sound. On the basis of the research summarized earlier, the presence of an animal has the potential to influence stress responses but does not do so uniformly.

Attitudes toward animals impact the stress-buffering effects of the presence of an animal; not all individuals respond similarly. Recognizing that there is variability in individuals' responses to the presence of animals, researchers addressed the role of attitudes toward animals in the antiarousal effects of animals of the same type (Friedmann *et al.*, 1990). Cardiovascular stress responses in the presence of a dog were significantly lower for people with a more positive attitude toward dogs than for those with a more negative attitude toward dogs (Friedmann *et al.*, 1990).

Research addressing the effects of implicitly watching or being in the presence of animals suggests that several factors may contribute to the effects of the presence of an animal on the stress response. These include the type and familiarity of the setting, type of stressor, perceptions about the type of animal, and relationship with the animal. For example, the stresses associated with either the setting itself or the nature of the task may overwhelm the stress-moderating effects of the presence of the pet.

Based on data presented, pet ownership is not necessary for individuals to receive stress-moderating benefits from the presence of a friendly animal. Positive perceptions of dogs promote dogs' effectiveness at reducing people's stress responses (Friedmann *et al.*, 1990). Because attitudes toward species are related to choice of pets (Serpell, 1981), particular effort will be required to separate the contributions of attitudes toward species and pet ownership itself to the stress-moderating effects of animals.

B. Effects of Interacting with Animals

Interacting with a friendly animal, not necessarily one's own pet, leads to direct antiarousal effects, but not necessarily to stress-moderating effects. Interacting with a pet by talking to and touching it was less stress inducing than talking or reading to other people (Baun *et al.*, 1984; Jenkins, 1986; Katcher, 1981; Wilson, 1987). Blood pressures of dog owners (n = 35) recruited from a veterinary clinic waiting room were measured while they rested without their pets in a private consultation room, interacted with their pets, and read aloud without their pets in the same room (Katcher, 1981). Similarly, BP and HR were measured while self-selected undergraduate students (n = 92) read aloud, read quietly, and interacted with a friendly but unfamiliar dog (Wilson, 1987) or pet owners (n = 20) read aloud or interacted with their pets (Jenkins, 1986). In all three studies, none of the cardiovascular levels increased while interacting with a pet, but they did increase significantly while reading aloud. The physiological effects of petting one's own pet and someone else's pet were compared (Baun *et al.*, 1984). Blood pressures decreased significantly from the first to the final assessment when dog owners (n = 24) petted their own dog, but not when the same individuals petted the unfamiliar dog. These differences disappeared if the initial greeting response when the owner's own dog entered the room was omitted.

The direct physiological consequences of touching animals that are uncommon pets or zoo animals were addressed in studies of touching snakes (Alonso, 1999; Eddy, 1996) and chimps (Eddy, 1995). In a case study of one snake owner, BP during 6 minutes of touching his pet were lower than in the periods of relaxing and looking at the snake that preceded it (Eddy, 1996). In a study of snake nonowners who were not fearful of snakes (n = 5), BP and HR were not different when holding the snake, watching the snake, or relaxing (Alonso, 1999). Physiological arousal assessed with BP and HR was higher when a chimpanzee's caretaker and assistants touched/tickled the chimp through a barrier than when they rested or observed the chimp through a barrier (Eddy, 1995). This occurred despite the subject's reported fondness for and lack of fear of the animals.

The stress-moderating effect of touching animals has been investigated in one study to date (Straatman *et al.*, 1997). After a baseline rest period, an unfamiliar small dog was placed in the laps of men preparing and presenting a 4-minute televised speech. There were no significant differences in cardiovascular stress responses between these men and men without a dog in their lap. Having a dog on the lap did not reduce the arousal associated with the tasks presented in this study.

The differences in arousal during interaction with animals suggest strongly that the individual's attitude toward an animal is of prime importance in determining whether touching that animal will enhance relaxation. The nonjudgmental aspect of interacting with an animal compared with the demands of interacting with other people is frequently cited as a possible reason for the difference in physiological arousal during human–human and human–animal interactions (Allen *et al.*, 1991, 2002; Friedmann *et al.*, 1990; Katcher, 1981; Locker, 1985).

The variety of ways of physically interacting with animals and the difficulty of standardizing interactions and responses also inhibit research in this area. It is particularly difficult to evaluate the relative contributions of the physical movement and exertion during interaction and the contributions of the calming influences of the interaction with animals. During vigorous interaction, the arousal-moderating effects of the animal may be more than counteracted by the effects of the exertion on BP and HR.

Results of the one study addressing the stress-moderating effect of interacting with animals (Straatman *et al.*, 1997) highlight the possibility that the demands of the stressor might counteract the stress-moderating effect of interaction with animals. A crucial factor appears to be the type of task the human–animal interaction was expected to moderate. Interaction with an animal may interfere with task completion and thus potentiate physiological arousal rather than relieving it.

C. Comparison of Effects of Presence of and Interaction with Animals

A final study specifically compared the stress responses of normotensive adults ($n = 50$) when a friendly animal (dog or goat) was present but the participants did not interact with it to when the animal was present and the participants were permitted to pat it. A third condition had no animal present. Blood pressure and HR increased during the cognitive stressor. Systolic BP, diastolic BP, and HR decreased more after the stressors if an animal was present than if it was not. The reduction was greater in the situation where the person observed the animal than when interaction with the animal was permitted (DeMello, 1999).

As with other areas of research, the outcomes of studies addressing the physiological impact of friendly animals on cardiovascular status are influenced by the design of the studies. In studies of the effects of implicitly watching animals and those of evaluation of AAT, those with crossover research designs, in which the same individuals are exposed to both the animal present and the animal absent conditions, revealed stress-moderating effects from the presence of friendly animals (Allen *et al.*, 1991, 2002; Friedmann *et al.*, 1990; Locker, 1985; Nagengast *et al.*, 1997), whereas those without crossover designs did not (Grossberg *et al.*, 1988; Hansen *et al.*, 1999; Havener *et al.*, 2001; Rajack, 1997). The ability of crossover designs, in which the same procedure is repeated both with and without an animal present, to evaluate both within subject and between subject variability is particularly important for dependent variables such as BP and HR, which vary tremendously from minute to minute and from person to person (Friedmann *et al.*, 2000; Moody *et al.*, 1996). This variability presents a significant challenge when moving to the natural setting. The combination of large variability and small sample size can make it very difficult to draw meaningful conclusions from studies, particularly those that appear to show that AAT, observing an animal, or interacting with an animal has no effect on the outcome of interest.

D. Clinical Trials of Pet Interventions

When people hear about the effects of pet ownership on health, they frequently ask whether they should obtain a pet. The gold standard for evaluating the effectiveness of interventions is the randomized double-blind clinical trial in which individuals are assigned randomly to an intervention or a control/usual care group. In the case of "prescribing a pet," a double-blind trial is not possible because the participant knows whether a pet has been prescribed. It is, however, possible to conduct randomized trials. Two small studies gave pets to elderly individuals and observed changes in health without random assignment of pets. Although both showed improvements in health status among those who received a pet, the results could be related to differences between those individuals choosing to have a pet bird (Mugford and M'Comisky, 1975) or an aquarium rather than to obtaining a pet (Riddick, 1985). More recently, Allen and colleagues (2001) conducted a randomized trial of dog ownership. Men in a high-stress occupation who were willing to keep dogs were assigned randomly to obtain dogs (therapy) or not (control/usual care). All patients received the usual medication, an angiotensin converting enzyme (ACE) inhibitor. Cardiovascular responses to mental stress were measured before the assignment of therapy and after 6 months of therapy. Resting BP for all participants was lower after therapy than before. While the cardiovascular responses to mental stress did not differ before intervention in those men assigned to the two groups, after intervention the responses were lower in those who received pets.

IV. DISCUSSION

Animal-assisted therapy is a promising intervention for the improvement of people's physical health. A limited amount of research directly evaluated the effects of AAT on health. More extensive documentation of the positive impact of animals on physical health comes from epidemiological studies that support long-term health effects of pet ownership, from experimental and quasi-experimental studies that support the short-term impact of people explicitly looking at or observing animals, people implicitly observing or being in the presence of animals, and people touching or interacting with animals, as well as from trials directly evaluating the impact of assignment to receive a pet.

Issues arising in reference to each category of human–animal interaction are addressed within the section devoted to that topic. Broader questions, which require further research, include: (1) What kind and magnitude of benefits can AAT be expected to provide? (2) Do the effects of different types of animals on people's health differ, and if so, what are the cultural, experiential, and attitudinal bases for these differences? (3) Are the short-term direct or stress-moderating physiological responses to animals the basis for the differences in health status found in the longer-term epidemiological studies? (4) Are there differences on the basis of sex or other demographic characteristics in the direct or stress-moderating short-term or long-term differences in the health effects of animals? (5) Are animals more effective at moderating the effects of certain types of stressors than others? The final and perhaps most important theme is the necessity for optimal research design in studies attempting to address these issues.

No studies directly compare the effectiveness of AAT with different species or even breeds within species. Behavioral studies of interactions of animals with people indicate that people respond differently to different animals. These data provide a concrete basis for testing a long-held assumption that individuals will have different physiological responses to different animals. Recent evidence, such as the epidemiological studies reported (Friedmann *et al.*, 1995; Rajack, 1997; Serpell, 1991), demonstrates that different types of pets might have different impacts on people's health and its underlying physiology.

Studies conducted to date focus primarily on the effects of friendly animals, dogs in particular, on individuals' physiology. The effects of specific animals on individuals' physiology are likely based on the individuals' previous direct and indirect experiences with as well as their beliefs, desires, and fears about specific species or even breeds. We cannot expect specific animals to evoke uniform physiological responses from different individuals (Friedmann *et al.*, 1990, 2000). The interpretation of an animal as safe or unsafe is expected to depend on early learning and/or personal experiences, even for animals that are culturally or innately defined as dangerous. Data presented suggest that individuals' responses to AAT with various species or even breeds are likely to differ according to the individuals' perceptions of different animals.

Even within species, compatibility with a specific animal can affect health outcomes. For example, people who are more compatible with their pets report fewer illness symptoms and better psychological well-being. Importantly, this was not the case for attachment to their pets (Budge *et al.*, 1998). In this study, pet attachment was not related to health outcomes. In a small survey of older Latino pet owners (n = 24) who indicated they were in good or excellent health, there was no relationship of pet attachment to self-perceived health or functional ability (Johnson and Meadows, 2002). Additional research directly addressing perceptions of and responses to a variety of animals and compatibility with specific animals would facilitate understanding in this area.

The physiological benefit from AAT will also depend on the recipient's psychological and health status at a specific time. Muschel (1984) reminds us of this in her quote from a terminal cancer patient in a nursing facility who did not wish to have another pet visit because "I've always had animals in my life. I love them. But I don't want one now because I would want to take it home with me and I'm not going home."

The research investigating the short-term effects of animals included investigation of two types of potential health benefits: direct effects on physiological stress indicators and stress-moderating or -buffering effects. The experimental and quasi-experimental studies provide evidence that explicitly and implicitly observing animals can lead to both direct antiarousal and stress-moderating effects. Interacting with a friendly animal, not necessarily one's own pet, also leads to direct antiarousal effects (Baun, et al., 1984; Katcher, 1981; Wilson, 1987; 1991) but not to stress-moderating effects (Straatman *et al.*, 1997). Studies conducted to date have not addressed the likely effects from different types of human–animal interaction in a systematic comparative manner. Too many variables have been varied between studies to draw meaningful conclusions.

Additional research evidence supports both direct antiarousal and stress-moderating effects of explicitly looking at or observing animals and of implicitly observing animals. Research supports direct antiarousal effects but not stress-moderating effects of interaction with animals. Many of the studies examining direct or stress-moderating benefits of animals differ from each other on the basis of two or more factors. Thus, while these studies provide important evidence that human–animal interactions have direct and stress-moderating effects, it impossible to attribute the observed effects to specific variables. Systematic research delimiting the mechanisms for and factors contributing to both short- and long-term health benefits from these types of human–animal interactions and the mediators of these effects is sorely needed.

Animals may be unpleasant or stressful to some individuals. These individuals are routinely and appropriately excluded from studies of the health benefits of companion animals through the informed consent procedure or of AAT through activity selection. When using AAT with individuals with dementia, sensitivity to the behavioral responses of the individual is particularly important. The individual may develop aversions to animals or the responsible party may be unaware of such aversions. In a study of the behavior of nursing home residents of a dementia unit during AAT, one resident indicated discomfort with a visiting dog by physically moving back in her chair and giving a startle response (Kramer *et al.*, 2005).

Addition of an animal to a stressful situation may increase the individual's distress rather than alleviate it. Exacerbation of the stress response would exacerbate the negative health effects of stress rather than ameliorate them. Two studies support the importance of attending to this possibility (Craig *et al.*, 2000; Straatman *et al.*, 1997).

Contact with animals or their refuse can also have severe detrimental physiological effects. Even small common companion animals can transmit infectious diseases, cause allergies, and inflict injuries such as bites and scratches (Centers for Disease Control and Prevention, 1997; Morrison, 2001; Plaut *et al.*, 1996). Several case reports indicate that pets may have negative health consequences for elderly owners, including rotator cuff injuries and falls (Nair *et al.*, 2004). The potential for physical injuries is generally minimized in AAT programs. There are few, if any, reports of zoonoses due to AAT. The dearth of reports could be due to a lack of such injuries, the lack of a central registry for making such reports, or poor recognition of the diseases. According to Brodie *et al.* (2002), the risks associated with zoonoses in the controlled environment of most medical or long-term care facilities are minimal. As AAT becomes more common and the number of immunocompromised individuals increases, infection control policies and procedures geared toward the management and prevention of zoonotic illnesses are crucial for all facilities that employ AAT (Guay, 2001; Robinson and Pugh, 2002).

V. CONCLUSION

A small but growing body of research supports the effectiveness of individual AAT for reducing stress, especially in children. The effectiveness of group AAT for reducing stress has not been substantiated. Research addressing the effects of animals on human health and indicators of physiological arousal conducted to date provide intriguing evidence that animals can be beneficial, particularly for cardiovascular health. Epidemiological studies indicate that owning pets is associated with a better 1-year survival rate of patients after myocardial infarctions, fewer health complaints, reduced use of medical resources, and fewer risk factors for cardiovascular disease. Owning or acquiring dogs may be more beneficial than having cats only. The complex interrelationships among cat ownership, dog ownership, other types of social support, life events, other aspects of psychological and physical health, and gender-related differences in mortality and morbidity must be addressed before firm conclusions are drawn.

REFERENCES

Allen, K., Blascovich, J., and Mendes, W. (2002). Cardiovascular reactivity and the presence of pets, friends and spouses: The truth about cats and dogs. *Psychosomat. Med.* **64**, 727–739.

Allen, K., Shykoff, B. E., and Izzo, J. L., Jr. (2001). Pet ownership, but not ace inhibitor therapy, blunts home blood pressure responses to mental stress. *Hypertension* **38**, 815–820.

Allen, K. M., Blascovich, J., Tomaka, J., and Kelsey, R. M. (1991). Presence of human friends and pet dogs as moderators of autonomic responses to stress in women. *J. Pers.Soc. Psychol.* **61**, 582–589.

Alonso, Y. (1999). Effect of pets on human health: Is there a correlation? *Gesundheitswesen* **61**, 45–49.

Anderson, W., Reid, C., and Jennings, G. (1992). Pet ownership and risk factors for cardiovascular disease. *Med. J. Austr.* **157**, 298–301.

Arato, M., Banki, C. M., Nemeroff, C. B., and Bissette, G. (1986). Hypothalamic-pituitary-adrenal axis and suicide. *Ann. N.Y. Acad. Sci.* **487**, 263–270.

Audy, J. R. (1971). Measurement and diagnosis of health. *In* "Environ/Mental Essays on the Planet as Home" (P. Shepard and D. McKinley, eds.), pp. 140–162. Houghton Mifflin, Boston, MA.

Banki, C. M., Karmacsi, L., Bissette, G., and Nemeroff, C. B. (1992). CSF corticotropin-releasing hormone and somatostatin in major depression: Response to antidepressant treatment and relapse. *Eur. Neuropsychopharmacol.* **2**, 107–113.

Barker, S. B., Knisely, J. S., McCain, N. L., and Best, A. M. (2005). Measuring stress and immune response in healthcare professionals following interaction with a therapy dog: A pilot study. *Psychol. Rep.* **96**, 713–729.

Baun, M. M., Bergstrom, N., Langston, N. F., and Thoma, L. (1984). Physiological effects of human/companion animal bonding. *Nurs. Res.* **33**, 126–129.

Baun, M. M., Oetting, K., and Bergstrom, N. (1991). Health benefits of companion animals in relation to the physiologic indices of relaxation. *Holistic Nurs. Pract.* **5**, 16–23.

Brodie, S. J., Biley, F. C., and Shewring, M. (2002). An exploration of the potential risks associated with using pet therapy in healthcare settings. *J. Clin. Nurs.* **11**, 444–456.

Budge, R. C., Spicer, J., Jones, B., and St. George, R. (1998). Health correlates of compatibility and attachment in human-companion animal relationships. *Soc. Anim.* **6**, 219–234.

Cole, K. M., and Gawlinski, A. (2000). Animal-assisted therapy: The human-animal bond. *AACN Clin. Issues* **11**, 139–149.

Corbalan, R., Verrier, R. L., and Lown, B. (1974). Psychological stress and ventricular arrhythmia during myocardial infarction in the conscious dog. *Am. J. Cardiol.* **34**, 692–696.

Craig, F., Lynch, J. J., and Quartner, J. L. (2000). The perception of available social support is related to reduced cardiovascular reactivity in phase II cardiac rehabilitation patients. *Integr. Physiol. Behav. Sci.* **35**, 272–283.

Dembicki, D., and Anderson, J. (1996). Pet ownership may be a factor in improved health of the elderly. *J. Nutr. Elder.* **15**, 15–31.

DeMello, L. R. (1999). The effect of the presence of a companion-animal on physiological changes following the termination of cognitive stressors. *Psychol. Health* **14**, 859–868.

DeSilva, R. A., Verrier, R. L., and Lown, B. (1978). The effects of psychological stress and vagal stimulation with morphine on vulnerability to ventricular fibrillation (VF) in the conscious dog. *Am. Heart J.* **95**, 197–203.

Eddy, T. J. (1995). Human cardiac responses to familiar young chimpanzees. *Anthrozoos* **4**, 235–243.

Eddy, T. J. (1996). RM and Beaux: reductions in cardiac activity in response to a pet snake. *J. Nerv. Ment. Dis.* **184**, 573–575.

Edwards, N. E., and Beck, A. M. (2002). Animal-assisted therapy and nutrition in Alzheimer's disease. *West. J. Nurs. Res.* **24**, 697–712.

Friedmann, E., Katcher, A. H., Lynch, J. J., and Thomas, S. A. (1980). Animal companions and one-year survival of patients after discharge from a coronary care unit. *Public Health Rep.* **95**, 307–312.

Friedmann, E., Katcher, A. H., Thomas, S. A., Lynch, J. J., and Messent, P. (1983). Social interactions and blood pressure: Influence of animal companions. *J. Nerv. Ment. Dis.* **171**, 461–465.

Friedmann, E., and Thomas, S. A. (1985). Health benefits of pets for families. *Marriage Family Rev.* **4**, 191–203.

Friedmann, E., and Thomas, S. A. (1995). Pet ownership, social support, and one-year survival after acute myocardial infarction in the Cardiac Arrhythmia Suppression Trial (CAST). *Am. J. Cardiol.* **76**, 1213–1217.

Friedmann, E., Thomas, S. A., and Eddy, T. J. (2000). Companion animals and human health: Physical and cardiovascular influences. *In* "Companion Animals and Us: Exploring the Relationships between People and Pets" (A. L. Podberscek, E. Paul, and J. A. Serpell, eds.), pp. 125–142. Cambridge University Press, Cambridge.

Friedmann, E., Zuck Locker, B., and Lockwood, R. (1990). Perception of animals and cardiovascular responses during verbalization with an animal present. *Anthrozoos* **6**, 115–134.

Globisch, J., Hamm, A. O., Esteves, F., and Ohman, A. (1999). Fear appears fast: Temporal course of startle reflex potentiation in animal fearful subjects. *Psychophysiology* **36**, 66–75.

Grossberg, J. M., Alf, E. F., Jr., and Vormbrock, J. K. (1988). Does pet dog presence reduce human cardiovascular responses to stress? *Anthrozoos* **2**, 38–44.

Guay, D. R. (2001). Pet-assisted therapy in the nursing home setting: Potential for zoonosis. *Am. J. Infect. Control* **29**, 178–186.

Hansen, K. M., Messenger, C. J., Baun, M., and Megel, M. E. (1999). Companion animals alleviating distress in children. *Anthrozoos* **12**, 142–148.

Havener, L., Gentes, L., Thaler, B., Megel, M. E., Baun, M. M., Driscoll, F. A., *et al.* (2001). The effects of a companion animal on distress in children undergoing dental procedures. *Issues Compr. Pediatr. Nurs.* **24**, 137–152.

Headey, B., Grabka, M., and Kelley, J. (2002). Pet ownership is good for your health and saves public expenditure too: Australian and German longitudinal evidence. *Aust. Soc. Monitor* **4**, 93–99.

Jenkins, C. D. (1976a). Medical progress: Recent evidence supporting psychologic and social risk factors for coronary disease. *N. Engl. J. Med.* **294**, 987–994.

Jenkins, C. D. (1976b). Recent evidence supporting psychologic and social risk factors for coronary disease. *N. Engl. J. Med.* **294**, 1033–1038.

Jenkins, J. (1986). Physiological effects of petting a companion animal. *Psychol. Rep.* **58**, 21–22.

Johnson, R. A., and Meadows, R. L. (2002). Older Latinos, pets, and health. *West. J. Nurs. Res.* **24**, 609–620.

Jorm, A. F., Jacomb, P. A., Christensen, H., Henderson, S., Korten, A. E., and Rodgers, B. (1997). Impact of pet ownership on elderly Australians' use of medical services: An analysis using Medicare data. *Med. J. Aust.* **166**, 376–377.

Julius, S., and Nesbitt, S. D. (1996). Sympathetic nervous system as a coronary risk factor in hypertension. *Cardiologia* **41**, 309–317.

Kaminski, M., Pellino, T., and Wish, J. (2002). Play and pets: The physical and emotional impact of child-life and pet therapy on hospitalized children. *Child. Health Care* **31**, 321–335.

Katcher, A. H. (1981). Interactions between people and their pets: Form and function. *In* "Interrelationships between People and Pets" (B. Fogle, ed.), pp. 41–67. Charles C. Thomas, Springfield, IL.

Katcher, A. H., Friedmann, E., Beck, A. M., and Lynch, J. J. (1983). Talking, looking, and blood pressure: Physiological consequences of interaction with the living environment. *In* "New Perspectives on Our Lives with Animal Companions" (A. H. Katcher and A. M. Beck, eds.), pp. 351–359. University of Pennsylvania Press, Philadelphia, PA.

Kramer, S., Friedmann, E., and Berstein, P. (2005). Comparison of the effect of animal-assisted therapy, human interaction, and AIBO-assisted therapy on long term care dementia residents. Presented at the International Society for Anthrozoology, Niagra Falls, NY.

Lampert, R., Jain, D., and Burg, M. M. (2000). Destabilizing effects of mental stress on ventricular arrhythmias in patients with implantable cardioverter-defibrillators. *Circulation* **101**, 158–164.

Locker, B. Z. (1985). "The Cardiovascular Response to Verbalization in Type A and Type B Individuals in the Presence of a Dog." Ph.D. New York University.

Lockwood, R. (1983). The influence of animals on social perception. *In* "New Perspectives on Our Lives with Animal Companions" (A. H. Katcher and A. M. Beck, eds.), pp. 64–71. University of Pennsylvania Press, Philadelphia, PA.

Long, J. M., Lynch, J. J., Machiran, N. M., Thomas, S. A., and Malinow, K. L. (1982). The effect of status on blood pressure during verbal communication. *J. Behav. Med.* **5**, 165–172.

Louis, W. J., Doyle, A. E., and Anavekar, S. N. (1975). Plasma noradrenaline concentration and blood pressure in essential hypertension, phaeochromocytoma and depression. *Clin. Sci. Mol. Med Suppl.* **2**, 239s–242s.

McEwen, B. S. (1998). Stress, adaptation, and disease: Allostasis and allostatic load. *Ann. N.Y. Acad. Sci.* **840**, 33–44.

Montague, J. (1995). Continuing care: Back to the garden. *Hosp. Health Netw.* **69**, 58, 60.

Moody, W. J., Fenwick, D. C., and Blackshaw, J. K. (1996). Pitfalls of studies designed to test the effect pets have on the cardiovascular parameters of their owners in the home situation: A pilot study. *Appl. Anim. Behav. Sci.* **47**, 127–136.

Morrison, G. (2001). Zoonotic infections from pets: Understanding the risks and treatment. *Postgrad. Med.* **110**, 24–30, 35.

Mugford, R. A., and M'Comisky, J. G. (1975). Some recent work on the psychotherapeutic value of cage birds for old people. *In* "Pet Animals and Society" (R. S. Anderson, ed.), pp. 54–65. Bailliere Tindall, London.

Muschel, I. J. (1984). Pet therapy with terminal cancer patients. *J. Contemp. Soc. Work* 451–458.

Musselman, D. L., Evans, D. L., and Nemeroff, C. B. (1998). The relationship of depression to cardiovascular disease: Epidemiology, biology, and treatment. *Arch. Gen. Psychiatr.* **55**, 580–592.

Nagengast, S. L., Baun, M., Megel, M. M., and Leibowitz, J. M. (1997). The effects of the presence of a companion animal on physiological arousal and behavioral distress in children during a physical examination. *J. Pediatr. Nurs.* **12**, 323–330.

Nair, B. R., Flynn, B., and McDonnell, M. (2004). Pet owners and risk factors in cardiovascular disease. *MJA* **180**, 144.

Nemeroff, C. B., Widerlov, E., Bissette, G., Walleus, H., Karlsson, I., Eklund, K., *et al.* (1984). Elevated concentrations of CSF corticotropin-releasing factor-like immunoreactivity in depressed patients. *Science* **226**, 1342–1344.

Parslow, R. A., and Jorm, A. F. (2003). Pet ownership and risk factors for cardiovascular disease: Another look. *Med. J. Aust.* **179**, 466–468.

Parslow, R. A., Jorm, A. F., Christensen, H., Rodgers, B., and Jacomb, P. (2005). Pet ownership and health in older adults: Findings from a survey of 2,551 community-based Australians aged 60–64. *Gerontology* **51**, 40–47.

Pasic, J., Levy, W. C., and Sullivan, M. D. (2003). Cytokines in depression and heart failure. *Psychosom. Med.* **65**, 181–193.

Plaut, M., Zimmerman, E. M., and Goldstein, R. A. (1996). Health hazards to humans associated with domestic pets. *Annu. Rev. Public Health* **17**, 221–245.

Raina, P., Waltner-Toews, D., Bonnett, B., Woodward, C., and Abernathy, T. (1999). Influence of companion animals on the physical and psychological health of older people: An analysis of a one-year longitudinal study. *J. Am. Geriatr. Soc.* **47**, 323–329.

Rajack, L. S. (1997). "Pets and Human Health: The Influence of Pets on Cardiovascular and Other Aspects of Owners' Health." Ph.D. University of Cambridge, Cambridge UK.

Riddick, C. C. (1985). Health, aquariums, and the non-institutionalized elderly. *In* "Pets and the Family" (M. B. Sussman, ed.), pp. 163–173. Haworth Press, New York.

Robinson, R. A., and Pugh, R. N. (2002). Dogs, zoonoses and immunosuppression. *J. R. SOC. Health* **122**, 95–98.

Rossbach, K. A., and Wilson, J. P. (1992). Does a dog's presence make a person appear more likeable? *Anthrozoos* **5**, 40–51.

Rozanski, A., Blumenthal, J. A., and Kaplan, J. (1999). Impact of psychological factors on the pathogenesis of cardiovascular disease and implications for therapy. *Circulation* **99**, 2192–2217.

Schwartz, A., and Patronek, G. (2002). Methodological issues in studying the anxiety-reducing effects of animals: Reflections from a pediatric dental study. *Anthrozoos* **15**, 291–299.

Serpell, J. A. (1981). Childhood pets and their influence on adults' attitudes. *Psychol. Rep.* **49**, 651–654.

Serpell, J. (1991). Beneficial effects of pet ownership on some aspects of human health and behavior. *J. R. Soc. Med.* **84**, 717–720.

Siegel, J. M. (1990). Stressful life events and use of physician services among the elderly: The moderating role of pet ownership. *J. Pers. Soc. Psychol.* **58**, 1081–1086.

Skinner, J. E. (1981). Blockade of frontocardial-brain stem pathway prevents ventricular fibrillation of ischemic heart. *Am. J. Physiol.* **240**, 156–163.

Skinner, J. E. (1985). Regulation of cardiac vulnerability by the cerebral defense system. *J. Am. Coll. Cardiol.* **5**, 88B–94B.

Sterling, P. (2003). Principles of allostasis: Optimal design, predictive regulation, pathophysiology and rational therapeutics. *In* "Allostasis, Homeostasis, and the Costs of Adaptation" (J. Shulkin, ed.), MIT Press, Cambridge, MA.

Straatman, I., Hanson, E. K. S., Endenburg, N., and Mol, J. A. (1997). The influence of a dog on male students during a stressor. *Anthrozoos* **10**, 191–197.

Thomas, S. A., Friedmann, E., Khatta, M., Cook, L. K., and Lann, A. L. (2003). Depression in patients with heart failure: Physiologic effects, incidence, and relation to mortality. *AACN Clin. Issues* **14**, 3–12.

Thomas, S. A., Friedmann, E., Wimbush, F., and Schron, E. B. (1997). Psychological factors and survival in the Cardiac Arrhythmia Suppression Trial (CAST): A reexamination. *Am. J. Crit-Care* **6**, 16–26.

Thomas, S. A., Liehr, P., DeKeyser, F., Frazier, L., and Friedmann, E. (2002). A review of nursing research on blood pressure. *J. Nurs. Scholarsh.* **34**, 313–321.

Tucker, J. S., Friedman, H. S., Tsai, C. M., and Martin, L. R. (1995). Playing with pets and longevity among older people. *Psychol. Aging* **10**, 3–7.

Veith, R. C., Lewis, N., Linares, O. A., Barnes, R. F., Raskind, M. A., Villacres, E. C., *et al.* (1994). Sympathetic nervous system activity in major depression: Basal and desipramine-induced alterations in plasma norepinephrine kinetics. *Arch. Gen. Psychiatr.* **51**, 411–422.

Wilson, C. C. (1987). Physiological responses of college students to a pet. *J. Nerv. Ment. Dis.* **175**, 606–612.

Wu, A. S., Niedra, R., Pendergast, L., and McCrindle, B. W. (2002). Acceptability and impact of pet visitation on a pediatric cardiology inpatient unit. *J. Pediatr. Nurs.* **17**, 354–362.

Wyatt, R. J., Portnoy, B., Kupfer, D. J., Snyder, F., and Engelman, K. (1971). Resting plasma catecholamine concentrations in patients with depression and anxiety. *Arch. Gen. Psychiatr.* **24**, 65–70.

SECTION II

Animal-Assisted Therapy

CONCEPTUAL MODEL AND GUIDELINES FOR QUALITY ASSURANCE

CHAPTER 7

The Art of Animal Selection for Animal-Assisted Activity and Therapy Programs

MAUREEN FREDRICKSON-MACNAMARA
MSW, Animal Systems, Ltd., Denver, Colorado 80210

KRIS BUTLER
American Dog Obedience Center, LLC, American Dog Obedience Center, Norman, Oklahoma 73026-8611

After the World Trade Center terrorist attacks, dogs with no previous testing or training for animal-assisted therapy (AAT) or animal-assisted activities (AAAs) demonstrated keen interest in and tolerance for high levels of human emotion and chaos. However, there were also reports of dogs with considerable training, screening, and experience that growled at other dogs or were so traumatized that they ignored everyone but their handler.

In countless AAT and AAA programs animals have responded to people in need with behaviors that made a significantly healing impact on the people with whom the animals were involved. There are also animals that once responded with grace and dedication to participants that became aloof, distant, and, in some instances, aggressive toward the very people that needed them.

This chapter reviews the development of AAT and AAA evaluation procedures for animals and their handlers and explores the context in which these procedures occur. Subsequently, it examines the extent to which current procedures reflect the settings in which animals actually work and whether these practices provide an accurate picture of the handler's and animal's "fit" with program expectations in many of today's more chaotic and unpredictable

Handbook on Animal-Assisted Therapy: Theoretical Foundations and Guidelines for Practice, 2e

settings. By understanding the assumptions and goals behind the development of screening procedures, one is better able to consider the extent to which these protocols are still meaningful.

Questions regarding the duration of evaluation results and whether screening and evaluation provide a reliable reflection of the handler's ways of interacting during AAT and AAA sessions are considered as well. It is equally important to address the impact of AAT and AAAs on the animals themselves. More chaotic and unpredictable settings challenge handlers to recognize the point at which the animal may become overwhelmed, threatened, or even traumatized during AAT or AAA sessions. This factor has the potential to extend or shorten the working life of therapy animals.

I. A HISTORICAL PERSPECTIVE OF ANIMAL SELECTION PROCEDURES

In the 1970s a majority of AAA programs incorporating companion animals were implemented by animal welfare organizations that encouraged volunteers to take animals in the shelter to visit people in nursing homes and other residential settings. The focus of the programs was to provide a recreational activity and a break from the monotony and isolation of residential living. However, by the 1990s concerns about health risks associated with animals (fleas, ticks, bacterial diarrhea, a propensity to bite or scratch or jump on people when startled) and any number of other hazards had reduced this practice greatly. In addition, concerns for the welfare and health of the animals themselves were raised. The A.S.P.C.A. reported that "visiting strange settings with unpredictable people and unusual noises stresses the animals, especially young animals that are awaiting adoption" (Shelter Animals, 1992).

Therapeutic riding programs, which provided riding lessons for people with disabilities, used screening developed in Europe. Horses were selected based on their tractability around unusual equipment and people with limited physical control and a steady nature. Horses were also evaluated in terms of the quality of their gaits in settings in which the goal was to provide physical or occupational therapy, hippotherapy, as the horse's movement directly effects the rider's movement (NARHA, 1994).

During the 1980s as more long-term care facilities acquired resident animals, risk management became the primary concern. In 1983, at the University of Minnesota Conference on the Human–Animal Bond, guidelines for animals in nursing homes were presented, recommending animal placement be preceded by careful evaluation. Hines *et al.* (1983) stated that prior to placing animals in the facility, a full assessment should be performed, including assessment of the social needs of residents, evaluation of the layout of the facility, and consideration of the role of the animals in the facility. The impact of the animals on residents and changes that might result from animal contact was only beginning to be explored.

Hines *et al.* (1983) provided the first written materials for including animals in human health care settings. While the materials were thorough, they did not address selection of animals that accompanied a volunteer or staff member for a short period of time or stayed during the staff member's shift. Health care providers, experienced volunteers, and animal care and welfare professionals created recommendations for companion animals that continued to focus primarily on the medical and physical safety of the residents. The minimum selection criteria for animals included medical screening, temperament/behavioral evaluation, and methods to monitor the animals over time (New, 1988). Visiting animals were screened most frequently using puppy temperament tests and other breed-specific temperament evaluations.

By the 1990s the focus of animal selection and screening had shifted as AAT and AAA programs developed more specific participant or program goals. Thus it became important not only to determine risk of contact with animals but also to identify the ways in which the animal influenced the participant. It was during this time that attention was given to the handler's role in AAT and AAAs. Screening procedures once designed with the animal as their exclusive focus now began to add items that addressed the interactions of the handler as well.

II. EVALUATION CRITERIA

"Standards of Practice for Animal-Assisted Therapy and Animal-Assisted Activities" was published in 1996 by the Delta Society to provide a structure for the development of programs. The Standards addresses both the role of the handler and the requirements for animals in broad terms. Handler requirements include continuing education, appropriate documentation of the animal's health, and demonstration of respect and an ability to advocate for the animal. The primary selection criteria for animals are reliability, predictability, controllability, and suitability.

The Standards require documentation of the criteria rather than detailed methods to test for each element. Definitions for each of the criteria provide a framework to guide the development of selection procedures. Taken as a group the criteria of reliability, predictability, controllability, and suitability were intended to address the majority of risk management concerns in a variety of settings (Fredrickson and Howie, 2000).

Reliability refers to the extent to which behavior can be repeated in a variety of situations and with a variety of participants. Predictability, as defined by the

Standards, means that behavior in specific circumstances can be anticipated in advance, and controllability means that behavior can be interrupted, guided, or managed. Suitability addresses concerns that the right animal be selected for the right job, including the participant's feelings of safety and comfort around various animals or different breeds and breed types.

Of the four criteria, controllability is addressed most uniformly by current AAT and AAA screening protocols. For companion animals, especially dogs, controllability is usually measured by the animal's response to various commands such as "sit" or "stay" and tends to be modeled after the Canine Good Citizen (CGC) test, developed by the American Kennel Club (AKC, 1989). Animals other than dogs are also required to follow basic commands, although these may be modified.

While the uniformity of this part of most screening procedures is helpful, questions are often raised as to the applicability of these tests. Obedience evaluations (and the CGC test) were designed to demonstrate that a dog is able to follow handler commands such that the dog does not pose a health and safety risk to the public. Obedience tests are designed to test dogs under fairly controlled situations. Usually held outdoors during a dog show, neither the CGC test nor obedience tests examine whether the dog is able to demonstrate behaviors under a variety of conditions. While the testing site itself could be seen as a distraction with many dogs and people moving around, the test site is always roped off from the crowd and one could argue that these distractions are actually quite peripheral to the dog.

In addition, a number of studies have found that behavior is governed by context. Boissy (1995) and Lanier (2000) found that tests of grazing animals' behavior was predictive of only certain types of behavior, such as shying, and that the behavior was related primarily to the context in which the animals were evaluated. In a study of interrelationships between various dog behaviors, Goodloe and Borchelt (1998) found only a limited link between obedience training and desirable behaviors. The authors suggested that owners willing to spend more time with their dogs may behave differently with their dogs and therefore reduce the dogs' fear in new and unusual situations.

Some screening procedures require a high degree of skill from the animal in terms of its ability to respond to verbal and hand signals. These requirements are found most often in programs that incorporate dogs to work in physical rehabilitation settings. Within this type of setting the dog is trained to stand still or wait at a distance or retrieve in a consistent manner. A common concern voiced by practitioners of this level of training is that the dog's spontaneous behaviors are eliminated and only animals with robot-like behaviors meet the criteria. These practitioners often point out that it is the spontaneity of animals that provides participants with some of the most healing interactions.

The criterion of suitability requires only that animals be selected with consideration for age, sex, size, and typical behaviors. The criterion also requires that the provider ensure a match between client needs, environment, animal skills and aptitude, and handler skills. Again, the standards do not elaborate on the method utilized to ensure the criterion is met.

Suitability is often evaluated in a very subjective manner and is frequently defined in terms of individual likes and dislikes. While one program may define suitability in broad terms, other programs narrow the definition to exclude certain animals and, in some instances, specific animal breeds. For example, the majority of screening procedures are targeted toward dogs. A number of therapy animal registration organizations such as Therapy Dogs International and Therapy Dogs, Inc. restrict their programs to dogs. When considering the needs of AAT and AAA participants, the subjectivity of this criterion may substantially reduce program outcomes.

Consider, for example, an educational program designed for adolescent boys. Boys of this age may be more motivated to learn about reptiles and arachnids than common household pets. Selecting dogs for this group because the organization only works with dogs may reduce participant motivation. In a medical facility where hallways are very narrow and crowded with equipment, the animal-handler team must be highly mobile and able to get out of the way quickly. Thus, given these dynamics, a rabbit in a basket may be more suitable than a golden retriever walking beside a handler.

Documentation of an animal's predictability in simulations of AAT and AAA situations is required by the standards. Program providers and indeed facilities themselves often overlook the additional caveat that the standards also require animals be observed on site by staff for their ability to meet this criterion. The requirement that animals be observed while working on site is often a neglected aspect of the standards. This issue is addressed further in this chapter.

The criterion for reliability is again very broad and requires documentation of a long-term relationship with the animal in a variety of "social contexts." For those that developed the standards, this requirement was used to address those programs that took dogs out of shelters to visit people in medically based residential settings. However, a number of programs provide AAT to youth diagnosed with a variety of emotional challenges, who teach dogs in shelters basic obedience skills. There are several factors operating in these examples that make the same animals appropriate in one situation and inappropriate in another situation.

Taking untrained or unscreened animals to visit medically fragile people presents increased risks of zoonotic infection or injury, yet these risks can be reduced by choosing to work with pets that have appropriate veterinary care and a certain level of training. In addition, the goal of this program may be related to providing residents with an opportunity to build relationships with the community. In this instance a handler and dog that return at regular intervals will address program goals better than a variety of dogs that come and go due to adoption.

However, the behavioral factors that may make dogs in shelters inappropriate for a medical facility may enhance the goals of a mental health program. In this situation the youth learn to control their own behaviors as they teach the dogs. Depending on the age and diagnosis of the youth, the experience of teaching impulsive, hyperactive adolescent dogs may provide a perfect metaphor for their own emotional challenges.

Because the Standards are voluntary and not linked to any national licensing or credentialing body, individual organizations interpret the Standards from the perspective of their own organization. This is also true for Standards for therapeutic riding programs or farm programs. The screening procedures developed to test for and document Standards criteria often reflect the biases of the particular organization. Selection methods and their relevance to therapeutic settings have long been debated by human service professionals, animal trainers, and indeed handlers themselves.

III. FIT OF SELECTION PROCEDURES

Nothing else animals do compares to the kind of intrinsically stressful social interaction that takes place when they work in AAT or AAA situations. No other animal-related event, no sport, and no competition requires animals to enter the intimate zones of unfamiliar humans and remain there for several minutes or longer while an unfamiliar person engages in petting, hugging, or directing (training, riding) the animal. The role is new, specific, and profound (Butler, 2004).

Author Gavin de Becker points out in his book *The Gift of Fear* that knowing the question is the first step toward knowing the answer. One must first have a clear expectation of the outcome to bring that possible outcome to mind. Any discussion of animal selection and evaluation must first consider the outcome or goal of participant–animal interaction. Because most job descriptions provide specific details regarding performance expectations, one has a vision of what is required of a plumber, an accountant, or a search-and-rescue dog, for example. While the expectations will vary with the specific setting and the experience level of the worker, the task expectations enable one to determine whether the task can be managed. By defining how the animal's presence or interactions will result in a therapeutic experience for the participant, selection and evaluation procedures can be targeted toward identifying the characteristics or behaviors that have a likelihood of affecting the stated outcomes.

In general, AAT and AAA sessions incorporate animals in ways that can be loosely categorized: implicitly observing or being in the presence of animals, explicitly looking at or observing animals, and interacting with animals. These parameters provide a context from which to consider participant interaction. The greater the degree of contact between the animal and participant, the greater the demand for clear definitions of appropriate screening outcomes.

In sessions that incorporate animals by creating opportunities for participants to observe or be in the presence of animals, there may be little need for evaluation of individual animals. For example, in residential centers for patients with Alzheimer's disease, an aviary built along hallways can help residents focus eternally. While it is important to select the appropriate animals (birds as opposed to sedentary reptiles), evaluating each finch for specific behaviors is less important. The expected outcomes of the interaction between participants and animals result in a passive role for the animal.

More explicit participant goals may be defined in a rehabilitation program in which the participant is specifically directed to look at a particular animal and describe it. The same role may be required in a mental health program for children with emotional disorders. A therapist may ask the participant to identify nonverbal behavior. In these types of interventions the goals of each program will demand more specificity in terms of the individual animal's behavior. A dog incorporated in the rehabilitation program may be required to lie quietly on a table, while a horse incorporated in the mental health program would be more effective if it was highly interactive with other horses in the environment.

AAT and AAA programs requiring the most rigorous definition of outcomes are those in which the participant interacts actively with animals. Animal-assisted rehabilitation programs provide an excellent example of those in which it is important to determine the performance expectations and it is critical to determine the most appropriate species as well as the individual animal. A participant who has head injuries may work with a dog during in-patient rehabilitation sessions. Once discharged the same participant may be referred to a hippotherapy program to continue to work on balance and coordination needs with a physical or occupational therapist.

In this case, participant goals must first be defined clearly. While the participant is a patient, goals may be standing balance and speech improvement. A quiet dog or even a cat or rabbit may be appropriate in this setting. It is possible that once discharged, intervention goals for the participant will change. Goals could be directed more toward social interactions and less toward physical rehabilitation. A therapeutic riding program that enables the participant to learn riding skills with the help of volunteers and a quiet, well-behaved horse has different performance expectations than the hippotherapy program that focuses on rhythmic balance changes and may require a horse that moves with more spark and energy.

In another example, consider a psychotherapy program in which a therapist works with a mentally ill adult regarding the effects of his aggressive behavior on others. The therapist may choose to work with a horse that will move away from the adult unless the adult speaks in a softer tone, moves more slowly, and minimizes gesturing. For this intervention to be effective as well as safe, the handler must have a clear understanding of the performance expectations for the horse and must not interfere with the horse's natural instinct to retreat or the therapeutic value is diminished greatly, if not lost. However, it is critical that the handler ensures that the interaction does not become too stressful for the horse.

SPECIFY OUTCOMES

Standards provided by national companion animal and horse organizations leave plenty of room for each program to define the outcomes expected from screening procedures. Few, if any, organizations have taken this step, crafting screening procedures that attempt to specify the expected outcome of the evaluation for potential participants. The American Hippotherapy Association (AHA) utilizes evaluation procedures that identify more specific outcomes. AHA's evaluation clearly measures the horse's gait in terms of balance, cadence, and rhythm, as these are directly linked to participant outcomes in terms of physical functioning.

Most evaluation procedures are not carried out in the setting or with the participants with which the team will interact. Animals' and handlers' abilities to demonstrate specific behaviors depend on environmental factors, as well as team skills and talents. The best way to determine if teams are appropriate for specific environments is by assessing their behaviors within those environments. Of most concern is the fact that few evaluation procedures regularly include children, and yet many dogs are involved in programs that bring unpredictable children and dogs together. This is particularly disturbing in light of the fact that most dog bites in the United States involve children and a dog that is familiar to them (Beck, 1985).

When considering whether a species is appropriate for AAT and AAA, it is critical that the animal be evaluated in terms of criteria described for domestic animals. Resolutions of the International Association of Human–Animal

Interaction Organizations (IAHAIO) state that only domestic animals will be involved in AAT and AAA (1998). It is generally recognized that domestic animals tend to possess a higher capacity for coping with people, their behaviors, and their inventions.

Differences between various animal species influence AAT and AAA interventions. Behavior patterns are vastly different between carnivorous and non-carnivorous animals. The fact that rabbits and guinea pigs need to eat more frequently than dogs may actually enhance their role in a setting with a goal of increasing patients' nurturing skills. In the same way, these animals require handling and techniques that will accommodate the animal's frequent need to eliminate.

It is important to determine to what degree the animal can be appropriately monitored for signs of stress. This is, perhaps, the most important consideration for any species involved in AAT and AAA programs. Although there are limited data regarding the impact of AAT and AAA on animals, handlers report a certain degree of changes in animals working in these programs. The handler must be able to monitor the animal's response to limited stress in order to avoid overstress. Often it is more difficult to monitor stress in exotic animals or wildlife, and lethal levels can be missed. With these concerns in mind, exotic animals and wildlife are suitable only in situations where the animal is not in direct contact with people, such as bird feeders or fish tanks. Even these situations, however, can be cause for concern if the animal's housing, social, and nutritional needs cannot be met.

Risk versus Uncertainty

Weimer and Vining (2005) write that risk involves contingencies with known probabilities, while uncertainty involves contingencies with unknown probabilities. Unclear outcomes of AAT and AAA screening procedures leave a great deal of uncertainty regarding the results of these evaluations. As programs work with increasingly more involved participants, screening procedures must begin to address risk in real terms. In developing screening procedures, providers are, in effect, trying to shift the uncertainty that comes with bringing animals and people together to a manageable level of risk. In other words, screening procedures have the potential of providing a way to shift contingencies with unknown probabilities to contingencies with known probabilities.

Selecting appropriate animals for incorporation into AAT and AAA interventions is for all intents and purposes a form of prediction. Through critical observation of handlers and the animals they work, evaluators seek to provide a prediction for the team's future performance in AAT and AAA. Prediction is trying to solve puzzles with logic. One may have great confidence in the answer by showing the methodology involved in the protocols, but that does not necessarily increase the accuracy of the methods.

As AAT and AAAs expand into ever more demanding settings, the prediction offered by team evaluations will be crucial to positive intervention outcomes. Effective predictions require more than value judgments. The world of high-stakes prediction, that which evaluates the potential for violence in individuals and nations, provides an updated and informed method for increasing the likelihood of success of animal evaluations.

de Becker's (1997) elements of prediction provide a model for screening animal/handler teams for AAT and AAA in a variety of settings where accuracy is critical. According to de Becker, accurate prediction is based on 11 elements. These elements are

- Measurability
- Vantage
- Imminence
- Context
- Experience
- Comparable events
- Objectivity
- Investment
- Replicability
- Knowledge
- Preincident indicators

Consideration of these elements or scoring these elements as part of animal screening can help determine if the given prediction (screening result) can be made successfully. In other words, by considering these elements, providers can determine the degree to which the team's performance in a given situation can actually be predicted.

Selection for the 21st Century

Measurability asks whether the outcome can be identified clearly. As stated earlier, determining whether a rabbit will be a good therapy animal is more difficult than predicting if the rabbit will stay in its basket while being passed between two people. One prediction has an increased likelihood of success because the outcome of staying in the basket while being passed is clearer than a more fluid notion of a "good" therapy rabbit. Weiss and Greenberg (1997) found that a dog's success in most commonly used selection test items for service work did not predict later success as a service dog. Success as a service dog is less obvious and is a value-laden judgment rather than predicting whether a dog will learn certain commands.

Success in prediction can be improved by understanding the role of vantage. One must be able to observe preincident indicators and the context. One's own perspective increases the likelihood of successful predictions, whereas reliance on the observation of others is less likely to provide successful predictions. In a study by Ledger and Baxter (1996) of family members' perception of the pet dog's temperament, it was found that family members varied considerably in their report of the dog's temperament. Observing the team in action in the setting with participants that the animal may actually encounter will provide a more relevant picture of the team than looking at the results of a test administered by an unknown person in an unknown setting (national screening tests) (see Wharton, 2005).

A number of organizations incorporate this element into evaluation procedures by observing the team on a number of visits before making final determinations. Teams go through a preliminary evaluation to determine if the animal meets health and training requirements before going on supervised visits. While this process may be cumbersome, it increases the likelihood of successful prediction.

Certainly imminence plays a significant role in the success of selection and evaluation outcomes. Determining whether an animal will respond to a specific situation that is about to occur is more certain than predicting behavioral outcomes over a longer period of time. In a study of horse temperament tests, researchers concluded that only a small number of behavioral parameters were consistent beyond the first year (Visser *et al.*, 2001). This raises concerns regarding current testing practices, as many animals require retesting at a variety of intervals ranging from only once in the animal's life to every 2 years.

By consistently observing and evaluating animals in an ongoing manner, handlers and programs can be alert to changes in the animals' response to different situations. Taking time to watch teams in action can also serve to alert handlers to potentially negative outcomes. An observer may, because of their vantage, notice that a cat is beginning to pin its ears when picked up by residents. Predicting a potential for the cat to scratch someone may give the handler a window in which to train the cat to stay in a basket rather than being picked up all the time, thus preventing a possible injury and loss of an otherwise successful therapy animal.

The context of the situation must be clear to the evaluator in order for the prediction to have any level of success. This element certainly addresses concerns about evaluation procedures in which the evaluator tests animals without a clear idea of the setting in which the team will work. When the outcome of the evaluation is also unclear, the reliability of the prediction is no better than mere chance. Most AAT and AAA programs need to provide participants and sponsors with a better degree of prediction than chance.

From economics we know that people tend to assess risk based on heuristics and estimate probabilities of events by the ease with which instances can be brought to mind (Weimer, 1999). The predictor must be experienced with the specific setting and species involved in order to make a successful prediction. It stands to reason that an evaluator who has limited experience with horses will understand less about things that can go wrong with horses than a person who has experience with horses in a variety of settings and under a variety of circumstances.

This factor brings into question the degree to which various evaluators have experience with the species of animal being evaluated and the quality of experience that they possess. An evaluator who is unfamiliar with cats, for example, might not know how to interpret a tail swishing back and forth. A person unfamiliar with llamas might think humming is a sign of pleasure. In the same way, evaluators who have experience with only their own pets lack the depth of experience of a person who has competed with dogs, worked as a veterinary technician, and spent time as a groomer. Working with animals other than one's own and under a variety of conditions builds one's understanding of the scope of an animal's potential behavioral responses.

Serpell (2001) reported a new method to test dogs for service dog work; however, the applicability of this evaluation to therapy dogs has not been investigated. Learning how the animal responds in comparable events is directly affected by the similarity between the events. Unfortunately, few events are substantively comparable to AAT or AAAs, except perhaps holiday family reunions! Any number of pet owners will readily admit that Fido and Fluffy spend the day of the family reunion hiding under a bed or in a closet yet happily carry the pet off to a nursing home to meet strangers in an even stranger setting.

Studying the way an animal responds in one AAT or AAA setting may provide important information about the animal's response in another setting. It is important to make careful observations of the animal in the familiar setting to understand how each behavior is related to subsequent responses.

Ideally, the evaluator should believe that the team is just as likely to fail as to succeed in the evaluation. The evaluator that believes golden retrievers make the best therapy dogs has completed their prediction before considering all the elements. Being objective enough to believe both outcomes are possible minimizes or prevents bias, whether positive or negative. Many teams participate in a series of training sessions provided by the organization, followed by an evaluation by the person involved in the training sessions or by another member of the organization.

This process can put evaluators in compromising situations. Imagine the evaluator faced with the task of screening a major donor's animal for participation in a visiting program. While one would hope that both parties would be able to overcome this obstacle, human behavior being what it is and funding being a significantly determining factor, this dilemma can reduce the integrity of the evaluation greatly.

Prediction depends to a great extent on the predictor's investment in the outcome. Personal or emotional investment can influence prediction significantly. It is a rare dog owner who willingly predicts that their dog will bite in any given instance; however, if it means the difference between being sued or participating in a rewarding experience, their prediction will be more successful. In much the same way an evaluator that has a reputation in the local community as a trainer may have more invested in the outcome of the prediction than someone who has a pet dog and provides evaluations for the fun of it.

Replicability is a significant element in scientific predictions because it tests the issue first in another setting. One can test whether there is helium in a tank by filling a balloon with the gas and watching to see if it floats. Although replicability is important in low-stakes prediction, it is marginally useful in high-stakes predictions. This is the concern when the only form of screening utilized by an organization is observing the dog in action. It is ethically inappropriate to test whether a dog will bite children by taking him to a classroom and watching what happens.

The success of projective tests is dependent on the expertise of the evaluator. The evaluator must have an accurate understanding of the dynamics of AAT and AAA interactions in order to make predictions regarding the appropriateness of the handler and animal. Understanding the unique interplay of the animal's abilities and aptitude and the handler's response to the animal is a crucial aspect in prediction. For example, an evaluator who shows dogs in competition obedience and is unfamiliar with AAT and AAAs might reject a dog unless it demonstrated precision obedience skills. These skills may not be relevant to the setting in which the dog will work.

Finally, de Becker writes that the most advanced concept of prediction has to do with determining how things are set in motion. Behavior is best predicted by preincident indicators, detectable factors that occur before the outcome being predicted. To understand preincident indicators, let us suppose you decide to rent a video. Walking between the rows of videos, you see a title that looks interesting and take the video home. As the video begins, the opening scene gives you the feeling that you have seen this video before. After running the video a little longer, some of the music makes you more certain that you have already watched it. During the next few minutes the tone of voice of the characters and specific action sequences convince you that you have seen this selection before.

All of these factors—music, colors, and voices—are preincident indicators of the end of the video. The more preincident indicators that can be detected and the more that is known about outcomes in any given situation, the more one can make predictions. Preincident indicators for animals involve subtle, nonverbal signals. Gross movement is the least predictive behavior. Anyone bitten by a dog that is wagging its tail will agree with this assertion. Behaviors such as licking lips, squinting, looking away, and even yawning are more predictive of an animal's comfort level and thus its potential for causing harm or injury.

Preincident indicators are part of the flow of behavior. In textbooks of animal behavior, still pictures are used to illustrate a wide range of animal emotions. This creates an image that animal behavior (and human behavior) occurs as a series of snapshots, discrete and separate actions. In actuality, behavior is more like a motion picture where one image blends into another. The wagging tail becomes a waving tail, and the ears become pinned back as a lip starts to curl. In watching the flow and totality of this picture, behavior can be very predictable.

These elements provide a way to think about how we incorporate animals in AAT and AAA rather than whether an animal has passed a test. By incorporating these elements in routine observation of AAT and AAA animals and their handlers, whether beginning teams or seasoned pros, the predictability and safety of any program are vastly enhanced.

MAINTAINING THE BALANCE

The human capacity to assess realistically the environments in which animals are being required to work and to respond ethically to what the animals are communicating within those environments has not kept pace with these new applications. Today, one of the most important challenges facing animals is human nonawareness of the complex, stressful environments in which the animals are being required to participate.

Early AAT and AAA practitioners recommended that criteria for selecting animals consider the following factors: physical characteristics, personality characteristics (particularly predictability of behavior and communicability of the animal's attitudes through its body language), the degree of bonding to humans, and the relationship between the working animal and its handler (Holmes, 1988). Current AAT and AAA selection procedures tend to focus on whether animals and their handlers have passed a performance test or evaluation at some point in their careers rather than considering whether the animal and handler, together, possess the capacity to enhance the therapeutic goals of a specific participant or program.

Effective interventions consist of handlers who appropriately present animals and animals that appropriately receive the participants with whom they are interacting. There are observable, identifiable animal behaviors that enhance therapeutic interventions. Animals that possess and demonstrate unique and necessary therapeutic behaviors have a talent or capacity for AAT and AAAs. Animals facilitate participant goals when they contribute to feelings of safety, comfort, and connection. The behaviors that are required to make people feel safe, comfortable, and connected to animals that interact with them remain consistent. However, animals' and handlers' abilities to demonstrate specific behaviors depend on environmental factors, as well as team skills and talents.

During AAT and AAAs the animal's role is to "receive" the person or people with whom the animal is interacting. The process of being received is what gives people the perception that there is a connection or bond between themselves and the animal. It is primarily that perception which motivates people to participate in therapy, learning, discussion, or other targeted activities. Animals that initiate physical contact, remain engaged, make eye contact, respect personal boundaries, and allow their behaviors to be redirected convey that a connection exists (Butler, 2004). Simply being able to cause an animal to make eye contact by saying its name is enough to create a sense of connection.

Animal behaviors that reduce the perception of a bond and hinder the therapeutic processes include disinterest, reluctance to engage, disregard for personal boundaries, and any conduct that might be interpreted as aggressive or stress related.

The reasons behind an animal's behavior are never as important as the effects of that behavior on the people being visited. For example, some vocalizations vocalize when they are excited, but the issue is not so much what the vocalizations mean as whether the targeted population feels threatened by the behavior. While friendliness and confidence are necessary qualities for AAT and AAAs, animals must also respect personal boundaries. Jumping, pawing, and licking (beyond the few quick and respectful face-to-face calming licks) can seem intrusive to people being visited.

Animals that demonstrate a capacity for AAAs and AAT might be referred to as "suitable" for the population and within the environment in which they are working. An often-neglected aspect of suitability is enjoyment. Dodging this criterion is not simply unfortunate, it can also be abusive. How the animal interacts in the setting is often indicative of the animal's comfort level. An animal consistently placed in untenable situations may eventually retaliate. Here is another example of how critical the handler's skills are. If a handler is not sensitive to and respectful of the needs of the animal, the handler can inadvertently place his/her needs over those of the animal. This may result in illness for a submissive animal or aggression in the case of an assertive or fearful animal.

Animals must be confident in their interactions with people to accept occasional rough handling due to arthritic joints or spastic muscles, they must be able to tolerate uncontrolled vocalizations from strangers, and they must be focused on people with whom they are working. This special relationship expands the handlers' responsibility to these animals.

The choice of suitability can also occur between individuals of the same species. Consider a vital man in his early sixties recovering from a stroke. He is relearning how to walk, but he forgets that he cannot walk so he gets up impulsively and then falls. He also neglects his right side and loses focus while walking and runs into things on his right side. A therapist wants him to walk supervised with a dog on his right, hoping that will encourage him to attend to the right. Although several dogs, a Chihuahua, a Sheltie, and a Labrador retriever, are available to the therapist, the Labrador is probably most suitable for work in this situation in terms of size, stability, and emotional impact.

Creating Balance within AAT Interventions

Butler (2004) stated that AAT and AAA programs can be viewed within the context of balance and compensation (Fig. 1).This concept of balance can inform AAT and AAA interactions. As children, we learned about balance and compensation on the playground. With a teeter-totter for a teacher, young children quickly figure out that it is not just size and strength that matter. The key to success on a teeter-totter lies in the ability and willingness of participants to compensate to achieve balance.

Participants in AAT and AAAs include the animal and handler as a team on one end of the scale and the environment on the other. When teams and environments are in balance, interventions can reasonably be expected to succeed.

Compensation can be viewed as either adding an equivalent to one side or decreasing/eliminating an undesired effect on the other. A dog might possess a talent for receiving young children and feel completely at ease listening to one child at a time reading out loud. However, it is possible for the same dog to be uncomfortable walking through the crowded, noisy halls of the school in which he works. The other students will make their presence known if given a chance, and so the students and their unsupervised (and so highly unpredictable) behavior must be considered on the environmental side of the balance scale. An example of compensation would be for the handler to walk the dog through the school only after the students were already in class or, if the dog were small, to use a carrier to transport the dog through the school.

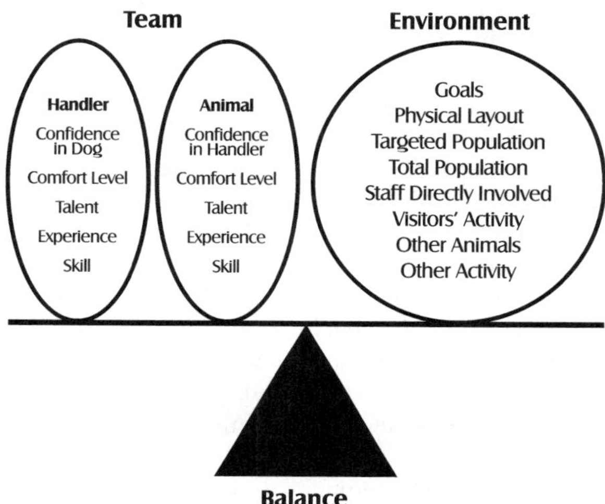

FIGURE 1 Graphic and corresponding text first published in *Therapy Dogs Today: Their Gifts, Our Obligation*. ©2004. Reprinted with permission of Kris Butler and Funpuddle Publishing Associates.

Team Elements of Balance

Butler (2004) also pointed out that although they work together as a team, each handler and animal come with individual levels of comfort, talent, skill, experience, and confidence in each other. Each team performs its own balancing act between the animal and the handler on its "team" end of the balance scale.

Comfort levels are dependent on each team member's individual ability to cope with the environment. Comfort is mostly an animal-related issue, simply because handlers do not repeatedly take the team into environments where the handler feels uncomfortable.

AAT and AAA environments are stressful to animals, perhaps for no other reason than the huge shift from settings and schedules that would be normal for the species. The key is in determining whether an animal has the capacity to recover from its perception of encroachments, cope comfortably in the environment, and enjoy interactions. AAT and AAAs are not appropriate if the emotional or activity levels of targeted populations are overwhelming to available animals. Experience is the teacher that causes animals and handlers to anticipate AAT and AAAs with either positive or negative expectations. Animals' perceptions can differ greatly from their handlers' perceptions of the same events. An animal's level of confidence in the handler is based both on their lifelong relationship and how the animal perceives the handler's behavior in the moment.

The most essential element an animal and handler possess is talent, yet it is often overlooked. Talent is a natural endowment. Some people are talented piano players; others simply play the piano. Talented handlers are able to deal with the reality of their current situation and act as their animals' advocates. Talented animals are able to demonstrate behaviors described previously as being therapeutic.

Skill refers to a team's trained or acquired behaviors. High levels of skill never compensate for absence of talent. Some animals can be trained to persevere despite distractions and sensory bombardment. Just because some animals are willing to tolerate overwhelming environments does not mean people have license to exploit the animals. Sometimes an environment imposes too much upon an animal.

The perception of a strong moment-to-moment connection between the handler and the animal increases everyone's confidence in the team. Handlers who talk in normal everyday tones and who make contact, either by touching or speaking, with their animals frequently demonstrate the bond that exists between themselves and their animals. Handler skill should reflect a loving partnership with the animal, while subtly suggesting that the handler is indeed in control and can easily redirect the animal's behavior when necessary (Butler, 2004). For example, a participant might not be able to identify that the handler kept a gentle hand on the dog, scratching behind the ears, during most of the AAT and AAA interaction, but the result is that the participant is left with a positive feeling about a strong, respectful relationship between the animal and the handler. When a handler physically places the animal into position and then does not touch the animal again except to reposition, it leaves an entirely different impression. Both gruff tone of voice and physical pushing/pulling can be distracting and create negative judgments about the relationship between handler and animal.

IMPACT OF ENVIRONMENTAL FACTORS OF ANIMALS

Together, an animal and a handler create a uniquely balanced team, but they do not visit in a vacuum. Within each facility are environmental elements that affect each team's talent and comfort levels, test each team's skill level, and draw from each team's experiences differently. An animal's and handler's abilities to demonstrate specific behaviors depend on environmental factors, as well as team skills and talents. The best way to determine if teams are appropriate for specific environments is by assessing their behaviors within those environments.

No matter where teams work, each environment includes a targeted population, specific goals for that population, a specific number of staff people involved, a total population, and perhaps visitor activity, other animals, and other activity. Assessments made through careful observation, not necessarily a formal process, will best determine whether an animal and handler team can remain in balance within a specific environment.

Staff participation carries more weight than any other element on the environmental side of the balance scale. Effective staffing mitigates risks associated with unpredictable populations and enables teams to address complex goals. Skill becomes an important issue when goals are complex and specific. Team skills must be adequate to meet the goals of the program. Gentle, talented animals without high levels of trained skill can provide effective opportunities for communication and socialization. In meeting the basic needs of traumatized people, an animal's skill is not as important as its ability to receive people unconditionally and increase their feelings of safety and security.

Some participant populations are not appropriate for hands-on AAT and AAAs with available animals, no matter how tolerant or talented the animals might be. AAT and AAAs are not appropriate for people who might harm the available animals or handlers, even inadvertently. The staff's role includes screening to determine which participants are appropriate for AAT and AAAs. Targeted populations cannot be changed, but there are often ways to compensate to achieve balance. For example, individual children who sit in chairs or on the floor are less threatening to small animals than groups of children who are playing throughout the environment. Sometimes balance is achieved through a selection of larger species of animals to compensate for more reactive populations.

Environments that facilitate AAT and AAAs often include other animals, such as residential animals, multiple visiting animals, visiting family pets, or service dogs. Some animals are, at best, unable to maintain focus in the presence of other animals and, at worst, aggressive toward or fearful of other animals. Balance is dependent on the working animal's ability to disregard other animals in the environment or the staff's ability to limit the access of other animals to selected areas of the facility.

Professional educators and therapists who work with their own animals within their professional environments are dual-role handlers who assume roles and responsibilities on both sides of the balance scale. Dual-role handlers present their animals and facilitate interventions. The attention required to fulfill the role of primary staff person leaves less attention available for the team handler position on the other end of the balance scale.

Dual-role handlers require animals that are able to fill any voids left by their multitasking handlers. Animals that work with dual-role handlers must be skilled to the degree that they behave appropriately even in the absence of direct handler attention. Length of workdays and workweeks are huge comfort-level issues for these animals. Because dual-role handlers do not enjoy the option of switching environments or changing targeted populations to achieve balance, it is important that they consider carefully the selection, training, and scheduling of their animals.

ANIMALS AS TOOLS OR COLLEAGUES IN THE THERAPEUTIC PROCESS

To ensure quality, respectful programs it is critical that animals are never "used" in AAT and AAAs, but treated as partners in a mutually beneficial relationship. The needs of animals must always be considered, accommodated, and balanced with the needs of participants within the scope of an AAT and AAA program. The challenge is to accept and appreciate each animal for what she/he is designed by nature to be and not project our human images of "success" onto them.

Sometimes there is no capacity for balance. Ethical handlers will remove their animals any time the environment is stacked against them. When it becomes impossible for an animal to work comfortably within the environment(s) available to the animal, it is the handler's responsibility to retire the animal from AAT and AAAs. When animals that live in the therapeutic setting such as resident pets or animals living on therapeutic farms are unable to cope with the environment in which they live, it is imperative that the handler or advocate rehomes the animals or, if rehoming is not realistic, consider euthanasia for the animals.

THE LANGUAGE OF PERSONAL SPACE

Proxemics is the study of personal space and the degree of separation that individuals maintain between each other in social situations. Each species has its own rules relating to personal territory. Animals participating in AAT and AAAs are no exception. Within each personal territory, there are zones. The zone at which an individual is first aware of another is the public zone. From there one enters the social zone. Although it is permissible to be in another's social zone, it is the nonverbal communication between the individuals that will make the situation either intimidating or acceptable. Moving still closer brings an individual into another's personal zone, which can be read as a sign of either

Proxemics
Personal Territory

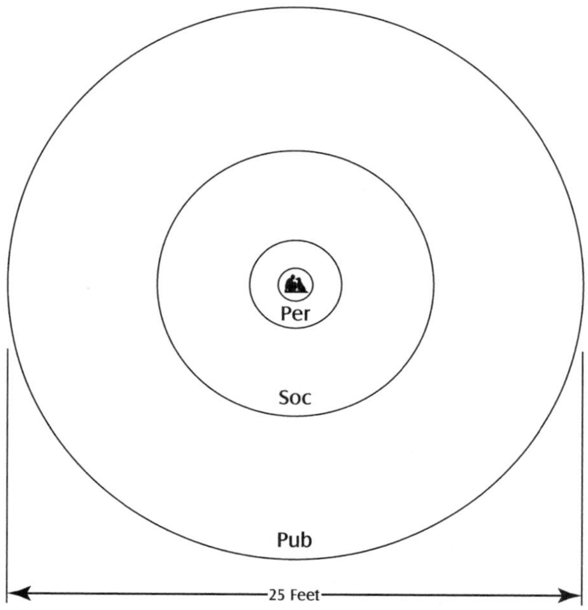

- Intimate Zone – 18 inches to contact
Per – Personal Zone – 4 feet to 18 inches
Soc – Social Zone – 12 feet to 4 feet
Pub – Public Zone – 25 feet to 12 feet

FIGURE 2 Graphic and corresponding text first published in *Therapy Dogs Today: Their Gifts, Our Obligation*. ©2004. Reprinted with permission of Kris Butler and Funpuddle Publishing Associates.

favor or manipulation. Closer than the personal is the intimate zone, which includes contact. An individual is overwhelmingly aware of another within one's intimate zone. Species maintain rigid rules of communication within this proximity. Ignoring or being unaware of those rules can be perceived as disrespect or intimidation. It is crucial to note that the great majority of AAT and AAA programs encourage participants to interact with animals in this zone (Fig. 2).

Whenever the barrier of an intimate zone is crossed, animals respond by signaling. These signals are obvious announcements of respect, appeasement, fear, defensiveness, or aggression; however, animals in AAT and AAA programs are routinely required to work in settings and with people for whom their language is completely foreign. The handler's ability to interpret and respond to each animal's important communiqués is a critical factor in mitigating the impact of these interactions.

Touching is the most intimate act of communication. Touching is an integral part of almost every animal-enhanced intervention, and while no one would suggest that people stop petting animals during AAT and AAAs, it is crucial that the animals are allowed to seek out this intimate contact. Animals that obediently tolerate an invasion of their intimate space may become overwhelmed or stressed.

In addition, small animals such as rabbits, guinea pigs, and tiny dogs bring with them unique intrinsic vulnerabilities associated with being prey. Predators often hover over, swoop in, grab their prey, and carry it off for consumption. Nature has endowed small prey animals with an intuitive sense of the seating arrangement at nature's dinner table. AAT and AAA setups often place a person or groups of people physically over an animal, in positions that suggest hovering, swooping, and grabbing at the animal. Warranted or not, animals' bodies respond to their intuition and signal their levels of discomfort.

Body language enables any species to send messages, note reception of messages, break through defenses, and avoid conflict. The process of communication is complicated and becomes even more so when different species have different interpretations for the signals included in their vocabulary. Often humans do not recognize the signaling of an animal or misinterpret the signals as disinterest or disobedience; however, each signal is part of a message an animal might be trying to convey about personal territory. Just as often, during AAT and AAAs people behave in ways that inadvertently signal tension to animals.

HUMAN HEALING OR ANIMAL STRESS: IS THERE A TRADE-OFF?

AAT and AAA environments are stressful to animals, perhaps for no other reason than the huge shift from settings and schedules that would be normal for the species. The key is in determining whether an animal has the capacity to recover from its perception of encroachments, cope comfortably in the environment, and enjoy interactions. AAT and AAAs are not appropriate if the emotional or activity levels of targeted populations are overwhelming to available animals. Experience is the teacher that causes animals and handlers to anticipate AAT and AAAs with either positive or negative expectations. Animals' perceptions can differ greatly from their handlers' perceptions of the same events. An animal's level of confidence in the handler is based on both their lifelong relationship and how the animal perceives the handler's behavior in the moment.

Individual behaviors will vary, but general signs of stress include changes in communication patterns and nonspecific body complaints. Shifts in communication patterns are detected through posture, body movement, head movement, and eye movement. Nonspecific body complaints that indicate stress reactions include sweating paws, salivating, panting, yawning, shaking off, sudden loss of hair, restlessness, withdrawal, muscle tenseness, suspiciousness, aggression, hyperalertness, intensified startle reflex, ducking behind handler, self-mutilation, and change in activity or appetite.

Most symptoms of stress are universal. People know stress when they see it, even in other species. Not only is it risky and abusive to visit with an animal that is stressed, but the people being visited will recognize the behaviors as stress related and ascertain that the animal does not wish to visit with them.

AT THE END OF THE DAY

Handlers make up 50% of working AAT and AAA teams but carry 100% of team responsibility for the process. The significance of adequate handler training and screening cannot be overemphasized. Handlers' experience, skill, and health are equally as important as animal assessment to minimize risk to all who participate in AAT and AAAs. The competence of the handler directly affects the degree of risk of injury, infection, or inappropriate interactions.

The handler's role in AAT and AAAs is to present the animal. Presenting an animal involves preparation (training, veterinary care, grooming), assessments prior to every intervention, moment-to-moment assessments, and actively working as the animal's advocate. Presentation skill includes a handler's knowledgeable and proactive handling to enhance the animal's ability to meet the needs of the targeted population and a basic knowledge of communication skills to enhance human-to-human interactions. Components of the handler's role include the ability to

- Demonstrate appropriate treatment of people and animals
- Demonstrate appropriate social skills (eye contact, smiles, confident posture, conversation) needed for interacting with people in AAT and AAAs
- Prepare for, conduct, and conclude a visit

- Demonstrate techniques for AAT and AAA interactions with a targeted population
- Maintain confidentiality
- Demonstrate pleasant, calm, and friendly reaction to and attitude toward the animal during various tasks and scenarios
- Demonstrate proactive (rather than reactive) animal handling skills
- Act as the animal's advocate in all situations
- Effectively read the animal's cues (stress, excitement, etc.) and act accordingly
- Protect and respect the animal's needs

The most effective handlers are knowledgeable about their role and responsibility in AAT and AAA interactions. They should understand the rationale behind requirements for the animal in order to anticipate the ways in which unpredicted behavior may affect outcomes. Handlers need to comply with documentation and facility administrative procedures and policies. Ultimately, handlers are responsible for infection control measures such as vaccinations and parasite control.

There is a strong social connection between handlers and their animals. The animals, after all, often hold the admission tickets to activities their handlers enjoy very much. It is understandable that some handlers measure a degree of their worth based on the recognition they receive from their animal-related services. Sometimes handlers want to keep the team intact, even when the animal is ready to break up the act (Butler, 2004). When denial keeps handlers from accepting the unwanted reality that their animals do not enjoy their work, handlers offer excuses—rationalizations, minimizations, and justifications—to remove any blame from a behavior.

"Yes, but he was abused."
"Yes, but you kept us waiting; we got hot."
"Yes, but I didn't see it that way."
"Yes, but that's just how terriers are."
"Yes, but he's never done that before."

M. Fredrickson-MacNamara wrote in the foreword to *Therapy Dogs Today*: "Effective handlers are capable of sublimating their own egos during AAT and AAA sessions. In traditional relationships with working with animals such as livestock work or competitions, handlers are congratulated for their skill and expertise. Handlers within AAT and AAA programs must be able to sublimate themselves to the developing intimacy between the participant and the animal. Those handlers who understand that the accolades belong to the person struggling to heal and not to their animal or themselves have reached a significant level of maturity and expertise in this work. Without this understanding, the handler remains in competition with the animal and the participant for reward and recognition" (Butler, 2004).

Animals have been moved to the front lines of successful treatment plans because of their capacity to motivate patients/students/participants to participate in a wide range of physical, cognitive, psychosocial, communication, and educational exercises. The experience of handlers in day-to-day settings such as school programs, rehabilitation centers, mental health programs, residential treatment programs, and others indicates that it is not specialized responses a team demonstrates but rather the depth of trust and breadth of relationship the team has that results in success within therapeutic settings. Successful handlers have a clear understanding of how their animal exhibits various degrees of stress and how to protect their animals from undue stress.

Today, AAT and AAA settings are never alike. Therefore, it is critical to go beyond training methods and one-time approaches developed years ago to screen therapy animal/handler teams for the brief nursing home and hospital visiting programs. Typical AAT and AAA programs go beyond merely offering participants opportunities to interact with animals. Metaphor created through interactions with animals is useful in developing self-awareness and understanding. That message must be considered carefully. Participant perception of the experience relates directly to the animal's perception of the same experience.

Selection and evaluation procedures have become separated from the important framework provided by standards of practice developed by national therapy animal organizations. These standards contain valid considerations for the selection of animals and handlers for AAT and AAAs. By combining this wisdom with a clear understanding of the elements of prediction, practitioners and organizations can develop evaluation processes that become an intrinsic part of each interaction rather than a single event. In chaotic and unpredictable settings, team evaluation must be as dynamic and fluid as the interactions themselves.

As we enter the 21st century, it is clear that there is much more to learn about the selection, training, and care of animals involved in AAT and AAAs. Expectations for animals involved in these settings have changed dramatically since the mid-1990s. AAT and AAAs have taken animals into settings and into close relationship with people never imagined by the crafters of the original standards and screening procedures. While this change in the place and role of animals in therapeutic interventions does not mean that previous work is irrelevant in today's practice, it does require that we step back and reassess the objectives of selection and evaluation procedures in light of new information and considerably more experience.

REFERENCES

American Kennel Club, Inc. (1989) The canine good citizen test. At Canine Good Citizen. http://www.akc.org/events/cgc/index.cfm

Beck, A. M., and Jones, B. A. (1985). Unreported dog bites in children. *Public Health Rep.* **100**(3), 315–321.

Boissy, A. (1995). Fear and fearfulness in animals. *Q. Rev. Biol.* **70**(2), 165–191.

Butler, K. (2004). "Therapy Dogs: Compassionate Modalities." Funpuddle Publishing Associates, Norman, OK.

Butler, K. (2004). "Therapy Dogs Today: Their Gifts, Our Obligation." Funpuddle Publishing Associates, Norman, OK.

de Becker, G. (1997). "The Gift of Fear: Survival Signals That Protect Us from Violence." Little, Brown and Company, New York.

Fredrickson, M. A., and Howie, A. R. (2000). Methods, standards, guidelines and considerations in selecting animals for animal-assisted therapy. Part B. Guidelines and standards for animal selection in animal-assisted activity and animal-assisted therapy programs. *In* "Handbook on Animal-Assisted Therapy: Theoretical Foundations and Guidelines for Practice" (A. Fine, ed.). Academic Press, San Francisco.

Goodloe, L. P., and Borchelt, P. L. (1998). Companion dogs temperament traits. *J. Appl. Anim. Welf. Sci.* **1**(4), 303–338.

Hines, L. M., Lee, R. L., Zeglen, M. E., and Ryan, T. (1983). "Guidelines: Placement of Animals in Nursing Homes." Paper presented at the Conferences on the Human-Animal Bond, University of Minnesota, Minneapolis, MN, and University of California, Irvine, CA.

IAHAIO Prague guidelines on animal-assisted activities and animal-assisted therapy (1998). Guidelines accepted at the IAHAIO General Assembly, September, Prague.

Lanier, J. L., Grandin, T., Green, R. D., Avery, D., and McGee, K. (2000). The relationship between reaction to sudden, intermittent movements and sounds and temperament. *J. Anim. Sci.* **78**, 1467–1474.

Ledger, R., and Baxter, M. (1996). A validated test to assess the temperament of dogs. *In* "Proceedings of the 30th International Congress of the ISAE" (I. J. H. Duncan, T. M. Widowski, and D. B. Haley, eds.), p. 111. Col. C.K. Centre for the Study of Animal Welfare, Guelph, Canada.

New, J. C., and Strimple, E. (1988). "Therapy Dog Criteria: Minimum Medical Criteria." Paper presented at the seventh annual Delta Society Conference, People, Animals and the Environment: Exploring Our Interdependence, Orlando, FL.

North American Riding for the Handicapped Association (1994). How to start a NARHA center. NARHA. http//www.NARHA.org

Serpell, J. A., and Hsu, Y. (2001). A novel approach to evaluating performance-related behavior in prospective guide dogs. *In* "Proceedings of the 35th Congress of the ISAE" (J. P. Garner, J. A. Mench, and S. P. Heekin, eds.). Center for Animal Welfare, UC Davis, Davis, CA.

Shelter animals inappropriate for visiting programs (1992). *Pet Partners Newslett.* **2**(6).

"Standards of practice for animal-assisted activities and animal-assisted therapy" (1996). Delta Society, Renton, WA.

Stephen, J. M., Ledger, R. A., and Stanton, N. (2001). Comparison of the perceptions of temperament in dogs by different members of the same household. *In* "Proceedings of the 35th International Congress of the ISAE" (J. P. Garner, J. A. Mench, and S. P. Heekin, eds.), p. 113. Center for Animal Welfare, UC Davis, Davis, CA.

Visser, E. K., van Reenen, C. G., Schilder, M. B. H., Knaap, J. H., and Blokhuis, H. J. (2001). Can behavioural parameters in young horses be used to quantify aspects of temperament? *In* "Proceedings of the 35th Congress of the ISAE" (J. P. Garner, J. A. Mench, and S. P. Heekin, eds.). Center for Animal Welfare, UC Davis, Davis, CA.

Wharton, T., Sercu, C., Malone, M., and Macauley, B. (2005). An analysis of equine stress levels after participation in therapy sessions. *Scientific and Educational Journal of Therapeutic Riding*, 25–30.

Weimer, D. L., and Vining, A. R. (2005). "Policy Analysis: Concepts and Practice." Pearson Prentice Hall, New Jersey.

Weiss, E., and Greenberg, G. (1997). Service dog selection tests: Effectiveness for dogs from animal shelters. *Appl. Anim. Behav. Sci.* 53, 297–308.

CHAPTER 8

Designing and Implementing Animal-Assisted Therapy Programs in Health and Mental Health Organizations

GERALD P. MALLON
Hunter College School of Social Work, New York, New York 10021

SAMUEL B. ROSS, JR., AND STEVE KLEE
Green Chimneys Children's Services, Brewster, New York

LISA ROSS
Touro University, Henderson, Nevada 89044

I. INTRODUCTION

Although health and mental health systems continually examine fresh and original approaches to serve their client constituents, new proposals are seldom greeted with enthusiasm within organizational structures (Bolman and Terrance, 1991; Brager and Holloway, 1978; Dutton, 1992; Ket de Vries and Miller, 1984; Morgan, 1986; Moss-Kanter, 1982, 1988). One relatively new approach that utilizes a variety of animals including companion animals, farm animals, and injured wildlife as adjuncts in the treatment of various populations has had or soon may receive greater acceptance and consideration by health or mental health organizations (Brooks, 2001; Hanselman, 2001; Mallon, 1994a,b, 1999). Utilizing animals in health and mental health organizations is a proposal that has engendered both the regard and the ire of administrators.

The emerging breadth of its applications and the involvement of skilled professionals from diverse disciplines have made animal-assisted therapy (AAT) more than a "therapeutic" intervention. Although AAT is beginning to be recognized as a treatment modality much like dance, music, art, and poetry therapy (Beck and Katcher, 1984), it is also important to note that the main difference between AAT and other adjunctive therapies is that the central "tools" in this intervention are living, breathing, interacting creatures. This is an important element because when animals are introduced into a health or mental health delivery system, unique organizational issues must be considered.

Utilizing a predominantly social work and psychological approach to organizational administration, this chapter contains advice to help organizations discern whether or not to utilize AAT and to aid implementation. What can be considered are equine experiential learning, equine-facilitated psychotherapy, and therapeutic riding as part of a program offering. In addition, horticultural activities should be considered as part of the introduction of the activities. Clarity as to whether the program is to provide therapy or psychotherapy must be part of any planning. Today dog training by students, in school gardens, minizoos, visiting animals, and handler and nature therapy combine elements that are seen in animal-assisted therapy and activity programs. With Green Chimneys Children's Services (see Ross, 1999) as our organizational model of choice, the authors, who are among the principal administrators of this program, focus on rules and principles that guide program development.

II. ANIMAL-ASSISTED THERAPY

Boris M. Levinson (1962) was the first professionally trained clinician to formally introduce and document the way in which companion animals could hasten the development of a rapport between therapist and patient and increase patient motivation (Mallon, 1994c). First termed *pet therapy* by Levinson, this approach is now known as animal-assisted therapy. Originally ridiculed by his colleagues for presenting such a "preposterous" technique, Levinson continued to research, write, and speak about the efficacy of this novel intervention throughout his life.

Levinson initially advocated utilizing animals with children in residential treatment and wrote extensively about it (Levinson, 1968, 1969, 1970, 1971, 1972; Levinson and Mallon, 1996). In an attempt to gather data on the utilization of animals in organizations, Levinson conducted the first survey documenting the use of pets in residential schools (Levinson, 1968). With a sample of 160 residential and day schools identified from the *Directory for Exceptional Children,* a response rate of 75.6% (N = 121) was obtained. Levinson found that 40.7% did not permit pets in the schools. State regulations, fear of diseases, the labor-intensive nature of caring for pets, and potential mistreatment by the children were all cited as reasons for barring animals in organizational settings.

In the 1970s the American Humane Education Society commissioned a survey to determine how many institutions in the country were using animals in facilitating the treatment of clients. The survey indicated results (48%) similar to those found earlier by Levinson. Several of the institutions surveyed reported disadvantages as well as advantages (Arkow, 1982). In many cases, these programs were developed in a surge of enthusiasm by well-meaning but overzealous and inexperienced individuals (Daniel *et al.*, 1984).

By the 1980s, then, the necessity of careful program design became clear. Although many other AAT programs are rapidly emerging both in this country and abroad, one organization that has thoughtfully and carefully crafted an animal-assisted program for children is Green Chimneys Children's Services, located in Brewster, New York, 60 miles outside of New York City.

III. THE GREEN CHIMNEYS MODEL

The main campus of Green Chimneys Children's Services is a temporary home for the 102 children and adolescents and 80 day students who share its rural environs with barnyard animals, domestic companion animals, and wildlife. The healing power of human–animal interactions has been an active component in this organizational therapeutic milieu for more than 50 years.

This former dairy farm was purchased in 1947 by the Ross family, and the organization was originally designed as an independent boarding school for very young children. Operating as Green Chimneys School for Little Folk, the educationally based facility incorporated the dairy farm into the children's daily lives. Initially, the staff did not know or appreciate the therapeutic part of this alliance. The staff saw the animals as merely providing companionship, socialization, pleasure, and education for the students. They soon realized, however, that they were providing much more.

In the early 1970s, the school evolved into a residential treatment center that specialized in the care of children with emotional and behavioral needs. Children came with histories of severe neglect; sexual, physical, and emotional abuse; homelessness; family substance abuse; and behavioral and educational difficulties. Many had learning disabilities and had experienced very limited success in school. Most were hospitalized for aggressive behaviors, suicide attempts, or chronic depression. The majority lived in poverty. Most had experienced significant psychosocial stressors at home, in school, and in their communities.

Although many changes occurred as the organization changed its program to meet the needs of a new population, the human–animal interactions component remained intact. The staff realized that these special children, mostly from urban environments, could truly benefit from interactions with animals.

IV. ORGANIZATIONAL ISSUES

The eventual success or failure of a proposed organizational innovation is a consequence of the interplay of power and politics at numerous levels: individual, intraorganizational, interorganizational, and societal (Frost and Egri, 1991). The Performance Improvement Committee, which is a board and staff committee, meets monthly. The executive council of Green Chimneys, which consists of the agency's executive director, the organization's founder, the clinical director, the clinical coordinator, the director of treatment, the chief fiscal officer, the director of education, and the director of fund development, meets on a weekly basis to monitor review agency practices and procedures and to ensure that all parts of the organization are functioning at optimal efficiency. This council provides leadership and direction and acts as a sounding board on major organizational issues, including the utilization of animals in the treatment programs.

Other health and mental health organizations that wish to implement an animal-assisted program component must consider the level of support that the innovation can amass on multiple levels. The following questions represent areas that the Green Chimneys executive council recommends as important considerations to be discerned by other organizational administrators who wish to implement an AAT program.

- Is there administrative support for the idea?
- Does the idea have board support, and will it need board approval?
- Does the innovation have staff that will support the idea?
- Will new staff have to be trained and hired?
- Has anyone asked the clients if they think this is a good idea?
- How will the innovation be funded, and what costs will be incurred throughout the process?
- What are the salient issues with respect to infection control?
- What are the issues with respect to safety and humane treatment of animals?
- What liability issues need to be considered?
- Is there family support for the program?
- Do the clinical staff accept and support the program?

Also, in the age of managed care:

- Are there measurable outcomes that will enable the organization to document and evaluate the program's effectiveness?
- How can this intervention be monitored for continuous quality improvements?

V. PROGRAM DESIGN ISSUES

A. Staff Issues

Because animals have always been a part of the Green Chimneys approach to working with children and families, we have always enjoyed the support of our organization's board of directors and agency administrators. However, as the agency has grown, we have often had to find ways to ensure that our animal focus is maintained.

Knowledgeable, experienced, and enthusiastic personnel greatly influence a program and ensure programmatic longevity. A consistent group of core staff make management easier. After a great deal of experimentation and trial-and-error logic, Green Chimneys has found that an animal-assisted program can be staffed by licensed and credentialed personnel (social workers, nurses, psychologists, physicians, occupational therapists, physical therapists, vocational therapists, teachers, certified therapeutic riding instructors, licensed wildlife rehabilitation staff) and other staff (child care workers, school personnel, recreation workers, nurse's aides, therapy aides) and that volunteers can provide animal-assisted activities (AAAs). It has been an ongoing challenge for our organization to determine which staff positions or responsibilities should be filled by professionals, which should be staffed by trained personnel, and which are suited for volunteers. Over the years we found that many of the staff currently employed by the agency came forward to fill roles in working with both children and animals. Staff may bring animals to work if there is a therapeutic purpose. Two key factors were their desire to incorporate animals into their work with people and their commitment to designing innovative approaches to working with people in need. An additional essential element was whether they had the support of their supervisors in this endeavor. Green Chimneys has historically recognized that those helping professionals who work with both people and animals need to be flexible, but there is also a need for structure, consistency, and limits. Many different philosophies are represented by those who are interested in developing approaches to working with animals and humans. Before any new program can be developed, it will need to be approved by the organization's board of directors and administrative staff. The first question that most boards of directors and administrators will want an answer to is this: How does this project relate to the organization's mission, vision, values, goals, and needs? On a secondary level, both bodies will want to know about costs, about maintaining the program, about agency personnel and client support, and about liability. At Green Chimneys we receive many calls and e-mails asking about insurance coverage and names of agents and carriers. When interviewing for positions, administrative staff must seek out the candidate's specific beliefs and personal stance and know where the candidate stands on issues that may come up in the workplace. Staff surveys may be another important step that can permit their voices to be heard when a new intervention is being considered.

B. Client Issues

Although it has been written that the human–animal bond is universal (Mallon, 1992; Senter, 1993), the reality is that not all people like animals. Some clients may be allergic to specific animals, some may have a phobia about a particular animal, and others may just not have had positive experiences with animals. At Green Chimneys, many of these issues are immediately addressed at intake, when the client first arrives for services. Clients are screened for allergies and asked about fears or dislikes for particular animals. It should be noted that there is evidence that youngsters with pets are less likely to develop allergies. At Green Chimneys, we have a high number of children diagnosed with asthma but we have not had any child hospitalized as a result of an asthma attack. The allergy information is integrated into the client's initial prospective treatment plan. Although Green Chimneys would like all of its clients to have a positive experience with animals, the organization respects the fact that not all children respond the same way to animal-assisted approaches to treatment.

Another means for assessing patient satisfaction or dissatisfaction is to conduct a survey of the clients' likes and dislikes about their treatment. This is more or less standard practice in most health and mental health organizations in today's managed care environment. A client-focused survey soliciting patient response toward animals is an important place to begin the process. In addition, it may be important to do a thorough assessment of any history of animal abuse. Most surveys of children, families, and staff give approval to animals, working at the farm, and gardening.

Concern for the physical well-being of the clients is a major priority in health and mental health care–related organizations. Cleanliness, infection control, and risk of illness related to zoonotic conditions claim a central focus in most health and mental health care systems. Organizations interested in adopting an AAT approach must research federal, state, and local regulations early in the planning process to consider possible limitations for such an intervention. It can be very disappointing for those interested in designing an AAT program to discover that rigid local health laws prohibit such techniques.

VI. ANIMAL SELECTION

Choosing animals at Green Chimneys to be part of our AAT program is an exciting endeavor, but animal selection can also be an imposing task. Again, we would caution that those wishing to introduce animals into an existing organization should start small. Zoning and health regulations will undoubtedly affect the location, nature, and size of programs incorporating animals. Geography also plays a large role in the selection of animals. Organizations in urban environments obviously need to consider restricting the program to smaller companion animals (see Senter, 1993; Serpell *et al.*, 2000). Some programs may choose to have a visiting AAA program rather than having animals in residence. Rural programs, such as our Green Chimneys program, utilize a wide variety of animals, including farm animals and captive wildlife. Our wildlife program is coordinated by an individual who is a licensed wildlife rehabilitator (see Senter, 1993). Most of our wild animals have sustained injuries and are placed only temporarily at the farm for rest, medical care, and eventual release. The size of the physical space needed for each animal is determined by the animal's physical size and need for space. An administrative policy should also be in place that ensures that all animals are healthy and have up-to-date vaccinations and a record kept on file of their health status.

Research and courses at colleges and universities have helped provide evidence of the value of such programs. Accrediting bodies have looked at the programs and have approved their place in hospitals, agencies, and schools. Foundations, corporations, and individuals have shown a real interest and are providing funding as it relates to the human–animal bond and related topics.

VII. COST EFFECTIVENESS

Initial start-up and continued financing, in any organization, plays a large role in the decision to develop a new program. This is particularly true for nonprofit organizations. Regardless of how useful an AAT program is deemed to be for an organization, the bottom line for most agency administrators and boards is how much is it going to cost and how will it be funded? Our Green Chimneys founder, Dr. Sam Ross, and our organization's development staff spend a great deal of time and energy on fund-raising efforts to keep all of our programs fiscally sound. Although this process can be a time-consuming enterprise, the good news is that incorporating animals does not have to be an expensive undertaking. There are many ways to raise money for programs. Innovative thinking and creativity are the keys.

All new programs have start-up costs, dictated by the size and nature of the innovation. "Start small" is a good maxim. Funds for animal upkeep and maintenance refer to the day-to-day expenses of keeping animals. These costs will vary from program to program but generally include food, shelter, veterinary costs, grooming costs, and staff salary costs.

At Green Chimneys we have found five ways to support an animal-assisted program: (1) use of present funds, (2) foundation or corporate support, (3) fee for service, (4) outright donations, and (5) sale of items. Where costs are minimal and programs are small, using present funds may be a quick-start solution. Many foundations or corporations, especially those with an obvious interest in animals, can provide possible seed money to start a program. Fees for services can be generated through visiting animal programs or by offering specialized training. Donations from the community and sales in the community not only help support the program but bring the organization's name out into the community. Linking the community to the program's efforts to help its constituents can be useful in many ways.

Since introducing the Farm-on-the-Moo-ve program, a mobile program providing animal contact with students as caregivers, the program has been replicated at many other places and has quite literally brought the farm into the community, in many cases to an urban community that is largely estranged from human–animal connections.

VIII. LIABILITY

All organizations are concerned about the potential for liability issues. Obviously there are risks inherent in having animals on site in a health or mental health organization. Green Chimneys has developed a documented safety plan for both clients and animals, and we would recommend that such a plan be considered a necessity for every organization. In the sections that follow, we discuss our Green Chimneys protocols for minimizing risk. These should be carefully considered and followed by organizational staff. The first place that organizations should start when considering liability issues is with a review of their current insurance carrier's policies about animals. If animals are included in the policy coverage and the organization's carrier is clear that the organization is launching a new initiative, then there is no need for further coverage. If animals are not included in the current coverage, then the organization must obtain coverage for staff, clients, and visitors.

IX. OUTCOMES

The widespread ardor about the almost universal efficacy of animal-assisted programs has, for many years, all but obscured any serious questioning of its possible risks. In the age of managed care, health and mental health organization administrators must evaluate the effectiveness of their interventions. Any program evaluation of a health or mental health organization must also include a review of the effectiveness of an organization's animal-assisted programs (Anspach, 1991; LaJoie, 2003). Although organizational administrators must develop stringent criteria for what constitutes a therapeutic gain, they must also develop criteria for what constitutes an effective programmatic intervention. Some suggested questions that should be assessed include the following. Is this intervention cost effective? Are there other interventions that are equally clinically appropriate and useful but more cost effective? How many clients are utilizing this service in a given cycle? What are the instruments used by program evaluators to determine clinical or program effectiveness with respect to this intervention? Therefore, guidelines for the implementation of an animal-assisted program need to identify conditions necessary to preserve the health and safety of both the animals and the clients and to ensure that the intervention is programmatically effective. Administrators should resist the attempt to rationalize the implementation of such programs as a kind of therapy that has universal benefits solely because of its appeal. Outcome studies are equally important in order to prevent outright rejection of the plan as unimportant or nontherapeutic. It is important to keep careful records on the children involved in the program.

X. INFECTION CONTROL ISSUES

Even in the best AAT programs, there is an element of risk. At Green Chimneys we have been aware of and respond to these risk factors on a daily basis. A medical services committee has the responsibility of including human and animal infection control. Animals bite, some produce allergic reactions, and some pass on zoonotic diseases. Therefore, an AAT program must develop infection control policies that address the need for some animals to avoid contact with certain people and develop surveillance procedures and responses. Every setting where pets or animals of any type are located must have some rules in place (Ross, 1989). At Green Chimneys we maintain a health record on each animal, and we recommend this task as an essential component of any planned AAA/T program.

XI. RULES THAT GUIDE ANIMAL-ASSISTED THERAPY PROGRAMS

Following Lewis's (1982) advice, rules that guide an intervention to action specify the practice. The Performance Improvement Committee and the executive council at Green Chimneys have focused a great deal of attention on the development of rules to guide practice in our AAT approaches to treatment.

These rules are enumerated for all Green Chimneys staff as a part of the agency's initial formal orientation process and are codified in writing in our organization's literature. We have found the following rules to be useful, and we believe they are adaptable for other organizations.

1. House animals are to be approved by the organization's administrator or designee.
2. Appropriate animals include dogs, cats, birds, fish, hamsters, gerbils, guinea pigs, rabbits, and, where appropriate conditions exist, farm animals such as goats, sheep, ducks, chickens, cows, and horses.
3. Wildlife are not permitted in the program unless they are cared for under the supervision of a licensed individual and then only in a rehabilitative circumstance, a previously injured status, or permanent injury.
4. At the time of admission, a medical record is started on each animal and is kept up-to-date as long as the animal remains in the organization.
5. Animals are to have up-to-date vaccinations by a licensed veterinarian.
6. Animals are to have an annual physical by a qualified veterinarian.
7. Animals who are ill are to be treated by a qualified veterinarian.
8. Aggressive animals will be removed immediately.
9. Dogs or cats are to be altered or spayed.
10. The administrator or designee is responsible for acceptable animal husbandry practices.
11. Animals are to be controlled by leash, command, or cage.
12. Animals are not permitted in the following areas: areas where food is cleaned, stored, or prepared; vehicles used for the transportation of food; patient/staff toilets, showers, or dressing rooms; and drug preparation areas, nursing stations, and sterile and cleaning supply rooms.
13. All pet utensils, food, and equipment used for maintenance of pets are to be kept in an area separate from clients' food preparation areas and are to be kept cleaned.
14. Animals are to be fed according to a schedule posted where the animals live and are cared for.
15. Animals are not to be fed human food.
16. Freshwater is to be made available for the animals at all times.
17. Food handlers are not to be involved in animal care, feeding, or cleanup of animal food or waste.
18. Dogs and cats are to be effectively housebroken.
19. Animal waste is to be picked up and disposed of in a trash receptacle made available for this purpose.
20. Any animal that bites a staff member or patient is to be quarantined for 10 days.

21. Animals who die on the premises are to be disposed of in accordance with the established organizational procedure.
22. Animals from outside the agency are permitted to visit the premises through a prearranged agreement under rules for visiting pets.
23. Animals are to be groomed daily.
24. All staff (except for kitchen workers, for sanitary reasons) is encouraged to be involved in actively caring for the animals.
25. Clients are to be involved in caring for the animals.
26. Animals are to be part of weekly sessions with the clients.
27. Issues related to death and dying must be handled appropriately.
28. Animal abuse issues need to be handled therapeutically and on a case-by-case basis.

XII. PRINCIPLES THAT GUIDE ANIMAL-ASSISTED THERAPY PROGRAMS

If a worker is "lacking a rule," the worker will search his or her own memory for a principle. This practice principle tells the worker what to do. Rules are clear cut and, therefore, can be recalled more rapidly from memory. The principle that is more abstract requires a more time-consuming and complex mental undertaking to recover from memory (Lewis, 1982). Principles are expressions of goals and permit staff to have leeway regarding the means by which they are carried out.

In identifying principles for the AAT practitioner, we offer the following, which are used at Green Chimneys.

1. All animals will be carefully selected and subject to behavioral assessment to determine their aptitude for working with people.
2. At time of hire, staff will be surveyed to determine allergies, fears, or dislike of animals. Attitudes of workers will be measured to evaluate former relationships with animals.
3. As part of screening at the time of intake or admission, clients will be surveyed to determine allergies, fears, dislike, or past abusive behavior toward animals. Attitudes of clients will be measured to evaluate former relationships with animals.
4. The rights of individuals who do not wish to participate in the program will be considered first, and off-limits areas for animals will be maintained for this purpose.
5. Companion animals should not pose a threat or nuisance to the clients, staff, or visitors.
6. Workers should integrate the patient interactions with animals into their comprehensive treatment plan, with specific and relevant goals.

7. The worker will strive to assure the patient the opportunity to choose his or her own goals in work with the animals and assist him or her in identifying and achieving this end.
8. Sessions that involve animal-assisted therapy must be documented in the weekly progress notes.
9. The worker will document any and all interactions that may be novel behavior as a result of the human–animal bonding.
10. The worker will closely supervise and monitor any patient who has a past history of animal abuse.
11. The worker will closely supervise and monitor the temperament of all animals that are utilized with patients. Animals will be permitted to rest every hour and a half and not be permitted to work more than 5 hours per day.
12. The worker should process animal-assisted activities to assist the patient in exploring new or possibly previously unexplored issues.
13. The worker should encourage the patient to work with her or him in settings other than offices, e.g., conduct a session while taking the dog for a walk.
14. The worker should utilize the animals with the patient to explore areas that can be seen as "dress rehearsal for life," e.g., birth, death, and pregnancy.
15. The worker should utilize the animal-assisted interaction to aid the patient in mastering developmental tasks.
16. The worker should utilize the animal to promote feelings of self-worth in the patient whenever possible.
17. The worker should utilize the animal to promote responsibility and independence in the patient.
18. The worker should utilize the animal to teach the patient the need to sacrifice or undergo inconvenience for the sake of a loved one.
19. The worker should make every effort to utilize the animal to promote companionship, warmth, and love with the patient.
20. The worker should remember that utilizing an animal is not an "open sesame" or a panacea to working with or uncovering the "inner world" of the troubled patient.
21. The worker should work to maintain the "therapy" component in animal-assisted therapy.
22. The worker should utilize the animal to teach lessons in life, thereby promoting and nurturing appropriate emotional responses from clients.
23. The worker should help the individual who has made contact and developed interest in the animals share this experience with a peer as a means of establishing peer relationships.

24. AAT needs to be integrated into the larger therapeutic milieu and to fit with the other adjunctive therapies the child is receiving as per their individualized treatment plan.

XIII. CONCLUSIONS

Encouraging well-designed, carefully evaluated interventions is essential to responsible current and future AAT program development. A diverse array of helping professionals are often in search of ways to improve the quality of life of persons who have overwhelming obstacles to overcome. To those clients who could benefit from an animal companion, a health or mental health care professional may be able to facilitate a new or support a long-established relationship by being sensitive to what is occurring in the field and by knowing which resources are available (Netting *et al.*, 1988). Another challenge is for health and mental health organizations to look for meaningful ways to incorporate animals into our human service organizations in mutually beneficial partnerships.

While what has been offered here is not, as Levinson pointed out, a panacea for the world's ills, it is a beginning. Animals can fulfill an important role for many people, but organizations that wish to set in motion such interventions must be careful to also initiate rules and principles to guide this practice. There is an ever-growing body of knowledge, information, and research that can help prepare interested persons to initiate a human–animal interaction program. Courses, workshops, and seminars are being held all over this country and in the global community. Although the labor-intensive nature of integrating animals into a health or mental health system may at first make it seem a daunting task, the organizational benefits of such an intervention are numerous (Mallon, 1994a). The introduction of animals into a human service system will not produce additional competitiveness or alienation but can, instead, provide that calming, unqualified attention and love that are needed to help some clients flourish, moving away from illness and toward health. As health and mental health organizations struggle to find their niche in an ever-expanding network of diverse services, we must be alert to novel and creative approaches to helping our clients, including, in some cases where indicated, utilizing an array of diverse animals as adjuncts in the treatment of various populations.

REFERENCES

Anspach, R. R. (1991). Everyday methods for assessing organizational effectiveness. *Soc. Probl.* **38**(I), 1–19.

Arkow, P. (1992). "Pet Therapy: A Study of the Uses of Companion Animals." Human Society of the Pikes Peak Region, Colorado Springs, CO.
Beck, A. M., and Katcher, A. H. (1984). A new look a pet-facilitated therapy. *J. Am. Vet. Med. Assoc.* **184**(4), 414–420.
Bolman, L., and Terrance, D. (1991). "Reframing Organizations." Josey-Bass, San Francisco.
Brager. G., and Holloway, S. (1978). "Changing Human Service Organizations: Politics and Practice." Free Press, New York.
Brooks, S. (2001). Working with animals in a healing context. *Reaching Today's Youth*, 19–22.
Daniel, S., Burke, J., and Barke, J. (1984). Educational programs for pet-assisted therapy in institutional settings: An interdisciplinary approach. *Vet. Techn.* 5(2), 394–397.
Datton, J. E. (1992). The making of organizational opportunities: An interpretive pathway to organizational change. *Res. Organ. Behav.* **15**, 195–226.
Frost, P. J., and Egri, C. P. (1991). The political process of innovation. *Res. Organ. Behav.* **13**, 229–295.
Hanselman, J. L. (2001). Coping skills interventions with adolescents in anger management using animals in therapy. *J. Child Adolesc. Group Ther.* **11**(4), 159–195.
Ket de Vries, M. F. R., and Miller, D. (1984). "The Neurotic Organization." Harper Business, New York.
LaJoie, K. R. (2003). "An Evaluation of the Effectiveness of Using Animals in Therapy." Unpublished doctoral dissertation, Spalding University, Louisville, KY.
Levinson, B. (1962). The dog as co-therapist. *Ment. Hyg.* **46**, 59–65.
Levinson, B. (1968). Household pets in residential schools. *Ment. Hyg.* **52**, 411–414.
Levinson, B. (1969). "Pet-Oriented Child Psychotherapy." Charles C. Thomas, Springfield, IL.
Levinson, B. (1970). Nursing home pets: A psychological adventure for the clients. *Natl. Hum. Rev.* **58**, 15–16.
Levinson, B. (1971). Household pets in training schools serving delinquent children. *Psychol. Rep.* **28**, 475–481.
Levinson, B. (1972). "Pets and Human Development." Charles C. Thomas, Springfield, IL.
Levinson, B., and Mallon, G. P. (1996). "Pet-Oriented Child Psychotherapy," 2nd Ed. Charles C. Thomas, Springfield, IL.
Lewis, H. (1982). "The Intellectual Base of Social Work Practice." The Lois and Samuel Silberman Fund and Haworth Press, New York.
Mallon, G. P. (1992). Utilization of animals as therapeutic adjuncts with children and youth: A review of the literature. *Child Youth Care Forum* **21**(1), 53–65.
Mallon, G. P. (1994a). Some of our best therapists are dogs. *Child Youth Care Forum* **23**(2), 89–101.
Mallon, G. P. (1994b). Cow as co-therapist: Utilization of farm animals as therapeutic aids with children in residential treatment. *Child Adolesc. Social Work J.* **11**(6), 455–474.
Mallon, G. P. (1994c). A generous spirit: The work and life of Boris Levinson. *Anthrozoos* 7(4), 224–231.
Mallon, G. P. (1999). Animal-assisted therapy interventions with children. *In* "Innovative Psychotherapy Techniques for Children and Adolescents" (C. E. Shaefer, ed.), pp. 415–434. Wiley, New York.
Morgan, G. (1986). "Images of Organization." Sage, Newbury Park, CA.
Moss-Kanter, R. (1982). Dilemmas of managing participation. *Org. Dyn.* **3**, 5–27.
Moss-Kanter, R. (1988). When a thousand flowers bloom: Structural, collective and social conditions for innovation in organization. *Res. Organ. Behav.* **10**, 169–211.
Netting, F. E., Wilson, C., and New, J. C. (1988). The human-animal bond: Implications for practice. *Social Work* **39**(1), 60–64.
Ross, S. B. (ed.) (1993). People and animals: Many benefits—some concerns. *N. Y. State Outdoor Educ. Assoc.* **23**(2), 2–13.

Ross, S. B. (1999). Green Chimneys: We give troubled children the gift of giving. *In* "Child Abuse, Domestic Violence, and Animal Abuse: Linking the Circles of Compassion for Prevention and Intervention" (F. R. Ascione and P. Arkow, eds.), pp. 367–379. Purdue University Press, IN.

Senter, S. (ed.) (1993). "People and Animals: A Therapeutic Animal-Assisted Activities Manual for Schools, Agencies and Recreational Centers." Green Chimneys Press, Brewster, NY.

Serpell, J., Coppinger, R., and Fine, A. H. (2000). The welfare of assistance and therapy animals: An ethical comment. *In* "Handbook on Animal-Assisted Therapy: Theoretical Foundations and Guidelines for Practice" (A. H. Fine, ed.), pp. 415–431. Academic Press, New York.

SECTION III

Best Practices in Animal-Assisted Therapy

GUIDELINES FOR USE OF ANIMAL-ASSISTED THERAPY WITH SPECIAL POPULATIONS

CHAPTER 9

Incorporating Animal-Assisted Therapy into Psychotherapy: Guidelines and Suggestions for Therapists

AUBREY H. FINE

College of Education and Integrative Studies, California State Polytechnic University, Pomona, California 91768

I. INTRODUCTION

Aaron came to his social skills group early each week so he could get Sasha's undivided attention. "Dr. Fine, can I bring in the cage and hold Sasha for a while? She is so cute," bellows Aaron as I enter the building. "Sure, why not," I reply. What he doesn't realize is that my eyes never leave him as he carries in my small gerbil, sits down in the classroom, and lets her out of the cage. Here is a 10-year-old child diagnosed with ADHD, sitting and giggling and smiling as Sasha crawls over his legs. So as not to frighten her, he sits calmly—something that is hard for him to do. He eventually begins to stroke her and tells her how beautiful she is. "You are a sweetheart, Sasha. I love you," he whispers, with a proud smile.

At these times, Aaron acts like a different child. Around Sasha he slows down, and she has a calming effect on him. Her nature transforms him. Perhaps it is her size. He does not want to overpower her, so he moves slowly and talks gently. She reciprocates by snuggling and allowing his tender touch. Over the course of the program, I often bring Sasha to Aaron so that he can learn to gauge his own activity level and perhaps be in more control. It is amazing to watch him transform. She immediately helps him regroup, and once he gets to hold her, his activity level is more in harmony with the others. "Holding Sasha is what he needs to have a calmer and more engaged session" (Fine and Eisen, in press).

This case study occurred over 30 years ago. Sasha eventually became my first therapy animal. Those preliminary observations helped develop my early understanding of the value of animal-assisted interventions (AAI). In particular, I began to appreciate how the integration of an animal into therapy promoted a more nurturing and safer environment for clients.

As has been articulated throughout this book, the value of the human–animal bond has been seriously investigated over many decades. Furthermore, popular culture reflects the bond between humans and animals as is seen in the popular press and the film industry. Most recently, various films in our pop culture have portrayed the importance of the human–animal bond as well as the impact of the bond. There has also been a proliferation of books focusing on the importance of wildlife to humans as recognition of the positive impact that animals have on the lives of people (Canfield *et al.*, 1998, 2005; Chernak-McElroy, 1996; Von Kreisler, 1997). It seems a logical next step that mental health professionals try and incorporate the human–animal bond connections, when applicable, into their practices where applicable. As Bern Williams once stated, "There is no psychiatrist in the world like a puppy licking your face."

II. THE NEED FOR RESEARCH

Despite positive anecdotal examples, the reader needs to recognize that there is limited empirical support and research validating the overall effectiveness of animal-assisted therapy (AAT) (Fine, 2002, 2003; McCulloch, 1984; Serpell, 1983). Voelker (1995) noted that the biggest challenge facing advocates of AAT can be summed up in two words: "prove it" (p. 1898). Voelker (1995) stressed that the major difficulties in obtaining outcome data in animal-assisted therapy is that many of the professionals applying these strategies do not see the necessity of conducting outcome research, or possibly, they do not take the time to validate outcomes. This lack of documentation and thorough investigation leaves a large void in demonstrating the efficacy of this approach. It seems that most clinicians persevere and incorporate the modality primarily on qualitative impressions that have been observed or heard about. However, a lack of empirical evidence may continue plaguing the acceptance of AAI, especially as many become more concerned about evidence-based forms of psychotherapy.

Barak *et al.* (2001) noted that research is also needed to identify the underlying mechanisms of AAT that produce therapeutic changes. The findings from these studies would be valuable to understand how the interventions work so that the best practice procedures can be implemented. Unfortunately, many outsiders have a limited awareness of how AAI are applied and there is a need to demystify the process. In addition, there also needs to be a more appropriate bridge between clinical practice and best practice research. Practitioners are encouraged to pay closer attention to the need for program evaluation and documentation. All of these efforts should assist the scientific community with the needed research priorities.

Many have pointed out that although the utilization of animals may be highly appealing, it needs to be understood that just because an interaction with an animal is enjoyable, it does not imply that the procedure is therapeutic (Katcher, 2000; Serpell, 1993).

Fine, in an interview with Kale (1992), pointed out that animals could have a therapeutic impact on children when the approach was integrated with other strategies. "To say that the therapeutic changes occur solely in isolation would perhaps be quite misleading." Fine (2005) explained that it is important to understand how animal-assisted interventions can be integrated alongside traditional psychotherapeutic approaches. Attention in future research must address this concern.

Therefore, it is strongly emphasized that over the next decade a concentrated effort be initiated to demonstrate the efficacy of this modality. The findings from quality designed studies will help clinicians as well as researchers answer a variety of questions, including (1) under what conditions are AAI most beneficial, (2) with what special groups do AAI appear to work the best, and (3) under which theoretical orientation (e.g., humanistic, cognitive, behavioral) does the incorporation of animals seem the most therapeutically effective?

III. OBJECTIVE OF CHAPTER

The objective for this chapter is to provide the reader with practical insight on how animals may be incorporated into a therapeutic practice. Within this context, the author also provides suggested guidelines to assure quality control for the client's and animal's safety. Case studies are incorporated to illustrate how the interventions can be applied logically.

IV. ROLE OF ANIMAL-ASSISTED THERAPY (AAT) IN PSYCHOTHERAPY: IS THERE SUCH A THING AS AN AAT Rx?

As discussed previously, one of my greatest reservations in recommending AAT has been the lack of published protocols. There is a definite lack of clarity of how a treatment regime can be replicated. Unfortunately, this lack of clarity makes it difficult to develop a clear-cut Rx for AAT. One should not look at AAT in isolation but rather observe how the animals support and augment the clinician's ability to work within his/her theoretical orientation (Fine, 2005). Fine (2005) has suggested that there are several basic tenets to consider when one incorporates animals into therapeutic practice. Therapists should consider utilizing a simple problem-solving template as they plan on applying AAT interventions with their various patients. The following three questions should be considered.

1. What benefits can AAT/animal-assisted intervention provide this client? The clinician needs to consider the benefits animals will have in the therapy. What benefits will the animals provide in the clinical intervention? Should therapists only expect the animals to act as social lubricants to promote a safer environment or can the animal's involvement be integrated more deeply within the clinical efforts?
2. How can AAT strategies be incorporated within the planned intervention? A clinician must begin to conceptualize the vast array of opportunities that the therapy animals can provide. Several of these alternatives are discussed later. A plan must be formulated so the outcome will not be purely serendipitous.
3. How will the therapist need to adapt his/her clinical approach to incorporate AAT? This perhaps is the most critical aspect to consider. A clinician must take into account how incorporating animals into therapy may alter his/her clinical orientation. Therapists must also mull over (even if they are an animal lover) whether they are comfortable practicing psychotherapy cojointly with their animals. If the animal's presence does not match the style of therapy practiced, it may cause more dissidence and become ineffective.

To assist the reader in better understanding how to apply AAT in traditional clinical practices, the following section briefly describes basic foundation strategies that should be considered.

V. CONSIDERATION 1: WHY CLINICIANS MAY FIND ANIMALS THERAPEUTICALLY BENEFICIAL

A. Animals as a Social Lubricant for Therapy

Early research investigating the incorporation of animals within outpatient psychotherapy was somewhat limited. Nevertheless, Rice *et al.* (1973) conducted a study to evaluate the extent to which animals were used by psychotherapists in the United States as a whole. Their study also attempted to classify the ways in which animals served in psychotherapeutic roles. One hundred and ninety members (64% of the sample) of APA division 29 (division of psychotherapy) responded to the survey. The findings of the study suggested that 40 clinicians (21%) indicated that they used animals or animal content in conjunction with their psychotherapy.

The most powerful finding from this study pertained to the specific uses of the animal within the therapeutic setting. The researchers reported that some therapists found some utility in actually having animals present in therapy, whereas others utilized animals in a conceptual manner. Common commentaries about the utilization of real animals pertained to employing an animal as a vehicle for cultivating or modeling the positive nature of interpersonal relationships. Most of the responders pointed out that animals were used to ease the stress of the initial phases of therapy to establish rapport. The researchers also reported isolated uses of animals, such as suggesting that a patient obtain a pet as a means of introducing practical caretaking responsibilities. The conceptual use of animals by most reporting clinicians was most frequently symbolic. Therapists often incorporate animal content to formulate interpretations of patient's fantasies or underlying themes in their discussions.

Mallon (1992) pointed out that the animals should not be considered as substitutes for human relationships but as a complement to them. It has been noted that animals appear to decrease the initial reservations that may develop from entering therapy. Arkow (1982) suggested that the animal may act as a link in the conversation between the therapist and the client. He called this process a "rippling effect." Others such as Corson and Corson (1980) described this process as a social lubricant. It appears that the presence of the animal allows the client a sense of comfort, which then promotes rapport in the therapeutic relationship.

Case Study

Fine and Eisen (in press) described how a gentle golden retriever aided a young girl with selective mutism in feeling more comfortable in therapy.

> For years, Diane's parents had told themselves their daughter was shy. However, after her first week at kindergarten, the teacher called the parents into school for a conference, where they were told that Diane needed professional help. In school she was not only unwilling to speak, but she cowered with fright when approached or spoken to and shrank from being touched. Diane's parents, concerned and upset by this evaluation, tried to work with Diane to overcome her selective mutism and fear when away from her home. However, nothing they said or did made any impression on Diane. She refused to talk and, at times, seemed incapable of speech, as though she physically either could not hear or speak.

My challenge, then, was to break through Diane's fear of strangers and the world beyond her home. The catch, however, was that I would be a stranger in a strange and new place. I first met Diane and her parents on a Friday afternoon, about 2:00 p.m.

They were all seated in the waiting room when Puppy and I walked out to greet them. Diane sat with her head down, her eyes directed to a spot on the floor directly in front of her. She made no move to look up or acknowledge our entrance. Puppy, walking ahead of me, made a beeline for Diane. Because Diane's head was bowed, Puppy was just 3 feet away when the girl finally caught sight of her. Startled by the unexpected sight of a large golden retriever, Diane's eyes grew huge and then her mouth curved into a smile. Puppy stopped directly in front of Diane and laid her head in the girl's lap. I introduced Puppy and myself, but Diane did not respond. She gave no indication that she had even heard me. Instead, she began to pet Puppy's head, running her hands over Puppy's ears, nose, and muzzle. She never changed her body posture, but she was smiling and enjoying her interaction with Puppy. This went on for several minutes as I spoke with Diane's parents. Then an idea hit me.

I turned toward the girl and the dog and spoke Puppy's name quietly. When Puppy looked up at me, I gave her a hand signal to come toward me and then to continue back into the inner office. Puppy started walking toward me, but I could tell she was still aware of what was happening behind her in the waiting room because she glanced back at Diane. As Puppy walked away, I watched Diane's face fall and her eyes take on a sad and disappointed look. I said, "Oh, I'm sorry. I didn't realize you wanted Puppy to stay with you. All you have to do for her to come back is to say, 'Puppy, come.' "

Diane's parents stared at me, a look of skepticism on their faces. For a few tense seconds Diane debated what to do, her lower lip quivering. Then, in a low voice, she called, "Puppy, come, please come, Puppy." The parents gazed at their daughter, and their jaws dropped in surprise. I gave Puppy the signal to go, and she ran over to Diane, who slid off of her chair and hugged Puppy tightly. We watched, her parents in tears, as Diane and Puppy snuggled together.

I knew that I had to seize the moment so I sent Diane's parents back into the office to wait for me. Sitting on the floor beside Puppy and Diane, I began to talk to her. I told her that I knew how hard it was for her to talk to people she didn't know and how happy we were that she had been brave enough to call for Puppy. Hoping to build on this small first step, I asked her what she liked about Puppy. She hesitated a moment and then answered, "She is so soft and cuddly." As we talked, Puppy sat leaning against Diane with the little girl's fingers laced through Puppy's fur.

When it was time for the session to end, I asked Diane to say goodbye to Puppy. She hugged the dog again and said, "Good-bye." Her voice was soft, but it was clear. Puppy reciprocated with a head nudging and a huge lick on her arm. She had made a remarkable breakthrough and could now begin her journey toward interaction with the world outside her home. I stroked Puppy's head, knowing that without her, the session could have gone quite differently.

Over the course of the next 5 months, Diane, Puppy, and I developed a wonderful relationship. Our simple first session eventually changed the lives of Diane and me forever. For Diane, her whole world opened up and she eventually developed the confidence to talk and interact with others, and in turn, her new confidence rippled throughout the family—they all could now grow and blossom. For myself, I learned to appreciate that a four-legged animal could be a cotherapist. Puppy was able to unlock Diane's silence in a manner that was impossible for me. She was able to nuzzle her and nonverbally reassure her that things were ok.

Kruger *et al.* (2004) and Beck *et al.* (1986) suggested that a therapist who conducts therapy with an animal present may appear less threatening, and consequently, the client may be more willing to reveal him/herself. A gentle animal helps a client view the therapist in a more endearing manner. This perception was also found by Peacock (1986), who reported that in interviews in the presence of her dog, children appeared more relaxed and seemed more cooperative during their visit. She concluded that the dog served to reduce the initial tension and assisted in developing an atmosphere of warmth. Numerous studies have elicited similar findings. Vrombrock and Grosser (1988) suggested that animals appear to have a calming effect on humans and to reduce arousal. In their study, data linked tactile contact with a dog with experimentally induced low blood pressures.

B. Benefits of Animals as an Extension to a Therapist: A Method for Rapport Building

Animals are known for the zealous greetings they provide to visiting clients they encounter. In a seminal article on the use of pets (in the treatment of children with behavior disorders), Levinson (1965) implied that bringing in the animal at the beginning of therapy assisted frequently in helping a reserved client overcome his/her anxiety about therapy. Many therapy dogs are more than willing to receive a client in a warm and affectionate manner.

For example, in most cases, animals can become an extension of the therapist. The animals that work with me are very responsive to greeting visitors. Children look forward to seeing PJ and Magic (golden retrievers), Hart (a black Labrador), Shrimp (mixed breed), Tikvah (a bare-eyed cockatoo), or Snowflake (an umbrella cockatoo). The dogs eagerly walk over to the children, encouraging attention. These initial encounters ease the tension at the beginning of every meeting. The animals are instrumental in regulating the emotional climate.

Levinson (1964), a pioneer of utilizing animals in therapeutic relationships, suggested that the animals may represent a catalyst in helping a child make more progress in a clinician's setting. It seems evident that the animals' presence may make the initial resistance easier to overcome.

Case Study

Several years ago, a 15-year-old boy who was diagnosed as being depressed was referred to my office. When he entered the waiting room he became very intrigued with the fish tanks. It seemed that over the years he had developed a strong interest in tropical fish. This common interest appeared to enhance our therapeutic rapport quickly. Over the next 6 months, our common interest went beyond talking about and observing the fish to a higher level of involvement. After careful consideration and planning, we both believed that putting together a 60-gallon salt water tank would be therapeutically beneficial for him. Indirectly and directly, his involvement and efforts in helping select the fish, plants, scenery, and rocks not only enhanced our bond but definitely appeared to reverse his sense of demoralization. Jeff had something to look forward to. His drive to fight off his lethargy and helpless thoughts seemed to be impacted by the sight of a new environment that he helped design and build. He would stop at the office frequently to check on the fish, taking pride in his accomplishments. Although Jeff continued to battle with his depression, he continued to find refuge and support in the tank he established. The partnership we established in developing the tank was a definite asset to our working relationship.

C. A Therapeutic Benefit of Animals in Therapy: A Catalyst for Emotion

Fine and Beiler (in press) pointed out that for many clients, the mere presence of an animal in a therapeutic setting can stir emotions. Simply interacting with an animal in a therapeutic setting can lighten the mood and lead to smiling and laughter. Animals may also display emotions or actions that may not be professionally appropriate for therapists to display. For example, the animal might climb into a client's lap or sit calmly while the client pets him. Holding or petting an animal may sooth clients and help them feel calm when exploring difficult emotions in treatment that might be overwhelming without this valuable therapeutic touch. For example, Fine and Eisen (in press) discussed the outcome of a meeting that was held at a colleague's clinic. A meeting was called to review the progress of a client who was severely struggling and to plan for his future treatment. The boy had been abused and traumatized in his early life and was removed from his biological family. He was eventually adopted, but the family members had become overwhelmed with their son's misbehaviors. Over the years, with only minimal gains, both the parents and the staff were becoming discouraged.

At this meeting, over 10 professionals (mental health, medical, and educational) gathered to discuss their perceptions. The boy was not present at the meeting, but his adoptive father was there. Also at the meeting was Teddy, the resident therapy dog, asleep on the floor.

For over an hour the father sat silently, overwhelmed with all the information and opinions he was hearing. Adding to his stress, the father was recovering from a stroke and was feeling fatigue. Unfortunately for him, the others in the room were oblivious to his condition, confusion, and fears as they continued with the discussion and commentary. It was only Teddy who was conscious of the father's uneasiness. She got up from her corner, sat next to him, and began licking his hand and tenderly tried to comfort him. She looked up and gazed at the rest of the people in the room. Some of the staff members in the room were embarrassed at Teddy's actions. At the father's insistence, though, Teddy was allowed to stay by his side for the rest of the meeting. He needed her reassurance and support. He noted that the meeting was quite stressful and having Teddy by his side made it easier for him to digest the information given. The presence of a Teddy or any trusted animal in therapy may also lend comfort and stability to the environment when a therapist must confront a client.

Animals within therapeutic settings can also elicit a range of emotions from laughter to sorrow. Often in the literature on animal-assisted therapy more attention has been given to the softer emotions which the human–animal bond instills. Nevertheless, recognition that animals can exhibit humorous behaviors is relevant. In his premier writing of *Head First: The Biology of Hope*, Cousins (1988) emphasized for decades that humor was beneficial in improving not only an individual's mental state but also his/her physical constraints. Laughter and joy are two ingredients that impact a person's quality of life positively. It seems apparent that not only do animals promote warmth within a relationship, but they may bring joy and a smile.

There are numerous examples that can be applied to illustrate this phenomenon. For example, a playful cockatoo or a puppy getting itself into mischief can always garner a smile. There have been numerous occasions where the animals incorporated therapeutically get themselves in comical/playful situations. It seems that when this occurs, the laughter generated has therapeutic value.

Selectively, animals are in a unique situation to display emotions and behaviors that may not be deemed professionally appropriate for a human service provider. For example, in difficult periods within therapy, a client may be in need of comforting and reassurance. The presence of an animal may become that catharsis. The holding of an animal or the petting of an animal (be it a cat, a dog, or a bunny) may act as a physical comforter and soothe many patients. The touching of the animal and the proximity to the animal may also represent an external degree of safety for many clients.

Moreover, an additional benefit of the animals may be their contribution in helping clients gauge excessive emotion and reactive behavior. On numerous occasions, I have witnessed that when a dispute would take place, the animal's presence seemed to lend some comfort and stability to the environment. The adults seemed to regulate their reactiveness, possibly because they were aware of the animal's presence. Furthermore, in working with children who were quite active and impulsive, it was amazing to observe how large birds (cockatoos and macaws) seemed to help promote decorum for what is or is not considered acceptable behavior. It seemed that most children gave tremendous respect to the birds' presence (possibly some unconscious intimidation), and the reduction in their disruptiveness was evident. Most children seemed to realize that their escalated behaviors would cause uneasiness in the birds, which they did not want to cause. In addition to this one benefit, as a follow-up to a child's outbursts and the birds' ability to help reduce the tension, discussions on self-control and behavioral regulation were introduced.

D. Animals Acting as Adjuncts to Clinicians

Mallon (1992) emphasized that animals must be considered as adjuncts in the establishment of a therapeutic relationship and bond. Hoelscher and Garat (1993) suggested that when relating to a therapist with an animal, people with difficulties sometimes find the animals the catalyst for discussion, which previously may have been blocked. For example, several years ago, an 8-year-old girl visited the office. She was very intrigued with the birds she saw and wanted to hold a few of the small lovebirds. Without asking if she could hold the bird, she eagerly put her hand toward the animal. To her dissatisfaction, the bird hissed at her. Shortly after this experience, I explained to the girl that she needed to ask the bird's permission (and mine) to touch the animal. Ironically, this was followed by the powerless response of "I know what you mean." Her response to my statement piqued my attention, since she was referred for depressive symptoms. I picked up the lovebird and began to scratch her head. I told the girl that the bird was very sensitive to touch, and there were certain spots that she didn't like to be touched. At this point, the girl became very teary eyed and responded by saying once again (very sadly this time), "I know what you mean." Shortly after, she began to reveal a history of sexual abuses by one of her grandparents. It was apparent the serendipitous use of the bird acted as a catalyst to promote a discussion on feelings that she had buried. Over the course of her treatment, we used the example of the bird to help her gain insight on the importance of giving people permission to embrace you and how you have the right to tell people that your body is private.

E. Use of the Relationship with Animals Vicariously: Role Modeling

A valued benefit of incorporating animals clinically is the vicarious outcomes that a client may develop as a consequence of the interaction between the clinician and the animals. For example, the loving relationship between the animal and the therapist may explain by example to the client some of the caring traits of the clinician. This outcome may enhance the development of the therapeutic relationship and alliance. Personally, over the years, I have been amazed with the comments I have received from clients observing my interaction with the animals. The most common response pertains to the interaction with the animals and how some clients compare these interactions with their own child/parent relationships (as most of my clients are children and their parents). Other clients comment on how well the animals are treated, including the elements of compassion, consistency, firmness, and love. These scenarios can be used to demonstrate to the client appropriate interactions and responses to behaviors.

Experienced clinicians will attest to the numerous occasions (during sessions) that boundaries need to be placed on the animals. This demonstration of limit setting should be a valuable teaching tool for the clients. The therapist can use these episodes as opportunities to model specific discipline or problem-solving strategies. For example, within my office, one of the many therapy birds that I use is an umbrella cockatoo. She periodically has a tremendous need for attention, and one approach that she uses is to screech. Parents are always amazed with my approach and the explanation that I give to them. The most common approach applied is extinction and the eventual reinforcement of the appropriate behavior when it is demonstrated (verbal praise and petting the bird). The outcome of this interaction eventually leads to an informal discussion on behavior management, which may have implications for their own child-rearing practices.

As can be seen, there are numerous episodes that a clinician could draw upon. It is of utmost importance that the therapist takes advantage of teachable moments and learning opportunities. Discussions with adults on boundary setting, the need to be loved and admired, and appropriate ways of interacting are all relevant.

VI. CONSIDERATION 2: THE THERAPEUTIC ENVIRONMENT—ANIMALS AS AN ASPECT OF MILIEU THERAPY

Modifications to the work environment may also be considered a valuable contribution that animals can influence. The perceived environment appears to be more friendly and comfortable to incoming clients. Barnard (1954) pointed out that it was Ernst Simmel's pioneer work that gave serious thought to the manipulation of the environment to meet the unconscious needs of clients. In her paper, Barnard (1954) reported that in ancient times even pagan temples (which promoted healing) provided an atmosphere of encouragement and hope. She noted that in an ancient institution in Cairo, patients were entertained daily with musical concerts as one source of their therapy. The underlying force within milieu therapy is recognizing the "climate" within the environment and its impact on the client. Sklar (1988) pointed out that there is constant interaction between the client and the therapist that is impacted by the physical and emotional environment created in the clinician's office. Sklar's writings, as well as Langs' (1979), suggest that the development of an effective therapeutic alliance may actually begin with the creation of a proper therapeutic environment. Sklar (1988) reported on how many outpatient clinics neglect giving attention to the physical environment in which the therapeutic process unfolds. Goldensohn and Hahn (1979) reported that clients' readiness for psychotherapy could be disturbed by the simplicity of a clinic's decor and perhaps by its disorder.

Sklar (1988) also reported that many facilities that provide mental health services appear to be proud of the happy, affectionate family atmosphere that the clinic attempts to create. He suggested that one must not only focus on the client's internal dynamics for treatment to become successful, but in addition the therapists also must address the clinical space within which treatment is ongoing.

As the research suggests, little attention appears to be given by most therapists to the elements which enhance their therapeutic environment. Light music, lighting, and climate control have always been intuitively associated with a more comfortable environment. These ingredients seem to promote a sense of security and comfort. It seems obvious that living beings could also be utilized to complement the work environment by making it more appealing and relaxing. Of utmost value is that animals appear to bring a certain sense of security and warmth into the environment. For example, in their study on anxiety and discomfort before and during dental surgery, Katcher and colleagues (1983) reported that subjects viewing an aquarium appeared more comfortable and less anxious than those subjects in a control group not viewing an aquarium. Watching a school of fish swim harmoniously can be quite relaxing for some. With proper lighting and an attractively designed tank, clients could feel more at ease when they enter an office or while undergoing a therapy session. Over the years, I have found fish tanks to be extremely enticing. The gentleness of the fish and the ambiance developed can be truly beneficial to a therapy session.

Unfortunately, when schools in a fish tank are not selected properly, the outcome can make people feel uncomfortable, especially if the fish incorporated are aggressive and hyperactive. For example, early in my own personal utilization of fish tanks for the ambiance they promote, my selection of fish was not appropriate. Two fish in the school were quite active and aggressive. They would often be observed fighting and chasing each other. Rather than finding the fish tank to be relaxing and comforting, many of the clients noted that they felt uneasy watching the fish. One adult was overheard saying that the activity level of the fish reminded her of the chaos that she witnesses within her own home, especially with her children. Although this event serendipitously led to a discussion about her concerns with her children, it did not put her at ease.

With the importance of a therapeutic environment now established, it is notable to appreciate how animals can be viewed within this dimension. Beck (1983) suggested that animals have the capacity to modify a person's environment. Friedman *et al.* (1983) demonstrated that people appear to exhibit lower blood pressure and verbally express feelings of relaxation in the presence of a dog, whereas Katcher and Beck (1983) have been able to correlate a similar phenomenon in the presence of viewing a tank of fish. Lockwood (1983) hypothesized that this outcome may occur because people perceive most situations with animals as safer and perhaps more benign.

Very few studies have been implemented investigating the impact that animals have in altering the therapeutic effects of an environment. Beck *et al.* (1983) initiated a study in Haverford, Pennsylvania, where the initial hypothesis speculated that animals would alter the therapeutic environment and make it less threatening to patients with various mental illnesses. These patients (who met in a room containing birds) attended sessions more faithfully and became more active participants in comparison to a control group. These researchers reported that the experimental group (who conducted their therapy in the presence of the birds) had a greater rate of attendance and demonstrated more frequent participation than the nonbird group. In addition, their findings from the Brief Psychiatric Rating Scale identified a reduction in hostility scores in clients within the experimental milieu. The researchers believed that this outcome was enhanced due to the impression the clients had about the birds (the animals were perceived by the patients as less hostile, and therefore, the clients felt more at ease in the presence of the animals).

Not only can animals be used to enhance the milieu, as well as enhance the relationship between the client and the therapist, but the therapist can also observe how the client relates and interacts with the animal. The client may unconsciously be overbearing and controlling to the animal or, for that matter, may act coldly and unresponsively. These experiences may provide the therapist with an alternate diagnostic window to view his/her client.

VII. CONSIDERATION 3: INCORPORATING THEORY INTO PRACTICE—AAT FROM A LIFE STAGE PERSPECTIVE

A clinician's theoretical orientation will have a strong bearing on the incorporation of animals within his/her therapeutic approach. An explanation that seems to naturally align itself is Erikson's theoretical orientation. Erikson views development as a passage through a series of psychosocial stages, each with its particular goals, concerns, and needs. Although the themes may repeat during a life cycle, Erikson noted that certain life concerns were more relevant during specific stages of life. For example, as people age and experience new situations, they confront a series of psychosocial challenges. I recommend that clinicians should consider the various eight stages of psychosocial development and reflect on how the application of animals may be appropriate. To articulate the various stages, I have incorporated Table I to illustrate the major elements found within each stage, which is followed by an interpretation of how Erikson's theory can be applied to animal-assisted therapy.

A. Suggested Developmental Goals and Treatment Purposes for Children

Within the first series of life stages, the primary goals that need to be achieved pertain to a child's need to feel loved, as well as to develop a sense of industry and competence. In a practical sense, animals can assist the clinician in promoting unconditional acceptance. Bowers and MacDonald (2001) pointed out that children over the age of 5 turn to their beloved companion animals when they feel stressed and are in need of unconditional love. This may hold true in a therapy environment. The animal's presence in therapy (as discussed previously) may assist a child in learning to trust. Furthermore, the animal may also help the clinician demonstrate to the child that he is worth loving. Unfortunately for some children, their reservoirs of life successes are limited and they feel incompetent. This sense of incompetence may be acted out aggressively toward others or internally against oneself. A therapist may utilize an animal to help a child see value in his life. Gonski (1985) further suggested that the presence of a therapy animal "enables the child to initially begin to trust in a safer, nonjudgmental object prior to placing their confidence in the worker or other significant adult" (p. 98).

TABLE I Erik Erikson's Eight Stages of Development

Stage 1: Basic trust vs basic mistrust (first year)
  Virtue—hope
  Estrangement, separation, and abandonment
Stage 2: Autonomy vs shame and doubt (second year)
  Virtue—will
Stage 3: Initiative vs guilt (3–5 years old)
  Virtue—purpose
Stage 4: Industry vs inferiority (sixth year to puberty)
  Virtue—competence (workmanship)
Stage 5: Identity vs identity confusion (adolescence)
  Virtue—fidelity
Stage 6: Intimacy vs isolation (young adulthood)
  Virtue—love
  Elitism
Stage 7: Generativity vs stagnation (middle adulthood)
  Virtue—care
  Generational (parental responsibilities toward the youth)
Stage 8: Integrity vs despair (older adulthood)
  Virtue—wisdom—integration of life experiences
  Ritual—integration
  Perverted ritual—sapientism (pretense of being wise)

Animal-assisted therapy can eventually go beyond the office visits. A clinician may suggest to a family the value of having a pet within the home. The animal may help a child in developing a sense of responsibility as well as importance in life. Triebenbacher (1998) pointed out that children perceive their pets as special friends and important family members. In her study, she pointed out that 98% of the participants viewed their pets as important family members. She also noted that children may use their pets as transitional objects. Results from the study support the position that pets may offer children emotional support and a strong source of unconditional love. The following case study discusses how a therapist could recommend an animal as a pet for a child in need.

The case study of Scott comes to mind when considering this position. Scott was 12 years old when I first met him. He could be described as functioning in the borderline range of intelligence as well as demonstrating a severe learning disability. Perhaps Scott's greatest barrier to successful integration was his inability to relate with peers. Scott lacked social savoir faire. He was constantly bullied by others and was the brunt of their vicious jokes. He was friendless. I worked with Scott over a 2-year period. Our visits were interrupted for a short while because he moved away. It was when he was 15 that he returned to my practice, still demonstrating many of the same undeveloped social behaviors.

Throughout our visits, our major treatment goal was to help Scott develop social insight. Unfortunately, he had difficulty generalizing the skills and continued to suffer. Over the course of the treatment, Scott became very intrigued with the birds that I had in my practice. He seemed attentive to their behaviors, especially their speech. Since all the birds were hand raised, they were receptive to Scott picking them up and stroking their heads gently. Eventually, Scott asked if he could take one of the birds home for a few weeks. The bird was great company for Scott. They were inseparable. Scott accepted his role graciously and took great care of the bird. After a month, Scott wanted his own pet. Through the assistance of a bird breeder, I was able to secure a bird for Scott. Over the next year, Scott started to come out of his shell. He joined an aviary club and also began breeding birds on his own. Although he still did not possess effective social skills, the birds allowed Scott to get out on his own. Through the birds, Scott was able to have some substance to talk about. He also had purpose in his life. The birds became Scott's counterparts. They gave him attention and made him feel worthwhile. As noted earlier, the primary goal of Erikson's stage for childhood is developing a sense of industry rather than a sense of inferiority. The birds in Scott's life helped him feel more competent and capable. Utilizing Erikson's terminology, the birds seemed to impact his sense of industry.

Therapists may use the experience of the interaction between the child and the therapy animal as an opportunity to observe and assess if a child may benefit psychologically from having a pet within the home. Levinson (1965) reported that a pet within the home may be an excellent extension to therapy. The pet could provide the child with constant solace and unconditional joy and warmth.

Bryant (1990) reported on how animal companions have been cited as providing important social support for children. He reported that animals within a home may assist children in developing a greater sense of empathy for others. Further studies, such as Poretsky and Hendrix (1990) and Covert *et al.* (1985), have documented similar outcomes. These researchers suggest that pet ownership may be extremely valuable in enhancing a child's self-esteem and social skills, as well as a sense of empathy. Although Paul and Serpell (1996) are in agreement with these findings qualitatively, they indicated that most of the research conducted has not demonstrated any firm causal relationship between childhood pet ownership and alterations in the psychological well-being of children. It is interesting to note that many researchers seem to agree that there appears to be qualitative support for the value of the animal–human bond but that there are difficulties in quantifying this value. Perhaps some of the challenges that researchers are being confronted with pertain not only to quality research protocols presently under investigation but also a possible measurement problem.

However, there have been some studies such as Bryant (1990) that do demonstrate some promise in promoting the therapeutic benefit of pets for children. In her study, Bryant (1990) studied the potential social–emotional benefits and liabilities of children having pets. Although the study and its implications were based on children, it is important for clinicians to consider some of the findings as being pertinent for adolescents and adults. Two hundred and thirteen children were surveyed as part of the sample under investigation. The outcome of the study identified four potential psychological benefits for children having animals. Furman's (1989) "my pet" inventory was utilized to assess the subjects' interests. A factor analysis of Furman's inventory indicated that from a child's perspective, there are four factors in which the child–pet relationship can be viewed as potentially beneficial. The factor of mutuality was defined by Bryant (1990) as having to do with the experience of both giving and receiving care and support for the animal.

Furman (1989) originally identified these variables as companionship and nurturance. The enduring affection factor identifies the child's perception of the lasting quality of their relationship with their pet. This factor focuses on the child's perception of the permanence of the emotional bond between the child and the animal. The third factor, which was entitled "enhanced affection," identifies the perception of the child that the child–pet relationship makes him/her feel good, as well as important. This factor is a crucial element that clusters the admiration and affection between the animal and the child. Finally, the factor of exclusivity focuses on the child's internal confidence in the pet as a confidant. This factor appears to be extremely crucial for therapists to underscore.

It is within this factor that a child may rely on the pet companion to share private feelings and secrets. This may be an important outlet, especially when there are limited friends and supports within the community or the home. Mallon (1994) also pointed out that evidence shows that a child may use an animal as a confidant. In his study on the effects of a dog in a therapeutic setting treating children with behavior disorders, the staff observed that the children would often utilize the dog as a sounding board or a safe haven to discuss their problems and troubles.

Bryant (1990) suggested that the viewing of the child–pet relationship may be extremely valuable in understanding the dynamics within the family. Negative relationships may also be indicative of existing or impending crises within the family. However, within the study, Bryant (1990) also pointed out some of the limitations to the child–pet relationship. Some of the constraints included distress associated with taking care of the pet, the unfair grief of a pet acting mean, or the rejection of the child by the pet. These data are in agreement with other researchers such as Kidd and Kidd (1980, 1985), who pointed out that the choice of the animal for the child has to be a proper match. Different breeds of animals (dogs, cats, and birds) may offer unsuitable physical and psychosocial benefits to their owners. Unfortunately, if the wrong animal or breed is selected as a pet for the child, there may not be an effective bond, which was described earlier.

B. Suggested Developmental Goals and Treatment Purposes for Adolescence

Erikson views adolescence as a time when the teenager must achieve a sense of identity. The teen goes through many physical and mental changes in his/her quest to secure an adult-like status. The developmental period appears to be the first time that there is a conscious effort in defining a sense of self. During this period, the teen begins to organize drives, beliefs, and ambitions toward a consistent and clear image of self. It is in this time frame that the emotional stability of the youth may be extremely fragile. Some teens may be unable to cope with the many physical, social, and developmental expectations that come with this passage. Their strong need for affiliations and the need to be wanted and to fit in with peers may become the primary goals within therapy. A clinician may find an animal's presence valuable in making the teen feel more at ease during his/her visit. The teen may be more willing to take down some of the barriers if she/he feels more comfortable. Furthermore, although a teen may project the need to be adult-like, the teen may appreciate the free spirit of an animal. The comfort the youth may receive may allow him/her to feel more appreciated.

The value identified earlier in regard to the psychosocial benefits of having a pet as a child may also be pertinent to a teenager. A therapist may strongly suggest to a family that having a pet may aid a teen in experiencing some social isolation. In their study on high school students and pets, Kidd and Kidd (1990) suggested that pet ownership may be beneficial to adolescents who are experiencing challenges in personal independence as well as mature interfamilial relationships.

C. Suggested Developmental Goals and Treatment Purposes for Adults

Therapists who focus more on adults may also find Erikson's insight beneficial. With young adults, their need to recognize that they can also take care of others may become a great starting point for discussion. A therapist may use a therapy animal as a starting point to discuss decisions about having children or, for that matter, child-rearing practices. It is not uncommon for some therapists to suggest to young couples that they try to rear a pet as a precursor to deciding if they are ready for children. The animal's presence may be an ideal introduction to this topic. Furthermore, adults experiencing parenting challenges and couples who are experiencing marital dysfunction may find the metaphors and the stories related to bringing up children and learning to share one's life with another person to be all appropriate topics. The presence of animals, and examples incorporating animals, may give some clarity to the subject of generativity versus self-absorption.

D. Suggested Developmental Goals and Treatment Purposes for the Elderly

Finally, animals may impact tremendously a clinician's ability to interact with elderly clients. Similar to the role that an animal may have in treating a child, a therapist may find an animal extremely useful in securing a positive relationship with an elderly client. Clients who have a history of animals in their lives may find the animal's presence extremely advantageous in reminiscing about past life events. Raina *et al.* (1999) have found that the daily activities for seniors who had pets increased dramatically in comparison to the elderly who did not live in the company of animals. Barak *et al.* (2001) believe that AAT "reawakens both memories of a former life" and a "need to continue interacting with animals" among seniors. It is astonishing how a lifetime of growing up with animals may make it easier, for some people, to reminisce and think about major milestones in their lives. Reflections of the past may become more apparent as a consequence of compartmentalizing specific life events, which may have revolved around or included pets. A clinician may ascertain that the presence of the animal may act as a catalyst for reliving past events.

Furthermore, the clinician may also recommend to an elderly patient that he or she consider purchasing a pet. Research done by Ory and Goldberg (1983), Friedman *et al.* (1980), Kidd and Fellowman (1981), Jenkins (1986), and Garrity *et al.* (1989), as well as information noted in the chapter on aging, suggests the inherent value of seniors having pets. A client's sense of value could be enhanced tremendously as a consequence of feeling needed once again. In addition, many individuals will thrive from the positive attention they will receive from their companion animal. In some cases, the animal–human relationship may become the necessary ingredient that alleviates a perceived sense of loneliness and isolation. Findings from research by Hunt *et al.* (1992) suggested that unobtrusive animals evoked social approaches and conversations from unfamiliar adults and children. It is apparent that the presence of an animal may become a social lubricant for spontaneous discussions with passing strangers. Furthermore, the walking of pets would also possibly enhance an individual's physical health and stamina. Kidd and Fellowman (1981) pointed out that because dogs require considerable energy in care, their survival rate might be associated with the greater physical activity on behalf of their owners.

VIII. CONSIDERATION 4: THE EXTENSION OF LIVE ANIMALS—UTILIZING SYMBOLISM AND METAPHORS OF ANIMALS

Mallon (1994) discovered that animals have been symbols of power and nurturance. The metaphors of flight with birds and strength of horses can be used therapeutically by therapists to help their clients uncover internal concerns. McMullen (in press), McMullen and Conway (1996), Close (1998), Battino (2003), Barker (1996), and Angus (1996) pointed out that metaphors are utilized extensively by clients in their conversations with therapists. Their research suggests that the incorporation of metaphor themes throughout the course of therapy may actually represent a productive indicator of the therapeutic relationship. Kopp (1995) pointed out that metaphors are similar to mirrors in their ability to reflect inner images within people. Metaphor therapy resides on the position that people in general structure their reality metaphorically. Both the client and the clinician can apply metaphors as a method of discovering and understanding the client's concerns. The imagery generated from the metaphors can be used to help the client uncover how she or he is coping or feeling. For example, a client could be talking to a therapist about feeling overwhelmed about her daily life. When asked what she plans to do about it, the client responds quickly by stating, "I really don't want to open that can of worms right now." The metaphor of the "opening of the can of worms" may represent the client's unwillingness to scramble and try to clean up the mess that she is in right now (rushing around trying to prevent the mess that would be made when the worms squirm out). She does not want to face the formidable task of putting her life in order. The metaphor helps accentuate that position.

Angus and Lawrence (1993) pointed out that in positive therapeutic outcomes, both the client and the therapist are able to draw upon a primary set of metaphoric scenarios in which the ongoing events within the client's life can be truly understood and integrated. For example, a mother of a child with a serious behavior disorder utilized the metaphor of feeling caged as an expression of the restrictions she felt as a consequence of her son's disruptive behavior. Throughout the course of her treatment, we embellished the metaphor not only with problem-solving strategies but also with stories, which edified similar scenarios. The stories were incorporated to lend some support or alternatives to strengthen the therapeutic discovery.

A poignant story of Eli Wiesel, the 1986 Nobel Peace Prize recipient, comes to mind when discussing the mother's metaphor of being caged. Wiesel was a keynote speaker in January of 1987 at an annual dinner of 600 survivors of the Holocaust. At the reception, he shared his insightful perceptions on the struggles of humanity to provide equal access to all its citizens. The audience was moved by an anecdote which captured his feelings. When Wiesel was a student, he once came across a man carrying a bird in a cage. The man was bringing his friend a birthday gift. "Does your friend like birds?" Wiesel asked. "I don't know," replied the man, "but come with me and see what happens." As the man was about to present the gift to his friend, the friend asked him to open the cage and set the bird free. The wish was granted and the man immediately beamed with internal joy. That was his gift. Wiesel went on to explain that there was no greater joy, no greater reward or act of faith, than setting another creature free or at least promoting its salvation or welfare. This was the woman's major goal. She wanted to feel free of her restraining emotional cage and more effective as a mother.

Throughout my years of utilizing birds therapeutically, I have also used birds metaphorically. None of my birds are ever caged, but with the clients we talk about cages as boundaries. Probably the most effective metaphors and stories about birds pertain to their grace in flight. Therapeutic discussions range from the majestic eagle soaring freely to the beauty in the flight of a flock of birds. Equally as beneficial are the sad metaphors that can be applied to a clipped (wings) or grounded bird.

Additional metaphors may include feeling chained or leashed, feeling smothered, or being in a cocoon. Clients may develop therapeutic gains when the metaphors applied also suggest a resolution. For example, the entire process of metamorphosis is an excellent example that illustrates a transformation. The caterpillar goes through the arduous task of spinning its cocoon, which initiates the metamorphosis from its present state to the magnificent butterfly. For months the caterpillar leads its sheltered existence as its body is transformed. Therapeutically, the process of metamorphosis can be valuable in explaining two challenges. Numerous insightful dialogues can be developed on either of these two themes. Some clients will benefit from a discussion of the process of transformation, whereas others may gain some insight into themselves while discussing the sheltering of a being in a protective environment. Furthermore, the short-lived life of a butterfly can also be related to the price that some will pay for the outcome.

A. Storytelling

Deshazer (1994) and Combs and Freedman (1990) implied that embellishing a client's thoughts through storytelling stems from the narrative psychotherapy tradition. From this approach, insights suggest that meaning is given to our lives and that movement occurs in therapy when we have transformational stories that help put our lives in a new context. The narrative approach to therapy suggests that some clients appear to be stuck in their lives and that the new stories generated help them gain a better understanding of their life conditions. Furthermore, the various stories may also lend credible approaches and insight for possible resolution. It seems that for some clients, the previous stories they rehearsed in their heads to cope with their challenges are not effective any longer or have lost their meaning. Therapeutic storytelling that takes advantage of thematic concerns can integrate narratives that pertain directly to the clients' concerns.

Experientially, because my practice incorporates animals, I also apply metaphors and use stories with animals to help clarify certain positions to my clients. Freeman (1991) pointed out that stories are appropriate in different manners at all stages of life. A clinician's ability to care for and maintain effective communication with his/her patients can be augmented and enhanced by the stories we hear and share. The use of tales can be utilized as a source of support and expression as a child or an adult works through a specific concern. The story may reflect a specific dilemma that the individual is attempting to confront and provide some insight on methods for resolution. Fine (1999) suggested that stories help us see the world from the inside perspective of other people. Through stories, outcomes and consequences of decisions are illustrated. Stories of events concerning people or animals can be an inspiring approach to apply with our clients. The stories can therapeutically illustrate and uncover specific concerns and issues and also help our clients unravel their concerns from other perspectives.

Metaphors, storytelling, and puppetry are definite extensions to traditional usage of animals. Nevertheless, it seems logical for therapists with training in storytelling as well as AAT to combine both procedures. When a carefully selected story is matched with a child's or an adult's needs, the process can be tremendously cathartic. Stories that incorporate animals may be easier for the child or client to identify with.

B. Puppetry

In addition to simple storytelling, the use of puppets to act out the stories seems to strengthen this process. For example, Haworth (1968) suggested that animal puppet characters appear to provide a basis for identification but, at the same time, allow a disguise so that a child has less of a need to be guarded. Linn *et al.* (1986) and Linn (1977) identified several attributes of puppetry that may contribute to its efficacy. Both articles advocate that the process of puppetry is immediately involving, active, and quite intimate. Puppets may serve as a catalyst for a child's interaction as she/he manipulates the puppet. Second, puppets can be used to talk with the child directly, and the child does not assume any other character. Therapists who have therapy animals within their practice could find puppets of the same breed as the animals. These puppets could act as "a talking extension" for the animal the child has bonded with. I have found this approach very valuable with my younger primary school–aged clients.

Irwin (1975) pointed out that although there is a wealth of qualitative writing regarding the diagnostic and therapeutic value of puppetry with children, there is little research on how it can be applied effectively in clinical settings. He does suggest that puppetry, because of its stimulating qualities and manipulative material, readily stimulates children in revealing both private symbols and thoughts. The scenarios applied and the fantasies acted out may provide the clinician with a clearer picture of the child's inner world and how she/he copes. The process may also be therapeutic in its release of expression and emotion, without the child having to take personal responsibility for what has been said. As stated earlier, the animated animals could be viewed as an extension of the live animals and could make discussing hard subjects an easier option.

The content of the puppet therapy sessions could be focused loosely on the recurring themes identified in previous therapy sessions. Themes for the puppetry should relate to the client's goals but could include scenarios that act out behavioral control, anger, fear, rejection, and social skills, as well as abandonment. The therapist should be observant of the types of animals the child selects in the puppet sessions. Diagnostically, this can shed a great deal of insight, e.g., does the child select timid or aggressive animals? Furthermore, the therapist can observe the child's interaction with the puppets and assess how the child is reacting to the topic. For example, if the puppet scenario were open ended, the child would have a choice of developing a fantasy that demonstrated a nurturing, caring personality versus an aggressive style. The style in which the child interacts with the puppets may shed tremendous clinical insight. Finally, a clinician could use the puppetry sessions as an opportunity to help the child develop problem-solving alternatives for various challenges.

IX. CONSIDERATION 5: THERAPEUTIC ALTERNATIVES UTILIZING ANIMALS—EXPANDING OUR CLIENTS' TRADITIONAL THERAPY

A. Walking Therapy

Serendipitously, I discovered what I have called "walking therapy." Clinicians may find many pleasant routes where they can walk with their clients and find privacy. Biophilia is a fundamental human need to affiliate with other living organisms (Kahn, 1997). Kahn (1997) revealed that children have an abiding affiliation with nature. Combining the therapeutic usage of animals along with nature exploration could be a powerful approach with some clients. A natural outcome of having a therapy animal is to walk the animal. While walking, one has the opportunity not only to engage in discussion but also to experience the surroundings. At times, the serendipitous observations may enhance or stimulate the ongoing conversation between the clinician and the client. I have found walking a productive part of therapy in some cases. When working with clients whose concerns are nonthreatening, the walk may put the client at ease. While working with children, most do not appear to become distracted while on a walk, but rather engage in discussions freely. While taking a walk, many life examples may be illustrated. For example, if the dog needs to relieve him/herself, the client must learn to be patient and understanding. Furthermore, the clinician can model responsible behavior and bring materials to clean up the mess.

The two types of animals that I utilize the most frequently on these sojourns are birds and dogs. While walking, children seem to display a great sense of pride leading the animal. In fact, on numerous occasions I stop the walk and make a point of how important the child appears leading the animal. This redirection emphasizes the importance of the special bond. They are stopped periodically by a pedestrian who may ask them a question about the animal, and in most cases, the interactions are quite pleasant.

Over the years, I have experimented with different variations of walking with the animals. Sometimes, it is just a casual stroll through the community, eventually returning to the office after a period of time. Sometimes our walks bring us to a school yard or a park, where we sit at a park bench or table and continue our therapeutic discussions. This alternative complements the therapeutic option by continuing the therapy and by taking advantage of the outdoors. Personal experience has found that some children begin to reveal their thoughts while our walk is starting, but the discussion is enhanced when concentrated attention is given to the dialogue while sitting at the park. Sitting at the bench or around the table gives both the client and the clinician a chance to elaborate on the specific topics as well as to problem solve the concerns. Practically, therapists will find it valuable to have a pad of paper and a pen to document discussions and appropriate goals to follow up. Combining utilizing the natural environment with the animals seems to be an added benefit in strengthening the rapport with the child.

B. Clinical Applications

Over the years, walking therapy has been applied with many of my clients. A population that seems to have had the greatest gains is children with selective mutism and those with separation and social anxiety. By using the walk as an excuse to leave the office, children who experience separation anxiety begin to practice leaving their parents. The ventures beyond the office can be used as true experiences for separation. The client can be instructed to develop alternative cognitive structures that promote optimal thinking.

In the several cases of treating children with selective mutism, walks with the dogs or birds are initially utilized as an opportunity to get the child to talk louder. While walking, there may be many competing sounds, which may impede our ability to hear each other. Requesting that the child speak louder is simply a reality of the environment. Amazingly, as the children become more comfortable with the animals and begin to enjoy our walks, their comfort and confidence seem to be increased. Bowers and MacDonald (2001) noted similar findings. They pointed out that affectionate animals have been found to elicit verbalizations in clients who refuse to speak or who are very withdrawn.

A natural occurrence during the walk is the occasional interruption from another pedestrian walking by. The animal seems to stimulate greetings from passersby. This outcome may eventually be a planned goal for the walk. Early in treatment, a clinician may select a route where there likely will not be any people on the road. However, as the client's confidence seems to build, a clinician may plan to take a route where interaction will be generated. A clinician may use some time prior to the walk to prepare the client with strategies in the event that a civilian may try to start up a conversation. The walk then could represent a true test to assess progress. The client then can return to the office and, with the clinician's support, evaluate the outcome.

Some clinicians may live in communities where there are established dog parks. It is now quite common to find, in various cities, parks where dogs interact. The clinician is advised to investigate and visit these parks (to learn about the protocol of entering the park as well as to observe the various dogs attending) prior to incorporating this procedure as part of his/her practice. This initial step could help avert unexpected pitfalls. The clinician could develop an action plan prior to therapeutically instituting this component. So much can be observed and learned vicariously in a dog park. The animals represent a small microcosm of the real world. There will be large and small dogs, hefty and lean dogs, playful and docile dogs, and finally aggressive and passive species. The observation of all of these animals can be applied to discuss the importance of understanding individual differences. Specific behaviors observed in any given dog may become valuable lessons for clarification with clients. For example, when observing an aggressive encounter between two dogs, a generalization can be formulated comparing this clash with human examples. A client may be more willing to initiate a personal exploration on the topic when it is initially disguised in discussing the observed battle. The framework of the discussion could eventually be modified to focus more directly on humans, and more specifically on the client. One of the most teachable lessons from the interactions at the dog park pertains to the compatibility of most of the dogs. In most cases, all the dogs get along. This outcome translates easily to a major lesson underlying the visit: that if all the dogs can learn to get along, so can children who may presently have social challenges.

The most pertinent discussions pertain to dogs that are overactive. Clinicians who primarily serve children will find the vicarious observations illuminating, especially when they are watching dogs that are hyperactive. The clinician can help the child observe how the impulsive and intrusive behavior of the dogs may agitate others. These observations may eventually be a catalyst for further personal discussion and problem solving.

Walks through the community or in the park may be useful for some clinicians. This option not only helps clients feel more relaxed, but the milieu may enhance their willingness to talk and reflect.

It is important that clinicians have the client sign a waiver consenting to go on walks with the animals. Tables II and III are examples of potential forms that can be used.

TABLE II **Permission Form for Animal-Assisted Therapy (AAT)**

I hereby give my consent that my child may be treated in individual psychotherapy that utilizes animal-assisted therapy (AAT). The AAT will be utilized as an adjunct to the prescribed treatment. I recognize that throughout my visit, my child and myself will come in contact with various species of animals (dogs, birds, fish, and various small lizards). Animal-assisted therapy is a goal-directed intervention where the animal/animals are an integral part of the treatment process.

As a parent, I will have the opportunity to discuss with Dr. Fine any concerns or reservations that I may have with this component of the treatment. The same opportunity will be given to the child. In addition, I (the parent) have identified to Dr. Fine that there are no allergies to the type of animals employed at this office.

I realize that my child will always be supervised at all times around the animals. Furthermore, if there are any health/personal concerns that come up during the course of treatment that would have an impact on the AAT, I will notify the therapist so that the AAT portion of the visit will be suspended for that session or future sessions.

____
Signature

____
Child's name

____
Date

TABLE III Consent Form for Taking Walks with Animals: An Aspect of AAT

I hereby give my consent that my child may go on therapeutic walks in the surrounding area with the therapist as an aspect of the animal-assisted therapy. I have been informed (by the therapist) of the purpose of such walks and also realize that a potential consequence of the walks is that my child's anonymity may be discovered (by a bystander walking by). All attempts will be made to keep the walks private, and no information about our visits will be disclosed on these walks.

I will always be informed of when a walk will be taken, as well as the route and duration. I have the right to refuse having my child take a walk with the animals at any given time period.

Signature	Client's Name	Date

FIGURE 1 The PAL Project.

C. Pets Are Loving Program

The PAL project (Fine 1992) was established to enhance the sense of responsibility and self-esteem of children with learning disabilities and an attention deficit (Fig. 1). The purpose of the program was to prepare and supervise children to become mentors with their animals for the elderly. The program was cosponsored by a local retirement community. Selected candidates for the program (the children) were screened with their animals to assess their com-

TABLE IV Major Components of the PAL Training Program

1. Elements of being a mentor:
   A. An overview of the PAL project. What should the mentors expect (e.g., when the program would meet, where the program would be held, the behavioral expectations, an explanation of their role, and duration of each visit)?
   B. An interactive discussion on how one interacts with the elderly. What should the mentor expect when interacting with the seniors? What should a typical visit be like?
   C. Skills of communication.
   D. The code of expected behavior: Guidelines for expected behaviors.
2. An explanation of aging:
   A. An interactive discussion on the myths and stereotypes of the elderly. How to positively understand and respect seniors (reducing stereotypical fears and anxieties).
   B. Methods of interacting with the seniors (e.g., learning how to talk quietly and move a little slower, how to help a senior with mobility).
3. Expected behaviors of the companion animals.
   A. Guidelines for how to introduce your pet to a senior.
   B. Guidelines for behavioral compliance.
4. Preparation for the session.
   A. Guidelines for grooming the animal as well as yourself.
   B. A discussion of reflective journal writing and weekly compulsory entries documenting the experience.
   C. Being an active member of the discussion group (reflection discussions held after every session).

patibility and suitability. All animals (in this case primarily dogs and cats) were evaluated to assess their efficacy in being viable companion animals. Those animals that did not meet the requirements were not incorporated. Their owners were encouraged to continue in the program but were paired with one of the project's animals.

After careful consideration, a training protocol was established for all participating mentors. The ratio of supervision within this program was five mentors to two staff members. Table IV identifies the highlights of the mentors' training.

The PAL program was designed to be 10 weeks long. At any given time, five children were enrolled with two group leaders supervising. The two staff leaders were selected due to their background in working with children as well as understanding animal behavior. The compatibility of the children, as well as their animals, was also taken into consideration. Each child was given a manual and a binder to help them collate their materials, as well as a writing space for their reflective thoughts. Qualitative evaluations suggested the program was effective for both the mentors and the elderly. Most children found the experience valuable. The experience seemed to alter their stereotypes about the aging process. The mentors also appeared to have experienced an enhancement of their behavioral control in public settings. The small group discussions appeared helpful in aiding the children in reflecting on the benefits and purposes of the experience.

There are many other unique options that therapists may consider. Project Read has become a popular alternative literacy program over the past decade. Within the project, dogs (highly trained in obedience) are paired with children who have reading difficulties. Satellite Project Read programs have been sponsored all over the world in libraries as well as in schools. Basically, the dogs' presence promotes a relaxing and accepting environment that appears to motivate children while reading aloud. Although not investigated thoroughly, the program seems to have its merits. Qualitative comments suggest some benefits, especially when the handler has experience in reading instruction.

Finally, projects such as a Second Leash on Life and Project Second Chance have become popular training programs for youth at risk (Duel 2000; Harbolt and Ward, 2001). Harbolt and Ward (2001) explained that Project Second Chance groups teenage offenders with shelter dogs who are being given a second chance to be adopted. During the training program the dogs are paired with youth mentors that work with them in basic obedience and becoming more comfortable with humans. The philosophy behind the intervention has led to tremendous outcomes, especially as it pertains to empathy building, kindness, and the acceptance of responsibility. In essence, both programs provide a second opportunity for life successes for both the animals and the youth. The participants eventually learn that compassion and consistency in training are more effective alternatives to aggression and anger. I have used aspects of training animals in some of my individual therapy sessions (Fine, 2005). Over the course of the last decade, I have adopted several puppies and have involved some of my patients in their training as an aspect of their therapy. To assist in generalizing the benefits, I give the clients homework, such as readings on dog behavior and training, as well as guided journal reflections. It is in the writing and the debriefing that I attempt to help clients crystallize the value of the experience. Emphasis is given to how the process of change in the animal has similar objectives to their own treatment goals.

X. CONSIDERATION 6: PRACTICAL SUGGESTIONS FOR CLINICIANS' USE OF ANIMALS

A. Training and Liability

Therapists considering incorporating animals within their practice must seriously consider the factors of liability and training, as well as the safety and welfare of both the animal and the client. Hines and Fredrickson (1998) and the Delta Society's Pet Partner Program strongly advocate that health care professionals must have training on techniques of AAT. Clinicians also need to be aware of best practice procedures ensuring quality, as well as safety, for all parties. Those clinicians living in North America should register through the Delta Society for a 1-day workshop or a home study course. In an effort to achieve the best possible qualitative results, Hines and Frederickson (1998) strongly suggest that health care staff receive training. They point out that without adequate training on how to apply AAT, therapists may incorporate animals inappropriately and get poor results. The Pet Partners Program developed by the Delta Society includes in-service training in a variety of areas, including an awareness of health and skill aptitude of the animals, as well as strategies to incorporate the animals with the clients. The Pet Partner Program should be considered as a valuable introductory course. All of the training will aid practitioners in gaining appropriate guidelines for quality practice (Hines and Fredrickson, 1998). There are numerous references that therapists should consider reading to help them understand dog behavior and possible training techniques. *The Other End of the Leash* by McConnell (2002) and *The Power of Positive Dog Training* by Miller (2001) are two excellent guides. There are many other good books on this area, including the many books written by Stanley Coren.

Fine and Stein (2003) identified several concerns that therapists should become aware of when selecting an animal for therapy. Table V identifies some of the suggestions given by Stein (2003) to therapists.

After completing the course successfully (which also includes a written test and an aptitude of the animal), one can become registered by the Delta Society. All those who are registered will receive continued education through bimonthly newsletters, as well as an opportunity to attend various seminars and workshops. A valuable benefit of being registered is the liability insurance program that is incorporated.

Finally, it is imperative that an animal's well-being is preserved and safeguarded. Tables VI and VII (adapted from Stein, 2003) represent the signs of stress that one should become familiar with so that fatigue and stress within the animals are avoided. Table V also identifies a few strategies that a therapist may consider in attempting to reduce stress.

B. Office Management and Decor

A lot of attention does not need to be given to the dimension of office management and decor, but it must be discussed. Having animals within one's therapeutic practice has an impact on the office's decor. One must make sure that the work environment still maintains a clean and orderly presence. This is not only a provision for ambiance but also for health requirements. Those who

TABLE V Guidelines for Incorporating Animals in AAT

Basic requirements:
- All dogs must have excellent temperament.
- The animals need to be calm and gentle and enjoy being around people.
- As therapy animals, the animals will be exposed to unusual sights, sounds, and smells. The therapist needs to be confident that the animals are prepared for these unusual circumstances.
- All therapy animals need to be obedient and follow directions of the therapist.
- Ability to regain self-control after play or excitement.
- Able to sit quietly for extended periods.
- Ability to navigate through crowded environments.
- Attentive to the handler.

Preparation:
All therapy dogs should have some certification in obedience training, such as meeting the standards of the American Kennel Club's canine good citizen's test. The test requires the dog to master the following skills:
- Be comfortable with a friendly stranger.
- Walk comfortably in a heel position on a leash.
- Sit, stay, come, and lie down on command.
- Be able to ignore a neutral dog.
- Practice self-control.
- Refrain from any aggressive responses.

Safety and comfort guidelines to consider:
- Major rule to follow: Always protect your therapy animal. Remove the animal from all stressful situations. Over time, you can continue to train the animal to overcome situations that were previously considered stressful.
- Give the animal constant breaks; providing walks and play breaks will allow the animal to be less stressed throughout the day.
- Always have fresh water available all day. On break times, have some of the animal's favorite toys available.
- On a daily basis have a pleasant grooming session.
- In the therapy environment, establish a safe space away from any stimulation. Within that area have the animal's favorite bed or cage.

may want to use birds in their practice should make sure that the cages are cleaned daily and that any food on the floor is cleaned up as quickly as possible. Other animals in cages or using litter boxes should also be monitored for cleanliness. Finally, dogs and cats should be able to access a fresh bowl of clean water whenever they have the need.

C. Animal Welfare

It is evident that the safety of one's patient would be the highest priority. Nevertheless, the therapist should and must consider the safety and welfare

TABLE VI Signs of Stress in a Dog

- Panting and salivating
- Pacing
- Shedding
- Diarrhea/bowel movements
- Inappropriate urination
- Licking the lips
- Coughing
- Sneezing
- Dilated pupils
- Trembling
- Shaking (as if the animal were shaking off water)
- Yawning
- Whining, excessive vocalizing
- Nipping
- Growling when approached to be handled
- Increased/decreased activity
- Excessive water consumption
- Food refusal
- Excessive scratching or licking repeatedly
- Loss of appetite
- Hiding behind handler or furniture
- Sweaty paws (leaving sweaty paw prints on the floor)
- Withdrawal and refusal to interact
- Willful disobedience
- Excessive sniffing
- Destructive behavior
- Redirected aggression toward people and other animals
- "Spacing out" by turning away or avoiding eye contact

for all of his/her animals used in therapeutic practice. In an earlier chapter, Frederickson discusses numerous concerns that should be addressed when selecting animals. She highlights (as do portions of this chapter) various symptoms that identify if an animal is becoming stressed. In lieu of repeating a similar commentary, only cardinal rules that should be adhered to by all clinicians planning to incorporate animals are identified. However, the clinician is strongly encouraged to review Chapter 7, as well as manuals such as the Pet Partners' program for further information.

To assist in identifying guidelines for animal safety and welfare, I have elected to incorporate some of the guidelines that Hubrecht and Turner (1998) highlighted when evaluating an animal's welfare in all living environments. The conditions noted were originally established by the United Kingdom Farm Animal Welfare Council. All of the categories emphasized by Hubrecht and Turner (1998) seem very applicable when evaluating the welfare and the safety of animals utilized in therapy. All clinicians must make a conscious effort to

TABLE VII Stress Signs in Cats

- Restlessness, distraction, agitation
- Listlessness, unusual passivity
- Defensive vocalizations
- Excessive shedding
- Dilated pupils
- Biting
- Inappropriate urination/defecation
- Clinging to handler
- Drooling
- Hiding/withdrawal and refusal to interact
- Water and food refusal
- Redirected aggression toward people and other animals
- Territorial marking
- Sitting in a fixed posture for long periods
- Psychogenic alopecia (excessive grooming)
- Pica (ingestion of inappropriate substances such as wool)
- Ritualized oral activities; sucking or chewing on inappropriate items (e.g., sweaters, people's fingers, different fabrics, or plastic)
- Kneading soft item

persevere and safeguard their animals' quality of life. Hubrecht and Turner (1998) argued adamantly that if an animal is not cared for properly or, for that matter, if the animal appears stressed while working, the human–animal relationship will not develop effectively. Furthermore, outcomes from the misuse of an animal will most likely jeopardize any therapeutic benefit or gain.

As clinicians our concerns must be with both our clients and the animals that work with us. We must certify that the physical, mental, and emotional care of our animals is irreproachable. This tenet must be followed at all times! Our animals' rights (for quality of life and safety) as active members on the therapeutic team must be addressed and protected (Fine *et al.*, 2001).

All animals need to be safe from any abuse and danger from any client at all times. Furthermore, the therapist must be aware of the animal's need for some quiet time and relaxation during any given therapeutic day. The animal must be able to find a safe refuge within the office that she/he can go to if she/he feels exhausted or stressed. Throughout the day, the animal needs to have a break from actual patient contact and be able to express normal animal behavior. The clients (especially children) need to learn to respect this decision and allow the animal a rest period. In cases of older animals, the animal may need the time to recoup his/her energy. When she/he is ready to return to the therapeutic area, she/he should be allowed. The therapist may need to inform some of his clients (especially children) that they have to respect the animal's need for privacy and rest. Some children may want to smother the animal with love and physical attention. When this occurs, instruct the client in the best manner to hug an animal without being confining.

Numerous other concerns may be thought of in relation to Hubrecht and Turner's (1998) third identified provision. Specifically, our therapy animals must be free from pain, injury, and disease. The therapist must practice good health procedures for all the animals being utilized. All animals should be up to date on all their inoculations and visually appear in good health. If the animal seems ill, stressed, or exhausted, medical attention must be given.

Care needs to be given to the animal's physical appearance. She/he should be groomed properly and look presentable. This can set a good example for all clients. The animals should be under the supervision of a veterinarian who is aware of the therapeutic dimension of the animals' life. The animals should be seen on an intermittent basis to assure that they are in good health. The veterinarian may also act as a medical advisor, guiding the clinician on any medical concerns that may pertain to the animals' welfare. There are so many variables that must be taken into consideration. For example, if an animal has not been well, how do you determine when she/he is ready to return to assisting with therapy?

Additionally, as an animal ages, his/her schedule for therapeutic involvement will have to be curtailed. This may cause some disruption and adjustment to the therapist's method of practice. Some therapists and clients may find this alteration a difficult transition to accept. However, this transition may also be emotionally difficult for the animal as well. A dog that is used to an active schedule may initially appear demoralized at the adjustment to his/her involvement. For example, my first therapy dog Puppy experienced some demoralization as she went into retirement. Eventually, I had her come to the office a few hours a day. She tired quickly and was often found napping throughout the day. To help her feel more comfortable, I set up one of her beds in a private office. When she got tired, she wandered to the office and fell asleep. Clients learned not to disturb her when she was sleeping, but some took a quick peek to see their beloved canine therapist. When she was ready to resume her duties, she wandered back to the treatment rooms. Puppy was able to follow this regime until a short time before she died. Making these accommodations, which supported her physical and mental well-being, allowed her to preserve her dignity and quality of life.

D. Precautions for Clients

Therapists must make wise choices in selecting animals for their practice. Not all pets make good adjunct therapists. A clinician who is considering incorporating animals within his/her psychotherapy must strongly consider what animals will serve the best purpose. This may mean further studying and purchasing animals that best suit his/her needs. Unfortunately, a good home pet may not be suitable for therapy.

Wishon (1989) pointed out that an underestimated problem that may occur in the animal–human bond is the pathogens that can be transmitted from animals to human beings. This process is now known as "zoonoses." Wishon (1989) reported that most cats and dogs carry human pathogens which, along with those carried by other animals, have been associated with more than 150 zoonotic diseases. However, Hines and Fredrickson (1998) pointed out that data regarding the transmission of zoonotic diseases in any AAT programs have been minimal. Practitioners are advised to work closely with veterinarians and other public health specialists to ensure the safety of the animals as well as the clients involved.

Brodie *et al.* (2002) suggested that although the potential to suffer some harm from AAI may exist, it can be minimized by taking simple precautions. These precautions include the careful selection of therapy animals, rigorous health care and monitoring for the animal, and informed consent by all those involved. When following good medical practices for both animals and patients, the risks for allergies, zoonoses, and potential injuries can be reduced tremendously. Finally, the clinician should be aware of any fears of animals or allergies before utilizing animals adjunctively with specific clients. This will ensure that the addition of the animal will not complicate the therapy.

E. Additional Concerns

There are numerous other concerns that a clinician should consider prior to introducing animals into his/her practice. Although some of the concerns cannot be planned for completely, the therapist must be aware of them. For example, a clinician should consider how to handle explaining an illness of the animal to his/her clients and how to explain the death of a beloved animal. Both of these variables are realistic concerns which will have to be considered seriously. Over the years, concerned attached clients have had difficulties accepting these inevitable problems. Furthermore, the introduction of new animals into a practice will also need attention. A suggestion is to transition all new animals gradually so that you are comfortable with the behavior. At times, young animals (specifically rambunctious young puppies) will need significant attention until they are capable of being more actively involved.

XI. CONCLUSIONS

With thought and planning, animals can make a major contribution to a therapist's arsenal in treating clients. Animals can enhance the therapeutic environment by making the milieu more emotionally and physically accessible to clients. Some clinicians may still be skeptical of the therapeutic value of the animal–human bond and may initially underestimate the clinical utility of animals as an adjunct to therapy. It is understood, as was discussed at the outset of this chapter, that the lack of documentation and thorough investigation of outcome research leave a large void in the efficacy of this approach. Interested clinicians may initially incorporate animals solely to develop rapport with clients. Nevertheless, after reading this chapter, a skilled and well-informed clinician should be able to recognize a multitude of benefits that animals can fulfill. A therapist may have to make some adjustments to his/her practicing philosophy to ease the incorporation of animals into one's professional repertoire.

Those clinicians who craft a place for animals into their therapeutic regimen will not be disappointed with their efforts. Their therapeutic milieu and approach will be richer as a consequence. As George Eliot (1857) writes in *Mr. Gilfil's Love Story*, "Animals are such agreeable friends. They ask no questions and they pass no criticism." The unconditional love and devotion that an animal will bring to a therapeutic practice will be an asset that may never be thoroughly understood but should be appreciated and harnessed.

REFERENCES

Argus, L. (1996). An intensive analysis of metaphor themes in psychotherapy. *In* "Metaphor: Implications of Applications" (J. Mio and A. Katz, eds.), pp. 73–85. Lawrence Erlbaum Associates, Mahwah, NJ.

Argus, L., and Lawrence, H. (1993). An intensive analysis of metaphor themes in brief dynamic therapy. *In* "Metaphor: Cognition and Application" (J. Mio, ed.). Symposium presented at the first annual meeting of the American Psychology Association, Toronto, Canada.

Arkow, P. (1982). "Pet therapy: A Study of the Use of Companion Animals in Selected Therapies." Humane Society of Pikes Peak Region, Colorado Springs, CO.

Barak, Y., Savorai, O., Mavashev, S., and Beni, A. (2001). Animal-assisted therapy for schizophrenic patients. *Am. Assoc. Geriatr. Psychiatr.* 117–132.

Barker, P. (1996). "Psychotherapeutic Metaphors: A Guide to Theory and Practice." Brunner/Mazel, New York.

Barnard, R. (1954). Milieu therapy. *Menninger Q.* 8(2), 21–24.

Battino, R. (2003). "Metaphoria: Metaphor and Guided Metaphor for Psychotherapy and Healing." Crown Publishers, New York.

Bazrad, S. (1993, June 6). Helping kids confidence take off, p. J-4. *Los Angeles Times*.

Beck, A., Hunter, K., and Seraydarian, L. (1986). Use of animals in the rehabilitation of psychiatric inpatients. *Psychol. Rep.* 58, 63–66.

Beck, A., and Katcher, A. H. (1983). Between Pets and People: The Importance of Animal Companionship. Putnam, New York.

Blue, G. F. (1986). The Value of Pets in Children's Lives. *Childhood Education*, December, 85–90.

Bowers, M. J., and MacDonald, P. (2001). The effectiveness of equine-facilitated psychotherapy with at risk adolescents. *J. Psychol. Behav. Sci.* **15**, 62–76.

Brodie, S., Biley Bnurs, F., and Sherwring, M. (2002). An exploration of the potential risks associated with using pet therapy in healthcare settings. *J. Clin. Nurs.* **11**, 444–456.

Brody, J. (1988, April 7). Personal health: Increasingly, laughter as potential therapy for patients is being taken seriously. *The New York Times*, B8.

Bryant, B. (1990). The richness of the child-pet relationship: A consideration of both benefits and costs of pets to children. *Anthrozoos* **3**, 253–261.

Canfield, J., Hansen, M., Becker, M., and Kline, C. (1998). "Chicken Soup for the Pet Lover's Soul." Health Communications, Inc., Deerfield Beach, FL.

Canfield, J., Hansen, M., Becker, M., Kline, C., and Shojai, A. (2005). "Chicken Soup for the Dog Lover's Soul." Health Communications, Inc., Deerfield Beach, FL.

Close, H. R. (1998). "Metaphor in Psychotherapy: Clinical Applications of Stories and Allegories." Impact Publishers, San Luis Obispo, CA.

Combs, G., and Freedman, J. (1990). "Symbol Story and Ceremony Using Metaphor in Individual and Family Therapy." Norton, New York.

Corson, S. A., and Corson, E. O. (1980). Pet animals as nonverbal communication mediators in psychotherapy in institutional settings. *In* "Ethology and Nonverbal Communication in Mental Health" (S. A. Corson and E. O. Corson, eds.), pp. 83–110. Pergamon Press, Oxford, U.K.

Cousins, N. (1979). "Anatomy of an Illness." Norton, New York.

Cousins, N. (1989). "Head First: The Biology of Hope." E. P. Dutton, New York.

Covert, A. M., Nelson, C., and Whiren, A. P. (1985). Pets, early adolescents and families. *Marriage Family Rev.* **8**, 95–108.

De Shazer, S. (1984). "Words Were Originally Magic." Norton, New York.

Duel, D. K. (2000). "Violence Prevention and Intervention: A Directory of Animal-Related Programs." The Humane Society of the United States, Washington, DC.

Fine, A. (1992). "The Flight to Inner Freedom: Utilizing Domestic Animals and Exotic Birds in the Psychological Treatment of Children with Unhealthy Self-esteem." Paper presented at the sixth International Conference on Human-Animal Interactions, Montreal, Canada.

Fine, A. (1993). "Pets Are Loving Project: A Manual and Resource Guide for Supporting Children." California State Polytechnic University Graphics, Pomona, CA.

Fine, A. (1999). "Fathers and Sons: Bridging the Generation." Diamond Communications, South Bend, IN.

Fine, A. H. (2002). Animal assisted therapy. *In* "Encyclopedia of Psychotherapy" (M. Hersen and W. Sledge, eds.), pp. 49–55. Elsevier Science, New York.

Fine, A. H. (2003). Animal Assisted Therapy and Clinical Practice. Psycho-Legal Associates CEU meeting, Nov. 1., Seattle, WA.

Fine, A. H. (2005). Animal Assisted Therapy and Clinical Practice. Psycho-Legal Associates CEU meeting, May 2, San Francisco, CA.

Fine, A. H., and Beiler (in press). Therapists and animals: Demystifying animal assisted therapy. *In* "The Handbook of Complementary Therapies" (A. Strozier, ed.). Haworth Press, New York.

Fine, A. H., and Eisen, C. (In press). "Afternoons with Puppy: Lessons for Life from a Therapist and his Animals." Purdue University Press, West Lafayette, IN.

Fine, A. H., Serpell, J., and Hines, L. (2001). The Welfare of Assistance and Therapy Animals: An Ethical Commentary. International Conference on the Human Animal Bond, Rio, Brazil, Sept. 14.

Fine, A. H., and Stein, L. (2003). Animal Assisted Therapy and Clinical Practice. Psycho-Legal Associates CEU meeting, Oct. 25, Pasadena, CA.

Fredrickson, M., and Hines, L. (1998). Perspective on animal-assisted activities and therapy. *In* "Companion Animals in Human Health" (B. C. Turner and C. C. Wilson, eds.), pp. 23–39. Sage, Thousand Oaks, CA.

Freeman, M. (1991). Therapeutic use of storytelling for older children who are critically ill. *CHC* **20**(4), 208–213.

Friedman, E., Katcher, A. H., Lynch, J. J., and Thomas, S. A. (1980). Animal companions and one-year survival of patients after discharge from a coronary care unit. *Public Health Rep.* **95**, 301–312.

Furman, W. (1989). The development of children's social networks. *In* "Children's Social Networks and Social Supports" (D. Belle ed.), pp. 151–72. Wiley, New York.

Garrity, T. F., Johnson, T. P., Marx, M. B., and Stallones, L. (1989). Pet ownership and attachment as supportive factors in the health of the elderly. *Anthrozoos* **3**, 35–44.

George, M. H. (1992). Child therapy and animals. *In* "Innovative Interventions in Child and Adolescent Therapy" (C. E. Schaefer, ed.), pp. 401–418. Wiley, New York.

Goldensohn, S., and Haan, E. (1974). Transference and countertransference in a third party payment system (HMO). *Am. J. Psychiatr.* **83**, 255–260.

Gomulkiewicz, R., Hart, L. A., and Hunt, S. J. (1992). Role of small animals in social interactions between strangers. *J. Soc. Psychol.* **132**, 245–256.

Gonski, Y. (1985). The therapeutic utilization of canines in a child welfare setting. *Child Adolesc. Social Work J.* **2**(2), 93–105.

Gunby, P. (1978). Pets for cardiac therapeutics. *J. Am. Med. Assoc.* **241**, 438.

Hall, C., and Lindzey, G. (1978). "Theory of Personality," 3rd Ed. Wiley, New York.

Harbolt, T., and Ward, T. (2001). Teaming incarcerated youth with shelter dogs for a second chance. *Soc. Anim.* **9**(2), 177–182.

Hoelscher, K., and Garfat, T. (1993). Talking to the animals. *J. Child Youth Care* **8**(3), 87–92.

Hubrecht, R., and Turner, D. C. (1998). Companion animal welfare in private and institutional settings. *In* "Companion Animals in Human Health" (B. C. Turner and C. C. Wilson, eds.), pp. 267–289. Sage, Thousand Oaks, CA.

Irwin, E. C., and Shapiro, M. I. (1975). Puppetry as a diagnostic and therapeutic technique. *Trans-cult. Aspects Psychiatr. Art* **4**, 86–94.

Jenkins, J. L. (1986). Physiological effects of petting a companion animal. *Psychol. Rep.* **58**, 21–22.

Kahn, P. H. (1997). Developmental psychology and the biophilia hypothesis: Children's affiliation with nature. *Dev. Rev.* **17**, 1–61.

Kale, M. (1992). How some kids gain success, self-esteem with animals. *InterActions* **10**(2), 13–17.

Katcher, A. H. (2000). Animal-assisted therapy and the study of human–animal relationships: Discipline or bondage? Context or transitional object? *In* "Handbook on Animal-Assisted Therapy: Theoretical Foundations and Guidelines for Practice" (A. Fine, ed.), pp. 461–473. Academic Press, San Diego.

Kidd, A. H., and Kidd, R. M. (1980). Personality characteristics and preferences in pet ownership. *Psychol. Rep.* **46**, 939–944.

Kidd, A. H., and Kidd, R. M. (1981). Pet ownership and self-perception of older people. *Psychol. Rep.* **48**, 867–875.

Kidd, A. H., and Kidd, R. M. (1985). Children's attitudes toward their pets. *Psychol. Rep.* **57**, 15–31.

Kidd, A. H., and Kidd, R. M. (1990). High school students and their pets. *Psychol. Rep.* **66**, 1391–1394.

Kidd, A. H., and Kidd, R. M. (1994). Benefits and liabilities of pets for the homeless. *Psychol. Rep.* **74**, 715–722.

Kopp, R. R. (1995). "Metaphor Therapy." Brunner/Mazel, New York.

Kruger, K., Trachtenberg, S., and Serpell, J. A. (2004). Can animals help humans heal? Animal-assisted interventions in adolescent mental health. Available at http://www2.vet.upenn.edu/research/centers/cias/pdf/CIAS_AAI_white_paper.pdf

Langs, R. (1978). "Technique in Transition." Jason Aronson, New York.

Langs, R. (1979). "The Therapeutic Environment." Jason Aronson, New York.

Langs, R. (1981). "Classics in Psychoanalytic Technique." Jason Aronson, New York.

Langs, R. (1982). "Psychotherapy: A Basic Text." Jason Aronson, New York.

Levinson, B. M. (1962). The dog as a "co-therapist." *Ment. Hyg.* **46**, 59–65.

Levinson, B. M. (1964). Pets: A special technique in child psychotherapy. *Ment. Hyg.* **48**, 243–248.

Levinson, B. M. (1965). Pet psychotherapy: Use of household pets in the treatment of behavior disorder in childhood. *Psychol. Rep.* **17**, 695–698.

Linn, S. (1977). Puppets and hospitalized children: Talking about feelings. *J. Assoc. Care Child Hosp.* 5(4), 5–11.

Lockwood, R. (1983). The influence of animals on social perception. *In* "New Perspectives on Our Lives with Companion Animals" (A. K. Katcher and A. M. Beck, eds.), pp. 351–362. University of Pennsylvania Press, Philadelphia.

Mallon, G. P. (1992). Utilization of animals as therapeutic adjuncts with children and youth: A review of the literature. *Child Youth Care Forum* **21**(1), 53–67.

Mallon, G. P. (1994). Cow as co-therapist: Utilization of farm animals as therapeutic aides with children in residential treatment. *Child Adolesc. Social Work J.* **11**, 455–474.

Mallon, G. P. (1994). Some of our best therapists are dogs. *Child Youth Care Forum* **23**(2), 89–101.

McCulloch, M. J. (1984). Pets in therapeutic programs for the aged. *In* "The Pet Connection" (R. K. Anderson, B. L. Hart, and L. A. Hart, eds.), pp. 387–398. Center to Study Human-Animal Relationships and Environment, Minneapolis, MN.

McElroy, S. (1996). "Animals as Teachers and Healers." Ballantine Books, New York.

McMullen, L. M. (2006). Putting it in context: Metaphor and psychotherapy. *In* "The Cambridge Handbook of Metaphor and Thought" (R. W. Gibbs, Jr., ed.). Cambridge University Press, New York.

McMullen, L., and Conway, J. (1996). Conceptualizing the figurative expressions of psychotherapy clients. *In* "Metaphor: Implications and Applications" (J. Mio and A. Katz, eds.), pp. 59–73. Lawrence Erlbaum Associates, Mahwah, NJ.

McConnell, P. (2002). "At the Other End of the Leash." Ballantine Books, New York.

Miller, P. (2001). "The Power of Positive Dog Training." Hungry Minds, New York.

Netting, F. E., Wilson, C., and New, J. C. (1987). The human-animal bond: Implications for practice. National Association of Social Workers, Inc., **60**(1), 60–64.

Ory, M. G., and Goldberg, E. L. (1983). Pet possession and life satisfaction in elderly women. *In* "New Perspectives on Our Lives with Companion Animals" (A. H. Katcher and A. M. Beck, eds.). University of Pennsylvania Press, Philadelphia.

Paul, E. S., and Serpell, J. A. (1996). Obtaining a new dog: Effects on middle childhood children and their families. *Appl. Anim. Behav. Sci.* **47**, 17–29.

Peacock, C. (1986). "The Role of the Therapeutic Pet in Initial Psychotherapy Sessions with Adolescents." Paper presented to Delta Society International Conference, Boston.

Poretsky, R. H., Hendrix, C., Mosier, J. E., and Samuelson, M. L. (1988). Young children's companion animal bonding and adults' pet attitudes: A retrospective study. *Psychol. Rep.* **62**, 419–425.

Raina, P., Waltner-Toews, D., and Bonnett B. (1999). Influence of companion animals on the physical and psychological health of older people: An analysis of a one-year longitudinal study. *J. Am. Geriatr. Soc.* 323–329.

Rice, S. R. (1973). Animals and psychotherapy: A survey. *J. Comm. Psychol.* **1**, 323–326.

Ross, S. B. (1983 March). The therapeutic use of animals with the handicapped. *Int. Child Welf. Rev.* **56**, 26–39.

Serpell, J. A. (1981). Childhood pets and their influence on adults' attitudes. *Psychol. Rep.* **49**, 651–654.

Serpell, J. A. (1983). Pet psychotherapy. *People–Animal–Environment*, 7–8.

Siegel, J. M. (1993). Companion animals: In sickness and in health. *J. Soc. Issues* **49**, 157–167.

Sklar, H. (1988). The impact of the therapeutic environment. *Hum. Sci. Press* **18**(2), 107–123.

Stein, L. (2003). Animal Assisted Therapy and Clinical Practice. Psycho-Legal Associates CEU meeting, Oct. 25, Pasadena, CA.

Triebenbacher-Lookabaugh, S. (1998). Pets as transitional objects: Their role in children's emotional development. *Psychol. Rep.* **82**, 191–200.

Voelken, R. (1995). Puppy love can be therapeutic, too. *J. Am. Med. Assoc.* **274**, 1897–1899.

Volth, V. L. (1985). Attachment of people to companion animals. *Vet. Clin. North Am. Small Anim. Pract.* **15**, 289–295.

Von Kreisler, K. (1997). "The Compassion of Animals." Prima Publishing Co., Rocklin, CA.

Wishon, P. M. (1989). Disease and injury from companion animals. *Early Child Dev. Care* **46**, 31–38.

CHAPTER 10

Animals in the Lives of Children

GAIL F. MELSON AND AUBREY H. FINE
Purdue University, California State Polytechnic University

All therapeutic interventions involving animals rest on a powerful assumption: There is something about animals that powerfully attracts and motivates humans. This assumption seems particularly compelling when children are involved. This chapter examines this assumption closely. First, we document the pervasiveness of animals, both real and symbolic, in children's lives. Second, we ask what the presence of such animals might mean for development. As a guide, we draw on four helpful conceptual approaches: psychodynamic, relational and self-psychologies, ecological psychology, and the biophilia hypothesis. We consider how existing research might support and also challenge hypotheses drawn from these approaches. Because well-designed research studies are limited, studies to date raise questions more than they provide answers. Finally, we use both conceptual frameworks and existing research to suggest implications for therapeutic practice with children and their families. (In doing so, we draw on case examples from the clinical practice of the second author, AHF.) Throughout this essay, we emphasize the importance of considering both children and animals within family systems and, when AAT occurs, within therapeutic systems. As children develop, they are embedded within complex social systems, the most important of which is the family. When

Handbook on Animal-Assisted Therapy: Theoretical Foundations and Guidelines for Practice, 2e

animals are added, both child and animal become part of a dynamic system, which almost always includes at least one adult (Melson, 2006). We must consider the entire system when we ask: What is the significance of animals in children's lives?

I. WHERE ARE ANIMALS IN CHILDREN'S LIVES?

The world of childhood in contemporary Western societies is "peopled" with animals. Overall in the United States, pet ownership rates are high; 62% of American households had one or more resident animals in 2002 (APPMA, 2003). Dogs and cats are found in at least one out of every three households. Among families with children under 18 years of age, 76% were pet owners in 2002, and most families report more than one pet. Thus, pets are more likely to be found in households with children than in any other household type (APPMA, 2003). Moreover, based on surveys, most parents acquire animals "for the children" in the belief that pets teach lessons of responsibility and nurturing while providing companionship and love (Melson, 2001). According to parents, children maintain high levels of daily involvement in caring for and playing with family pets as the children grow from preschoolers to teens, even though children's (human) family time decreases as they age (Melson and Fogel, 1996). While children's own attachments to pets vary depending on many factors, in general, children report a strong bond with at least one resident animal.

The demographics of pet ownership become more striking when juxtaposed with the changing demographics of human family structure. Since the Baby Boom generation, within-home family size has been shrinking, as declining birth rates and rising divorce rates strip away additional children and adults from the household. To be sure, children have been adding "sometime" family ties—noncustodial parents, half-siblings, stepparents, longer living grandparents—but they often juggle commitments within and outside the family. When we search for affective bonds present 24/7 for children within their homes, pets may well be the most available.

Beyond pets in the home, children encounter animals in their classrooms, especially in the early years of school. A survey of 431 Indiana public elementary school teachers found that over a quarter (26.1%) had resident pets in their classrooms, while an additional 46% had animal "visitors" (Rud and Beck, 2003). Teachers who incorporated animals in their classrooms echoed pet-owning parents in extolling the benefits of fish, rabbits, gerbils, hamsters, and other "pocket pets" in teaching children responsibility and caring, providing enjoyment, and generally enhancing children's psychological well-being. Given the pervasiveness of pets in children's homes, it is not surprising that teachers view animals as lending their classroom a more "homey" atmosphere.

Children's encounters with animals are not limited to those species kept as pets. Although children's everyday contact with wildlife has been shrinking as Western societies become more urbanized, what one might call *intentional wildlife experiences* persist. Families and schools set up birdfeeders, take children to zoos and aquariums, and organize nature walks in parks. For example, the American Zoo and Aquarium Association (AZA) estimates that AZA-accredited zoos and aquariums draw more visitors—disproportionately families and groups with children—than the NFL, NBA, and major league baseball combined (www.aza.org).

The animal world of children extends beyond direct contact with living animals to encompass mediated exposure through print, audio, and visual media such as Animal Planet. This involvement is gaining in importance; for many children, it is the dominant mode of gaining knowledge about wild animals. For example, in one study of rural 8- to 14-year olds living next to a national park and protected wilderness, over 60% said they had seen more animals on television and in the movies than in the wild (Nabhan and Trimble, 1994).

Finally, anyone who remembers childhood is likely to recall fanciful animal characters—Peter Rabbit, Barney the dinosaur, Curious George, or Nemo the clownfish. Children's picture books, stories, toys, games, and media are saturated with animal symbols, reflecting, in part, the cultural assumption that animals and children naturally go together. Thus, when Swedish, Hungarian, and Chinese researchers wanted to examine how 6- and 7-year olds in their cultures made up stories, they asked each child to tell a story about a dog (Carlsson *et al.*, 2001). There is also ample evidence from children themselves of interest in animals. For example, in a study of 8- to 13-year-old Dutch children's Internet use, "seeking information about animals" was one of the four most common descriptions of positive experiences with the Internet (Valkenburg and Soeters, 2001). In sum, wherever one looks, animals, particularly those species kept as pets, are an integral part of children's lives.

II. WHAT DO ANIMALS MEAN IN CHILDREN'S LIVES?

The pervasiveness of animals—pets, wildlife, and story characters—raises the question of their significance. A number of conceptual frameworks are helpful in suggesting some answers. These answers (more cautiously, one might call them clues) have implications for animal-assisted therapy (AAT) with children.

A. Psychodynamic Theories

Freud (1965) was struck by children's fascination with animals, noting how frequently animals appeared in the dreams of children (and adults). For him, animal figures represented projections of powerful adults, usually parents, who were too threatening to the child to pop up undisguised in the dream world. From a psychoanalytic perspective, children and animals share a natural kinship, as biological urges rather than human reason holds sway over both of them. Even more than Freud, Jung stressed that animal symbols often express facets of the self. As one Jungian psychologist argued, "The self is often symbolized as an animal, representing our instinctive nature and its connectedness with one's surroundings" (von Franz, 1972).

Such was the frequency of animal imagery in children's dreams and associations that psychoanalytically oriented psychologists developed a variety of projective tests using animal images for children and even for the purported "inner child" of adult patients. One of the latest versions is the animal attribution storytelling technique (Arad, 2004), in which family members assign an animal counterpart to each member of the family and then tell a short story about the animal protagonists. The technique has been applied to family therapy with families that have a child diagnosed with conduct disorder or ADHD; according to its developer, "the animal name attribution to family members creates a fun, non-threatening atmosphere that helps to promote the description of personality traits and interpersonal relationships through the various animal counterparts" (p. 249).

Play therapists often advocate the use of animal toys. A recently developed therapeutic technique, "My family as animals," was designed "to interest and maintain the attention of children so that therapists will become more comfortable with the presence of young ones in the room" (Rio, 2001).

There are many therapists who employ animal puppets in their work with children. It appears that most children relate more easily to animal puppets and seem to open up more naturally. Perhaps this is due to the nature of the puppets, as children do not see them as an extension of themselves. Fine (2005) and Fine and Lee (1996) recommend that clinicians utilizing this modality consider incorporating animal puppets in their work because such puppets could be considered less threatening than human representations. It appears that children can act out their conscious and unconscious feelings more freely with animal versus human figures (Fine, 2005).

Fine (2005) reports that puppetry can be quite clinically revealing, especially as it relates to observing how clients select their puppets and how they act with them. Specific themes can be played out that relate directly to the challenges a child is experiencing. Fine and Lee (1999) point out that while observing the child during puppet play, the clinician can develop a clearer diagnostic understanding of the child. The medium of puppetry can help the child verbalize certain conscious-associated feelings or act out unconscious feelings, thereby relieving underlying tensions. For example, Adam (all client names have been changed to protect confidentiality) is a 6-year-old boy who has a mild learning disability. He was referred for therapy because of being constantly bullied by others and feeling left out. An aspect of his cognitive therapy was AAT. He responded well to the animals in the office, especially the young golden retriever. At times puppets were also integrated, and he felt very comfortable when the therapist presented a group of animal puppets. In fact, several of the puppets had been purchased because of their similarities to the therapy animals within the practice.

Clinically, it was diagnostically fascinating to observe how Adam selected specific animal puppets. Although traditionally gentle in nature in the office, when the medium of puppetry was applied, he acted out aggressively toward the therapist's puppets. Growls and hostile tone accompanied his actions. It soon became apparent that his behavior in the play session was cathartic, allowing him to vent his frustrations in a constructive manner. Outside the therapy context, in his classroom, playground, and other settings, he was always being picked on. Within this session, he was rebelling against his victimization by acting out. When the therapist redirected the session, he had his puppet reveal hurt feelings and beg the other puppet to exhibit kindness. Immediately, Adam's puppet acted more compassionately and became more accepting. The puppet session led to a discussion of how to handle bullies. The medium provided an excellent entry into this discussion, allowing Adam to feel less threatened about confronting his feelings.

Bibliotherapy, especially books about animals, can be an effective adjunct to traditional AAT (Fine and Lee, 1996). The reading materials may serve as a springboard for discussing sensitive issues "while at the same time giving the child an opportunity to explore these issues in an indirect and more comfortable manner" (Fine and Lee, 1999, p. 261). There are many books on subjects ranging from death to divorce that have animals as their main characters. The indirect use of the animals as stand-ins for the self and other humans makes these books easy to read and follow without arousing the child's defenses. Appropriate books can be found through a variety of sources, including searches on the Internet and resource books such as the Bookfinder, published by the American Guidance Services.

Implications for AAT

Because animals slip under the radar of human defense mechanisms, an animal presence in the therapeutic setting, either direct or indirect (e.g., as a story character), may help open a window into the person's or family's underlying issues. However, a skilled therapist is required to help the client make sense of this "unleashed" (if one may permit the pun) material. Moreover, psychodynamic theory cannot specify the forms of animal contact considered most helpful in various circumstances. Would a therapist's dog in the therapy room be preferred to a storytelling exercise involving animal characters? When and under what circumstances?

Clinically, the answers to these questions are complex. For some children, the live animal will be an appropriate therapeutic choice, whereas for other clients, storytelling or perhaps puppetry will be a powerful alternative. Fine (2005) suggested that both of these two alternatives—living animals and symbolic representations—seem to fit naturally in a practice that is centered on AAT or animal-assisted intervention. Clinical experience suggests that child clients readily accept approaches that involve animals, but the specific modality and approach must be individualized.

Another implication of the psychodynamic approach for AAT stems from the view that children are instinctively drawn to animals because both are subject to the sway of id, biological urges untamed by the strictures of civilization. As Freud (1980) put it: "The child unhesitatingly attributes full equality to animals; he probably feels himself more closely related to the animal than to the undoubtedly mysterious adult, in the freedom with which he acknowledges his needs." Thus, Boris Levinson (1997), the great pioneer of animals within child therapy contexts, liked to observe child clients as they watched Jingles, the dog Levinson dubbed his "cotherapist." Jingles went about being a dog, therapy or no therapy—shedding fur, taking a nap, licking his genitals, and slopping up water from his dish. How children responded to this essential dogginess gave Levinson clues to the internal struggles being fought.

Having several animals in my practice (AHF), I find this previous comment particularly apposite. On various occasions, all of the animals have acted in ways that generate a smile, laughter, or an endearing feeling. For example, when the birds begin to talk to the clients, it often catches them off guard. Snowflake, an umbrella cockatoo, tends to greet clients when they enter the room with a soft "hi." The greeting usually prompts children to head toward the bird and to begin a conversation. The cockatoos frequently act in mischievous ways. Periodically, they sneak off their perches and wander to a nearby computer. When not monitored closely, they have pecked off all the keys of the computer keyboard, while the therapy dogs sat and watched. (Surprisingly, the keyboards were not destroyed and could be reassembled quite easily.) Children have been easily amused by the behaviors of the birds. Such incidents illustrate the role that animal behavior can play in providing moments of humor and distraction. What appears to be animal "misbehavior" can provide an opening for discussion of a child's feelings of "badness."

B. Relational and Self-Psychologies

Social connections were of paramount importance for psychologists such as George Herbert Mead and Charles H. Cooley, who argued that a child's sense of self and indeed all thought and emotion emerge through relationships with others, called "objects" by object psychologists such as Margaret Mahler and Heinz Kohut. Cooley coined the term "looking glass self" to capture how the self is built from the qualities seen reflected in the eyes of others. Among the interpersonal experiences that these relational and self-psychologists contended were building blocks for a cohesive and balanced sense of self were mirroring (feeling recognized and affirmed), merging (feeling one with another), adversary (being able to assert oneself against an available and responsive other), efficacy (feeling able to elicit a response from the other), and vitalizing (feeling the other is attuned to one's shifting moods) (Wolf, 1994). It was assumed that only other humans were eligible to provide such relationship benefits. However, more recent research finds that many children report these building blocks in their relationships with their pets (Melson, 2001). Thus, the range of "self–object" experiences now includes other species, not just human–human bonds.

Attachment theory singles out one type of relationship as particularly significant. In the secure attachment relationship, another individual provides the child with a sense of security and safety, particularly under conditions of perceived threat. The founding father, John Bowlby (1969), and mother, Mary Ainsworth (1979), of attachment theory began with the assumption that mothers were the primary attachment figures, but since then, attachment theory and research gradually have expanded the list of potential "attachment objects" to fathers, older siblings, grandparents, and child care providers, among others. Human–animal bond researchers have suggested that pets can sometimes function as attachment "objects" for children (Melson, 1991) by giving them as sense of reassurance, calm, and security.

Implications for AAT

A cornerstone of relational and self-psychologies is that only *relationships*, as contrasted to interactions or contacts, contribute to the self. Thus, children must develop an ongoing relationship with a specific individual animal before these "building blocks" of self can be activated. The ingredients of relationship involve commitment over time. Moreover, specific qualities of a relationship predict which building blocks can come into play. For example, children are most likely to develop a secure attachment bond to another when, over an extended period, that individual has been promptly responsive to the child's needs (Ainsworth, 1979). Beyond that, it is unclear how long, broad, and deep contacts with another individual need to be for a therapeutic relationship to emerge. This poses challenges for AAT, which generally lasts for a limited period per session over a limited number of sessions. The more limited the contact with an individual animal or the more different animals participate interchangeably, the less likely building blocks of self will emerge.

Some self–object experiences—merging, vitalizing, and secure attachment—may be more likely with animal species such as dogs that are highly responsive to humans (and within species, individuals who are most responsive). However, the well-known human propensity to anthropomorphize animals—think of a child looking at a fish in an aquarium and exclaiming, "He likes me!"—might make self–object experiences even more likely with animals than with humans!

C. Ecological Systems Psychology

This perspective emphasizes the importance of contexts of development, radiating outward from the most intimate—the family—to neighborhood, school, region, and culture (Bronfenbrenner, 1979). In this view, a nuanced, multilayered depiction of children's environments is as essential as a detailed anatomy of a child's internal physiology and psychology. In other words, we understand children "from the outside in" as well as "from the inside out." Like relationship psychologists, ecological systems view relationships as important within all the settings of a child's many worlds. However, relationships themselves do not tell the whole story. A detailed description of physical contexts is also needed.

The term "systems" signifies that contexts are interrelated so that one context affects every other, forming a system of interacting parts. Thus, families are affected by (and contribute to) the neighborhood crime rate, which city and regional law enforcement policies also influence. While the immediate family is of primary importance as a context for child development, ecological approaches also focus on school, peer groups, neighborhood play groups, religious settings, after-school activities, and extended family members. From these contexts, individuals draw their *social network*, all those with whom they interact regularly (Cochran *et al.*, 1990). This social network, in turn, provides the potential for *social support*, the provision of material, psychological, informational, and practical assistance (Cohen and McKay, 1984). Hundreds of studies have documented the power of social support to help both adults and children weather stress. Social support shows up as a strong predictor of everything from adults' recovery from stroke, cancer, and heart attacks to children's risk of abuse and their success in school. Why is social support so potent? Researchers believe that when we receive social support, we feel loved, accepted unconditionally, esteemed, and interconnected. These feelings, more than practical assistance, such as a loan, or information, such as a doctor referral, are the "magic bullet" of social support in ameliorating stress.

Despite the fact that social support research studies usually ask only about "the people in your life who support you," evidence shows that many children turn to pets for reassurance and a sense of emotional support during stress. In interviews with German fourth graders, 79% said that when they were sad, they sought out their pets (Rost and Hartmann, 1994). A study of Michigan youngsters 10 to 14 years old found that when they were upset, 75% turned to their pets (Covert *et al.*, 1985). Pet-owning preschoolers in Indiana about to enter public school were less likely to be anxious and withdrawn during that transition if they turned to their pets for support when they were feeling sad or angry (Melson and Schwarz, 1994). Some children in residential therapeutic settings with animals reported that when they needed comforting, they sought out resident animals to talk to, touch, or just be near (Mallon, 1994).

In Chapter 15, Gorczyca and colleagues cite Bronfrenbrenner's ecological model and explain how animals complement and support the lives of persons with AIDS. It is within the microsystem of the family that animals may play the most crucial role, as children tend to view their pets as a peer or family member (Nebbe, 1991). The ready availability of companion animals means that they can provide a feeling of support and compassion when humans are unable to or are unavailable. In addition, because pets generally have shorter life spans than human family members, children are likely to witness important life cycle events, such as birth, serious illness, and death, through experiences with family pets.

1. Helping Children Cope with Animal Loss

When clinicians have a good understanding of the human–animal bond, they may be more likely to lend sensitive support to children and other family members coping with animal loss. Nieburg and Fischer (1996) point out that the death of a pet is usually a child's first experience with loss. It is crucial that the animal's illness or eventual death is explained to children truthfully and sensitively. Therapists and parents should allow children to share their feelings about their loss. Clinicians should help children express their grief and let them realize that it is a natural emotion.

Unfortunately, some parents try to hide information about an animal's illness and death, particularly when the pet is euthanized, out of desire to "protect" their child from an upsetting loss. Clinically, this is not a good option. Nieburg and Fischer (1996) point out that children have active imaginations and may fantasize about the death of their pet in a manner much worse than what really happened. The writers strongly recommend that parents not be afraid of answering children's questions, but use simple, clear, and accurate information so the child does not get overwhelmed or confused. Phrases such as "putting to sleep" can confuse young children and even scare them as they prepare to go to bed at night.

During the grieving process, family members at various age levels will react differently. Children 2 to 5 years old have an inaccurate understanding of death, viewing the process as reversible. They may still wait for the animal to return back to life. As children enter the concrete operations stage, at about age 7, according to Piagetian theory, they begin to see death as final and irreversible. It is important for families to allow the child to be bereaved and to express loss. For example, if the child wants to have a burial ceremony, parents should respect the child's wishes. These rituals may help resolve the loss (Probst, 1998).

There are many therapeutic interventions appropriate for families who are experiencing a loss of an animal. As noted earlier, reading books about pet loss is one comforting alternative to consider. Books such as "I'll Always Love You" (Wilhelm, 1988), "Lifetimes" (Mellonie, 1983), "Dog Heaven" (Rylant, 1995), and "Cat Heaven" (Rylant, 1997) are valuable resources to begin discussing death with younger children. Databases such as the Bookfinder or other bibliographic searches are useful in order to find other resources. Art activities and other mediums, such as scrapbooking or journaling, are also dynamic and sensitive techniques to help support children. Finally, within many communities throughout the country, humane societies offer support groups for pet loss. Some universities also have "hotlines" to call for guidance and emotional support.

2. Animals in the Family System

Another tenet of ecological systems psychology holds that within a single context, all relationships and elements interact in what is called a "dynamic system." Thus, a child's relationship with a parent is affected by (and affects) the mother–father tie, sibling bonds, and the child's relationship with the other parent. Because of this web of mutual influence, family systems therapy considers a child entering therapy as the "presenting problem" of the family system and generally insists on working with all family members, as therapeutic intervention must be at the level of the family system. Most therapists work on the assumption that all members of the family system are human beings.

It may surprise the reader to learn that, with few exceptions, descriptions of children's ecologies or their family systems remain restricted to an inventory of human–human ties, despite the prevalence of pets in households with children, the ubiquity of animals in children's lives, and the evidence that animals often function as social support. In part, these blinders derive from a persistent "humanocentric" perspective that recognizes only intraspecies contacts as significant. Melson (2001) has argued that a paradigm shift to a "biocentric" approach, which encompasses other species and the natural world, is needed.

With such a biocentric perspective, one notes that the majority of pet owners say they consider their animals to be "family members." This does not (usually) mean that parents value the family gerbil, bird, or cat as much as their children, but their use of "family member" to describe the animal is not just a figure of speech either. It is likely that pets are drawn into the web of intersecting relationships that make up a family system. In a pioneering study, Cain (1983) reported frequent use of "triangling" with pets in the family systems of 60 pet-owning families. Triangling occurs when two family members transfer intense interpersonal feelings onto another family member. Thus, a father might yell at the dog when he was angry with his wife, a mother might say something to the cat that her daughter would overhear, or two pets would begin fighting when family members are distant or tense.

3. Implications for AAT

Therapeutic interventions from a family systems perspective would do well to follow Cain's (1983) lead and consider family pets or other animals as part of that system. Where possible and appropriate, home observation might reveal patterns ripe for therapeutic interpretation. When the animals in the therapy room are similar to those a child has at home, these animals may "trigger" associations to themes involving the family pet and other (human) family members.

For example (from a clinical case in AHF's practice), a client with a language processing disorder was frequently overheard saying, "I wish my dog would listen as well as yours." This became a springboard for future discussions about why he felt his dog did not listen as well. He eventually explained that his father was not as friendly with the dog as the boy wished. He would describe how his father gave very little attention to the family dog and only barked out orders when convenient to him. When children recount episodes such as this about their animals at home, they also may reveal information about their relationships with other family members or the climate within the home. Returning to the previous example, it was common for this young man to disclose similarities between himself and the dog in relation to his father. It appeared that his dad frequently ignored him and gave both him and the dog limited attention. Once the boy disclosed these feelings, I (AHF) spent time reflecting how he felt and talking about his desire to get his father's approval and positive attention. At the end of one session, the client looked at one of the golden retrievers who sat next to him and stated, "When you give them love and attention, they grow up stable and loving like your dogs."

As the aforementioned example illustrates, a systems approach prevents us from considering the child in isolation. Whatever we learn about a child's relationships with animals must be integrated with knowledge about human–human ties. It is still unclear whether a close bond with a pet functions as a compensatory relationship when human bonds are frayed. Another possibility is that interspecies and intraspecies ties tend to be positively correlated. This would mean that children with strong parental bonds and good peer relations would be more likely to respond positively to animals, whether their own or a therapy animal. A child's sense of support from a pet's presence or behavior may be a reflection of the child's social skills, empathy, or social adjustment.

D. The Biophilia Hypothesis

This idea, first advanced by the biologist E. O. Wilson, suggests that a predisposition to attune to animal life is part of the human evolutionary heritage, a product of our coevolution as omnivores with the animals and plants on which our survival depends (Kellert and Wilson, 1993; Wilson, 1984). Biophilia implies not a love of animals but simply an innate interest in living things. During human evolution, this interest was fueled not only by the need to consume animals and plants for food and clothing but also because animals served as sentinels of the environment. Some animals (poisonous snakes, lions, bears) might pose a direct danger to humans or compete with humans for food and use of an environment (Barrett, 2005). Animal behavior also was diagnostic of environmental conditions: birds circling lazily in the sky or cows grazing contentedly function much like clear blue skies in telling us that environmental threats are absent. Like darkening clouds, the alarm cries of other animals communicate a nearby danger.

As with other aspects of evolutionary psychology, the biophilia hypothesis recognizes that environmental and cultural influences, the "nurture" of the "nature/nurture debate," shape and channel the expression of biophilia (Kahn, 1997, 1999). Thus, the biophilia hypothesis is consistent with evidence of children's abuse of, fear of, and dislike for animals, as well as children's attachment to their pets and fascination with wildlife and dinosaurs.

The biophilia hypothesis that we evolved to respond to animals as environmental sentinels of danger or safety implies that friendly, calm animals are likely to have a calming effect upon human mood, while agitated, aggressive animals are likely to have the opposite effect. There is some evidence to support this view. Watching, for only 10 minutes, tropical fish swimming in an aquarium was shown to be as effective as hypnosis in reducing the anxiety and discomfort of adult patients about to undergo dental surgery (Beck and Katcher, 1996). Children ages 9 to 16 who sit quietly next to a friendly dog have lower heart rates and blood pressure than when sitting alone. When the child is asked to read aloud some poetry, heart rate and blood pressure predictably rise, but when the dog is present, the increase is significantly lower than when the child is reading alone (Friedmann *et al.*, 1983). Healthy children who undergo a simulated physical medical examination in the presence of a friendly dog versus without an animal present have less behavioral distress (Nagergost *et al.*, 1997).

Implications for AAT

The biophilia hypothesis provides a powerful rationale for including animals in a therapeutic context. If the hypothesis is correct, children are more likely to notice and respond to animals than other items, such as toys or dolls. In other words, animals are predicted to be an attention grabber that may help engage the child. Fine (2005) reported incorporating a robotic dog in his practice (an Icybe) to assess how children would respond to the robot in comparison to his therapy dogs. Although the children were initially very curious about the robotic dog, all of them considered it a toy rather than an animal. Unfortunately, the robot did not seem to have any calming effects and, in fact, when it seemed to wander around the office, some of the clients became more active but in an unfocused way. Most clients found it as interesting to watch how the therapy dogs and birds reacted to the Icybe's movements as it was to watch the robot move. In most cases, the animals did not know what to make of the robot and seemed uncomfortable with its random movements. Although research on AAT applications of robotic pet technology is needed, it appears that children tend to perceive robotic pets more as fancy and complex toys than as analogues for living animals. Studies of children's behavior toward and perceptions of the robot dog AIBO support this conclusion. In a free-play, nonclinical setting, both preschool age and older (7–15 years) children treated the robot dog as a complex artifact and judged its potential as a social companion to be much lower than that of a living dog (Melson *et al.*, 2004, 2005).

A second implication of the biophilia hypothesis is that a friendly animal presence may convey that the therapeutic setting is a safe place. A child may feel calmer and therefore more open to therapeutic intervention. Both the attention-getting and calming components of AAT were documented in a well-controlled "crossover" design study conducted by Aaron Katcher, called the "companionable zoo" (Katcher and Wilkins, 2000). The intervention targeted 12- to 15-year-old boys with severe conduct disorder who were in residential treatment. Half the boys were assigned randomly to the "zoo" and half to an Outward Bound nature program. At the zoo program, boys attended 5 hours of classes weekly. They first learned how to hold and care for the resident rabbits, chinchillas, guinea pigs, iguanas, turtles, doves, finches, cockatiels, goats, and Vietnamese pot-bellied pigs. Only after mastering the biology, characteristics, and care requirements of an animal could a child adopt it as a pet and name it. The child could then earn "skill cards" by learning more about the animal. Field trips to special education classes and rehabilitation hospitals allowed the children to show their animals and demonstrate their expertise in public settings. Two cardinal rules reigned at the zoo: to speak softly and be gentle with the animals and to respect the animals and each other.

After 6 months, "zoo" staff found that remarkably, not a single incident requiring physical restraint occurred. (On the basis of the boys' histories, the staff expected that these boys would have to be physically restrained because of conduct disorder 35 times over a 6-month period.) Behaviors at the "zoo"—nurturing, affection, play, lowered aggression, peer cooperation, accepting responsibility, teaching others, and responding to adult authority—were in sharp contrast to the boys' problematic profiles. For the boys who were attending the Outward Bound program, however, aggression did not diminish and rates of physical restraint held steady. Katcher and Wilkins report that in subsequent replications over a 6-year period at three other treatment centers, staff members have never reported an incident requiring physical restraint (Katcher and Wilkins, 2000). Thus, this intensive, supervised animal care experiment produced greater focused attention and calming in these boys with severe emotional and behavioral disorders.

Fine and Eisen (in press) discuss several case examples of how animals help cultivate a more accepting environment. The following are some clinical case notes from a session with a child in AHF's practice.

> Mary is an 11-year-old who has been diagnosed with a bipolar disorder. She often arrives for her weekly visit bursting with anger. For years she has been the brunt of everyone's jokes and feels like an outcast in school. On one of her therapy sessions she enters the office ranting at her parents and myself. "I want to go home! I told you I didn't want to come today. I'm tired and fed up with everybody! What can you do anyways? You cannot stop them from bugging me! They aren't fair. Everyone blames me for the problems. They always just start up with me."
>
> It takes a while until she is convinced to walk back to one of the therapy rooms. Once she leaves the waiting room, Mary's anger continues to fester. She is resistant to conversation and avoids our discussion by covering her face with her hands. Although one can sense her irritation and frustration, you begin to wonder if she is trying to provoke a confrontation deliberately. Is she hoping to alienate me, and, therefore, build more walls? Being unpopular and being aware of it is hard for her, or any child, to cope with. She sits with her head down, hopeless of any resolution. She doesn't want to talk, and only tears and the sound of sobbing can be heard throughout my office.

> Luckily, PJ, one of the therapy dogs, is around and engages Mary by resting her head in Mary's lap. Mary resists PJ's affection and so PJ trots over to her bed. But PJ's big brown eyes are tranquilizing and inviting, even from across the room. Mary walks over to PJ's bed and curls up next to her. This outcome usually doesn't occur and I decide to sit and just watch what will occur. Mary is like a child holding onto a beloved teddy bear, and PJ seems to sense Mary's pain and lies still as she is being held. Her brown eyes gaze into Mary's and for the next few moments they communicate in silence. Not a word is said between them, but in their silence comfort is found. I allow this contact to continue for several minutes. Finally, I join them and sit down on the carpet nearby. I speak to her of loneliness and feeling left out. At first my voice is the only one heard, but as I began to chip away at her barriers, she opens up. She never leaves PJ's side, on the bed, but with PJ's help I am able to help Mary open up and verbalize some of her feelings of demoralization and loneliness. "Why me, why me?" she repeats out loud. "Even when I try, they never give me a chance. The teachers never believe me when I complain. They always take the other kids' side." I listen without commenting, allowing Mary the opportunity to vent now that she is calm and acknowledge my presence as a sounding board rather than an antagonist. The session proves more productive than I anticipated, but we still have much more to resolve.

Fine, in Chapter 9, discusses how a therapeutic office is altered by having animals present. From a clinical standpoint, fish tanks, vivariums, terrariums, and plants are all ingredients that promote a sense of relaxation. Although discussed in the context of milieu therapy, the biophilia orientation contributes to understanding why these alternatives work. All of these options introduce elements of the living environment into the built environment of an office, thereby making it more appealing. This "greener" milieu may help generate conversations about birth, the food chain, gentleness, or aggression because of the presence of animals and other living things.

However, the biophilia hypothesis sounds a cautionary note to those who hope that contact with animals will generalize to positive changes when children are in other contexts. Biophilia predicts only transient mood changes when in the presence of animals and other living things but does not predict long-term changes, particularly when animals are no longer there. In the companionable zoo experiment, boys attending the "zoo" continued to struggle with aggression and conduct disorder in their dorms, classrooms, and other activities. Only toward the end of the 6-month program did regular classroom teachers (who did not know the boys' group assignments) note lowered aggression in that context and dorm counselors find that episodes of out-of-control behavior in the dorms began to decline. Thus, generalization to contexts where animals were not present was slow to happen, even while children were participating in the intervention. Moreover, the "crossover" design switched the groups after 6 months; those who had been at the "zoo" now entered the Outward Bound program, whereas those who had been in Outward Bound began attending the "zoo." Once out of the AAT environment of the "zoo," the symptoms of the former "zoo boys" began to worsen. Because of this, Katcher and Wilkins (1998) speculated that any beneficial therapeutic outcomes of AAT may require continuing "doses" of animal presence to maintain children's positive mood and behavior changes.

In addition, biophilia does not give priority to animals but sees them as part of the fabric of life, including trees and plants. Therapists who integrate AAT into their practice often also provide a "greener" environment, including houseplants, flowers, and artwork that depicts nature. From a research perspective, changes in the child in such an environment cannot be traced solely to the animals. From the biophilia perspective, there may be multiple routes to attunement to life, with some children more responsive to flora and others to fauna.

Biophilia posits that distressed animals will convey "messages" that the environment is *not* safe and hence may even increase a child's discomfort. This makes the animal's own behavior and temperament all the more important and places special responsibility on the animal's owner (and the therapist) to monitor the animal. Of course, animal welfare concerns mandate vigilance against stressing therapy animals.

III. GENERAL ISSUES FOR AAT WITH CHILDREN AND THEIR FAMILIES

AAT rests on the foundation of animal welfare. Responsible clinicians give equal priority to the welfare of participating animals *and* children. Animal welfare is not limited to issues of good medical care, proper training, and certification as an assistance animal. In addition, as any therapist knows, anyone who has sustained contact with highly stressed populations is at risk of stress and burnout. This makes AAT animals at risk, by definition. When therapists are also owners and enthusiastic about the therapeutic benefits of their animals, the therapist–owner may not always pick up on early signs of stress.

As the field of AAT matures and moves toward "best practices," more attention to individual differences is warranted. The first source of individual differences is the therapy animal. Assuming all animals are certified and not at risk for stress, there remain individual differences in temperament, activity level, size, and so on that may make a particular animal a good or poor choice to interact with a particular child or family. There is currently more art than science to the task of matching animal to client in terms of maximizing AAT treatment benefits.

The second source of individual differences is the child and family. Biophilia recognizes individual differences, as personal history, culture, and upbringing shape our innate interest in life forms. Some children and family members do not respond to animals, have had negative experiences with animals, or are afraid of animals. We can probably locate any human on an approach–avoidance gradient with respect to animals in general or particular animal species. It is likely that individuals who come into AAT with positive predispositions toward animals, especially those similar to the therapy animal, will be more responsive in therapy and will have better outcomes.

Results of the companionable "zoo" study and other data support this hypothesis. Friedmann (2000) found that adults with more positive attitudes toward dogs experienced significantly lower blood pressure when reading aloud in the presence of an unfamiliar dog than adults with more negative attitudes toward dogs. Similarly, among boys who completed the "zoo" experience, there was variation in learning and behavior change. "Zoo" personnel identified "high performers," boys who showed especially high motivation, lots of learning about animals, and particularly gentle, responsive treatment of the animals, as well as "low performers," who were minimally engaged in the "zoo". Although both high and low performers had completed the intervention, the high performers still maintained lower aggression in their regular classrooms 6 months after the "zoo" ended, whereas the low performers had returned to the high preintervention rates of classroom disruption (Katcher and Wilkins, 2000). Thus, the same AAT intervention will have different effects on different children, in part because of the predispositions they bring into the therapy at the outset.

The final source of individual differences to consider is that of the therapist. Beyond the usual variations in training, experience, and skill level, therapists who incorporate AAT may differ in their enthusiasm and commitment to this therapy. Like clients of AAT, therapists who are more motivated are likely to achieve better outcomes. However, one caution that highly motivated AAT therapists might consider is that enthusiasm for AAT, particularly with a "wonderful" therapy animal, perhaps the therapist's own pet, may make it difficult to recognize clients who are unresponsive to AAT or better suited to another type of intervention or, perhaps most difficult for the therapist, simply dislike the therapist's animal. Like everything else that occurs in the therapy room, the therapist's reactions to both positive and negative client behavior toward the therapy animal should be material for therapy supervision. Therapists working in the psychodynamic tradition should be attentive to countertransference processes triggered by clients' treatment of the therapy animal.

In sum, diverse theoretical frameworks provide conceptual underpinning for AAT with children and their families. These frameworks see animals as freeing up repressed thoughts and feelings, providing an affirming and supportive relationship, reflecting the dynamics of the family system, and focusing and calming the child and family in the therapeutic context. However, each framework also suggests cautions and limitations, which may inform the development of "best practices" as AAT continues to expand and become institutionalized.

REFERENCES

Ainsworth, M. (1979). Attachment as related to mother-infant interaction. *In* "Advances in the Study of Behavior" (R. Hinde and J. Rosenblatt, eds.). Academic Press, New York.

APPMA (2003). "2003–2004 APPMA National Pet Owners Survey." APPMA Greenwich, CT.

Arad, D. (2004). If your mother were an animal, what animal would she be? Creating play-stories in family therapy: The animal attribution story-telling technique (AASTT). *Family Proc.* **43**, 249–263.

Barrett, H. C. (2005). Cognitive development and the understanding of animal behavior. *In* "Origins of the Social Mind: Evolutionary Psychology and Child Development" (B. J. Ellis and D. F. Bjorklund, eds.), pp. 438–467. Guilford Press, New York.

Beck, A. M., and Katcher, A. H. (1996). "Between Pets and People: The Importance of Animal Companionship." Purdue University Press, West Lafayette, IN.

Bowlby, J. (1969). "Attachment." Basic Books, New York.

Bronfenbrenner, U. (1979). "The Ecology of Human Development." Harvard University Press, Cambridge, MA.

Cain, A. O. (1983). A study of pets in the family system. *In* "New Perspectives on Our Lives with Companion Animals" (A. H. Katcher, and A. M. Beck, eds.), pp. 72–81. University of Pennsylvania Press, Philadelphia, PA.

Carlsson, M. A., Samuelsson, I. P., Soponyai, A., and Wen, Q. (2001). The dog's tale: Chinese, Hungarian and Swedish children's narrative conventions. *Int. J. Early Years Educ.* **9**, 181–191.

Cochran, M., Larner, M., Riley, D., Gunnarsson, L., and Henderson, C. R., Jr. (eds.). (1990). "Extending Families: The Social Networks of Parents and Their Children." Cambridge University Press, New York.

Cohen, S., and McKay, G. (1984). Social support, stress, and the buffering hypothesis: A theoretical analysis. *In* "Handbook of Psychology and Health" (A. Baum, J. E. Singer, and S. E. Taylor, eds.), pp. 253–267. Erlbaum, Hillsdale, NJ.

Covert, A. M., Whirren, A. P., Keith, J., and Nelson, C. (1985). Pets, early adolescents and families. *Marriage Family Rev.* **8**, 95–108.

Fine, A. H., and Eisen, C. (In press). Afternoons with Puppy: Lessons for Life from a Therapist and his Animals. Purdue University Press, West Lafayette, IN.

Fine, A. H. (2005). "Animal Assisted Therapy and Clinical Practice." Psycho-Legal Associates CEU Meeting, May 2, San Francisco, CA.

Fine, A., and Lee, J. (1996). Broadening the impact of services and recreational therapies. *In* "Therapeutic Recreation for Exceptional Children" (A. Fine and N. Fine, eds.), pp. 243–269. Charles C Thomas, Springfield, IL.

Freud, S. (1965). "The Interpretation of Dreams." Avon/Basic, New York.

Freud, S. (1980). "Totem and Taboo" (trans. James Strachey). Norton, New York.

Friedmann, E. (2000). The animal–human bond: Health and wellness. *In* "Handbook on Animal-Assisted Therapy: Theoretical Foundations and Guidelines for Practice" (A. Fine, ed.). Academic Press, New York.

Friedmann, E., Katcher, A., Thomas, S., Lynch, J., and Messent, P. (1983). Social interaction and blood pressure: Influence of animal companions. *J. Nerv. Ment. Dis.* **171**, 461–465.

Kaduson, H. G., and Schaefer, C. E. (eds.). (2001). "101 More Favorite Play Therapy Techniques." Jason Aronson Inc., Northvale, NJ.
Kahn, P. H., Jr. (1997). Developmental psychology and the biophilia hypothesis: Children's affiliation with nature. *Dev. Rev.* **17**, 1–61.
Kahn, P. H., Jr. (1999). "The Human Relationship with Nature: Development and Culture." MIT Press, Cambridge, MA.
Katcher, A. H., and Wilkins, G. G. (1998). Animal-assisted therapy in the treatment of disruptive behavior disorders in children. *In* "The Environment and Mental Health: A Guide for Clinicians" (A. Lundberg, ed.), pp. 193–204. Erlbaum, Mahwah, NJ.
Katcher, A. H., and Wilkins, G. G. (2000). The centaur's lessons: Therapeutic education through care of animals and nature study. *In* "Handbook on Animal-Assisted Therapy: Theoretical Foundations and Guidelines for Practice" (A. Fine, ed.). Academic Press, New York.
Kellert, S. R., and Wilson, E. O. (eds.). (1993). "The Biophilia Hypothesis." Island Press, Washington, DC.
Levinson, B. (1997). "Pet-Oriented Child Psychotherapy," 2nd Ed. Charles C Thomas, Springfield, IL.
Mellonie, B. (1983). "Lifetimes." Bantam, New York.
Melson, G. F. (2006). Children in the living world: Why animals matter for children's development. *In* "Human Development in the 21st Century: Visionary Policy Ideas from Systems Scientists" (A. Fogel and S. Shanker, eds.). Council on Human Development, Bethesda, MD.
Melson, G. F. (2001). "Why the Wild Things Are: Animals in the Lives of Children." Harvard University Press, Cambridge, MA.
Melson, G. F., and Fogel, A. (1996). Parental perceptions of their children's involvement with household pets. *Anthrozoos* **9**, 95–106.
Melson, G. F., Kahn, P. H., Jr., Beck, A. M., Friedman, B., Roberts, T., and Garrett, E. (2005). Robots as dogs? Children's interactions with the robotic dog AIBO and a live Australian Shepherd. *In* "Extended Abstracts of CHI 2005." ACM Press, New York.
Melson, G. F., Kahn, P. H., Jr., Beck, A. M., Friedman, B., and Roberts, T. (2004). "Children's Understanding of Robotic and Living Dogs." Paper presented to the Tenth International Conference on Human-Animal Interactions, Glasgow, Scotland.
Melson, G. F., and Schwarz, R. (1994). "Pets as Social Supports for Families with Young Children." Paper presented to the annual meeting of the Delta Society, New York City.
Nabhan, G. P., and Trimble, S. (1994). "The Geography of Childhood: Why Children Need Wild Places." Beacon Press, Boston, MA.
Nagergost, S. L., Baun, M. M., Megel, M., and Leibowitz, J. M. (1997). The effects of the presence of a companion animal on physiologic arousal and behavioral distress in children during a physical examination. *J. Pediatr. Nurs.* **12**, 323–330.
Nebbe, L. (1991). The human-animal bond and the elementary school counselor. *School Counsel.* **38**, 362–371.
Nieburg, H., and Fischer, A. (1996). "Pet Loss." Harper Perennial, New York.
Probst, S. (1998). Pet Column for the week of July 13, 1998, Office of Public, College of Veterinary Medicine. Retrieved on August 20, 2005 from http:// www.cvm.uiuc.edu.
Rio, L. M. (2001). "My family as animals": A technique to promote inclusion of children in the family therapy process. *J. Family Psychother.* **12**, 75–85.
Rost, D., and Hartmann, A. (1994). Children and their pets. *Anthrozoos* **7**, 242–254.
Rud, A. G., and Beck, A. M. (2003). Companion animals in Indiana elementary schools. *Anthrozoos* **16**, 241–251.
Rylant, C. (1995). "Dog Heaven." The Blue Sky Press, New York.
Rylant, C. (1997). "Cat Heaven." The Blue Sky Press, New York.

Valkenburg, P. M., and Soeters, K. E. (2001). Children's positive and negative experiences with the Internet: An exploratory survey. *Commun. Res.* **28**, 652–675.

Von Franz, M. L. (1972). The process of individuation. *In* "Man and His Symbol" (C. G. Jung and M.-L. von Franz, eds.), pp. 158–229. Dell, New York.

Wilhelm, H. (1988). "I'll Always Love You." Dragonfly Books, New York.

Wilson, E. O. (1984). "Biophilia." Harvard University Press, Cambridge, MA.

Wolf, E. (1994). Self-object experiences: Development, psychopathology, treatment. *In* "Mahler and Kohut: Perspectives on Development, Psychopathology, and Technique" (S. Kramer and S. Akhtar, eds.), pp. 65–96. Jason Aronson, Northvale, NJ.

CHAPTER 11

A 4-Year Trial of Animal-Assisted Therapy with Public School Special Education Students

AARON KATCHER AND SUE TEUMER
The Our Farm Program, Arlington, Texas 76017

I. INTRODUCTION

The purpose of this chapter is to report the results of an animal-assisted therapy (AAT) and nature study program for children in public school special education. The program was modeled on the one reported in the previous edition of this book and other publications (Katcher and Wilkins 1993, 1998, 2000), which was proven effective in a controlled clinical trial with children with behavior disorders in residential treatment. This chapter describes how the original program was modified to adapt it for public school students and reports results both for the whole special education population and for children with autism, attention deficit hyperactivity disorder (ADHD), and emotional disability (ED). It also draws some conclusions about the problems of bias in measurement, mechanism of the therapeutic effect, the moral obligations to both students and animals that this kind of a program requires, and the value of the program in public school education.

Handbook on Animal-Assisted Therapy: Theoretical Foundations and Guidelines for Practice, 2e

II. PROGRAM METHOD

The teaching program is structured around animals at the farm, nature study, and gardening. Small lesson plans for each animal were generated that contained information about the biological and social needs of the animal, proper method of care, skills required in caregiving, and the rationale for the particular requirements of each animal. There were also similar lesson plans for gardening and nature study. To obtain the privilege of caring for and playing with an animal with relative independence, the child must master these standards and be able to both verbalize the correct answers and demonstrate the requisite skills. For the last several years we have been calling these collections of skills and knowledge "requirements for a license," implying that the child's possession of the right to care for the animal is temporary and needs to be "renewed" from time to time to demonstrate that the skills and knowledge are still present. The "requirements for a license" were the same for all children who were not autistic; however, for the autistic children and those with limited verbal or cognitive skills, the license requirements were modified in several respects. In some instances, the regular license forms were augmented with pictures so that children who did not read and, in some instances, did not speak could decode the pictures and still follow the instructions. The requirement that the child should be able to verbalize the instructions was sometimes relaxed for nonverbal or poorly verbal children.

The second general characteristic of the program is what we call, somewhat pedantically, judicious heuristic anthropomorphism: The definition of the animal as a social other and the relationship between child and animal is a social one, governed by rights and obligations. We assume that the child can decode the animal's signals and anticipate the animal's needs—and as well has a duty to respect them and protect the animal from harm, pain, and excessive fear. We also teach that the child's right to play with the animal derives from his obligation to care for its needs. We also ask the child to draw inferences from the needs of animals to his own needs and the needs of other children and adults.

The program was housed on a working farm and gave services to children from surrounding school districts. Children were bussed to the farm program for one day a week for a 2-hour session. Some children were also seen as part of various after-school programs, but they are not included in the analysis. Almost all of the children were formally designated as being in special education and, as a result, had an individual education plan (IEP).

The farm contained an education building, which housed the small animals, various pens and barns, which sheltered farm animals, an irrigated garden area with raised beds, two permanent ponds, and areas of relative "wilderness," which were used for nature study. On arriving at the farm, children were received in the education building and for a brief period of time sat in a circle and planned the day's activities with the farm's lead teacher and their accompanying aides, teachers, and counselors. Licenses were awarded at this time and other student achievements discussed. The events of the day were varied depending on the season, weather, and new events at the farm. At this time children were helped to decide which license they would work on with the help of the lead teacher, teachers, or other students. At the conclusion of the session there was another meeting in the round to discuss the accomplishments of the day.

The original program (Katcher and Wilkins 1993, 2000) was designed for residential treatment in which the children's school teachers had no interaction with the program. Institution staff that was recruited from residential staff delivered the animal-centered education. At Our Farm, the special education teachers participated actively, both at the farm and back in the children's regular classroom. The teachers were given an evening's orientation to the program in which they played the role of their students and worked briefly with the animals. There were longer courses of orientation offered, but these were attended only by a few interested teachers. For the most part the teachers learned their roles through watching the lead teacher (the coauthor of this chapter) working with the children during their regular visits. Teachers and aids participated to varying degrees: Some were highly enthusiastic and adapted easily to the active kind of more diffusely focused learning experiences at Our Farm, whereas others were more passive, turning more of the work over to the lead teacher and participating only at the request of the children or lead teacher. While it was determined the learning expectations at the farm closely matched the state's educational standards in science, geography, and other subjects as well as the school districts' character development programs, integration of principles learned at the farm into the school program was quite varied. Some teachers were quick to plan joint projects, whereas others did not take advantage of the opportunity. The best integration was achieved with the contained classroom whose regular teachers and aides accompanied the children to the farm program. We also provided children who were taken out of their regular classrooms a chance to participate in "demonstration days" in which the animals were transported to the school and they could show and tell their regular classmates about the animals with some assistance from the teachers.

III. INFORMED CONSENT

All children were referred by their local school districts and sent to the program during the regular school day. The child's parents signed a consent form indicating their willingness for their child to participate in the program and to have the school share information about their child with the program's staff.

An additional consent form was signed to permit the program to take pictures of their children and to share aggregated research data with others. When the child arrived at the program, he or she signed an animal integrity contract that indicated his or her willingness to participate in the program.

IV. RESEARCH METHODOLOGY

For the first year student progress was tracked with the Achenbach TRF (Achenbach, 1991). The classroom teacher completed the baseline measurement of school performance sometime in September. Another measurement was made in the farm school context in November after the teachers who brought the children to the farm school had a chance to observe their initial behavioral adjustment. At the end of the school year, in May or early June, the classroom teacher completed a second inventory for behavior in the classroom. Also around this time the teacher who brought the child to the farm school completed a TRF for his/her comportment at the farm school. Because many of the children were in self-contained classrooms, the same teacher completed evaluations for both regular classroom behavior and behavior at the farm school.

After the first year of the project, the school district switched to the BASC inventory, and to take advantage of teacher training in that method, we switched as well. For the next 3 years the children were tracked with the BASC teacher rating scales (TRF) (Reynolds and Kamphaus, 1998). Children's achievement in the farm school was measured by recording the number of animal licenses they earned during the course of a year's participation.

We also asked the schools to provide us with the children's IEP but were not always successful. In the absence of an IEP we attempted to obtain formal diagnoses by asking teachers and school counselors. Because children frequently had multiple diagnoses, we assigned them to groups for analysis in a way that tended to maximize the size of the most frequent categories. Thus if a child had both ADHD and Tourette's, we assigned him/her to the ADHD group. We had sufficient numbers to do a statistical analysis for autism, ADHD, and ED. For purposes of analysis, all other children were placed in a residual group and analyzed separately. There were a substantial number of children in this latter group that had no formal diagnosis but were sent to the program for problems with classroom socialization.

In addition we accumulated a large volume of qualitative information, including written evaluations of the students' response to the program completed at the end of the year, progress notes written by the project's lead teacher, incident reports, and notes from a formal group evaluation held at the end of the year with the lead teacher from the project and Round Rock special education teachers and one of their psychologists. This chapter reports statistical data and only alludes to the more qualitative material, which is reported elsewhere (Katcher and Teumer, 2005).

There were some problems with the execution of the research methods. We were not successful in obtaining all research data from every student. Teachers left the district at the end of the year and did not complete their evaluations or managed to delay completing the forms so that we could no longer trust the data. As a result we do not have data on every child who was seen in the program, but the only children left out of the analysis were those who lacked the appropriate evaluation.

It was at times difficult to ensure that the teachers completed the evaluations of the students' behavior in the farm school at the farm school and the classroom behavior in their regular classroom. Teachers tended to want to complete them at their convenience. As a result we cannot be sure that data always accurately reflected the students' behavior in each context.

As noted earlier, many students were in self-contained classrooms and one teacher would fill out both evaluations. We were, however, able to test for the effects on the number of raters, and having one or two raters had no significant influence on the magnitude or the distribution of results, but because the children could not be assigned to be evaluated by one or two raters, the results could not be considered definitive.

Data provided by the teachers were entered into a computer and scored with programs provided by the originators of the tests. The statistical analysis employed the SPSS MANOVA program.

V. RESULTS

With the relatively small number of students followed for the entire first year of the program and evaluated with the Achenbach TRF, we found that there were significant changes in total symptom score for both place (farm vs school) and time (first and second administration of the TRF in farm and school environments; see Fig. 1. In the 3 subsequent years children were evaluated with the BASC TRS. The results of children followed for a complete year were pooled for the 3 program years, and we tested for all 19 variables of the BASC TRS and observed a significant effect of place (school vs farm) that was present on both the first and second administrations, but no effect of time (subjects = 95, variables = 19, $F = 9.87$, $P < 0.000$). The effect of place was present and significant for all BASC factor and summary problem scores, but not for the four adaptability scores. The magnitude of the change in the problem score was a t score difference of 6–10 between school and farm for the summary problem scores. The end of school year farm scores were no lower at the end

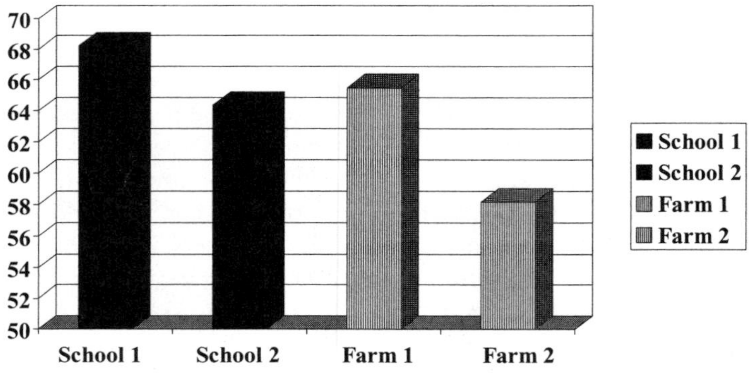

FIGURE 1 Achenbach TRF (total symptom score) of 14 students followed for 1 year at **Our Farm**.

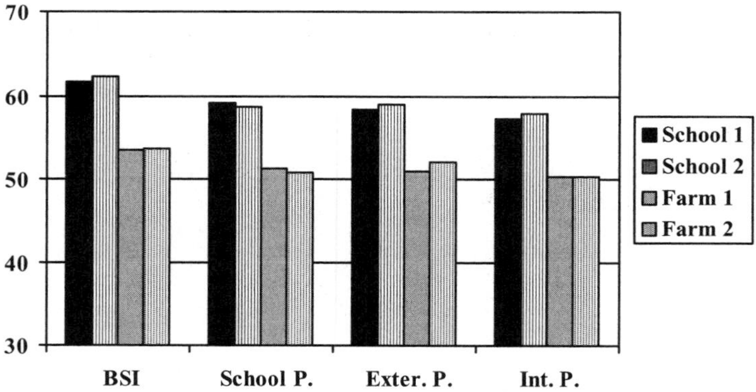

FIGURE 2 All differences for place (school vs farm) were significant at the $P > 0.000$ level. All differences for time were not significant. Subjects were pulled for 3 years that the BASC was used. N = 95.

of the school year than they were at the end of the first term. There was also no change in the school scores—either positive or negative—from the baseline measured in September to the year-end administration given in May (see Fig. 2).

Because there was no improvement in the scores over time from the start to the end of the school year, we could include in our analyses children who were only seen for part of a year. When we looked at the pooled results of the observations for all children for whom we had end of the year measurements,

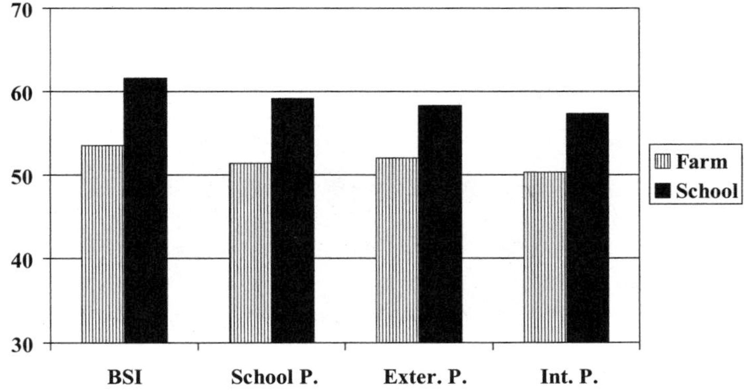

F=94.6, P<0.000 F=106, P<0.000 F= 57.7, P<0.000 F=66.9, P<0.000

FIGURE 3 All children in school and farm environments: end of year contrast BASC summary scores ($N = 163$).

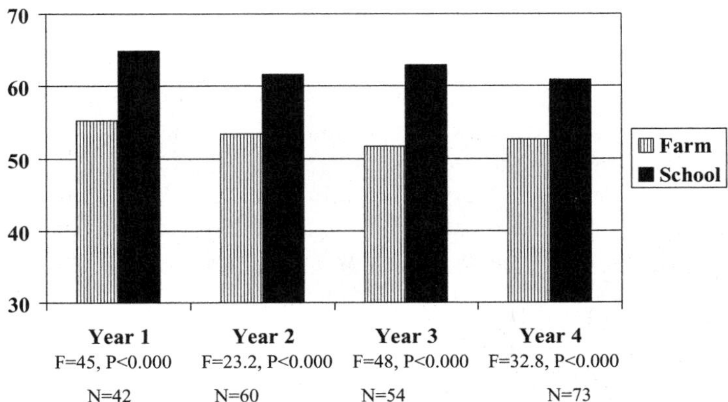

FIGURE 4 Total symptom score in farm and school environments: end of year contrast years (year 1, Achenbach TRF; years 2–4, BASC TRS).

we observed the same differences with place (subjects = 120, variables = 19, $F = 9.23$, $P < 0.000$). All factor scores and problem scores were lower in the farm program compared to the regular classroom, but the adaptability scores did not change significantly for the group considered as a whole. The decrease in symptoms when the child was in the farm program not only was significant for the whole group but was consistently large each year (Fig. 4).

TABLE I Summary Scores in School and Farm Program for Different Diagnostic Groups[a]

	Autism School	Autism Farm	ADHD School	ADHD Farm	ED School	ED Farm	Others School	Others Farm
External problems	57	53**	67	56***	62	53***	64	52***
Internal problems	53	49*	61	50***	60	50***	60	48***
School problems	54	50***	62	51***	62	51***	59	48***
Total problems	57	52**	67	55***	64	52***	64	51***

[a]Farm–school differences significant at $*P < 0.05$, $**P < 0.01$, and $***P < 0.005$. Autism N = 39, ADHD $N = 26$, ED $N = 30$, Others $N = 50$.

We next examined the response of students with autism, who constituted the largest group of students with a single diagnostic category in the program. This high prevalence of students with autism in our group did not represent their frequency among the special education students in the district schools but stemmed from the referral patterns of one school district where the teachers thought that students with autism in contained classrooms were most suitable for the farm program. The MANOVA for the summary problem scores, but not the adaptability scores, was significantly lower in the farm environment compared to the school (subjects = 39, variables = 14, $F = 1.954$, $P < 0.032$). Results for the summary scores for the children with autism are given in Table I. Unlike the other categories of students, their symptom scores are relatively low, with averages being below the "at-risk" level (t score equaling 60 or greater was defined as "at risk") for all of the summary scores. Nonetheless all of the summary scores were significantly lower in the farm environment. The relatively low level of the problem scores is a bit hard to explain, as some of these children were mute and others needed one-to-one attention from an aide. The only factor score that was elevated consistently in these children was the "atypical factor," the one found to be associated most closely with autism by the authors of the BASC system of tests (Reynolds and Kamphaus, 1998). It was the only score in which the average in the school was above the "at-risk" level (defined as a t score of 60 or over). However, the atypical factor score did not decrease significantly in the farm environment. The only factor scores that did were depression, learning problems, and conduct problems (Table II).

The atypical factor was elevated in other diagnostic groups as well as the autistic children. It was almost as great in the children with ADHD. The difference between students with autism and others in their response on the

TABLE II Factor Scores in School and Farm Program for the Different Diagnostic Categories[a]

	ADHD School	ADHD Farm	ED School	ED Farm	Autism School	Autism Farm	Others School	Others Farm
Hyperactivity	64	57**	61	54***	53	50	62	52***
Aggression	67	57***	65	57***	51	48	65	53***
Conduct	65	52***	58	41***	50	46*	60	50***
Anxiety	61	50***	59	47***	51	48	56	48***
Depression	64	54***	63	52***	56	50**	62	52***
Attention problem	63	55***	61	52***	56	50	60	52***
Learning problem	60	48***	61	50***	51	45***	57	44***
Atypical	64	53***	62	50***	66	61	61	48***
Withdrawal	57	53*	60	52**	58	53	60	52**

[a]Farm–school differences significant at $*P < 0.05$, $**P < 0.01$, and $***P < 0.005$. Autism $N = 39$, ADHD $N = 26$, ED $N = 30$, Others $N = 50$.

atypical factor was that in all other diagnostic categories there was a significant decrease in the atypical factor in the farm environment compared to the school. This was true for even the small number of students with Asperger's syndrome we saw in the program (Fig. 5). The highest summary and factor scores in the school program were seen in the ADHD students (Tables I and II); however, there were no significant differences among the diagnostic characteristics of ADHD, ED (Tables I and II), and the residual group of students with various diagnoses or no diagnoses at all other than "social problems." In all of these groups, most of the average summary and factor scores were elevated above the "at-risk" level in school. All of the scores were significantly lower in the farm environment compared with the school.

The BASC teacher rating scale also has factors measuring adaptability. There are factor scores for adaptability, leadership, social skills, and study skills. An adaptability score below 40 is considered to place the child "at risk" by the test authors. For children with ADHD and ED there were significant increases in the adaptation and social skills factor but not in the leadership and study skills factor or the summary adaptability score. For children in the residual category, there were increases in the adaptability factor score and a decrease in the study skills factor score in the farm environment and no significant changes in the other adaptability scores. There were no changes in adaptability in the autistic students (see Table III).

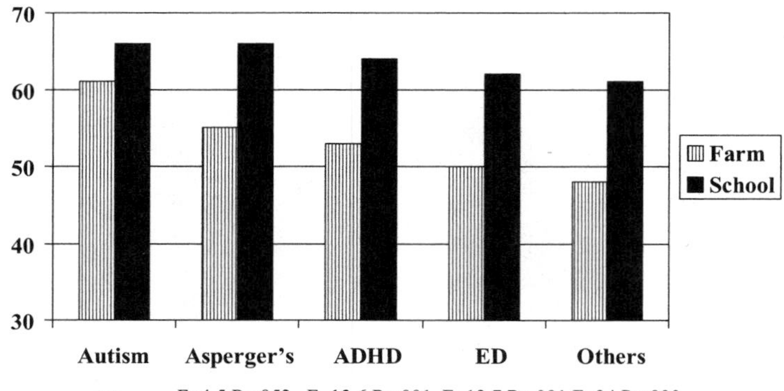

FIGURE 5 Autistic children compared with children with other diagnoses for the BASC atypical scale in school and farm environments.

TABLE III Adaptive Factor Scores[a]

Adaptive scores	Autism School	Autism Farm	ADHD School	ADHD Farm	ED School	ED Farm	Others School	Others Farm
Adaptation	37.3	39	36.5	41.7*	36.7	42.1*	36.5	46.7***
Social skills	37.4	37	41.6	46.1*	44.7	48.3*	43.5	45.2
Leadership	38.5	37.8	40.5	41.7	40	42	42.4	41.8
Study	37	35.8	38.9	38.1	39	39	41	36.7***
Adaptive summary	36.1	36.2	38.1	40.4	40.2	42.7	39.9	40.8

[a]Farm–school differences significant at $*P < 0.05$, $**P < 0.01$, and $***P < 0.005$. Autism N = 39, ADHD N = 26, ED N = 30, others N = 50.

We had only one quantitative measure of success in the farm program: The number of licenses earned during the year. However, there was no relationship between the number of licenses earned and the difference between farm and school scores (Fig. 6). We also kept track (Table IV) of the animals chosen by the students to earn their licenses during the last 2 years of the study. It is of practical interest that reptiles such as the tortoise, bearded dragon, and gecko and birds such the cockatiel were chosen with a frequency just about as high as more conventional "furry" pets such as the rabbit, guinea pig, ferret, and miniature donkey. This suggests that animals lower down the philogenetic tree may have the same therapeutic potential as "anointed" animals such as dogs, cats, and horses.

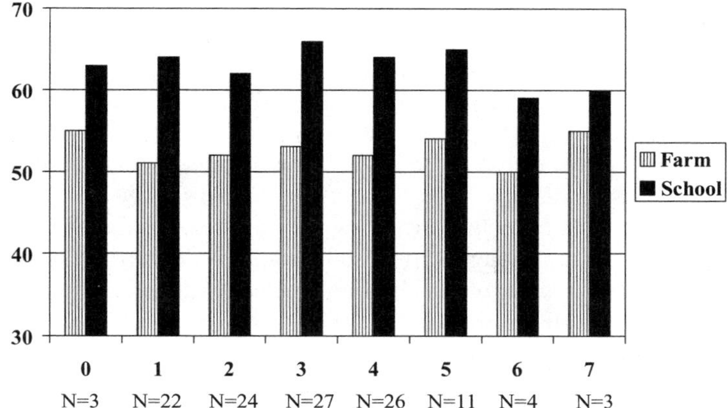

FIGURE 6 For nonautistic children, contrast between farm program and school related to number of licenses earned. End of year contrast for BASC summary score BSI (N = 120).

TABLE IV Frequency with which Children Chose Different Animals to Earn Licenses (2004–2005)

Cockatiel[a]	Gecko[b]	Rabbit[a]	Tortoise[b]	Ferret	Bearded dragon	Barn cat[a]	White tree frog
39	38	37	33	22	20	14	13
Sand boa	Domestic rat[a]	Tropical fish[b]	Conure	Hermit crab			
12	9	8	7	5	1		
Miniature donkey	Pot-bellied pig	Farm pig	Goat[b] pig	Llama	Alpaca		
32	30	15	15	4	2		

[a]Multiple animals same species or breed.
[b]Multiple species or breeds.

VI. DISCUSSION

There are a number of aspects of data that are of interest from a theoretical perspective. The biophilia hypothesis (Beck and Katcher, 1996; Katcher, 2002; Katcher and Wilkins, 1993) holds that our cognitive apparatus is more likely to focus attention outward toward the outside world and less likely to be distracted by an internal thought stream in the presence of a natural environment and animals. This hypothesis is premised on the long history of hunting and gathering that paralleled the development of the brain in our hominid ancestors. We observed in all students, not just the autistic ones, a high frequency of elevated *t* scores on the factor labeled "atypical" in the BASC (Table II). This factor indexes statements such as "babbles to self," "complains about being unable to block out unwanted thoughts," "daydreams," "seems out of touch with reality," "stares blankly," and "repeats one activity over and over." Thus this factor scores indexes being turned away from the immediate environment and engaged by private thoughts. It was elevated not only in autistic and psychotic students but in most of the children in special education, so that paying attention to the outside world while in school seems to be a common problem for almost all special education students. The atypical factor score decreased from school to farm in all categories of students observed except those with autism. That decrease indicates that in the presence of the farm, children are more attentive to their environment and less encapsulated in their own world. As a result, they are more amenable to instruction and learning and have a higher capacity for social interaction. This inference is also supported by the much lower levels of the factor scores for attention problems, learning problems, and the summary score for school problems in the farm environment. To use a metaphysical term, the children could be said to be more "mindful" in the farm program than they are in their regular classrooms. This result is highly compatible with the inference one would make from the biophilia hypothesis.

The nonautistic special education students were perceived by their teachers to be in a state of high negative arousal. Scores for the ADHD children for hyperactivity, aggression, conduct problems, anxiety, and depression were on average at or above the "at-risk" level in their regular classrooms. Scores for the ED children and children in the residual category were only slightly lower. All of these factors decreased significantly in the farm environment. There may be several alternative explanations for the decrease in negative and dysphoric arousal. The farm may have been perceived as less demanding and less threatening than their regular classroom, and this impression would be reinforced by their ability to learn real skills and earn rewards in the farm context. However, if that were the case, we would expect that differences between farm and school would increase over time. Instead there was no significant change between first and second farm measurements. Moreover, we would expect that the children who were rewarded the most as a result of accomplishing more—earning more licenses—would do better, i.e., have larger differences between school and farm. Again this was not the case; when autistic students were eliminated from the comparison, there was no relationship between numbers of licenses earned and school–farm differences. The effects of the farm environment on the children's emotional state and behavior must have been relatively rapid, and the rapidity of change—in the absence of any regression due to a novelty effect wearing off—suggests another cognitive mechanism. When attention is directed outward, there is an immediate decrease in arousal and awareness of symptoms (Katcher *et al.*, 1983). This effect of directing attention outward is the basis of the calming effect of hypnosis, meditation, and mindfulness (Katcher and Wilkins, 1993). If the painful arousal seen in the school environment was not generated by events in the school day but was a result of the children's internal arousal mechanism, based on the salience of past experience; then the program, by making the internal thought stream and its attendant emotion less salient, would be expected to produce the observed effects on arousal. This is another finding that one would have predicted from the biophilia hypothesis.

Although there is considerable and perhaps misguided interest in the use of animals to treat autism within the field of AAT (200,000 hits on an Internet search), there is no evidence that AAT produces any substantial improvement in the behavior of children with autism that persists over time and is manifest outside of the treatment context. This negative conclusion is not remarkable, as most of the treatment programs using AAT have been of very short duration, and autism is a lifelong disorder that requires extended and persistent treatment. This study reports the largest number of autistic students studied with a well-accepted and standardized test measurement. Moreover, the students studied were observed for at least 1 year. We observed a small but statistically significant positive effect of the program on autistic students. We also observed that teachers who had the autistic students in contained classroom were enthusiastic, consistent, and persistent in their evaluation of the farm program. They preferred to have their autistic students at the farm. This shared enthusiasm could have created a positive bias in their evaluation of the student's behavior at the farm. However, it is more probable in view of the consistency of the objective measures employed that the changes were small but real. We would conclude that a farm environment might be an optimal long-term teaching strategy for these children. However, before we would suggest AAT as a viable treatment for autistic children, it would have to be tested against an established treatment method for autism (Strain, 2001).

Bias is always a problem in the study of AAT. In conventional AAT in which the therapist is a volunteer using her own animal or a professional who is identified with AAT, as in the case of most practitioners of equine therapy, the therapist is hopelessly biased (Katcher, 2000). Unless a third party is evaluating the results of the interaction with some kind of an objective measure or at least a defined and well-standardized behavioral checklist, it is difficult to be confident of the results. Even when well-standardized instruments are used, as in the case of this and our previous study, expectancy effects can bias the results.

We know that the teachers liked their time in the farm almost as much as the children. Could they have biased their own reporting, especially in many instances where the same teacher was reporting on the child in both environments? We have negative evidence that the number of raters did not influence the results in an analysis of variance. However, that militates against but does not eliminate the possibility of bias. There is, in fact, no way to eliminate all doubt, as it is not possible to disguise the nature of the treatment. The best one can do is to field a controlled experiment in which some equally attractive activity is contrasted with an animal care and nature study program. That is what we attempted to do in previous research when the AAT program was contrasted with the effect of an Outward Bound–like program (Katcher and Wilkins, 2000).

Previous work emphasized that the largest effect observed was an effect of context, not a change that perpetuated itself across different contexts. In this study the effect of the AAT program was established at the baseline measurement some 2 months after the children started in the program. We observed no increase or decrease in the difference between school and AAT contexts after that time. The simultaneous measurements of contextual difference made at the end of the school year were as great as the sequential baseline measurements. These results indicate a rapidly established effect that was not increased with the passage of time. The questionnaire study of Kuo and Taylor (2004) also suggested that the effect of nature on the behavior of children with ADHD may very well be a rapidly mediated contextual effect.

In our teaching method we used anthropomorphism in a constructive manner, defining the relation between the child and the animal as a social one and asking the child to make inferences about what the animal wants and needs and to reason, back and forth, from the animal to the child. It may be poor ethology, but it is good training in social skills. This study provided the first evidence that in comparison to the classroom, the program increased social skills. To make the definition of the animal as a social animal meaningful to the children, there has to be a real commitment to moral and ethical treatment of the animals. One cannot expect children to think of an animal as a person, equivalent in some very real way to human persons, if the animals are treated cruelly, neglected, or unduly stressed by the students. Proper care of animals is not, however, an easy or inexpensive goal to attain. Animals need to be cared for on weekends and holidays, which requires considerable staff devotion and a proper budget for care outside of school hours. The veterinary bills can be quite large when animals are given optimal care and even larger when heroic measures are used to save a particularly beloved animal. School programs frequently do not budget sufficient funds for animal care and rely on euthanasia to solve problems of small animal illness. In any program where animals are anthropomorphized, it is difficult to answer the question of "How much will we spend on veterinary care for an animal?" It is not the purpose of this chapter to give answers to those problems or even social mechanisms for their solution. What we suggest is that there may be an interdependence of the ethical basis of the program and the outcome of the program.

VII. CONCLUSIONS

1. An environment that permits children in special education to interact with animals and nature decreases the amount and frequency of pathological and disruptive behavior manifested by these students while they are in that environment.
2. Since the children's regular classroom was used as a comparison, it can be said that animal interaction and nature study provide an environment that elicits more adaptive behavior than the constraints imposed by conventional classroom work. This is the first study that demonstrated an increase in adaptive behavior as measured by a standardized instrument.
3. The salutary effects of the program have been seen in all symptom groups studied but are most pronounced in those children who are characterized by symptoms of aggression, hyperactivity, and lack of attention to the environment.
4. The magnitude of the effect observed, a *t* score change in the range of 8 to 12, is comparable to the range of change seen in trials of stimulant medication for ADHD, as well as the range of change observed in a previous study of residential children with ADHD and other behavioral disorders (Katcher and Wilkins, 1993).
5. The improvement in the context of the farm environment was consistent from year to year and across the major diagnostic categories studied, as well as the residual group of children with diagnoses too infrequent to be studied as an independent entity.
6. Autistic students benefit from the environment provided by the farm program. The benefits are small but significant.
7. Programs of this type that teach by defining the animal as a person to whom the participants have duties and obligations are effective in improving social skills and reducing symptoms; however, they demand a highly developed commitment to the animals welfare.

ACKNOWLEDGMENTS

Support for this project was provided by the Animal Therapy Association now located at 727 Tenna Loma Court, Dallas, Texas, 75208. The authors also wish to acknowledge the cooperation of the Round Rock and Taylor I.S.D.

REFERENCES

Achenbach, T. M. (1991). "Manual for the Child Behavior Checklist 14–16 and 1991 Scoring Profile." University of Vermont, Burlington, VT.

Beck, A., and Katcher, A. (1966). "Between Pets and People: The Importance of Animal Companionship." Purdue University Press, West Lafayette, IN.

Katcher, A. (2000). Animal-assisted therapy and the study of human–animal relationships: Context or transitional object? *In* "The Handbook on Animal Assisted Therapy: Theoretical Foundations and Guidelines for Practice" (A. Fine, ed.). Academic Press, New York.

Katcher, A. (2002). Learning to talk people by learning to talk animal. *In* "Children and Nature: Theoretical and Scientific Foundations" (P. Kahn and S. Kellert, eds.). MIT Press, Cambridge.

Katcher, A., Friedmann, E., Beck, A., and Lynch, J. (1983). Looking, talking, and blood pressure: The physiological consequences of interaction with the living environment. *In* "New Perspectives on Our Lives with Companion Animals" (A. Katcher and A. Beck, eds.). University of Pennsylvania Press, Philadelphia, PA.

Katcher, A., and Teumer, S. (2005). A study of 39 autistic children in animal assisted therapy.

Katcher, A., and Wilkins, G. (1993). Dialogue with animals: It's nature and culture. *In* "The Biophilia Hypothesis" (S. Kellert and E. O. Wilson, eds.), pp. 173–200. Island Press, Washington, DC.

Katcher, A., and Wilkins, G. (1998). Animal assisted therapy in the treatment of disruptive behavior disorders. *In* "Environment and Mental Illness" (A. Lundberg, ed.). Lawrence Erlbaum Associates.

Katcher, A., and Wilkins, G. (2000). The centaur's lessons: Therapeutic education through care of animals and nature study. *In* "The Handbook on Animal-Assisted Therapy: Theoretical Foundations and Guidelines for Practice" (A. Fine, ed.). Academic Press, New York.

Kuo, F. E., and Taylor, A. F. (2004). A potential natural treatment for attention-deficit/hyperactivity disorder: Evidence from a national study. *Am. J. Public Health* **94**(9), 1581–1586.

Reynolds, C. R., and Kamphaus, R. W. (1998). "BASC Behavior Assessment System for Children: Manual Including Preschool Norms for Ages 2–6 through 3–11." American Guidance Service, Circle Pines, NM.

Strain, P. (2001). Empirically based social skill intervention: A case for quality-of-life improvement. *Behav. Disord.* **27**(1), 30–36.

CHAPTER 12

Clinical Approaches to Assessing and Utilizing Animal-Related Experiences in Therapeutic Interventions with Children, Adolescents, and Their Caregivers

BARBARA W. BOAT
Department of Psychiatry, University of Cincinnati, Cincinnati, Ohio 45267

I. INTRODUCTION

It has long been recognized by clinicians who work with children and adolescents that the entire family of the "identified patient" is relevant to the intervention whether or not the family members are actually present in the room. Only recently, however, are clinicians becoming aware that animals, especially companion animals, are an integral and important part of the family system as well. As a result, clinicians are beginning to ask about relationships with animals and incorporate aspects of these relationships into their interventions. In most cases there is no direct contact by the clinician with the animal but the animal is, nonetheless, "present" and acknowledged in many ways. Companion animals may be spontaneously described when the child is talking about daily routines or events ("I was late because my dog, Bitsy, hid my shoe," "Mom was mad because I forgot to change my gerbil's litter," "My cat scratched me"). Companion animals may be invoked by children to describe an aspect of themselves ("I'm a real cat lover," "I hate yippy little dogs. My dog is really big").

Frequently, however, the child's experiences that are relevant to the well-being of both the child and the animal go undetected by clinicians because

Handbook on Animal-Assisted Therapy: Theoretical Foundations and Guidelines for Practice, 2e

we do not ask specific questions about animal-related experiences. Typical "screening" questions among mental health providers are often as follows: "Do you have any pets? Oh, you have a dog. That's nice. What is your dog's name? Snoopy? That's a nice name." Thus ends the exploration and conversation about pets in the child's life. Asking focused questions can provide very useful information about the environment that the child and the animal share and be the impetus for developing more effective interventions.

I work in the area of childhood trauma and maltreatment. Not surprisingly, my focus is on early detection of settings where children are at risk for abuse or neglect. Adding the animal dimension to assessment and treatment of children and families has been invaluable in fostering awareness and developing interventions that prevent further victimization of both the child and the pet. This chapter discusses the following:

- Why it is important for clinicians to routinely assess for the child's animal-related experiences.
- Use of a questionnaire to assess for animal-related experiences.
- Clinical examples of interventions that have addressed the animal-related experiences of children and adolescents in the larger context of therapy.

II. WHY IT IS IMPORTANT FOR CLINICIANS TO ROUTINELY ASSESS FOR THE CHILD'S ANIMAL-RELATED EXPERIENCES

A. Most Children Have Pets or Live in Homes Where There Are Pets

A recent survey reports that pets, which can be defined as companion animals that live inside the home with an individual or family and are not used primarily for work purposes, are found in approximately 63% of homes in the United States (American Pet Products Manufacturers Association, 2005). Pet ownership has risen during the past decade from 54 million households to 64.2 million households. Ninety million cats and 74 million dogs are companion animals, an increase of 17 and 18%, respectively, from 1998 to 2005.

Nearly 75% of American families with school-age children have at least one companion animal (Humane Society of the United States, 2004), and the majority of pet-owning households contain children. Indeed, one study found that families with children present were the most likely to own pets (Bulcroft, 1990). In another report, approximately 90% of school children had pets (Kidd and Kidd, 1985). Thus, clinicians who work with children will frequently encounter children who have had experiences with pets.

B. Pets Share the Daily Lives of Household Members

Pets often are considered to be members of the family (Bonas *et al.*, 2000; Cain, 1983; Enders-Slegers, 2000; McNicholas and Collins, 2001; Sable, 1995). In a recent survey, 84% of American pet owners regarded their animals as family members. Forty-one percent of dogs share their owners' beds, as do up to 51% of cats. Americans spent a record $34 billion on pet products and services according to a census bureau tracking of retail sales, exceeding spending on hardware and jewelry (American Pet Products Manufacturers Association, 2005).

Holidays are celebrated by giving pets presents or treats. Birthdays and funerals of pets are memorialized (Davis, 1987; Dresser, 2000; Serpell, 1986). Pet owners have photographs of their pets, and frequently, children are photographed with the family pet. The environment in which the pet lives is usually the same environment in which the child lives. As a result, the clinician is afforded a valuable opportunity to obtain relevant information about the family setting by asking a series of questions about the pets in the household. Thus, I recommend that clinicians seek information from children or teenagers about their experiences with pets and other animals as routinely as we ask about their experiences with siblings or parents or grandparents.

C. Children Often Will Talk about Their Pets' Experiences before They Disclose Their Own Experiences

Children's animal-related experiences are a bonus for the clinician because often children will talk about what happens to pets in their homes more willingly than they will share what happens to other family members, especially to themselves. Because children are less likely to censor the information they give about their pets, they inadvertently reveal incidents or settings that put them at risk for abuse or neglect. A 15-year-old boy was asked if there was a stressful time when his favorite dog had been a source of comfort to him. He replied, "Yeah. After my stepdad beats me, my dog jumps up and licks my tears." The clinician had no idea that the boy's stepdad was beating him.

Sharing the experiences of a pet can become a window on the world that the child inhabits. For example, during a school-based presentation on domestic violence and safety, fourth grade students were asked only one animal-related question: "Do you think your pet is safe at home?" One boy volunteered that he and his older brother each had a cat. He became teary as he shared that his older brother would tease and hurt the younger boy's cat, sometimes strangling it and often throwing the cat at the boy. Then the fourth grader went on to reveal that the older brother would hit and strangle him when their mother was not home. The teacher reported these concerns to the school counselor. Clinicians who do not inquire about animal-related experiences are missing potentially critical information about a child's environment and experiences that place their client at risk for abuse or neglect (Boat *et al.*, 2006).

D. The Behavior That Harms the Animal Is the Same Behavior That Harms the Human

Since the mid-1990s, the links among animal cruelty, child abuse, and domestic violence have received important attention both in professional literature and in the media. Anecdotal and research evidence links acts of cruelty to animals with acts of cruelty to humans (Arkow, 1996; Felthous and Kellert, 1987; Kellert and Felthous, 1985). One study noted that in homes where children were physically abused, pets were significantly more likely to be abused. Furthermore, and importantly, inhabitants of these physically abusive homes were 10 times more likely to be bitten by the family dog (DeViney *et al.*, 1983). Clinicians must be aware of these data on dog bites because currently in the United States, dog bites to children ages 5 to 9 have been designated as a major public health problem (Centers for Disease Control, 2000). The statistics on dog bites in the United States are alarming! Fifty percent of dog bite victims are children under the age of 12, 70% of fatal dog bite attacks involve children, and dog bites are the third leading cause of emergency room admissions in children (American Veterinary Medical Association, 2001). The important point for clinicians is that dog bites to children that occur in the family home may be an indicator of a physically abusive or otherwise chaotic household.

Knowing the breed of the dog that resides in the child's home has implications for risk assessment and intervention. Recent research demonstrates that ownership of high-risk (vicious) dogs, such as pit bulls, is a significant marker for general deviance as measured by a number of convictions in a court of law (Hulsmann *et al.*, in press). For example, owners of dogs that were unlicensed and cited as vicious by breed or behavior had an average of 5.9 criminal convictions compared to an average of 0.6 convictions for owners of dogs that were licensed and not deemed vicious by breed or behavior. Ownership of high-risk cited dogs is part of a high-risk lifestyle and appears to be a significant marker for general deviance.

The Huelsmann *et al.* (2006) study also found that failure to license a dog was predictive of other deviant behaviors, including child endangerment, harm to a juvenile, violation of safety restraint of a child, and contributing to juvenile unruliness. Both failure to license a dog and owning a high-risk breed of dog should be included in professional assessments of risk to children or other vulnerable individuals.

Because the behavior that harms the animal is the same behavior that harms the human, it is not surprising that research documents that both children and animals are at risk in homes where there is domestic violence (Ascione *et al.*, 1998). In two studies in different locales, the majority of pets in homes where battering occurred were threatened with harm or actually killed by the batterer and the majority of children witnessed the abuse to the pet. In addition, in 21–40% of these homes the children continued to be exposed to potential harm because their mothers remained in the home to protect the pet rather than seek safe shelter for themselves and their families (Ascione, 1998; Thomas and McIntosh, 2001).

Clinicians, including medical personnel, who treat children should routinely screen for domestic violence and the safety of pets (Boat, 2000). The following questions can be useful.

1. Parent Screening (Interview the Parent Alone)

1. "Do you ever feel unsafe at home?"
2. "Has anyone at home hit you or tried to injure you in any way?" [Questions 1 and 2 have a sensitivity of 71% and a specificity of 85% in detecting domestic violence (Eisenstat and Bancroft, 1999).]
3. "Has anyone ever threatened or tried to control you?"
4. "Have you ever felt afraid of your partner?"
5. "Has your partner ever hurt, or threatened to hurt, any of your children?"
6. "Do you have pets? If so, has your partner ever hurt or said they would hurt your pets?"
7. "Where do you keep the guns in your house?" (This question is deliberately phrased as a presumptive question. The respondent can always deny that there are guns in the house.)

2. Child Screening (Interview the Child Alone)

1. "What happens in your house when your mother and (father figure or partner) get angry with each other?"
2. "Is there any hitting in your house?"
3. "Have you (or siblings) ever been hurt?"
4. "Do you have any pets?" "Has anyone ever hurt or threatened to hurt your pet?"
5. "Do you ever worry about bad things happening to your pet?"

Just as the majority of children in violent homes witness domestic violence, the majority of children also witness pet abuse (Ascione, 1998). Exposure to animal cruelty can have a significant impact on the developing child, including promoting desensitization and decreasing empathy, reinforcing the idea that the child, like the pet, is expendable, damaging the child's sense of safety and confidence in the ability of adults to protect him or her from harm, teaching acceptance of physical harm as part of allegedly loving relationships, fostering the seeking of empowerment by inflicting pain and suffering, and leading to the imitation of abusive behaviors. Indeed, children exposed to domestic violence are almost 3 times more likely to be cruel to animals (based on maternal report) than nonexposed children (Currie, 2005).

Again, clinicians must take into account that some of the disturbed and disturbing behaviors exhibited by children may be related to witnessing cruelty to animals. A particularly pernicious and vicious form of child and animal abuse is forcing the child to kill or maim a pet. In a poignant video titled "Both Sides of the Coin" (1991), a man who is in treatment for his violent temper describes getting his first dog, Lassie, when he was 3 years old. Lassie was his best friend. Each year Lassie would have puppies, and each year, as the puppies began to be noisy and move around, his brutal uncle would kill them. The man recalls that when he was 12 years old, his uncle made him kill the puppies himself. The man describes holding the puppies underwater until they quit moving, putting their bodies in a gunny sack, and hiding them in the barn. He says, with a breaking voice, that he will never forget the pain and the guilt he felt. He could no longer relate to being a child and began burning down grain elevators and derailing trains. "I started acting out my pain!"

Exposure to pet abuse in the context of domestic violence can also contribute to the recently documented neurobiological deficits occurring in children who witness domestic violence. One result is that the brains of children exposed repeatedly to traumas such as witnessing domestic violence are significantly smaller, resulting in serious problems in social, emotional, and intellectual functioning (DeBellis, 1999; DeBellis *et al.*, 1999). As clinicians we cannot afford to miss these important animal-related connections that place our clients at risk for abuse or neglect.

E. Attachment to a Pet Is Both a Positive and a Potentially Negative Experience for a Child

The child's experience of attachment to a companion animal provides important information to the clinician. When a child reveals that he or she has a favorite pet, we know that this is a positive sign of an ability to connect with another living creature. However, clinicians must be aware that caring about a pet can make the child more vulnerable to loss. Bulcroft (1990) describes an interview with a 70-year-old man in a senior center, an interview that was assessing intellectual functioning, not targeting animal-related experiences. The author asked the man to recall one of his most vivid childhood memories. With tears in his eyes, the man related that when he was 8 years old, he saw his dog, Ben, killed by a stray bullet while they were hunting. An attachment to, and loss of, pets can have a lasting impact.

A teenager described how her beloved dog was killed by her stepfather after the dog tried to protect her from this man, who was raping her. Another child had to give his dog away when he was moved into foster care. Sometimes the story includes threats of harm or harming the pet in order to coerce the child to comply: "If you tell anyone what I did, I will kill your kitty." "If you don't have sex with me, I will sell your horses." "You have been a bad boy and to punish you, one of your puppies must die. You choose the puppy that I will kill or I will kill all of them."

In the aftermath of the gulf coast's Hurricane Katrina in September 2005, we have been poignantly reminded of the intensity of attachment and the fear of losing a pet. Many survivors endangered their own lives by refusing to evacuate unless they could take their pets.

Attachment is good. Clinicians can build on the caring feelings that a child has for a favorite pet and promote empathy and gentleness. But clinicians must also be aware of the downside of attachment and assess whether the child has experienced loss of a pet or threats of loss of a pet. Sometimes the loss, especially if it is repeated, overwhelms the child's coping abilities, and the child may detach from any investment in animals in order to protect him or herself from feeling such pain again.

F. Use of a Questionnaire to Assess for Animal-Related Experiences

The Childhood Trust Survey on Animal-Related Experiences

It is useful to have a set of questions available to guide the assessment of the child's experiences with animals. The Childhood Trust Survey on Animal-Related Experiences (CTSARE) is a 10-item screening questionnaire for children, adolescents, and adults that asks about experiences of ownership, attachment, loss, cruelty, and fears related to pets and other animals (see Boat, 2002; Boat *et al.*, in press). A longer version of the CTSARE has been adapted for use in several studies (Baker *et al.*, 1998; Flynn, 1999; Miller and Knutson, 1997) and is available in a chapter by Boat (1999). However, the validity and reliability of CTSARE have not been established. This instrument should be used as an interview guide and administered orally so the interviewer can use follow-up questions to obtain additional information as appropriate. The questions that are found in the CTSARE (see Appendix A) are described here.

- Questions 1 and 2 inquire about past and present ownership of pets. Data support that pets rarely survive more than 2 years in homes that are chaotic, have few resources, and have several risk factors for abuse or neglect (DeViney *et al.*, 1983). Frequently, the inhabitants of these homes list many pets and a high mortality and turnover rate. When asked what happened to all the pets he had listed, one teenager shrugged and said, "I don't know. Either grandma got rid of them or they're dead." When several pets have "just disappeared," a caution flag should be raised that the family may be in need of help. Frequently the inability to care for pets adequately is an indicator of an inability or lack of resources to care for the rest of the family members.
- Question 3 seeks information about whether the child has, or has had, a favorite pet as an indicator of attachment. Lack of any special relationship with a pet may signal a child who is divested from, or has never formed, close relationships.
- Question 4 asks about a difficult or stressful time when a pet was a source of comfort or support. Children often readily disclose situations where they felt vulnerable, sad, or frightened when they are focused on their pet (Doyle, 2001).
- Questions 5, 6, and 7 address issues of the pet having been hurt, worries about something bad happening to the pet, managing a pet's behavior, and losing a pet. Responses to these questions can offer a window into the child's home environment and assist in focusing the intervention.
- Questions 8 and 9 focus on seeing someone hurt an animal or hurting an animal. Sometimes a child or adult is prevented from helping a sick or injured animal. This is a potentially devastating experience. It may be important to question others to get adequate information about the child himself hurting animals or pets. Parents, neighbors, or teachers with classroom pets may observe harsh treatment of an animal. Teachers may overhear a child talking about seeing or committing cruel acts or read about concerning behaviors around animals in the writings of their students.
- Question 10 underscores the need to know if a child has ever been badly frightened or hurt by a pet or other animal. The trauma of being chased, pinned, or bitten by a dog can shape a lifelong negative response to dogs. This question also can reveal a home or neighborhood where a child may be at greater risk of being harmed by an animal. Elements of such neighborhoods include the child having access to dogs that are chained

outdoors, dogs that are running freely, and the presence of higher risk dogs such as pit bulls.

III. CLINICAL EXAMPLES OF INTERVENTIONS THAT ADDRESS THE ANIMAL-RELATED EXPERIENCES OF CHILDREN AND ADOLESCENTS IN THE LARGER CONTEXT OF THERAPY

Effective interventions for both children and animals can be informed by knowing and understanding the impact of the child's animal-related experiences. Effective interventions utilize knowledge of the child's animal-related experiences with the aim of reducing risk, addressing loss, and creating safe ways for the child to attach to another living being.

A. Foster Care Placements: Preserving the Child's Connection to the Pet

One difficult adjustment for children who must go into foster care is the loss of their companion animal. Many adults who were in foster care as children describe this loss as very difficult, especially if the only place their pet could go was the local animal shelter, where it would be euthanized if not adopted. A wonderful program in Florida resulting from a collaboration between the Hurlburt Field Family Advocacy Office and the Humane Society and Adoption Center at PAWS (Safe People, Safe Pets) will care for the pets of foster children, including their "pocket pets" (hamsters, guinea pigs, etc.). The children can visit, see photos, and otherwise stay connected to their pets. If reunion is not possible, the program facilitates the adoption of the pet and the child is usually reassured that the pet is safe and receiving good care.

Unfortunately, such foster care programs for children's pets are rare. More often the clinician's role is to support the child's feelings of loss and help the child preserve mementos and positive memories of the pet. If no photos of the pet are available, often children will find pictures in magazines that look somewhat like the pet or they can draw pictures. They can write about what made the pet so special and in other ways memorialize the positive aspects of their attachment (Raphael *et al.*, 1999). Similar approaches can be used with all family members together when they share the loss of a companion animal.

Sometimes knowing about a child's attachment to a pet happens because an adult is tuned in and "hears" the child's concerns about a pet. A moving example is portrayed in the video "Battered Hearts: A Story of Family Violence" (1995). A taped 911 call to report domestic violence is played. The caller is a terrified 6-year-old girl who says that her mother's old boyfriend is trying to hurt her mother. Her next sentence to the dispatcher is, "I think my cat's scared!" During the call her mother is shot by the boyfriend and the child sobs into the phone, "My mommy's dead." It is hoped that the professionals who intervened were aware of the child's concern about her cat and made sure that her cat was included in the plan of care. Preserving the girl's attachment to her cat in the aftermath of the trauma of her mother's death would be an important therapeutic intervention, even if they needed to be housed separately.

B. Domestic Violence: The Realities of Finding Shelter for Pets and for Families

Asking about experiences with animals is especially important when working with children or adults who have histories of trauma or maltreatment. We know that it is not uncommon for pets to be harmed in families where there is battering, and witnessing brutal abuse of pets can be a terrifying event that contributes to feelings of helplessness and guilt. Some battered mothers and children who must leave pets behind to seek shelter have an option to put their pets in foster care. Realistically, however, many mothers and children may not be able to reclaim their pets because they cannot find pet-friendly housing after leaving the battered-women's shelter. The clinician must help frame their decision to put their pet up for adoption as an act of caring and kindness. Sometimes the children will be able to have a different pet or a "pocket pet" in the new setting, a recommendation that the clinician can make if the children are invested in pets, are gentle with pets (the clinician can observe this if the pet comes for a visit), and have adequate supervision. Based on responses to the CTSARE, the clinician should note any instances of cruelty by the children or other adults and gauge the appropriateness of animals living in this household at this time. For some very stressed families there is not enough energy or resources to care for themselves, much less another living creature. Failure to thoroughly assess and advise the family at this point can contribute to another round of battered pets and subsequent guilt and hopelessness.

C. Empowering Youth to Protect Their Pets

Empowerment of youth to protect animals, even if those animals belong to others, is another intervention strategy. Kathy, 15, had witnessed severe domestic violence for years. She remembered her parents drinking and then having terrible fights. Kathy recalled that during the fights, when she was 5 years old, she would grab her little sister from her high chair and flee to a closet. In tears, Kathy confessed that it was her fault that her parents fought because if she had hidden the liquor bottles her parents would not drink and subsequently fight. Kathy revealed on the CTSARE that she loved cats. Kathy had recently moved after she had been severely beaten by her father. She could not take her cat with her, so it was left with her father. She worried about the safety of her beautiful white cat, as well as the wolf–dog mix that lived on a short chain in her father's back yard. Soon after she left, Kathy found out that her cat was dead. Unable to prove that her father had been the one to break her cat's leg, leading to the cat being euthanized, she focused on trying to help the dog. Kathy called the animal humane society to investigate the dog's living conditions. The call was empowering as the humane office responded immediately and the dog subsequently was removed to a new home. Kathy was so relieved. She had one less creature to worry about. Later Kathy was able to move to a setting where she could have a kitten. She brought the kitten to therapy, a kitten that was as powerless to care for itself as she had been to care for herself and her sister when she was little. Now Kathy was older and able to intervene to keep animals safe. In addition, her sense of empathy and caring for animals could be reinforced as there was little positive happening in her current life that could promote empathy and caring for people. One essential point about the Kathy case: The clinician knew about her animal-related experiences because the clinician asked about her animal-related experiences. Remember, if we do not ask, we will never know.

D. Proactive Interventions When Working with Abused and Neglected Children and Their Caregivers

Physically and sexually abused children have a higher incidence of abusive behavior to animals (Ascione, 2001), which can involve several different motivations, including their lack of boundaries, witnessing and imitating violence towards animals, or desire for revenge. Some sexually abused children are sexually reactive and seek sexual stimulation. They may masturbate excessively, fondle other children or adults, or seek stimulation from the family pet. Sometimes the sexual abuse of the child has involved being sexual with an animal, especially a dog. If the clinician knows that a child is sexually reactive, it is imperative to talk about the possibility that the child may use the family pet in a sexual way. Creating a safety plan for both the pet and the child may avert the tragedy that occurred in the following example.

A 5-year-old girl had recently disclosed prolonged and significant molestation by a man who had been a trusted neighbor and friend to her family. Naturally, her mother was extremely upset by this revelation. One day the mother was walking by the closed door of her child's bedroom and heard moaning sounds inside. Upon opening the door the mother discovered that her daughter had the family pet cat between her legs and the cat was licking the child's genitals. The mother was so distraught and enraged by this scene that she grabbed the cat and slammed the cat against the wall, killing the cat. Clinicians who anticipate and problem-solve these potential situations with caregivers can ensure that neither child nor pet is harmed further. A first step in preventing such a sad occurrence is to screen the family for animal-related experiences.

E. Management of Cruel Behaviors Toward Animals

Cruel behaviors toward animals may not be the primary referral concern. Unless we routinely ask about animal-related experiences, we may miss this important target for an intervention. Consider the following case.

The divorced mother of the almost 4-year-old boy called me after the Head Start teacher became concerned about his aggressive behaviors toward the other preschoolers. Josh would hit, try to strangle, and even tackle a peer unexpectedly. He was rough and tough, and his placement in Head Start was in jeopardy.

Josh lived with his mother and his older half-brother during the week and spent most weekends with his father. The mother's concern was about his aggressive behavior with other children. However, asking about pets in the family revealed additional concerning behaviors. Josh's mother disclosed that she had a cat that had recently given birth to three kittens. She went on to state that when Josh was just 3 years old, he had stomped on the back of a kitten from the last litter and the kitten had died. Recently she caught him holding a kitten by the neck over the toilet, ready to drop it in the water.

Further inquiry revealed that Josh's father "loved to play rough." During his weekends with Josh he would pretend to strangle him, engage Josh in very physical wrestling, and expose Josh to videos depicting scary violence. The father stated that he was training Josh to be tough and not cry, no matter how much he was hurt. Josh's older brother was also very rough with him.

The intervention in this home was two-pronged and focused on protecting both the child and the cats. The parents agreed to participate in Parent–Child Interaction Therapy, a relationship enhancement, evidence-based intervention that taught them effective play and discipline skills (Eyberg, 1988; Hembree-

Kigin and McNeil, 1995). In addition, the mother agreed to institute a safety plan for the mother cat and her kittens until she found homes for the kittens. In this case, she had a locked room where they could be safe if the mother was not home to supervise Josh. The mother also agreed to have her cat spayed, understanding that it was unfair to put Josh in a position where he could harm vulnerable pets such as kittens until his aggressive behavior was under control. Josh's behaviors improved as his parents learned new management skills, and the cats were now safe as well.

F. Community Service for Youths Adjudicated for Cruelty to Animals

There are several ways in which clinicians may find knowledge of animal-related experiences useful in assisting the court in assessment and disposition of cases involving children and families. Children who have been charged with animal cruelty should be evaluated by a clinician. Depending on several factors (see Lewchanin and Zimmerman, 2000), the severity of the cruelty can be determined and appropriate interventions ordered by the judge or magistrate.

A teenager who has been adjudicated for cruelty to animals may be remanded by the courts to perform community service at a humane society. However, clinicians should insist that no child or adolescent be in a humane society unless they are first screened for animal-related experiences. Charles was adjudicated for animal cruelty after setting fire to a kitten. Charles was 13 and in the sixth grade. His history included witnessing many episodes of domestic violence, a substance-abusing father, intense physical punishment, a larceny charge, and school failure. Charles had "closed down" his feelings in the manner of many traumatized children, and he felt no empathy for the kitten. He stated, "It was just a cat" and "I thought the cat was a stray." On the CTSARE, Charles related that his family had many pets in the past, including 14 dogs and numerous rabbits, gerbils, and birds. They had no cats because his father "hated cats." However, Charles did describe having 2 dogs that were special and a source of comfort to him. Clinically, this admission of attachment to a companion animal was useful. Charles might be an appropriate candidate for supervised community service in an animal shelter where his attachment to dogs could be used to bridge positive interactions with the feline community at the shelter.

Under no circumstances should children who have been adjudicated as cruel to animals be assigned only to clean-up jobs at shelters. They need positive supervised interactions with the animals, such as learning to clicker train dogs in "good shelter dog manners" (Pryor, 2003). Children who are fearful of dogs or cats or report no attachments to a pet or other animal are usually inappropriate for this type of community service. Most importantly, clinicians involved in treatment recommendations for adjudicated youth must remember that humane societies are short-staffed and often unable to provide the mentoring and supervision these referrals require.

G. Management of Dog Bites to Children

Dog bites can be traumatizing to both the child and the caregiver (Bernardo *et al.*, 1998, 2000; Rossman *et al.*, 1997). The sequelae are often more severe than is recognized in the medical and mental health communities. In developing therapeutic interventions with children who have been bitten and with their caregivers, clinicians need to obtain a thorough history of the child's and the caregiver's experiences with animals. Dealing with the pain, fears, and physical recovery of the child can be very difficult for families. In addition, if the companion animal in the home has done the biting, difficult decisions must be made about the fate of the pet. Finally, the trauma of the bite may be an ongoing concern in the family if the child develops severe avoidance reactions to dogs as a consequence of being badly frightened and injured. The child may develop posttraumatic stress disorder (PTSD). Unrecognized and untreated symptoms of PTSD in children can lead to well-documented impairment in brain development and cognitive, behavioral, and social skills (DeBellis et. al, 1999; Siegel, 1999; Van der Kolk, 1994).

Joey was almost 4 when he was bitten by the neighbor's Akita. According to Joey's father, when Joey was outdoors the dog came into their yard and attacked Joey. The father was unaware of the attack until he heard his son scream and come running in the house. Joey suffered 21 bites to his head and arm and spent 5 days in the hospital. Two months later Joey and his parents were referred for therapy. Joey exhibited classic symptoms of PTSD: waking frequently during the night, clinging to adults, regressing to baby talk, refusing to go outside to play, and avoiding all contact with dogs. The neighbor who owned the Akita was aggressive and combative, threatening to go to court to avoid having his unlicensed dog euthanized. The parents had to hire an attorney with money they could not spare and felt extremely guilty for being unable to prevent this trauma.

In my office Joey played out his fears, aggressively growling and grabbing a toy bear in his teeth, shaking it furiously while I described his behavior and his desire to be big and strong and do back to the dog what the dog had done to him. We made a book about the bite incident and coping skills he could use, and he also put in pictures of lots of "nice dogs." Joey and his parents learned the rules about how to be safer around dogs. We practiced standing still like a tree if a strange dog approached him or crouching like a rock if a dog jumped on him. He practiced approaching a toy dog on a leash and asking, "Is your dog friendly? May I pet your dog?" Joey's grandmother had an old, almost blind little dog. The parents noted how much Joey had liked that dog, especially putting it on a leash and tugging it all over the yard. We discussed the importance of modeling gentleness to all animals and providing constant supervision.

Perhaps the hardest thing for the parents was the amount of time it took until some of Joey's fears began to diminish. They needed substantial education about the impact of a life-threatening trauma on Joey's nervous system. His hypervigilant responses would take considerable time to abate.

H. Bringing Family Pets to the Clinician's Office

How fortunate is the clinician who can say to a family, "Bring your dog or cat or gerbil or rat or guinea pig when you come for the next appointment. I would love to meet it!" Hearing family members talk about their pets and observing their pet interactions are additional venues for gathering valuable information. Obviously, this is not an option for many clinicians or families. However, if the opportunity is present, I urge clinicians to invite companion animals to the therapy session.

Families can bring a pet to my office. I do not have any office pets, but I do have pigeons (rock doves) outside a window that can be opened. It only takes a few safflower seeds to convince a pigeon that he or she should visit regularly. For some of my clients an integral part of coming to see me is to feed—and name—the pigeons. For one traumatized and highly dissociative teenager, every therapy session began with her feeding the pigeons. This contact with the pigeons helped her make the transition into my office. She later told me that knowing she could feed the pigeons made it possible for her to come to my office when she was feeling particularly distressed and confused.

IV. CONCLUSION

Routinely asking about animal-related experiences can provide important and useful information that clinicians can incorporate in their therapeutic interventions with children, adolescents, and their caregivers.

APPENDIX A

CTSARE

The Childhood Trust Survey on Animal-Related Experiences 10 Screening Questions for Children, Adolescents and Adults

1. **Have you or your family ever had any pets? . . . . Y N**

	How many?		**How many?**
a. Dog(s)	_____	g. Rabbits, hamsters, mice, guinea pigs, gerbils	_____
b. Cat(s)	_____	h. Wild animals (describe) _________	_____
c. Bird(s)	_____	i. Other (describe) _________	_____
d. Fish	_____		
e. Horse(s)	_____		
f. Turtles, snakes, lizards, insects, etc.	_____		

Do you have a pet or pets now? . . . . Y N

	How many?		**How many?**
a. Dog(s)	_____	g. Rabbits, hamsters, mice, guinea pigs, gerbils	_____
b. Cat(s)	_____	h. Wild animals (describe) _________	_____
c. Bird(s)	_____	i. Other (describe) _________	_____
d. Fish	_____		
e. Horse(s)	_____		
f. Turtles, snakes, lizards, insects, etc.	_____		

2. **Who takes care of your pet(s)?**

   ____

3. **Do/did you ever have a favorite or special pet? . . . . Y N**

   What kind? ________________________________
   What made the pet special? __________________
   ____

4. **Has a pet ever been a source of comfort or support to you—even if you did not own the pet? (e.g. When you were sad or scared?) . . . . Y N**

How old were you? ______________________________

Tell me about the pet ______________________________
What happened? ______________________________

5. **Has your pet ever been hurt?** . . . . Y N

What happened? ______________________________

____

____

a. Accidental? (hit by car, attacked by another animal, fell, ate something, etc.)
b. Deliberate? (kicked, punched, thrown, not fed, etc.)

Have you ever felt afraid for your pet or worried about bad things happening to your pet? (describe) . . . . Y N

____

____

Are you worried now? . . . . Y N

6. **How do you teach your pet(s) to "be good"? (example)** __________

____

____

What happens when your pet misbehaves? (example) __________

____

____

7. **Have you ever lost a pet you really cared about? (e.g. Was given away, ran away, died or was somehow killed?)** . . . . Y N

If your pet died, was the death:

a. Natural (old age, illness, euthanized)	**b.** Accidental (hit by car)	**c.** Deliberate (strangled, drowned)	**d.** Cruel or violent (eg. pet was tortured)

What happened?

____

____

____

8. **Have you ever <u>seen</u> someone hurt an animal or pet?** . . . . Y N

What happened?______________________________

____

____

Have you ever seen an organized dog fight? . . . . Y N
How old were you? ____________________
Tell me about it ____

____

____

9. **Have <u>you</u> ever hurt an animal or pet?** . . . . Y N

How old were you? ________________
Tell me about it ____

____

____
What kind of animal? ____
Were you alone when you did this? . . . . Y N
Did anyone know you did this? . . . . Y N
What happened afterwards? __________________________________

____

10. **Have you ever been frightened—really scared or hurt by an animal?** . . . . Y N

What happened? ____

____

Are you still afraid of this kind of animal or other animals? . . . . Y N
(Describe) ____

____

REFERENCES

American Animal Hospital Association (2004). Pet owner survey. American Animal Hospital Association, www.aahanet.org.

American Pet Products Manufacturers Association (2005–2006). National Pet Owners Survey, http://www.appma.org/press_releasedetail.asp?v=ALL&id=52.

Ascione, F. R. (1998). Battered women's reports of their partners' and their children's cruelty to animals. *J. Emotion. Abuse* **1**(1), 119–132.

Ascione, F. R. (2001). "Animal Abuse and Youth Violence." OJJDP Juvenile Justice Bulletin, U.S. Department of Justice, Washington, DC.

Ascione, F. R., Friedrich, W. N., Heath, J., and Hayashi, K. (2004). Cruelty to animals in normative, sexually abused, and outpatient psychiatric samples of 6- to 12-year-old children: Relations to maltreatment and exposure to domestic violence. *Anthrozoös* **16**(3), 194–212.

Arkow, P. (1996). The relationship between animal abuse and other forms of family violence. *Family Viol. Sex. Assault Bull.* **12**(1–2), 29–34.

Baker, D., Boat, B. W., Grinvalsky, M. D., and Geracioti, T. (1998). Interpersonal and animal-related trauma experiences in female and male military veterans: Implications for program development. *Milit. Med.* **163**(1), 20–25.

Battered Hearts: A Story of Family Violence (1995). S.A.F.E. Place, P.O. Box 199, Battle Creek, MI 49016.

Bernardo, L. M., Gardner, M. J., and Amon, N. (1998). Dog bites in children admitted to Pennsylvania trauma centers. *Int. J. Trauma Nurs.* **4**, 121–127.

Bernardo, L. M., Gardner, M. J., O'Conner, J., and Amon, N. (2000). Dog bites in children treated in a pediatric emergency department. *J. Soc. Pediatr. Nurs.* **5**, 87–95.

Boat, B. W., Loar, L., and Phillips, A. (in press). Collaborating to assess, intervene and prosecute animal abuse: A continuum of protection for children and animals. *In* "International Handbook of Theory, Research, and Application on Animal Abuse and Cruelty" (F. R. Ascione, ed.), Purdue University Press, West Layfayette, IN.

Boat, B. W. (1999). Abuse of children and abuse of animals: Using the links to inform child assessment and protection. *In* "Child Abuse, Domestic Violence and Animal Abuse: Linking the Circles of Compassion for Prevention and Intervention" (F. R. Ascione and P. Arkow, eds.), pp. 83–100. Purdue University Press, West Layfayette, IN.

Boat, B. W. (2000). Children exposed to domestic violence. *In* "Pediatric Primary Care: Well-Child Care" (R. C. Baker, ed.), pp. 236–239. Lippincott, Williams & Wilkins, Philadelphia, PA.

Boat, B. W. (2002). Links among animal abuse, child abuse and domestic violence. *In* "Social Work and the Law: Proceedings of the National Organization of Forensic Social Workers 2000" (I. Neighbors, ed.), pp. 33–45. Haworth Press, Binghamton, NY.

Bonas, S., McNicholas, J., and Collis, G. M. (2000). Pets in the network of family relationships: An empirical study. *In* "Companion Animals and Us: Exploring the Relationships between People and Pets" (A. L. Podberscek, E. S. Paul, and J. A. Serpell, eds.), pp. 209–237. Cambridge University Press, New York.

Both Sides of the Coin (1991). Varied Directions International. 18 Mt. Battie Street, Camden, ME 04843.

Bulcroft, K. (1990). Pets in the American family. *People Anim. Environ.* **8**(4), 13–14.

Cain, A. O. (1983). A study of pets in the family system. *In* "New Perspectives on Our Lives with Companion Animals" (H. Katcher and A. M. Beck, eds.), pp. 72–81. University of Pennsylvania Press, Philadelphia, PA.

Centers for Disease Control (2000). Healthy people 2010: Animal control. www.healthypeople.gov.

Currie, C. L. (2005). Animal cruelty by children exposed to domestic violence. *Child Abuse and Neglect*, **30**, 425–435.

Davis, J. H. (1987). Preadolescent self-concept development and pet ownership. *Anthrozoös* **1**(2), 90–94.

De Bellis, M. D. (1999). Developmental traumatology: Neurobiological development in maltreated children with PTSD. *Psychiatr. Times* **16**, 11.

De Bellis, M. D., Keshavan, M. S., Clark, D. B., Casey, B. J., Giedd, J. N., Boring, A. M., Frustaci, K., and Ryan, N. D. (1999). Developmental traumatology. II. Brain development. *Soc. Biol. Psychiatr.* **45**, 1271–1284.

DeViney, E., Dickert, J., and Lockwood, R. (1983). The care of pets within child abusing families. *Int. J. Study Anim. Probl.* **4**, 321–329.

Doyle, C. (2001). Surviving and coping with emotional abuse in childhood. *Clin. Psychol. Psychiatr.* **6**, 387–402.

Dresser, N. (2000). The horse bar mitzvah: A celebratory exploration of the human-animal bond. *In* "Companion Animals and Us: Exploring the Relationships between People and Pets" (A. L. Podberscek, E. S. Paul, and J. A. Serpell, eds.), pp. 90–107. Cambridge University Press, New York.

Eisenstat, S. A., and Bancroft, L. (1999). Domestic violence. *N. Engl. J. Med.* **341**(12), 886–892.

Enders-Slegers, M. (2000). The meaning of companion animals: Qualitative analysis of the life histories of elderly cat and dog owners. *In* "Companion Animals and Us: Exploring the Relationships between People and Pets" (A. L. Podberscek, E. S. Paul, and J. A. Serpell, eds.), pp. 237–256. Cambridge University Press, New York.

Eyberg, S. (1988). Parent-child interaction therapy: Integration of traditional and behavioral concerns. *Child Family Behav. Ther.* **10**, 42–51.

Felthous, A. R., and Kellert, S. R. (1987). Childhood cruelty and later aggression against people: A review. *Am. J. Psychiatr.* **144**(6), 710–717.

Flynn, C. P. (1999). Exploring the link between corporal punishment and children's cruelty to animals. *J. Marriage Family* **61**, 971–981.

Hembree-Kigin, T., and McNeil, C. (1995). "Parent-Child Interaction Therapy." Plenum Press, New York.

Hulsmann, J. E., Boat, B. W., Putnam, F. W., Dates, H. F., and Malhman, A. (in press). Ownership of high-risk ("vicious") dogs as a marker for deviant behaviors: Implications for risk assessment. *J. Interpers. Viol.*

Humane Society of the United States, Animal Cruelty and Family Violence: Making the Connection (2004). www.hsus.org.

Kellert, S. R., and Felthous, A. R. (1985). Childhood cruelty toward animals among criminals and noncriminals. *Hum. Relat.* **38**, 1113–1129.

Kidd, A. H., and Kidd, R. M. (1985). Children's attitudes toward their pets. *Psychol. Rep.* **57**(1), 15–31.

Lewchanin S., and Zimmerman, E. (2000). "Clinical Assessment of Juvenile Animal Cruelty." Biddle Publishing Co. and Audenreed Press, Brunswick, ME.

Loar, L., and Colman, L. (2004). "Teaching Empathy: Animal-Assisted Therapy Programs for Children and Families Exposed to Violence." Latham Foundation, Alameda, CA.

McNicholas, J., and Collins, G. M. (2001). Children's representations of pets in their social networks. *Child Care Health Dev.* **27**(3), 279–294.

Miller, K. S., and Knutson, J. F. (1997). Reports of severe physical punishment and exposure to animal cruelty by inmates convicted of felonies and by university students. *Child Abuse Neglect* **21**, 59–82.

Pryor, K. (1999). "Clicker Training for Dogs." Sunshine Press, Boston, MA.

Raphael, P., Loar, L., and Colman, L. (1999). Teaching compassion: A Guide for Humane Educators, Teachers, and Parents. Latham Foundation, Alameda, CA.

Rossman, B. R., Bingham, R. D., and Emde, R. N. (1997). Symptomology and adaptive functioning for children exposed to normative stressors, dog attack, and parental violence. *J. Am. Acad. Child Adolesc. Psychiatr.* **36**, 1089–1096.

Sable, P. (1995). Pets, attachment, and well-being across the life cycle. *Social Work* **40**(3), 334–341.

Safe People, Safe Pets, Hurlburt Field Family Advocacy Office, 113 Lielmanis Avenue, Bldg. 91020, Hurlburt Field, FL.

Serpell, J. (1986). "In the Company of Animals: A Study of Human-Animal Relationships." Basil Blackwell Ltd., New York.

Task Force on Canine Aggression and Human-Canine Interactions (2001). A community approach to dog bite prevention. *J. Am. Vet. Med. Assoc.* **218**, 1732–1749.

Thomas, C., and McIntosh, S. (2001). Exploring the links between animal abuse and family violence as reported by women entering shelters in Calgary communities. Presentation at Our Children, Our Future: A Call to Action, International Conference on Children Exposed to Domestic Violence, London, Ontario, Canada, June 7.

Van der Kolk, B. (1994). The body keeps the score: Memory and the evolving psychology of posttraumatic stress. *Harv. Rev. Psychiatr.* Jan–Feb, 250–260.

CHAPTER 13

Characteristics of Animal-Assisted Therapy/Activity in Specialized Settings

BEN P. GRANGER
School of Social Work, Colorado State University, Fort Collins, Colorado 80523

LORI R. KOGAN
Department of Clinical Sciences, Colorado State University, Fort Collins, Colorado 80523

When I'm with Dillon, I feel happy.
When I'm with Dillon, I feel content.
When I'm with Dillon, I feel refreshed.
When I'm sad, he makes me forget about it.
If I'm hated, he changes the way I feel.
Altogether, he's the best dog I know.

This poem was written by an 11-year-old boy who experienced animal-assisted therapy (AAT) in a residential treatment setting. The human–animal team worked with this youth for a year and a half, with the basic comment from facility staff that they did not know if he had anything soft within him. He was asked to express his thoughts about Dillon, a golden retriever. Dillon was able to find a way inside the protective shield, enabling the child to be his true self and to enjoy the time spent with his special friend.

I. INTRODUCTION

This chapter continues to use the terms *animal-assisted therapy* and *animal-assisted activity* (AAA) as a context for discussing the therapeutic use of

Handbook on Animal-Assisted Therapy: Theoretical Foundations and Guidelines for Practice, 2e

companion animals, the depth and level of human–animal interventions, and the settings in which these take place. It is noted that there are additional developing terms such as "animal-assisted intervention," which is defined as "any therapeutic intervention that intentionally includes or incorporates animals as part of the therapeutic process or milieu" (Kruger, *et al.*, 2004).

Animal-assisted therapy is regarded as a goal-directed intervention in which an animal that meets specific criteria is an integral part of the treatment process. AAT is directed and/or delivered by a health/human service professional with specialized expertise and within the scope of practice of his/her profession. Key features include specified goals and objectives for each individual and measured progress. In contrast, animal-assisted activity provides opportunities for motivational, educational, recreational, and/or therapeutic benefits to enhance the quality of life. AAAs are delivered in a variety of environments by specially trained professionals, paraprofessionals, and/or volunteers in association with animals that meet specific criteria. Key features include absence of specific treatment goals; volunteers and treatment providers are not required to take detailed notes; and visit content is spontaneous (Delta Society, n.d.).

These definitions are ongoing efforts to help clarify and understand the essence of this therapeutic human–animal intervention. However, despite these efforts there continues to be considerable confusion in practice settings as well as with the public regarding exactly what animal-assisted therapy/activity or animal-assisted interventions are and what they are suppose to accomplish. In addition, the term "pet therapy" is used commonly to convey forms of human–animal interaction, without differentiating between animal-assisted therapy and activity. Without a formative definition it is difficult to clearly state what one is doing and how well.

A contributing factor to the current status of AAA/AAT is the lack of research, evaluation, and articles in the literature that help clarify and validate how this intervention is conducted and its effectiveness with various populations and settings. Little effort has been extended to detail AAA/AAT parameters, protocols, and methods of evaluation (Granger and Kogan, 2000). Also, the fact that AAA/AAT is interdisciplinary (e.g., without a professional identity) further complicates defining and therefore evaluating the effectiveness of this intervention. There have been some recent efforts to incorporate AAA/AAT as a professional practice modality, as animal-assisted social work, and as specialized certificate programs. However, AAA/AAT as delivered in a number of specialized settings can still be regarded as being in its early professional development. To some it is considered one of the complementary therapies, and by others, a helpful volunteer activity.

While a number of critical questions regarding the validity of AAA/AAT remain, support from those who have experienced the positive effects of AAA/AAT is increasing. It is both a challenging and encouraging time for increasing the understanding and appreciation of the human–animal bond, the therapeutic use of companion animals, and specifically AAA/AAT.

II. VARIATION OF ANIMAL-ASSISTED THERAPY AND ANIMAL-ASSISTED ACTIVITY (AAA/AAT) IN SPECIALIZED SETTINGS

There are numerous reasons for the variations in AAA/AAT, including the species, breed, and training level of the animals involved in AAA/AAT programs; the level of training and characteristics of the human partner and/or professional; the nature and purpose of the setting and client population; and the knowledge level of AAA/AAT by individual programs or facilities. Each of these reasons is discussed next.

A. Variety of Animals

Domesticated about 30,000 years ago, dogs have a long history of coexisting in a mutually beneficial manner with humans. Beginning as early as the 9th century, dogs have been used to provide therapy (Catanzaro, 2003) and are still the most common species used in AAA/AAT. There are no specific breeds or size requirements that work best for AAA/AAT; instead, successful therapy is dependent on the individual dog's temperament, level of training, and setting in which it will work. Small and large dogs and pure and mixed breeds all can work well with different populations.

Careful screening is essential in assessing the therapeutic potential of a particular dog. A thorough screening involves veterinary/medical screening, temperament testing, and skills or training testing. Veterinary screening, usually provided by the owner's veterinarian, should include a complete physical examination, necessary vaccinations, and an assessment for internal and external parasites. Documentation of a clean bill of health should be a requirement before beginning any AAA/AAT program. The next aspect of screening involves temperament testing, conducted to determine how a dog will react in new and/or startling situations. Although some dogs are simply not suited for therapy work, other dogs can become great therapy dogs with practice and exposure to situations in which they first appear nervous or stressed.

Temperament testing usually includes several situations that have the potential to be stressful or novel to a dog.

Skill testing and/or training is also a critical component in determining the success of a therapy dog. One commonly used skills test is the American Kennel Club's canine good citizen (CGC) test (American Kennel Club, 2004). Most aspects of the test involve learned behaviors and not actual personality traits. The 10 components of the CGC test include accepting the approach of a friendly stranger, allowing a stranger to pet them, allowing a stranger to groom and examine them, walking on a loose leash, walking through a crowd of people, sitting on command as well as staying in place, coming when called, behaving politely when exposed to other dogs, not panicking when faced with distractions, and maintaining training skills when handled by someone other than their owner.

All three components of testing (i.e., veterinary screening, temperament testing, and skills training) are equally important to adequately screen and certify a dog for AAA/AAT. Furthermore, periodic checks in each area should be done to monitor any changes that might occur over time, as some dogs may become less suitable as therapy dogs as they age.

Cats as therapy animals have been documented in a variety of settings, and while many people prefer dogs because of their personalities, some people enjoy cats' more aloof demeanor. Cats also work well with people who are afraid of or allergic to dogs. Cats, like dogs, can become certified as animal partners. AAA/AAT with cats, in addition to providing tactile stimulation, can help clients improve their gross and fine-motor skills through playing with toys, brushing, petting, and feeding activities.

The ideal therapy cat is one that enjoys being petted, seeks out human attention, gets along with dogs and other cats, and is able to accept new environments. Additionally, therapy cats should tolerate being transported and not become overly fearful when exposed to loud noises or unexpected behaviors.

During most types of cat certification testing, the animal's behavior is assessed while being held by several strangers, with the owner both present and absent. More advanced skills that cats can exhibit for therapy include walking on a leash, permitting strangers to hold them on their laps, playing with toys, tolerating hugs, and coming when called (Burch, 1996). Some therapy cats, through operant training techniques, can actually be taught several commands. Most cats, however, due to their level of trainability, are used for AAA rather than AAT.

In situations unsuitable for a dog or cat, a rabbit may be the solution (Adbill and Juppe, 1997). Rabbits can become certified animal partners after going through a careful screening process. To pass certification testing, a rabbit must tolerate being transported and should enjoy being held. Therapy rabbits are tested to ensure they tolerate being passed from the owner to strangers, being placed on a table (in a carrier) for 30 seconds, and being held by a stranger for 2 minutes. The rabbit should also permit variations of traditional petting, including basic or clumsy petting, petting by numerous people at once, or petting on all parts of its body (e.g., mouth, ears, and paws).

Good therapy rabbits do not become stressed around individuals with disabilities and walkers, crutches, or wheelchairs. They should also remain calm when confronted with loud noises (including raised voices) and crowds of people. Rabbits that pass these requirements can be used with a variety of populations and have been found to be a favorite among small children (Mallon, 1994). They provide variation to the usual AAA animals and can be used to improve fine-motor skills through holding and petting the animal. If the client is placed in a position to care for the animal, this can give them an opportunity to learn responsibility and empathy.

Birds have been used in a variety of settings to alleviate depression and to provide an impetus for social interaction (Holcomb *et al.*, 1997). The most commonly used birds are parakeets, finches, and canaries (Bernard, 1995). By encouraging clients to help in the daily care and maintenance of these animals, birds can be used to enhance self-esteem and a sense of responsibility. Larger birds can be used outside of cages within a safe setting. Although some birds are used in AAA/AAT, most birds are used as visual stimulation similar to fish tanks. They can, however, serve in an AAA/AAT capacity with the proper supervision, goals, and implementation.

AAA/AAT with horses offers many unique aspects that are not available with smaller animals. The use of horses within a therapeutic setting falls under four broad categories: hippotherapy, riding therapy, riding for rehabilitation, and vaulting (Biery, 1985). Hippotherapy literally means "therapy with the help of a horse" (Copeland, 1998). Because a horse's gait closely resembles that of a person's walk, by sitting on a walking horse, a rider's body is taken through the physical motions of walking without placing any weight on the legs (Engel, 1992). The rhythmic, dynamic movement of a horse can positively impact a client's posture, balance, and mobility without the necessity of controlling the horse. Positive results of hippotherapy have been documented in clients with one-sided paralysis; cerebral palsy; spastic and rigid muscles; and coordination, balance, and posture problems (Biery, 1985; Lehrman and Ross, 2001; McCowan, 1984).

Although similar to hippotherapy, which is classified as a passive therapy, riding therapy can be either passive or active. Therefore, riding therapy can include times when the rider allows the horse to lead and times when the rider takes an active role in the exercises. Benefits of riding therapy include increased flexibility, balance, gross motor coordination, and cardiorespiratory function, as well as speech and language abilities (Biery, 1985; Macauley and Gutierrez, 2004). Riding for rehabilitation, when the rider takes active control over the horse, can be used to help improve coordination and ameliorate psychological or social problems (Copeland, 1998). In addition, riders can work on sequential tasks by practicing the activities that must take place prior to riding, thereby enhancing long-term memory skills. The ability to control one's behavior is taught naturally during riding as the rider learns what behaviors will result in positive responses from the horse.

Vaulting, defined as "gymnastic exercises on horseback," is one variation of riding therapy (Biery, 1985). In order to perform vaulting activities correctly, the rider and horse must establish good communication and a high level of trust. Most riding programs combine different types of horse therapy, thereby offering a wide range of benefits, including improved balance and arm and leg coordination and increased muscle strength, mobility, self-esteem, attention span, and self-control (Biery, 1985).

Because the goals for each type of riding therapy differ, the selection of the proper horse for each activity is paramount. Because hippotherapy is designed to improve a rider's posture, balance, mobility, and function (Sayler, 1992), the movements of the horse are extremely important. The horse must move with a symmetrical, balanced, rhythmic gait. As with all types of AAA/AAT, the personality of the animal is a key component to successful therapy. To help ensure a positive experience for the rider and horse, care should be taken to select a therapy horse that is patient and gentle. Successful therapy horses are those screened carefully in both behavior and skill level. They must exhibit reliability and predictability and follow basic commands (Burch, 1996). As with other therapy animals, a good fit should be made between the individual horse's temperament and abilities and the needs of the rider.

Farm animals, including cattle, poultry, and pigs, have been used for many years with a variety of different populations, including those with physical, mental, and emotional impairments (Diesch, 1984). All animals should be medically screened and temperament tested before being exposed to clients to ensure a safe interaction for all involved. Any animal that appears nervous or unpredictable in simulated therapy settings should not be used for therapy.

Through interactions with farm animals, numerous skills can be taught or enhanced. Examples of cognitive skills include species care and information, measuring abilities practiced when feeding, and time management used for feeding and exercising schedules. The enhancement of gross and fine-motor skills can be accomplished through such activities as sweeping, feeding, shoveling, brushing, and milking. While caring for the animals, clients learn about responsibility, the ability to be consistent and punctual, and following a schedule. Additionally, interaction with these animals can increase self-worth and empathy.

Although many people do not get the opportunity to work with dolphins, these animals can provide a unique AAA/AAT experience due to their intelligence level and the stress-reducing qualities of water. Dolphins are thought to be closer to humans in their multimodal learning style and cognitive abilities than most other animals (Nathanson, 1989). It is therefore probable that dolphins have a greater capacity to sustain interest in a task and can provide a powerful reinforcement for therapeutic interventions (Nathanson and de Faria, 1993). Because water has been shown to be a useful tool in many areas (i.e., increasing motor skills, providing greater flexibility in movement, and alleviating anxiety and depression), dolphin AAA/AAT provides an alternative to traditional AAA/AAT and has been shown to improve motivation and attention span; gross and fine-motor skills; speech and language; and psychoemotional states (Lukina, 1999; Nathanson, *et al.*, 1997). Nathanson (1998) found that short-term dolphin-assisted therapy can help children with severe disabilities move up to a new level of functioning in a relatively short period of time.

The characteristics, level of training, and care of any animal obviously impact the delivery and success of AAA/AAT. After one decides what type of animal would work best for the situation at hand, it is important to remember that each animal is a unique being, with its own temperament, strengths, and weaknesses. A successful AAA/AAT program is one that blends the needs of the client with the strengths and abilities of the animal. This variability, however, makes exact replication of studies difficult as one attempts to study the impact of AAA/AAT. This is one of the difficulties faced by the field in evaluating the effectiveness of AAA/AAT with various client populations.

B. Level of Training and Characteristics of the Human Partner and/or Professional

Of equal importance are the humans engaged in AAA/AAT; the persons who are frequently regarded as "on the other end of the leash." These persons can include the owner, trained volunteer, professional, staff member of the setting, or a combination of these persons in a team arrangement. The knowledge and skill base, the training and understanding level of AAA/AAT, and the personal characteristics of these persons all present important factors that bring about variation. Frequently the term "handler" is used to convey the role of the human member of the team. This person is usually the one who has been involved in the training of the animal. While "handler" is commonly used, it may understate the function and purpose of the human participating with the animal in either AAA or AAT.

Persons volunteering from varying levels of education, training, and experience tend to have one main characteristic in common. They all are believers in the importance and uniqueness of the human–animal bond and the therapeutic use of companion animals. While these differences may challenge the suitability of volunteering for AAA/AAT, in many ways the human–animal bond factor provides a focal point for training, volunteering, and maintaining commitment and the level of enjoyment/satisfaction of participating in AAA/AAT in partnership with a companion animal.

Because volunteers come from such wide backgrounds, providing AAA/AAT requires ongoing professional guidance, direction, and coordination with the specific organization where this takes place. An understanding of human and animal behavior, and how these interface in providing AAA/AAT, is essential. Where these components are insufficient, this unique intervention, with the use of human and animal volunteers, can be ineffective or viewed as not important in the delivery of rehabilitation and supportive services.

Similarly, while the commitment to the human–animal bond exists, for the most part professionals have not had formal preparation for conducting AAA/AAT. Frequently, students in the various disciplines are more interested than faculty in incorporating this into their professional careers. Furthermore, most disciplines do not have content in this area in their curriculum, and universities have not taken into consideration the interdisciplinary nature of the human–animal bond and how this can impact separate majors and professions. Practicum opportunities are also limited for students wanting "hands-on" experience.

Staff members within an organization frequently seek opportunities to participate in AAA/AAT. While this should be encouraged, there are the issues of how to provide necessary training and credentialing and how to carry out AAA/AAT as part of their job responsibility or in another capacity (i.e., volunteer of a community organization providing these services). Whether the companion animal is a horse, cat, or dog, and regardless of what role the human plays, she/he must be qualified and trained to work with that animal. This involves in-depth and ongoing training for both the human and the animal. When working as an AAA or AAT team, the human and animal must feel comfortable and confident in working together and with the population or client group receiving the therapy or intervention. For example, working in a hospice setting can be stressful on both the human and the animal.

C. Nature and Purpose of the Setting and Client Population

There are numerous specialized settings with a variety of populations that can benefit from AAT. These include the elderly, patients with terminal illnesses, hospital patients, children, and inmates in correctional facilities.

The use of AAA/AAT with the elderly has expanded rapidly in long-term care facilities, adult day care centers, and private homes. For those that reside in long-term care facilities, therapies that enhance social, psychological, and physical well-being are necessary to combat the negative effects that often accompany relocating to a facility. AAT offers the opportunity for nonjudgmental social interaction as well as providing an avenue for sensory stimulation (Struckus, 1991).

Animal interactions with the elderly have proven beneficial in a multitude of areas, including physiological benefits such as decreased blood pressure and increased survival rate of coronary care patients. Furthermore, the physical activities involved in caring for an animal (e.g., walking, grooming) can help residents release excess energy and maintain muscle strength and joint mobility (Beyersdorfer and Birkenhauer, 1990; Boldt and Dellmann-Jenkins, 1992; Manor, 1991).

In addition to physiological aspects, numerous social and psychological benefits of animals have been observed. These include companionship for withdrawn and isolated people, decreased depression, anxiety, and loneliness, and increased socialization and vigor (Arkow, 1990; Baun *et al.*, 1984; Friedmann *et al.*, 1980). Animals also help the elderly gain a renewed sense of purpose and an increased sense of self-worth (Elliot, 1991). Through performing tasks such as feeding, walking, or brushing, an elderly client can gain increased self-respect, independence, and perceived control over his/her environment (Corson *et al.*, 1975).

Communication skills are another important component in AAA/AAT involving the elderly. Animals enhance verbal communication by offering opportunities for patients to vocalize and reminisce (Levinson, 1972). Another way animals facilitate communication is through their ability to foster social interaction (Messent, 1983). People often perceive social interaction as less threatening in the presence of an animal. This allows patients the opportunity to practice and maintain social skills, thereby increasing connections with others (Savishinsky, 1985). For many elderly, especially those who experience memory deficits, nonverbal communication becomes increasingly important. Due to the fact that people often maintain nonverbal communication skills after the loss of verbal abilities, the nonverbal acceptance and communication of animals have recognized benefits and importance (Beck and Peacock, 1988). Physical contact with an animal (holding, stroking, and hugging) provides sensory experiences that are difficult to replicate on a consistent basis with people.

People with a terminal illness can work through the five stages described by Kubler-Ross (denial, anger, bargaining, depression, and acceptance) most smoothly when others around them are seen as supportive and are able to remain emotionally and physically close (Kubler-Ross, 1969). However, because death makes most people uncomfortable, even caretakers can unconsciously give signals that increase patients' anxiety and fear levels. For this reason and others, patients with terminal illnesses can benefit from AAT. Animals, with their unconditional acceptance, have been found to be useful in helping people with terminal illnesses work through their feelings. Additionally, Muschel (1984) found that patients with terminal cancer felt more in control when they were able to care for an animal. When patients have another living creature to care for, they are able to shift some of the focus from their own illness. These animals can lessen fears, despair, loneliness, stress levels, and isolation for people with numerous types of terminal illnesses, including AIDS (Haladay, 1989). The hospice environment offers another avenue in which terminally ill patients can access AAA/AAT. For example, a human–animal team, consisting of a hospice social worker and trained dog, can work effectively with the patient and family with this special intervention. With the therapeutic use of the dog, relationships can often be established quickly and palliative care provided.

The presence of AAA/AAT in medical centers, with a wide variety of patients, has been increasing over the last several years, even though hospitals, due to zoonoses concerns, have traditionally been difficult places to initiate AAA/AAT programs. Zoonoses are diseases that can be transferred from animals to people, but with proper care, the chances of zoonoses remain rare (Burch, 1996). Although the risks of zoonoses are always present, Barba (1995) suggested that they tend to be overestimated and are actually low, even for immunosuppressed patients with cancer or HIV.

Hospitalized clients have shown improvement from AAA/AAT in such areas as impaired communication, ineffective coping, impaired physical mobility, self-concept problems, sensoriperceptual alteration, impaired social interactions, and altered thought processes (Barba, 1995). AAA/AAT sessions can help patients with verbal abilities and with memory and motor skills. A reduction of stress level is another benefit often witnessed in hospital settings, as animals provide a distraction for the patients. This is especially beneficial for patients with pain, anxiety, hyperactivity, or high blood pressure (Bernard, 1995). Because animals make people appear less sick to others (Rossbach and Wilson, 1992), animals can also improve social interactions with visitors. By giving families and friends something else to focus on, communication can become less strained and forced.

Because animals are nonjudgmental, a person's self-confidence and self-esteem can improve with animal contact. People are often self-conscious about physical differences during (or after) an illness or accident. These differences could range from speech problems to a lack of muscle coordination or movement. Patients can quickly sense when their changes make other people uncomfortable. Animals allow people to relax and just enjoy the direct physical contact of holding and petting a living creature. Cole and Gawlinski (1995) found that patients described their feelings after AAT sessions as happier, calmer, and less lonely. Furthermore, almost half of the patients in one survey indicated that the opportunity to participate in AAT sessions would help determine their choice of hospitals (Voelker, 1995).

AAA/AAT in school and residential settings, both for healthy and for impaired students, can be of benefit. Caring for animals can help children learn to nurture and increase motivation (Beck *et al.*, 2001; Katcher and Wilkins, 2000). AAT also allows children an outlet for the loving part of themselves and helps them control and regulate their own behavior while developing empathy toward other living creatures (Gonski, 1985; Ross, 1992). Through successes with the animal, many children are able to increase their self-esteem and thereby have more confidence when approaching new tasks. AAA/AAT provides a different approach in working on the same educational and social skills goals/objectives within a school setting.

Levinson (1964) was one of the first pioneers to report the benefits for children with various disabilities, including those who are nonverbal, inhibited, autistic, withdrawn, or schizophrenic. Although one of the first to actually document his use of animals, Levinson found that 33% of practitioners surveyed utilized animals at some point in their practice (Beck and Katcher, 1984). AAT has also demonstrated success with children who have emotional or physical problems, as well as those who have been abused or neglected. One way in which this is accomplished is to introduce the animal as a topic of conversation and mutual interest point. Whereas many children are reluctant to talk about what is going on at home, for instance, they are usually open to talking about how an animal looks or feels. Some AAT sessions begin with the therapist/animal handler talking to the animal instead of directly to the child. In this way, the child does not feel threatened and oftentimes will join in the conversation. The use of AAT has also been used successfully with autistic children in addressing self-esteem, socialization, and language skills (Law and Scott, 1995).

As of June 30, 2004, there were 2,131,180 prisoners in federal or state prisons or local jails. This constitutes approximately 486 inmates per 100,000 U.S. residents (U.S. Department of Justice Bureau of Justice Statistics, 2004). While the aim for this population has traditionally been one of punishment, many communities are looking more toward creative rehabilitative programs to help these individuals become contributing members of society. This has led to the establishment of several different types of inmate–animal programs. Reported by Strimple (2003), animal programs have been utilized by the department of corrections in a minimum of 15 states and one federal penitentiary. Oakwood Forensic Center (formally the Lima State Hospital for the Criminally Insane) in Lima, Ohio, is credited as the first successful animal therapy program in a U.S. prison (Strimple, 2003). After noticing changes in inmates who had cared for an injured bird, the center proposed a study to investigate the impact of animals on the inmates. When they compared two identical wards, one with and one without the presence of animals, they found that the ward with animals had a reduced number of violent incidents and fewer suicide attempts and required half the amount of medication (Lee, 1984).

These types of positive effects were also found at the Washington Correction Center for Women (WCCW) in Gig Harbor, Washington. Together with Tacoma Community College, WCCW trains shelter dogs to be service dogs to people in the community (Bustad, 1990). In this way, the benefits of the Prison Pet Partnership are threefold. The inmates acquire a marketable skill of dog training, gain self-esteem, and earn college credits. The community benefits by helping dogs that would have otherwise been destroyed, and finally, the recipients of the service dogs benefit. At present, 100% of the inmates who participated in the program have found employment upon release, and no one has reoffended in the past 3 years. (Schwartz, 2003). These two programs give new meaning to restorative justice, whereby prisoners simultaneously gain new skills as they give back to the community. These program developers have inspired other, like-minded individuals to develop similar programs around the country.

At the federal level, Coleman Federal Complex in Coleman, Florida, has partnered with Southeastern Guide Dogs, Inc. Together, they have worked to train the female inmates as dog handlers. These women train and socialize the dogs, after which the dogs are returned to Southeastern Guide Dogs for more advanced training before being given to individuals with impaired vision (Brink, 2001). Military Helping Individuals (AIMHI), established in 1994, is located in Fort Knox, Kentucky. In this program, dogs are trained as service dogs, hearing dogs, or social therapy dogs by U.S. Army inmates who, as a result, learn animal husbandry, human and animal behavior, and dog training. The success of this program can be noted through the decision to expand it to Fort Leavenworth in 2000 (Strimple, 2003).

Ohio leads the country in terms of developing and implementing dog training programs. The state currently has programs in 26 state and 2 private prisons. Part of this is likely due to the fact that in 1991, the governor mandated that all inmates must do some type of community service (Suber, 2002). These animal training programs are an excellent way to meet this requirement. Dogs in these programs are trained to assist people with mobility difficulties, as well as hearing, neurological, emotional, and visual problems [Ohio Department of Rehabilitation and Corrections (ODRC), 2000]. Pilot Dogs, Inc. of Ohio is one example of an ongoing successful program. Located in Columbus, Ohio, the program began at the Ohio Reformatory for Women in Marysville, Ohio, in 1992. Since that time, it has expanded to include seven prisons in Ohio and one in West Virginia. The program has reported success in training dogs and in improvements with inmates (Strimple, 2003).

Incarcerated juveniles can also benefit from animal training programs. Project Pooch was one of the first programs created to target juvenile offenders. Created in 1993, at McLaren Juvenile Correctional Facility in Woodburn, Oregon, the program teaches students such things as dog grooming and training, as well as how to care for dogs' health needs. The adolescents learn these skills by running a boarding kennel where the dogs receive training and grooming. These marketable skills are ones that can be utilized in many different settings (Hill, 2001). Assessment of this program found marked adolescent behavior improvements in areas of respect for authority, social interaction, and leadership. They also found evidence of growth in honesty, empathy, nurturing, social growth, understanding, confidence level, and pride in accomplishment. Additionally, there was zero recidivism among the participants (Merriam-Arduini, 2000). Similar findings were also made at the Colorado Boys Ranch with their "New Leash on Life" program (Seiz, 2003).

In addition to training dogs, visitation programs can be beneficial to adolescent and adult inmates. Pen Pals is an animal visitation program at Central New Mexico Correctional Facility in Los Lunas, New Mexico. In this program, volunteers visit with a variety of animals. They found that inmates who were reluctant to participate in other programs, through the desire to see the visiting animals, became more familiar with the staff and other settings on the campus. As a result, they were more likely to participate in other mental health programs. While some programs have volunteers who bring in animals that have been trained and screened for this purpose, other facilities have planned how to successfully implement animals into inmates' lives by allowing staff to bring their own animals into work. Obviously, these animals need to be screened and trained, and proper attention to their care must be made prior to these kinds of arrangements.

Another option for the inclusion of animals in correctional facilities includes allowing residential animals to live at the facility. Usually, the inmates are responsible for the care of the animals (with direct supervision). The success of this type of program relies on extensive planning and structure. Animals that require less care might be one way to slowly implement such a plan. Beginning with fish, birds, or small pocket pets (i.e., guinea pigs, hamsters) allows the staff and inmates to ensure the safety of all involved. After the basic program has been created, it can then be modified to include higher maintenance animals.

The Wild Mustang program, although terminated in 1992, demonstrated success in a multitude of areas. This program initially involved taming and training wild horses that were in danger of dying from starvation or thirst. The horse problem began when the New Mexico Bureau of Land Management

(NMBLM) began removing wild horses from public rangelands because of overcrowding. Because the Wild and Free-Roaming Horse and Burro Act of 1971 required humane care and treatment for these horses, the NMBLM created a partnership with the New Mexico Department of Corrections in which inmates would halter break the mustangs and prepare them for sale to the general public (New Mexico Bureau of Land Management, 1989). Handling the horses allowed inmates the opportunity to do meaningful work with tangible rewards. This program was a win–win situation. The horses were handled humanely, the NMBLM was able to improve its public image, and the correctional facility was able to offer work to its inmates that did not threaten any private industry. The Wild Mustang program helped the inmates in several ways. The opportunity to work with the wild mustangs gave the inmates an opportunity to assume a nurturing role, practice autonomy, and gain a sense of responsibility. Inmates that participated in the program had fewer disciplinary reports and an increased ability to handle stress. The recidivism rate for inmates in the program was significantly lower than the overall rate for New Mexico state correctional facilities (Cushing and Williams, 1995).

AAT with individuals is also increasing in correctional and residential treatment settings. A trained human–animal team, in collaboration with a professional staff member, works with the inmate/patient toward specific rehabilitative goals and objectives. By working through the animal, this is regarded as a more enjoyable and rewarding experience.

These different populations and their use of AAT demonstrate the wide range in which AAT is appropriate and useful. Because each setting has its own unique needs and population, each type of AAT focuses on different goals and strategies.

D. Program Level of Understanding AAA/AAT

Related to the preceding discussion is the variation in AAA/AAT that is based on the level of understanding that the agency or program has relative to this intervention. Efforts in providing in-service training for staff have proven useful. However, factors such as staff turnover and the difficulty of including all staff members in training opportunities (including the director and administrative staff) challenge agencies' ability to understand AAA/AAT and how these can be components of their therapeutic program.

As noted, to a large extent AAA/AAT is viewed as a volunteer activity. While volunteers are important to any social service organization, frequently this impacts how and to what extent AAA/AAT is incorporated into the professional therapeutic services provided by an agency.

A program fee for AAA/AAT often depends on whether organizations acknowledge that this is a useful and important service. Whether this is regarded as a volunteer activity or as a professional intervention, there are costs involved in delivering AAA/AAT effectively. Like many nonprofit organizations, AAA/AAT programs suffer from insufficient funding, with too much time and energy used to locate the funds necessary to operate. Presently, the majority of AAA/AAT is not third-party reimbursable, even though it may be a component of a client's care plan or student's individual education plan.

III. DESCRIPTION OF THE STRUCTURES AND APPROACHES OF AAA/AAT

Other considerations relative to AAA/AAT are the structures through which these services are provided and the particular approaches used. Structures can include the following: a university-affiliated or -based program; an autonomous nonprofit organization; an agency-based program; an individual volunteer; and the independent practitioner. AAA/AAT approaches include the human–animal team; volunteer and companion animal; professional and companion animal; and staff member and companion animal. A brief description of these structures and approaches is presented. It is important to recognize that the context in which AAA/AAT is delivered impacts quality, effectiveness, and accountability issues.

Some universities have been successful in developing human–animal bond interdisciplinary programs or centers. A university-based program is a well-established structure for responding to special practice and research areas. However, there are only a few such programs around the country that focus on the delivery of AAA/AAT services and the training of human–animal teams. There is merit to this approach, including having the interdisciplinary resources of a university available and students interested in learning about this intervention for their future professional practice.

AAA/AAT programs are related more frequently to organizations that obtain nonprofit status and have varying degrees of organizational structure, including a board of directors, paid and volunteer staff, and a budget. An advantage of this approach is that AAA/AAT is conducted under an auspice that provides guidance and some level of ongoing supervision and interaction among its members. These organizations also have the capacity to compete for external funding and to maintain volunteer commitment through training and ongoing team-building experiences.

Some service delivery organizations, such as a long-term care facility, develop their own AAA/AAT programs through staff that have some expertise in the human–animal bond field. Frequently it is the activities' coordinator/director, or another staff member, who initiates an AAA/AAT program as part of her/his responsibilities. Obviously, to be successful there must be administrative and staff support.

Another delivery mode of AAA/AAT is a person who wants to use the human–animal bond experience as a part of her/his volunteer or professional responsibilities. The level and quality of this can vary considerably based on such factors as the degree of training of the animal and human partner, ongoing supervision, and support from the organization where this takes place.

Private practitioners or therapists may use their companion animals in their work. The therapist determines when and under what conditions the animal could facilitate treatment. Under these circumstances AAA/AAT can vary considerably based on knowledge and skill of the therapist and training/temperament of the animal. This is less likely to be reported in the literature or evaluated systematically. It is more of an adjunctive intervention that is determined by the therapist as beneficial to the client.

A human–animal team approach is used frequently, consisting of the trained animal (usually a dog), the owner/handler, and a staff professional. The intent is a team effort in the delivery of the intervention. This is basically used in AAT, as there are identified goals and objectives determined, along with ongoing evaluation of effectiveness. There is significant merit to this team approach, with each team member having special contributions to make. For example, the staff member brings the understanding of the client, treatment goals, and organizational context; the owner/handler brings the expertise of the training; and the dog brings the uniqueness of the human–animal bond.

IV. AAA/AAT AND THE HUMAN–ANIMAL TEAM MODEL

As noted, it is critical to define and clarify AAA/AAT in order to validate this intervention and to evaluate its effectiveness. An illustration is provided as a way to encourage this development, using the dog as the companion animal (Table I).

V. RESEARCH AND EVALUATION

A number of current issues relate to implementing successful AAA/AAT programs. One of the most crucial ones is the provision of research and evaluation. Research and evaluation are important defining characteristics of AAA/AAT. Many persons and programs refer to what they do with animals as pet therapy but are not able to define its parameters and protocol clearly. There is an inability to properly evaluate the effectiveness of their programs. In

TABLE I The Human–Animal Team Model[a]

Animal-assisted therapy	Animal-assisted activity
Qualifications/training of human team member Behavioral screening and training of canine/dog Qualifications/training of agency staff member Endorsement/support of host organization	Similar requisites are required, but within the dimensions of AAA activity
Assessment of the participant (e.g., student, resident, patient, client)	Less is needed to be known in conducting AAA
Clarification of purpose of AAT, with specified goals and objectives Plan of sessions Monitoring, supervision, evaluation	Clarification of the purpose of AAA, with some need for monitoring, supervision, evaluation
Unique characteristics required include the ability to function as human–animal team; work through the animal; understand the human–animal bond; carry out AAT in the context of normalization, enjoyment, compassion, sensitivity; engage in ongoing dog and human training; be the dog's advocate	These characteristics are also necessary for AAA

[a]For these requisites it is necessary to examine the level or extent required for competent practice. For example, it is questionable that a sufficient level of training of the human and animal can be completed in a short, limited time frame. Further, it is important that the human–animal team is provided with ongoing supervision. Without some agreement on what is required for these requisites, AAA/AAT will continue to have wide variation and its worthiness will be regarded differently. Having the ability to "work through the animal" as the unique intervention factor is critical to the human–animal team.

addition, most studies are descriptive and do not make use of qualitative or quantitative measures. To a large extent, monitoring is achieved through periodic meetings with those involved to reflect on the progress seen and make any necessary modifications. However, there is limited formal evaluation.

There have been some recent gains in evaluation and research in this field. For example, a review of the literature on animal-assisted interventions in adolescent mental health was provided by the Center for the Interaction of Animals and Society, University of Pennsylvania, School of Veterinary Medicine (Kruger *et al.*, 2004). This was followed with a conference called "Can Animals Help Humans Heal? Animal-Assisted Interventions in Adolescent Mental Health." The intent of the conference was to bring together leading practitioners and scholars in the field to present relevant research findings. It was noted that some of the existing studies demonstrate the important potential benefits of animal-assisted interventions in the treatment of adolescent mental disorders. These include anxiety reduction in the therapeutic situation; expedited rapport between patients and therapists; improved attendance at, compliance with, and retention in therapy; improved interactions between patients and therapists; and improved behavior outside the context of therapy. Within the therapeutic milieu, animals also appear to serve as catalysts for learning, as sources of contact comfort, as outlets for nurturance, and as models of positive interpersonal behavior (Kruger *et al.*, 2004).

There are other illustrations of improvement in research and evaluation. Two other studies presented findings that noted improvement in the social skills of youth who were in specialized school and residential settings. One study, conducted in 2002–2003, involved evaluating the effectiveness of AAT approaches in an alternative high school for expelled youth (Granger and Granger, 2004). Individual and group AAT interventions were incorporated into selected students' individual educational plans. Qualitative and quantitative data measures were used, including pre- and posttest use of standardized teacher and student behavior rating scales. Analysis of data collected suggested the following results in terms of the outcome variables listed in the study.

- Socialization: Students participating in AAT exhibited a gain in social skills as a result of their involvement in the project.
- Social-peer behavior: Staff was supportive of the project and felt there was an overall positive impact.
- Educational adjustment: Participating students showed improvement in the areas of trust, communication, and pet–student interactions.

Students involved in the project said they enjoyed the experience. Staff members involved were supportive of the program, with some reservation about scheduling and time away from academics. All participants agreed the project had a positive impact on the students.

A second study took place in a residential treatment setting for boys (Seiz, 2004). The purpose of the project was to evaluate the effectiveness of an on-campus dog training program. For each 10-week training period, five dogs were selected from local humane shelters and, under supervision of a teacher/dog trainer, five youth individually cared for and trained the dogs for eventual adoption into the community. Qualitative and quantitative measures were used, including the canine bonding scale for specialized settings and the balanced emotional empathy scale. Conclusions of the study revealed that bonding played an increasing role in the boys' emotional life (e.g., helped the boys through tough times, comforted them when they were upset, helped them to relax, and helped them feel responsibility for the dog). There was also improved personal and social development (social skills), which augurs well for the boys' future.

A third study focused on providing AAT for children with autism (Leech *et al.*, 2004). Three cases were studied individually; behavioral change was measured against the individual students' own past measurements. Common themes were then determined. The study used several methods of observation to capture each individual's behavioral measures during each session. Goal areas included social and academic functioning levels. The social category included observations made around the students' interactions with their animals, their therapists, the researchers, their teachers, and their peers. Subthemes were connection to animal, following social norms and expectations, experiencing and expressing emotions, and empathizing. The academic category included observations of those behaviors that would enhance academic performance and success in the classroom environment.

Establishing a connection to the child's animal proved an important part of the AAT experience for all three participants. All three children consistently demonstrated a strong connection to their animals through hugs, petting, grooming, and talking to their animals. They also showed that they could use the connection with their animals for comfort. Learning to follow social norms and expectations was evident across participants. This included improved eye contact, remembering names, increased polite manners, and using appropriate voice tone and inflection. Empathy was evidenced through attempting to understand what their animals were feeling and how their own actions affected others. In addition, all three participants showed progress toward academically oriented goals. For example, one student had an increased ability to use present-tense verbs ending in "ing" and increased comprehension of prepositional phrases. Another participant improved in following multitask directions that could aid him in more complicated classroom tasks. Another student worked on listening skills that were initially creating difficulty for her academically. The study suggests that giving autistic students individual attention, individualized goals, and the opportunity to build relationships with animals can have therapeutic benefits.

A fourth study was in a restorative nursing program, with the primary goal of assisting older adults in reaching their highest functional ability (Bennet *et al.*, 2004). The participants were residents of a long-term care setting and were referred to restorative care when they reached their rehabilitative goals or were no longer improving within rehabilitation services. Group size ranged from four to eight participants. The human–animal teams were observed by graduate students, with data collected on participation in level of activity, including group physical, group cognitive, independent physical, independent social, and independent cognitive. Five common themes were found characterizing the sessions: serving to increase verbalizations, increasing socialization/interaction among participants, increasing attention to or participation with the dog or the leader, providing opportunities to be physically active, and providing perceptive, assistive leadership that enhanced opportunities for participation. An increase in happiness (smile/laugh) was also observed. The study provided additional parameters for measuring effectiveness and demonstrating benefits of AAT.

There are other research and evaluation efforts as presented in the journal *Anthrozoos*, as well as in specific disciplinary journals. However, to date most of the research efforts have been small scale and underfunded.

VI. CONCLUSIONS

We have described the current status of AAA/AAT in specialized settings. It continues to be a picture of considerable variation in levels of quality. Much of this is related to the very nature of AAA/AAT, understanding the uniqueness of the human–animal bond, and the ability to work through the animal. Other factors influencing this intervention include the variety of animals involved, their temperament and level of training, and the human team member and her/his level of training and personal characteristics. The setting or organization where AAA/AAT takes place and the variety of clients also influence how this intervention is conducted.

The interdisciplinary nature of AAA/AAT in many respects enriches its content but also contributes to different ways of conducting or implementing it. Professionals, staff, and volunteers engage in AAA/AAT based on their understanding of and personal commitment to the human–animal bond and their level of training in this intervention. Efforts have been made to establish guidelines for AAA/AAT, but to date these have fallen short of addressing the wide variation that presently exists. The "how to" or the procedure for conducting this intervention needs standardization. Despite these factors, the therapeutic use of companion animals, specifically AAA/AAT, is continuing to expand into multiple areas of service. Whether it gains the necessary creditability as a vital therapeutic intervention and receives sufficient funding for direct services, evaluation, and research remain to be seen.

REFERENCES

Adbill, M. N., and Juppe, D. (1997). "Pets in Therapy." Ravensdale, Idyll Arbor, Inc., WA.

American Kennel Club (2004). AKC evaluator's guide: Canine good citizen program. Retrieved August 5, 2005 from http://www.akc.org/events/cgc/program.cfm?page=3.

Arkow, P. (1990). "Pet therapy: A Study and Resource Guide for the Use of Companion Animals in Selected Therapies," 6 Ed. Humane Society of the Pikes Peak region, Colorado Springs, CO.

Barba, B. E. (1995). A critical review of the research on the human/companion animal relationship: 1988–1993. *Anthrozoos* **8**(1), 9–14.

Baun, M. M., Bergstrom, N., Langston, N. F., and Thoma, L. (1984). Physiological effects of human/companion animal bonding. *Nurs. Res.* **33**(3), 126–129.

Beck, A. M., and Katcher, A. H. (1984). A new look at pet-facilitated therapy. *J. Am. Vet. Med. Assoc.* **184**(4), 414–421.

Beck, A. M., Melson, G. F., da Costa, P. L., and Liu, T. (2001). The educational benefits of a ten-week home-based wild bird feeding program for children. *Anthrozoos* **14**(1), 19–28.

Beck, C., and Peacock, P. (1988). Nursing interventions for patients with Alzheimer's disease. *Nurs. Clin. North Am.* **23**(1), 95–124.

Bennet, A., Goldstein, S., Pettigrew, L., and Cecil, M. S. (2004). "Animal-Assisted Therapy in Restorative Care: A Comparison of Three HABIC (Human-Animal Bond in Colorado) Animal-Assisted Therapy Groups." Unpublished manuscript, Department of Occupational Therapy, Colorado State University.

Bernard, S. (1995). "Animal Assisted Therapy: A Guide for Health Care Professionals and Volunteers." Therapet, Whitehouse, TX.

Beyersdorfer, P. S., and Birkenhauer, D. M. (1990). Therapeutic use of pets on an Alzheimer's unit. *Am. J. Alzheimers Care Relat. Disord. Res.* **5**(1), 13–17.

Biery, M. J. (1985). Riding and the handicapped. *Vet. Clin. North Am. Small Anim. Pract.* **15**(2), 345–354.

Boldt, M. A., and Dellmann-Jenkins, M. (1992). The impact of companion animals in later life and considerations for practice. *J. Appl. Gerontol.* **11**(2), 228–239.

Brink, G. (2001). Time to train. Retrieved August 2, 2005 from http://www.sptimes.com/News/022501/State/Time_to_train_.shtml.

Burch, M. R. (1996). "Volunteering with Your Pet: How to Get Involved in Animal Assisted Therapy with Any Kind of Pet." Howell Book House, New York.

Bustad, L. K. (1990). Prison programs involving animals. "Compassion, Our Last Great Hope" *In* (L. K. Bustad, ed.), pp. 72–73. Delta Society, Renton, WA.

Catanzaro, T. E. (2003). Human-animal bond and primary prevention. *Am. Behav. Sci.* **47**(1), 29–30.

Cole, K. M., and Gawlinski, A. (1995). Animal-assisted therapy in the intensive care unit: A staff nurse's dream comes true. *Nurs. Clin. North Am.* **30**(3), 529–537.

Corson, S., Corson, E., Gwynne, P., and Arnold, L. (1975). Pet facilitated psychotherapy in a hospital setting. *Curr. Psychiatr. Ther.* **15**, 277–286.

Cushing, J. L., and Williams, J. D. (1995). The Wild Mustang program: A case study in facilitated inmate therapy. *J. Offend. Rehab.* **22**(3-4), 95–115.

Delta Society. (n.d.). About Animal-Assisted Activities and Animal-Assisted Therapy. Available at http://www.deltasociety.org/aboutaaat.htm.

Diesch, S. L. (1984). Companion animals on the farm. *In* "Dynamic Relationships in Practice: Animals in the Helping Professions" (P. Arkow, ed.), pp. 257–270. Latham Foundation, Alameda, CA.

Elliot, V., and Milne, D. (1991). Patients' best friend? *Nurs. Times* **87**(6), 34–35.

Engel, B. T. (1992). Therapeutic riding programs: Instruction and rehabilitation. *In* "A Handbook for Instructors and Therapists." Barbara Engel Therapy Services, Durango, CO.

Friedmann, E., Katcher, A., Lynch, J., and Thomas, S. (1980). Animal companions and one-year survival of patients after discharge from a coronary care unit. *Public Health Rep.* **95**, 307–312.

Gonski, Y. A. (1985). The therapeutic utilization of canines in a child welfare setting. *Child Adolesc. Soc. Work J.* **2**(2), 93–105.

Granger, B., and Granger, G. V. (2004). "Evaluating the Effectiveness of Animal-Assisted Therapy Approaches in an Alternative High School for Expelled Youth: A Qualitative/Quantitative Analysis." Paper presented at the Can Animals Help Humans Heal? Animal-Assisted Interventions in Adolescent Mental Health conference, Philadelphia, March. Available at http://www.vet.upenn.edu/research/centers/cias/pdf/Proceedings.pdf.

Granger, B., Kogan, L., Fitchett, J., and Helmer, K. (1998). The human-animal team approach to animal assisted therapy. *Anthrozoos* **11**(3), 172–176.

Granger, B., and Kogan, L. (2000). Animal-assisted therapy in specialized settings. *In* "Handbook on Animal-Assisted Therapy: Theoretical Foundations and Guidelines for Practice" (A. H. Fine, ed.), pp. 213–236. Academic Press, San Diego, CA.

Haladay, J. (1989). Animal assisted therapy for PWA's: Bringing a sense of connection. *AIDS Patient Care* 3(1), 38–39.

Hill, N. (2001, March 1). Project pooch offers a second chance. *Dog Nose News* 8–9.

Holcomb, R., Jendro, C., Weber, B., and Nahan, U. (1997). Use of an aviary to relieve depression in elderly males. *Anthrozoos* **10**(1), 32–36.

Katcher, A. H., and Wilkins, G. (2000). The centaur's lessons: Therapeutic education through care of animals and nature student. *In* "Handbook on Animal-Assisted Therapy: Theoretical Foundations and Guidelines for Practice" (A. H. Fine, ed.), pp. 153–177. Academic Press, San Diego, CA.

Kruger, K., Trachtenberg, S., and Serpell, J. (2004). Can animals help humans heal? Animal-assisted interventions in adolescent mental health. Center for the Interaction of Animals and Society, University of Pennsylvania School of Veterinary Medicine. Retrieved September 2, 2005 from http://www2.vet.upenn.edu/research/centers/cias/publications.html.

Kubler-Ross, E. (1969). "On Death and Dying." Macmillan, New York.

Law, S., and Scott, S. (1995). Tips for practitioners: Pet care: A vehicle for learning. *Focus Autist. Behav.* **10**(2), 17–18.

Lee, D. (1984). Companion animals in institutions. *In* "Dynamic Relationships in Practice: Animals in the Helping Professions" (P. Arkow, ed.), pp. 229–236. Latham Foundation, Alameda, CA.

Leech, N., Foster, A., Granger, B., Granger, V., and Bender, K. (2004). "Animal Assisted Therapy with Children with Autism." Unpublished manuscript, Research and Development Center for the Advancement of Student Learning, Colorado State University.

Lehrman, J., and Ross (2001). Therapeutic riding for a student with multiple disabilities and visual impairment: A case study. *J. Vis. Impairm. Blindn.* **95**(2), 108–109.

Levinson, B. (1964). Pets: A special technique in child psychotherapy. *Ment. Health* **48**, 243–248.

Levinson, B. M. (1972). "Pets and Human Development." Charles C Thomas, Springfield, IL.

Lukina, L. N. (1999). Influence of dolphin-assisted therapy sessions on the functional state of children with psychoneurological symptoms of diseases. *Hum. Physiol.* **25**(6), 676–679.

Macauley, B. L., and Gutierrez, K. M. (2004). The effectiveness of hippotherapy for children with language-learning disabilities. *Commun. Disord. Q.* **25**(4), 205–217.

Mallon, G. P. (1994). Cow as co-therapist: Utilization of farm animals as therapeutic aides with children in residential treatment. *Child Adolesc. Social Work J.* **11**(6), 455–474.

Manor, W. (1991). Alzheimer's patients and their caregivers: The role of the human animal bond. *Holist. Nurs. Pract.* **5**(2), 32–37.

McCowan, L. L. (1984). Equestrian therapy. *In* "Dynamic Relationships in Practice: Animals in the Helping Professions" (P. Arkow, ed.), pp. 237–256. Latham Foundation, Alameda, CA.

Merriam-Arduini, S. (2000). "Evaluation of an Experimental Program Designed to Have a Positive Effect on Adjudicated Violent, Incarcerated Male Juveniles Age 12–25 in the state of Oregon." Unpublished doctoral dissertation, Pepperdine University in California.

Messent, P. (1983). Social facilitation of contact with other people by pet dogs. *In* "New Perspectives on Our Lives with Companion Animals" (A. Katcher and A. M. Beck, eds.). University of Pennsylvania Press, Philadelphia, PA.

Muschel, I. J. (1984). Pet therapy with terminal cancer patients. *Soc. Casework.* **65**(8), 451–458.

Nathanson, D. E. (1989). Using Atlantic bottlenose dolphins to increase cognition of mentally retarded children. *In* "Clinical and Abnormal Psychology" (P. Lovibond and P. Wilson, eds.), pp. 233–242. Elsevier, North Holland.

Nathanson, D. E. (1998). Long-term effectiveness of dolphin-assisted therapy for children with severe disabilities. *Anthrozoos* **11**(1), 22–32.

Nathanson, D. E., de Castro, D., Friend, H., and McMahon, M. (1997). Effectiveness of short-term dolphin-assisted therapy for children with severe disabilities. *Anthrozoos* **10**(2-3), 90–100.

Nathanson, D. E., and de Faria (1993). Cognitive improvement of children in water with and without dolphins. *Anthrozoos* **6**(1), 17–29.

New Mexico Bureau of Land Management (1989). A winning combination: Wild horses and prison inmates (BLM-NM-GI-89-022-4370). Bureau of Land Management, Santa Fe, NM.

Ross, S. B. (1992). Building empathy to reduce violence to all living things. *J. Soc. Compan. Anim. Stud.* **4**(1), 4–5.

Rossbach, K. A., and Wilson, J. P. (1992). Does a dog's presence make a person likable? Two studies. *Anthrozoos* **5**(1), 40–51.

Savishinsky, J. (1985). Pets and family relationships among nursing home residents. Special Issue: Pets and the family. *Marriage Family Rev.* **8**(3-4), 109–134.

Sayler, P. (1992). Selecting the hippotherapy horse. *In* "Therapeutic Riding Programs Instruction and Rehabilitation: A Handbook for Instructors and Therapists" (B. T. Engel, ed.), pp. 86–87. Barbara Engel Therapy Services, Durango, CO.

Schwartz, B. K. (2003). The use of animal-facilitated therapy in the rehabilitation of incarcerated felons. *In* "Correctional Psychology: Practice, Programming, and Administration" (B. K. Schwartz, ed.), pp. 16:1–16:9. Civic Research Institute, Kingston, NJ.

Seiz, R. (2003). "Evaluation Research Project on the New Leash on Life Program: Colorado Boys Ranch." Unpublished manuscript, School of Social Work, Colorado State University.

Strimple, E. O. (2003). A history of prison inmate-animal interaction programs. *Am. Behav. Sci.* **47**(1), 70–78.

Struckus, J. E. (1991) Pet-facilitated therapy and the elderly client. *In* "Handbook of Clinical Behavior Therapy with the Elderly Client: Applied Clinical Psychology" (P. A. Wisocki, ed.), Vol. xviii, pp. 403–419. Plenum Press, New York.

Suber, W. (2002). Prisoner community service. Ohio department of rehabilitation and corrections. Retrieved August 15, 2005 from http://www.drc.state.oh.us/web/commserv.htm.

U.S. Department of Justice Bureau of Justice Statistics (2004). Prison Statistics retrieved August 10, 2005 from http://www.ojp.usdoj.gov/bjs/prisons.htm.

Voelker, R. (1995). Puppy love can be therapeutic, too. *J. Am. Med. Assoc.* **274**(24), 1897–1899.

CHAPTER 14

Human–Animal Interaction and Successful Aging

MARA BAUN
University of Texas, Health Science Center at Houston School of Nursing, Houston, Texas 77030

REBECCA JOHNSON
University of Missouri–Columbia, MU Sinclair School of Nursing, Columbia, Missouri 65211

BARBARA MCCABE
University of Nebraska Medical Center, College of Nursing, Lincoln, Nebraska 68588

I. SUCCESSFUL AGING

Rapid expansion in the numbers of persons over age 65 in general and over age 80 in particular is an accepted reality in the United States and many other countries. This longevity is possible through advances in treating disease, improving nutrition, and expanding fitness and health education. In recent years, as greater longevity has become a distinct possibility for most older adults, the question of how to live and age "successfully" has arisen and received great attention.

There are varying definitions of "successful" or "healthy" aging. Commonly these involve not only living longer but remaining able to function with varying degrees of independence (Haveman-Nies *et al.*, 2003) and maintaining physical, mental, and social well-being (Vaillant and Mukamal, 2001). One of the most recognized definitions of successful aging, described by Rowe and Kahn (1998), forms the basis for content of this chapter. This definition includes three components: absence of chronic disease and disability, high cognitive and physical functioning, and active engagement with life. The components, while useful, are altered slightly in this chapter by our interpretation and clarification. We do not suggest that aging is either "successful" or "unsuccessful," but rather that success occurs along a continuum between the two. Thus older adults may view themselves and be viewed by others as aging successfully, despite living with chronic illness, having cognitive and physical limitations, and being limited in their engagement with the outside world.

Given that older adults suffer from chronic diseases at rates higher than their younger counterparts, it would be unrealistic to declare that no one with any of these conditions could age successfully. Their most common chronic conditions include arthritis, heart disease, hypertension, osteoporosis, and diabetes. Successful aging can occur when one prevents these conditions as long as possible through a healthy lifestyle and/or controls the symptoms and progression of these conditions after they arise so as to continue functioning as independently as possible. Older adults with disabilities can age successfully given modifications in their environment and behavior to accommodate their disabilities.

Most older adults live, on average, 17.4 years past age 65 and spend 10.5 of these without any disability (Crimmins *et al.*, 2003). On average, women (the largest group of older adults) live 77 years without any limitation in their ability to take care of themselves (Crimmins *et al.*, 2003). However, despite the fact that most older adults age with one or more chronic illnesses, they assess their health as good or better than good. This suggests that they may believe that something is compensating for or minimizing existing symptoms and preventing worsening of their health. For example, Seeman and Chen (2003) reported various risk and protective factors for older adults' physical functioning based on a national sample of 1066 people they studied for over 2 years. They found that engaging in regular physical exercise seemed to exert a protective effect over declines in health among older adults whether or not they had chronic illnesses. They also found that among those with chronic illnesses, psychosocial support limited a decline in function. This effect is believed to occur by reducing the stress of dealing with these illnesses via lowering physiologic arousal (the "fight-or-flight" response to stress). There are many actions that older adults can take to lower this arousal, and also many situations in a given day that have the same effect.

II. HEALTH-PROMOTING BEHAVIOR AND SUCCESSFUL AGING

The benefit of health-promoting lifestyle behaviors continues to mount. There is ample evidence demonstrating there is no chronological age limit to maintaining and/or increasing one's active engagement with life. In fact, one can hardly escape the mantra of "use it or lose it" in scientific as well as lay literature (Rowe and Kahn, 1998). Nightly news shows feature special reports disavowing the stereotypical thinking that older individuals must "slow down" and "take it easy" in order to avoid injury and protect their health. The National Institute on Aging (NIA) has a web site (http://nihseniorhealth.gov/exercise/toc.html) directed to informing and encouraging the older adult to "get in shape." Specific exercises to improve strength and flexibility are featured on the web site as well as information about healthy nutrition. The essence of this web site and companion booklet—"Exercise: A Guide from the National Institute on Aging" (National Institute on Aging, 2001)—is that "it's never too late" to engage in healthy lifestyle behaviors.

There is clear and convincing evidence that engaging in physical activity can lead to improvement in overall physical health, muscular and bone strength (Thompson, 2002), cardiovascular endurance (Houde and Melillo, 2002), and cognitive functioning (Reuter-Lorenz and Lustig, 2005). Physical activity has become the "magic elixir" that brings the promise of functional health and successful aging.

Opportunities abound for persons of all age groups to make health-promoting lifestyle behavior changes in such areas as physical activity, nutrition, stress management, interpersonal relationships, and spirituality (Pender *et al.*, 2005). This is especially good news for older individuals who typically have more leisure time available to pursue activities that lead to improved health outcomes and ultimately quality of life. The challenge is to find ways to support older adults in their efforts to replace sedentary lifestyle behaviors with behaviors consistent with active engagement with life.

There is increasing evidence that social support is an integral component of healthy lifestyle behaviors. For older adults there are fewer contemporaries to provide support to take on new behaviors. A relationship with a companion animal can serve as a motivator to try out lifestyle behaviors that lead to greater involvement with life.

III. HUMAN–COMPANION ANIMAL INTERACTIONS AND SUCCESSFUL AGING

Research has demonstrated that physiologic arousal lowers in response to human–companion animal interaction. Early research showed lowering of blood pressure when people interacted with dogs to which they were attached (Baun *et al.*, 1984). More recently, Odendaal (2000) found that stress hormone (cortisol) levels decreased most when people interacted quietly with their own pet dog. Cortisol levels also decreased (but less) when people interacted with an unfamiliar, but friendly, dog. Elevated cortisol levels have been linked with memory loss (Greendale *et al.*, 2000) and listed as one component of "allostatic load," in which the body develops cumulative effects of repeated adaptations to stressors (Seeman *et al.*, 1997). Allostatic load has been associated with overall physical and cognitive decline in older adults (Seeman *et al.*, 1997). Long-term recurrent stress, activating the "fight-or-flight" response, has been linked to the most common chronic illnesses experienced by older adults, including high blood pressure, diabetes, and heart disease. Thus, it is essential for older adults to reduce their allostatic load so as to prevent chronic illnesses and to minimize the negative effects of illnesses when they do occur in order to maintain physical and mental functioning.

Interacting with a companion animal may be one way to reduce allostatic load. Allen and colleagues (2002) found that people had significantly smaller increases in blood pressure and heart rate when a dog was present while they completed arithmetic tasks and that pet owners had significantly lower blood pressure and heart rate levels than non–pet owners to begin with. Hertstein (1995) found that pet saliency or importance was a significant predictor of physical health in older adults.

Psychosocial support–mediated stress and allostatic load reduction may be the main mechanism by which older pet owners have been found to have better functioning in activities of daily living than nonowners when studied over a 1-year period (Raina *et al.*, 1999) and to have fewer physician appointments than non–pet owners even in the face of stressful life events (Siegel, 1990). While merely interacting with pets may produce some of the benefits described, they may also be due to healthier lifestyles among pet owners. Dembicki and Anderson (1996) found that older adult pet owners walked longer and also had lower triglyceride and cholesterol levels than non–pet owners. Commitment to pets, particularly dogs, involves exercising them and thus may lead to healthier exercise patterns among dog owners, but these patterns may differ across ethnic groups. For example, Johnson and Meadows (2002) found that while Latino elders expressed a very strong bond with their pet dogs, they did not necessarily exercise with them. The implications for maintaining function among older adults who do exercise with pets have yet to be tested. Investigators have found that modifiable impairment, such as lower extremity impairment, was a strong predictor of declining function among older adults (Tinetti *et al.*, 2005). Based on this finding, walking (e.g., with a pet) may have an impact on preventing disability and functionally limiting effects of chronic illnesses.

Other investigators have found that pets influence older adults' health indirectly by improving morale (Lago *et al.*, 1989). This mind–body connection has been well established in research and can be a factor in maintaining older adults' health and preventing or minimizing disability. There is reason to believe that older adults' interaction with companion animals may activate this connection and be a powerful tool for health care providers, family members, and older adults themselves in promoting successful aging by preventing chronic illnesses or, when they do occur, by minimizing their disabling effects. For example, elderly women having a pet to which they were attached were more likely to report higher levels of happiness than those who either did not have a pet or were not attached to their pets (Ory and Goldberg, 1983). This effect of pets, however, was related to the socioeconomic status (SES) of the women, with those of higher SES having higher levels of happiness than those of lower SES.

Among the institutionalized elderly, animals have been found to be therapeutic in a number of ways. The presence of therapy animals has been particularly useful in reducing agitated behaviors (Churchill *et al.*, 1999; Richeson, 2003), in decreasing episodes of verbal aggression and anxiety (Fritz *et al.*, 1995), and in increasing social interaction (Fick, 1993; Kongable *et al.*, 1989) in institutionalized elderly with dementias, including Alzheimer's disease.

Aquariums have had interesting effects on persons with Alzheimer's disease. Edwards and Beck (2002) demonstrated significant increases in nutritional intake among residents of specialized Alzheimer's units by simply placing aquariums in the dining rooms. The increases in nutrition were accompanied by significant weight gain among the residents.

While many areas of companion animal interaction with older adults need further research to substantiate their effectiveness, there are studies to support positive benefits from this intervention. These interventions, however, need to be planned carefully, considering not only characteristics of the older adults themselves but also of their environment.

A. Facilitating Relationships between Pets and Older Adults "Aging in Place"

The notion of "aging in place" is not a new concept. Most investigators and others who work with older adults routinely hear their participants/clients express a desire to remain living "in my own home." Often older adults want to remain in their own homes so that they can keep their pets. Staying in their own homes can present particular challenges given the rapidly expanding demographic group that older adults constitute and their needs for health care services. Approximately one-third of all older adults need some form of supportive care and services to remain living in the community. This care can range from homemaker services to assist with housework and bathing to professional services, such as medication management, regular monitoring of health conditions, and full-scale coordinating of many health care providers. Aging in place aims, as an alternative to relocation to a nursing home, to provide needed care and prevent relocation-associated trauma.

As the aging in place movement has grown, so have the number of options for these types of places in which to live. A wide variety of alternatives exist including subsidized apartments designed for older adults, where care and services are not provided, retirement communities, assisted living facilities where older adults may have their own room or apartment, with limited services typically including congregate meals and housekeeping, or a combination of these. These models provide only partial versions of aging in place. The fear of having to move, even to a different part of the building, can be so intense for older adults that they may attempt to hide their growing needs and thus do not receive care that could facilitate their health and functioning.

A group of faculty at University of Missouri–Columbia (MU) Sinclair School of Nursing whose expertise is in gerontology recognized the need for a new model of aging in place in which the threat and stress of relocation would not impede proper care provision for older adults. This aging in place project was formulated with two components: A home health agency—Senior Care—was formed to provide care coordination and direct care to older adults. The second component required a corporate partner to build and manage TigerPlace, a 32-apartment residential facility. The partnership was formed with Americare Systems, Inc., of Sikeston, Missouri. Americare is the "landlord" of the facility and provides meal service, housekeeping, and concierge-type activity planning. At TigerPlace, a resident need not relocate when even advanced levels of care are needed. The facility is equipped with sensors to detect and report falls and monitoring devices for those with dementia that are used to ensure their safety. Staff of Senior Care monitor the residents' health and care needs and implement treatment plans within the facility.

TigerPlace features efficiency one- and two-bedroom apartments, a large community room, classroom, congregate and private dining rooms, hair salon, sports bar, exercise room, and clinic space for resident use with health care providers. Situated on several acres, the facility includes walk trails and outside exercise areas.

TigerPlace has a strong relationship with University of Missouri–Columbia and is host to students from nursing, physical therapy, social work, occupational therapy, medicine, law, journalism, engineering (who were heavily involved in developing the building with state-of-the-art technology), and education. TigerPlace residents are encouraged to participate in the myriad of activities, lectures, concerts, and exhibits that the university has ongoing, and transportation is provided.

TigerPlace is a pet-inclusive, pet-encouraging facility. This philosophy is based on research showing that human–pet interaction provides visual, auditory, olfactory, and tactile stimulation and that this interaction may stimulate well-being through chemical processes. For example, Odendaal (2000) found that in response to a quiet petting interaction with a dog, people had significant improvements in serum oxytocin, prolactin, β-endorphin, norepinephrine, phenylethylamine, dopamine, and cortisol levels. These neurochemicals are believed to enhance feelings of well-being, positive mood, and relaxation. Knowing that pets are beneficial for older adults, engineers considered pets throughout the design and construction of the TigerPlace facility. Each apartment has a screened porch, wide windowsills, an outside entrance, and tile entry to accommodate pet needs. Perhaps the most unique and compelling feature is the veterinary clinic within the building, specially designed to provide care for the pet residents of TigerPlace.

B. TigerPlace Pet Initiative (TiPPI)

TiPPI is a cross-disciplinary, collaborative program between the MU Sinclair School of Nursing and the MU College of Veterinary Medicine. The underlying principle of TiPPI is the belief in the health benefits of human–animal interaction and the human–animal bond for older adults and pets. This belief is based on research showing that older adults live longer, healthier, and happier lives when they own or interact regularly with pets.

The goals of TiPPI are to provide the following benefits.

- Foster a pet-inclusive environment at TigerPlace. An admission and periodic screening process is in place for residents' pets, and residents who do not have pets are assisted to adopt pets as they would like.
- Facilitate excellent veterinary care of TigerPlace residents' pets, while simultaneously providing an invaluable learning experience for veterinary students to work with older adult clients. The facility features a fully equipped veterinary exam room with equipment enabling preventive health care and treatment for noncritical illnesses. Residents need only walk down the hallway with their pets to visit the veterinarian. The clinic is staffed on a periodic basis with students and clinicians from the MU College of Veterinary Medicine. Pets are transported (either by the residents or TigerPlace staff) to the veterinary medical teaching hospital if they need more intense treatment.
- Promote research into the benefits of human–animal interaction and the human–animal bond. TigerPlace provides an ideal place to study the role of pets in older adults' lives.
- Provide foster care and adoption services for bereaved pets. An endowment is in place so that when a TiPPI pet's owner is deceased or can no longer care for the pet, funds are available to support the pet's care in a foster home with another resident of TigerPlace or, if this is not possible,

in a foster home in the community. The funds support food and medical care of the pet until it is placed in a permanent home.

Taken in total, TigerPlace offers a remarkable change in the usual model of aging in place. It eliminates mandatory relocation as older adults' care needs increase and thus minimizes the fear associated with this. TigerPlace residents enjoy meals bordering on the gourmet prepared by a formally trained executive chef and regular activities and excursions, and most importantly, they can bring their pets and know that these beloved companions will also be cared for.

IV. PET SELECTION

A. Community-Dwelling Elderly

Recommending a pet for an elderly person is a challenging opportunity. Even though a number of studies have demonstrated that pets can be beneficial to the elderly, e.g., in alleviating depression and in increasing socialization, finding the right pet for a particular person can be difficult. The primary consideration is the health and safety of the person.

Many older adults have mobility difficulties. It is not uncommon for elderly persons to walk with canes or walkers and to be somewhat unsteady on their feet. While a young dog can provide much affection and entertainment, it may be too strong for the elderly person to walk on a leash or it might be able to cause a fall by jumping against the legs or tripping the person. The elderly may not be able to move quickly enough to get a puppy house broken. Thus, an older dog, particularly one who has been obedience trained, socialized, and housebroken, may be a good alternative. Often dog breeders, especially those who show their dogs, have adult dogs who are still young but are no longer going to be shown and whom they would like to place in loving homes. These purebred dogs usually are excellent examples of the breed, have been bred for good temperament, have been socialized to dog shows where they had to perform in front of hundreds of people and dogs, and thus make excellent pets.

Other sources of well-trained dogs are the agencies who train dogs as service dogs, e.g., seeing eye, hearing, and assistant dogs for people with handicaps. At present, there is a 75% dropout rate for these dogs, i.e., three-quarters of the dogs who have been specially reared do not succeed in their formal training program. Generally, they make excellent pets because they have had systematic socialization and obedience training since they were young puppies. There are, however, long lists of people waiting to adopt these dogs, and the puppy raisers generally have the first option to adopt the dog if it is rejected during the formal training program.

Many humane societies have adopt-a-pet programs, some designed specifically for the elderly. While there are many animals at humane society shelters who can become excellent pets, careful consideration needs to be given to the elderly person's abilities and the pet's needs. If the animal was brought to the shelter for behavior problems, an elderly person may not be able to provide the appropriate behavior modifications. However, sometimes wonderful pet animals are available for adoption.

Elderly persons seeking to acquire a dog will have individual needs and likes and dislikes. Sometimes as individuals age, their self-concept does not change as their bodies become more limited, and they may be unrealistic in assessing what they can and cannot do. Their memories of a loved dog may not include the difficulties encountered during puppyhood, and they may only remember the docile, well-behaved older dog in the last years of its life. Thus, seeking advice on the type of dog to be acquired from an experienced dog person and health care provider may be very useful in matching the individual with the right dog.

Most major cities have one or more kennel clubs and dog training clubs. Often these clubs provide public service through maintaining a telephone to assist persons with dog-related questions. Some purebred dog clubs participate in rescue programs where they take unwanted dogs of their breed, rehabilitate them if necessary, and place them in good homes. Some of these rescued dogs might make excellent pets for the elderly. Also, veterinarians can provide advice about the care requirements of various breeds. Another avenue of information on purebred dogs is the American Kennel Club, which has an excellent web site (http://www.akc.org) and can refer inquiries to the national breed clubs. In addition, there are numerous home pages on various breeds of dogs and other dog-related activities that can be accessed through one of the search engines on the Internet. Most libraries have sections on dogs.

It is a good idea for anyone, particularly the elderly, not to be impulse driven in the acquisition of a pet. In addition to the monetary investment, there may be a 10- to 15-year commitment involved. A few weeks of investigation and planning can be a good investment in making sure that the acquisition of the pet is a positive experience. Sometimes, it is useful if an adult child partners with the elderly person in the process of pet adoption. It is hoped then that the adult child will have some commitment to assisting the elderly person throughout the process. The elderly need to recognize their current and potential limitations that could occur during the life of the pet. If there is a strong potential that the person will not be able to care for the pet throughout its entire life, an arrangement might be made with a family member or other responsible person to take the pet if the elderly person becomes unable to provide care either temporarily or permanently. In Houston and other cities there are groups of volunteers who will care for pets of low-income hospitalized or incapacitated elderly (http://www.pawshouston.org/).

A few retirement homes allow elderly residents to bring their pets with them, but the elderly have to be able to care for the pet, and there may be restrictions on the size and species of the pets allowed. It is hoped that the number of institutions allowing personal pets will increase in the future. Most nursing homes do not have facilities for personal pets. One of the greatest sources of distress for the institutionalized elderly can be the loss of their beloved pets. Many nursing homes do have regular pet visitation programs and allow individuals' pets to visit on a regular basis. Family members or friends can keep the pet and bring it to see its owner. A particularly sad occurrence is for the pet to be taken to the local humane society when its owner is institutionalized and then euthanized or placed with strangers so that the elderly person experiences not only the loss of personal independence but also the loss of a real significant other.

Sometimes, the choice of a pet other than a dog is ideal for an elderly person. Cats, for example, require less personal care than dogs. Nonetheless, the elderly person needs to be mobile enough to change the litter box and responsible enough to feed and care for the cat. Eyesight needs to be good enough to avoid tripping over any pet who has access to the floor.

Sometimes, a caged animal, such as a bird, might be a better choice if the elderly person has difficulty with mobilization. Birds can be excellent companions. Most domestic birds can be hand trained, thus providing physical contact, but also can be kept in cages. The elderly person needs to be able to provide food and water and clean the cage regularly.

Many other small animals could provide touch and affection for elderly persons. Gerbils, guinea pigs, mice, rats, rabbits, hamsters, turtles, and snakes are but a few of the potential small animals that could be wonderful pets. Sometimes it is not possible to predict to which animal strong bonds can develop. Physical contact with the animal is extremely important in the choice of a pet for some people but is not a strong consideration for others. For example, some elderly may find that watching fish in a tank can provide many hours of intense enjoyment.

A major consideration in the acquisition of pets by the elderly is access to veterinarian care. Frequently, elderly persons are no longer able to drive. Finding someone to take the pet to the veterinarian's office may be problematic. Even though there are many ways for the elderly to get transportation for their own health care appointments, there are no similar services for animal health care. In addition, many elderly are living on fixed incomes and may not be able to afford the additional costs of health care for pets. A few cities provide low-cost clinics for animal health care, some particularly for animals belonging to the elderly, but again the elderly have to find transportation to the clinics. Some veterinarians practice in mobile vans. The availability of such a veterinarian for pets of the elderly would be of great assistance in allowing the elderly to maintain pets in their homes. Provision for the animal's health care needs to be a critical part of the planning that takes place prior to the acquisition of a pet. Sometimes, if it is not feasible for the elderly to have personal pets, wild animals, such as birds and squirrels, can fill the gap. The elderly can get many hours of enjoyment from watching birds and squirrels at feeders.

B. Pets in Long-Term Care Facilities

A variety of animals can be used in institutions either as residents or as regular visitors. The most common are dogs, cats, rabbits, small rodents, birds, and fish. Dogs, cats, and rabbits generally visit on a regular basis, although some institutions have acquired them as residents.

The success of a resident animal in a long-term care facility depends on a number of factors. Probably the most important is careful planning prior to the acquisition of the animal. The first step is to review the regulations of review boards and accrediting organizations about resident or visiting animals. If there is no contradiction to the acquisition of an animal, the next step is to decide which animal is best for that facility.

Staff need to consider who will be responsible for the animal. It is generally overly optimistic to assume that the elderly will care for resident animals. Responsibility needs to be assigned to staff members. If some aspects of care can occasionally be done by elderly residents, that care needs to be accomplished under the supervision of staff members. Thus, staff need to be willing to assume additional duties in relation to a resident animal. The nature of the animal to be acquired, therefore, has implications for staff workload. A dog, for example, needs food, toileting, and exercise on a regular schedule 24 hours a day 7 days a week. Thus, staff from all shifts will need to make provision for its care. It is possible for the day shift staff to be excited about the acquisition of a resident animal and the night shift staff to resent the added responsibilities. In such a facility, a caged bird, which requires less care that can be given on only one shift, might be a good choice.

Part of the planning for the acquisition of a resident pet is to consider potential allergies among residents and staff. It may be necessary to specially treat the animal to reduce the disbursement of allergens, e.g., dander, that can trigger allergic reactions. Also, toenails need to be kept well trimmed and blunt to prevent injury to frail skin. Likewise, a plan needs to be in place for flea and other parasite prevention.

The potential for zoonotic infections, i.e., infections that can be transmitted between species, needs careful consideration. Any animal brought into a long-term care facility should be given a complete examination by a licensed veterinarian prior to introduction. There should be a plan for regular examinations to ensure that it remains free of parasites and infections, that immunizations are current, and that preventatives, such as heartworm pills, are administered appropriately.

There may be some older adult residents who should not interact with the pet, such as those who are immunocompromised or allergic. The plan for the resident animal needs to include provisions for protecting these residents. However, as Johnson and colleagues (2002) reported, there is little, if any, research evidence reporting zoonotic infections in such situations. The risks to older adult residents are minimal and potentially outweighed by the benefits if facilities adhere to published guidelines (Centers for Disease Control and Prevention Healthcare Infection Control Practices Advisory Committee, 2001).

Another consideration in acquiring a resident animal is the location of the facility. Residents coming primarily from rural settings often have very different views of animals than those who have been city dwellers all of their lives. Even animals traditionally regarded as companions, such as dogs and cats, may be considered as appropriately living outside and performing some instrumental function. Retired farmers may prefer interactions with farm animals, such as sheep and chickens, to dogs and cats. They can get a great deal of satisfaction watching these animals through the window as opposed to petting or cuddling companion animals.

The age of the animal also is a significant factor to be considered in planning. Puppies, although cute and appealing, need housebreaking and training. Older animals have the potential to have training completed before placement. One important consideration is that the animal needs to be temperament tested to ensure that it is suitable for interaction with older adults. Most cities have animal trainers who can perform this function.

Another consideration is that the animal needs time alone away from constant interaction with humans. While staff are not expected to work 24 hours a day, neither should such "work" be expected from the resident animal. In some instances, resident animals have actually developed stress-related illnesses in response to overstimulation. Planning for a place where the animal can be away from people for part of each day and get its proper rest is essential. Such planning requires an understanding of the behavior of the species. Dogs, for example, generally are most active in the morning and evening and sleep a great deal in between. Planning for a resident dog might include an enclosure with a shelter on the grounds where the dog can be placed in the middle of the day as well as for the night. An alternative might be for the dog to have a resting place designated within the building that is kept free from other activities and purposes.

Some institutions have found that a more satisfactory arrangement for having a therapy animal, particularly for animals such as dogs and cats, is to have the animal reside with one of the staff. Then, the animal comes to "work" with the staff member and goes home at the end of the shift to a more normal living arrangement where it can get its own needs met. Such an arrangement also negates the need for staff to provide 24-hour, 7-days-a-week care for the animal.

The need for careful planning prior to the acquisition of an animal for a long-term care facility cannot be overemphasized. It would be well to have a committee of stakeholders formed to consider aspects of acquisition of the animal and to generate a written set of guidelines that would become part of the facility's policies and a budget for care of the animal. Such careful planning should result in a happy and therapeutic relationship among the animal, staff, and residents.

V. GUIDELINES FOR ANIMAL-ASSISTED THERAPY WITH OLDER ADULTS

Many institutions for the elderly have resident pets, and many have regular pet visitation programs. While many studies have demonstrated the beneficial effects of contact with pets for a variety of persons, including the elderly, the long-term effects of resident pets and pet visitation programs have not been examined. Nonetheless, the idea of bringing pets into contact with institutionalized elderly has become quite popular in the United States and elsewhere.

There is no doubt that the presence of pets in a setting such as a nursing home, where one ordinarily does not expect to see them, provides a source of distraction and novelty. All one has to do is witness the attention a dog gets as it walks into a unit. Residents, staff, and visitors descend on the dog almost like it is a magnet. However, the question of what the long-term effects are of contact with a companion animal for the institutionalized elderly has yet to be answered.

Distraction from one's ordinary daily life in a nursing home is not without merit. Also, pets provide a source of affectionate physical contact that often is lacking in an institutional setting. Perhaps these effects are enough to justify the cost of maintaining these programs. There are important factors to consider in instituting an animal-assisted therapy program.

1. Choice of animal. Most pet visitation programs utilize companion animals such as dogs, cats, rabbits, and Vietnamese pot-bellied pigs.

These animals can be transported easily to the institution and walked or carried to interested residents. One criterion for animals being included as regular visitors is that they be tested for their suitability to interact with strangers. Many pet therapy groups have established their own testing programs. National organizations such as the Delta Society (http://www.deltasociety.org/) have standardized testing that can be done by a local person who is certified. Once the animal has passed the test, it receives a certificate that it can be an institutional visitor. Often it is eligible to wear some sort of symbol of this certification so that persons who see it in the institution know that has been tested.

2. Orientation of pet handlers. Persons bringing the animals to the institution need to have an orientation to that institution. They need to know in which sections of the building, generally eating areas, animals are not allowed. Also, they should be informed about the types of persons they will encounter and how to deal with problems if they should arise. The safety both of the residents and of the persons and animal visiting is of utmost importance. It is possible for cognitively impaired elders to behave in strange ways and to attempt to injure animals and their handlers. Animals visiting an institution should be under the direct physical control of the handler at all times.

Many persons who participate in animal visitation programs continue to do so for many years because it is so personally rewarding for them to be a part of the human–animal team. One has only to see the delight and interest on so many otherwise sad or blank elderly faces when allowed to interact with a companion animal to be "hooked" forever and convinced that animals truly are good for the elderly!

REFERENCES

Allen, K., Blascovich, J., and Mendes, W. (2002). Cardiovascular reactivity and the presence of pets, friends and spouses: The truth about cats and dogs. *Psychosom. Med.* 64, 727–739.

Banks, M. R., and Banks, W. A. (2002). The effects of animal-assisted therapy on loneliness in an elderly population in long-term care facilities. *J. Gerontol.* 57(7), 428–432.

Baun, M., Bergstrom, N., Langston, N., and Thoma, L. (1984). Physiological effects of human/companion animal bonding. *Nurs. Res.* 33(3), 126–129.

Centers for Disease Control and Prevention Healthcare Infection Control Practices Advisory Committee. (2001). Draft guideline for environmental infection control in healthcare facilities. Retrieved from http://www.cdc.gov/ncidod/hip/envior/env_guide_draft.pdf.

Churchill, M., Safaoui, J., McCabe, B. W., and Baun, M. M. (1999). Using a therapy dog to alleviate the agitation and desocialization of people with Alzheimer's disease. *J. Psychosoc. Nur.* 37(4), 16–22.

Crimmins, E., Kim, J., and Hagedorn, A. (2003). Health expenctancy: An indicator of successful aging and a measure of the impact of chronic disease and disability. *In* "Successful Aging and Adaptation with Chronic Diseases" (L. Poon, S. Gueldner, and B. Sprouse, eds.), pp. 70–82. Springer, New York.

Dembicki, D., and Anderson, J. (1996). Pet ownership may be a factor in improved health of the elderly. *J. Nutr. Elderly* **15**(3), 15–31.

Edwards, N. E., and Beck, A. M. (2002). Animal-assisted therapy and nutrition in Alzheimer's disease. *West. J. Nurs. Res.* **24**(6), 697–712.

Fick, K. M. (1993). The influence of an animal on social interactions of nursing home residents in a group setting. *Am. J. Occupat. Ther.* **47**(6), 529–534.

Fritz, C. L., Farver, T. B., Kass, P. H., and Hart, L. A. (1995). Association with companion animals and the expression of noncognitive symptoms in Alzheimer's patients. *J. Nerv. Ment. Dis.* **183**(7), 459–463.

Greendale, G. A., Kritz-Silverstein, D., Seeman, T., and Barrett-Connor, E. (2000). Higher basal cortisol predicts verbal memory loss in postmenopausal women: Rancho Bernardo Study. *J. Am. Geriatr. Soc.* **48**(12), 1655–1658.

Haveman-Nies, A., De Groot, L. C., and Van Staveren, W. A. (2003). Dietary quality, lifestyle factors and healthy ageing in Europe: The SENECA study. *Age Ageing* **32**, 427–434.

Hertstein, V. (1995). "The Relation between Pet Ownership and Physical, Psychological, and Functional Health Disorders among Community-Based Elderly Residents." Unpublished doctoral dissertation. Columbia University Teachers College, New York.

Houde, S. C., and Melillo, K. D. (2002). Cardiovascular health and physical activity in older adults: An integrative review of research methodology and results. *J. Adv. Nurs.* **38**(3), 219–234.

Johnson, R. A., and Meadows, R. L. (2002). Older Latinos, pets and health. *West. J. Nurs. Res.* **24**(6), 609–620.

Johnson, R. A., Odendaal, J. S., and Meadows, R. L. (2002). Animal-assisted interventions research: Issues and answers. *West. J. Nurs. Res.* **24**(4), 422–440.

Kanamori, M., Suzuki, M., Yamamoto, K., Kanda, M., Matsui, Y., Kojima, E., Fukawa, H., Sugita, T., and Oshiro, H. (2001). A day care program and evaluation of animal-assisted therapy (AAT) for the elderly with senile dementia. *Am. J. Alzheim. Dis. Other Dement.* **16**(4), 234–239.

Kongable, L. G., Buckwalter, K. C., and Stolley (1989). The effects of pet therapy on the social behavior of institutionalized Alzheimer's clients. *Arch. Psychiatr. Nurs.* **3**(4), 191–198.

Lago, D., Delaney, M., Miller, M., and Grill, C. (1989). Companion animals, attitudes toward pets, and health outcomes among the elderly: A long-term follow-up. *Anthrozoos* **3**(1), 25–34.

National Institute on Aging (2001). Exercise: A guide from the National Institute of Aging.

Odendaal, J. S. J. (2000). Animal-assisted therapy: Medicine or magic? *J. Psychosom. Res.* **49**(4), 275–280.

Ory, M. G., and Goldberg, E. L. (1983). Pet possession and well-being in elderly women. *Res. Aging* **5**(3), 389–409.

Pender, N. J., Murdaugh, C. L., and Parsons, M. A. (2005). "Health Promotion in Nursing Practice." Prentice Hall, Upper Saddle River, NJ.

Raina, P., Waltner-Toews, D., Bonnett, B., Woodward, C., and Abernathy, T. (1999). Influence of companion animals on the physical and psychological health of older people: An analysis of a one-year longitudinal study. *J. Am. Geriatr. Soc.* **47**(3), 323–329.

Reuter-Lorenz, P. A., and Lustig, C. (2005). Brain aging: Reorganizing discoveries about the aging mind. *Curr. Opin. Neurobiol.* **15**, 245–251.

Richeson, N. E. (2003). Effects of animal-assisted therapy on agitated behaviors and social interactions of older adults with dementia. *Am. J. Alzheim. Dis. Other Dement.* **18**(6), 353–358.

Rowe, J. W., and Kahn, R. L. (1998). "Successful Aging." Pantheon Books, New York.

Seeman, T., and Chen, X. (2003). Risk and protective factors for physical functioning in older adults with and without chronic conditions: The MacArthur study of successful aging. *In* "Successful Aging and Adaptation with Chronic Diseases" (L. Poon, S. Gueldner, and B. Sprouse, eds.), pp. 83–103. Springer, New York.

Seeman, T., Singer, B., Rowe, J., Horwitz, R., and McEwen, B. S. (1997). The price of adaptation: Allostatic load and its health consequences. *Arch. Intern. Med.* **157**, 2259–2268.

Siegel, J. (1990). Stressful life events and use of physician services among the elderly: The moderating role of pet ownership. *J. Personal. Soc. Psychol.* **58**, 1081–1086.

Thompson, L. V. (2002). Skeletal muscle adaptations with age, inactivity, and therapeutic physical activity. *J. Orthoped. Sports Phys. Ther.* **32**(2), 44–57.

Tinetti, M. E., Allore, H., Araujo, K. L. B., and Seeman, T. (2005). Modifiable impairments predict progressive disability among older persons. *J. Aging Health* **17**(2), 239–256.

Vaillant, G. E., and Mukamal, K. (2001). Successful aging. *Am. J. Psychiatr.* **158**, 839–847.

CHAPTER 15

History, Development, and Theory of Human–Animal Support Services for People with AIDS/HIV and Other Disabling/Chronic Conditions

KEN GORCZYCA

Pets Are Wonderful Support, San Francisco, California 94107

AUBREY H. FINE

College of Education and Integrative Studies, California State Polytechnic University, Pomona, California 91768

C. VICTOR SPAIN

Philadelphia Department of Public Health, Division of Disease Control, Philadelphia, Pennsylvania 19146

DANA CALLAGHAN

University of North Texas, Counseling Program, Denton, Texas 76203-0829

LAURA NELSON

Pets Are Wonderful Support, San Francisco California 94107

LORI POPEJOY

Boone Hospital Center, Columbia, Missouri 65201

BELINDA WONG

University of California, San Francisco, California 94118

STEPHANIE WONG

U.S. Navy Marine Mammal Program, San Diego, California 92152

People come to visit but they can only stay an hour and then they have to go; my cat, she's always there.

Bob, pet owner with AIDS

Afraid of infection, I fear the birds (Tuberculosis), the cats (Toxoplasmosis), my dog, my horse (Mycobacterium avium), and people. For weeks I was reluctant to leave the house. I didn't ride my horse for several months. Walking in the park or at the beach was unpleasant because of the birds. My doctors gave contradictory advice—Dr. (A) said to get rid of all animals. Dr. (B) said it didn't matter and enjoy what life I had left. My cousin asked if I couldn't get a bubble like the bubble boy.

Stephen Yarnell, M.D., "When Doctors Get Sick," 1987

Eric knows that animal companionship can be powerful medicine. Thirteen years ago as he was struggling with HIV, high blood pressure, depression, addiction, and cancer, he rescued Emily from the street. A domestic shorthair kitten, Emily stood by Eric through his struggle with disease.

Three years later, Eric received Boner, a vivacious Jack Russell terrier, as a Christmas present. From his garden apartment in the Castro, Eric took Boner for regular walks, which helped him establish a healthy exercise routine and build community with other dog owners. Emily and Boner became Eric's family, bringing more joy and happiness than he had ever experienced (Fig. 1).

A few years after Boner entered his life, Eric's health declined, turning into full-blown AIDS. Financially and physically unable to care for his pets, Eric turned to PAWS. From the PAWS food bank, Eric received pet food and cat litter assistance. The veterinarian program helped Eric cover medical bills for his family. PAWS volunteers took Boner for walks when Eric was unable to do so.

"What people may not realize is that many PAWS clients suffer from multiple disabilities and disadvantages," said Eric. "PAWS is really there to help in so many ways. The staff and volunteers are courteous and helpful. PAWS makes such a big difference."

Although his health has improved, Eric continues to suffer from a range of medical issues and is on a rigorous regime of medicines. "Through it all, my pets have provided me with such support," said Eric. "They make me want to get up even when I am depressed. Boner's unconditional love gives me the will to live. It's like having a child, a brother, or a sister."

FIGURE 1 PAWS client Eric Skiver and his two saviors, Boner the dog and Emily the cat. Photo credit: Yan Liu.

Eric now volunteers to raise awareness and funds for PAWS so that others can enjoy the healing love of their pets for as long as possible.

I. INTRODUCTION

People who suffer from terminal or chronic illness often find that their physical condition impacts how they live their daily life and influences the quality of their life. For some, the physical and often psychological barriers manifested by their medical condition lead to a decrease or an end to previously enjoyed social opportunities and relationships. For many their relationships with their pets offer an opportunity for unconditional love and acceptance, as well as increased socialization brought about by the need to take care of another living creature.

This chapter reviews the prevalence of AIDS and other chronic and terminal diseases, as well as possible obstacles facing people living with these conditions. We focus on the AIDS epidemic, which spawned the field known today as human–animal support services (HASS; see Table I) and pet-associated zoonoses education (see Appendix 1). This background information is followed by evidence of how animals can enhance the quality of life for people

TABLE I Definitions of HASS, AAA, and AAT

- Human–animal support services (HASS) are programs that help keep a person with a chronic/terminal illness or disability together for as long as possible with their current animal companions in a mutually beneficial relationship. HASS services include financial, emotional, and practical assistance to the disabled pet owner. HASS programs can be independent, volunteer run, or nonprofit organizations or can be programs under the umbrella of other organizations, such as humane associations or societies, veterinary hospitals, schools or associations, AIDS organizations, or other similar human or animal community service organizations.
- Animal-assisted activities (AAAs) are goal-directed activities designed to improve the patients' quality of life through utilization of the human–animal bond. Animals and their handlers must be screened and trained, but are not guided by a credentialed therapist.
- Animal-assisted therapy (AAT) utilizes the human–animal bond in goal-directed interventions as an integral part of the treatment process. Working animals and their handlers must be screened and trained and meet specific criteria. A credentialed therapist working within the scope of practice of his/her profession sets therapeutic goals, guides the interaction between patient and animal, measures progress toward meeting therapy goals, and evaluates the process.

living with these illnesses. The authors use an ecosystem model to explain how support systems and animals may contribute to an increased quality of home life for those living with chronic disease that are able to live at home. [Note: traditional animal-assisted therapy (AAT) programs and the benefits of animals in hospital-based programs are discussed elsewhere in this book.] The second part of this chapter is practice oriented. This section focuses on the development of HASS guidelines, showcases existing HASS organizations, and discusses in detail one such successful HASS organization called Pets Are Wonderful Support, a program founded in San Francisco, California, and how others can develop and implement similar programs and services in their area. The goal of both AAT and HASS is to work in parallel, encouraging positive health benefits from human–animal interaction (see Table I).

The AIDS epidemic helped produce a movement of volunteer-based social services. Many of the people living with AIDS were also pet guardians who required help to take care of their animals. Traditionally, social services supported the financial, physical, and emotional assistance that this population required. Social services has since evolved to include human–animal support services.

Our society's understanding of the importance of the human–animal bond can be seen most recently by Hurricanes' Katrina and Tina evacuations. The latter evacuation allowed for the evacuation of animal companions with their human guardians, after the first evacuation exposing those that would not leave their pet behind.

TABLE II Leading Causes of Death in 2004[a]

Total deaths	2,443,387
Diseases of the heart	696,947
Cancer	557,271
Cerebrovascular diseases	162,672
Chronic lower respiratory diseases	124,816
Accidents (unintentional injuries)	106,742
Diabetes mellitus	73,249
Influenza and pneumonia	65,681
Alzheimer's disease	58,866
Nephritis, nephronic syndrome, and nephrosis	40,974
Septicemia	33,865

[a]Total deaths per category in the United States.
From U.S. National Center of Health Statistics, National Vital Statistics Reports, Vol. 53, No. 17, 2004.

II. CHRONIC AND TERMINAL ILLNESS

A. An Overview

Chronic and terminal conditions affect people's physical and mental health, their social life, and their employment status in radically different ways. While terminal conditions, by definition, lead to death, chronic conditions persist over a long period of time (see Table II). Many chronic conditions can be highly disabling, while others are less so. Some chronic conditions, such as diabetes, may not disable a person initially, but may lead to severe disabling effects if they are not treated and controlled. Terminal conditions such as acquired immune deficiency syndrome have, over time, become more chronic in nature, as new and more effective treatments become available. Alternatively, it is also not unusual that some people with chronic illness return to former levels of daily activity after recovery (e.g., heart attack or a stroke). Many people with chronic conditions live full, productive, and rewarding lives; however, others experience isolation, depression, physical pain, and other outcomes (Hoffman and Rice, 1995). There is a myriad of middle points on this continuum.

Chronic conditions affect people of all ages and socioeconomic levels. Contrary to popular misconceptions, the elderly are not the only ones to develop chronic and debilitating conditions (see Table III). In fact, data show that about 90 million people in the United States have one or more chronic illnesses (U.S. Census Bureau, 2004). For example, arthritis affects 32 million people; high blood pressure affects 22.5 million; some 16 million have

TABLE III Percentage of Noninstitutionalized Persons with Chronic Conditons by Age Group (1987)[a]

0–17 years	14%
18–44 years	31%
45–64 years	29%
65+ years	26%
88.5 million people	

[a]From Hoffman and Rice (1995).

diabetes, while heart disease afflicts 14 million. More than 5 million people have asthma (seniornet.org). In 1995, one in six people in the United States (41 million) had a chronic condition that inhibited their lives to some degree. In 1993, 8 million working-age adults were prevented from working due to a disability caused by a chronic condition. At least 9 million people with disabilities need help with either personal care or home management. Of these, 40% are under 65 years of age.

In addition, 15% to 18% of all children in the United States have a chronic health condition. Each year, an estimated 50,000 children acquire a permanent disability as a result of injury or acute illness. Asthma is the leading chronic illness among those 18 and younger in the United States, affecting approximately six million children (Judson, 2004). The child who is chronically ill or has a chronic condition will experience one or more of these sequelae: (1) limitation of functions appropriate to age and development; (2) disfigurement; (3) dependency on medical technology for functioning; (4) dependency on medication or special diet for normal functioning or control of condition; (5) need for more medical care or related services than usual for the child's age; and (6) special ongoing treatments at home or in school (Jackson and Vessey, 2000). As has been discussed throughout this book, the animal–human bond can dramatically enhance the quality of life for all those involved. Table IV identifies many benefits to people with chronic/terminal illnesses.

B. AIDS: An Overview

Acquired immune deficiency syndrome is one of the most serious and complex health problems humanity has ever has faced. AIDS is caused by the human immunodeficiency virus (HIV). HIV attacks the immune system and eventually reduces an infected person's ability to resist other infections and diseases. An estimated 1 million U.S. citizens are infected with HIV, with as many as 44,000 new infections each year in the United States (UNAIDS/WHO,

TABLE IV Benefits That Animal Companions Can Give to People with Chronic Illnesses

Provide companionship
Decrease feelings of loneliness
Act as a surrogate for other relationships
Decrease stress
Provide a reason to exercise
Give the human caregiver a sense of purpose
Ease social interactions in public
Provide a sense of security to children and adults

TABLE V Global Summary of the HIV/AIDS Epidemic (December 2004)[a]

People newly infected with HIV in 2004	4.9 million
North America	44,000
Sub-Saharan Africa	3.1 million
Western Europe	21,000
Number of people living with HIV/AIDS	39.4 million
North America	1 million
Sub-Saharan Africa	25.4 million
Western Europe	610,000
AIDS deaths in 2004	3.1 million

[a]From UNAIDS/WHO 2004 report on the global AIDS epidemic, United Nations Program on HIV/AIDS (www.unaids.org).

2004). Although the epidemic has appeared to slow somewhat in the developed world, AIDS has reached pandemic levels in developing countries such as South Africa and India (United Nations AIDS/WHO, 2004). Worldwide, there have been 4.9 million new infections in 2004 alone (Table V). Ninety-five percent of all HIV-infected people now live in developing countries (UNAIDS/WHO 1998). AIDS has killed at least 26 million people, has orphaned more than 12 million children, and currently infects over 40 million people (Garrett, 2005).

HIV is transmitted in various ways: sexually, through contact with infected body fluids; from mother to child during pregnancy or breast-feeding; through the sharing of infected needles; or via blood transfusions. The progression from HIV to AIDS is usually a slow process, and it may be 10 years or longer from the time of initial infection with HIV until symptoms of AIDS appear. Once immunosuppression has occurred, people with AIDS (PWAs) become susceptible to opportunistic infections and cancers. These opportunistic infections typically cause minimal disease in healthy persons but can lead to death in PWAs.

As more effective and less toxic treatments become available, AIDS is becoming a chronic condition. However, many of the therapies used to treat AIDS are experimental and have unknown toxicities when used for a lifetime. Already serious complications such as liver and kidney failure and heart disease are on the increase in individuals using the AIDS treatments for long periods. In addition, these therapies are expensive and are not generally available to populations in the developing world or to the uninsured or underinsured in the developed world. This obstacle has led to the evolution of two distinct epidemics.

C. The Psychosocial Impact of Illness: The AIDS Virus

The psychological burden produced by AIDS and HIV infection can exceed that produced by any other medical condition (Maj, 1991). PWAs are faced with the disease process and also the psychological ramifications of this serious but chronic illness. Primary among these obstacles are HIV's incurability and the associated public hysteria and misunderstanding (Cherry and Smith, 1993). A wealth of information suggests that PWAs are targets of stigmatization (Bennett, 1990). Individuals with AIDS often describe feelings of isolation, alienation, and estrangement and loneliness (Carmack, 1991). Two categories of loneliness have been described: emotional isolation and social isolation (Weiss, 1973). Emotional isolation appears to develop as a direct result of absence of an attachment figure, such as a partner or close friend. Social isolation, however, occurs when an individual lacks (or perceives a lack of) an effective social network. Research reported by Christ *et al.* (1986) suggests that the PWAs may be especially susceptible to the experience of loneliness. They reported that 75% of patients with AIDS have diminished social support from friends, family, and significant others.

III. HOW ANIMALS HELP CHILDREN AND ADULTS ADAPT TO THEIR ILLNESS

A. Theoretical Model

Research has shown that the quality of life for children and adults with chronic or terminal illnesses is highly dependent on the support mechanisms available to them. Quality of life is defined as an overall well-being that encompasses physical, material, social, and emotional well-being (Felce and Perry, 1993). It is believed that perceived quality of life for persons with an illness depends, in part, on how an individual attempts to cope with his or her medical chal-

FIGURE 2 PAWS client Pali Boucher and her sweetheart, Memphis Minnie. Photo credit: Alison Bank.

lenges. When one feels supported and perceives fewer challenges, his or her quality of life may be enhanced (Fig. 2).

For this chapter, the authors selected a definition of social support—one measure of quality of life—that includes meaningful social contact, availability of confidants, and companionship (Dean and Lin, 1977). An individual's quality of life cannot be enhanced in a vacuum or in isolation. Schalock (1996) suggested that the use of social supports is an efficient and effective way to maximize someone's independence, productivity, and life satisfaction. These social supports can include family members, other people, technology, in-home living assistance, and animal companionship. Wilson (1991) suggested that more scientific investigation is needed to study the interaction between animals and humans. Little is known about the role animals can play in social support. What is known is generally positive about the role that animals play in the lives of humans. Nebbe (1991) pointed out various studies that suggested that families with pets appear to be more emotionally secure. Another study conducted by Levine and Bohn (1986) found that children in families with pets appeared to show greater empathy for other human beings.

The authors have considered many models in an attempt to describe how companion animals and animal-assisted activities can be understood as an important dimension of support. A theoretical "ecosystem" model developed by Bronfenbrenner (1989) seems applicable in describing the support mechanisms that people use for overcoming the stresses of having a chronic and/or terminal illness (Fig. 3). This model consists of a series of nested contexts called a microsystem, exosystem, and macrosystem. The original model has been utilized to describe many significant challenges confronting families, including divorce and child abuse (Belsky, 1980). This model views a person's life as a social unit embedded within various formal and informal social units (Shea and Bauer, 1991).

Bronfenbrenner's model explains behavior similarly to the way a naturalist would view nature. An individual's ecosystem may be visualized as a series of layers that are all connected. The most central layer is what he called the microsystem. This system incorporates all the variables that can either support or contaminate the growth of an individual within his or her home. A child or adult who has a functioning support system at home may adapt more effectively to his/her illness. The impact of the medical challenge on any family appears dependent on the number of factors affected by the condition. These factors may include the family resources (e.g., financial, job), the relationships within the family, and the social support system within both the family and the community.

The exosystem consists of all other support systems found outside the home. Financial, medical, and emotional supports found in formal and informal neighborhood opportunities can make the life of a person with a chronic illness more livable or less of an ordeal. These options may be found formally at a work site, clinics, and various religious institutions, as well as numerous community social service agencies. Informally, a person's sense of well-being may be lifted as a direct result of the contributions made by extended family members and close friends. Having good neighbors and family members who visit or call frequently can impact one's perceived quality of life tremendously. Also, support groups, social clubs, and churches can help enlarge the support from the person's exosystem.

Finally, the macrosystem is the outermost layer of a human being's ecosystem and incorporates the larger culture of the world in which we all live. This macrosystem may represent the culture's bias and reaction to various illnesses and conditions; it is within the cultural macrosystem that the stigma of an illness is developed. According to the tenets of an ecosystem model, there is a

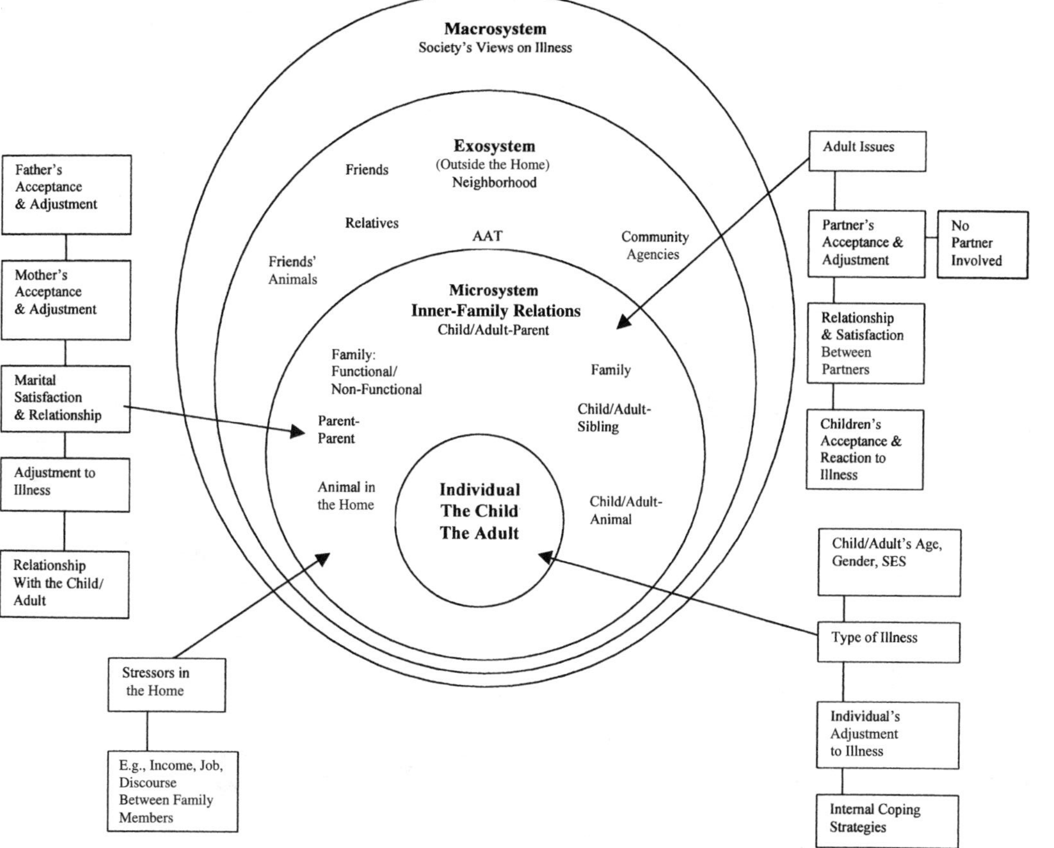

FIGURE 3 The ecosystem model displaying the various layers within the ecosystem and how they are all interrelated.

positive correlation between the resources secured and an individual's ability to function and adapt more effectively.

Bronfenbrenner urges mental health professionals to view the psychological health of any individual as a direct result of the forces operating within the systems that he or she lives within. The model permits simultaneous consideration of numerous factors within the microsystem, the exosystem, and the macrosystem that can help an individual adapt to illness.

As discussed earlier, the strength within a microsystem is related directly to the relationships that have been cultivated within a person's immediate family and household. As would be expected, the microsystem for any individual differs from one to another. Persons with various illnesses may find themselves being responded to differently as a consequence of their specific illness, age, gender, and sexual orientation. Specifically, people with AIDS may face losing the support network they hold most dear—their family and friends (Cherry and Smith, 1993). Many PWAs find that their families or significant others do not understand or do not want to deal with the physical, emotional, and social challenges associated with AIDS. Maj (1991) reported numerous incidents in which families refused to talk to their children with AIDS, denied financial assistance, and even returned correspondence unopened. Conversely, there are many PWAs who have supportive microsystems in which their families and significant others have been heroic in helping the PWA live and die with dignity. When individuals live in a supportive and harmonious environment, they are apparently better at handling the stresses related to their illness.

B. Palliative Care

Living in a harmonious and supportive environment is desirable in any part of the life span, but is especially significant toward the end of life. Palliative care is characterized as care that helps people live fully until they die (see Table VI). This assistance can occur in the microsystem and exosystem. The World Health Organization (WHO, 2005) defines palliative care as "an approach that

TABLE VI Goals of Palliative Care (World Health Organization, 2005)

Providing relief from pain and other distressing symptoms
Affirming life and regarding dying as a normal process
Neither hastening nor postponing death
Integrating the psychological and spiritual aspects of patient care
Offering a support system to help patients live as actively as possible until death
Offering a support system to help the family cope during the patient's illness and in their own bereavement
Using a team approach to address the needs of patients and their families, including bereavement counseling, if indicated

improves the quality of life of patients and their families facing the problems associated with life-threatening illness, through the prevention and relief of suffering by means of early identification and impeccable assessment and treatment of pain and other problems, physical, psychosocial, and spiritual." According to the National Hospice and Palliative Care Organization (2005), palliative care extends the principles of hospice care so that a broader population of people can receive beneficial care earlier in their disease process, prior to the last 6 months of life when hospice typically begins. In addition to enhancing the quality of life, applying palliative care early in the course of illness in conjunction with other therapies may also positively influence the trajectory of the patient's illness.

IV. THE ROLE OF PETS

The U.S. Human Society indicates that more than half of U.S. households have pets (HSUS, 2003). Pets are more common in households with children, yet there are more pets than children in U.S. households (HSUS, 2005). An estimated 45% of Americans infected with HIV own pets (Spencer, 1992) (see Figs. 1 and 2), and many other PWAs have contact with animals through traditional AAT programs while hospitalized or in a hospice. Imagine the possible benefits all of these animals can provide for their human companions. It is this caveat of living with AIDS or another chronic illness that the importance of finding meaning and joy in life through the positive interactions with pets may be particularly cogent. Therefore, using the ecosystem theory, it is inside the microsystem that an animal may play the most crucial role. It is not uncommon for a child or an adult to perceive an animal as a peer or family member (Nebbe, 1991). Pets provide a valuable source of comfort and companionship for many individuals, including children (Wilson, 1991). According to Veevers (1985), animals may act as surrogates when they take the place of people. He suggested that "almost all interaction with companion animals involves some anthropomorphism and can in some way be construed as a surrogate for human relationships." Serpell (1983) further suggested that animals can supply compassion in cases where humans are unable to or are unavailable.

Persons with AIDS may perceive a companion animal as a family member and a direct source of emotional support, which is particularly important for someone who may feel isolated and perhaps neglected. In an article on companion animals for PWAs, Carmack (1991) noted that animal companions decrease feelings of isolation and provide a perceived reduction of stress. She also reported findings that suggest that PWAs perceive that their companion animals help reduce their stress levels. Stress reduction can, in turn, improve immune system function. Because animals require affection and companionship, they can enhance feelings of being needed and valued ("I care for them, and it lets me forget about things"). Castelli and colleagues (2001) found that pet cats, but not dogs, offered comfort and companionship to people with AIDS and enhanced their relationships with family and friends. Similarly, Siegel *et al.* (1999) found that men with AIDS who had close attachments with their pets were significantly less likely to suffer from depression than those men who did not have pets as companions. Chinner and Dalziel (1991) found that a resident poodle in a hospice setting facilitated interactions between people and improved both staff and patient morale. However, attachment to the pet does seem to make a difference to how much effect the animal has on the person. Those who were isolated or lonely did not develop affection for the poodle. Early work by Rynearson (as cited in Cookman, 1996) supports the importance of attachment and notes that the reciprocal nature of the relationship between pet and owner is crucially important. It is wise to keep in mind that not all people desire to develop an attachment to an animal.

Alternatively, Volth (1985) indicated there may be a biological predisposition for humans to develop a strong attachment bond to animals. It is not uncommon to see many companion animals that may, for example, sleep in their owners' rooms and accompany their owners on short trips and holidays. Many companion animals are recipients of special treats and gifts, just like other family members. Volth's research pointed out that both dog and cat owners can become equally attached to their animals. Jorgenson (1997) observed that pets are a constantly available source of direction of attention and affection. In a study about pets functioning as family members, Cohen (2002) found that pets do function within the family circle and that they give back as much as they receive from their owners. Within the animal–human relationship there is an unambivalent exchange between pet and owner that may not exist in other relationships. Pets may allow people to express deep feelings and offer a way to nurture another living being (Cohen, 2002). Nevertheless, caution is warranted again, as Cohen also found differences in how males and females view their relationship with a pet; men were less expressive of their relationship with the pet than were women.

According to Siegel (1993), companion animals within the home appear to acquire the ability to elicit positive emotional responses from their owners. Positive responses are initially elicited from the good feelings that are derived from tactile and emotional contact with the animal, and this continued pairing usually leads the owner to view the animal as a source of comfort. Interestingly, a social worker in England pointed out that companion animals appear to demonstrate some of the same attributes that are seen as being favorable in social workers (Hutton, 1982). Companion animals, for example, tend to help people use their own strengths to help themselves; animals tend to have the ability to form and establish relationships quickly; and animals are sensitive to people's feelings and emotions, thus recognizing those occasions when they are needed or wanted. Cusak (1988) suggested that animals can function as human surrogates in a number of roles, including as friends and confidants. Persons who are secluded within their homes may find the companionship of animals more meaningful. They can act as true friends, not only to pass time with but also to engage in true relationships. Pets can bring laughter and tenderness into a home. They can bring comfort at times when loneliness may be overbearing.

A good illustration of how pets support patients resulted from a study by Muschel (1985), who looked at the effects of animals on enhancing the quality of life of patients with cancer. Animals visited 15 hospitalized patients. Twelve of the 15 patients seemed very concerned about the "visiting" animals' welfare and would go out of their way to reassure the pets. They also seemed more content and outgoing in the presence of the animals and were observed to sing to and play with the animals. Interestingly, Muschel also alluded to how the animals seemed to be valuable as companions while the patients were struggling with facing death: "The animal's quiet, accepting and nurturing presence strengthens, and frees the patient to resolve his or her final experience successfully." In much the same way, having a companion animal in a patient's home would seem to elicit the same responses.

Companion animals in the home may also help to improve physical health by increasing the amount of exercise in which chronically ill people may engage (Meer, 1984). Pet ownership also has been shown to improve cardiovascular health by reducing anxiety, loneliness, and depression (Freidman *et al.*, 1983; Katcher, 1981; Katcher et al., 1983). Animals can be used to support and enhance many levels of more healthy living patterns.

V. THE ROLE OF COMMUNITY AND FAMILY

While we recognize the important role that companion and therapy animals can play for people with chronic illnesses, these people may need assistance in caring for their companion animals from within their exosystem. In most cases, research has been conducted addressing the importance of human contemporaries and their relationships in enhancing quality of life. Shea and Bauer (1991) pointed out that relatives, neighbors, friends, and community organizations may provide tremendous support to the individual. An effective exosystem can provide much needed assistance and opportunities for an individual. There can be people outside one's immediate microsystem who can make life more meaningful and easier. Friends and relatives may make it possible for some people to continue living on their own by providing intermittent help with cooking, shopping, cleaning, and pet care. Isolation may be prevented or decreased as a consequence of this external support system. Programs such as PAWS (Pets are Wonderful Support; described later in this chapter) or friends within the community can be a viable resource for helping an individual keep a pet companion at home. Although a person with a chronic/terminal illness may not have the support within his/her microsystem to help take care of a companion animal, there may be people within the exosystem who can fill this void. Close relationships outside the home may provide ongoing support, as well as a sense of stability, in the lives of PWAs (Jue, 1994). Supportive relationships with friends or visiting animals can contribute to the individual's quality of life. These connecting experiences contribute indirectly and directly to offsetting the effects of isolation and enhancing a sense of self-worth. These findings support the role of companion animals and visiting animal programs in decreasing a person's sense of social isolation. However, those caring for PWAs and others with compromised immune systems need to also understand some of the risks of animal companionship, such as pet-associated zoonoses (see Appendix 1).

VI. THE HISTORICAL SIGNIFICANCE OF PET-ASSOCIATED ZOONOSES AND AIDS

Several million people in the United States have compromised immune systems, including an estimated one million people living with HIV (CDC, 2005). Other immunosuppressive illnesses and treatments include chemotherapy, some cancers, dialysis, congenital diseases, and others (see Table VII). Immunosuppressed persons are susceptible to a number of opportunistic infections, including zoonoses. Zoonoses are diseases that can be transmitted to humans by other vertebrate animals or shared by humans and other vertebrate

TABLE VII Immune-Compromising Diseases/Conditions

Alcoholism/liver cirrhosis
Cancer (some)
Chronic renal failure
Congenital immunodeficiencies
Diabetes mellitus
HIV/AIDS
Immunosuppressive treatments for
Autoimmune diseases
Cancer
Transplant recipients
Long-term hemodialysis
Old age
Malnutrition
Pregnancy
Splenectomy

animals. Angulo (1994) reported that about 45% of immunosuppressed individuals might own pets, and few immunosuppressed individuals are offered information about zoonoses prevention by health care providers. Although AIDS helped create the need for pet-associated zoonoses education, the information is important for all immunosuppressed populations (see Table VII).

AIDS was first identified in 1981, when a cluster of case reports in New York City emerged describing a rare pneumonia in young, previously healthy homosexual males. This specific infection, caused by an opportunistic parasite known as *Pneumocystis carinii*, had previously been seen only in patients with immune system dysfunction, cancer, or those undergoing chemotherapy treatments. Suddenly, because of AIDS, a large number of people were developing previously rare opportunistic infections, including some that are considered zoonotic. The swiftness of the spread of the virus and the large number of deaths in previously healthy individuals were unprecedented in modern medicine. Although we knew that companion animals could not transmit AIDS, at the time, many questions about the risks of other infections remained unanswered.

The medical community in general was not prepared to answer esoteric questions about catching diseases from "Fluffy" the cat. Veterinarians knew about animal-borne diseases, but little about the degree of increased risk to immunosuppressed humans. Many physicians, unfamiliar with the details of zoonotic transmission, often chose to err on the side of caution and simply advised their immunosuppressed patients to relinquish their pets to minimize any possible risks.

Was there a real risk, or was there an overreaction by overzealous physicians? In the mid-1980s there was very little in the veterinary or medical literature about the increased risk of zoonoses to immunosuppressed individual pet owners. What made this situation so controversial and complicated was that there was a concurrent cerebral toxoplasmosis epidemic in PWAs. Toxoplasmosis is a parasitic disease seen mostly in cats, but humans and other mammals can acquire it. PWAs were developing symptoms from this infection at previously unknown rates. In addition, infected cat feces were known to be one source of transmission of this infection to people. Because most physicians were unfamiliar with zoonoses (Gorczyca, 1989), a real crisis of misinformation about AIDS and zoonoses developed within the health care system. In actuality, the cause of the toxoplasmosis epidemic was mostly from previous infections that recurred as the person's immune system deteriorated. Toxoplasmosis is more likely to be acquired from eating undercooked meat or contact with a contaminated environment rather than directly from pet cats. Unfortunately, at the time clinicians did not understand this and chose instead to recommend that patients have reduced contact with pet cats.

The recommendation for PWAs to find their pets a new home created a particular new dilemma. People with HIV typically face many losses, including loss of employment, friends, and family, and often feel isolated, rejected, and stigmatized. However, it is the special relationship with their pets that provides them with constancy, love, and affection, and now these people were being separated from their beloved pets, often due to medical advice. Unfortunately, many of these people were the very people who most needed the emotional and psychological benefits provided by their animal companions.

Soon, veterinarians began taking the lead in educating the public and health care fields about zoonotic risk for PWAs. These veterinarians questioned the value of separating animal companions from the people who seemed to need the companionship the most. Veterinarian Malcolm Kram, for example, moved the New York State Veterinary Medical Association to develop the first recommendations in 1986 on how to minimize the risks of transmitting zoonoses from animals to people. However, not all veterinary organizations were willing to assume responsibility for educating the public. In some cases, it was the AIDS support organizations, such as the Shanti Project in San Francisco, that were willing to help (Gorczyca, 1991). These efforts eventually led to the publication of the PAWS' safe pet guidelines in 1988. These were the first published guidelines to explain how to minimize zoonotic risks and support the importance of the human–animal bond for people with AIDS.

Today, there is still little evidence in the literature that supports people contracting diseases from their companion animals, except for reptiles and some other exotic animals (Wong, 1998). In fact, for many physicians who treat AIDS patients, zoonoses have become a nonissue relative to other concerns about treatment and survival (D. Abrams, personal communication, 1998). However, there is still confusion and misinformation about pet-associated zoonoses. Is it the physician's or veterinarian's role to educate? Today, information about zoonoses in immunosuppressed populations is more readily available. The Healthy Pets, Healthy People (HPHP) project was created in 1997 by Stephanie Wong (as the first PAWS veterinary student extern). The Lesbian and Gay Veterinary Medical Association then took the lead and sponsored the HPHP initiative and published the recommendations on their web site (www.lgvma.org). Today, the Centers for Disease Control (CDC) officially sponsors and hosts the initiative at www.cdc.gov/healthypets (see Appendixes 1 and 2).

VII. HOW PAWS DEVELOPED TO PROVIDE SUPPORT FOR PEOPLE WITH AIDS WITH PETS

Around the same time that zoonoses emerged as an issue for pet guardians with AIDS, the San Francisco community recognized that there were many other unfulfilled needs crucial to helping keep the family together. Many

TABLE VIII Problems PWAs Face in Caring for Their Pets

PWAs may have limited ability to care for their companion animals because of
Limited financial resources
Limited family and/or social support
Impaired physical ability
AIDS-related dementia
Risk of zoonotic disease
Loss of housing
Lack of "reasonable accommodations"

individuals were finding that the devastating effects of AIDS made it increasingly difficult for them to feed and care for their pets. PWAs who chose to keep their pets often faced, for example, financial burdens and physical constraints (see Table VIII). Many of these people lacked family support. As highlighted previously within Bronfenbrenner's model, these individuals' microsystems were no longer functioning in ways to help them with pet care. Thus, community programs evolved in the exosystem to fill this void and help keep people and pets together by maintaining the existing relationship for those who already had pets in the home.

Initially, existing animal-oriented or AIDS support organizations were not set up to provide the kind of in-home services PWAs needed to care for their pets. No single group was prepared to cope with this particular dilemma. Clients of the San Francisco AIDS Foundation (SFAF) food bank began to request pet food. Unfortunately, pet food was not initially available, and some clients were forced to use their human rations to feed their animal companions. In response, the food bank began carrying pet food in 1985. While the financial needs associated with veterinary care and pet food were obvious, it soon became apparent that pet owners required other services, including assistance with dog walking, boarding services if the person became hospitalized, and adoption services if the person died. Except for carrying pet food at the food bank, the SFAF and other AIDS organizations in San Francisco were not equipped to put resources into the care of companion animals. The AIDS epidemic quickly overwhelmed social services in San Francisco.

In 1986, a group of people, including founding veterinarian Ken Gorczyca, banded together to help PWAs keep their pets for as long as possible. In recognition of the importance of the human–animal bond, they called their group "Pets Are Wonderful Support," nicknamed "PAWS." Since its founding, the organization has sought to fill in the gaps between other AIDS service– and animal-related organizations to address the particular problems and questions faced by immunosuppressed pet owners. Utilizing the terminology discussed

TABLE IX HASS Services

Veterinary care (preventative health and emergency care)
Pet food bank
Foster care
Adoption planning
Grooming and flea control
In-home pet care (dog walking; aquarium, bird cage, and cat litter box cleaning)
Pet transportation
Administration of medication
Pet-associated zoonoses education (brochures, talks, education booths, referrals)
Veterinary externship program
Public health externship program
Housing advocacy
Education on service animal rights
Hospital pet visitation program (such as personal pet visitation offered by PAWS Houston)
Senior program (such as PAWS/LA and recently PAWS in San Fransisco)

in our previous applied model, PAWS is an example of how a contributing member within the exosystem can help keep the companion animal and person together. In comparison to traditional animal-assisted therapy programs in which animals are brought into the hospital or home for short periods, the PAWS services allowed, in essence, 24-hour therapy using an individual's own companion animals. PAWS evolved to keep the "family" together.

PAWS became an independent nonprofit, volunteer-operated organization in 1987. The main client services have evolved to include financial, emotional, and practical assistance. These include veterinary care, a pet food bank, foster care and adoption planning, in-home pet care, and pet transportation (see Table IX). PAWS has also become a leader in education on the human–animal bond and pet-associated zoonoses education.

PAWS' purpose has been to deliver support services to keep PWAs and their animal companions together for as long as possible in mutually healthy environments. Over the past two decades, similar organizations and programs in other communities worldwide have filled this niche. The authors use PAWS as a model to describe the various services offered by HASS. Each community is diverse, and the services offered vary among the different programs, depending on the local funding, volunteer base, community need, and macrosystem/exosystem support. Some HASS organizations, including PAWS, have expanded their services to include other disabled or elderly populations as well as PWAs. In 2002, PAWS expanded its services to qualifying low-income people with disabling conditions, including AIDS, in the PAWS expansion program (PEP) (see Table X).

TABLE X Breakdown of the Types of Illnesses of Non-AIDS/HIV Clients Compared to Those with AIDS/HIV (PAWS 2005)

AIDS	264
Disabling HIV	112
Mental illness	30
Heart dysfunction	3
Brain trauma	5
Cancer	3
Visual impairment	2
Hepatitis C	2
Diabetes	1
Chronic fatigue syndrome	1
Lung disorder	1
Mobility impairment	11
Dual diagnosis	15
Multiple diagnosis	12

VIII. SERVICES PROVIDED BY PETS ARE WONDERFUL SUPPORT (PAWS)

A. Veterinary Care

The veterinary care program is one of the most important functions of PAWS because keeping a pet healthy is important in keeping the human companion healthy. The program provides an annual physical examination and vaccinations to each client's animal. The visit with a veterinarian also allows the client to ask questions about zoonoses. The annual examination, vaccines, and advice are provided free of charge by Pets Unlimited, a local veterinary hospital and shelter. To help defray the costs of emergency or other essential medical treatments, PAWS offers an annual veterinary (vet) fund to each client. Vet fund amounts are determined each year in the budgeting process. Local veterinary hospitals also help by offering discounts to PAWS clients. If the client is unable to take their pet to the veterinarian, PAWS also provides volunteers to take the pet. In addition, PAWS encourages and helps to pay for spay/neuter surgeries.

B. Pet Food Bank

The PAWS food bank provides monthly allotments of pet food, litter, flea treatments, and pet accessories. The pet food bank is open every weekend and may be accessed once a month by PAWS clients, with delivery provided for homebound clients. Most of the products are donated by pet food manufacturers and distributors, by local supermarkets, or by individual donors. Veterinary clinics also offer discounts on "special diets" for pets with special dietary needs. Additional food is purchased with funds raised by PAWS development staff and volunteers.

C. Foster Care

Many times, a family member or friend will take care of the person's companion animals if a PAWS client goes into the hospital or is unable to care for the animal. However, early in the AIDS epidemic, several pets were found in people's homes unattended when a pet owner went unexpectedly into the hospital. Through the years, there have been many instances in which individuals refused necessary hospital care until they were absolutely sure that their animal would receive proper care. PAWS' foster care program was created to fill this need. For example, if a client needs hospitalization, PAWS attempts to find a temporary foster home for their pets. If no foster home is available, PAWS will make arrangements with local kennels, veterinary clinics, or shelters to board the pet until a foster home can be provided or until the pet can be returned to its owner. If appropriate, PAWS will also attempt to provide in-home care of the animal if foster care is not immediately available.

D. Adoption

Many clients are fearful of what will happen with their pet if they die. When a client registers with PAWS, they are encouraged to make an adoption plan, including a living will. The living will addresses clients' fears by designing a plan of action to secure their pet a good home if and when the person cannot provide it themselves. Individuals are asked to notify PAWS of the future adopting "parent" to ensure that the pet will be transferred to the appropriate person in the event of the pet guardian's death. If an individual is isolated and has no family or friends willing to adopt their companion animal, PAWS helps identify possible alternative sources for adoption of their pets. PAWS has extensive networks within the animal welfare system and local animal adoption programs. It is important for any adoption program to have screening policies for new "adoptive parents" to help prevent mismatching.

E. In-Home Services

PAWS volunteers offer litter box cleaning, dog walking, aquarium and aviary cleaning, administration of a pet's medications, pet grooming, and flea control. Volunteers help bathe animals and trim their nails. Local groomers have also been generous in donating their services to PAWS clients.

F. Pet-Associated Zoonoses Education: Safe Pet Guidelines

From the inception of PAWS, zoonoses education has been a priority. In response to the lack of information on the risk of contracting zoonoses for PWAs, PAWS developed the safe pet guidelines (see Appendix 2), which were first presented at a Delta Society meeting of humane educators in 1988. The first challenge was to educate physicians treating PWAs about the benefits of animal companionship, the "small" risk of zoonoses, and how to make pets even safer for their patients with AIDS. In the 1990s, many other veterinary organizations and schools, humane societies, and the CDC published guidelines modeled after those published by PAWS. Currently, the Healthy Pets, Healthy People project, now run by the CDC, brings all of these resources together in one place (see www.cdc.gov/healthypets).

All PAWS clients receive a copy of the safe pet guidelines brochures (see Appendix 2). These guidelines help educate individuals on which animal-handling behaviors are risky and how to reduce those risks. Consultations with veterinarians also allow questions about zoonoses to be answered.

A primary goal of PAWS is preventative education, which has led to continued outreach to physicians, veterinarians, and other health care workers about the benefits and risks of animal companionship for PWAs and other immunocompromised populations. The organization provides community education at local and national medical and veterinary conferences. This includes information booths, posters, zoonoses talks, a web site, and referrals (see Fig. 4).

G. A PAWS Externship Program

The development of the PAWS veterinary extern program has allowed interested veterinary students the opportunity to get experience in public health, the human–animal bond, and nonprofit organizations. In turn, the extern also

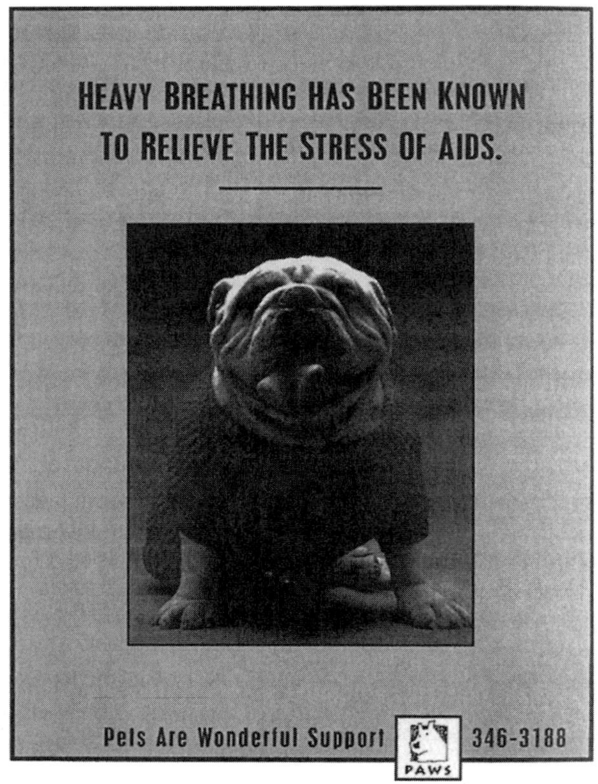

FIGURE 4 An example of an educational poster produced and distributed by PAWS (reprinted courtesy of Pets Are Wonderful Support).

helps the PAWS education program evolve. One of the first externs, Stephanie Wong, helped establish the Healthy Pets, Healthy People project in 1998 (see previous section on zoonoses). The PAWS veterinary externship program continues to publish booklets and a web site and staff educational booths at veterinary, medical, and other professional conferences. The student externs answer questions about the benefits of the human–animal bond and the risks of zoonoses. HASS organizations can also offer externship opportunities for students of other professions. HPHP is working to bring together the medical and veterinary communities in a common effort to improve animal and human health.

PAWS San Francisco has introduced a public health externship program to complement its veterinary externship program. Public health externs work in conjunction with vet externs to help bridge the communication gap between the two disciplines. In 2005, Belinda Wong, an MPH student, completed an applied research project examining the role of pets in health promotion using the PAWS organization as a case study. The purpose of the project was to assess the overall quality of the PAWS program. Ms. Wong surveyed PAWS clients using an anonymous mail survey, and results indicated high satisfaction with PAWS' operation and services. Clients confirmed the importance of their pets and the role of the PAWS program in their lives. One client revealed, "The help given is wonderful. I am disabled mentally, physically, and emotionally, this food and vet assistance helps me get by on a very limited fixed income. I can keep my little family member and (me) in a healthy state of well-being." Both veterinary and public health externships provide important information to the community and anyone working in the human or animal health field.

H. National Conference Series

In 2000, PAWS led a national effort to produce a conference, "The Healing Power of the Human–Animal Bond: Lessons Learned from the AIDS Epidemic." As part of PAWS' ongoing commitment to help educate community providers about the importance of the human–animal bond for people living with HIV/AIDS and other disabling illnesses, PAWS presented, in partnership with PAWS Los Angeles, "The Healing Power of the Human–Animal Bond: Companion Animals and Society" on June 2–4, 2005. This conference program explored the social, psychological, and physical benefits that animals provide people living with HIV/AIDS and other disabilities and the rights and roles of service animals. Presented information included data supporting positive benefits to both renters and landlords for allowing pets in buildings, housing law regarding companion and service animals, roles of psychiatric service dogs, and the health benefits of companion animals. Conference proceedings are available from the PAWS web site (http://www.pawssf.org/conference/2005/).

I. Client Advocacy Program

Many disabled, low-income San Franciscans with service animals (including emotional support animals) face housing problems, including eviction or lack of reasonable accommodation. All of these individuals have animals that meet the Americans with Disabilities Act definition of a service animal, i.e., an "animal individually trained to work or perform tasks for an individual with a disability" (49 CFR 37.3). The right to emotional support animals was decided in a 2002 case before the California Department of Fair Employment and Housing and was upheld in a 2004 ruling by the court of appeals. For many people who are homebound, isolated, and critically ill, the emotional support that animals provide may be the only affection they receive on a daily basis.

The Client Advocacy Program provides consultation, direct advocacy, and access to pro-bono legal assistance to low-income, disabled San Francisco residents who are having housing-related difficulties because they have a service animal. The program also educates service organizations and community leaders about housing and service animals.

J. Emotional Support

Perhaps one of the most important functions of PAWS is the provision of caring emotional support. Both staff and volunteers often provide friendship and guidance to clients in the most difficult of times, such as with the loss of a beloved companion animal. Oftentimes, clients relish the opportunity to simply share a heartwarming story about their animal with someone who understands their intense bond. They know that their connections to their animals will never be belittled or dismissed and will always be taken seriously.

Ms. Wong, public health extern, asked PAWS clients what was the best thing about PAWS. Clients revealed (in this order) the food bank, the organization itself, veterinary care fund, staff, and volunteers. The practical and financial support of the food bank and vet care fund—and the idea of the organization itself, along with the singled out staff and volunteer commendations—shows the unequivocal importance of financial, practical, and emotional support.

K. Personal Pet Visitation

PAWS Houston provides a program that enables hospital patients to receive visits from their own animal companions on a case-by-case basis (currently with programs at Methodist and CHRISTUS St. Joseph's Hospital). PAWS Houston arranges and coordinates the hospital administration logistics and necessary pet transportation for these visits. Many medical professionals are trying to install these programs in other hospitals as well because of the tremendous research supporting the positive health benefits of having a pet close by. This is different from AAT programs described elsewhere in this book. This program can also be used to help people in hospices who can no longer keep their pet with them.

TABLE XI HASS Program Types and Examples[a]

1. Independent not-for-profit programs: PAWS in San Francisco, PAWS/LA in Los Angeles, and PETS, DC, in Washington, D.C.
2. Collaboration with local AIDS organization: PAWS NY Capital Region program with Albany Damien Center in Albany, New York, and Pet Project at the Monterey County AIDS Foundation
3. Collaboration with local animal shelters: Phinny's Friends with MSPCA in Boston and SHARE Program with Marin Humane Society in Novato, California
4. Collaboration with veterinary schools and veterinary hospitals: Philly PAWS and Mercer Clinic in Sacramento, California
5. Entirely volunteer not-for-profit: Pets Are Loving Support, Guerneville, California, and Veterinary Street Outreach Services (VetSOS) in San Francisco

[a]All HASS programs are only loosely connected by purpose. See www.pawssf.org for a current listing of HASS programs.

IX. EXAMPLES OF HUMAN–ANIMAL SUPPORT SERVICE PROGRAMS

Since the mid-1980s, the HASS/PAWS movement has provided health education, services, and emotional support to marginalized members of the community. Each community has its own resources and needs and produces its own unique response. Various examples of programs have evolved nationwide to include independent nonprofits to programs of existing animal or human service organizations (see Table XI).

PAWS in San Francisco started out as an initiative to help pet guardians with AIDS/HIV. In 2002, after extensive planning and feasibility studies, PAWS expanded its services to include other needy disabled members of the San Francisco community. PAWS was careful to create the new program in a way that would not affect its original client base and level of services. Other programs across the United States have, unfortunately, closed down due to the changing nature of the AIDS epidemic and available community resources. Subsequently, PAWS also has led to the development of other innovative programs to help other marginalized members of our community, such as low-income elderly (PAWS/LA) and homeless pet guardians (SOS in San Francisco). There are many populations that can benefit from HASS services.

X. GETTING STARTED

If an individual or group is interested in starting a human–animal support program in their own community, a great deal of planning is required. Each community typically has resources to help developing nonprofit organizations. Additionally, existing human and animal service organizations, including other HASS organizations, may offer assistance for the initiative. PAWS offers a "start up" packet for individuals wanting a blueprint (www.pawssf.org).

XI. CONCLUSION

Companion and therapy animals reach people on many life-improving and life-enhancing levels. Companion animals have been used in community and health care settings to "reach" those who have a reduced capacity to interact with others (Fine, 2002). PAWS makes it possible for people with chronic or terminal illnesses to stay together at home with their valued animal companions for as long as possible. In both realms, animals provide affection and companionship that are not dependent on cognitive or physical capacity (Baun and McCabe, 2003). For those who have pets and care for them, this relationship can truly provide a method to enhance physical and emotional healing. The HASS models presented in this chapter represent guidelines and provide blueprints designed to assist persons with chronic/terminal illnesses with pets in enhancing their quality of their life while they live within their homes (or the homes of others). Clinicians, veterinarians, and community members interested in enhancing the lifestyles of these individuals may consider using the HASS model as a starting point to build upon.

APPENDIX 1: EDUCATING PEOPLE ABOUT PET-ASSOCIATED ZOONOSES, BY STEPHANIE WONG, DVM

While pets can provide many health benefits, pets may also transmit diseases (zoonoses) to people. The benefits of animal companionship still outweigh risks in most cases. Some people have a greater risk of acquiring pet-associated zoonoses; examples of higher risk groups include children less than 5 years old, elderly persons, pregnant women, people with AIDS/HIV, organ transplant recipients, and people using some types of chemotherapies. As such, there is a need to educate people about pet-associated zoonoses (diseases) to (1) minimize a person's risk of getting diseases from pets, (2) prevent a person from giving up pets unnecessarily, and (3) correct misinformation.

Having an appropriate healthy animal companion can provide companionship and health benefits. The risk of picking up an infection from a healthy pet is small and can be reduced further by following good hygiene and the guidelines listed here. If you have questions, always talk to your veterinarian and doctor.

Who Is Providing Zoonosis Education?

In 1999, physicians and veterinarians were surveyed about their perceived roles as zoonosis educators. Interestingly, physicians believed that zoonosis education was the veterinarian's responsibility because it involved animal diseases, and veterinarians believed that zoonosis education was the physician's responsibility because it involved human health. As a result, people who need to be educated about zoonosis prevention may not be receiving information from their physicians or their veterinarians. Instead, information about zoonoses may be provided by health care workers, social workers, volunteers, and groups such PAWS. Misinformation can sometimes be presented by the media, family members, and the health care team.

How Should Zoonosis Prevention Be Taught to Patients and Clients?

To effectively teach patients and clients about zoonoses prevention, it is important to understand how people best *learn* health guidelines. People are most likely to understand and follow zoonosis prevention guidelines if

- They believe that they may be at risk of acquiring pet-associated zoonoses.
- They believe that pet-associated zoonoses can be severe.
- They believe that they can follow the zoonoses prevention guidelines effectively.
- They believe that zoonoses prevention guidelines are easy to access.
- They believe that following zoonoses prevention steps will truly decrease their risk of getting sick.

The reader can use information from the following five sections to effectively educate people about preventing pet-associated zoonoses.

Risks of Acquiring Pet-Associated Zoonoses

Humans coexist in a world filled with bacteria, fungi, parasites, and viruses (microbes). These microbes can be found throughout our environment, including our pets. As such, everyone is at some risk of acquiring diseases (zoonoses) from pets; the good news is that the risk is usually very small. For example, while the Centers for Disease Control and Prevention have developed specific guidelines for pet-associated zoonoses prevention, they do *not* recommend that people with compromised immune systems give up their pets (especially if the pets are adult dogs or cats).

Two factors may increase the risk of acquiring zoonoses from pets, if: (1) The person may have a compromised immune system, or (2) the pet is more likely to carry a harmful bacterium, fungus, parasite, or virus. The following groups may have a higher risk of acquiring zoonoses:

- Children less than 5 years old
- Elderly persons
- Pregnant women
- People with AIDS/HIV
- People with organ transplants
- People being treated with some chemotherapies

The following animals are more likely to carry *significant* zoonoses:

- Reptiles, including lizards, snakes, and turtles
- Baby chicks and ducklings
- Puppies and kittens
- Farm animals, including animals in petting zoos
- Exotic animals such as prarie dogs
- Wild animals

When providing zoonoses prevention tips, people should be informed about the risks of acquiring zoonoses from their pets, including who may be at higher risk and which animals may be more likely to make them sick.

Severity of Pet-Associated Zoonoses

While most pet-associated zoonoses are limited to mild illness in people, some zoonoses can cause severe disease. People with the conditions listed in the previous section are more likely to have more severe illness than the general population. Some examples of pet-associated zoonoses with potentially severe outcomes are provided here.

- *Campylobacter* infections, which may be acquired from farm animals, puppies, and kittens, can cause Guillain–Barre syndrome, a painful disorder that affects the peripheral nervous system.
- Cat-scratch disease is caused by a bacterium, *Bartonella henselae*, and can lead to a severe skin disease called bacillary angiomatosis.
- *Salmonella* infections, including those from pet reptiles, may cause septicemia (blood stream infection) and death in infants.
- *Cryptosporidium* infection from animal feces (stool) can cause severe diarrhea and death in people with compromised immune systems.
- *Toxoplasma* infections from cats can cause abnormalities in fetus development during pregnancy and may lead to death in people with compromised immune systems.

It is important to remember that, aside from the high-risk animal groups provided in the previous section, the CDC does not recommend that people with compromised immune systems give up their pets; instead, people should decrease their risk of severe zoonoses by following simple prevention guidelines (see Appendix 2).

Zoonosis Prevention Guidelines: User-Friendly and Accessible

To effectively educate a person about zoonosis prevention, the person needs to believe that he/she can easily access and follow the zoonosis prevention guidelines. User-friendly guidelines have been developed by multiple institutions, including Pets Are Wonderful Support and the Centers for Disease Control and Prevention. These prevention guidelines are easily accessible on the Internet and can be printed for distribution as needed. Information to access these guidelines is provided here.

- Safe pet guidelines from PAWS San Francisco: http://www.pawssf.org/library_safepetguidelines.htm
- Healthy Pets, Healthy People from the Centers for Disease Control and Prevention: www.cdc.gov/healthypets
- Lesbian and Gay Veterinary Medical Association's Healthy Pets, Healthy People Project: www.lgvma.org

While there are specific guidelines for zoonosis prevention by animal, human medical condition, and zoonoses, general and user-friendly guidelines are provided.

1. People with the following conditions and categories should avoid contact with reptiles (including lizards, snakes, and turtles), baby chicks and ducklings, puppies and kittens, and farm animals: pregnant women, children aged less than 5 years old, elderly, people with AIDS/HIV, organ transplant recipients, some chemotherapy recipients, and people with other conditions that may compromise the immune system.
2. People with compromised immune systems should avoid contact with animal feces. Organizations such as PAWS may be able to provide volunteers who can help clean cat litter boxes, walk dogs, and clean bird cages. If a person cannot avoid handling animal feces, he/she should wash his/her hands thoroughly with warm water and soap or an alcohol-based hand sanitizer after contact with feces.
3. Avoid contact with animals that may lead to scratches or bites (e.g., rough play with kittens).

4. All people should wash their hands thoroughly with warm water and soap after contact with animals.
5. Avoid keeping exotic or wild animals as pets.

Zoonoses Prevention Guidelines: Effectiveness

When educating people about zoonoses prevention, it is important to tell them that the simple guidelines provided in the previous section will *effectively reduce their risk of getting diseases from animals*. While few formal studies have been conducted to measure the effectiveness of these guidelines, the risk factors for pet-associated zoonoses are well known. Therefore, by reducing the known risks of animal scratches, bites, and exposure to animal feces, a person will effectively reduce his/her risk of getting a pet-associated disease. Additionally, studies conducted by the CDC during outbreaks associated with animal contact (i.e., petting zoo outbreaks and reptile-associated outbreaks) have documented that hand washing was a significant protective factor against becoming ill.

In summary, educating patients and clients about pet-associated zoonosis prevention is everyone's job. To educate people about zoonosis prevention effectively, one must do more than provide an informational handout; the educator needs to ensure that the people believe they (1) are susceptible to pet-related zoonoses, (2) may acquire severe disease, (3) have access to zoonosis prevention guidelines, (4) can follow the guidelines easily, and (5) if they follow the guidelines, they will truly decrease their risk of infection. Benefits of animal companionship outweigh the risk of pet-associated zoonotic infection.

More information about pet-associated zoonoses and prevention guidelines can be found at Pets Are Wonderful Support, San Francisco (http://www.pawssf.org/library_safepetguidelines.htm) and the Centers for Disease Control and Prevention (www.cdc.gov/healthypets).

APPENDIX 2: SAFE PET GUIDELINES FOR PREVENTING ZOONOTIC INFECTIONS (2006)[1]

These preventative measures will help reduce the risk that an animal used in AAT or those living in a home will carry or transmit a disease.

[1] Adapted with permission from PAWS (Pets Are Wonderful Support), San Francisco, 2002. Printable versions of the Safe Pet Guidelines are available at http://www.pawssf.org/library_safepetguidelines.htm.

PETS ARE WONDERFUL!

Anyone who has ever lived with a companion animal knows that the unconditional love and acceptance we receive from them is unlike what we generally experience with our human relationships. This is especially important to us when our human contacts diminish through, for example, aging or isolation because of disease.

Animals can bring a unique sense of continuity, stability, and love to our lives; studies demonstrate that companion animals have a positive influence on the quality of life for the aging and ill. However, if our immune system becomes suppressed through disease, age, or medical treatments, we become more vulnerable to infections and may become fearful of contact with other living creatures, including our companion animals.

Zoonoses

Zoonoses (pronounced ZO-uh-NO-seez) are diseases that humans can catch from other animals. This section reviews general guidelines for minimizing your risk of catching a disease from a companion animal. If you are immunocompromised and either have an animal companion or want to adopt one, carefully review these guidelines with your doctor and your animal's veterinarian (http://www.pawssf.org/library_safepetguidelines.htm-top#top).

Am I at Risk for Catching a Disease from My Pet?

Current evidence supports the fact that most pets pose little or no health risk to their owners. An individual's risk may be slightly higher if he or she has a compromised immune system. This includes the following:

- People with HIV/AIDS, especially if their CD4 count is low
- People on chemotherapy or high doses of steroids
- People who are aged
- People born with congenital immune deficiencies
- Pregnant women and the children they carry
- People who have received organ or bone marrow transplants
- Children 5 years of age or younger

Zoonoses and HIV/AIDS

While there are a number of diseases we can catch from animals, there are only rare instances when people with HIV or AIDS have caught infections from their pets. The Centers for Disease Control and Prevention also states that there is no evidence that dogs, cats, or any other nonprimate animals can contract HIV or transmit it to humans.

Benefits of Animal Ownership Outweigh the Risks

Follow these guidelines to help keep your pets healthy and as safe as possible. Keep in mind that a little preventive care can go a long way in maintaining your animal's health and that a healthy animal is less likely to pick up diseases and transmit them to you. A healthy pet is a safe pet.

General Guidelines for Your Animal

Diet

- Feed your pet a high-quality commercial diet that is designed for your animal and his or her stage of life.
- Do not feed your animal raw or undercooked meats or unpasteurized milk. Keep in mind that microwaving may not heat the meat sufficiently to kill organisms in it.
- Prevent your animal from eating his or her own or another animal's or human feces.
- Provide plenty of clean, fresh water. Do not let your animal drink from the toilet or standing water outside.
- Prevent your animal from raiding the trash.
- Prevent your animal from hunting or eating other animals.
- Keep cats indoors so they cannot catch diseases from mice, birds, or other animals. If your cat does go outdoors, consider placing two bells on its collar to help warn potential prey.

Veterinary Care

- Have all new animals examined by a veterinarian.
- Take your animals to the veterinarian for a checkup at least once each year and whenever your animals develop diarrhea or become ill.
- Keep your pet up to date on vaccines (shots). Consult with your veterinarian about the best protocol for your area.
- Keep your pet free of worms and other parasites. Ask your veterinarian about the best testing and treatment protocol for your area.
- Have your cat (particularly a new cat or an outdoor cat) checked for the feline leukemia virus (FeLV) and feline immunodeficiency virus (FIV),

because while not transmittable to humans, these diseases suppress the cat's immune system, making him or her more susceptible to diseases that could be passed on to you.

Grooming/Flea Control

- Have your animal bathed, brushed, and combed as needed to keep the skin and coat healthy.
- Keep your animal's toenails trimmed to minimize the risk of your being scratched. If necessary, ask your vet about rubber caps that can be placed on your cat's nails as an alternative to declawing.
- Use good flea control. Consult with your veterinarian about the best available products.
- Have your pet examined if there is any hair loss.
- A clean environment is important. Keep your pet's living and feeding areas clean. Wash your pet's bedding regularly.

Safe Litter Box Guidelines

- Keep the box away from the kitchen and eating areas.
- If possible, have someone who's not at risk change the litter box. Otherwise, change the litter box daily using disposable gloves. It takes the *Toxoplasma* parasite at least 24 hours to become infectious.
- Use disposable plastic liners and change them each time you change the litter.
- Do not dump the litter! If inhaled, the dust could possibly infect you. Gently seal the plastic liner with a twist tie and place in a plastic garbage bag for disposal.
- Disinfect the litter box at least once a month by filling it with boiling water and letting it stand for 10 minutes. This will kill the *Toxoplasma* organism, which can normally persist in the environment. Do not use disinfectants like Lysol as they are toxic to young cats.
- Always wash your hands with soap and warm water after cleaning the litter box, even if you wear gloves.

Adopting a New Animal

Adopting a new animal companion is always exciting, but keep in mind that new pets, especially puppies and kittens, present more of a risk. If you are going to adopt a new pet, an adult animal is safer. Consult with your veterinarian and doctor before adopting a new animal. Your veterinarian may recommend some tests for parasites and other diseases on a new animal. It is best not to take a new animal into your home until you know that he or she is healthy.

Animals to Avoid

Unfortunately, some animals simply present too much risk to immunosuppressed people and should be avoided altogether.

- Stray animals
- Animals with diarrhea
- Reptiles (turtles, lizards, and snakes) and amphibians
- "Exotic" pets, such as pot-bellied pigs, sugar gliders, and prairie dogs
- Wild animals and birds, including pigeons, baby chicks, and ducklings
- Farm animals, including baby chicks and ducklings
- Nonhuman primates (monkeys). Nonhuman primates carry the greatest risk because of their close genetic relationship to humans and should not be pets under any circumstances. It is also good to remember that humans in the household pose many risks to the animal as well (http://www.pawssf.org/library_safepetguidelines.htm-top#top).

Human Health Measures

First Aid for Bites/Scratches

Rinse a bite wound or scratch right away with plenty of running water. Wash the area with a mild soap or with a tamed iodine solution such as Betadine solution that has been diluted with water. Contact your doctor.

Hygiene

- Wash your hands frequently, especially before eating or smoking.
- Avoid contact with your pet's bodily fluids such as vomit, feces, urine, or saliva. In the event of an accident, clean up the mess with a disinfectant (an ounce of bleach in a quart of water works nicely to kill many infectious organisms) and then wash your hands thoroughly. Better yet, wear gloves or have someone not at risk clean it up.
- Do not let your pet lick a wound on your face or body.
- Never walk barefoot or contact the soil where it is likely to find feces in the soil or sand.
- Control mice or rats living in your home.

About Dogs

Most healthy dogs carry little or no health risk to people. Some dogs, particularly puppies, however, do carry some diseases that could be harmful to someone at higher risk. Parasites that dogs can transmit to people include roundworms, hookworms, *Cryptosporidium,* and *Giardia.* In rare instances, dogs can also transmit bacteria such as *Salmonella* and *Campylobacter.* These parasites and bacteria are most often associated with puppies or with adult dogs that live in unsanitary environments. Any new dog or any dog having diarrhea should have his or her stool tested for these infections by a veterinarian.

Can I Reduce the Risk of Catching a Disease from My Dog?

Yes. PAWS recommends that people at risk only get dogs older than 9 months of age. Puppies are more likely to harbor infections than healthy adult dogs. Following the general guidelines listed earlier will help reduce your risk of catching any infections your dog may have.

About Cats

Can I Reduce the Risk of Catching a Disease from My Cat?

Yes. Most cats pose a minimal risk for transmitting a disease. Indoor cats have the lowest risk of carrying a disease that can spread to a person. Following the guidelines in this section will help you reduce your risk of contracting a disease from a cat. If you are at an increased risk, you should review these recommendations with your doctor and your veterinarian (http://www.pawssf.org/library_yourcatyourhealth.htm-top#top).

What Is Cat Scratch Disease (CSD)?

CSD is a bacterial infection caused by *Bartonella henselae.* The infection usually causes fever, fatigue, and swollen lymph nodes. Most cat scratches do not develop into CSD.

What Is Bacillary Angiomatosis (BA)?

BA is a rare complication of *B. henselae* infection, which usually occurs in people with HIV/AIDS. Patients with BA may have skin lesions, which sometimes resemble Kaposi's sarcoma. BA can also affect internal organs such as the liver or spleen.

What Is *Bartonella*?

Both CSD and BA appear to be caused by the same bacteria, *B. henselae*. Human *Bartonella* diseases are the most common zoonotic disease in the United States today.

How Is My Cat Affected by This Organism?

Cats that carry the bacteria are generally not ill and show no signs of infection. Research shows that cats acquire the *Bartonella* organism from fleas.

How Is This Organism Transmitted to People?

Cats may transmit *Bartonella* to people by scratches or possibly bites. Fleas may also be involved with transmission to people. Kittens are more likely to be associated with transmission of CSD or BA to humans than adult cats.

Should I Have My Cat Tested?

Although tests are available to determine if your cat has been exposed to *Bartonella*, testing is not recommended because test results can be confusing and would not change recommendations.

Is It Treatable in People?

It is extremely important to see a doctor if you think you may have BA. The condition is very treatable (and curable). CSD in people with healthy immune systems is usually benign. If you are concerned about CSD, consult your doctor. If you are scratched or bitten by a cat and develop a wound that will not heal, a fever, unusual skin lesions, or are otherwise ill from unknown causes, you should let your doctor know that you were scratched or bitten.

Can I Prevent Myself from Getting This Disease?

- Follow the general guidelines listed earlier.
- Minimize contact with kittens.
- Wash your hands after handling a cat.
- Wash all bites or scratches immediately with soap and water. If you are bitten, contact your doctor.
- Discourage your cat from scratching or biting you. Avoid rough play.

- Keep your cat's nails trimmed short. If your cat tends to scratch frequently, talk to your veterinarian about behavior modification or nail caps for cats to help minimize scratches.
- Do not allow a cat to lick open wounds on your body.

What Is Ringworm?

Ringworm is not actually a worm. It is the common name for a group of fungal infections that affect the skin of a large variety of animals, including cats and people.

How Will I Know if My Cat Is Carrying Ringworm?

Most cats with ringworm will lose hair and have crusty skin where the infection is. This can look very similar to many other skin conditions so contact your veterinarian if you are concerned that your cat may have ringworm. Some cats, particularly certain purebred cats, can carry ringworm without showing any symptoms. Ask your veterinarian if your cat may be at risk.

Can I Catch Ringworm from My Cat?

The rate of transmission is low, but anyone, including someone with a healthy immune system, can potentially contract ringworm from a cat (or other animal) that is carrying the disease.

What if I Catch Ringworm?

Ringworm is treatable. Contact your doctor if you are concerned about possible exposure. There is no evidence that ringworm is more severe or more common in people with compromised immune systems (http://www.pawssf.org/library_yourcatyourhealth.htm-top#top).

What Is Toxoplasmosis?

Toxoplasmosis is an infection caused by the single-celled parasite *Toxoplasma gondii*. It can infect most mammals (including humans) and some birds.

Why Are Cats Blamed for Toxoplasmosis?

Cats are the only species of animal to shed the infectious stage in their feces. Other animals, however, can disseminate *T. gondii* if their infected meat is eaten without proper cooking. Humans most commonly contract toxoplasmosis by eating undercooked infected meat.

How Do Cats Get Toxoplasmosis?

Cats acquire toxoplasmosis by eating rodents, undercooked meat, the feces of other cats, or contaminated soil. Cats can acquire the infection easily if they are allowed to hunt or are fed raw or undercooked meat; as many as 90% of cats are exposed to *T. gondii* during their lives.

How Will I Know If My Cat Has Toxoplasmosis?

Most infected cats show no symptoms of the disease. Sometimes there is a short episode of diarrhea, pneumonia, or ongoing eye problems or problems of the nervous system. Healthy cats pass the infectious stage in their feces only during the first 2 weeks after they are exposed. After that time, the cat's immune system will usually prevent passing of the organism.

Should I Test My Cat for Toxoplasmosis?

No. Although a test is available to measure a cat's antibody response to toxoplasmosis, testing cats is not recommended because the test results would not change the recommendations.

How Do I Prevent My Cat from Getting It?

To minimize your cat's chance of infection, follow the general guidelines listed earlier.

Should I Worry about Getting Toxoplasmosis from My Cat?

Humans will only rarely acquire toxoplasmosis from an infected cat. More commonly, people are exposed by eating undercooked meat and unwashed fruits or vegetables, congenitally (from an infected mother to her fetus through the placenta), or by accidental ingestion of contaminated soil when gardening. About 15–50% of the U.S. population (depending on where you live) has already been exposed.

What Happens If I Get Toxoplasmosis?

A healthy adult person is unlikely to get sick when exposed to *T. gondii*; most commonly they will only exhibit mild flu-like symptoms. If you are pregnant, however, and if and only if it is your first exposure, infection can lead to birth defects and possible miscarriage. If you have a compromised immune system due to conditions such as HIV/AIDS or chemotherapy, toxoplasmosis can be life-threatening, often leading to central nervous system disorders. Most cases of toxoplasmosis in immunocompromised people are due to a reactivation of a previous infection and not a new infection.

Should I Be Tested for Exposure to Toxoplasmosis?

A test is available to determine if you have been exposed to *T. gondii*. This test is currently recommended for all immunocompromised people. Consult your doctor if you are concerned.

If You Have a Compromised Immune System:

1. If you test positive, your doctor may put you on therapy.
2. If you test negative, be sure to follow the general guidelines listed earlier.

If You Are Pregnant:

1. If you test positive, you have built up antibodies to protect you and the fetus from a new infection.
2. If you test negative and you become infected with *T. gondii* during your pregnancy, you risk having a baby with birth defects, so be sure to follow the safe litter box guidelines listed earlier.

How Can I Reduce My Risk of Catching Toxoplasmosis?

- Use caution around the litter box (see safe litter box guidelines listed earlier).
- Cook all meats well (this means cooking to an internal meat temperature of 165° F). Microwaving may not always cook meat well enough.
- Wash hands and food-preparation surfaces thoroughly after contact with raw meats.
- Wash vegetables well.
- When gardening, wear gloves and avoid touching your mouth (do not smoke or drink).

What Is Plague?

Plague is a rare disease caused by the bacteria *Yersinia pestis*. It is found most commonly in the southwestern United States (e.g., Colorado and New Mexico).

Do Cats Carry the Plague Bacteria?

Yes, in very rare cases cats do carry *Y. pestis*, but most often, fleas living on rodents (mice and rats) are the source of infection for humans and cats.

How Do I Keep My Cat from Catching Plague?

Keep your cat indoors (http://www.pawssf.org/library_yourcatyourhealth.htm-top#top) at all times, and use good flea control measures in your home and on your cat. Eliminate rats or mice living in your home.

How Would I Know if My Cat Is Infected with Plague?

Cats typically will be very tired and have swollen lymph nodes and a fever. Sometimes they may also have lung problems.

Can I Catch Plague from My Cat?

Most human plague infections occur when the person is bitten by an infected flea from a mouse or rat. If your cat becomes infected, however, it is possible for you to also become infected from your cat.

How Do I Protect Myself from Catching Plague?

Do not handle or pick up dead animals from your home, work, or recreation areas. Treat your pets with flea control products regularly.

What Happens If I Get Plague?

People usually show symptoms 2–6 days after being infected. The initial symptoms usually include fever, chills, weakness, swollen and painful lymph nodes, and headaches. Plague can be cured, so consult with your doctor if you may have been exposed to plague.

What Other Diseases Can I Catch from Contact with My Cat's Feces?

Cats can occasionally be the source for a variety of intestinal ailments, including some bacterial infections (*Salmonella* and *Campylobacter*) and some intestinal parasites (*Giardia*, *Cryptosporidium*, hookworms, and roundworms). These diseases can be spread to people by direct contact with the feces of an infected cat or by contact with soil that has been contaminated by the feces of an infected cat. Many animals other than cats also can carry these infections. *Salmonella* and *Campylobacter* are spread most often through undercooked meat or improperly prepared food.

How Will I Know If My Cat Is Carrying One of These Diseases?

Cats that are carrying one of these infections will sometimes, but not always, have diarrhea. Cats at highest risk for one of these infections are stray cats, young kittens, cats recently adopted from an animal shelter, or cats that are immunocompromised themselves.

What Will Happen If I Catch One of These Diseases?

This group of bacterial and parasitic infections will usually produce only temporary symptoms in someone with a healthy immune system. For people who are immunocompromised, however, these infections can be life-threatening, often resulting in prolonged diarrhea.

Feline Leukemia Virus and Feline Immunodeficiency Virus

Both of these viruses are different from the human AIDS virus (HIV). Both FeLV and FIV are contagious between cats, but neither of them can infect humans, nor can the human virus infect cats. These diseases do, however, suppress the cat's immune system, making it more susceptible to diseases that could be passed on to you. If you are immunocompromised, it is best not to keep a cat with FeLV or FIV. If you do keep a cat with one of these diseases, be extra careful about following the general guidelines listed earlier.

About Birds

Can Bird Diseases Make Me Sick?

Most healthy pet birds pose little or no health risk to humans, but some bird diseases can cause illness in people. *Mycobacterium avium* complex (MAC), psittacosis (parrot fever), cryptococcosis (*Cryptococus*), and salmonellosis (*Salmonella*) are the primary diseases associated with pet birds that can be potentially transmitted to humans. Allergic alveolitis can also develop in sensitive humans. It is unlikely that you will acquire an infection from your bird, but caution is always advised, especially for higher risk groups (http://www.pawssf.org/library_yourbirdyourhealth.htm-top).

What Are the Chances That My Bird Has One of These Infections?

That depends on the species of bird and its source, age, and general health status. Newly adopted birds and birds undergoing other stresses are always more risky. A veterinarian experienced in avian medicine should be consulted to evaluate your particular situation.

How Can I Tell If My Bird Has an Infection?

There are no specific symptoms characteristic of each disease. If your bird stops eating, loses weight, has vomiting or diarrhea, appears fluffed up and chilled, or just is not right, then your bird should be seen by a veterinarian immediately.

How Do I Get These Diseases from My Bird?

These diseases can be transmitted by direct contact with stool and nasal discharges or by breathing dried, powdered droppings.

Can I Acquire These Diseases from Sources Other Than My Bird?

Yes. In fact, it is much more common to acquire these diseases from the environment, from undercooked or contaminated foods, or in some cases, from other people. Complete avoidance of all zoonoses is impossible.

What Happens If I Get Any of These Diseases?

MAC (also known as atypical mycobacterium, a disease similar to tuberculosis) is acquired most commonly from the environment, can cause a variety of symptoms (including night sweats, weight loss, abdominal pain, fatigue, diarrhea, and anemia), and is suspected to be involved with AIDS wasting syndrome. MAC is a lifelong infection that can be reactivated as the immune system deteriorates. There are now drugs that can help control human infections of MAC.

Psittacosis (parrot fever) produces flu-like symptoms and is usually accompanied by a dry cough and fever. Psittacosis can be acquired multiple times. People catch this infection by breathing dried secretions from infected birds. To date, there are no reported cases of psittacosis in people with HIV/AIDS. Those at greatest risk are pet bird owners, pet shop employees, veterinarians, and employees in poultry processing plants.

Salmonella infections cause fever and gastrointestinal symptoms, including stomach cramps and diarrhea. Sometimes, the symptoms are so severe that medical treatment is required. *Salmonella* infections can occur repeatedly, and an infected person can become a chronic carrier without showing any symptoms.

Cryptococcosis is a fungal infection that rarely causes any signs of illness in healthy individuals, but for those that are immunocompromised, severe brain and spinal cord disease can occur. The disease is spread by breathing the droppings of wild birds, including pigeons. Dogs and cats can also contract cryptococcosis from birds, but they cannot transmit it to humans. Those with compromised immune systems should avoid areas where wild birds congregate.

Allergic alveolitis produces coughing and difficulty breathing. Allergic alveolitis is a progressive respiratory disease and can be alleviated by total avoidance of bird dander, feathers, and in some cases, poultry products.

If you are diagnosed with any of these diseases, your doctor will outline a treatment plan. Once again, it is important to emphasize that the likelihood of acquiring these infections from your pet bird is quite low (http://www.pawssf.org/library_yourbirdyourhealth.htm-top).

Are There Other Bird-Associated Illnesses?

Yes, but the aforementioned five diseases are by far the most common. Good sanitation and keeping your bird healthy are the best prevention for most infectious diseases.

Can a Pet Bird Catch Bird Flu?

As of 2005, the H5N1 strain of avian influenza (often called *bird flu*) was found only in wild birds (especially wild ducks) and in farmed chickens. This virus is found mostly in Asia, although it is possible that it will eventually infect wild birds in North America. If bird flu comes to your locality, the best way to protect your pet bird is to prevent it from coming in contact with any wild birds or their droppings. In general, it is a good idea for any person to avoid unnecessary contact with wild birds and farmed birds (check with the CDC or the PAWS websites for updated precautions and current information).

How Do I Prevent My Bird from Getting These Diseases?

- Never expose your bird to other birds that have not been tested for psittacosis and quarantined for 45 days. It is especially important to avoid contact with pigeons and other wild birds.

- Avoid situations in which your bird will have casual contact with other birds (such as going to the pet store for wing clips and nail trims). Ideally, birds should be cared for at home rather than in boarding facilities.
- All sick birds should be seen by a veterinarian as soon as possible.

How Can I Prevent Myself from Getting These Diseases?

- Good sanitation and hygiene. See *Human Health Measures* listed earlier.
- Clean your bird's cage liner daily.
- If you are in a higher risk category, use a surgical mask when cleaning your bird's cage.
- Wash your hands after contact with birds.
- Avoid contact with wild birds, including pigeons.
- Avoid farmed birds and baby ducklings or chicks.

How Can I Adopt a Safe Bird?

- In accordance with the 1992 Wild Bird Conservation Act, PAWS recommends only buying birds from a reputable breeder. Even though importation of wild birds for the pet trade has been illegal in the United States since 1992, theses illegally imported birds are commonly sold at flea markets and by street vendors for a much reduced price. Illegally imported birds have a higher risk for carrying infectious diseases.
- Do not buy birds that have been housed with imported birds.
- Avoid pet store birds and any bird that appears sick.
- Always set up a postadoption veterinary visit to have your bird examined and to get all of your questions answered.

Should My Bird Be Tested for Any of These Diseases?

Because each situation is different, your veterinarian will be better able to make recommendations for your particular situation. In general, we do not recommend routine screening for MAC or *Salmonella* because even some birds carrying these diseases will have a negative test result. In general, all newly acquired birds in the parrot family should be tested for psittacosis, but it is important to keep in mind that no single test or combination of tests can definitively rule out psittacosis in any bird or human.

How Do I Locate a Veterinarian Who Has Experience with Birds?

Contact your state or local veterinary medical association or the Association for Avian Veterinarians (AAV) at P.O. Box 811720, Boca Raton, FL 33481, or call AAV at 561/393-8901 or find them on the web at http://www.aav.org/. AAV also publishes a great brochure on psittacosis.

About Aquarium Fish and Amphibians (Frogs, Toads, and Salamanders)

Aquarium fish can occasionally be the source of infectious diseases. Mycobacterial infections (a type of tuberculosis) can be transmitted by aquarium fish, and some skin infections can be spread by contact with infected aquarium water. People can catch *Salmonella* infections from contact with infected amphibians and aquarium water.

What Can I Do to Reduce My Risk If I Decide to Keep Aquarium Fish or Amphibians?

Wear gloves when cleaning an aquarium or when handling fish or amphibians. Fish suspected of having mycobacterium or any fish showing unusual lumps should be removed from the tank, and the aquarium should be disinfected before new fish are introduced. Follow the general guidelines listed earlier.

About Reptiles (Snakes, Turtles, and Lizards, Including Iguanas)

We do not recommend that people at risk keep or handle reptiles. *Salmonella* infection can be transmitted by almost any reptile. Many reptiles are carriers of *Salmonella* without showing any signs of illness. Because reptiles have a tendency to lie in or move through their own feces, these bacteria can be found anywhere (and everywhere) on the animal's body. Treating the reptile with antibiotics is not a reliable method to rid the animal of *Salmonella* and is not recommended.

What Can I Do to Reduce My Risk If I Decide to Keep a Reptile in My Home?

Use gloves and a face mask when handling or cleaning these animals or their habitat. Better yet, have someone not at risk do the cleaning. Never wash your reptile in your kitchen sink or bathtub. Wash your hands thoroughly after handling a reptile. Feed a reptile a commercial diet and avoid feeding raw meat and eggs to reduce your animal's risk of acquiring *Salmonella*. If possible, dead prey rather than live should be offered to your reptile.

About Ferrets

Zoonoses transmitted by pet ferrets are rare. Intestinal parasites are common in young ferrets and can potentially be spread to people. PAWS does not recommend that people at risk come in contact with an immature ferret. Ferrets are also susceptible to human influenza and can easily pass it back to the human. Following the general guidelines will help reduce your risk of acquiring any infections your ferret may have.

About Horses

Zoonoses transmitted by horses are rare. Intestinal parasites and infections such as *Salmonella* can potentially be spread to people. PAWS does not recommend that people at risk come in contact with an immature horse, a horse with diarrhea, or areas where horses are raised. Most adult horses kept in a clean environment pose little or no risk for transmitting a disease.

About Rabbits and Rodents

Zoonoses transmitted by pet rabbits and rodents (rats, mice, guinea pigs, hamsters, or gerbils) are rare. The most common problems usually stem from reactions to rabbit scratches or infections from rabbit or rodent bites. The *Pasteurella* bacteria carried by most rabbits may infect scratches or bite wounds. Scratches and bite wounds should be washed and disinfected immediately. Some external parasites of the rabbit, including fur mites and ringworm (a type of fungal infection), may be transmitted to humans. Tuleriemia and rabbit hemorrhagic fever have occasionally been associated with rabbits also.

Guinea pigs, mice, and rats can occasionally be the source for a variety of intestinal ailments, including some bacterial infections (*Salmonella* and *Campylobacter*) and some intestinal parasites (*Giardia* or *Cryptosporidium*). These diseases can be spread to people by direct contact with the feces of an infected animal or by contact with soil that has been contaminated by the feces of an infected animal. Lymphocytic choriomeningitis (LCMV) is a potentially serious virus that humans can catch from infected mice and hamsters. Pet mice and hamsters can get LCMV from other animals in a pet store or from exposure to wild mice in your home.

How Can I Reduce the Risk of Catching a Disease from My Rabbit or Rodent?

Do not feed your animal raw eggs or raw meat. Be diligent about washing your hands after handling your animal. Use disposable gloves when cleaning your animal's cage, or better yet, have someone who is not at risk care for the animal. Follow the general guidelines listed earlier. If you are adopting a new rabbit or rodent, be sure that the animal is healthy and has not recently been exposed to any ill rabbits or rodents (http://www.pawssf.org/library_safepetguidelines.htm-top#top).

About Rabies

What Is Rabies?

Rabies is a virus that can infect the brain of some animals, including dogs, cats, and ferrets. In rare situations, it can also infect people.

Can I Get Rabies from My Pet?

In the United States, human rabies cases are usually picked up from bats, raccoons, skunks, foxes, and coyotes; it can be acquired from bites from dogs in other countries. It has been more than 30 years since someone caught rabies from a dog or cat in the United States.

How Can I Protect My Pet from Catching Rabies?

Rabies vaccinations (rabies shots) are available for dogs, cats, and ferrets to keep them from catching rabies. Ask you veterinarian about the best protocol for rabies vaccination. If possible, keep your cat indoors so that it will not come into contact with other animals that can carry rabies. If your dog or cat is bitten by a wild or stray animal, call your veterinarian.

How Can I Protect Myself from Catching Rabies?

Prevent bats from entering your home, and if one does enter your home, call a professional service to have it removed. Consult with your doctor right away if you are ever bitten by any animal or have had a bat in your home. Many bat bites go unnoticed because the wound is small and painless.

If I Have Further Questions, Who Can I Contact?

Pets Are Wonderful Support, 645 Harrison St., Suite 100, San Francisco, CA 94103, or call 415-979-9550. Additional information on specific zoonotic diseases can be found at the CDC web site (http://www.cdc.gov/healthypets/).

ACKNOWLEDGMENTS

Thanks to the following original contributors—Vic Spain, DVM; Karen Blount, DVM; Fred Angulo, DVM; Ken Gorczyca, DVM; James M. Harris, DVM; Alan Stewart, DVM, and Carol Glasser, DVM, MD—and to the following 2005 contributors—Gail Hansen, DVM, MPH; Patricia Payne, DVM, Ph.D.; Chip Wells, DVM; Stepahine Wong, DVM, MPH; Dr. Heather Bair-Brake; Kathy Gervais, DVM; Ken Gorczyca, DVM; Vic Spain, DVM, Ph.D.; James Carpenter, DVM, DAZM; Michelle Hawkins, DVM, DAZM; and Joshua Freng.

REFERENCES

Angulo, F., and Glasser, C. (1994). Caring for pets of immunocompromised persons. *J. Am. Vet. Med. Assoc.* **205**, 12.

Belsky, J. (1980). Child maltreatment: An ecological integration. *Am. Psychol.* **35**, 320–335.

Belsky, J. (1980). Early human experience: A family experience. *Devel. Psychol.* 17, 3–24.

Bennet, M. J. (1990). Stigmatization: Experiences of persons with acquired immune deficiency syndrome. *Issues Ment. Health Nurs.* **11**, 141–154.

Bronfenbrenner, U. (1977). Toward an experimental ecology of human development. *Am. Psychol.* **32**, 513–531.

Bronfenbrenner, U. (1979). "The Ecology of Human Development." Harvard University Press, Cambridge, MA.

Carmack, B. J. (1991). The role of companion animals for persons with AIDS/HIV. *Holist. Nurs. Pract.* 5(2), 24–31.

Castelli, P., Hart, L. A., and Zasloff, R. L. (2001). Companion cats and the social support systems of men with AIDS. *Psychol. Rep.* **89**, 177–187.

Cherry, K., and Smith. (1993). Sometimes I cry: The experience of loneliness for men with AIDS. *Health Commun.* **5**, 181–208.

Chinner T. L., and Dalziel F. R. (1991). An exploratory study on the viability and efficacy of a pet-facilitated therapy project within a hospice. *J Palliat Care.* 7(4), 13–20.

Christ, G., Wiener, L., and Moynihan, R. (1986). Psychosocial issues in AIDS. *Psychiatr. Ann.* **16**, 173–179.

Cookman, C. A. (1996). Older people and attachment to things, places, pets, and ideas. *Image: J. Nurs. Sch.* **28**, 227–231.

Cusack, O. (1988). "Pets and Mental Health." The Haworth Press, New York.

Dean, A., and Lin, N. (1977). The stress buffering role of social support; problems and prospects for systematic investigation. *J. Nerv. Ment. Dis.* **165**, 408–417.

Felce, D., and Perry, J. (1993). Quality of life: A contribution to its definition and measurement. Mental Handicap in Wales Applied Research Unit, Cardiff, Wales, UK.

Garrett, L. (2005). The Lessons of HIV/AIDS. Foreign Affairs.

Gorczyca, K. (1991). Special needs for the pet owner with AIDS/HIV. *In* "The Bond between All Living Things," pp. 13–20. R and E Publishers, Saratoga, CA.

Gorczyca, K., Abrams, D., and Carmack, B. (1989). Pets and HIV Disease: A Survey of Provider's Knowledge and Attitudes, V International Conference on AIDS Proceedings.

Gortmaker, S. L. (1985). Demography of chronic childhood diseases: Prevalence and impact. *Pediatr. Clin. North Am.* **31**, 3–18.

Healthy Pets, Healthy People (1998). "Healthy Pets, Healthy People Resource Guide." San Francisco.

Hoffman, C., and Rice, D. (1995). 1997 National Medical Expenditure Survey. University of California, San Francisco. Institute for Health and Aging.

Humane Society of the United States (2003). U.S. pet ownership statistics. Retrieved on February 21, 2005 from http://www.hsus.org/pets/issues_affecting_our_pets/pet_overpopulation_and_ownership_statistics/us_pet_ownership_statistics.html.

Hutton, J. S. (1982). Social workers act like animals in their casework relations. Society for Companion Animal Studies Newsheet **3**, 30.

Jackson, P. L., and Vessey, J. A. (2000). "Primary Care of the Child with a Chronic Condition," 3rd Ed. Mosby, St. Louis, MO.

Johnson, R. (2003). Human animal interaction, illness prevention, and wellness promotion. Editorial. *Anim. Behav. Sci.* **47**(1), 5–6.

Judson, L. (2004). Global childhood chronic illness. *Nurs. Administr. Q.* **28**(1), 607.

Jue, S. (1994). Psychosocial issues of AIDS long-term survivors. *J. Contemp. Hum. Serv.* **43**, 324–332.

Levine, M. M., and Bohn, S. (1986). Development of social skills as a function of being reared with pets. *In* "Proceedings of Living Together: People, Animals, and the Environment," p. 27. Delta Society International Conference, Boston, MA.

Maj, M. (1991). Psychological problems of families and health workers dealing with people infected with human immunodeficiency virus. *Acta Psychiatr. Scand.* **83**, 161–168.

Meer, J. (1984). Pet theories. *Psychol. Today* **18**, 60–67.

Muschel, U. (1985 October). Pet therapy with terminal cancer patients. *J. Contemp. Soc. Work* 451–458.

Nebbe, L. L. (1991). The human-animal bond and the elementary school counselor. *School Counselor* **38**, 362–371.

Pets Are Wonderful Support (2005a). Healing power of the human-animal bond: Conference proceedings. Hollywood, CA.

Pets Are Wonderful Support (2005b). "Safe Pet Guidelines," 3rd Ed. Blount and Spain, San Francisco.

Pets Are Wonderful Support (1998). "Questions You May Have about Your Bird and Your Health." Ed. Blount and Spain, San Francisco.

Pets Are Wonderful Support (1998). "Questions You May Have about Your Cat and Your Health." Ed. Blount and Spain, San Francisco.

Perrin, J. M., and MacLean, W. E., Jr. (1988). Children with chronic illness: The prevention of dysfunction. *Pediatr. North Am.* **35**, 1325–1337.

Seniornet (n.d.). Chronic conditions. Retrieved May 10, 2005, from http://www.seniornet.org/php/default.php?PageID=5541&Version=0&Font=0.

Serpell, J. A. (1983). Pet psychotherapy. People-Animals-Environment, 7–8.

Shea, T. M., and Bauer, A. M. (1991). Parents and teachers of children with exceptionalities: A handbook for collaboration. Allyn and Bacon, Needham Heights, MA.

Siegel, J. M. (1993). Companion animals: In sickness and in health. *J. Soc. Issues* **49**, 157–167.

Siegel, L. J. (1993). Psychotherapy with medically at-risk children. *In* "Handbook of Psychotherapy with Children and Adolescents" (T. R. Kratochwill and R. J. Morris, eds.), pp. 472–501. Allyn and Bacon, Boston, MA.

Siegel, J. M., Angulo, F. J., Detels, R., Wesch, J., and Mullen, A. (1999). AIDS diagnosis and depression in the multicenter AIDS Cohort Study: The ameliorating impact of pet ownership. *AIDS Care* **11**(2), 157–170.

Spencer, L. (1992). Study explores health risks and the human/animal bond. *J. Am. Vet. Med. Assoc.* **201**(11), 1669.

UNAIDS (n.d.). Regional HIV and AIDS estimates 2004. Retrieved May 1, 2005, from http://www.unaids.org/EN/default.asp.

United Nations AIDS/World Health Organization (1998). Report on the Global HIV/AIDS Epidemic.

United States National Center of Health Statistics (n.d.). 2004 National Vital Statistics Reports Vol. 53 (17). Retrieved June 15, 2005, from http://www.cdc.gov/nchs/data/dvs/nvsr53_17table E2002.pdf.

Veevers, J. E. (1985). The social meaning of pets: Alternate roles for companion animals. *In* "Pets and the Family" (M. B. Sussman, ed.), pp. 11–30. Haworth Press, New York.

Volth, V. L. (1985). Attachment of people to companion animals. *Vet. Clin. North Am.* **15**, 289–295.

Weiss, R. S. (1973). "Loneliness: The Experience of Social and Emotional Isolation." MIT Press, Cambridge, MA.

Wilson, C. C. (1991). The pet as an anxiolytic intervention. *J. Nerv. Ment. Dis.* **179**, 482–489.

Wong, B. (2005). Role of pets in health promotion: A PAWS case study. Poster session presented at the 133rd annual meeting of the American Public Health Association, Philadelphia, PA.

Wong, S. (1998). Report from World AIDS Conference in Geneva. Lesbian and Gay Veterinary Medical Association's Good News, **6**(3).

Wrongdiagnosis (n.d.). Statistics about chronic illness. Retrieved May 10, 2005 from http://www.wrongdiagnosis.com/c/chronic/stats.htm.

CHAPTER 16

Animal Abuse and Developmental Psychopathology: Recent Research, Programmatic, and Therapeutic Issues and Challenges for the Future

FRANK R. ASCIONE
Department of Psychology, Utah State University, Logan, Utah 84322

SUZANNE BARNARD
Annie E. Casey Foundation, Bethesda, Maryland 20817

SUSAN BROOKS AND JULIE SELL-SMITH
Green Chimneys, Brewster, New York 10509

I. OVERVIEW

As animals become a more significant component of therapeutic interventions with children and adolescents, greater attention is being paid both to the benevolent and to the problematic relations that exist between animals and young people. The field of animal welfare has a long history of attempts to enhance children's attitudes toward and treatment of animals (for overviews, see Ascione, 1997, 2005b). However, as society focuses on the persistent challenge of violence in human relationships, renewed attention is being given to animal abuse as a correlate of and potential precursor to human mental health problems (Green and Gullone, 2005). The role of animals in preventing and treating psychological dysfunction in children and adolescents is also receiving increased scrutiny.

This chapter provides (a) an overview of research on the relation between animal abuse and interpersonal violence, (b) a discussion of efforts by animal

Handbook on Animal-Assisted Therapy: Theoretical Foundations and Guidelines for Practice, 2e

and human welfare organizations to use this information to expand their scope to areas of common interest, and (c) an illustration of the unique role animals may play in assessment and therapeutic intervention with young people who are psychologically at risk. Each of us approached this project from our own varying perspectives of developmental psychology, child and animal welfare, and child clinical intervention and animal-facilitated therapy. However, a common thread in all of our work is the belief that collaboration among professionals is the most fruitful avenue to solving complex human (and animal!) problems.

II. THE CONFLUENCE OF ANIMAL MALTREATMENT AND INTERPERSONAL VIOLENCE

A. How Do We Define Animal Abuse?

Throughout this chapter, nonhuman animals are referred to as "animals" for simplicity. Defining animal abuse is a challenging endeavor due to the variety of statuses that animals acquire in different human cultures (Kaufmann, 1999). When we define animal abuse, are we referring to farm animals that provide food for humans, animals used in research (in human and veterinary medicine), wildlife, animals maintained in zoological parks, assistance animals, or companion animals? As cultures, we condone or condemn various practices depending on which status an animal occupies. Clearly, we are faced at the outset with a task more difficult than defining human abuse and one in which international and cross-cultural comparisons must be approached with caution.

Agnew (1998) has suggested that attempts to define animal abuse share a number of features: ". . . the harm inflicted on animals should be (1) socially unacceptable, (2) intentional or deliberate, and/or (3) unnecessary" (see Kellert and Felhous, 1985; Baenninger, 1991; Ascione, 1993; Vermuelen and Odendaal, 1993). Animal abuse may include acts of commission or omission, paralleling types of child maltreatment such as child physical abuse and neglect of a child's nutritional needs. In fact, we can easily borrow classifications of child maltreatment and apply them to animals (Munro, 1996; Munro and Thrusfield, 2001a,b,c,d): physical and sexual abuse, neglect, and emotional abuse [see Beetz and Podberschek (2005) for an extensive exploration of the sexual abuse of animals and McMillan (2005) for an analysis of the emotional maltreatment of animals].

In judging the significance of animal abuse by young people, we must always determine whether the youth's behavior violates community and cultural standards and whether sufficient cognitive maturity is present to indicate that the behavior was intentionally harmful. Both of these factors are relevant for clinical assessment and may also be related to legal statutes pertaining to the treatment of animals.

B. How Have Scientists Attempted to Measure Animal Abuse, Especially Since This Behavior Often Occurs Secretively?

In some jurisdictions, especially those where animal abuse may be a felony offense, one could examine official records to determine the incidence of animal abuse reported to authorities. However, animal abuse is most often a misdemeanor offense that may not be recorded separately or cannot be extracted from official criminal records (H. Snyder, personal communication, 2001). Animal welfare organizations also vary widely in their tracking of animal abuse cases. The current situation is similar to our inability to track the incidence of child maltreatment before mandatory reporting became law.

In cases where official records are available, checklists of different types of maltreatment can be used for categorization, a method employed in South Africa by Vermuelen and Odendaal (1993). A similar process can be applied to the clinical case records of children and adolescents. However, as noted later, it is only in the past decade that animal abuse has been highlighted as a symptom of certain psychiatric disorders in young people. Prior to this, clinicians may not have asked about the presence of animal abuse in a child's history. A clinical history that does not contain animal abuse may reflect that no one asked about this symptom as distinct from its actual absence.

Structured interviews about animal abuse have also been used with respondents old enough for verbal questioning. This method has most often used retrospective reporting and been applied to adult clinical and criminal samples (e.g., Felthous and Kellert, 1987; Merz-Perez and Heide, 2004; Schiff *et al.*, 1999). As with all self-report methods, especially with sensitive topics, issues of social desirability, reluctance to disclose, or false disclosure to enhance one's reputation for violence must be considered in evaluating such reports. These cautions also apply to the use of a structured interview protocol for children and adolescents developed by Ascione and colleagues (1997): the Cruelty to Animals Assessment Instrument (CAAI).

The CAAI is designed to elicit reports of abusive and kind treatment of pet, farm, wild, and stray animals either observed or performed by children at least 5 years of age. A rating system based on CAAI responses attempts to quantify a child's animal abuse in terms of frequency, severity, chronicity, and level of empathy. However, it has yet to be applied to large samples of young people at risk for psychological disorders.

More recently, three questionnaires based, in part, on the CAAI have been developed by Australian researchers (Dadds *et al.*, 2004; Guymer *et al.*, 2001; Thompson and Gullone, 2003). These assessments show great promise for the more efficient and standardized assessment of animal abuse, as well as the positive treatment of animals (see also Baldry, 2003).

Unstructured interviews and qualitative methods (Fitzgerald, 2005) have also been applied to assessing animal abuse. Examples include a police interview of a pedophile who admitted to repeatedly trying to suffocate and then revive a cat by sealing it a plastic garbage bag and the 1998 Herbeck case where the convicted perpetrator said he used animal abuse to soothe himself (Milwaukee Journal Sentinel Online, July 6, 1998).

The most commonly used clinical checklist that contains information, albeit meager, on animal abuse is the Child Behavior Checklist (CBCL) developed by Achenbach and Edelbrock (1981). One form of this assessment is administered to parents/guardians and asks about a number of symptoms, including "physical cruelty to animals" over the past 6 months. Respondents rate children on whether each symptom is never, sometimes, or often true of their child. Unfortunately, a youth self-report and a teacher report form of the CBCL do not ask about cruelty to animals. This makes assessment of correspondence between parent and child reports problematic. Offord and colleagues (1991) found poor correspondence using a variation of the CBCL. One factor that may account for the lack of correspondence is that animal abuse may occur covertly, especially for older children, and parents may be unaware of such acts. In addition, because "cruelty" is not defined for respondents, we do not know the standards they use in making their judgments. Teachers may not see animal abuse but may hear reports of it from their students.

A cruelty to animals item is also included in Kazdin and Esveldt-Dawson's (1986) interview for antisocial behavior, and responses to this item differentiate conduct-disordered (see description later) from non-conduct-disordered children.

Two other instruments have been developed specifically for assessing animal abuse in domestic violence situations. The Battered Partner Shelter Survey (Ascione and Weber, 1997) and the Children's Observation and Experience with Pets (Ascione and Weber, 1997) assessment were designed for use with women and children who have entered a shelter for women who are battered. These structured interviews allow assessment of threatened and actual animal abuse as well as other information about pet care.

C. How Prevalent Is Animal Abuse in Adults?

Because national records on animal abuse are not available, we must rely on clinical case control studies to estimate its prevalence (i.e., any incidents of abuse within a particular time frame) in adult samples. Felthous and Kellert's (1987) review suggests that in psychiatric and criminal samples, animal abuse is reported by up to 57% of respondents in contrast to near-zero rates for respondents in normative comparison groups. In a study of serial sexual homicide perpetrators, prevalence rates approached 70% for men who said they themselves had been sexual abuse victims (Ressler *et al.*, 1988). These estimates must be viewed with caution, as definitional and measurement variations between studies may affect self-reports. The Minnesota Multiphasic Personality Inventory (MMPI) also contains some items related to the treatment of animals, but we are not aware of any investigations on animal abuse using this instrument (Hathaway and McKinley, 1989).

D. How Prevalent Is Animal Abuse in Children and Adolescents?

Ascione (1993) reported that between 14 and 22% of adolescent delinquents at facilities in Utah admitted to torturing or hurting animals in the past year. Using norming data from the CBCL (Achenbach and Edelbrock, 1981), children and adolescents seen at mental health clinics display rates of animal cruelty between 10 and 25%, depending on the sex of the child. Comparable rates for nonclinic children are under 5%. Recall that animal abuse is not measured on the self-report form of the CBCL. That these percentages may be underestimates is suggested by data from Offord *et al.* (1991) in which maternal reports of cruelty to animals in a nonclinic sample of 12–14 year olds was 2%, but the children's self-reports yielded a prevalence rate of 10%. Again, definitional issues, reduced parental surveillance as children get older, and parental reluctance to admit their children's animal abuse may all contribute to such discrepancies.

E. Do Children and Adolescents "Outgrow" Abusing Animals?

Behaviors that emerge and then "disappear" with increasing age are usually the result of complex interactions between maturational and experiential processes. Animal "abuse" by an older infant or toddler may be a matter of poor motor and impulse control that can be dealt with easily by parental monitoring and intervention. More recalcitrant animal abuse by a child may require more intensive assessment and treatment. An important theoretical analysis of adolescent antisocial behavior may be applicable here. Moffit (1993) suggested that adolescents who engage in antisocial behavior likely fall into one of at least two groups: adolescence-limited and life-course persistent. In the former group, acting out only becomes prominent during the adolescent period and might even be considered normative. When adolescents leave this period of development, they also leave their antisocial behavior behind. In the latter group, antisocial behavior emerges early in childhood and, if untreated, may persist into adolescence and adulthood. This categorization may also be true for animal abuse as a specific form of antisocial behavior. It should be noted that abusive behavior could shift from an animal to a human victim and/or may become more covert as a child gets older.

When a young child abuses animals, it may allow for early intervention but may also be an indicator that a child may be on a life-course persistent path for antisocial behavior. Therefore, early detection is critical both for separating normative from pathognomic animal abuse and for targeting scarce intervention resources.

F. What Is the Significance of Animal Abuse as a Symptom of the Childhood and Adolescent Psychological Disturbance Known as Conduct Disorder?

Although animal abuse has been considered potentially symptomatic of psychiatric disturbance for centuries (see Pinel, 1809), it was only since 1987 that animal abuse has been included in standard psychiatric classification manuals. "Cruelty to animals" made its first appearance in the revised third edition of the "Diagnostic and Statistical Manual of the American Psychiatric Association" (DSM-IIIR) in 1987 and has been found to be one of the earliest symptoms of conduct disorder to appear in childhood (Frick *et al.*, 1993). At that time, it was unclear whether animal abuse, as a symptom of conduct disorder,[1] was more similar to property destruction or interpersonal violence. This confusion was resolved in DSM-IV and DSM-IV-TR (American Psychiatric Association, 1994, 2000) in which physical cruelty to animals was listed among the symptoms under the heading, "aggression toward people and animals." This change makes intuitive sense, as animal abuse involves harm to sentient creatures capable of experiencing pain, distress, and death and speaks to potentially impaired capacity for empathy in the perpetrator. Animal abuse is also listed as a correlate of antisocial behavior in the International Classification of Diseases (World Health Organization, 1996). Gleyzer and colleagues (2002) reported that criminal defendants who abused animals were

[1] Conduct disorder "is a repetitive and persistent pattern of behavior in which the basic rights of others or major societal norms or rules are violated" (American Psychiatric Association, 1994, p. 85).

more likely to receive a diagnosis of antisocial personality disorder (37%) than those who did not abuse animals (8%).

These developments now make it more likely that clinicians and other mental health professionals will attend to this symptom during assessment and diagnostic work. Although research has not specifically addressed how often animal abuse is one of the symptoms present in diagnoses of conduct disorder, one estimate suggests that animal abuse may be present in 25% of conduct disorder cases (Arluke *et al.*, 1999). This estimate received confirmation in a study by Luk *et al.* (1999).

G. What Biological Factors Appear Related to Animal Abuse?

Although no research, to our knowledge, has been specifically addressed regarding physiological and biochemical processes that may underlie animal abuse, the importance of such research should not be overlooked. As noted by Lockwood and Ascione (1997), "we will need to attend to brain-behavior relations as we seek a better understanding of the phenomenon of cruelty to animals" (p.151). This information will be valuable for both diagnosis and intervention and would also help identify circumstances when engaging in animal abuse causes significant biochemical change in the perpetrator or cases where pharmacological agents may prompt animal abuse (Jimenez-Jimenez *et al.*, 2002). Pharmacological interventions for violent behavior in general should also be examined for their effectiveness in reducing animal abuse.

H. How Is Animal Abuse Specifically Related to the Physical and Sexual Abuse of Young People?

Although attention to the overlap between animal abuse and child maltreatment is increasing, few existing studies have addressed this issue. DeViney *et al.* (1983) found a 60% pet abuse and neglect prevalence rate in a sample of families with substantiated child maltreatment. Friedrich (cited in Ascione, 1993) found that 27 to 35% of female and male child sexual abuse victims displayed cruelty to animals (the rate was less than 5% in the nonabused samples). More recently, Ascione and colleagues (2003) reported a study of 1433 children 6 to 12 years of age, some of whom were victims of sexual abuse and others who were psychiatrically disturbed. Subsamples of these children had also been physically abused and exposed to domestic violence. In these cases, cruelty to animals was as high as 60%. These data support anecdotal reports of the overlap and case study examples (see Tapia, 1971; Section IV of this Chapter).

I. What Might Motivate a Young Person to Abuse Animals?

Understanding the motivations underlying animal abuse will be essential for designing effective prevention and intervention programs. Ascione and colleagues (1997) discovered a variety of motivations in a sample of at-risk children. These included identification with the aggressor and imitation, modifying one's mood (animal abuse creating excitement), peer-facilitated and -forced animal abuse, and sexually reactive animal abuse. The question "Why is the child doing this?" cannot be answered using behavioral checklists [for an extensive discussion of both adult and child/adolescent motivations for abusing animals, see Ascione (2005b)]. More in-depth assessment will be required as illustrated in the case study in Section IV.

J. What Role Does Empathy Play in Preventing Animal Abuse?

We are only beginning to explore human capacity for empathizing with other species. The development of empathy between humans is believed to have its roots in early infancy (Eisenberg, 1992; Goleman, 1995) and to be dependent on the quality of relationships a child experiences. It is believed that empathy enables humans to help each other and that its absence makes harming others easier. We must explore these phenomena and their applicability to human–animal relations. For example, Magid and McKelvey (1987) note that children with distortions in their attachments may lack empathy and be likely to abuse animals; the relation between empathy and a lower likelihood of violence toward others has been documented by developmental psychologists (Hastings *et al.*, 2000). Empathy to people and empathy to animals are not identical but are sufficiently correlated to command our attention (Ascione, 2005b; Pagani, 2000; Weber and Ascione, 1992).

K. Is There a Relationship between Domestic, or Family, Violence and Animal Abuse?

Research on the overlap between violence between intimate partners and animal maltreatment is still in its infancy (Ascione, 2005a,b). Despite numerous anecdotal references to this overlap, Renzetti's (1992) research was the first to document the overlap in a study of violent lesbian relationships. In this study, 38% of abused respondents reported that their pets had been hurt by their partners. Ascione (1998) studied this phenomenon in 38 women seeking safety at a shelter for women who are battered. Nearly three-quarters of the women had pets (currently or in the past year), and over half of these women reported that their pets had been hurt or killed by their partner [similar results were reported in studies from Wisconsin and Colorado (Arkow, 1996)]. A recent replication with 101 women who were battered (see Ascione *et al.*, 2006) found similar results. In the replication study, over 60% of the children in these homes had witnessed animal abuse, suggesting one mechanism by which some children might acquire and imitate animal abuse. However, it is also important to note that many children tried to intervene on behalf of their pets when violence erupted in their homes. [For more extensive discussions of animal abuse and domestic violence, see Ascione (2006).]

L. Why Is Information about Animal Abuse as a Form of Domestic Violence Important for the Welfare of Animals as Well as the Welfare of Women and Children?

The studies just described suggest that women, children, and animals are at risk in families experiencing domestic violence. In fact, Ascione *et al.* (2006) found that nearly one-quarter of the women reported that concern for their pets' welfare had kept them from seeking shelter sooner. In some cases, women may be forced to endanger themselves and their children because they do not know how to ensure their pets' safety if they decide to leave a violent partner. This issue is reinforced by the inclusion of pet abuse on a number of instruments used to assess risk of danger from a violent partner.

M. Is Information about Domestic Violence and Animal Abuse Being Applied and, if so, How?

The results cited earlier have prompted a number of animal welfare agencies to collaborate with domestic violence programs to provide free or low-cost pet sheltering (either at the shelter facility or with foster caretakers) when a woman decides to leave an abusive partner. The degree of need for such programs is still difficult to determine, as only a minority of domestic violence shelters may ask women clients about pet abuse (Ascione *et al.*, 1997).

As these sheltering programs emerge, a number of practical, programmatic, and ethical issues arise (Ascione *et al.*, 1997; Ascione, 2000; Kogan *et al.*, 2004). For example, funding such programs may become problematic if pets are left for significant periods of time (e.g., months), designating personnel to direct these programs may divert animal shelters from other missions, and animal welfare/human welfare conflicts may arise, such as how long should sheltering last before adoption or euthanasia is considered? What if a woman is reclaiming her pet but is returning to her abusive partner who had harmed the pet? How does the animal shelter deal with reports that the children in these homes have abused pets?

Other animal-related issued have yet to be addressed. Although we know that children growing up in violent homes may display behavior disorders, how are the pets affected by such an environment? Are these pets less adoptable if given up by their owners? Will domestic violence shelters accept an assistance animal if a client has a handicap such as blindness? Since many battered women will return to their partners, can we assist them in developing a safety plan that will keep the women and their children's welfare paramount but also consider pet safety? Davidson (1998) noted that an animal abuse history was used in a parental rights termination case. Is such information relevant for a woman if she is considering a permanent break from her partner but hopes to retain custody of the family pet(s)? Should she have on file a detailed complaint against her partner that could be used at a later time? Are there ways of easing the pain of separation from their pets when women and children must enter a shelter? A strategy developed by the Baltimore Police Department was to take photos of the pets as a reminder that the pets will be well cared for (Ascione, 2005). Can animal welfare programs assist women to find transitional housing that allows pets? What is the extent of training about domestic violence issues, such as confidentiality and safety factors, that should be provided to animal shelter personnel and foster caretakers?

N. When Children and Adolescents Abuse Animals, What Steps Should Be Taken to Address this Behavior?

We recommend that animal abuse by young people be addressed like any of the other serious symptoms of conduct disorder. Comprehensive and developmentally sensitive assessment will help determine the context of the abuse and its seriousness as well as the child's level of culpability (Hindman, 1992). One could model animal abuse interventions on programs for dealing with childhood fire setting (Kolko, 2002). Curiosity fire setters will likely respond to educational interventions, and humane education can be effective with some children who maltreat animals. Pathological fire setters require more intensive therapy similar to the therapy for animal abuse illustrated by the case study described at the end of this chapter (see Section IV). Interventions will need to consider exposure to family and community violence as well as a child's possible victimization (physical, sexual, emotional) by parents, other caretakers, and siblings.

O. In What Ways Can Child Welfare, Domestic Violence, Animal Welfare, and Law Enforcement Professionals Collaborate in Dealing with Animal Abuse?

Each of these organizations includes among its goals the prevention and reduction of violence to vulnerable victims. Either directly or indirectly, they share interests in both human and animal welfare and safety. Given these shared agendas, areas of collaboration have emerged and are flourishing. Cross-training of child and animal welfare professionals and law enforcement officers (addressed in more detail in Section III) is becoming common and should be extended to include domestic violence professionals. When animal welfare organizations seek to strengthen animal abuse laws, coordination with human welfare programs is critical. Because it would be counterproductive to propose stiffer penalties for abusing an animal than for abusing a child, animal welfare agencies must be familiar with legislation on all forms of abuse, human and animal.

California and Colorado have now passed legislation incorporating evaluation and counseling, either mandated or recommended, for individuals convicted of animal abuse. It is hoped that these efforts will help reduce recidivism. Both prosecutors and judges need training about these programs, especially if the programs' effectiveness can be documented through outcome studies that indicate benefits, such as reduced recidivism in states having such programs.

These organizations may also collaborate when developing public service posters and announcements (PSAs). The Baltimore Police Department has developed an ad campaign depicting a woman, child, and pet cowering in the shadow of a batterer. The American Humane Association has produced a series of PSAs highlighting the link between animal and human abuse. Other examples include the case study described by Ascione *et al.* (2000) in which animal-facilitated therapy was used with a disturbed child. Would a similar animal-facilitated component be effective in certain forms of intervention for batterers? Clearly, there are a number of unexplored areas of collaboration between agencies involved with human and animal welfare.

P. What Are the Continuing Needs for the Assessment and Tracking of the Problem of Animal Abuse?

In the United States, the child welfare movement benefited dramatically from public acknowledgment of child maltreatment and legislative attention. We can now obtain documentation of the number of child maltreatment cases reported each year and the percentage that are substantiated. Similar data are unavailable, on a national basis, for animal abuse cases. Without such data, we will never know if animal abuse is becoming more or less prevalent and we will lack a baseline against which to measure the effectiveness of prevention and intervention programs.

Congressional legislation resulted in a national system for reporting child maltreatment, including designation of mandated reporters. This model is currently absent for animal abuse. Likewise, the Uniform Crime Report tracks incidents of juvenile perpetrated crimes, such as vandalism, but does not track animal abuse. Thus, those interested in animal welfare cannot use these reporting systems to assess animal maltreatment.

It would be an advantage if animal welfare professionals, such as veterinarians and organizations such as animal shelters, at a minimum, were required to keep nationally comparable records on animal abuse reports and investigations. Other sentinels who may note animal abuse include groomers, postal workers, meter readers, and other neighborhood workers. Their watchfulness could also be used to document cases of animals at risk. The standard inclusion of questions about animal abuse on all risk of danger assessments for domestic violence cases would also be valuable. Because research on animal abuse and domestic violence has relied exclusively on the reports of women who are battered, there is a critical need for questioning batterers about their treatment of animals; to date, only one such study has been reported (Ascione and Blakelock, 2003).

In the area of research, the need for longitudinal analysis of animal abuse, especially in childhood and adolescence, is critical. We need to be able to differentiate transient from chronic animal abuse, as animal abuse may only predict serious mental health disturbance when observations are aggregated over time (see Loeber *et al.*, 1993). Recent retrospective research also suggests that the age of onset for animal abuse may be related to its seriousness and persistence (Henry, 2004a,b; Hensley and Tallichet, 2005).

Finally, despite the inclusion of animal abuse in the most current version of the "Diagnostic and Statistical Manual of the American Psychiatric Association," there are indications that mental health professionals do not always ask about this symptom of conduct disorder. In a study by Nelson (2001), only

14% of clients were queried about animal abuse. Similar results have been reported by Bell (2001) when she surveyed child welfare and mental health agencies in England.

III. PROGRAMMATIC RESPONSES TO THE "LINK" BETWEEN VIOLENCE TO PEOPLE AND ANIMALS

The good news about human experience is that we can cope with almost anything. The bad news is that we will tolerate almost anything—that we have become accustomed to almost anything.

–James Garbarino

A. Introduction

Our willingness to "tolerate almost anything" when it comes to victimizing children and animals has decreased dramatically in recent years. Thanks in part to increased awareness of the etiology of early childhood cruelty to animals and its implications for criminal behavior in adulthood, professionals in fields that treat family violence are taking a serious look at animal cruelty and its linkages to other forms of violence.

This increased attention to the seriousness of animal abuse is evidenced in many ways. In 1993, only 6 states had felony penalties for animal cruelty. By 2004, 41 states and the District of Columbia made it a felony to abuse animals. Across the country, social workers, animal protection practitioners, members of the legal and medical communities, and ordinary citizens have formed community coalitions to address the need for cross-reporting. By working together, they are removing system barriers that cause fragmented service delivery between human services and animal welfare agencies and are helping to craft stricter laws that address the need to punish malicious acts of cruelty to animals more adequately.

Veterinarians and other animal welfare professionals are recognizing the importance of creating standardized definitions of animal cruelty, developing assessment instruments for use in cruelty investigations, and working with the judicial system to develop model statutes that address the need to treat juvenile and adult perpetrators of violence to animals.

Child welfare workers have also gained a better understanding of the implications of animal cruelty. In child protection caseloads, they look for warning signs and evidence that women and children may have been intimidated into silence about sexual or other abuses through threats made toward a favorite pet. Sometimes pets are hurt or killed to punish a child. An abused child might act out aggression and frustration on the family pet. In most of these cases, the animal is the first victim in a chain of abusive behaviors that research shows increasingly is perpetrated on the weakest family member by the one most in control.

There is a growing recognition in both child and animal welfare fields that animals, especially pets, can get caught up in the cycle of family violence and that each profession has an important role to play in recognizing and addressing the shared roots of violence affecting children and animals (American Humane Association, 1997, 2004). However, despite the increased awareness of this problem, the systems designed to protect these populations continue to operate largely independently from each other.

Human services workers, primarily child welfare workers, have been especially slow at initiating ways to work in concert with animal protection professionals to develop collaborative responses to cruelty. This section of the chapter looks at the different ways that human services professionals can work together with animal protection professionals to broaden protection for both children and animals.

B. Defining the Problem

We cannot solve a problem or even study it in depth until it is clearly defined. While every state has animal cruelty laws, there is currently no common terminology for animal abuse. Even the term "animal abuse" has widely varying definitions and interpretations. Therefore, it is difficult to know the true extent of the problem.

In the years before the definitions of child abuse were more clearly defined, the legal line between child abuse and child discipline was never clearly drawn and communities were reluctant to become involved in family matters except when presented with the most abhorrent circumstances. That began to change in 1962 with the publication of Dr. C. Henry Kempe's landmark study, "The Battered Child Syndrome," which appeared in the Journal of the American Medical Association in July of that year. For the first time, a prestigious medical journal had set forth a scientific framework within which child abuse and neglect could be addressed. Shortly after that study was published, model statutes dealing with child abuse and child abuse reporting were prepared based on the presumption that when parents or caretakers are unwilling or unable to protect children, the government must intervene to keep children safe.

An increasing number of prestigious entities began to lead the debate regarding child protection; every state in the union had passed laws by 1966 that required physicians to report suspected child abuse. Once these laws were enacted, other professionals working with children (nurses, teachers, day-care providers) were required by law to report suspected maltreatment. The definition of child abuse was subsequently broadened to include emotional and sexual abuse and various forms of neglect.

Gradually, child abuse and neglect programs, in order to meet federally mandated requirements of accountability for service provision, have developed technological means to collect data necessary to define the extent of the problem of child abuse and to measure the outcomes of child welfare work. Accurate information about the scope of the problem benefited research and set the stage for enhanced public awareness and education.

Fortunately, following the lead from those early years in child protection when the field was defining itself, some important research is being done in the animal welfare field to identify those factors that contribute to defining "battered pet" syndrome. Modeled after Dr. Kempe's methods of defining diagnostic criteria for identifying battered children, Dr. Helen Munro, with support from the Royal Society for the Prevention of Cruelty to Animals of England and Wales and the Scottish Society for Prevention of Cruelty to Animals, is working in concert with other animal welfare professionals to define and describe clinical signs of animal cruelty. It is hoped that her work will act as a springboard for the eventual identification of various clinical and behavioral signs that will one day define what we mean when we use the term *animal abuse* and lead to the development of laws and treatment modalities for perpetrators of that form of abuse.

C. Setting Standards

There are other ways that child welfare professionals can use what they have learned about recognizing, reporting, and treating child abuse to help inform the field of animal protection. The data collection methods, terminology, and best practice standards that child welfare workers rely on can be adapted and applied to set practice standards for animal welfare workers. Moreover, it would enhance Dr. Munro's research if those who worked to protect animals and educate the nation regarding the harmful effects of cruelty to animals would find common research ground and agree to establish common terminology and set standards to better define animal abuse for the field.

Just as the child welfare community has relied on members of its professional, medical, and legal communities to help define abuse of children and set practice standards, so should the animal welfare field rely on the combined wisdom of its national, medical, and legal experts to create similar practice standards around animal cruelty. Once common terms are agreed upon, limits regarding the treatment of animals can be set. When those limits are breached, the community will have grounds to demand intervention.

Longitudinal studies are also needed to track the histories of children who abuse animals. Residential treatment centers and child protection agencies should be collecting detailed histories of animal cruelty when treating children.

Child welfare agencies and domestic violence shelters could contribute to this body of knowledge by using instruments, such as the Boat Inventory on Animal-Related Experiences (BIARE), to gather more detailed information. The BIARE contains a series of specific questions that can be asked of children and their caregivers to provide important information about the treatment of animals living in a family that is at risk of abuse or neglect. The instrument is used to determine the extent to which animal-related violence is prevalent within a family. The BIARE is particularly valuable for child welfare professionals because information from the instrument can be included with information from the standardized risk/safety assessments made during investigations of child maltreatment.

Further research into the similarities and dissimilarities of cruel acts would also provide valuable information for identifying perpetrator profiles and for developing treatment modalities specifically tailored for animal cruelty perpetrators. In this way, when animal abuse is recognized as a serious crime, specific treatment programs can be created that will treat this type of cruelty as a *disorder* rather than the way it is currently treated, simply as a *symptom* of some other disorder.

D. Treatment Responses

As increasing numbers of states pass legislation that requires convicted adolescent and adult perpetrators to engage in therapeutic interventions, it is important to ensure that effective treatment programs are available.

Many court systems have the misperception that animal cruelty perpetrators can be "treated" by performing community service at the local animal control agency or shelter or by attending anger management classes. Neither of these options is considered effective or even acceptable by animal welfare practitioners. Most animal welfare agencies are not equipped to deal with the presenting problems of animal cruelty perpetrators. These agencies are frequently understaffed and overtaxed with trying to provide care for the many animals that are placed in their shelters and do not have the resources to keep track of or rehabilitate an offender.

AniCare and AniCare Child Models of Treatment for Animal Abuse (see Section IV), developed by the Doris Day Animal Foundation and the

Psychologists for the Ethical Treatment of Animals (Doris Day Animal Foundation, undated), are examples of developing treatment models. AniCare Child is a cognitive-behavioral approach to treatment that is intended for short-term use with young children in an outpatient setting. It can be used to assess the quality of any child's attachment to animals and is an important vehicle for teaching self-management and for fostering empathy in all children.

The AniCare model is used to assess and treat individuals who abuse animals and who are not so severely disturbed that they cannot be expected to respond to treatment. Both models are valuable tools for use by those professionals to whom the court refers offenders for assessment and treatment.

Another emerging approach to treatment and assessment that shows promise is the work of social worker Philip Tedeschi. Tedeschi is developing guidelines (Tedeschi, undated) for assessing the seriousness of animal cruelty acts as a predictor of future harm to animals and humans through the use of a structured clinical interview process. In an unpublished paper developed through a grant from the Park Foundation, Tedeschi states his belief that the preliminary focus of treatment should be on programs that stress prevention of violence toward animals, such as humane education programs that are tied in with healthy family and child development initiatives. Although it will require in-depth research and data to validate, Tedeschi has developed a comprehensive clinical assessment tool for identifying different levels of risk in an abuser once abuse has occurred. Once it is completed and validated, this tool will provide valuable information needed to craft specific treatment programs for individuals who are at risk for continued abuse.

E. Programmatic Responses

Since the mid-1990s there have been increased efforts by many family-serving agencies, with assistance from their communities, to develop programmatic responses to the link between violence to people and animals. Many of these programs have a common focus on using the lessons learned in human services treatment programs combined with animal assistance programs to strengthen interventions. Some of these promising intervention programs include (1) the Mississippi Children's Advocacy Center, which uses a trained therapy dog to attend child therapy sessions to help children feel less stressed during a forensic investigation or to accompany a child on the witness stand; (2) the New Mexico–based Project Second Chance, which provides youth offenders with animal-assisted therapy and life skills training through the temporary placement of shelter animals in the youth treatment facility; (3) the Chicago Anti-Cruelty Society outreach program, which works with urban youth to discourage the use of dog fighting (one of the chief motivators for childhood cruelty to animals); and (4) Green Chimneys, one of the early pioneers in the use of animal-assisted therapy for at-risk youth based in New York City (see later).

There are also several examples of community-based responses that rely on a combined network of social workers, prosecutors, domestic violence advocates, animal welfare professionals, and ordinary citizens to address issues of violence to people and animals. They include (1) the Colorado Springs–based Domestic Violence Emergency Response Team, which includes the humane society of the Pike's Peak region as one of the second-tier responders to domestic violence; (2) the Michigan Humane Society in Detroit, one of many animal care agencies that has undertaken community relations–building efforts by creating awareness of the link between animal abuse and human violence; (3) the Delaware Attorney General's Task Force, which meets regularly to discuss cooperative solutions to child and animal abuse–related issues; and (4) the Toledo Humane Society (1994), one of the first groups to offer child abuse recognition training to animal cruelty investigators.

F. Conclusion

Child and animal welfare practitioners have much to offer each other in the ongoing struggle to understand and treat the root causes of violence. Child welfare practitioners in particular can (1) contribute knowledge from lessons learned in over a century of child protection work; (2) recognize that animal welfare practitioners are critically important as observers, interveners, and witnesses in child cruelty cases; and (3) work in concert with other child-serving professionals to include animal protection professionals in the business of protecting children (Phillips, 2004). Following are some additional recommendations for both types of practitioners.

- Convene a national meeting of animal and child welfare experts with the specific purpose of creating recommendations for commonly accepted terminology and practice standards regarding the recognition and reporting of animal abuse.
- Encourage child welfare practitioners to familiarize themselves with local animal cruelty statutes and include, as a part of the ongoing training curriculum, coursework in the identification and reporting of suspected animal cruelty.
- Amend state child abuse and reporting statutes to mandate animal welfare practitioners, including veterinarians, to report suspected child abuse and provide training to facilitate this process.
- Advocate for all states to pass legislation requiring cross-reporting of child and animal abuse. San Diego, California, has a cooperative agreement

between its child and animal welfare agencies to report abuse. They have had, since the mid-1990s, a simple and effective system in place for training and reporting that does not overburden workers and which can be used as a model for implementation in other states.

- Advance the study of the etiology of early childhood cruelty to animals using the large body of scientific knowledge already available about early childhood development. Systematically gathering data on the incidence and frequency of this type of cruelty will encourage more research.
- Consider animal cruelty as an integral part of family violence and address any incidence of violence to animals, within the family, during forensic evaluations, when filing petitions for temporary custody of a child, when filing for termination of the parent–child legal relationship, and/or when investigating complaints of child abuse in domestic violence situations (Davidson, 1998).
- Consider previous acts of animal cruelty during sentencing reviews or parole/probation hearings. Tracking numbers should be assigned to animal cruelty convictions to support research into connections between early childhood cruelty to animals and later juvenile delinquency and adult criminal patterns.
- Promote additional development of assessment tools and animal cruelty perpetrator treatment protocols. Animal control agencies would also benefit from on-site therapeutic assistance from social workers and/or psychologists. The New York City–based American Society for the Prevention of Cruelty to Animals has a clinical psychologist on staff who provides treatment for perpetrators of animal cruelty.
- Include examples of successful interventions for treating animal abuse in the training curricula for foster parents and other youth caretakers in order to help stabilize placements and provide support for foster and adopting families (Zero to Three, 2005).

Although we are less likely to "tolerate anything" when it comes to the abuse of children and animals in our society, we must link the substantial advancements made by individuals and organizations to each other and to similar efforts. When we set aside whatever it is that prevents us from coordinating our efforts to build a stronger, more cohesive response network for both children and animals, we are most likely to achieve our greater goal of eliminating family violence.

IV. CLINICAL CASE STUDY

Green Chimneys, a nationally renowned residential treatment center for children with severe emotional and behavioral challenges located on 160 acres of farmland in Brewster, New York, is a unique facility that focuses on animal-assisted and nature therapies. The agency is considered to have one of the strongest and most diverse therapy programs in the world, involving specific farm, animal, plant, and wildlife–assisted activities, in addition to more conventional intervention programs such as outdoor education, job training, and sports activities. Green Chimneys' mission is to help children reclaim their youth and make strides toward a bright future through specialized therapeutic treatment, as well as educational and recreational services.

Children are placed into Green Chimneys' care after the public school system or the state's social service system deems their community setting unable to meet their special needs. Children often enter the facility with unhealthy patterns of interaction with others that are unacceptable in society. They may also enter with the effects of severe trauma such as abuse and neglect. In addition, children can be admitted with serious psychological disturbances such as mood and anxiety disorders and psychosis. No matter the reason for referral, the youth soon integrate into the ego-supportive nature of the Green Chimneys farm program and begin treatment within the human–animal bond. These children quickly learn the importance of developing relationships—not only with people, but with animals, plants, and nature. Within the structured therapeutic milieu of the farm setting, these thoughtful relationships provide children a means for healing and an opportunity for unparalleled learning.

In order to design an appropriate program for each child, the facility screens children thoroughly for instances of animal aggression during the admission and intake process. The Green Chimneys farm center administers specific corrective interventions and programs designed for children who exhibit a range of negative behaviors toward animals. These children are carefully introduced to the farm and wildlife centers with one-to-one supervision and are never more than an arm's length away from staff at all times. It is estimated, however, that less than 1% of new admissions present with episodes of severe animal cruelty. In these very rare cases, a child with a recent or extremely severe animal abuse history may be judged to be better suited for an alternate placement.

All children admitted to Green Chimneys undergo a thorough farm assessment by the farm psychologist. The clinical psychologist completes an animal-related mental status examination that includes assessing the child's previous experience with animals, the child's moral and cognitive functioning, and the child's mood and behavior as he or she explores the farm. Also included in this assessment is the manner in which a child touches an animal or the refusal to initiate touch at all. Once the child has matured to the age of 7 or 8 years, touch becomes an important diagnostic indicator for children who struggle with issues of neglect, trauma, and lack of nurturance. A child's touch with an animal serves as a "window" into how a child has experienced physical contact. *How* a child touches an animal, how he holds an animal, whether or not he attempts to build a relationship with the animal, and the animal's response to the child are all significant diagnostic indicators for the clinician. It is imperative to complete this assessment prior to beginning any form of animal-assisted therapy or activity to ensure safety for the child and for the animal (Brooks, 2006).

At times, children who have no previously documented signs of aggression toward animals "act out" once they adjust to the safety and security of the Green Chimneys environment. Unfortunately, animals may become the target of a child's anger, frustration, and anxiety. Children can project negative feelings onto an animal. For some children, this projection acts as a personally safe emotional discharge, allowing the child a release of difficult feelings they are having trouble expressing. Children may also act aggressively toward an animal because they subconsciously feel that the animal is a subordinate being over which they can have "power." When children have been dominated and abused by adults, they may act out toward a subordinate being in order to release their own feelings of powerlessness. In addition, many children have connected inappropriately to animals in their prior life experience in the community through observing cock fighting, training dogs to be aggressive, or watching others abuse an animal. Some aggressive behaviors and attempts at aggression observed at Green Chimneys include throwing stones at animals, kicking at and hitting animals, and verbally encouraging animals to fight one another. These incidents are always examined and processed with the utmost level of precaution and detail.

Green Chimneys maintains a highly developed program for processing instances of animal aggression. First, an incident report is completed for all children who display aggression toward an animal (see Appendix). This report goes into a child's file and is reviewed by staff from different departments. The report outlines the specific incident, triggers to the behavior, the child's reaction, and identification of witnesses present. The farm psychologist processes all incidents and fills out an animal aggression review form. Immediate short-term interventions include an assessment of the child's level of emotional and cognitive development and moral meaning-making system, talking the incident through with the child, usually with any staff who had observed or intervened, and the identification of repercussions and restitution. The psychologist may reiterate basic points of humane education that the child is already learning in his daily school and farm activities. Long-term interventions almost always include a referral for animal-assisted psychotherapy. In these sessions, the farm psychologist is able to address and explore certain issues at a deeper level. Such issues may include feeling-identification and expression through working with animals; anger control; empathy; and boundary work (Ascione *et al.*, 2000). Children are always encouraged to admit their wrongdoing and to play an active role in developing a suitable course of reconciliation. Many children identify ways to assist the very animal they acted out against, e.g., cleaning the animal's stall, drawing the animal a picture, apologizing directly to the animal, or feeding the animal a special treat.

A. AniCare Group Model and the Green Chimneys Program

The authors of this chapter section developed a therapeutic group model targeting latency-aged boys who were displaying fear aggression toward animals. This group, known as the "animal group" to its participants, was a synthesis of the Green Chimneys program for processing instances of animal aggression combined with concepts presented in *AniCare Child*, a treatment model for childhood animal abuse (Randour *et al.*, 2001).

The group's aim was to teach children with a history of fear aggression toward animals to develop alternate methods of coping with stress and fear of animals through the therapeutic tasks of connecting with others, identifying and expressing feelings, and teaching corrective interventions. The overarching goal of this group was to reduce aggressive behaviors toward animals and to identify emotions and triggers that lead to such behavior, as well as to increase the children's comfort level with animals in general.

B. Group Demographics

The "animal group" described earlier consisted of four male residents between the ages of 8 and 12 years. Each member had engaged in at least one incident of fear aggression toward an animal within the past 6 months. Fear aggression toward animals is defined as an underlying tension, which manifests itself in the forms of taunting and teasing an animal; a hasty or rough, macho manner when approaching, retreating from, or reaching out to touch an animal; and verbally degrading or threatening an animal, as well as an outright physical attack in response to feelings of fear. The children in this group who present with fear of animals in an aggressive manner can display a kind of bravado in an attempt to overcompensate for this underlying tension based in deep-rooted feelings of fear and unease. Fear aggression is a behavior observable in the animal world; e.g., an animal may respond with a snap, bite, or verbal complaint to a human or animal stimulus they perceive as threatening. Brooks (2006) has documented that being with an animal in a structured facilitated interaction can allow a child to overcome aggressive and fearful behavior and can enhance his or her sense of self-efficacy, despite a child's previous negative connection to animals.

Before the members of the animal group were selected, staff determined that the size of the group should remain small in number due to the high level of risk presented by possible participants and the need for intensive, individualized treatment. The farm psychologist and each child's treatment team, which included the child's social worker, dorm supervisor, and teacher, conferred together about the appropriate placement of each child into the group. Children who were already receiving intensive, individual animal-assisted therapy were best suited as referrals, as any material that arose during group sessions could be processed further during individual sessions as part of the ongoing treatment process. The children selected for the group were informed of the decision by the treatment team and also given the choice to participate or not. Additionally, families and referral sources were notified prior to the advent of the group.

The four children chosen to participate in the group presented with low intellectual functioning, in the borderline range. In addition, each child possessed a limited attention span, which was estimated to be less than 3 minutes. Therefore, all group activities needed to be concrete in nature and short in duration. If feeling safe in the company of adults, the children were observed to engage more easily with animals at the farm. During follow-up review of the group, it was determined that for these children and their special limitations, experiential exercises incorporating auditory, visual, and kinesthetic learning situations were the most effective in illustrating and teaching concepts.

Prior to the sessions, it was critical for the staff to review a detailed psychosocial history of all participants in the group, as well as a history of behavior for each animal incorporated in the sessions. Knowledge gleaned by the group leaders from these histories of behavior only enhanced the effectiveness of the sessions and protected participants, both human and animal. For example, knowing that a child has a history of sexual abuse allows a facilitator to structure sessions in a manner to prevent potentially "retraumatizing" participants. Similarly, if it is known that an animal has been exposed (or has never been exposed) to a particular stressor, facilitators can establish an environment that reduces such stress factors and potential negative behaviors. All the animals chosen were physically sturdy, exhibited predictable behaviors, and had a high tolerance for various stress factors.

C. Group Sessions

The animal group met once a week for a 50-minute session over the span of 8 weeks. This program was designed to be a short-term, intensive curriculum with carefully planned aftercare procedures. Each week, a particular concept outlined in the AniCare Child model was highlighted and taught as a concrete skill the children could practice through a series of exercises.

During the first session, the concept of connecting to others, also referred to as "being with," was emphasized and remained a basic underlying concept for all the other sessions. "Being with" refers to the process of beginning to establish a relationship with another being while remaining fully open to and aware of what another being is expressing in a quiet, gentle manner. In the process of "being with," a child learns to release his or her energy, become profoundly aware of the other creature's mood and behavior, and remain in a calm, present-centered state of responsiveness to the other being. Rather than forcing an interaction, clouding it with an agenda or unsettled emotions, or confusing or ignoring signals from the animal, the child learns to bring their whole self to the presence of another and—*through* that process—gain better control over their own internal state. Inherent in the "being with" process is learning the behavior of others and how those others are "speaking" their behavior. For example, if an animal moves away when a child approaches, it may mean she is afraid or does not want to be touched at that moment. Before a second approach is attempted, a facilitator encourages the child to consider his or her own energy level, speed and intensity of movement, body position, eye contact, and intent of purpose. In a successful experience of "being with," the animal will willingly tolerate the presence of the child or even display its own species-specific behaviors that indicate an attempt to make a connection with the child.

On the first day of animal group, the facilitators picked up each participant from his classroom, greeted him, and escorted the group of boys to the meeting room. Along the walk, which lasted approximately 10 minutes, the children had casual conversation with the facilitators and were introduced to a carefully chosen basset hound named Molly. A similar walk back to the school was conducted at the conclusion of each session, which helped create a sense of transition back to the regular school day for the boys. Upon arrival in the meeting room, the facilitators began the session by acknowledging that although the children cared deeply for animals, the reason they were chosen for this group was because they had some difficulty interacting with animals. The facilitators explained that the group would help them improve these relationships. During the session, ground rules for behavior and basic expectations for the group were established by the children and facilitators together.

Molly the basset hound was present throughout this first session, as well as all subsequent sessions, and served as a transitional object for participants' feelings. Staff ensured that Molly had a comfortable bed, available water, and a place to retreat to if and when the children became too loud and overwhelming for her. Molly's presence during the initial walk to group became a reminder to the children that they were about to enter a session. She helped engage the children as they began to ask for turns to walk her and to pet her. When the children interacted with Molly, she provided a context for immediate learning, as children were encouraged to practice the skills of voice and body movement regulation and touch. The children observed Molly's reactions to high-pitched, loud voices, sudden movements, and rough touches and adjusted their behaviors accordingly. Molly gave immediate feedback to the participants by "mirroring" back calm, steadfast behavior when the children demonstrated the ability to control themselves. Perhaps because of the safe and gentle supervised manner in which Molly was introduced to the group context, the comfort level of the children within the group context, and the modeling of the adult–animal interactions, the children did not exhibit fear aggression in any of their interactions with Molly. They began to practice and demonstrate behaviors appropriate for the concept of "being with."

The next four sessions focused on the tasks of identifying and expressing feelings. Many children who have a history of aggression or abuse toward animals are unable to identify and express their feelings and are therefore unable to articulate the underlying basis of their behavior. However, many children who have spoken about abusing animals *are* able to recognize and distinguish specific feelings of boredom and anger in their interactions. Upon further inquiry, and years of work exploring this subject, clinical staff have determined that identified feelings of boredom and anger are not only closely connected, but boredom is actually, in this context, an obscured perception of shut-down (latent) anger.

Inherent in teaching young children how to build a relationship with an animal is teaching children how to relate to others different from themselves. Part of the child's work is learning how to identify and express a wider range of emotions. The therapeutic task of expression explores the child's emotional life and how he communicates. Expression of feelings entails the following functions: recognizing, identifying, owning, and regulating emotions (Randour *et al.*, 2001). One of the exercises included during these sessions was an "emotional choices" task (Randour *et al.*, 2001) where participants listened to emotionally charged stories involving animals and were asked how they would respond to the dilemmas presented. A specific exercise, known as the Animals at Risk Thematic Apperception Test (from Friedmann and Lockwood, 1991), was also administered. This exercise, based on the classic Thematic Apperception Test model used for eliciting unconscious material, provided a series of pictures depicting scenes in which children, animals, and adults appear to be in situations of risk. Afterward, participants were encouraged to create stories about the presented pictures. Facilitators used this projective tool to explore a child's attitude toward animals and prior experiences with animals and to uncover incidents a child may have observed or participated in that heavily influence their relationships with animals, particularly around content that encompassed fear aggression. During one of these sessions, we read a book about a child who is afraid of dogs but learns to overcome her fear. This book, "Dog Magic" by Carla Golembe, was useful as a springboard for a discussion with the children about their fears of animals and how to manage this fear without being aggressive.

During one of the last sessions within this phase of treatment, we brought the group to interact with live animals. Participants were taken to a goat pen to spend time with a mother goat and her babies. Participants were asked to sit in the pen and simply spend time with the animals. The leaders were positioned inside the pen with the children and were actively supervising, supporting, and participating in the experience. As the babies crawled on top of the participants, the children were observed to exhibit a range of emotions—fear, anxiety, and unease, along with joy and delight. The children were able to manage these feelings without aggressive responses. The group facilitators intervened at certain moments and processed out loud what they observed going on in the pen for the children and the animals. Participants were encouraged to process their thoughts and feelings at the end of the session. Additionally, participants exhibiting a tendency for power and dominance in their animal interactions were encouraged to discuss what it feels like to give up some control. The facilitators helped children displaying fear aggression to learn that they can interact with animals in a way that is calm, nurturing, and mutually reassuring.

One of the most compelling exercises during this phase of the group was a series of puppet shows the group facilitators designed and presented addressing the issue of fear aggression. The puppet role plays illustrated situations such as a child getting angry and taking out his frustrations on an animal; a child wanting to pet an animal when the animal does not want to be touched; a child taunting an animal; and a child witnessing animal abuse. The children were encouraged to decide how the puppets should react to those situations. As children's thoughts and feelings were explored, they began to recall their own experiences of animal aggression. Upon further exploration, it was determined that all of the children in the group had, at some point, perpetrated aggression against an animal as part of a fear-based reaction. The facilitators' comments to the children on this subject were geared toward helping the children understand that fear-based behavior toward animals (such as teasing) actually keeps animals away from them, when in fact the underlying desire of the children exhibiting this behavior is to establish a safe connection. As a follow-up aftercare program for this particular subject, each child continued to explore these ideas through individual animal-assisted therapy and through therapeutic animal-assisted activities in the format of a tailored farm job designed to reinforce this learning.

Also during this phase of treatment, as the children began to feel more comfortable around the farm animals, the children participated in a "trust walk" at the farm where each child was paired with another participant. The first step of this exercise was to introduce the children to minihorses by having the children spend time with them and by going over basic horse safety rules. The trust walk challenge involved one of the two children leading his blindfolded partner through a small paddock of two miniature horses. The "seeing" participant was encouraged to lead his partner safely into the pen and guide the "blind" participant through the tasks of brushing and petting one of the horses. Participants were supervised closely by one of the group facilitators in the paddock. This group leader had knowledge of equines as well as these particular horses. The other facilitator remained outside of the pen with Molly the basset hound. Molly's presence was very valuable in this exercise because of the way the facilitator cast her in the role of outside observer to the activity. The staff sitting with Molly was able to create a running commentary or "conversation" with Molly about how and what the boys were doing in the exercise—praising, encouraging, admiring, and supporting them in positive comments to Molly. By choosing to share such comments with Molly, which the boys could certainly overhear, the facilitator could support the boys without interrupting the flow of the boys' activity by speaking to them directly.

Most of the children struggled with this trust walk activity. One child, who had high dominance aggression in his fearfulness, was unable to wear the blindfold. For this child, the blindfold overwhelmed him with feelings of being out of control, so he chose instead to simply cover his eyes with his hand. At times, the boys struggled to keep their eyes closed and peeked at the animal and their partner. This response was not surprising considering the children's histories of trauma and their need for high levels of control. However, during processing time at the end of the session, participants indicated that they felt the exercise was helpful and assisted in building their trust in others and themselves.

The sixth and seventh sessions of the animal group focused on the task of corrective intervention. Corrective intervention refers to the final phase of treatment, where the child is encouraged actively and directly to replace destructive behaviors with healthy methods of coping. As recommended in the AniCare Child model, two forms of corrective intervention are critical: empathy development and self-management (Randour *et al.*, 2001).

The animal group participants were actively encouraged to take the perspective of an animal victim throughout this phase of treatment. A number of stories and vignettes outlining animal abuse were presented to the participants.

They were then encouraged to identify how the animal might "feel" about the abuse. Puppet role plays were again utilized for problem solving and promoting empathy for the animal victims. The children sat in front of the stage and called out their opinions on how the puppets should behave in order to do the "right thing." The children now interacted with each other, supporting or teaching each other and speaking about what each thought was the "right thing" to do. All participants in the group appeared to express a high level of caring and understanding for the animals abused in these stories and role plays.

Self-management skills, such as regulation of feelings, impulse control, and positive decision making, allow children to change their behavior constructively. These skills can be taught with a number of cognitive-behavioral interventions with animals. The AniCare Child model presents several examples of self-management activities, including problem-solving exercises, anger management, and impulse control activities (Randour*et al.*, 2001). Due to the low cognitive functioning of the animal group participants, examples had to be clear, simple, and concrete in order to maximize learning.

For example, during this phase of treatment in the animal group, participants interacted with various farm and companion animals. The boys were encouraged to identify the skills they needed in order to remain calm and in control during their interactions with animals prior to their actual interaction. During the interaction, the boys were asked to think about which behaviors were most successful at inviting the animals to approach them and helping the animals feel safe. The facilitators also constantly encouraged the boys to reflect on ways to manage unwanted feelings rather than acting them out. When the boys were calm throughout their activities, they were rewarded with permission to sit with Molly the bassett hound and spend some extra time with her. In these ways, the coping skills for fear management were identified, utilized, discussed, and reinforced throughout each session.

This phase of treatment allowed facilitators to emphasize the importance of establishing boundaries between individuals, in this case between humans and animals. Children were taught to recognize and respect physical and emotional boundaries in a relationship. Teaching children about animal behavior was a key piece of this work. One child had to learn that Molly the bassett hound had her own "rules" for interaction based on canine behavior. Molly, who wore a harness rather than a neck collar for the group, did not appreciate having her long ears pulled or having her leash tugged. On one occasion, when this child was unable to express his needs verbally, he acted out his frustration with his predicament in an aggravated gesture toward the dog, giving her a short push away from him with the palm of his hand at her shoulder. He was immediately required to meet with Molly and explain to her about what he did that was wrong (as best he could given his cognitive limitations). In addition, he had to decide how he could "repay" Molly for his wrongdoing. He was asked to consider what it would be like if someone hit him, pushed at him, or violated his personal boundaries. He later "apologized" to Molly and gave her a hug, which was an acceptable form of touch.

During the seventh session, participants were asked to consider how they would accept personal responsibility for their actions and make amends for the hurt they had inflicted or fear they had engendered in an animal. They were encouraged to discuss the harm they perpetrated against an animal victim and how they might express remorse. Many children identified ways to help an animal, either the one they had behaved poorly with or another. Some examples included drawing a picture for an animal, giving the animal a special treat, cleaning the animal's stall, or doing community service. Facilitators encouraged participants to follow through with their proposed plan of action as a form of "homework."

This "homework" assignment was processed during the eighth and final session of group treatment. Participants were encouraged to consider all concepts explored throughout the course of treatment during this last meeting and discussed those they considered helpful and those not. They were encouraged to express their feelings about the group's conclusion and "saying good-bye." Everyone was encouraged to discuss feelings about the group with Molly the bassett hound and to give her a hug. The group concluded with a special lunch, celebrating a successful completion. Molly, too, ate a healthy dog treat that the children fed her for "lunch." Participants received certificates of achievement along with a special stuffed animal to serve as a transitional object for memories about the group.

D. Follow-Up

A short questionnaire was administered to the participants' caregivers at two different intervals after the group. The questionnaire asked respondents to indicate any further acts of aggression, especially those perpetrated against animals, and how they were handled. As specific postgroup aftercare, each child began therapeutic animal-assisted activities, most often in the format of a tailored "farm job" that incorporated an individualized treatment program. In addition, the farm psychologist continued individual animal-assisted psychotherapy with several of the children. No further incidents were reported with any of the children while staying at Green Chimneys. Long-term follow-up data on the participants could not be obtained, as each participant was discharged from the care of Green Chimneys within the year, either to another facility or to their community setting, and was unavailable for interviewing.

APPENDIX: FORMAT FOR TRACKING ANIMAL CRUELTY

A. Reporting cruel, abusive, or aggressive behavior.
   1. An incident report is filled out on all children who are cruel to an animal.
   2. Verbal aggression or threats to hurt an animal are given to the farm psychologist verbally.
   3. The farm psychologist processes all incidents and fills out an animal aggression review form.

B. Immediate short-term intervention.
   1. The child's level of emotional, cognitive, and moral development is assessed.
   2. Attempts are made to process the incident with the observer.
   3. Repercussions for the child's actions.
   4. Restitution.
   5. Humane education.

C. Considerations in long-term intervention.
   1. Referral for treatment.
      a. Acceptance of the child's feelings and level of functioning.
      b. Humane education in the form of hands-on work.
      c. Learning about feelings through working with animals; what is a feeling, location of feelings in the body.
      d. Anger work.
      e. Empathy work, boundary work, projections, and the reciprocity of a relationship.
      f. Termination.

REFERENCES

Achenbach, T. M., and Edelbrock, C. S. (1981). Behavioral problems and competencies reported by parents of normal and disturbed children aged four through sixteen. Monographs of the Society for Research in Child Development, 46, Serial No. 188.

Agnew, R. (1998). The causes of animal abuse: A social-psychological analysis. *Theor. Criminol.* 2, 177–209.

American Humane Association (1997). Child abuse and animal cruelty: Linked in the cycle of violence. *Protecting Children* Vol. 13 (2).

American Humane Association (1998). Operational guide for animal care and control agencies: Handling the pets of domestic violence victims. Author, Englewood, CO.

American Humane Association (2004). Understanding and addressing the link between child maltreatment and animal abuse: A cross-systems approach to protecting children and supporting families. *Protecting Children* Vol. 19 (1).

American Psychiatric Association (1994). "Diagnostic and Statistical Manual of Mental Disorders," 4th Ed. Author, Washington, DC.

American Psychiatric Association (2000). "Diagnostic and Statistical Manual of Mental Disorders," 4th Ed. (text revision). Author, Washington, DC.

Arkow, P. (1996). The relationship between animal abuse and other forms of family violence. *Family Viol. Sex. Assault Bull.* **12**, 29–34.

Arluke, A., Levin, J., Luke, C., and Ascione, F. (1999). The relationship of animal abuse to violence and other forms of antisocial behavior. *J. Interpers. Viol.* **14**, 963–975.

Ascione, F. R. (1998). Battered women's reports of their partners' and their children's cruelty to animals. *J. Emotion. Abuse* **1**, 119–133.

Ascione, F. R. (1993). Children who are cruel to animals: A review of research and implications for developmental psychopathology. *Anthrozoos* **6**, 226–247.

Ascione, F. R. (1997). Humane education research: Evaluating efforts to encourage children's kindness and caring. *Genet. Soc. Gen. Psychol. Monogr.* **123**(No.1), 57–77.

Ascione, F. R. (1999). The abuse of animals and human interpersonal violence: Making the connection. *In* "Child Abuse, Domestic Violence, and Animal Abuse: Linking the Circles of Compassion for Prevention and Intervention" (F. R. Ascione and P. Arkow, eds.), pp. 50–61. Purdue University Press, West Lafayette, IN.

Ascione, F. R. (2000). "Safe Havens for Pets: Guidelines for Programs Sheltering Pets for Women Who Are Battered." Author, Logan, UT.

Ascione, F. R. (2005a). Children, animal abuse, and family violence: The multiple intersections of animal abuse, child victimization, and domestic violence. *In* "Victimization of Children and Youth: Patterns of Abuse, Response Strategies" (K. A. Kendall–Tackett and S. Giacomoni, eds.), pp. 313–334. Civic Research Institute, Inc., Kingston, NJ.

Ascione, F. R. (2005b). "Children and Animals: Exploring the Roots of Kindness and Cruelty." Purdue University Press, West Lafayette, IN.

Ascione, F. R. (ed.) (2006). "International Handbook of Research, Theory, and Application on Animal Abuse and Cruelty." Purdue University Press, West Lafayette, IN.

Ascione, F. R., and Arkow, P. (eds.) (1999). "Child Abuse, Domestic Violence, and Animal Abuse: Linking the Circles of Compassion for Prevention and Intervention." Purdue University Press, West Lafayette, IN.

Ascione, F. R., and Blakelock, H. H. (2003). Incarcerated men's reports of animal abuse: A study of the perpetrator's perspective. Paper presented at the 8th International Family Violence Conference, Portsmouth, NH.

Ascione, F. R., Friedrich, W. N., Heath, J., and Hayashi, K. (2003). Cruelty to animals in normative, sexually abused, and outpatient psychiatric samples of 6- to 12-year-old children: Relations to maltreatment and exposure to domestic violence. *Anthrozoös* **16**, 194–212.

Ascione, F. R., Kaufmann, M. E., and Brooks, S. M. (2000). Animal abuse and developmental psychopathology: Recent research, programmatic, and therapeutic issues and challenges for the future. *In* "Handbook on Animal-Assisted Therapy: Theoretical Foundations and Guidelines for Practice" (A. Fine, ed.), pp. 325–354. Academic Press, New York.

Ascione, F. R., Thompson, T. M., and Black, T. (1997). Childhood cruelty to animals: Assessing cruelty dimensions and motivations. *Anthrozoös* **10**, 170–177.

Ascione, F. R., and Weber, C. V. (1997a). "Battered Partner Shelter Survey (BPSS)." Utah State University, Logan, UT.

Ascione, F. R., and Weber, C. V. (1997b). "Children's Observation and Experience with Pets (COEP)." Utah State University, Logan, UT.

Ascione, F. R., Weber, C. V., Thompson, T. M., Heath, J., Maruyama, M., and Hayashi, K. (in press). Battered pets and domestic violence: Animal abuse reported by women experiencing intimate violence and by non-abused women. *In Violence Against Women* **12**.

Ascione, F. R., Weber, C. V., and Wood, D. S. (1997). The abuse of animals and domestic violence: A national survey of shelters for women who are battered. *Soc. Anim.* **5**, 205–218.

Baenninger, R. (1991). Violence toward other species. *In* "Targets of Violence and Aggression" (R. Baenninger, ed.), pp. 5–43. North-Holland, Amsterdam.

Baldry, A. C. (2003). Animal abuse and exposure to interparental violence in Italian youth. *J. Interpers. Viol.* **18**, 258–281.

Beetz, A. M., and Podberschek, A. L. (eds.) (2005). "Bestiality and Zoophilia: Sexual Relations with Animals." Purdue University Press, West Lafayette, IN.

Bell, L. (2001). Abusing children–abusing animals. *J. Social Work* **1**, 223–234.

Brooks, S. M. (2006). Animal assisted psychotherapy and equine facilitated psychotherapy. *In* "Working With Traumatized Youth in Child Welfare". (N.B. Webb, ed.), pp. 196–218. Guilford Press, New York, NY.

Dadds, M. R., Whiting, C., Bunn, P., Fraser, J. A., Charlson, J. H., and Pirola-Merlo, A. (2004). Measurement of cruelty in children: The Cruelty to Animals Inventory. *J. Abnorm. Child Psychol.* **32**, 321–334.

Davidson, H. (1998). On the horizon: What lawyers and judges should know about the link between child abuse and animal cruelty. *ABA Child Law Pract.* **17**(No. 4), 60–63.

DeViney, E., Dickert, J., and Lockwood, R. (1983). The care of pets within child abusing families. *Int. J. Study Anim. Probl.* **4**, 321–329.

Doris Day Animal Foundation (undated). The violence connection: An examination of the link between animal abuse and other violent crimes.

Eisenberg, N. (1992). "The Caring Child." Harvard University Press, Cambridge.

Felthous, A. R., and Kellert, S. R. (1987). Childhood cruelty to animals and later aggression against people: A review. *Am. J. Psychiatr.* **144**, 710–717.

Fitzgerald, A. J. (2005). "Animal Abuse and Family Violence: Researching the Interrelationships of Abusive Power." Edwin Mellen Press, Lewiston, NY.

Frick, P. J., Van Horn, Y., Lahey, B. B., Christ, M. A. G., Loeber, R., Hart, E. A., Tannenbaum, L., and Hanson, K. (1993). Oppositional defiant disorder and conduct disorder: A meta-analytic review of factor analyses and cross-validation in a clinical sample. *Clin. Psychol. Rev.* **13**, 319–340.

Friedmann, E., and Lockwood, R. (1991). Validation and use of the Animal Thematic Apperception Test. *Anthrozoös* 174–183.

Gleyzer, R., Felthous, A. R., and Holzer, C. E., III (2002). Animal cruelty and psychiatric disorders. *J. Am. Acad. Psychiatr. Law* **30**, 257–265.

Goleman, D. (1995). "Emotional Intelligence." Bantam Books, New York.

Golembe, C. (1997). "Dog Magic." Houghton Mifflin, Boston, MA.

Green, P. C., and Gullone, E. (2005). Knowledge and attitudes of Australian veterinarians to animal abuse and human interpersonal violence. *Austr. Vet. J.* **83**, 17–23.

Guymer, E. C., Mellor, D., Luk, E. S. L., and Pearse, V. (2001). The development of a screening questionnaire for childhood cruelty to animals. *J. Child Psychol. Psychiatr.* **42**, 1057–1063.

Hastings, P. D., Zahn-Waxler, C., Robinson, J., Usher, B., and Bridges, D. (2000). The development of concern for others in children with behavior problems. *Dev. Psychol.* **36**, 531–546.

Hathaway, S. R., and McKinley, J. C. (1989). Minnesota Multiphasic Personality Inventory. University of Minnesota Press, Minneapolis, Minnesota.

Henry, B. C. (2004a). The relationship between animal cruelty, delinquency, and attitudes toward the treatment of animals. *Soc. Anim.* **12**, 185–207.

Henry, B. C. (2004b). Exposure to animal abuse and group context: Two factors affecting participation in animal abuse. *Anthrozoös* **17**, 290–305.

Hensley, C., and Tallichet, S. E. (2005). Learning to be cruel? Exploring the onset and frequency of animal cruelty. *Int. J. Offend. Ther. Comp. Criminol.* **49**, 37–47.

Hindman, J. L. (1992). "Juvenile Culpability Assessment." Alexandria Associates, Ontario, OR.

Jimenez-Jimenez, F. J., Sayed, Y., Garcia-Soldevilla, M. A., and Barcenilla, B. (2002). Possible zoophilia associated with dopaminergic therapy in Parkinson disease. *Ann. Pharmacother.* **36**, 1178–1179.

Kaufmann, M. E. (1999). The relevance of cultural competence to the link between violence to animals and people. *In* "Child Abuse, Domestic Violence, and Animal Abuse: Linking the Circles of Compassion for Prevention and Intervention" (F. R. Ascione and P. Arkow, eds.), pp. 260–270. Purdue University Press, West Lafayette, IN.

Kazdin, A. E., and Esveldt-Dawson, K. (1986). The interview for antisocial behavior: Psychometric characteristics and concurrent validity with child psychiatric inpatients. *J. Psychopathol. Behav. Assessm.* **8**, 289–303.

Kegan, R. (1982). "The Evolving Self: Problem and Process in Human Development." Harvard University Press, Cambridge, MA.

Kellert, S. R., and Felthous, A. R. (1985). Childhood cruelty toward animals among criminals and noncriminals. *Hum. Relat.* **38**, 1113–1129.

Kogan, L. R., McConnell, S., Schoenfeld-Tacher, R., and Jansen-Lock, P. (2004). Crosstrails: A unique foster program to provide safety for pets of women in safehouses. *Viol. against Women* **10**, 418–434.

Kolko, D. (ed.) (2002). "Handbook on Firesetting in Children and Youth." Academic Press, New York.

Lockwood, R., and Ascione, F. (eds.) (1998). "Cruelty to animals and Interpersonal Violence: Readings in Research and Application." Purdue University Press, West Lafayette, IN.

Loeber, R., Keenan, K., Lahey, B., Green, S., and Thomas, C. (1993). Evidence for developmentally based diagnoses of oppositional defiant disorder and conduct disorder. *J. Abnorm. Child Psychol.* **21**, 377–410.

Luk, E. S. L., Staiger, P. K., Wong, L., and Mathai, J. (1999). Children who are cruel to animals: A revisit. *Austr. New Zeal. J. Psychiatr.* **33**, 29–36.

Magid, K., and McKelvey, C. A. (1987). "High Risk: Children without a Conscience." Bantam Books, New York.

McMillan, F. D. (2005). Emotional maltreatment in animals. *In* "Mental Health and Well-Being in Animals" (F. D. McMillan, ed.), pp. 167–179. Blackwell, Ames, IA.

Merz-Perez, L., and Heide, K. M. (2004). "Animal Cruelty: Pathway to Violence against People." AltaMira Press, Walnut Creek, CA.

Moffit, T. E. (1993). "Life-course persistent" and "adolescence-limited" antisocial behavior: A developmental taxonomy. *Psychol. Rev.* **100**, 674–701.

Munro, H. (1996). Battered pets. *Irish Vet. J.* **49**, 712–713.

Munro, H. M. C., and Thrusfield, M. V. (2001a). "Battered pets": Features that raise suspicion of non-accidental injury. *J. Small Anim. Pract.* **42**, 218–226.

Munro, H. M. C., and Thrusfield, M. V. (2001b). "Battered pets": Non-accidental physical injuries found in dogs and cats. *J. Small Anim. Pract.* **42**, 279–290.

Munro, H. M. C., and Thrusfield, M. V. (2001c). "Battered pets": Sexual abuse. *J. Small Anim. Pract.* **42**, 333–337.

Munro, H. M. C., and Thrusfield, M. V. (2001d). "Battered pets": Munchausen syndrome by proxy (factitious illness by proxy). *J. Small Anim. Pract.* **42**, 385–389.

Nelson, P. (2001). "A Survey of Psychologists' Attitudes, Opinions, and Clinical Experiences with Animal Abuse." Unpublished doctoral dissertation, Wright Institute Graduate School of Psychology, Berkeley, CA.

Offord, D. R., Boyle, M. H., and Racine, Y. A. (1991). The epidemiology of antisocial behavior in childhood and adolescence. *In* "The Development and Treatment of Childhood Aggression" (D. J. Pepler and K. H. Rubin, eds.), pp. 31–54. Lawrence Erlbaum Associates, Hillsdale, NJ.

Pagani, C. (2000). Perception of a common fate in human-animal relations and its relevance to our concern for animals. *Anthrozoös* **13**, 66–73.

Phillips, A. (2004). American Prosecutors Research Institute, Reasonable Efforts Vol. 1, Number 4.

Pinel, P. (1809). "Traite medico-philosophique de la alientation mentale," 2nd Ed. Brosson, Paris.

Randour, M. L., Krinsk, S., and J. Wolf (2001). The AniCare child: Assessment and Treatment Approach for Childhood Animal Abuse.

Renzetti, C. M. (1992). "Violent Betrayal: Partner Abuse in Lesbian Relationships." Sage, Newbury Park, CA.

Ressler, R. K., Burgess, A. W., and Douglas, J. E. (1988). "Sexual Homicide: Patterns and Motives." Lexington Books, Lexington, MA.

Schiff, K., Louw, D., and Ascione, F. R. (1999). Animal relations in childhood and later violent behaviour against humans. *Acta Criminol.* **12**, 77–86.

Tapia, F. (1971). Children who are cruel to animals. *Child Psychiatr. Hum. Dev.* **2**, 70–77.

Tedeschi, P. (undated). MSSW, LCSW Animal Abusers Interview and Risk Assessment Tool (AARAT).

Thompson, K. L., and Gullone, E. (2003). The Children's Treatment of Animals Questionnaire (CTAQ): A psychometric investigation. *Soc. Anim.* **11**, 1–15.

Toledo Humane Society (1994). "Animal Advocates for Children: Training Manual for Cruelty Investigative Agents." Author, Toledo, OH.

Vermuelen, H., and Odendaal, J. S. J. (1993). Proposed typology of companion animal abuse. *Anthrozoös* **6**, 248–257.

Weber, C. V., and Ascione, F. R. (1992). Humane attitudes and human empathy: Relations in adulthood. Keynote address at the Sixth International Conference on Human Animal Interactions, Montreal, Canada, July 23.

World Health Organization (1996). "International Classification of Mental and Behavioral Disorders (ICD-10)." Cambridge University Press, Cambridge, MA.

Zero to Three Policy Center (2005). Restructuring the federal child welfare system: Assuring the safety, permanence and well-being of infants and toddlers in the child welfare system, Fact Sheet, January.

SECTION IV

Special Topics and Concerns in Animal-Assisted Therapy

CHAPTER 17

Measuring the Bond: Instruments Used to Assess the Impact of Animal-Assisted Therapy

DAVID C. ANDERSON
Owner, RockyDell Resources, Lincoln, California 95648

Measuring the Bond presents a selection of the principal measures (e.g., surveys, questionnaires, scales) recently used by researchers to study attachment between humans and companion animals. No attempt is made to include attitude scales. Daniel Kossow, while a graduate student in the Tufts Center for Animals and Public Policy, compiled a bibliography of surveys on public attitudes toward animals and animal-related issues.[1] In 2000 Harold Herzog and Lorna Dorr published an article on electronically available surveys of attitudes toward animals.[2] It has been estimated that 40% of the human–animal studies literature focuses on human attitudes toward animals.

The measures presented here have been selected from the author's *Assesment Tools for Researching the Human-Companion Animal Bond* (Purdue University Press, forthcoming) for their generally wide use. Typically, the selected meas-

[1] Kossow, Daniel. Attitudes towards animals and animal issues: A historical perspective in the US. www.tufts.edu/vet/cfa/surveys.html (accessed January 28, 2005).

[2] Herzog, Harold A.; Dorr, Lorna B. Electronically available surveys of attitudes toward animals. *Society & Animals*, 8(2) 2000:183–190. www.psyeta.org/sa/sa8.2/herzog.shtml (accessed August 20, 2005).

Handbook on Animal-Assisted Therapy: Theoretical Foundations and Guidelines for Practice, 2e

ures have been used to determine the relative attachment of a subject or group of subjects to their companion animals. However, the Measurement of Pet Intervention, MOPI, is included as it measures change in the behavior of people who have been through controlled animal-assisted therapy sessions. MOPI is included here in the expectation that it may lead to further use or modification.

Each section is devoted to a single measure and begins with a citation to its initial publication. In some cases, additional citations are given in which the measure is developed or validated further. Notes and a copyright notice appear on the page before the measure.

Both the International Society for AnthroZoology and Society & Animals Forum plan for their respective journals, *Anthrozoös* and *Society & Animals*, to be readily available on the World Wide Web. Where applicable, the reader may turn to their web sites, http://www.vetmed.ucdavis.edu/CCAB/isaz.htm and http://www.psyeta.org/sa/index.html, for a particular article or individual measure published in their journals.

Late in the publication process, two additional tools specifically designed to assess the impact of animal-assisted therapy were identified. They are:

Lawrence, Marilyn. *Animal-assisted therapy: therapy effectiveness evaluation.* (Rev. ed.) [Fort Myers, FL]: M. K. Lawrence, c2002, c2004, one compact disc (4-3/4 inches) of 44 pages (mostly forms). Contents: Overview—Objectives—Client assessment—Therapy session documentation—Therapy session summary—Document samples. This instrument was validated for use with adults in: Glacken, Joan; Lawrence, Marilyn K. "Content validation and pilot studies of the Therapy Effectiveness Evaluation for Animal-Assisted Therapy instrument." American Journal of Recreation Therapy, 4(3) 2005 Summer: 21–24. $US 19.95 incl s&h (USA): orders to Marilyn K. Lawrence, 16031 South Pebble Lane, Fort Myers, FL 33912 USA; email: mklaw@earthlink.net

Velde, Sarah. *The development and validation of a research evaluation instrument to assess the effectiveness of animal-assisted therapy*. 2005. [viii], 202 leaves. Dissertation—Ph.D. in Health Administration, Kennedy-Western University, 2005. The final version of the tool is Appendix L, Template for Guiding & Evaluating Animal-Assisted Therapy, pages 198–202. The thesis is available through the Delta Society website, at www.deltasociety.org/AnimalsResourcesResources.htm# (Accessed 23 April 2006).

The author's thanks and deep appreciation go to the authors and publishers of these measures and their willingness to permit their publication or reprinting here. Thanks are also due to Purdue University Press for permission to reprint portions of the book, *Assessment Tools for Researching the Human-Companion Animal Bond.*

CENSHARE PET ATTACHMENT SCALE, PAS

Published In:

Holcomb, Ralph; Williams, R. Craig; Richards, P. Scott.

The elements of attachment: Relationship maintenance and intimacy. *Journal of the Delta Society,* 2(1) Winter 1985:28–34.

Also describes validation efforts.

Table 2: "The CENSHARE Pet Attachment Survey," a 27-item self report, Scale 1, Relationship Maintenance, and Scale 2, Intimacy, appears on page 31.

Notes:

Reverse score items 2, 13, 19, and 20.

The CENSHARE Pet Attachment Survey is also available from the Behavioral Measurement Database Services, BMDS, producer of the Health and Psychosocial Instruments (HaPI) database. Phone 412/687-6850, fax 412/687-5213, or email bmdshapi@aol.com for ordering information. Supply the HaPI accession number 52474 and the title, CENSHARE Pet Attachment Survey.

CENSHARE Pet Attachment Survey

	Almost Always	Often	Sometimes	Almost Never
1. Within your family, your pet likes you best.	1	2	3	4
2. You are too busy to spend time with your pet.	1	2	3	4
3. You spend time each day playing with or exercising your pet.	1	2	3	4
4. Your pet comes to greet you when you arrive.	1	2	3	4
5. You talk to your pet as a friend.	1	2	3	4
6. Your pet is aware of your different moods.	1	2	3	4
7. Your pet pays attention and obeys you quickly.	1	2	3	4
8. You confide in your pet.	1	2	3	4
9. You play with your pet when he/she approaches.	1	2	3	4
10. You spend time each day training your pet.	1	2	3	4
11. You show photos of your pet to your friends.	1	2	3	4
12. You spend time each day grooming your pet.	1	2	3	4
13. You ignore your pet when he/she approaches.	1	2	3	4
14. When you come home, your pet is the first one you greet.	1	2	3	4
15. Your pet tries to stay near by following you.	1	2	3	4
16. You buy presents for your pet.	1	2	3	4
17. When you feel bad, you seek your pet for comfort.	1	2	3	4
18. You prefer to be with your pet more than with most people you know.	1	2	3	4
19. When your pet misbehaves, you hit him/her.	1	2	3	4
20. Your pet is a nuisance and a bother to you.	1	2	3	4
21. You consider your pet to be a member of your family.	1	2	3	4
22. When you feel bad, you seek your pet for comfort.	1	2	3	4
23. You feel sad when you are separated from your pet.	1	2	3	4
24. You like to have your pet sleep near your bed.	1	2	3	4
25. You like to have your pet sleep on your bed.	1	2	3	4
26. You have your pet near you when you study, read, or watch TV.	1	2	3	4
27. You don't like your pet to get too close to you.	1	2	3	4

The CENSHARE Pet Attachment Survey has been reproduced here courtesy of the Delta Society, www.deltasociety.org; Ralph Holcomb, MSW, Ph.D., LISW; and R. K. Anderson, DVM, Director, Center for the Study of Human-Animal Relationships and the Environment (CENSHARE), University of Minnesota.

COMPANION ANIMAL BONDING SCALE, CABS

CABS is an eight-item instrument used to measure the extent of child–animal activities. CABS focuses on the quality of the relationship between the human and the pet based on evidence that shows bonding between humans and animals can have a positive effect on humans, such as reducing feelings of alienation and loneliness.

Published In:

Poresky, Robert H.; Hendrix, Charles; Mosier, Jacob E.; Samuelson, Marvin L. The Companion Animal Bonding Scale: internal reliability and construct validity. *Psychological Reports,* 60(3, pt1) 1987:743–746.

CABS is given on p. 744. ". . . is an 8-item behavioral scale describing the extent of child-animal activities. . . . The Cronbach alpha estimates of internal reliability were 0.82 and 0.77, respectively. Construct validity was indicated by significant correlations between scores on the Pet Attitude Scale [Templer *et al.* 1981] for the childhood and contemporary bonding scale of 0.39 and 0.40, respectively" (p. 743).

". . . developed to provide an accurate measure of a person's interaction with or attachment to a pet by asking behavioral questions. . . . The CABS focuses on eight actual behaviors or events (Table 1) that an observer might see. . . . It appears to have face validity because the eight behaviors all reflect an individual's interaction with a pet. The items must be understood by the anticipated respondents. The items used in the CABS were intended for older children and adults and do not contain difficult words." (Poresky, Robert H. Analyzing human-animal relationship measures. *Anthrozoös* 2(4) 1989: 236).

CABS exists in two forms: contemporary form and past form, in which the verbs are, respectively, in the present and past tense. Both are presented here.

Validated In:

Poresky, Robert H.

Analyzing human-animal relationship measures. *Anthrozoös* 2(4) 1989: 236–244.

"The Companion Animal Bonding Scale and the Companion Animal Semantic Differential meet the basic requirements described herein for internal reliability, face validity, and construct validity" (p. 244).

Poresky Robert H.

The Companion Animal Bonding Scale: internal consistency and factor structure when administered by telephone. *Psychological Reports* 80(3) 1997 Jun:937–939.

Poresky, Robert H.; Hendrix, Charles.

Young Children's Companion Animal Bonding and adults' pet attitudes: a retrospective review. *Psychological Reports* 62 1988:412–425.

Triebenbacher, Sandra Lookabaugh.

Re-evaluation of the Companion Animal Bonding Scale. *Anthrozoös* 12(3) 1999:169–173.

Notes:

Also available in: Fischer, Joel; Corcoran, Kevin. "Measures for clinical practice: a sourcebook". Vol. 1: Couples, families, and children. 2nd ed. New York: The Free Press, c1994, pp. 457–458.

Also available in: Corcoran, Kevin; Fischer, Joel. "Measures for clinical practice: a sourcebook". Vol. 1: Couples, families, and children. 3rd ed. New York: The Free Press, c2000, pp. 528–529.

Also available on the Educational Testing Service web site http://sydneyplus.org/ (Accessed 22 October 2004).

The total score is the sum of the answers.

The contemporary version can be obtained by changing the verb tense in each statement from past to present. Both the retrospective and the contemporary versions are included here.

Companion Animal Bonding Scale

1. How often were you responsible for your companion animal's care?
   5___Always 4___Generally 3___Often 2___Rarely 1___Never
2. How often did you clean up after your companion animal?
   5___Always 4___Generally 3___Often 2___Rarely 1___Never
3. How often did you hold, stroke, or pet your companion animal?
   5___Always 4___Generally 3___Often 2___Rarely 1___Never
4. How often did your companion animal sleep in your room?
   5___Always 4___Generally 3___Often 2___Rarely 1___Never
5. How often did you feel that your companion animal was responsive to you?
   5___Always 4___Generally 3___Often 2___Rarely 1___Never
6. How often did you feel that you had a close relationship with your companion animal?
   5___Always 4___Generally 3___Often 2___Rarely 1___Never
7. How often did you travel with your companion animal?
   5___Always 4___Generally 3___Often 2___Rarely 1___Never
8. How often did you sleep near your companion animal?
   5___Always 4___Generally 3___Often 2___Rarely 1___Never

Companion Animal Bonding Scale

1. How often are you responsible for your companion animal's care?
   5___Always 4___Generally 3___Often 2___Rarely 1___Never
2. How often do you clean up after your companion animal?
   5___Always 4___Generally 3___Often 2___Rarely 1___Never
3. How often do you hold, stroke, or pet your companion animal?
   5___Always 4___Generally 3___Often 2___Rarely 1___Never
4. How often does your companion animal sleep in your room?
   5___Always 4___Generally 3___Often 2___Rarely 1___Never
5. How often do you feel that your companion animal is responsive to you?
   5___Always 4___Generally 3___Often 2___Rarely 1___Never
6. How often do you feel that you have a close relationship with your companion animal?
   5___Always 4___Generally 3___Often 2___Rarely 1___Never
7. How often do you travel with your companion animal?
   5___Always 4___Generally 3___Often 2___Rarely 1___Never
8. How often do you sleep near your companion animal?
   5___Always 4___Generally 3___Often 2___Rarely 1___Never

Robert H. Poresky, Ph.D., and Jacob E. Mosier, D.V.M., are deceased.

LEXINGTON ATTACHMENT TO PETS SCALE, LAPS

Published In:

Johnson, Timothy P.; Garrity, Thomas F.; Stallones, Lorann.

Psychometric evaluation of the Lexington Attachment to Pets Scale (LAPS). *Anthrozoös,* 5(3) 1992:160–175.

"Table 1. Wording of LAPS Items": p. 163.

". . . [A] final 23-question instrument . . . was developed, having excellent psychometric properties. The scale is suitable for use with dog and cat owners. Data on internal consistency, factor structure, and item response theory (IRT) modeling are presented, along with correlations between the LAPS and several domains of variables known to relate to pet attachment" (p. 160). The scale remains unrevised since 1992.

Developed and Validated In:

Garrity, Thomas F.; Stallones, Lorann; Marx, Martin B.; Johnson, Timothy P.

Pet ownership and attachment as supportive factors in the health of the elderly. *Anthrozoös,* 3(1) 1989 Summer:35–44.

Used scales of recent life events (Appendix 1, p. 44), of pet attachment (Appendix 2, p. 44), of illness behavior, demographic characteristics, and the Center for Epidemiological Studies' Depression Scale (CES-D).

Stallones, Lorann; Johnson, Timothy P.; Garrity, Thomas F.; Marx, Martin B.

Quality of attachment to companion animals among U.S. adults 21 to 64 years of age. *Anthrozoös,* 3(3) 1990 Winter:171–176.

Eight items of the scale appear in Table 1 "Distribution of Responses to Pet Attachment Questions . . ."

Notes:

The category "Don't Know or Refused" includes "Not Asked."

Lexington Attachment to Pets Scale

Telephone interviewer: I'd like to ask you whether you agree or disagree with some very brief statements about your favorite pet. For each statement, please tell me whether you strongly agree, somewhat agree, somewhat disagree, or strongly disagree. You may refuse to answer.

	Agree Strongly	Agree Somewhat	Disagree Somewhat	Disagree Strongly	Don't Know or Refused
a. My pet means more to me than *any* of my friends.	1	2	3	4	5
b. Quite often I confide in my pet.	1	2	3	4	5
c. I believe that pets should have the same rights and privileges as family members.	1	2	3	4	5
d. I believe my pet is my best friend.	1	2	3	4	5
e. Quite often, my feelings toward people are affected by the way they react to my pet.	1	2	3	4	5
f. I love my pet because s/he is more loyal to me than most of the people in my life.	1	2	3	4	5
g. I enjoy showing other people pictures of my pet.	1	2	3	4	5
h. I think my pet is just a pet.	1	2	3	4	5
i. I love my pet because s/he never judges me.	1	2	3	4	5
j. My pet knows when I'm feeling bad.	1	2	3	4	5
k. I often talk to other people about my pet.	1	2	3	4	5
l. My pet understands me.	1	2	3	4	5
m. I believe that loving my pet helps me stay healthy.	1	2	3	4	5
n. Pets deserve as much respect as humans do.	1	2	3	4	5
o. My pet and I have a very close relationship.	1	2	3	4	5
p. I would do almost anything to take care of my pet.	1	2	3	4	5
q. I play with my pet quite often.	1	2	3	4	5
r. I consider my pet to be a great companion.	1	2	3	4	5
s. My pet makes me feel happy.	1	2	3	4	5
t. I feel that my pet is a part of my family.	1	2	3	4	5
u. I am not very attached to my pet.	1	2	3	4	5
v. Owning a pet adds to my happiness.	1	2	3	4	5
w. I consider my pet to be a friend.	1	2	3	4	5

MEASUREMENT OF PET INTERVENTION, MOPI

Created by Chrisann Schiro-Geist and her graduate assistants, MOPI evaluates the effect of animal-assisted therapy on client or student functioning. It has four items (attention span, physical movement, communication, and compliance) evaluated on a Likert scale of one to seven. One indicates no evidence and a seven indicates strong evidence of the specified behavior. The students were assessed over time, from beginning of the trial to the end of treatment.

Training of the evaluators is critical.

Used In:

Heimlich, Kathryn.

Animal-assisted therapy and the severely disabled child: a quantitative study. *Journal of Rehabilitation,* 67(4) 2001 Oct–Dec:48–54.

Used the Direct Observation Form (DOF) and the Teacher's Report Form of the Child Behavior Checklists (Achenbach, 1991), the Behavior Dimensions Rating Scale (Bullock, Wilson, 1989) and the MOPI.

Heimlich, Kathryn; Schiro-Geist, Chrisann; Broadbent, Emer.

Animal-assisted therapy and the child with severe disabilities: a case study. *Rehabilitation Professional*, 11(2) 2003 Apr/May/Jun:41–53.

"The instruments employed to assess changes in behavior were not subjected to tests of internal validity and reliability measures. The case study presented is believed to be representative of the changes across multiple participants in two groups of children studied . . ." (page 45).

Measurement of Pet Intervention

Evaluator: ______________
Title: ______________
Date: ___/___/_______
Subject: ______________

Please rate the subject on the following behaviors based on your interactions with the subject. You are being asked to rate the subject's behavior on a 7-point Likert scale where:

1 = no evidence of this behavior
7 = strong evidence of this behavior

Please circle the corresponding number:

	No evidence					Strong evidence	
Attention Span	1	2	3	4	5	6	7
Physical Movement	1	2	3	4	5	6	7
Communication	1	2	3	4	5	6	7
Compliance	1	2	3	4	5	6	7

Attention Span: This involves attention and concentration, as well as "time on task" for a particular activity; the uninterrupted time the student devotes to an activity until being distracted.

Physical Movement: This involves both gross and fine motor skills, and encompasses mobility, task-oriented movement; observably intentional movement by the student.

Communication: This involves verbal expression only; observably intentional attempts to communicate verbally by the student.

Compliance: This involves the students following directions both implicit and direct; the completion of assigned tasks.

Comments: ____

____

____

The Measurement of Pet Intervention (MOPI) is reproduced by the kind permission of Chrisann Schiro-Geist, Ph.D., Director, Program in Disability and Rehabilitation Education and Training, University of Illinois at Urbana-Champaign, and Kathryn Heimlich, M.S., C.R.C.

PET ATTITUDE SCALE–MODIFIED, PAS-M

Published In:

Templer, Donald I.; Salter, Charles A.; Dickey, Sarah; Baldwin, Roy; Veleber, David M.

The construction of a Pet Attitude Scale. *Psychological Record,* 31(3) 1981:343–348.

Also used the Marlowe-Crowne Social Desirability Scale and an acquiescent response measure of Couch and Keniston (1960).

Table 1 (p. 344) reproduces the 18-item Pet Attitude Scale items and key.

Modified In:

Munsell, Kathleen L.; Canfield, Merle; Templer, Donald I.; Tangan, Kimberly; Arikawa, Hiroko.

Modification of the Pet Attitude Scale. *Society & Animals* 12(2) 2004:137–142.

Used both the 1981 PAS and the modified 2004 PAS. The recommended modifications are presented in the PAS-Modified. This study will become available on the Society and Animals Forum web site.

Comments:

The PAS "is one of the few published scales with reliability information (Cronbach alpha of .93, and 2-week test–retest stability of .92) in the undergraduate sample ($N = 92$) used to develop the scale. The PAS contains 18 items that represent three factorially derived subscales—"love and interaction," "pets in the home," and "joy of pet ownership"—taken from Lago *et al.* (1988). Assessment of favorable attitudes toward pets: development and preliminary validation of self-report pet relationship scales. *Anthrozoös* 1(4) 1988 Summer: 41–42.

Notes:

Reverse score items 4, 6, 9, 12, 13, and 17 (that is, if the subject used a 7, change it to a 1, for a 6 make it a 2, etc.) and total them. Sum the remaining 18 item responses to obtain total scale scores. Add the two totals together; the sum is the person's pet attitude score. Scores can range from 18 to 126. The higher the score, the more positive the person's feelings are toward pets.

Also cited in the web site, Educational Testing Service, ETS Test Collection Service, www.ets.org/testcoll/ (revised 3 Oct 2003; accessed 18 May 2004).

The alternative web site is http://sydneyplus.ets.org/ (accessed October 23, 2004).

This measure is also available from the Behavioral Measurement Databases Services, producer of the database Health and Psychosocial Instruments (HaPI), phone 412/687-6850, fax 412/687-5213, or email bmdshapi@aol.com for ordering information. Provide the BMDS accession number, 13718, and the title, Pet Attitude Scale.

The unmodified form is also available in William Langston, "Research Methods Laboratory Manual for Psychology". Pacific Grove, CA: Wadsworth Group, c2002. Chapter 3, supplement 1, p. 33.

Pet Attitude Scale–Modified

Age ____
Sex ____

Please answer each of the following questions as honestly as you can, in terms of how you feel right now. This questionnaire is anonymous and no one will ever know which answers are yours. So, don't worry about how you think others might answer these questions. There aren't any right or wrong answers. All that matters is that you express your true thoughts on the subject.

Please answer by circling one of the following seven numbers for each questions.

1	2	3	4	5	6	7
Strongly Disagree	Moderately Disagree	Slightly Disagree	Unsure	Slightly Agree	Moderately Agree	Strongly Agree

For example, if you slightly disagree with the first item, you would circle the number three.

Thank you for your assistance.

1. I really like seeing pets enjoy their food.

1	2	3	4	5	6	7
Strongly Disagree	Moderately Disagree	Slightly Disagree	Unsure	Slightly Agree	Moderately Agree	Strongly Agree

2. My pet means more to me than any of my friends (or would if I had one).

1	2	3	4	5	6	7
Strongly Disagree	Moderately Disagree	Slightly Disagree	Unsure	Slightly Agree	Moderately Agree	Strongly Agree

3. I would like to have a pet in my home.

1	2	3	4	5	6	7
Strongly Disagree	Moderately Disagree	Slightly Disagree	Unsure	Slightly Agree	Moderately Agree	Strongly Agree

4. Having pets is a waste of money.

1	2	3	4	5	6	7
Strongly Disagree	Moderately Disagree	Slightly Disagree	Unsure	Slightly Agree	Moderately Agree	Strongly Agree

5. House pets add happiness to my life (or would if I had one).

1	2	3	4	5	6	7
Strongly Disagree	Moderately Disagree	Slightly Disagree	Unsure	Slightly Agree	Moderately Agree	Strongly Agree

6. I feel that pets should always be kept outside.

1	2	3	4	5	6	7
Strongly Disagree	Moderately Disagree	Slightly Disagree	Unsure	Slightly Agree	Moderately Agree	Strongly Agree

7. I spend time every day playing with my pet (or would if I had one).

1	2	3	4	5	6	7
Strongly Disagree	Moderately Disagree	Slightly Disagree	Unsure	Slightly Agree	Moderately Agree	Strongly Agree

8. I have occasionally communicated with my pet and understood what it was trying to express (or would if I had one).

1	2	3	4	5	6	7
Strongly Disagree	Moderately Disagree	Slightly Disagree	Unsure	Slightly Agree	Moderately Agree	Strongly Agree

9. The world would be a better place if people would stop spending so much time caring for their pets and started caring more for other human beings instead.

1	2	3	4	5	6	7
Strongly Disagree	Moderately Disagree	Slightly Disagree	Unsure	Slightly Agree	Moderately Agree	Strongly Agree

10. I like to feed animals out of my hand.

1	2	3	4	5	6	7
Strongly Disagree	Moderately Disagree	Slightly Disagree	Unsure	Slightly Agree	Moderately Agree	Strongly Agree

11. I love pets.

1	2	3	4	5	6	7
Strongly Disagree	Moderately Disagree	Slightly Disagree	Unsure	Slightly Agree	Moderately Agree	Strongly Agree

12. Animals belong in the wild or in zoos, but not in the home.

1	2	3	4	5	6	7
Strongly Disagree	Moderately Disagree	Slightly Disagree	Unsure	Slightly Agree	Moderately Agree	Strongly Agree

13. If you keep pets in the house, you can expect a lot of damage to furniture.

1	2	3	4	5	6	7
Strongly Disagree	Moderately Disagree	Slightly Disagree	Unsure	Slightly Agree	Moderately Agree	Strongly Agree

14. I like house pets.

1	2	3	4	5	6	7
Strongly Disagree	Moderately Disagree	Slightly Disagree	Unsure	Slightly Agree	Moderately Agree	Strongly Agree

15. Pets are fun, but it's not worth the trouble of owning one.

1	2	3	4	5	6	7
Strongly Disagree	Moderately Disagree	Slightly Disagree	Unsure	Slightly Agree	Moderately Agree	Strongly Agree

16. I frequently talk to my pets (or would if I had one).

1	2	3	4	5	6	7
Strongly Disagree	Moderately Disagree	Slightly Disagree	Unsure	Slightly Agree	Moderately Agree	Strongly Agree

17. I hate animals.

1	2	3	4	5	6	7
Strongly Disagree	Moderately Disagree	Slightly Disagree	Unsure	Slightly Agree	Moderately Agree	Strongly Agree

18. You should treat your house pets with as much respect as you would a human member of your family.

1	2	3	4	5	6	7
Strongly Disagree	Moderately Disagree	Slightly Disagree	Unsure	Slightly Agree	Moderately Agree	Strongly Agree

The Pet Attitude Scale is reproduced here in the recommended modified form, with the permission of Donald I. Templer, Ph.D., David M. Veleber, Ph.D., and Charles E. Rice, Editor, The Psychological Record, from: Templer, D. I.; Salter, C. A.; Dickey, S.; Baldwin, R. & Veleber, D. M. The construction of a Pet Attitude Scale. *Psychological Record,* 1981, 31, 343–348.

PET RELATIONSHIP SCALE, PRS

The best source of information on this scale is found on Dan Lago's faculty web site: http://www.personal.psu.edu/faculty/d/j/djl/research.htm. Under the Attitudes toward Animals: Scales for Empirical Research, there are three links to the broad set of 17 scales (116 items), carefully translated and back-translated into both French and Spanish, along with the English version. The three Pet Relationship Scales are subscales 14–16 of the Animal Relationship Scales.

Published In:

Kafer, Rudy; Lago, Dan; Wamboldt, Patricia; Harrington, Fred.

The Pet Relationship Scale: replication of psychometric properties in random samples and association with attitudes toward wild animals. *Anthrozoös*, 5(2) 1992:93–105.

Table 2, "Factor Structure of Pet Relationship Scales (random sample, Nova Scotia, N = 1451)," p. 98, and Table 3, "Pet Relationship Scale, Subscale Structure and Reliability (Nova Scotia, random sample, N = 1451)," p. 99.

Developed In:

Lago, Dan; Kafer, Rudy; Delaney, Mary; Connell, Cathleen.

Assessment of favorable attitudes toward pets: development and preliminary validation of self-report pet relationship scales. *Anthrozoös*, 1(4) 1988 Spring:240–254.

Described development of the PRS along with preliminary reliability and validity information. Validation studies were based on comparison of the PRS with the Pet Attitude Scale (Templer *et al.*, 1981).

Notes:

A four-point Likert scale may be used but will likely produce lower item to total correlations. We do not recommend a scale with a neutral point.

Pet Relationship Scale

Instructions. This set of questions asks about your feelings, opinions, and behavior about your pets. Please answer every question. There are no right or wrong answers. We simply seek your honest opinion of how much you agree or disagree with each statement. Thank you very much for your help.

Pet Relationship Scale 1 Items (Affectionate Companionship)

1. There are times I'd be lonely except for my pet.

Strongly Disagree	Moderately Disagree	Mildly Disagree	Mildly Agree	Moderately Agree	Strongly Agree
1	2	3	4	5	6

2. My pet and I watch TV together frequently.

Strongly Disagree	Moderately Disagree	Mildly Disagree	Mildly Agree	Moderately Agree	Strongly Agree
1	2	3	4	5	6

3. I give gifts to my pet for birthdays and special occasions.

Strongly Disagree	Moderately Disagree	Mildly Disagree	Mildly Agree	Moderately Agree	Strongly Agree
1	2	3	4	5	6

4. My pet is a valuable possession.

Strongly Disagree	Moderately Disagree	Mildly Disagree	Mildly Agree	Moderately Agree	Strongly Agree
1	2	3	4	5	6

5. I talk to my pet about things that bother me.

Strongly Disagree	Moderately Disagree	Mildly Disagree	Mildly Agree	Moderately Agree	Strongly Agree
1	2	3	4	5	6

6. Making me laugh is part of my pet's job.

Strongly Disagree	Moderately Disagree	Mildly Disagree	Mildly Agree	Moderately Agree	Strongly Agree
1	2	3	4	5	6

7. I miss my pet when I am away.

Strongly Disagree	Moderately Disagree	Mildly Disagree	Mildly Agree	Moderately Agree	Strongly Agree
1	2	3	4	5	6

8. My pet gives me reason for getting up in the morning.

Strongly Disagree	Moderately Disagree	Mildly Disagree	Mildly Agree	Moderately Agree	Strongly Agree
1	2	3	4	5	6

Pet Relationship Scale 2 Items (Equal Family Member)

9. My pet is a member of the family.

Strongly Disagree	Moderately Disagree	Mildly Disagree	Mildly Agree	Moderately Agree	Strongly Agree
1	2	3	4	5	6

10. I share my food with my pet.

Strongly Disagree	Moderately Disagree	Mildly Disagree	Mildly Agree	Moderately Agree	Strongly Agree
1	2	3	4	5	6

11. My pet knows when I'm upset and tries to comfort me.

Strongly Disagree	Moderately Disagree	Mildly Disagree	Mildly Agree	Moderately Agree	Strongly Agree
1	2	3	4	5	6

12. My pet is constantly at my side.

Strongly Disagree	Moderately Disagree	Mildly Disagree	Mildly Agree	Moderately Agree	Strongly Agree
1	2	3	4	5	6

13. My pet is an equal in this family.

Strongly Disagree	Moderately Disagree	Mildly Disagree	Mildly Agree	Moderately Agree	Strongly Agree
1	2	3	4	5	6

14. I treat my pet to anything I happen to be eating if he/she seems interested.

Strongly Disagree	Moderately Disagree	Mildly Disagree	Mildly Agree	Moderately Agree	Strongly Agree
1	2	3	4	5	6

15. In many ways my pet is the best friend I have.

Strongly Disagree	Moderately Disagree	Mildly Disagree	Mildly Agree	Moderately Agree	Strongly Agree
1	2	3	4	5	6

Pet Relationship Scale 3 Items (Mutual Physical Activity)

16. My pet helps me to be more physically active.

Strongly Disagree	Moderately Disagree	Mildly Disagree	Mildly Agree	Moderately Agree	Strongly Agree
1	2	3	4	5	6

17. I spend a lot of time cleaning and grooming my pet.

Strongly Disagree	Moderately Disagree	Mildly Disagree	Mildly Agree	Moderately Agree	Strongly Agree
1	2	3	4	5	6

18. I take my pet along when I go jogging or walking.

Strongly Disagree	Moderately Disagree	Mildly Disagree	Mildly Agree	Moderately Agree	Strongly Agree
1	2	3	4	5	6

19. My pet goes to the veterinarian for regular checkups and shots.

Strongly Disagree	Moderately Disagree	Mildly Disagree	Mildly Agree	Moderately Agree	Strongly Agree
1	2	3	4	5	6

20. I enjoy having my pet ride in the car with me.

Strongly Disagree	Moderately Disagree	Mildly Disagree	Mildly Agree	Moderately Agree	Strongly Agree
1	2	3	4	5	6

21. I bathe my pet regularly.

Strongly Disagree	Moderately Disagree	Mildly Disagree	Mildly Agree	Moderately Agree	Strongly Agree
1	2	3	4	5	6

22. My pet and I often take walks together.

Strongly Disagree	Moderately Disagree	Mildly Disagree	Mildly Agree	Moderately Agree	Strongly Agree
1	2	3	4	5	6

The Pet Relationship Scale is reproduced here from Dan Lago's web site by the kind permission of Dan Lago and Rudy Kafer. Dr. Lago's permission extends to all 17 scales of attitudes toward animals on his web site. The PRS reproduced here is a slight revision of the version published in *Anthrozoös*, 5(2) 1992:98–99. Anthony L. Podberscek, Editor-in-Chief for the International Society of AnthroZoology, also granted permission to reproduce the scale.

LIST OF SIMILAR MEASURES

Childhood Pet Ownership Questionnaire (Paul and Serpell, 1983)
Children's Attitudes and Behaviors toward Animals, CABTA (Guymer *et al.*, 2001)
Children's Treatment of Animals, CTAQ (Thompson and Gullone, 2003)
Comfort from Companion Animals Scale, CCAS (Zasloff, 1996)
Companion Animal Semantic Differential, CAS (Poresky *et al.*, 1988)
Dog Care Responsibility Inventory (Davis, 1987)
Human/Pet Relationships Measures (Siegel, 1990)
Miller-Rada Commitment to Pets Scale (Staats *et al.*, 1996)
People's Experiences Following the Death of a Pet (Adams, 1996)
Pet Attachment Scale–Revised (Melson, 1988)
Pet Attitude Inventory, PAI (Wilson *et al.*, 1987)
Pet Bonding Scale, PBS (Angle *et al.*, 1993)
Pet Expectations Inventory, PEI (George, 1992)
Pet Friendship Scale (Davis, 1995)

CHAPTER 18

Techniques for Searching the Animal-Assisted Therapy Literature

MARY W. WOOD

UC Center for Animal Alternatives, School of Veterinary Medicine, University of California, Davis, California 95616

While animals have been used in human therapy for decades, the scientific research and literature in the area are still developing and getting established. There has been significant growth in recent years, and the trend continues. However, animal-assisted therapy (AAT) remains on the frontier with strong practitioner interest, while academic institutions and publishers catch up with the research required for the assessment of efficacy of this therapy.

As the research literature on AAT is so widely dispersed, the interested scholar does well to create a personalized strategy for searching and regularly keeping apprised of the evolving literature of particular interest. Such a goal can be implemented efficiently by using appropriate sources on the web to conduct user-friendly searches on a regular basis.

The information is not voluminous, and valuable resources and publications are available; however, locating material, particularly peer-reviewed, research-quality publications relevant to the licensed practitioner, remains difficult to unearth. How does the practicing psychologist or clinician locate scientifically sound information on animal-assisted therapy? How does a student in these fields identify and obtain reliable resources? The techniques and strategies for searching for this information are described in this chapter. The

Handbook on Animal-Assisted Therapy: Theoretical Foundations and Guidelines for Practice, 2e

focus is on the discipline of animal-assisted therapy, specific therapies, and data as might be useful to the practitioner incorporating the therapeutic uses of animals.

The most obvious challenge to finding research literature is sorting through the abundant anecdotal information, stories, and personal narratives that are first retrieved when doing a quick Google search. While the anecdotal information is more plentiful, scientific-quality material on the topic does exist.

Few published scientific data corroborate the long-term therapeutic benefits of animal-assisted therapy (Rowan and Thayer, 2000). While the anecdotal information supports the value of a therapy animal, the lack of scientific study and documentation delays the acceptance and development of the academic discipline. The therapeutic use of animals needs to be systematically researched more extensively, and the results published (Serpell, 2000), advancing knowledge and improving practice through a scientific process (Duncan and Allen, 2000). This process is realized via publication, which consists of primary sources, discussing current research, theories, methodologies in journal articles and books by original authors, and secondary sources, such as reviews, edited books, and references cited in research reports (Kidd and Zasloff, 1995).

I. WHO WANTS WHAT INFORMATION

Practicing therapists and academic researchers require access to the research literature. Finding the appropriate information when it is needed and identifying and locating research studies, both for information and for general interest, are basic to practitioners and academics. Learning how to implement animal-assisted therapy, discovering the current research interests, learning what has been studied, and finding out about current recommendations are all important. The best approach to locating reliable, useful, and quality information requires the searcher to consider both *how* to search, including the approach and terminology, and *where* to search, among the many options.

Practitioners incorporating animal-assisted therapeutics into their work include such health and service professionals as marriage, family, and child counselors, alcohol counselors, school counselors, speech pathologists, speech therapists, occupational therapists, physical therapists, physicians, psychologists, psychotherapists, vocational rehabilitation counselors, social workers, pastoral counselors, RNs, recreational counselors, and others (Arkow, 2004). These clinicians and counselors all have a need for AAT and related information, such as animal behavior, animal welfare, service animals, health issues, methodology, and research.

II. HOW TO BEGIN A SEARCH

Before beginning a search, it is important to spend some time thinking about just what exactly is wanted and to make notes of terms used commonly in the area. By considering all of the synonyms, the search is expanded significantly, improving the likelihood of retrieving more of the relevant information. Search terms are much more than simply the topic, such as "animal-assisted therapy and children." While that will work as a search string in many databases, the results will be neither comprehensive nor precise. If breadth is desired, additional broad search terms include "interspecies interaction," "human–animal interactions," "pet-facilitated therapy," "animal–human interaction," "pet therapy," "human–animal bond," "animal companions," "pet-assisted therapy," "animal-assisted visitation," "pet–client relationship," "service dogs," "assistance dogs," "animal intervention," "human–animal relationships," "pets and companion animals," "anthrozoology," "bonding, human–pet," "pets, therapeutic use," and "animals, therapeutic use."

Depending on the specificity desired or the area being studied, additional search terms may be added or used instead. This is where synonyms are essential. The field is still undefined, and therefore the subject headings, indexing standards, and mapping of terms are still weak, or nonexistent. As an example, if a psychologist or therapist were interested in using horseback riding in their practice, they might search using the terms "equine-assisted therapy," "equine-facilitated psychotherapy," "therapeutic riding," "therapeutic horseback riding," "therapeutic recreation," and/or "hippotherapy." There are undoubtedly others, as well.

Synonyms, or a list of possible terms, are necessary for every aspect of the topic. This would include the type of animal-assisted therapy or activity proposed, the animal to be used, and the treatment or goal. This list of terms can then be used to search as keywords, subject headings, descriptors, or identifiers, depending on the individual database search protocol.

III. WHERE TO SEARCH

There are many options, dependent on both interest and availability. Those with access to an academic or research library will have more choices than the solo practitioner in a rural setting. However, both have the ability to locate relevant quality materials. Over time, a person can develop a searching strategy that is tailored to specific targets of interest and easily keep apprised of new research developments in the literature.

A. Journals

There are professional peer-reviewed journals that regularly publish research in the area of animal-assisted therapy. These journal titles include *Anthrozoos* (International Society of Anthrozoology), *Animal Law* (Lewis and Clark Law School), *Society and Animals: Journal of Human–Animal Studies*, *Latham Letter*, and *Applied Animal Behaviour Science*. While it may be productive to search these titles by browsing through their tables of contents, most animal-assisted therapy articles appear irregularly in a wide range of diverse nursing, psychology, medical, and veterinary journal titles. Representative examples include *International Journal of Aging and Human Development, Animal Behaviour, Nursing Research, Journal of Social Psychology, Journal of the Royal Society of Medicine, Journal of Applied Animal Welfare Science, Childhood Education*, and many more.

In order to effectively search for journal articles in this broad spectrum of publications, search tools must be used. These tools include traditional bibliographic databases and bibliographies, but also other web-based guides and resources. Fortunately, most everything is now available online, even if not freely accessible.

B. Books

There are a limited number of books dedicated to the topic of animal-assisted therapy and only a few reference books. Other than this volume, two reference books of particular value are noted here. Phil Arkow's "Animal-Assisted Therapy and Activities: A Study, Resource Guide and Bibliography for the Use of Companion Animals in Selected Therapies" is a 195-page spiral-bound book that covers everything the title promises. In addition to providing a short history of animal-assisted therapy and activities, it also provides guidelines. "institutional applications of AAT/AAA," "how to become an AAT/AAA specialist," and "how to organize an AAT/AAA program" provide guidance and insight difficult to find elsewhere. However, its "resource guide for further information" makes this book valuable to the researcher and scientist; the research and resource guides therein provide access to a hundred pages of citations, capably and carefully divided by subject and application (Arkow, 2004).

The other reference book is the Delta Society's "Standards of Practice for Animal-Assisted Activities and Therapy." It provides suggested standards for every aspect of AAT and AAA, such as "standards for AAA/AAT providers," "standards for provider organizations," "standards for service delivery," and "standards for animals." The "guidelines for educational curricula," "sample forms," and the "annotated bibliography" are also helpful (Delta Society, 1996).

C. Databases

Finding current, relevant journal articles and identifying useful books and resource guides remains challenging. While bibliographies are extremely valuable, especially in a new field such as this, unfortunately they become dated almost as soon as they are published and obsolete soon thereafter. A bibliography older than five years would retain its historical value but no longer be of use for finding current research literature. In order to keep up to date and learn what others are doing in the field, databases are needed. Direct links to a wide array of databases described here are available from the UC Center for Animal Alternatives web site (Hart and Wood, 2005).

1. Searching for Books

Melvyl is the comprehensive catalog of the University of California libraries and the California State Library, containing records for books, journals, movies, maps, music scores and recordings, computer files, dissertations, and government documents. The catalog is available worldwide via the web and may be searched by title, author, keyword, or subject, with pertinent subject headings being "bonding, human-pet"; "pets—therapeutic use"; "human–animal relationships"; and "animals—therapeutic use." Users anywhere can use this valuable resource to scan and identify the available literature of interest (Regents of the University of California, 2005a).

WorldCat (the OCLC Online Union Catalog) is a catalog of millions of records for books, journal titles, and materials in other formats from approximately 12,000 libraries worldwide. It provides good coverage of animal-assisted therapy publications, accessible by using keyword searching. This valuable tool is available at most libraries. (OCLC, 2005)

2. Searching for Articles

a. Free

Ageline provides abstracts of social gerontology and aging-related articles, books, and reports. It is available free from the AARP web site, and the AAT information is most relevant to those working with the elderly (AARP, 2005).

AGRICOLA is a free database published by the National Agricultural Library. The database describes books and journal articles encompassing all aspects of agriculture and allied disciplines, including animal science and veterinary science. As a result, animal-assisted therapy is covered through that filter, using Library of Congress subject headings "pets—therapeutic use" and "human–animal relationship" (National Agricultural Library, 2005).

GoogleScholar searches for scholarly literature on the web, including peer-reviewed papers, theses, books, preprints, abstracts, and technical reports, from a variety of academic publishers, professional societies, preprint repositories, and universities. Advanced Scholar Search allows searching by a specific phrase, authors, dates, or subject areas. The resources it indexes, however, are usually not readily or freely available in full text (Google, 2005).

PubMed, by the U.S. National Library of Medicine, provides citations and abstracts for articles published in journals in medicine, life sciences, health administration, veterinary medicine, and others. The relevant medical subject headings (MeSH) include "bonding, human-pet" and "complementary therapies." Keyword searching is also effective, allowing the search to narrow to the specified area of interest (National Library of Medicine, 2005).

b. Subscription Based

BIOSIS indexes all life science areas and indexes journals, serials, and conference proceedings. It is an extensive database with a complex indexing system and, as a result, covers this topic fairly well (Thomson, 2005).

CAB Abstracts provide citations and abstracts to the international agricultural literature, including veterinary medicine and human and animal nutrition. It indexes journals, conference proceedings, and selected books. There is good coverage of this topic, with a strong emphasis on the veterinary perspective. Identifiers such as "anthrozoology" and descriptors such as "pets" or "therapy" improve retrieval (CAB International, 2005).

CINAHL references and abstracts nursing, biomedical, allied health, and consumer health literature. It covers the area of pet therapy, human–pet bonding, and animal-assisted therapy extremely well. This database is found most commonly at schools that offer a nursing or similar medical program (Cinahl Information Systems, 2005).

HealthIndex provides information on prevention, wellness, and therapy so it includes material on animal-assisted therapies. It is available at many public and hospital libraries (Action Potential, 2005).

LexisNexis is a large web-based, full-text database for current business and legal information, which includes state and federal laws and regulations. Its Quick News Service provides access to current news in newspapers and on television and radio news programs. It is a unique and valuable resource for locating specific animal-related regulations (LexisNexis, 2005).

PsycInfo is produced by the American Psychological Association. It provides citations to articles in professional journals, along with conference proceedings, books, reports, dissertations, and even important Internet sites. It is unusual in its inclusion of books and book chapters and in indexing historical material back to 1840. With descriptors (similar to subject headings) such as "animal-assisted therapy" and "interspecies interaction," it clearly covers the subject seriously (American Psychological Association, 2005).

D. Web Sites

Faculty members who are teaching topics related to animal-assisted therapy may desire to facilitate students searching in this literature. They have an option to create their own web sites with links to relevant sources, thus making it easier for students to get started in searching the refereed literature rather than getting submerged in the anecdotes that are pervasive in Google. One simple step, of course, is for them to shift over to Google Scholar, but additional sources can be recruited and offered on a web page. For this type of instructional tool in searching for animal-assisted therapy, partnership with a librarian offers particular benefit.

Organizations and professional societies often develop resources and provide access to information that might be otherwise unavailable. These may be self-published resources, such as health tips written by UC Davis veterinarians in the Companion Animal Behavior Program (Hart, 2005), or access to materials, such as abstracts from conference proceedings available at the International Society for Anthrozoology (ISAZ) (International Society for Anthrozoology, 2005) site. Other web sites provide simplified or directed access to publications, as is found at the UC Center for Animal Alternatives. In addition to developing regularly updated bibliographies on specific topics related to human–animal interactions, the UCCAA web site also has created links to embedded searches, or search templates, which, when clicked, will initiate a current search in the associated database (Hart and Wood, 2005). These templates facilitate an easy and quick search of the current literature.

1. Organizations

Anthrozoology is a site supported by Petcare Information and Advisory Service Australia, offering an online information service intended to promote interest in the human–companion animal bond. It maintains a searchable database of human–animal interaction citations, as well as links to scholarly research programs, courses, institutions, and events (Petcare Information and Advisory Service Australia Pty Ltd., 2005).

The ISAZ supports the scientific and scholarly study of human–animal interactions. It promotes the study of human–animal interactions and relationships by publishing research in the journal *Anthrozoos*, holding annual international conferences, and disseminating information via its newsletter and web site (International Society for Anthrozoology, 2005).

The People, Animals and Nature, Inc. mission is to improve the safety and quality of clinical practice in the field of animal-assisted therapy and to disseminate information via their newsletter, meetings, workshops, courses, and publications (People, Animals and Nature, 2005).

The Society and Animals Forum (formerly Psychologists for the Ethical Treatment of Animals) works with social scientists, mental health providers, and other animal protection organizations to produce educational programs and materials on the relationship between human and nonhuman animals. They publish the journal *Society and Animals*, as well as professional manuals and other educational materials. A recently added resource available on their web site is the "Dissertation Database: Human-Animal Studies, 1967–2003," developed by David Anderson and Kathy Gerbasi. With the goal of promoting the development of the academic field of human–animal studies, it provides access to otherwise invisible research (Society and Animals Forum, 2005).

2. Academic Centers

CENSHARE, located in the School of Public Health at the University of Minnesota, supports the study of human–animal relationships and environments via education, research, and service. They support a separate section devoted to animal-assisted therapy (Regents of the University of Minnesota, 2005b).

The Center for Animal Human Relationships (CENTAUR) is part of the Virginia–Maryland Regional College of Veterinary Medicine. They provide educational services and support collaborative research programs in the study of the animal–human interface (Suthers-McCabe, 2005).

The Center for Animals in Society at the University of California, Davis, studies human–animal relationships and interactions. Their service animals and animal ambassador programs are representative of the research and outreach focus of the center (Timmins, 2005).

The Center for the Human–Animal Bond in the School of Veterinary Medicine at Purdue University supports research, education, and service programs, with a goal of communicating their findings to scientists and the public (Purdue University, 2005).

The Center for the Interaction of Animals and Society Research (CIAS) is a multidisciplinary research center within the school of veterinary medicine at the University of Pennsylvania. It was established to provide a forum for addressing the many practical and moral issues arising from the interactions of animals and society. Its interdisciplinary approach encourages the involvement of scholars and researchers from a wide variety of different backgrounds and interests (Serpell, 2005).

The UC Center for Animal Alternatives at the University of California, Davis, gathers and disseminates information concerning animal alternatives with the goal of improving the well-being of research animals and optimizing their contribution to education and research. Consideration of service animals and animal-assisted therapies has emerged as one of the related fields and resulted in several useful publications and informative web sites. One in particular is "David Anderson's literature of human–animal studies," an online resource relevant to almost every aspect of human–animal interactions (Anderson, 2005; Hart and Wood, 2005).

IV. CONCLUSION

More than in most research areas, an effective search in the field of animal-assisted therapy requires regular review of a variety of sources; even two or three searching sources are not enough to review the evolving literature in this field. The array of user-friendly databases that can be searched freely from around the world makes it feasible for anyone to compile a list of sources of probable interest. Searching Melvyl for books and other databases for journal articles is free and available to all users. Thus, one can scan information on the available books and research papers, usually including abstracts, even without access to a university library. From this information, it is possible to print out the specifics on the promising resources and then seek to acquire them from sources that are available, such as local academic libraries, web-based book sales sources, interlibrary loan services, reprint requests from the authors, or reprint requests at a fee. Working closely with a librarian can always enhance the repertoire of pertinent searching possibilities. Ultimately, each scholar does well to develop and continue refining a personalized strategy for searching that is efficient and comprehensive for the particular research emphasis of interest, one that can be adapted and modified for each occasion. A variety of useful tools and approaches are set forth in this chapter that can supplement the user's art in locating the particular literature of interest in the field of animal-assisted therapy.

REFERENCES

AARP (2005). AgeLine Database. Retrieved October 7, 2005, from http://www.aarp.org/research/ageline/.

Action Potential (2005). Health Index. Retrieved October 7, 2005, from http://www.healthindex.com/.

American Psychological Association (2005). PsycINFO. Retrieved October 7, 2005, from http://www.apa.org/psycinfo/.

Anderson, D. C. (1997). The pursuit of better science: A personal view of the search for alternatives. *In* "Animal Alternatives, Welfare and Ethics" (L. F. M. van Zutphen and M. Balls, eds.). Elsevier, Amsterdam.

Anderson, D. C. (2005). David Anderson's Literature of Human-Animal Studies. Retrieved October 7, 2005, from the University of California, Davis, School of Veterinary Medicine web site http://www.vetmed.ucdavis.edu/ccab/haibooks.htm.

Arkow, P. (1986). "Pet Therapy: A Study and Resource Guide to the Use of Companion Animals in Selected Therapies," 4th Ed. Humane Society of the Pikes Peak region, Colorado Springs, CO.

Arkow, P. (ed.) (1987). "The Loving Bond: Companion Animals in the Helping Professions." R&E Publishers, Saratoga, CA.

Arkow, P. (2004). "Animal-Assisted Therapy and Activities: A Study, Resource Guide and Bibliography for the Use of Companion Animals in Selected Therapies," 9th Ed. Author, Stratford, NJ.

Beck, A., and Katcher, A. (1996). "Between Pets and People: The Importance of Animal Companionship." Purdue University Press, West Lafayette, IN.

Bernard, S. (1995). "Animal-Assisted Therapy, A Guide for Healthcare Professionals and Volunteers." Therapet LLC, Whitehouse, TX.

CAB International (2005). CAB Abstracts. Retrieved October 7, 2005, from http://www.cabipublishing.org/AbstractDatabases.asp?SubjectArea=&PID=125.

Chandler, C. K. (2005). "Animal Assisted Therapy in Counseling." Routledge, New York.

Cinahl Information Systems (2005). Cinahl Database. Retrieved October 7, 2005, from http://www.cinahl.com/prodsvcs/cinahldb.htm.

Companion Animal Behavior Program (2004). Human Animal Interactions Literature: An Introductory List of Resources. Retrieved October 7, 2005, from the University of California, Davis, School of Veterinary Medicine web site http://www.vetmed.ucdavis.edu/CCAB/hailit~1.htm.

Delta Society (1992). "Handbook for Animal-Assisted Activities and Animal-Assisted Therapy." Author, Renton, WA.

Delta Society (1996). "Standards of Practice for Animal-Assisted Activities and Animal-Assisted Therapy." Author, Renton, WA.

Delta Society (2005). Health benefits of animals bibliography. Retrieved October 7, 2005, from http://www.deltasociety.org/AnimalsHealthGeneralBibliography.htm.

Duncan, S. L., and Allen, K. (2000). Service animals and their roles in enhancing independence, quality of life, and employment for people with disabilities. *In* "Handbook on Animal-Assisted Therapy: Theoretical Foundations and Guidelines for Practice" (A. H. Fine, ed.), pp. 303–323. Academic Press, New York.

Fine, A. H. (ed.) (2002). "Handbook on Animal-Assisted Therapy: Theoretical Foundations and Guidelines for Practice." Academic Press, New York.

Firestein, K., and Hart, L. A. (2000). Unobstrusive study of animals in the wild: Database search strategies. *In* "Progress in the Reduction, Refinement and Replacement of Animal Experimentation" (M. Balls, A.-M. van Zeller, and M. E. Halder, eds.). Elsevier, Amsterdam.

Google (2005). Google Scholar Beta. Retrieved October 7, 2005, from http://scholar.google.com/.

Hakkinen, P. J., and Green, D. K. (2002). Alternatives to animal testing: Information resources via the Internet and world wide web. *Toxicology* **173**, 3–11.

Hart, B. L. (2005). Companion Animal Behavior Program. Retrieved October 7, 2005, from the University of California, Davis, School of Veterinary Medicine web site http://www.vetmed.ucdavis.edu/CCAB/main.htm.

Hart, L. A., and Wood, M. W. (2005). UC Center for Animal Alternatives. Retrieved October 7, 2005, from the University of California, Davis, School of Veterinary Medicine web site http://www.vetmed.ucdavis.edu/Animal_Alternatives/main.htm.

International Society for Anthrozoology (2005). ISAZ home page. Retrieved October 7, 2005, from the University of California, Davis, School of Veterinary Medicine web site http://www.vetmed.ucdavis.edu/CCAB/isaz.htm.

Kidd, A. H., and Zasloff, R. L. (1995). Research methods in animal assisted therapy. Unpublished guidelines, Center for Animals in Society, University of California, Davis.

LexisNexis (2005). Retrieved October 7, 2005, from http://www.lexisnexis.com/.

National Agricultural Library (2005). AGRICOLA Article Citation Database. Retrieved October 7, 2005, from http://agricola.nal.usda.gov/.

National Library of Medicine (2005). PubMed. Retrieved October 7, 2005, from http://www.ncbi.nlm.nih.gov/entrez/query.fcgi.

Online Computer Library Center (2005). WorldCat. Retrieved October 7, 2005, from http://www.oclc.org/worldcat/default.htm.

People, Animals and Nature, Inc. (2004). PAN. Retrieved October 7, 2005, from http://www.pan-inc.org/.

Petcare Information and Advisory Service Australia Pty Ltd. (2005), Anthrozoology. Retrieved October 7, 2005, from http://anthrozoology.org/index.html.

Purdue University (2005). Center for the Human-Animal Bond. Retrieved October 7, 2005, from the Purdue University School of Veterinary Medicine web site http://www.vet.purdue.edu/chab/.

Regents of the University of California (2005a). Melvyl: The Catalog of the University of California Libraries. Retrieved October 7, 2005, from the California Digital Library web site http://melvyl.cdlib.org.

Regents of the University of Minnesota (2005b). CENSHARE. Retrieved October 7, 2005, from the University of Minnesota web site http://www.censhare.umn.edu/.

Rowan, A. N., and Thayer, L. (2000). Foreword. *In* "Handbook on Animal-Assisted Therapy: Theoretical Foundations and Guidelines for Practice" (A. H. Fine, ed.), pp. xxvii–xlv. Academic Press, New York.

Serpell, J. A. (1996). "In the Company of Animals: A Study of Human-Animal Relationships." University Press, Cambridge.

Serpell, J. A. (2000). Animal companions and human well-being: A historical exploration of the value of human-animal relationships. *In* "Handbook on Animal-Assisted Therapy: Theoretical Foundations and Guidelines for Practice" (A. H. Fine, ed.), pp. 3–20. Academic Press, New York.

Serpell, J. A. (2005). Center for the Interaction of Animals in Society. Retrieved October 7, 2005, from the University of Pennsylvania School of Veterinary Medicine web site http://www2.vet.upenn.edu/research/centers/cias/.

Society and Animals Forum (2005). Retrieved October 7, 2005, from the Psychologists for the Ethical Treatment of Animals web site http://www.psyeta.org/.

Suthers-McCabe, M. (2005). CENTAUR Center for Animal Human Relationships. Retrieved October 7, 2005, from the Virginia-Maryland Regional College of Veterinary Medicine web site http://www.vetmed.vt.edu/centaur/index.html.

Thomson (2005). BIOSIS. Retrieved October 7, 2005, from http://www.biosis.org/.

Timmins, R. (2005). Center for Animals in Society. Retrieved October 7, 2005, from the University of California, Davis, School of Veterinary Medicine web site http://www.vetmed.ucdavis.edu/Animals_in_Society/main.htm.

University Library at UC Davis (2005). Retrieved October 7, 2005, from the University of California, Davis, web site http://www.lib.ucdavis.edu/.

CHAPTER 19

"Old Wine in a New Bottle": New Strategies for Humane Education

PHIL ARKOW
American Humane Association, Englewood, CO
The Latham Foundation, Alameda, CA

[The ability] to understand the hopes and aspirations of others . . . was the beginning of all morality. If you knew how a person was feeling, if you could imagine yourself in her position, then surely it would be impossible to inflict further pain. Inflicting pain in such circumstances would be like hurting oneself.

—Alexander McCall Smith
Morality for Beautiful Girls

It has been axiomatic for hundreds of years, in a variety of cultures, that children who are taught to respect animals will develop empathy and compassion and grow up to be kinder to their fellow human animals. A wide array of philosophers and writers, including Ovid, St. Thomas Aquinas, Montaigne, John Locke, William Hogarth, Immanuel Kant, and Margaret Mead, have argued that harming animals is the first step down the slippery slope of desensitization against interpersonal violence. These writers have extolled the virtues of being kind to animals not just out of consideration for animals' well-being, but out of concern for what animal maltreatment says about the human condition (ten Bensel, 1984; Wynne-Tyson, 1990).

Moralistic tracts of the Victorian era, in particular, are filled with lofty sentiments about harming animals as being a precursor to antisocial behaviors:

> A worm, a fly, and all things that have life, can feel pain: if we learn to be cruel while boys, we shall not grow up to be good men. (Cobb, 1832)
>
> One who is cruel to a cat or a dog, a bird or a fish, will be cruel to his fellow-man, and such cruelty dulls all those finer feelings which make a true gentleman or lady. (Johnson, 1900)

Beginning in the 1790s, growing comprehension of the importance of how childhood experience can impact character development fueled a robust transatlantic publishing industry infused with a humane didactic. What became known as "humane education" presented one means of insulating young boys against the tyrannical tendencies that might undermine civic life were their violent natures to go unchecked. Animals were nicely suited for instruction and became important means of inculcating such standards of gentility as self-discipline, Christian sentiment, empathy, and moral sensitivity. Humane education helped separate refined middle- and upper-class standards from the coarser behaviors of the lower classes and immigrants who were implicitly seen as the sources of much brutality (Ritvo, 1987; Saunders, 1895; Unti and DeRosa, 2003).

As early as 1868, the newly emerging humane movement in the United States, where the term "humane society" (as an animal welfare organization) appears to have nothing in common with its British counterpart (an organization dedicated to the rescue and resuscitation of drowning victims), identified humane education as the intervention of choice for guiding wayward youths into a righteous path in which animals were well regarded, respected, and cared for, not just for the animals' welfare, but to improve human behavior. George Angell, founder of the Massachusetts SPCA, argued that although animal abuse should be a concern in its own right, society should heed animal abuse as an omen of violence among people (cited in Ascione, 2004).

Angell stressed humane education's utility for ensuring public order, suppressing anarchy and radicalism, smoothing relations between the classes, and reducing crime: it would be a valuable means for socializing the young (especially of the lower socioeconomic classes) and the solution to social unrest and revolutionary politics. The promotion of humane education as an antidote for depraved character and a panacea for societal ills aligned the fledgling animal protection movement with other social reform and justice movements concerned with cruelty, violence, and the social order (Unti and DeRosa, 2003).

The early history of the Latham Foundation, founded in 1918 for the promotion of humane education, exemplifies this paradigm. A poster from the 1930s, still widely used by the foundation today, depicts two children with a puppy approaching a set of steps leading to "world friendship." The first step up this hill is "kindness to animals," which will subsequently take the voyagers to kindness to each other, other people, our country, other nations, and the world. This sentiment echoed the writings of Boston activist Sarah J. Eddy (1899), who wrote:

> The humane education movement is a broad one, reaching from humane treatment of animals on the one hand to peace with all nations on the other. . . . It implies character building. Society first said that needless suffering should be prevented; society now says that children must not be permitted to cause pain because of the effect on the children themselves.

Embedded in this philosophy is the premise that kindness to animals has a benefit to human beings as well. A century later, advocates still promote the virtues of humane education as a broad approach that can address everything from at-risk animals to global peace. Weil (2004), for example, described humane education as offering a solution to war, bigotry, cruelty, environmental disaster, terrorism, species extinction, human oppression, ecological degradation, racism, sexism, homophobia, and global warming. Antoncic (2003) declared "humane education can offer society hope for an active, independent, self-thinking future citizenry."

I. ORIGINS OF A PARADIGM

How did this irrepressible, albeit largely unproven, faith in the power of humane education emerge, and why has it not been institutionalized in education systems? It would appear to be self-evident that empathy toward human beings can be fostered through greater appreciation of and respect for nonhuman animals. Humane education proponents believe fervently in the power of didactic instruction to effect compassionate attitudinal and behavioral changes. Animal protection organizations conduct classroom programs in hopes of effecting societal value shifts to treat animals with greater kindness. An underlying subtext, often overlooked in presentations focusing on responsible pet care, has always been that kindness to animals has ancillary benefits to the human species as well.

On the surface, humane education should show much potential. Kellert (1989) reported direct correlations between higher education levels and support for moralistic, humanistic, and ecologistic attitudes consistent with animal rights, animal welfare, and environmental causes. Bjerke and Ostdahl (2004) argued that although it is difficult to see how higher education unequivocally could directly influence our attitudes toward nature and biological diversity, as only a minority study biological and ecological disciplines, education could contribute to a biocentric value orientation by influencing more fundamental life values such as egalitarianism.

However, it is not clear how humane education compares and contrasts with other more accepted curricula that also seek to inspire appreciation of, and respect for, the natural world, such as environmental education, natural studies, zoo education programs, or high school biology classes. Similarly, it is not clear why humane education remains a largely marginalized activity of animal organizations and has not been institutionalized in school systems, while the more contemporary instructional programs of "values education" or "character education," which arguably seek to effect similar outcomes among students, are flourishing with federal dollars flowing to school districts across the United States.

Support for humane education came relatively early. In 1933, the National Congress of Parent–Teacher Associations espoused the value of inculcating children with the higher principles of kindness to animals (Arkow, 1990; Wishnik, 2003):

> Children trained to extend justice, kindness, and mercy to animals become more just, kind and considerate in their relations to each other. Character training along these lines will result in men and women of broader sympathies, more humane, more law-abiding—in every respect more valuable citizens. Humane education is teaching in all the schools and colleges of the nation the principles of justice, goodwill, and humanity toward all life. The cultivation of the spirit of kindness to animals is but the starting point towards that larger humanity which includes one's fellow of every race and clime. A generation of people trained in these principles will solve their difficulties as neighbors and not as enemies.

Several generations have come and gone since the National Congress of Parent–Teacher Associations made this prediction, yet it would appear to many that we are no further along in raising nonviolent, law-abiding, empathetic children. Where did we go wrong, or have we just not applied enough humane education to the curriculum?

II. SQUANDERED OPPORTUNITIES

Beginning in 1905, state departments of education began imposing compulsory humane education instruction; by the 1930s, almost half of American states had mandated some form of humane education. This instruction, however, was rarely enforced and was implemented haphazardly at best. In ensuing decades, support for humane education dwindled, even as schools instituted similar character education and values education curricula.

Today only 13 states are believed to mandate humane education (Antoncic, 2003).

At the peak of the humane education movement, Bands of Mercy, started by the Massachusetts SPCA for elementary school students and modeled after the English temperance movement's Bands of Hope, which rallied children against the evils of alcohol consumption, claimed as many as 265,000 children in 1912. Writer Jack London started animal rights clubs for older students, but interest in these humane education vehicles, as with the Bands of Mercy, also died out.

Clifton (2004a) criticized the squandering of this "lost opportunity":

> The mandates, as adopted, were forthright in equating humane education as moral education and in expecting the curriculums to challenge students to think—but by 1930 the onset of the Great Depression and shrinking budgets both for education and for humane work brought the collapse of youth groups and visiting teacher corps who had been entrusted with doing humane education, and the whole notion vanished from most U.S. schools for decades.

Today, school educators and humane educators often overlook the opportunity presented by the sheer ubiquity of pets in the lives of children. Children are surrounded by animal presences, from the stuffed animals in their cribs to the decorations on their clothing, from the cartoon characters on their TV screens to the plastic animals in their baths. Most children learn their numbers by counting animals and learn to read from picture books filled with animals (Doris Day Animal Foundation, 2005). The American Veterinary Medical Association (2002) estimated that pets are present in 64.1% of U.S. households with children under the age of 6 and in 74.8% of households with children aged 6 or over. About 69 million homes have pets, and the average dog owner will spend approximately $11,500 on the animal over its life span, leading, perhaps, to a proliferation of veterinarians: the number of practitioners in the United States increased from 32,000 in 1980 to over 70,000 in 2005 (Finkelstein, 2005).

Melson (2001) observed that words for such common animals as *dog*, *cat*, *duck*, *horse*, *bear*, and *bird* are among the first 50 words that most American toddlers say and that more children say these words than any other words except *mama* and *daddy* or their equivalents. Fairy tales have more animals in them than fairies. For many children in contemporary America, pets are more likely to be a part of growing up than are siblings or fathers. And 80 to 90% of American children first confront the loss of a loved one when a pet dies, disappears, or is abandoned. However, traditional education renders animals as objects to be analyzed apart from the texture of daily experience. Even though many classrooms have animals, teachers are largely unaware of the impact of animals on children's development.

Even today, humane education is often limited to a single 45-minute classroom presentation by a visitor from an animal shelter. The impact of such a program has been calculated as comprising only 4/10,000ths of 1% of a student's 12-year classroom contact time; the impact of such a program against the influence of students' peers, family, and the media is impossible to measure.

Debbie Duel, the former humane educator in neighborhoods in inner-city Washington, DC, which are marked by high levels of violence, once asked me: "How can I go into a classroom and teach children to be kind to their puppies when they're afraid to *go* to school because of drive-by shootings?"

After 800 years of philosophical thought and 140 years of classroom instruction, society has never been able to prove the simple assumptions underpinning humane education. Developing a sense of empathy for animals is assumed to be a bridge to caring about human beings, but this premise and the programs spawned by this assumption have been difficult to assess (Ascione, 2004). The corpus of literature on the effectiveness of humane education is meager and inconclusive at best (O'Brien, undated).

It has been argued, even by foundations promoting humane education, that fundamental values are best taught at home by parents: public schools merely fill in the formal education (Tebault, 2004). Meanwhile, some educators ardently believe it is a school's job to focus on "the 3 R's" and to not get embroiled in politically volatile issues of character building in their students, despite research showing that successful learners are knowledgeable, self-determined, strategic, and empathetic. Children who develop a sense of empathy tend to be more resilient, more socially competent, more popular with their peers, and less aggressive (Doris Day Animal Foundation, 2005).

Still, professional and volunteer humane educators soldier on, nobly attempting to teach children a sense of responsibility, respect, and compassion for animals and their needs in hopes of developing good character, self-awareness, and greater respect for all living things (Yao, 2003).

III. CHALLENGES TO HUMANE EDUCATION

However, unlike similar movements such as environmental education, character education, or values education, humane education continues to be a good idea that has not quite caught on (Alberta SPCA, 2004). Efforts to institutionalize the teaching of humane treatment of animals within the larger framework of the educational establishment have had only limited success. In many respects, humane education is best seen as an arena of untapped potential rather than one of unfulfilled promise. Humane educators face numerous challenges.

A. Inadequate Definitions

The terms "cruelty to animals" and "humane education" are like "pornography": impossible to define, but we know it when we see it. What is called "humane education" in an animal welfare context has also been called environmental education, character education, values education, moral education, and humanistic education in other venues. Zoo educators, conservation groups, pet food companies, veterinarians, and associations in support of biomedical research all conduct animal welfare education programming, but are these "humane education"?

Numerous definitions of "humane education" have been proposed but never accepted universally. Arkow (1992) summarized humane education as being composed of the "5Rs."

1. *Respect* for the other animals that share our homes, our cities, and our planet.
2. *Reverence* for the life force of which we are but a small part.
3. *Responsibility* toward those other animals that we have chosen to domesticate and bring under our dominion.
4. *Realistic* awareness of animals for what they are and are not.
5. *Relevance* of fellow and accessible creatures with which we are intimately familiar but who are worlds apart, whose "us-ness" and "other-ness" may teach us much about ourselves as we study their uniqueness.

Weil (2004) described humane education as instilling reverence, respect, and responsibility through providing accurate information and fostering curiosity, creativity, and critical thinking. Students are offered positive choices that empower them to create a world that benefits themselves, other people, the Earth, and animals.

Meanwhile, the statutory definitions of "cruelty to animals" vary widely among the 50 states (Frasch *et al.*, 1999; Lacroix, 1999) and from country to country, and they do not necessarily align with what many researchers now prefer to call "animal abuse" (Arkow, 1996) or with what the general public may consider objectionable behavior. What is not clearly defined cannot be measured reliably (Merz-Perez and Heide, 2004).

B. Marginalization of the Victims

Only one country, Canada, is believed to have considered (but has still not enacted) legislation that would redefine animal abuse as a crime of violence rather than an offense against property. Although 12 cities and one county in the United States have redefined animal "owners" as "guardians" (Finkelstein,

2005), this movement is small and shows no signs of changing common law and a societal paradigm that has existed for hundreds of years. Ultimately, animal abuse can be faced head-on as a crime only when all concerned embrace the perception that animals can indeed be victims (Merz-Perez and Heide, 2004).

C. Insufficient Knowledge of the Etiology of Violence against Animals

Animal abuse is a complex and multideterminate event based on many confounding social, personal, familial, societal, cultural, and psychological factors. Kellert and Felthous (1985) identified nine motivations for cruelty to animals. Animal cruelty should be seen as a process rather than an act, and its motivations are as diverse and complicated as those for interpersonal violence (Merz-Perez and Heide, 2004).

D. Inadequate Financial Resources to Sustain Concerted Efforts

According to the American Association of Fundraising Counsel (Giving USA Foundation, 2005), Americans donated $248.52 billion to charity in 2004. Of this amount, $7.61 billion, or only 3.1%, was donated to environmental and animal causes—a percentage that has remained relatively constant since statistics were first compiled in 1987. (By comparison, religion received 35.5%, education 13.6%, health 8.7%, human services 7.7%, and arts/culture/humanities 5.6%.) While there is no accurate breakdown of how these donations are apportioned, it is widely believed that environmental and wildlife causes comprise the most substantial part, with companion animal organizations receiving minuscule amounts. Similarly, of an estimated 60,000 foundations in the United States, less than two dozen are believed to support companion animal welfare interests as a primary interest area.

The practical and financial burdens of animal shelter operations, hospital services, animal control obligations, and humane law enforcement continue to push humane education to the periphery of animal protection activities. In a survey of 213 animal care and control organizations in Illinois and Indiana, 69.8% of organizations claimed to be operating humane education programs, but only 41.1% of those educators held full- or part-time paid positions and 97.8% of educators also had other duties. When asked to rank the importance of humane education, 55% of organizations ranked it of extreme importance, but 72.1% of these organizations allocated zero dollars for paid humane educators and 31.6% allotted zero dollars for humane education supplies (Senechalle and Dunn, 2004). Although animal protection advocates universally extol the importance of humane education as being mission critical, these programs maintain at best a peripheral importance for local animal care and control agencies. Youth education continues to be a marginal, if not entirely dispensable, facet of animal protection work, support for which has been called "anemic" (Unti and DeRosa, 2003). Clifton (2004b) observed that animal shelters obtain most of their funding for tangible, emotionally appealing activities such as direct services to animals in need; lobbying and litigation inspire donors much less, and humane education attracts the least support relative to long-term importance.

E. Inadequate Legal Mandates

Currently, 13 U.S. states are believed to mandate humane education in curricula. Yet in none of these states is this mandate enforced, nor do data indicate whether students in these states are kinder and gentler than in the nonmandating 37 states. Few of these statutes have compliance or penalty provisions, and none includes a budgetary allocation, thereby reducing humane education to merely a statement of legislative intent regarding kind treatment of animals and preservation of the environment (Antoncic, 2003). These laws address such varied issues as preventing hate violence, improving human relations, fostering appreciation for people of different ethnicities, conservation of natural resources, promotion of diversity, recognition of arbor and bird days, recycling, waste management, and, almost incidentally, kindness to animals (Antoncic, 2003).

F. Unknown Effectiveness

Humane education has not achieved significant acceptance over the past 140 years due, in part, to the absence of longitudinal studies and mechanisms to evaluate its effectiveness. Since the early 1990s, little research analyzing the impact of programs, approaches, or teaching materials has been published (O'Brien, undated). The following core question has never been adequately answered: does kindness to animals lead to empathy toward humans? (Winiarskyj, 2001). Relatively little empirical evidence exists showing that humane education programs increase children's knowledge about or improve their attitudes and behavior toward animals; none exists showing that such gains are carried into adulthood. Research investigating the transference theory—the tacit assumption that positive attitudes toward animals are transferable, or will generalize, to humans—is inconclusive (Unti and DeRosa, 2003). Even education programs addressing arguably the most potentially serious human health and safety issues related to pet ownership—the prevention of dog bites—are difficult to assess. In a randomized, controlled trial in Sydney, Australia, Chapman *et al.* (2000) evaluated the efficacy of "Dog Safe" interventions among 346 seven- and eight-year-old children. Although the children who received the instruction clearly demonstrated safer animal interaction skills 7 to 10 days following the interventions, the long-term efficacy of these programs is unknown.

G. Inadequate Strategies

To be effective, educators must impart cognitive awareness of facts, which may lead to affective emotional responses, which may result in behavioral changes among their students. Humane educators have rarely had the resources necessary to address these three components adequately.

This challenge is exacerbated by the segmentation of animal instructional programming among six distinct philosophical contingents: animal exploitation, animal use, animal control, animal welfare, animal rights, and animal liberation (Morgan, 1983). This instruction is further challenged by the presence of 10 distinct value systems (Kellert, 1989) among students, who furthermore are at various stages of developmental receptivity, in a multicultural society. Numerous strategies integrate humane education into existing teaching modules and learning subjects, but these programs are introduced haphazardly and simplistically and have not been evaluated (Cavanaugh *et al.*, 1998).

As examples of strategic dilemmas that have not been addressed adequately, consider the following:

- Given the evidence that perpetrators of domestic violence and animal abuse are overwhelmingly male (Flynn, 2004), and research suggesting that it is not the mere presence of pets but rather a high degree of caring for pets that leads to more empathic values (Arluke, 2003; Ascione and Weber, 1996), should humane educators not concentrate their limited resources on giving young boys positive experiences in caring for animals rather than conducting broad-brush programs for all students (Robertson, 2004)?
- Should the goal of humane education be to inspire *empathy* (which would be facilitated greatly by teaching animal behavior and an ethological appreciation of animals) or *sympathy* (which is based on compassion)?

- Although anthropomorphism has been described as "demeaning to animals, confusing and inaccurate" and is generally discouraged as being politically incorrect, could anthropomorphism help facilitate young persons' abilities to relate to and establish emotional connectedness to animals (Dawson *et al.*, 2004)?
- If the human–animal bond is so powerful and animals are catalysts for communication who offer tactile stimulation and enhance the therapeutic milieu (Arkow, 2004), does the value of including animals in classroom presentations outweigh the risk to animals' well-being in such programs?
- Given research showing limited success with short-term humane education programs presented by outsiders (Ascione, 1997), should animal protection organizations focus their limited resources on training school educators to conduct teacher-facilitated instruction?
- Can the research in moral development and character education inform practices in humane education, or are the two fields mutually exclusive? Are humane educators, with their traditional focus on companion animals, willing or able to expand their horizons to integrate character education strategies?
- What are the best practices in humane education, and how are these disseminated and replicated?
- Is there a threshold effect for humane education? How much exposure and participation are necessary to be worthwhile in the long term?

H. Cultural Illiteracy

Many issues facing animal protection organizations—from proliferation of fighting dogs to effective deployment of veterinary resources to understanding the ecology of animal populations in urban habitats—are heavily affected by inner-city and minority populations. Yet diversity is lacking at animal care and control facilities where staff, leadership, and board positions are largely white and middle class.

I. No Room at the Inn

Animal advocates must compete against hundreds of other special-interest groups that also seek to have their programs introduced into school curricula. Many of these interests, such as agricultural and industrial associations and science education groups, promote consumptive uses of animals that are in opposition to the humane imperative (Antoncic, 2003).

J. Lack of Credentials

What qualifications and philosophical perspectives are necessary to be a "humane educator"? There are no requisite certification procedures, and humane educators represent such diverse viewpoints as animal welfare, animal rights, rescue groups, advocacy activists, nonprofit shelters, and municipal agencies.

K. Lack of Professional Development

There are few university-level humane education opportunities. Some animal protection organizations train classroom teachers to convey the humane message through newsletters and in-service/continuing education training; these strategies show great promise and may be effective, but they are not applied systematically through the humane movement.

L. Lack of Public Support

Parents and the general public, who continually expect schools to do more with less, have never provided the critical mass that would impel systemic changes in support of humane education.

M. Lack of Teacher Support

Elementary education teachers routinely conduct lessons about the biological differences between spiders and insects yet fail to teach that humans are animals or why dogs bite. Teachers rarely recognize that the dogs and cats who reside in three-fourths of their students' homes are a teaching resource to develop an ethological appreciation for animals. Although educators resist additional instructional mandates to already crowded curricula, Antoncic (2003) observed that humane and character education, especially when integrated into existing subject materials, is an effective way to enhance learning rather than an additional burden upon teachers. "Character education is not one more thing to add to the plate—it is the plate," Antoncic noted. Nevertheless, while education reforms may be started by advocates outside the education profession, reforms become institutionalized only when the reforms are taken up by educators themselves (Finch, 1989). To date, few teachers or school districts have provided this necessary support.

N. Bureaucratic Obstacles to Curriculum Change

The teacher who is interested in humane education is frequently confronted with institutional stasis and legal restrictions that impede curriculum change. The difficulty of penetrating school district bureaucracies has proven to be insurmountable for many advocates.

O. Lack of Media Reinforcement

Until the debut of *Animal Precinct* and the Animal Planet cable TV network, most children's mainstream media awareness was limited to anthropomorphized movies and cartoons.

P. What Does the Audience Want?

Humane educators attempt to impart their value systems without asking the students what messages and media would resonate most successfully with them.

> Kids are not interested in ideas. They like puns, cruel jokes, amazing statistics, monsters, the subversion of authority, brute strength, complicated pictures, and perverse nonsense. In short, anything, no matter how veiled in metaphor, that suggests to them that they are getting a no-bullshit glimpse of the silly but dangerous universe that adults inhabit and that they will have to, bit by bit, adapt themselves to. (Gosnell, 1975)

IV. OVERCOMING THE CHALLENGES

Because of these challenges, humane education has never achieved the critical mass necessary for widespread implementation. However, one way to jump-start the movement and to gain research, funding, evaluation, and credibility would be to revise an old paradigm into new language appropriate for the 21st century—what Ascione (2004) called, in a related context, putting "old wine into a new bottle." The key to this is to use the growing recognition of animal-assisted therapy and the links between animal abuse and interpersonal violence as rationales for introducing humane education into school curricula.

Research into the links among animal abuse, child abuse, domestic violence (Ascione and Arkow, 1999; Ascione, Kaufmann, and Brooks, 2000), and, to a lesser extent, elder abuse (Boat and Knight, 2000) are drawing scholarly and public attention to the implications of violence against animals as it portends a risk to the human species. Building upon this increased awareness, humane education is an intervention that may prevent abuse to animals and people. Humane education offers an effective vehicle to prevent violence by fostering respect, responsibility, and empathy in youth toward all forms of life and the environment. Several studies support this proposition and validate humane education as a deterrent to violence (Antoncic, 2003). On the basis of the assumption that children exposed to domestic violence are at an elevated risk of eventually committing violence, many advocates view humane education as an applicable tool for violence intervention and prevention (Merz-Perez and Heide, 2004).

With a growing body of research about the sociological and psychological dimensions of animal abuse and about linkages among animal abuse and heterosexual partner abuse, lesbian partner abuse, child physical abuse, child sexual abuse, and sibling abuse, cultivation of empathy for nonhuman animals is beneficial not only for animals' well-being but also because informed interaction with animals can aid healthy character development in children. Discussion of and involvement with animal-assisted therapy (AAT), which likewise is becoming widely accepted for its human health benefits, should be crucial components of a humane education curriculum. Educators, particularly counselors, should use humane education to help identify and prevent animal abuse and offer remedial and preventive strategies for adverse human–animal interactions (Thomas and Beirne, 2002).

Childhood offers us a brief window of opportunity to redirect future sociopaths. It is a chance to intervene with a child at a critical juncture. Vachss (2004), who called animal abuse "the Rosetta Stone of predatory psychopathology," wrote, "The young child who throws a rock at a flock of pigeons isn't so much endangering a bird as he is giving us the chance to intervene at the crossroads. We can teach empathy, or we can encourage cruelty."

Contemporary research (www.animaltherapy.net, 2005) is confirming centuries of conventional wisdom that children who are not kind to animals have a high risk of developing serious antisocial behaviors. Boys will be boys, but violent boys have a great risk of becoming dangerous men.

Animal abuse, when perpetrated or witnessed by youths, is a significant risk factor that portends serious consequences for society; puts other creatures at risk; and has implications for educators, law enforcement personnel, social workers, parents, the health care field, the network of community caregivers, the animal protection community, and, not least, the animals themselves.

Animal protection laws have traditionally been enacted not because legislators feel an affinity toward animal welfare or animal rights but rather because of the impact that animal maltreatment is perceived to have on the human condition (Animal Welfare Institute, 1990; Frasch *et al.*, 1999; Lacroix, 1999). For today's legislators, "being kind to animals" is not a priority; lawmakers are, however, interested in reducing bullying, school violence, and family violence. Humane education, predicated upon link research, can fit these agendas.

While being kind to animals is certainly a *nice* thing to do and the *right* thing to do, it is only when leaders recognize that animal abuse has adverse effects on the *human* animal that animal maltreatment will become culturally unacceptable and that real, lasting changes, including curriculum development, will be made.

When animals are abused, people are at risk, and when people are abused, animals are at risk. What should be a warning marker for parents and teachers is all too often dismissed as "boys will be boys" or "it was only a rabbit." Numerous intersections of animal abuse and risk factors for youth have been identified:

- Thirty-one percent of cases of intentional abuse against animals are committed by boys under age 18. Twenty-one percent of intentional animal abuse cases involve domestic violence, child abuse, or elder abuse (Humane Society of the United States, 2001).
- Seventy percent of animal abusers also have records for crimes of violence, drugs, property destruction, or disorderly conduct (Arluke and Luke, 1997).
- Sixty percent of families under investigation for child abuse also had incidents of animal abuse; the incidence of dog bites in these households was 11 times greater than in nonabusive homes, creating serious public health risks (DeViney *et al.*, 1983).
- The cycles of violence are intergenerational and handed down as malevolent family values: 71% of women seeking shelter from abusive partners reported their husband or boyfriend killed, harmed, or threatened an animal. Seventy-five percent of these incidents occurred in the presence of the children. Thirty-two percent of these women reported their children had hurt or killed animals (Ascione, 1998).
- As many as 40% of battered women cannot seek shelter in a safe house because they fear what their batterer will do to their animals. In response, women's shelters have begun offering foster care for these women's pets (Ascione, 2000).

Conversely, the act of caring for pets may be significant in helping children to achieve prosocial values:

- Youths who have pets have greater self-concept and self-esteem, are better integrated socially, have wider social networks, and are more popular with their classmates (Endenburg and Baarda, 1995).
- High school students who have pets perform better on college entrance examinations and have higher grade point averages (American Pet Products Manufacturers Association, 1999).

- Because attachment to pets is a gender-neutral expression of caring, pets may be especially important for the development of empathy among young boys (Melson, 1988).

V. SHIFTING A PARADIGM: THREE KEY ELEMENTS

What these findings tell us is that we must take cruelty to animals and humane education out of their Victorian-era context and reframe violence against animals into a 21st-century context with which contemporary legislators, educators, and courts are more comfortable. The three key elements of this shift can be summarized as follows.

A. Animal Abuse Is Family Violence

Traditionally, we have thought of acts of violence against animals as isolated acts, but animal abuse rarely occurs in a vacuum. It frequently indicates other emotional, familial, economic, or social problems. In today's society, 98% of Americans see pets as "companions" or as "members of the family" (AVMA, 2002). As pets come to be seen less as "property" and more as "members of the family," acts of animal abuse often intersect acts of child abuse and/or domestic violence. We must redefine animal abuse as family violence.

B. Animal Abuse Is a Human Welfare Concern

American anticruelty laws are the oldest in the world and date to 1641 (Animal Welfare Institute, 1990). These statutes have been enacted because animal maltreatment is perceived primarily as an affront to a civilized society's mores or as a threat to others' private property–human welfare concerns. We should expand the legal concept of "cruelty to animals" as a human welfare issue by reclassifying it as a more contemporary "animal abuse" where it is not necessary to prove criminal intent in order to obtain convictions.

C. Community Caregivers Must Be Cross-Trained

The network of humane and human social service agencies must learn to recognize telltale warning signs of all forms of family violence outside their immediate purview and to cross-report to their counterparts in other agencies. A multidisciplinary approach to family violence, rather than "silos" of bureaucratic isolationism, holds greater promise in making earlier identifications, timelier interventions, and more effective preventions of animal abuse, child abuse, domestic violence, and elder abuse.

VI. HUMANE EDUCATION INNOVATIONS

The mere presence of pets is neither necessary nor sufficient for children to develop empathy (Arluke, 2003). However, if animals are present, especially if there is attachment to those animals, there is an opportunity for children to develop a healthy sense of compassion for others (Ascione, 2004), higher measures of social competence and empathy (Poresky, 1990), greater orientation toward social values and greater likelihood of entering a helping profession (Vizek-Vidovic *et al.*, 2001), greater empathy toward people (Ascione and Weber, 1996), higher self-esteem (Bierer, 2001), and less aggression (Hergovich *et al.*, 2002).

Consequently, educational programs in traditional classrooms, schools for emotionally disturbed and behaviorally challenged students, youthful offender programs, classes for at-risk youth, and numerous other venues are achieving breakthroughs by using animals to soften harsh environments, to remind us of our universal kinships, and to inspire empathy. The newest and most promising of these animal-assisted interventions are implementing humane education programs based on links between animal abuse and human violence (San Diego Humane Society and SPCA, 2005; Soltow and Shepherd, 1992).

A. A National Humane Education Curriculum

In South Africa, whose constitution requires the inclusion of environmental education in schools, widespread awareness of the animal abuse/family violence connections resulted in the Humane Education Trust developing a national multilingual humane education component that will comprise 9% of this environmental instruction. Link training will also be available to every police station in the country (Humane Education Trust, 2003; L. Van der Merwe, personal communication, 2004).

B. Professional Development for Educators

In Canada, the Alberta SPCA obtained federal funding to publish a guide for teachers based on the link between animal abuse and other violent behaviors. This guide to resources and curriculum design is used in the Alberta

Teachers' Association's Safe and Caring Schools Project. The guide includes the symbiotic relationship between children and animals and offers recommendations for teachers whose students disclose incidents of animal abuse (Battle, 2003).

In Pennsylvania, the extensive Humane Education Guidebook is predicated on the animal abuse/child abuse connection (Federated Humane Societies of Pennsylvania, 2000).

The Association of Professional Humane Educators (2004) has published a directory of humane education resources in keeping with its development and networking activities for educators.

In response to opposition from the American Lung Association and People for the Ethical Treatment of Animals against the use of classroom animals due to the absence of veterinary, humane, science, or health protocols, the Pet Care Trust, a nonprofit foundation established by pet food and supply companies, offers workshops to help teachers select and manage classroom animals using veterinary technicians as mentors. The Pet Care Trust estimates that 25% of teachers use pets in their classrooms.

C. Revitalization of Kindness Clubs

Long after the Bands of Mercy and Jack London White Fang clubs disappeared, there is renewed interest in organizing groups of youngsters dedicated to protecting animals. In Bloemfontein, South Africa, an area described as "a rural area with a Wild West mentality," "Ubuntu" clubs to promote "better life for all living beings" are being launched with the enthusiastic support of the provincial department of education, based on the inseparable link between violence toward women and children and violence toward animals. The head boy of one school wrote, "During Apartheid, whites treated animals better than they treated blacks because whites thought animals were better than blacks. As black people became aware of that, some of them started hating pets such as dogs and cats" (B. Wiltshire, personal communication, 2004).

D. Advanced Degrees in Humane Education

The International Institute for Humane Education launched the first Humane Education Certificate Program in the United States and later affiliated with Cambridge College to offer a distance learning master of education degree program in humane education. Animal protection is one of five modules in the five-semester course, along with human rights, environmental ethics, cultural issues, and education and communication.

Humane Society University (HSU), a program of the Humane Society of the United States (HSUS), in conjunction with Webster University, offers an online master of arts in teaching degree with a focus on character development and humane education. The fully accredited program teaches teachers to develop, implement, and evaluate educational programs that emphasize character development and respect for animals and the environment. HSU also offers online professional development coursework in humane education and character development, nonprofit organizational management, shelter operations, shelter animal health and behavior, and humane community solutions (Humane Society University, 2004).

In conjunction with HSUS's National Association for Humane and Environmental Education (NAHEE) division, HSU also offers a certified humane education specialist program and numerous other distance learning courses to help humane educators reach teachers and to create service learning opportunities. This trend toward credentialization may be part of a larger pattern of certification and training programs now available, although not mandated, for other professionals in the animal field, including AAT specialists, animal welfare administrators, cruelty investigators, euthanasia technicians, kennel technicians, and animal control officers using chemical immobilization, disaster response, and technical rescue techniques.

E. Specialized Humane Education Schools

The world's first humane education charter school has opened in Harmony, Florida, with a second one planned in Citrus Heights, California. These schools feature humane education–based learning environments that foster the development of ethical children who conduct service learning programs (Wishnik, 2004). The goals of these schools include promoting community involvement and activism; rejecting all forms of cruelty, exploitation, and oppression; developing critical thinking skills; respecting human rights; and appreciating the natural community. Students are expected to learn compassion from their relationships with nonhuman animals and to transfer these skills to their human relationships (Wishnik, 2003).

F. Professional Classroom Materials

The American Society for the Prevention of Cruelty to Animals publishes an annual "Learning to Care Catalog" featuring videos, bilingual programs, handouts, activities sheets, resource guides, pet care flyers, and books. NAHEE publishes *KIND News*, a monthly classroom newspaper with articles, puzzles, and celebrity interviews that teach children the value of showing kindness and respect to animals, the environment, and one another. NAHEE's numerous other resources include books and online reviews of children's literature and movies.

G. Targeted Humane Education Interventions

In 1987, the American Psychiatric Association added cruelty to animals to the list of indicators for a diagnosis of conduct disorder to the "Diagnostic and Statistical Manual of Mental Disorders." The median age of onset of animal abuse is 6.5 years, is often noticed before other indicators of conduct disorder are manifest, and may forecast major dysfunction in adulthood. Identifying animal abuse early and intervening before a child is seven years of age may be a way to stop maladaptive behavior. Elementary school programs in the United States, Japan, and elsewhere are introducing animals into curricula to help solve social problems, including animal abuse and neglect (Matoba and Coultis, 2004).

Preliminary evidence indicates that animal-based interventions in mental health settings for adolescents have many potential benefits (Kruger *et al.*, 2004). Humane organizations are augmenting traditional broad-spectrum classroom presentations with specialized animal-assisted interventions for at-risk youth. In Los Angeles, SPCALA developed TLC (Teaching Love and Compassion) for at-risk youths with histories of disruptive or violent behavior. The youths attend a four-week workshop during the prime-risk after-school hours. Boys and girls work together learning nonviolent resolution of conflicts as they make shelter dogs more adoptable through obedience training based on positive reinforcement techniques and humane animal husbandry (Yao, 2003). East Coast Assistance Dogs' Pet Assisted Learning Services (PALS) in New York teaches at-risk youth in four residential schools to train service dogs. Similar programs include the Wisconsin Humane Society's Project PAL, Project Pooch in Oregon, and Project Second Chance in New Mexico (Arkow, 2003).

In Ft. Lauderdale, Florida, the Humane Society of Broward County created Pet Clubs in nine Boys and Girls Clubs in high-risk neighborhoods where children are regularly exposed to feral cats and dogs who are chained and trained to be dangerous. Because few of these children have had positive experiences with animals and many are terrified of dogs, the Pet Clubs provide AAT/AAA visits that allow children to interact in positive ways while learning the correct ways to approach, handle, and care for pets. The Humane Society also developed a "No Bones About It" badge for local Girl Scouts (Katz, 2004).

The South African Red Cross Society has launched the first program in Africa, if not the world, that trains school dropouts in first aid skills for animals to become part of an animal ambulance service. The program in Strandfontein, Western Cape province, takes at-risk youths off the streets and away from crime, drugs, and dog fighting. The program rescues animals in distress and provides transportation for economically disadvantaged families taking their pets to veterinarians (Animal Voice, 2005).

The Latham Foundation has published "Teaching Empathy: Animal-Assisted Therapy Programs for Children and Families Exposed to Violence." This handbook for therapists, humane educators, and teachers uses the link as the keystone for humane education and AAT interventions (Loar and Colman, 2004).

H. Nonclassroom Education Outreach

A number of SPCAs conduct summer camps with curricula based on humane themes. The Animal Rescue League in Rhode Island designed a "Pets and People" exhibit at the Providence Children's Museum that teaches 120,000 children and their grown-ups each year about pet responsibility and kindness.

I. Recognitions

NAHEE issues annual awards for the Humane Teen of the Year, National KIND Teacher, Children's Book Award, and a national humane education achievement award. The Latham Foundation biennially recognizes outstanding humane education videos.

J. Literacy Programs

Many animal welfare organizations have begun partnering with libraries to inspire children to read by having them read stories aloud to dogs. The Barks and Books reading enrichment program at the Pasadena Humane Society and SPCA offers children in southern California the opportunity to read animal-related short stories of their choice to dogs in the society's Companion Animal Program: the activity makes reading fun and builds children's confidence in reading aloud. A training video to teach therapy teams how to implement a reading education assistance dogs program is available from Intermountain Therapy Dogs (P.O. Box 17201, Salt Lake City, UT 84117) or www.therapyanimals.org.

K. Electronic Learning

An innovative educational web site called "Learning and Living Together: Building the Human–Animal Bond Online Curriculum" has been designed by the People Pet Partnership at the Center for the Study of Animal Well-Being at the College of Veterinary Medicine at Washington State University. The web site, with three grade-specific modules, promotes science and general education, encourages humane care of pets, and builds leadership skills through relationships with companion animals (Martin and Taunton, 2004).

VII. CONCLUSION

Mankind's earliest known works of art, dating back 32,000 years, are cave paintings of animals (Associated Press, 2001). Our earliest ancestors had primeval affinities with the animals that shared their environment. Over the last 320 centuries, we have feared animals, partnered with them, worshiped them, domesticated them, and made some of them members of our families. In the future we may take them with us into outer space (Levinson, 1984).

Animals can capture children's attention, imagination, and emotions in ways that people-focused subject matter cannot. Teaching abstract concepts such as compassion can be easier, more engaging, and more fun when animals are the springboard for discussion. As animal-assisted therapists have long known, animals are catalysts for communication, and people often find it easier to talk about animals than about other topics, particularly if the other person is a stranger or an authority figure or if the subject is uncomfortable. Animals can be introduced more easily into curricula by using the growing evidence about AAT and interest in the links between animal abuse and human violence.

"When we show [kids] that they can help animals, they learn that they can make a real difference in the world," said Bill Samuels, former director of humane education at the ASPCA. "Humane education allows children to do more than learn about other animals—it helps children learn from them" (Samuels, 2004).

A confluence of federally funded mandates for character education to promote core moral values, coupled with widespread awareness of the human health benefits of animal-assisted therapy and the links between animal abuse and interpersonal violence, has created a unique opportunity to portray an age-old message in a new light. At least 28 states have adopted some form of character education law, and 21 others without specific legislation have indicated support for character education (Antoncic, 2003). The U.S. Department of Education tripled its budget for character education as part of the "No Child Left Behind" mandate (Lord, 2001). Faculty chairs in character education and centers for the advancement of ethics and character are proliferating at universities. Advocates for humane education, working with their counterparts in the animal-assisted therapy and violence prevention fields, should work together using these models to target at-risk individuals.

Although some may argue that the appropriate place for humane, character, morals, or values education is in the home, widespread concern about rates of violence, substance abuse, teen pregnancy, dropout rates, and bullying is energizing efforts to introduce preventive measures through classroom instruction. Humane education should be an equal partner in this activity. Humane education is especially relevant at a time when the connection between childhood acts of cruelty to animals and interpersonal violence is widely known, and the perceived moral decline of our nation's youth is a common and increasingly fervent lament (Unti and DeRosa, 2003).

Human–companion animal bond and link research should lead to a reassessment and renaissance of animal-assisted education programs based on concrete data rather than abstract moral philosophies. A greater understanding of the ambassadors from the natural world, and of the human implications of animal abuse using a 21st-century paradigm that other professions can accept, will protect animals better and reduce the violence harming the two- and four-legged members of our families.

Perhaps Alan Beck expressed our humane educational mandate as succinctly as anyone when he said, "Companion animals are our children's children, and the best thing we can do for our children is to help them be better parents" (Dickstein, 1999).

REFERENCES

Alberta SPCA (2004). Humane education: An idea whose time has come. *AnimalWise* 5(2), 4–5.

American Pet Products Manufacturers Association (1999). Cited in *Time*, Nov. 8.

American Veterinary Medical Association (2002). "U.S. Pet Ownership and Demographics Sourcebook." AVMA, Schaumburg, IL.

Animal Voice (2005). "Red Cross launches first ambulance for animals in Africa." Autumn, p. 1.

Animal Welfare Institute (1990). "Animals and Their Legal Rights." Washington, DC.

Antoncic, L. S. (2003). A new era in humane education: How troubling youth trends and a call for character education are breathing new life into efforts to educate our youth about the value of all life. *Anim. Law* 9, 183–213.

Arkow, P. (1990). "Humane Education." American Humane, Englewood, CO.

Arkow, P. (1992). Humane education: A historical perspective. *In* "Progress in Humane Education" (M. E. Kaufmann, ed.), pp. 2–3. American Humane, Englewood, CO.

Arkow, P. (1996). The relationships between animal abuse and other forms of family violence. *Family Viol. Sex. Assault Bull.* 12(1–2), 29–34.

Arkow, P. (2003). "Breaking the Cycles of Violence: A Guide to Multidisciplinary Interventions." Latham Foundation, Alameda, CA.

Arkow, P. (2004). "Animal-Assisted Therapy and Activities: A Study, Resource Guide and Bibliography for the Use of Companion Animals in Selected Therapies," 9th Ed. Author, Stratford, NJ.

Arluke, A. (2003). Childhood origins of supernurturance: The social context of early humane behavior. *Anthrozoös* **16**(1), 3–27.

Arluke, A., and Luke, C. (1997). Physical cruelty toward animals in Massachusetts, 197 1996. *Soc. Anim.* **5**(3), 195–204.

Ascione, F. R. (1997). Humane education research: Evaluating efforts to encourage children's kindness and caring toward animals. *Genet. Soc. Gen. Psychol. Monogr.* **123**, 59–77.

Ascione, F. R. (1998). Battered women's reports of their partners' and their children's cruelty to animals. *J. Emot. Abuse* **1**, 119–133.

Ascione, F. R. (2000). "Safe Havens for Pets: Guidelines for Programs Sheltering Pets for Women Who Are Battered." Utah State University, Logan, UT.

Ascione, F. R. (2004). "Children and Animals: Exploring the Roots of Kindness and Cruelty." Purdue University Press, West Lafayette, IN.

Ascione, F. R., and Arkow, P. (1999). "Child Abuse, Domestic Violence and Animal Abuse: Linking the Circles of Compassion for Prevention and Intervention." Purdue University Press, West Lafayette, IN.

Ascione, F. R., Kaufmann, M. E., and Brooks, S. M. (2000). Animal abuse and developmental psychopathology: Recent research, programmatic and therapeutic issues, and challenges for the future. *In* "Handbook on Animal-Assisted Therapy: Theoretical Foundations and Guidelines for Practice" (A. Fine, ed.), pp. 325–354. Academic Press, San Diego, CA.

Ascione, F. R., and Weber, C. V. (1996). Children's attitudes about the humane treatment of animals and empathy: One-year follow-up of a school-based intervention. *Anthrozoös* **9**(4), 188–195.

Associated Press (2001). Prehistoric engravings found in France. Reported in *Philadelphia Inquirer*, July 12, 1.

Association of Professional Humane Educators (2004). "Directory of Organizations with Humane Education Resources." Latham Foundation, Alameda, CA.

Battle, T. (2003). "Learning to Care through Kindness to Animals: A Guide for Teachers." Alberta Teachers' Association, Edmonton, Canada.

Bierer, R. E. (2001). The relationship between pet bonding, self esteem, and empathy in preadolescents. *Dissert. Abstr. Int.* **61**(11-B), 6183.

Bjerke, T., and Ostdahl, T. (2004). Animal-related attitudes and activities in an urban population. *Anthrozoös* **17**(2), 109–129.

Boat, B. W., and Knight, J. C. (2000). Experiences and needs of adult protective services case managers when assisting clients who have companion animals. *J. Elder Abuse Neglect* **12**(3/4), 145–155.

Cavanaugh, K., Kaufmann, M., and Moulton, C. (eds.) (1998). "Humane Education at the Crossroads: Visions for the Future." American Humane, Englewood, CO.

Chapman, S., Cornwall, J., Righetti, J., and Sung, L. (2000). Preventing dog bites in children: Randomised controlled trial of an educational intervention. *Br. Med. J.* **320**, 1512–1513.

Clifton, M. (2004a). Humane education materials from South Africa. *Animal People*, April, 20.

Clifton, M. (2004b). Fundraisers and pro-animal strategy. *Animal People*, November, 3.

Cobb, L. (1832). "Cobb's Juvenile Reader No. 2 Containing Interesting, Moral, and Instructive Reading Lessons Composed of One, Two, and Three Syllables." Thomas L. Bonsal, Philadelphia, PA.

Dawson, S., Taso, A., Cehic, E., Campbell, B., and Johnson, M. (2004). Empathy, sympathy, emotional identification? Reflections on an animal focused story-making method within a school-based therapy programme in Bosnia and Herzegovinia. Presented at conference, "The Magic of the Human-Animal Bond: Professionals Working Together," Undergraduate Student Training Day, International Association of Human-Animal Interaction Organizations, Glasgow, Scotland. Oct. 6, 2004.

DeViney, E., Dickert, J., and Lockwood, R. (1983). The care of pets within child abusing families. *Int. J. Study Anim. Probl.* **4**, 321–329.

Dickstein, C. L. (1999). The family pet: Tiger's hungry, Dodger needs walking, whose responsibility is it, anyway? *ASPCA Animal Watch*, Fall, 23.

Doris Day Animal Foundation (2005). "The Empathy Connection." Washington, DC.

Eddy, S. J. (1899). "Friends and Helpers." Publisher unknown.

Endenburg, N., and Baarda, B. (1995). The role of pets in enhancing human well-being: Effects on child development. *In* "The Waltham Book of Human-Animal Interaction: Benefits and Responsibilities of Pet Ownership," pp. 7–17. Pergamon, Exeter, UK.

Federated Humane Societies of Pennsylvania (2000). "Humane Education Guidebook." Bensalem, PA.

Finch, P. (1989). Learning from the past. *In* "The Status of Animals: Ethics, Education and Welfare" (D. Paterson and M. Palmer, eds.), pp. 64–72. CAB International, Oxon, UK.

Finkelstein, S. I. (2005). High noon for animal rights law: The coming showdown between pet owners and guardians. *Bellwether* **62**, 18–21.

Flynn, C. P. (2004). Gender, power and control: A sociologist looks at the link between animal abuse and family violence. *In* "Linking Violence: An Interdisciplinary Conference on the Relationship between Violence against Animals and Humans," pp. 5–14. University College of Cape Breton, Sydney, NS, Canada.

Frasch, P. D., Otto, S. K., Olsen, K. M., and Ernest, P. A. (1999). State animal anti-cruelty statutes: An overview. *Anim. Law* **5**, 69–80.

Giving USA Foundation (2005). "Giving USA 2005." American Association of Fund Raising Council/Trust for Philanthropy, Glenview, IL.

Gosnell, S. (1975). Leave the kid alone. *Esquire*, March, 97.

Hergovich, A., Monshi, B., Semmler, G., and Zieglmayer, V. (2002). The effects of the presence of a dog in the classroom. *Anthrozoös* **15**(1), 37–50.

Humane Education Trust (2003). Why humane education is crucial to society. Cape Town, South Africa.

Humane Society of the U.S. (2001). "2000 Report of Animal Cruelty Cases." Washington, DC.

Humane Society University (2004). Educational opportunities. Accessed online Apr. 3 at http://www.hsus2.org/hsu/webster1.htm

Johnson, I. T. (ed.) (1900). Young people's natural history: A popular story of animals, birds, reptiles, fishes and insects, describing their structure, habits, instincts and dwellings, with thrilling stories of adventure and amusing anecdotes of wild and tame animals. A. B. Kuhlman and Co., Chicago, IL.

Katz, L. (2004). Join the club! Humane society shares a wealth of knowledge. *ASPCA Anim. Watch* **24**(3), 40.

Kellert, S. R. (1989). Perceptions of animals in America. *In* "Perceptions of Animals in American Culture" (R. J. Hoage, ed.), pp. 5–24. Smithsonian Institution Press, Washington, DC.

Kellert, S. R., and Felthous, A. R. (1985). Childhood cruelty toward animals among criminals and noncriminals. *Hum. Relat.* **38**, 1113–1129.

Kruger, K. A., Trachtenberg, S. W., and Serpell, J. A. (2004). Can animals help humans heal? Animal-assisted interventions in adolescent mental health. University of Pennsylvania School of Veterinary Medicine Center for the Interaction of Animals and Society, Philadelphia, PA.

Lacroix, C. A. (1999). Another weapon for combating family violence: Prevention of animal abuse. *In* "Child Abuse, Domestic Violence and Animal Abuse: Linking the Circles of Compassion for Prevention and Intervention" (F. R. Ascione and P. Arkow, eds.), pp. 62–82. Purdue University Press, West Lafayette, IN.

Levinson, B. (1984). Foreword. *In* "Dynamic Relationships in Practice: Animals in the Helping Professions" (P. Arkow, ed.), pp. 1–20. Latham Foundation, Alameda, CA.

Loar, L., and Colman, L. (2004). Teaching empathy: Animal-assisted therapy programs for children and families exposed to violence *In* "A Handbook for Therapists, Humane Educators, and Teachers". Latham Foundation, Alameda, CA.

Lord, M. (2001). Morality goes to school. *U.S. News World Rep.* **130**, 50–51.

Martin, F., and Taunton, A. (2004). Center for the study of animal well-being at Sashington State University educates the public about the HCAB. *Latham Lett.* **25**(1), 10–11.

Matoba, M., and Coultis, D. (2004). Fostering cooperation between the United States and Japan: Japanese elementary school program teaches reverence for all life. *Latham Lett.* **25**(4), 12–15.

Melson, G. F. (1988). "Attachment to Pets, Empathy and Self-Concept in Young Children." Presentation at 7th annual Delta Society conference, Orlando, FL.

Melson, G. F. (2001). "Why the Wild Things Are: Animals in the Lives of Children." Harvard University Press, Cambridge, MA.

Merz-Perez, L., and Heide, K. M. (2004). "Animal Cruelty: Pathway to Violence against People." AltaMira Press, Walnut Creek, CA.

Morgan, K. B. (1983). An overview of animal-related organizations with some guidelines for recognizing patterns. *Comm. Anim. Contr.* **2**(2), 18–19.

O'Brien, H. (undated). "An Annotated Bibliography of Research Relevant to Humane Education". National Association for the Advancement of Humane Education, East Haddam, CT.

Poresky, R. H. (1990). The young children's empathy measure: Reliability, validity and effects of companion animal bonding. *Psychol. Rep.* **66**, 931–936.

Ritvo, H. (1987). "The Animal Estate: The English and Other Creatures in the Victorian Age." Harvard University Press, Cambridge, MA.

Robertson, J. (2004). Sex differences in the effects of caring value orientation, pet care experience and pet attachments on animal use attitudes. *In* "Linking Violence: An Interdisciplinary Conference on the Relationship between Violence against Animals and Humans," pp. 15–24. University College of Cape Breton, Sydney, NS, Canada, MA.

Samuels, B. (2004). Learning to care, love and learn: Why we need humane education. *ASPCA Anim. Watch* **24**(2).

San Diego Humane Society and SPCA (2005). Teaching children to respect animals has far-reaching effects. *Anim. Fare* **40**(2), 1.

Saunders, M. (1895). "Beautiful Joe: The Autobiography of a Dog." Jarrold and Sons, London.

Senechalle, J. A., and Dunn, R. M. (2004). University of Illinois students evaluate use and effectiveness of humane education materials. *Latham Lett.* **25**(3), 6–8.

Soltow, W. A., and Shepherd, J. (1992). Justifying humane education as a means to prevent child abuse and other violence. *Shelter Sense*, November, 3.

Tebault, H. (2004). Expectations, June 2004. *Latham Lett.* **25**(3), 4.

Ten Bensel, R. (1984). Historical perspectives of human values for animals and vulnerable people. *In* "The Pet Connection: Its Influence on Our Health and Quality of Life" (R. K. Anderson, B. L. Hart, and L. A. Hart, eds.), pp. 2–14. University of Minnesota/CENSHARE, Minneapolis, MN.

Thomas, S. C., and Beirne, P. (2002). Humane education and humanistic philosophy: Toward a new curriculum. *J. Human. Counsel. Educat. Dev.* **41**, 190–199.

Unti, B., and DeRosa, B. (2003). Humane education past, present, and future. *In* "The State of the Animals II 2003" (D. J. Salem and A. N. Rowan, eds.). Humane Society of the United States, Washington, DC.

Vachss, A. (2004). Foreward. *In* "Children and Animals, Kindness and Cruelty" (F. R. Ascione, ed.). Purdue University Press, West Lafayette, IN.

Vizek-Vidovic, V., Arambasic, L., Kerestes, G., Kuterovac-Jagodic, G., and Vlahovic-Stetic, V. (2001). Pet ownership in childhood and socio-emotional characteristics, work values and professional choices in early adulthood. *Anthrozoös* **14**(4), 224–231.

Weil, Z. (2004). "The Power and Promise of Humane Education." New Society Publishers, Gabriola Island, BC, Canada.

Winiarskyj, L. (2001). Kindness to people and animals: Are the two connected? *KIND Teacher*, September.

Wishnik, Y. (2003). Humane education learning community: A California public charter school. A charter school proposal presented to the governing board of the San Juan Unified School District. California Teachers Association Humane Education Learning Community Charter School Development Team, Citrus Heights, CA.

Wishnik, Y. (2004). Humane-education school set to open. *PsyETA News*, Winter, 3–5. www.animaltherapy.net (2005). Bibliography of materials about animal abuse, child abuse and domestic violence. Accessed July 7, 2005.

Wynne-Tyson, J. (1990). "The Extended Circle: An Anthology of Humane Thought." Sphere Books, London.

Yao, S. (2003). A valuable lesson: SPCALA's humane education department works to break the cycle of violence and abuse. *Latham Lett.* **24**(4), 18–19.

CHAPTER 20

Welfare Considerations in Therapy and Assistance Animals

JAMES A. SERPELL
Department of Clinical Studies, School of Veterinary Medicine, University of Pennsylvania, Philadelphia, Pennsylvania 19104

RAYMOND COPPINGER
Hampshire College, Amherst, Massachusetts 01002

AUBREY H. FINE
College of Education and Integrative Studies, California State Polytechnic University, Pomona, California 91768

I. INTRODUCTION

Throughout history, people have used animals—whether for food, fiber, sport, adornment, labor, or companionship—as a means of satisfying human ends and interests. However, animals also have interests—in avoiding pain, fear, distress, or physical harm and in pursuing their own needs (DeGrazia, 1996). Relations between human and nonhuman animals become morally problematical where there is a conflict of interests between the two: where the human use of the animal either causes the latter pain, fear, or harm or it in some way thwarts or prevents the animal from satisfying its own needs.

Since the mid-1980s, purveyors and proponents of animal-assisted interventions (AAI)[1] such as the Delta Society have made concerted efforts to professionalize the "industry" and establish selection and training standards

[1] Animal-assisted interventions are defined here as "any intervention that intentionally includes or incorporates animals as part of the therapeutic process or milieu" (see Kruger *et al.*, 2004).

that aim to minimize the risks of harm to all concerned, including the animals (Hines and Fredrickson, 1998). However, the field has experienced explosive growth in recent years, and in many cases these standards have been established in the absence of any systematic or empirical evaluation of the potential risks to animals imposed by current practices. Indeed, the general but unsubstantiated feeling across the industry is that these are "good" activities for animals to be engaged in. The fact that a large number of animals fail to respond to the nurturing and training they receive has not generally been taken as evidence that they do not want to, or are unable to, participate. Instead, practitioners tend to respond to failure by changing the selection or the training procedures, as if the animals are theoretically capable of responding positively to any demands made of them. Indeed, with the laudable exception of some contributions to this volume, it is unusual to find more than a passing reference to animal welfare concerns in any recent review of risk factors in the AAI field (see, e.g., Brodie *et al.*, 2002).

Much of the rest of this handbook has been devoted to demonstrating how the use of therapy and assistance animals significantly enhances human health and well-being. The primary question addressed in this chapter is whether this end morally justifies the means of achieving it. Specifically, the goal is to reexamine the animal–human partnership from the animal's viewpoint to see what the benefits might be for the animal or to see if the raising, training, and use of therapy and assistance animals are causing significant degradation in their welfare.[2] In doing so, however, we recognize that there is a serious shortage of reliable scientific evidence to reinforce some of our claims and suggestions.

Behnke (2005) points out that the ability to use ethical judgment and discretion is a defining feature of the helping professions and that arriving at an ethical course of action implies weighing and balancing the values of professional knowledge and realizing that complex situations do not necessarily result in simplistic solutions. With these observations in mind, we urge practitioners and clinicians to examine their ethical responsibilities for the welfare of their therapeutic adjuncts and ensure that the safety and well-being of these animals are safeguarded at all times.

[2] The concept of welfare or "poor" welfare has been variously defined by animal welfare scientists as the presence of unpleasant mental or emotional states such as pain, fear, frustration, or suffering (Dawkins, 1980); as impairments to an animal's biological fitness (Broom and Johnson, 1993; McGlone, 1993); and as the extent to which environmental stresses and strains exceed the animal's ability to cope or adapt (Fraser and Broom, 1980). For the purposes of this chapter, we consider welfare as comprising elements of all three.

II. GENERAL WELFARE CONSIDERATIONS

A. The Five Freedoms

Although different kinds of welfare problems attend the specific roles and activities performed by different classes of therapy or assistance animals, there are some basic welfare considerations that tend to apply to all of them regardless of how they are used. Most authorities accept that these basic considerations are reasonably well summarized by the following "five freedoms," originally formulated by the so-called Brambell report (Command Paper 2836, 1965).

1. Freedom from thirst, hunger, and malnutrition by ready access to fresh water and a diet to maintain full health and vigor.
2. Freedom from discomfort by providing a suitable environment, including shelter and a comfortable resting area.
3. Freedom from pain, injury, and disease by prevention and/or rapid diagnosis and treatment.
4. Freedom from fear and distress by ensuring conditions that avoid mental suffering.
5. Freedom to express most normal behavior by providing sufficient space, proper facilities, and company of the animal's own kind.

Of these "freedoms," the fifth is the probably the hardest to define and the easiest to overlook or ignore. While it is obvious to most people that animals have physical requirements for adequate food, water, protection from the elements, and so on, it is much less widely acknowledged that animals also have social and behavioral needs (Dawkins, 1983; Hughes and Duncan, 1988) and that these needs differ markedly between species (Mendl and Mason, 1993). Understanding animals' social and behavioral needs by primary caregivers is part of the ethical obligation attending animal ownership and use. It is of some concern, therefore, that few practitioners in the AAI field receive adequate ethological training on such matters. Judging the value of a particular behavior or social interaction to an animal may sometimes be difficult. However, in general, if an animal is strongly motivated internally to perform a particular behavior or social interaction and if its motivation to perform appears to increase following a period of deprivation, it is an indication that the activity or interaction is probably important to the maintenance of that animal's welfare. Common indications of deprivation include animals performing abnormally high frequencies of displacement or vacuum[3] activities, repetitive or stereotypic behavior, apathy and prolonged inactivity, and/or self-mutilation (Broom and Johnson, 1993).

In contrast to free-living animals, most therapy and assistance animals are trapped in systems where they have little control over their social lives and where they cannot avoid or escape unwelcome or unpleasant social intrusions. Denying animals control over their physical and social environment is also known to have adverse effects on their physical and mental well-being (Hubrecht *et al.*, 1995).

For service and therapy animals, problems of basic welfare are most likely to arise in circumstances where animals are either residential within health care settings or spend large amounts of time in holding facilities such as kennels or stables. In the former context, inadequate advance planning, selection, and staff commitment and oversight can lead to animals being cared for improperly (Hines and Fredrickson, 1998). Small mammals, birds, and reptiles that are caged or confined are probably at greater risk of neglect or improper care, and nondomestic species that tend to have more specialized requirements than domestic ones are also likely to be at greater risk. "Cared for improperly" in these contexts should have the broadest definition. Most often it is defined as animals that are fed, watered, or cleaned inadequately. However, any failure to attend to individual needs should be regarded as improper care. Overfeeding animals to the point of obesity is just as negligent as underfeeding. Giving an animal the opportunity to exercise or interact with conspecifics is not enough without ensuring that the individual takes advantage of the opportunity.

B. Aging and Retirement Issues

Further welfare challenges arise when therapy and assistance animals begin to age. Many dogs, for instance, display clear evidence of progressive cognitive as well as physical impairment associated with aging, including disorientation, failure to recognize familiar individuals, restlessness, and house soiling (Neilson *et al.*, 2001). Naturally, under these circumstances, an animal's schedule for therapeutic involvement will need to be curtailed. This may cause some

[3] Displacement activities involve the performance of seemingly irrelevant acts, such as grooming, scratching, yawning, or feeding, out of context in situations that excite conflicting motivational tendencies, thwarting, or frustration. A vacuum activity is the performance of a particular behavior pattern in the absence of its normal eliciting stimulus (e.g., sham feeding in the absence of food) (Hinde, 1970).

disruption and adjustment for both the clinician and the animal, although careful planning may help to mitigate this.

C. The Problem of Stress

As defined originally by Selye (1956), stress is the body's natural physiological response to environmental stressors. The processes underlying this stress response are now reasonably well understood: when humans and other animals are subjected to unpleasant or painful stimuli, their bodies respond by secreting a group of hormones from the hypothalamus and the pituitary and adrenal (HPA) glands. These hormones ordinarily serve to prepare the body for so-called fight or flight reactions, and once the emergency is over, hormone secretion generally declines to a normal baseline level. However, under certain circumstances, particularly when the source of pain, anxiety, or distress cannot be avoided or controlled readily, the stress response of the HPA system may become prolonged or "chronic," thereby producing a number of deleterious consequences for the health and welfare of the individual. It is essentially impossible to know precisely what levels of stress an individual is experiencing at any given moment. Instead we are reliant on various indirect measures or "indicators," including levels of stress hormones (cortisol, catecholamines, etc.) in body fluids—blood, saliva, urine, etc.—and outward manifestations of stress involving overt changes in behavior. Behavioral indicators of stress vary greatly between species, and in many they have never been studied or described in any detail. In the dog, studies and anecdotal observations suggest that sweating paws, salivating, panting, muscle tension, restlessness, body shaking, paw lifting, yawning, aggression, hypervigilance, and intensified startle reflex may all be behavioral manifestations of stress (Beerda *et al.*, 1998, 1999; Butler, 2004), whereas in cats, alert inactivity, tense muscle tone, crouching posture, and pupil dilation may be indicative (McCobb *et al.*, 2005).

There are many potential sources of chronic stress in the lives of assistance and therapy animals. Trainers, practitioners, and end users of these animals should be educated to recognize the warning signs and act accordingly. As part of routine veterinary visits and physical examinations, HPA activity should also be monitored regularly.

D. Use of Nondomestic Species

Most domestic animals have been selected to show a higher degree of tolerance of stressful situations and stimuli compared with nondomestic species, even those reared entirely in captivity (Hemmer, 1990). The implications of this are that if a particular animal-assisted intervention or activity is stressful or potentially stressful for a domestic species, such as a dog, cat, or horse, it is likely to be even more so for a nondomestic one. The majority of wild animals kept in captivity also have more specialized nutritional and husbandry needs than their domestic counterparts, greatly increasing the likelihood that they will receive inadequate care unless practitioners, staff, and consulting veterinarians are versed properly in their particular species-specific requirements. Nondomestic species are also harder to train, and their entrained responses extinguish more quickly in the absence of appropriate reinforcement. Some species, such as parrots and many nonhuman primates, are also highly intelligent and socially manipulative (Cheney and Seyfarth, 1990), which tends to make them potentially unreliable or disruptive as social companions. All of these factors render nondomestic species less suitable for use in AAA/T and assistance animal programs and more likely to experience welfare problems if used.

Among therapy animals, this point is well illustrated by the increasing use of parrots in residential settings, such as hospices, long-term care facilities, and correctional institutions. Recent advances in avian medicine, nutrition, and behavior reveal that most of these birds have highly specialized needs relating to air quality, nutrition, lighting, housing, sleep, and both environmental and social enrichment. Because avian wellness and welfare are difficult to maintain in institutional contexts due to a lack of centralized, informed, and consistent care, it should be questioned whether it is ethically appropriate to place birds in these settings at all (Anderson *et al.*, 2005).

Similar concerns are raised by recent efforts to train and use capuchin monkeys (*Cebus* sp.) to assist profoundly disabled people. In most cases, these programs have found it necessary to neuter and surgically extract the canine teeth from the monkeys before they can be used safely with such vulnerable human partners. Monkeys may also be required to wear remote-controlled electric shock collars or harnesses in order to provide the user with a means of controlling their potentially aggressive and unreliable behavior. Clearly, the necessity of using such extreme and invasive measures raises doubts about the practical value of such programs, as well as serious ethical questions concerning the welfare of the animals involved.

III. ANIMALS USED IN THERAPY

Although the boundary may at times seem blurred, particularly with respect to so-called emotional support animals,[4] a reasonably clear distinction exists

[4] See Grubb (2005). http://www.gdui.org/cado.html, Dec. 6, 2005, and http://www.bazelon.org/issues/housing/infosheets/fhinfosheet6.html, Dec. 6, 2005.

between therapy animals and service (or assistance) animals, at least in the United States. However, whereas service animals are relatively strictly defined under federal law [Americans with Disabilities Act (ADA), 1990], therapy animals form a heterogeneous category that can encompass everything from pet visitation to swim with dolphins programs (Iannuzzi and Rowan, 1991). The particular welfare issues confronting therapy animals are therefore correspondingly diverse.

A. Animal Visitation Programs

The majority of therapy animals are personal pets (usually dogs) that, together with their owners, provide supervised visitation programs to hospitals, nursing homes, special-population schools, and other treatment centers (Duncan, 2000). Such animals (and their human partners) are typically certified as being suitable for the task of visiting based on their responses to simplified temperament tests. However, while most such tests evaluate the animal's reaction to acute stressors and its willingness to tolerate intimate or invasive handling by strangers, rarely (if ever) do they attempt to ask the animal if it is actually motivated to interact socially with unfamiliar humans given the choice. As one author on the subject points out, the distinction is a crucial one:

> Nothing else dogs do compares to the kinds of intrinsically stressful social interactions that take place when they visit clinical, educational, or post-trauma situations. No other canine-related event, no sport nor competition requires a dog to enter the intimate zones of unfamiliar humans and remain there for several minutes of petting and hugging. . . . Most dogs have been bred for generations to distinguish between outsiders and the family, and to act accordingly. There has never been a breed of dog designed to enjoy encroachment from strangers. Dogs who actually enjoy interactions in clinical and educational settings are very rare, and the uniqueness of their talent should be appreciated (Butler, 2004, p. 31).

Even if this last sentence might be considered exaggerated by some, the fact remains that visiting animals rarely enter therapeutic settings of their own volition, and many of them are likely to find the experience of being constantly approached and handled by strangers—often strangers with abnormal behavior or demeanor—stressful and/or anxiety provoking. If this is the case with dogs, it is reasonable to conclude that other species used occasionally in visitation programs are even more likely to experience welfare problems. Having said this, however, much will depend on the individual animal's age and developmental experience. In most cases, a properly socialized puppy, exposed frequently to novel persons, dogs, and situations during the formative early weeks and months of its life, will be able to cope with the stresses of therapy and assistance work far better than a dog that has spent most of its early life in a kennel or chained in a yard.

Signs of stress-related fatigue are commonly reported in visiting therapy animals, leading some practitioners to conclude that such visits should be limited to one hour or less (Iannuzzi and Rowan, 1991). As one author notes, "[E]thical handlers develop time frames and environmental policies that allow their dogs to visit only within environments that are comfortable for them, and they leave before, not after, their dogs develop major symptoms of stress" (Butler, 2004, p. 37). Unfortunately, many handlers appear oblivious to the stress signals emitted by their animals, perhaps because they enjoy the social aspects of visitation more than their dogs do.

B. Residential Programs

Although reliable evidence is lacking, the potential for stress-related fatigue or "burnout" in therapy animals is probably greatest among residential programs—prisons, nursing homes, inpatient psychiatric hospitals, long-term care facilities, etc.—where the animals are potentially "on duty" all day, every day of the year (Iannuzzi and Rowan, 1991). Animals housed in residential settings must therefore be provided with adequate "downtime" as well as access to comfortable and safe havens where they can escape entirely from the attentions of residents should they wish to.

While the goals of therapy or rehabilitation may be enhanced by encouraging inmates and residents to participate in the care and training of such animals, it is essential that these activities are supervised appropriately and that one or more staff persons are fully committed to accepting primary responsibility for ensuring the welfare and well-being of the animals. The lack of a clear "chain of command" with respect to animal care responsibilities is the most frequently cited reason why animals' needs are sometimes neglected in residential facilities. Regular, routine veterinary examinations should also be required both to monitor the animals' health and to evaluate their stress status by monitoring HPA activity (Iannuzzi and Rowan, 1991).

The potential for serious animal abuse and cruelty is probably also greatest in residential programs, particularly those based in correctional or psychiatric facilities. Although thankfully rare, occasional cases of outright cruelty to therapy animals have been reported or alluded to in the literature, usually in situations in which the human–animal interactions have not been supervised closely (Doyle, 1975; Levinson, 1971; Mallon, 1994a, b). Once again, this speaks to the necessity of establishing clear and careful guidelines regarding staff oversight and control of all animal-based interventions.

C. Animals in Individual Counseling and Psychotherapy

As in most animal visitation programs, the animals used in individual counseling and therapy are usually the therapists' own pets. The ethical responsibilities and obligations attending this type of AAI are therefore comparable to those attending pet ownership, although with additional risks associated with exposure to potentially unpredictable clients. For obvious reasons, most clinicians would be ill-advised to employ any animal as a cotherapist unless they are already very familiar with, and confident about, its particular characteristics and temperament and possess sufficient knowledge, time, and resources to ensure that its welfare needs can be accommodated at all times.

Budding animal-assisted therapists should also be cautious about how animals are introduced to their clients. They should make a special point at the outset of therapy to discuss with patients the importance of demonstrating kindness to the animals and of avoiding behavior that might disturb or frighten them, such as sudden or erratic movements, loud noises, or overvigorous physical interactions. Animals should never be placed in any situations where they could be at risk either physically or emotionally. This kind of orientation sets the stage for proper integration of the animal in a safe therapeutic partnership based on mutual respect.

D. "Ecotherapy"

Along with the expanding popularity of ecotourism, the idea of restoring human health through contact with nature—or "ecotherapy"— is acquiring a growing following among alternative and complementary therapists. While in many such programs therapy involves contributing directly to wildlife rehabilitation or conservation projects, others promote recreational contact with wild animals, chiefly dolphins and other cetaceans, in natural, seminatural, or captive settings (Burls and Caan, 2005). So-called dolphin swim programs of various kinds are proliferating worldwide at an alarming rate, and because the majority are based in developing countries, they are largely unregulated from an animal welfare perspective.[5] Several detailed studies have documented serious risks to the welfare and survival of cetaceans involved in these programs, particularly those involving captive animals that must be captured in the wild and, in some cases, transported for thousands

[5] http://www.onevoice-ear.org/english/campaigns/marine_mammals/victory_caribbean.html, Dec. 6, 2005. http://csiwhalesalive.org/csi05303.html, Dec. 6, 2005.

of miles to established aquaria (Samuels *et al.*, 2000; Samuels and Bejder, 2004). Given the high costs and limited evidence of therapeutic efficacy of dolphin swim programs (Humphries, 2003; Marino and Lilienfeld, 1998), it is difficult to find any ethical justification at all for supporting these kinds of interventions.

IV. SERVICE/ASSISTANCE ANIMALS

The Americans with Disabilities Act (1990) defines a service animal as any guide dog, signal dog, or other animal individually trained to provide assistance to an individual with a disability. If they meet this definition, animals are considered service animals under the ADA regardless of whether they have been licensed or certified by a state or local government. Service animals typically perform some of the functions and tasks that the individual with a disability cannot perform for him- or herself (e.g., guiding people with impaired vision, alerting persons with hearing impairments to sounds, pulling wheelchairs, carrying and picking up things for persons with mobility impairments, and assisting persons with mobility impairments with balance). Because of their relatively specialized functions, assistance animals are subjected to a more refined level of "processing" (e.g., controlled breeding, rearing, selection, and training) compared with the average therapy animal, which creates a set of particular welfare problems that are more or less unique to this class of animals.

A. Changes in Social and Physical Environment

The life cycle of the typical assistance animal generally involves a series of relatively abrupt changes in its social and physical environment. For such sociable and sensitive animals as dogs, these disruptions may give rise to welfare problems—a good example being the practice of rearing guide and service dogs in the enriched environment of a human foster home and then kenneling them individually for months at a time as part of their final training (Hubrecht and Turner, 1998). Such sudden and extreme changes in the animals' social and physical milieu appear to be highly stressful for some individuals (Coppinger and Zuccotti, 1999), not only affecting their immediate welfare but also potentially fostering obnoxious behaviors that may preclude successful training and placement later in life.

Assistance animals may also be at risk because of the changing nature of their relationships with successive human owners and handlers throughout their lives. Most of these animals are picked because they seek out social interactions with others and because they form strong bonds of attachment for their human partners. Having to endure a succession of different handlers with different characteristics, experience, and motivations for "ownership" is likely to be particularly stressful for these individuals. Unfortunately, many assistance animal practitioners have little firsthand knowledge of animal needs other than hygienic veterinary or training considerations, and with many agencies there is confusion as to who is responsible for the animals' social requirements. The organizations keeping and rearing these animals should recognize their ethical obligations by doing everything possible to minimize the distress caused by these difficult transitions.

B. Selecting and Breeding Animals for Assistance Work

Not all domestic animal species are practical for becoming assistance animals. Without belaboring the point, it would be difficult to conceive of a guiding cat or a hearing ear donkey. In practice, dogs may be the only domestic species that can be trained reliably to perform a wide variety of household tasks for a disabled person, but within the dog population as a whole there is considerable individual variation in the suitability of dogs for this type of work.

Some assistance dogs, such as hearing ear dogs, are often obtained from animal shelters, partly out of a desire to rescue some of these otherwise forsaken animals. Recycling animals relinquished to shelters clearly has a beneficial welfare impact. Some practitioners, however, doubt the reliability of these reconditioned pets, fearing that latent unacceptable behavior will emerge and cause injury to the person using the animal (Weiss and Greenberg, 1997). About half of all assistance animal agencies currently rely on shelter dogs, although identifying suitable dogs among the 4 to 5 million relinquished each year is a major problem. Hearing ear and therapy dogs are perhaps the easiest to locate, as there are no size restrictions, but it is important to identify the animal before the abandonment and confinement process has a permanent damaging effect on its personality (Coppinger and Coppinger, 2001). Agencies using these dogs often have a prescribed test that the dog is required to pass in order to be accepted into a program (e.g., Weiss and Greenberg, 1997). However, personnel vary widely in their ability to interpret test results, and few of the tests have been validated properly (Weiss, 2002). Given the industry's need for qualified dogs, and the ethical benefits of using shelter animals, there is considerable room for improvement in the identification and distribution of serviceable animals from shelters.

In-house breeding programs are favored by guide dog and wheelchair dog organizations. Both kinds of agencies will also purchase dogs and accept donated dogs. The primary reason for producing and buying dogs is to obtain animals of relatively uniform size. It is not necessarily that other breeds are temperamentally unsuited, but the task to be performed requires a dog with particular physical characteristics. Within the industry, most of the emphasis is on just three breeds: Labrador retrievers, German shepherds, and golden retrievers. Recently, more interest has also been shown in using crossbred retrievers.

The vast majority of our modern sporting and working dogs originated from the results of random matings accomplished by the animals themselves and accompanied by postzygotic culling of unwanted animals. Just prior to the beginning of the 20th century, breeds were created by hybridizing strains in order to achieve working excellence. In the 19th century, a shift toward prezygotic selection began, which has intensified ever since. The assumption behind this process is that excellence of form and behavior can be purified and preserved within a breed. Unfortunately, although such breeding practices do tend to produce uniformity of appearance and behavior within breeds, in the absence of periodic outcrossing, dogs generated by these systems tend to be more vulnerable to infectious disease, as well as being more likely to show inbreeding depression and the phenotypic expression of deleterious mutant alleles. Overall, these kinds of issues raise doubts about the wisdom of maintaining exclusively purebred strains of dogs for assistance work.

In some agencies there is considerable attention paid to inbreeding depression, but it is mostly in terms of how to slow the rate rather than discussions of how to prevent it. There has been some suggestion that sharing breeding stock between agencies could revitalize inbred stock. Progress made at one agency at eliminating genetic defects could then be helpful to other breeders.

C. The Importance of Early Development

There is confusion among many assistance animal programs concerning the difference among genetic, environmental, and developmental effects. The embryological definition of development is the interaction between a gene and its environment (Serpell, 1989). Therefore, a dog with the condition known as hip dysplasia is a product of an inherited (genetic) predisposition interacting with the environment at various stages in its development. Precisely the same is true of behavior. It is well established from research on canid development that early experiences have more profound and longer-lasting effects on behavior than those occurring at later stages of the life cycle (Serpell and Jagoe, 1995). It is not difficult to understand why. When a German shepherd puppy is born, it has a brain volume of about 8 cm^3, and at this stage it has all the brain cells it is ever going to have. By 8 weeks its brain has grown to 80 cm^3, and by 16 weeks the brain is approaching its adult size of 120 cm^3. Because the brain increases 15 times in volume during this short period but maintains the same cell number, most of the growth is clearly occurring due to the development of connections between the cells. This matrix of cells is constructed during the first 16 weeks in response to electrical stimulation and activity patterns. How the animal moves, what it perceives with its senses, and the kinds of stresses it endures all determine the pattern of growth of the connective matrix. Human children growing up in orphanages not only have smaller brains (not as many connections) than "normal" children, but they do not show the same electrical patterning, even though they presumably have the same number of brain cells. This is what is meant by a developmental effect—a synergism between genes and the environment.

In the sense that they tend to insulate puppies from varied stimuli, many breeding kennels for assistance dogs may be equivalent to orphanages. Although kennel workers are very good at keeping puppies clean and healthy, it would probably be fair to say that few are familiar with the profound effects of early environment on brain development. Why is it that a substantial proportion of agency-bred dogs are unable to perform the tasks assigned to them? Is it because of genetic flaws, or is it because of the developmental effects of spending the first eight weeks in an impoverished environment? If it is the latter, then the "industry" may be predisposing puppies to be ill-equipped to cope with the demands made on them later in life. The behavioral result of environmental impoverishment during this critical period is relatively permanent. Depending on how the dog was wired in those early sensitive periods largely predetermines how it will behave as an adult.

Agencies and programs raising animals for service have a duty to ensure that the animals they produce are correctly prepared for their adult roles. At every stage of growth and development, dogs should be shaped and molded to perform their adult tasks. If particular tasks are required of an assistance dog (e.g., turning on a light), then the puppy's developmental exposure should prepare it for such a task. Food boxes could require similar tasks in such a way that the dog achieves a cognitive awareness of what is being performed. How dogs handle novel situations and stimuli is another major cause of rejection. A fearful dog cannot be trained to deal with novelty. For example, sidewalk grates that are common in cities may be an insurmountable problem for a dog. Many such problems might be eliminated by paying attention to the early (4–16 week) developmental environment.

If early rearing is done properly, a dog might even learn to enjoy performing its work simply because it has developed the cognitive ability to transcend operant conditioning and understand what it is doing and why. However, the "industry" may also have to face the morally uncomfortable possibility that the only way to raise a "good" assistance dog is to raise it in a deprived environment. It may be that the most successful dogs are products of particular kinds of environmental impoverishment and that the more cognitively developed animals are actually ill-suited to perform this kind of repetitive and tedious daily work (Coppinger and Coppinger, 2001).

D. Use of Inappropriate or Aversive Training Methods

The underlying assumption of operant conditioning is that any animal can learn any performance by external reward or external punishment. For example, a moving animal is rewarded for going in the correct direction and punished for going in the wrong direction. There is a lengthy and complex literature on when, how much, and how often the animal should be rewarded or punished and about what is actually reinforced. This is essentially the learning paradigm used to train many assistance animals, but two important elements are often missing. First, one of the reasons dogs have been so successful as companions is that they are prepared to work for the reward of social interaction with people. Second, because particular dog breeds innately "like" to search for game or to herd sheep, it is not essential to reward such performances. Working dog specialists generally consider it impossible to train an animal that does not show the internal motivation to perform the specific task. Furthermore, most traditional working dog trainers do not use aversive conditioning as the primary training strategy. Nor do they need to. Dogs tend to "sour" with aversive conditioning, and because many performances depend on stamina and willingness to work, dog trainers avoid associating performance with any form of punishment. On a sled dog team, severe punishment might be used to stop a dog fight, but no experienced driver would attempt to persuade a dog to run by punishing it (Coppinger and Coppinger, 2001).

In contrast, aversive conditioning is the primary method of instruction for many assistance dogs. It may be the only method that is practical, as many assistance dog tasks are not discrete; nor is the significance of the task necessarily understood by the dog. "Find the bird" is a discrete task, regardless of how long it takes. It has a beginning and an end of which the dog is aware. Pulling a wheelchair is fundamentally different because there is no intrinsic reward nor is it socially facilitated in the manner, say, of a sled dog performing with other dogs. Tasks like these are difficult to reward because performance is an ongoing event. You cannot reward the cessation of activity at the end of the pull, and punishment is equally inappropriate (Coppinger *et al.*, 1998). There has recently been much interest in "click and treat" training methodologies as trainers adapt the ideas of Pavlov and Skinner specifically to dogs. This approach has been shown to be effective in training some assistance dogs and is used extensively in hearing dogs and therapy dogs. The training of wheelchair and guide dogs has not kept up with these modern techniques to the same extent, and this is an area that is ripe for experimentation on ways of eliminating the more aversive and protracted procedures currently employed.

E. Unrealistic Expectations

Assistance animals are expected to obey complex commands and perform relatively challenging physical activities that also create a potential for welfare problems. In one study, Coppinger *et al.* (1998) were critical of the unrealistic expectations that some assistance dog programs have of their protégés. Superficially simple activities, such as pulling a wheelchair or opening a swing door, may impose excessive physical strains on a dog that could result in physical injury over time. Furthermore, because the tasks themselves are potentially aversive and because the dogs have not been specifically selected for performing these tasks the way most traditional working dogs have, they lack any internal motivation to perform and may, as a consequence, have difficulty meeting the goals of conventional reward-based training or retaining responses once they have been entrained (Coppinger *et al.*, 1998).

F. Use of Poorly Designed Equipment and Facilities

By analyzing the "physics" of some of the tasks that service dogs are asked to perform, Coppinger *et al.* (1998) drew attention to inherent design flaws in some of the equipment used by disabled persons that may result in discomfort or injury to the dogs. Harnesses, for example, suggested that the designers did not understand the basic principles of harness design. Some had pulling webs crossing moving parts, thus chafing the dog badly as it moved. Trying to get a dog to pull a wheelchair that is designed to be pushed forces the dog into awkward positions, thereby increasing the difficulty of the task. Some of the tasks, such as pulling a wheelchair or pulling open a door with the teeth, reach the limits of what a dog is physically able to perform.

Various studies have also been critical of conventional kennel housing for dogs, most of which has been designed to reduce labor costs and facilitate hygiene rather than designed with the welfare of the animals in mind. Kennels used to house service dogs during training are often cell-like in appearance, with opaque barriers separating adjacent pens. Dogs are usually housed singly or, less often, in pairs, and often there is little in the way of toys or other forms of enrichment to relieve the tedium of kennel existence. Dogs housed in these sorts of conditions for long periods display a range of abnormal, repetitive, or "stereotypic" behavior, such as circling, pacing, "wall bouncing," and barking (Fox, 1965; Hite *et al.*, 1977; Hubrecht *et al.*, 1992; Hughes *et al.*, 1989; Sales *et al.*, 1997). Noise levels from barking in some facilities may also be sufficiently loud to cause permanent damage to dogs' hearing (Sales *et al.*, 1997).

V. END-USER PROBLEMS

Although there have been few systematic studies of the problem, anecdotal observations suggest that some therapy and assistance animal users may have negative attitudes toward animals or be insufficiently experienced with handling or training them. As a consequence, the people are likely to derive less satisfaction and therapeutic benefit from the animals (Lane *et al.*, 1998), and the animals may be ignored or neglected, given inappropriate or ill-timed commands, punished for failing to respond to these commands, rewarded at inappropriate times, and so on (Coppinger *et al.*, 1998; Iannuzzi and Rowan, 1991). Not surprisingly, animals may become confused and apathetic as a result of such inept handling, and the problems are likely to multiply with the use of less trainable and more socially manipulative species such as nonhuman primates. Some agencies provide refresher courses for their clients or can send a trainer to the person's home to correct special problems. However, greater continuing education efforts by agencies would certainly help ensure improved quality of life for animals used in this way.

The issue of continuing education is also a significant concern for clinicians applying AAA/T in their own practices. As stated in earlier chapters, although clinicians may be very cognizant of treatment goals with their clients, they may be in need of further training on how to incorporate animals into their practice (therapeutically and safely). Hines and Frederickson (1998) point out that without training on how animal interactions impact various user groups, therapists may incorporate inappropriate animals and procedures that fail to maximize treatment outcomes. The Pet Partners Program developed by the Delta Society includes in-service training in a variety of areas, including an awareness of health and skill aptitude of the animals, as well as strategies to incorporate the animals with the clients. The Pet Partners Program should be considered a valuable introductory course for practitioners in this field. Educational programs should be interdisciplinary in nature and must combine sound theory along with good practical training. Topics that should be covered include ethology and human–animal interactions, the psychosocial benefits of animals as social support providers, and risk management concerns (Turner, 1999).

Clinicians will also be able to find continuing education opportunities at conferences and workshops sponsored by organizations such as the International Association of Human–Animal Interaction Organizations,[6] the International Society for Anthrozoology,[7] and the Delta Society.[8] Further opportunities may also be available at conferences and workshops sponsored by local and regional humane societies, as well as many other professional organizations interested in the therapeutic utility of human–animal interactions.

VI. CONCLUSIONS AND RECOMMENDATIONS

The concept of using trained and socialized animals to assist people with disabilities or as therapeutic adjuncts has great intrinsic appeal, exemplifying, as it does for many people, the ultimate in mutually beneficial animal–human partnerships. Nevertheless, while the advantages to the humans in these relationships may be obvious, the benefits to the animals are by no means always self-evident. Indeed, the use of animals for animal-assisted activities and therapy imposes a unique set of stresses and strains on them that the "industry" has only begun to acknowledge recently.

This chapter has tried to identify a number of potential sources or causes of animal welfare problems in AAA/T and assistance work. In doing so, it is not our intention to criticize particular programs or practitioners but rather to focus attention on specific practices that may give rise to ethical concerns and that should therefore be subjected to further scrutiny and study. This is, after all, a new field of animal exploitation, and a certain number of "growing pains" are only to be expected.

While it is still in its early days and much of what can be said is necessarily somewhat speculative, the following preliminary recommendations are appropriate.

1. Those involved in preparing or using animals for service and therapy need to educate themselves regarding the particular social and behavioral needs of these animals, both to avoid the consequences of social and behavioral deprivation and to permit animals a degree of control over the levels of social and environmental stimulation they receive.

[6] http://www.iahaio.org/
[7] http://www.vetmed.ucdavis.edu/CCAB/isaz.htm
[8] http://www.deltasociety.org/

2. AAI practitioners need to understand that close physical contact with strangers may be inherently stressful for many animals and recognize the signs of stress when they appear. Ideally, visitation and therapy sessions should be terminated before, rather than after, such symptoms are manifested.
3. In residential programs, one or more staff persons should be held primarily accountable for the care and welfare of any therapy animal and for supervising all interactions with inmates/residents. No animal should be left unsupervised in a situation where its welfare might reasonably be considered at risk.
4. Nondomestic species should not be used for AAA/T or assistance work except under exceptional circumstances (e.g., wildlife rehabilitation) and where appropriate care can be guaranteed.
5. On the basis of current evidence, so-called dolphin swim programs cannot be ethically justified.
6. During the process of rearing and training assistance animals, transitions between successive handlers or owners should be carried out in such a way as to cause minimal distress due to the disruption of preexisting social bonds.
7. Efforts and resources should be dedicated to developing methods of accurately identifying and distributing suitable assistance animals from among those relinquished to animal shelters. These efforts should include research into appropriate behavioral screening methods.
8. The present level of assistance dog "failure" is ethically unacceptable and needs to be reduced. The "industry" should be more aware of the problems inherent in the use of closed purebred populations of service and assistance dogs. The potential benefits of outcrossing to other populations and of crossbreeding should be explored to reduce the prevalence of deleterious genetic diseases, as well as improving infectious disease resistance.
9. The "industry" should give more attention to ensuring that assistance and service animals are prepared adequately during development for the tasks and roles assigned to them as adults.
10. Alternatives to the use of aversive conditioning in the training of assistance animals need to be investigated and developed wherever possible, particularly with respect to the training of wheelchair dogs. If necessary, the "industry" should consider discontinuing the use of animals for particular purposes if alternatives to aversive conditioning cannot be found.
11. More attention should be given to the design and construction of animal-friendly equipment and holding facilities for AAA/T and assistance animals.

12. Continuing education programs for animal practitioners and end users should be available to ensure that animals are handled, cared for, and used correctly.

To assist in organizing some of our thoughts pertaining to the psychosocial concerns and needs of therapy animals, an Appendix has been formulated to identify specific guidelines for consideration. These guidelines are pertinent to services provided in large-scale institutionally based programs as well as small clinical practices.

APPENDIX: ETHICAL GUIDELINES FOR THE CARE AND SUPERVISION OF ANIMALS WHILE UTILIZED IN AAT OR AAA

Goal: Incorporating animals therapeutically to assist human clients.
Issue: How to balance the needs of human clients with respect for the needs of the animals.

Basic Ethics Principles for Use of the Therapy Animal

1. All animals utilized therapeutically must be kept free from abuse, discomfort, and distress, both physical and mental.
2. Proper health care for the animal must be provided at all times.
3. All animals should have access to a quiet place where they can have time away from their work activities. Clinicians must practice preventative health procedures for all animals.
4. Interactions with clients must be structured so as to maintain the animal's capacity to serve as a useful therapeutic agent.
5. A situation of abuse or stress for a therapy animal should never be allowed except in such cases where temporarily permitting such abuse is necessary to avoid a serious injury to, or abuse of, the human client.

Procedures for Ethical Decision Making Regarding Therapy Animals

1. Identify the human needs: What does the client need from the therapy animal, how much time does the client need to spend with the animal, and what is the nature of the contact/time spent with the animal?

2. Identify the animal's most basic needs: proper care, affection, and quiet time.
3. Compare the human and animal needs: only the most compelling of human needs (e.g., avoiding serious mental or physical injury) should ever be allowed to take priority over the basic needs of the animal.

Implications of Procedure for Ethical Decision Making Regarding Therapy Animals

1. If the intervention is unduly stressing the animal, the clinician should suspend the session or the interaction.
2. Therapists using therapy animals must provide downtime for the animal several times a day.
3. Animals that due to age are unduly stressed, should have their service scaled back or eliminated entirely. Attention should also be given to transition the animal as s/he begins to retire. This will help with the animal's sense of wellness.
4. In a situation where a client, whether intentionally or unintentionally, subjects a therapy animal to abuse, the basic needs of the animal must be respected, even if this means terminating the animal's relationship with the client. In a case where a therapist suspects that a client may be likely to abuse the animal, a therapist must take precautions to protect the animal's welfare. When any evidence of stress or abuse becomes evident, the therapist must terminate the animal's relationship with the client.
5. Clients who severely abuse a therapy animal may thereby destroy the animal's capacity to help others. Clients in this situation thus violate principle 4.

REFERENCES

Anderson, P. K., Coultis, D., and Welle, K. R. (2003). Avian wellness: The proper care of birds in institutional settings. International Society for Anthrozoology Conference, Canton, OH, 2003.

Beerda, B., Schilder, M. B. H., Van Hooff, J. A. R. A. M., De Vries, H. W., and Mol, J. A. (1998). Behavioural, saliva cortisol and heart rate responses to different types of stimuli in dogs. *Appl. Anim. Behav. Sci.* **58**, 365–381.

Beerda, B., Schilder, M. B. H., Van Hooff, J. A. R. A. M., De Vries, H. W., and Mol, J. A. (1999). Chronic stress in dogs subjected to social and spatial restriction. 1. Behavioral responses. *Physiol. Behav.* **66**, 233–242.

Behnke, S. (2005). Reflecting on how we teach ethics. *Monit. Psychol.* **36**, 64–65.

Brodie, S. J., Biley, F. C., and Shewring, M. (2002). An exploration of the potential risks associated with using pet therapy in healthcare settings. *J. Clin. Nurs.* **11**, 444–456.

Broom, D. M., and Johson, K. (1993). "Stress and Animal Welfare." Chapman and Hall, London.

Burls, A., and Caan, W. (2005). Human health and nature conservation. *Br. Med. J.* **331**, 1221–1222.

Butler, K. (2004). "Therapy Dogs Today: Their Gifts, Our Obligation." Funpuddle Publishing, Norman, OK.

Cheney, D. L., and Seyfarth, R. M. (1990). "How Monkeys See the World." Chicago University Press, Chicago, IL.

Coppinger, R., and Coppinger, L. (2001). "Dogs: A Startling New Understanding of Canine Origin, Behavior and Evolution." Scribner, New York.

Coppinger, R., Coppinger, L., and Skillings, E. (1998). Observations on assistance dog training and use. *J. Appl. Anim. Welf. Sci.* **1**, 133–144.

Coppinger, R., and Schneider, R. (1995). Evolution of working dogs. *In* "The Domestic Dog: Its Evolution, Behaviour, and Interactions with People"(J. A. Serpell, ed.), pp. 21–47. Cambridge Press, Cambridge, MA.

Coppinger, R., and Zuccotti, J. (1999). Kennel enrichment: Exercise and socialization of dogs. *J. Appl. Anim. Welf. Sci.* **2**, 281–296.

Dawkins, M. (1980). "Animal Suffering: The Science of Animal Welfare." Chapman and Hall, London.

Dawkins, M. (1983). Battery hens name their price: Consumer demand theory and the measurement of behavioural needs. *Anim. Behav.* **31**, 1195–1205.

Dawkins, M. S. (1988). Behavioural deprivation: A central problem in animal welfare. *Appl. Anim. Behav. Sci.* **20**, 209–225.

DeGrazia, D. (1996). "Taking Animals Seriously: Mental Life and Moral Status." Cambridge University Press, Cambridge, MA.

Doyle, M. C. (1975). Rabbit: Therapeutic prescription. *Perspect. Psychiatr. Care* **13**, 79–82.

Duncan, S. L. (2000). APIC state-of-the-art report: The implications of service animals in health care settings. *Am. J. Infect. Contr.* **28**, 170–180.

Fox, M. (1965). Environmental factors influencing stereotyped and allelomimetic behavior in animals. *Lab. Anim. Care* **15**(5), 363–370.

Hemmer, H. (1990). "Domestication: The Decline of Environmental Appreciation." Cambridge University Press, Cambridge, MA.

Hinde, R. A. (1970). "Animal Behaviour: A Synthesis of Ethology and Comparative Psychology," 2nd Ed. McGraw-Hill, London.

Hines, L., and Fredrickson, M. (1998). Perspectives on animal-assisted activities and therapy. *In* "Companion Animals in Human Health"(C. C. Wilson and D. C. Turner, eds.), pp. 23–39. Sage, Thousand Oaks, CA.

Hite, M., Hanson, H., Bohidar, N., Conti, P., and Mattis, P. (1977). Effect of cage size on patterns of activity and health of beagle dogs. *Lab. Anim. Sci.* **27**, 60–64.

Hubrecht, R. (1993). A comparison of social and environmental enrichment methods for laboratory housed dogs. *Appl. Anim. Behav. Sci.* **37**, 345–361.

Hubrecht, R. (1995). The welfare of dogs in human care. *In* "The Domestic Dog: Its Evolution, Behaviour, and Interactions with People" (J. Serpell, ed.), pp. 179–195. Cambridge Press, Cambridge, MA.

Hubrect, R., Serpell, J., and Poole, T. (1992). Correlates of pen size and housing conditions on the behaviour of kenneled dogs. *Appl. Anim. Behav. Sci.* **34**, 365–383.

Hubrecht, R., and Turner, D. C. (1998). Companion animal welfare in private and institutional settings. *In* "Companion Animals in Human Health" (C. C. Wilson and D. C. Turner, eds.), pp. 267–289. Sage, Thousand Oaks, CA.

Hughes, B. O., and Duncan, I. J. H. (1988). The notion of ethological needs, models of motivation and animal welfare. *Anim. Behav.* **36**, 1696–1707.

Hughes, H. C., Campbell, S., and Kenney, C. (1989). The effects of cage size and pair housing on exercise of beagle dogs. *Lab. Anim. Sci.* **39**(4), 302–305.

Humphries, T. L. (2003). Effectiveness of dolphin-assisted therapy as a behavioral intervention for young children with disabilities. *Bridges* **1**, 1–9.

Iannuzzi, D., and Rowan, A. N. (1991). Ethical issues in animal-assisted therapy programs. *Anthrozoös* 4, 154–163.

Lane, D. R., McNicholas, J., and Collis, G. M. (1998). Dogs for the disabled: Benefits to recipients and welfare of the dog. *Appl. Anim. Behav. Sci.* **59**, 49–60.

Levinson, B. M. (1971). Household pets in training schools serving delinquent children. *Psychol. Rep.* **28**, 475–481.

Mallon, G. P. (1994a). Cow as co-therapist: Utilization of farm animals as therapeutic aides with children in residential treatment. *Child Adolesc. Soc. Work J.* **11**(6), 455–474.

Mallon, G. P. (1994b). Some of our best therapists are dogs. *Child Youth Care Forum* **23**(2), 89–101.

Marino, L., and Lilienfeld, S. O. (1998). Dolphin-assisted therapy: Flawed data, flawed conclusions. *Anthrozoös* **11**, 194–200.

Mason, G., and Mendl, M. (1993). Why is there no simple way of measuring animal welfare? *Anim. Welf.* **2**, 301–320.

McCobb, E. C., Patronek, G. J., Marder, A., Dinnage, J. D., and Stone, M. S. (2005). Assessment of stress levels among cats in four animal shelters. *J. Am. Vet. Med. Assoc.* **226**, 548–555.

McGlone, J. (1993). What is animal welfare? *J. Agricult. Environ. Ethics* **6**(Suppl. 2), 28.

Neilson, J. C., Hart, B. L., Cliff, K. D., and Ruehl, W. W. (2001). Prevalence of behavioral changes associated with age-related cognitive impairment in dogs. *J. Am. Vet. Med. Assoc.* **218**, 1787–1791.

Sales, G., Hubrecht, R., Peyvandi, A., Milligan, S., and Shield, B. (1997). Noise in dog kennelling: Is barking a welfare problem for dogs? *Appl. Anim. Behav. Sci.* **52**, 321–329.

Samuels, A., and Bejder, L. (2004). Chronic interaction between humans and free-ranging bottlenose dolphins near Panama City Beach, Florida, USA. *J. Cetacean Res. Manag.* **6**, 69–77.

Samuels, A., Bejder, L., and Heinrich, S. (2000). "A Review of the Literature Pertaining to Swimming with Wild Dolphins" (Contract Number T74463123). Marine Mammal Commission, Bethesda, MD.

Serpell, J. A. (1987). The influence of inheritance and environment on canine behaviour: Myth and fact. *J. Small Anim. Pract.* **28**, 949–956.

Serpell, J., and Jagoe, J. A. (1995). Early experience and the development of behaviour. *In* "The Domestic Dog: Its Evolution, Behaviour, and Interactions with People" (J. A. Serpell, ed.), pp. 80–102. Cambridge University Press, Cambridge, MA.

Turner, D. (1999). The future of education and research on the human–animal bond and animal assisted therapy. *In* "Handbook on Animal-Assisted Therapy: Theoretical Foundations and Guidelines for Practice" (A. H. Fine, ed.). Academic Press, New York.

Weiss, E. (2002). Selecting shelter dogs for service dog training. *J. Appl. Anim. Welf. Sci.* **5**, 43–62.

Weiss, E., and Greenberg, G. (1997). Service dog selection tests: Effectiveness for dogs from animal shelters. *Appl. Anim. Behav. Sci.* **53**, 297–308.

CHAPTER 21

Role of the Veterinary Family Practitioner in Animal-Assisted Therapy and Animal-Assisted Activity Programs

RICHARD TIMMINS

Center for Animals in Society, School of Veterinary Medicine, University of California, Davis, California 95616

AUBREY H. FINE

College of Education and Integrative Studies, California State Polytechnic University, Pomona, California 91768

I. THE ORIGIN OF VETERINARY FAMILY PRACTICES

The evolution of the relationship between humans and companion animals has had a marked effect on the practice of veterinary medicine during the past few decades. A prime indicator of the changing role of pets in human society is the extent to which humans have welcomed companion animals into their homes. One survey reported that 85% of pet owners considered their pet a member of the family (Brown and Silverman, 1999).

Historically, the legal status of animals supported society's perception of animals as chattel, considered primarily in terms of their economic value. That perception is changing. Some communities seek to alter that status through statutes (e.g., replacing the term "pet owner" with the word "guardian" or outlawing certain procedures perceived to be inhumane) (Fiala, 2005; Sapperfield, 2002). The courts are confirming the noneconomic value of animals, issuing awards to pet owners for suffering and loss of companionship (Fiala, 2004; Lofflin, 2004). As the emotional attachment to companion animals becomes stronger, veterinary clients demand technologically advanced health care for their pets and show an increasing willingness to spend more money to

Handbook on Animal-Assisted Therapy: Theoretical Foundations and Guidelines for Practice, 2e

TABLE I Objectives of Veterinary Family Practice

- Serve as a community resource for information about the well-being of animals.
- Advocate for the physical health and the emotional well-being of companion animals in the context of their roles in the family and in society.
- Develop a lifelong health plan for individual patients, taking into account genetics, environmental exposures, and functional expectations.
- Provide preventive and therapeutic medical and surgical services to patients, referring to specialists when appropriate.
- Provide information and resources to help clients manage the health and well-being of their pets.

maintain the health of their animal companions (Grieve *et al.*, 2003). The veterinary profession has responded with a revolution in medical and surgical technology and knowledge. In urban and suburban America, the number and type of veterinary specialty services offered have grown dramatically in the past few decades.

The need to advocate for the well-being of animals in the context of their roles in the family necessitates specific skills and knowledge. Some of these are not currently taught in most schools or colleges of veterinary medicine (e.g., life stage health management, attachment issues, risk assessment, and community outreach). Special expertise is required in other topics of study that can often be found in the veterinary curriculum, including behavior, nutrition, clinical genetics, and preventative medicine. Enhanced interpersonal skills are also essential. The need to identify and teach these concepts has resulted in the development of the discipline of veterinary family practice. Through veterinary school coursework or continuing education, the veterinary family practitioner (VFP) seeks to acquire the skills and knowledge necessary to meet the objectives of veterinary family practice, as described in Table I.

II. ROLE OF VETERINARIANS IN ANIMAL-ASSISTED THERAPY (AAT)/ANIMAL-ASSISTED ACTIVITY (AAA)

Often, the most important role identified for veterinarians in AAT/AAA programs is ". . . the need for careful behavioral and medical (zoonotic) screening of animals . . ." (Johnson and Meadows, 2000). The American Veterinary Medical Association (2001) expands this role in the wellness guidelines for animals used in AAA, AAT, and resident animal programs. These guidelines recommend that the veterinarian should work closely with the individual with primary responsibility for the animal, the therapist, and a qualified behaviorist to develop a wellness plan that will enhance the health and welfare of the animal. The guidelines also state that "Total wellness encompasses the physical and behavioral attributes of the animal, as well as the characteristics of interaction between people and animals participating in the program." This is in accordance with the concept of veterinary family practice, in which the veterinarian is an active member of a team that includes the hospital staff, the pet owner, and area specialists, all of whom are focused on the well-being of the pet. A major aspect of well-being is enabling the pet to perform a particular function effectively without stress or discomfort. When the function is participation in an AAT or AAA program, the VFP can be a valuable partner with the therapist and the individual responsible for the care of the animal. The following discussion assumes that the therapist is the individual responsible.

A. Animal Selection

The first opportunity for the VFP to facilitate the work of the therapist is to counsel the therapist on the species or breed of animal appropriate for the therapeutic objectives. It is important that the therapist be specific about the work expected of the animal during therapy. A discussion of these expectations will lead to identifying the characteristics essential to therapeutic success. A list of possible expectations can be found in Table II.

TABLE II Possible Expectations of Animals Employed in AAT

1. Provide an atmosphere of acceptance.
2. Offer a nonjudgmental social interaction.
3. Reinforce a sense of responsibility and accountability in the patient.
4. Induce a calm, nonstressful environment.
5. Provide reassurance to patients in difficult moments.
6. Follow directions from therapist to interact with patients in specific ways.
7. Act as a model of positive behavior.
8. Act as a sounding board to some clients.
9. Assist the therapist in developing rapport with the client.
10. Support the therapist in establishing limits in a session. The animal will act as a calming agent.
11. The animal will need to follow very simple directions and commands. It is imperative that the animal–human team is in tandem so the attention is given to the client(s).
12. The animal's behavior must be reliable. Younger animals and those that are active will have a hard time in a therapeutic setting.
13. Some animals will be involved in taking therapeutic walks with clients. The behavior of the selected animals must be reliable. The animals have to be able to handle the sounds and be comfortable navigating throughout the community.
14. When involved in group settings, a therapy animal should be comfortable moving among groups of people, as well as being handled. It is imperative that the clinician safeguard the safety of the animal so that inappropriate handling and treatment are prevented.
15. The animal should be accepting of all humans it is in contact with.

Mental, social, or physical qualities of the patient or client may determine the appropriateness of a given species or breed. Is the patient immunocompromised? Does the patient have allergies or phobias? Are there aspects of the patient's history that suggest a positive or negative value of a particular choice of species or breed? Are there limitations due to a physical disability or the patient's age?

If the therapist is seeking a relaxing environment, freshwater or saltwater aquariums have been shown to have calming and other beneficial effects on humans. Although there are now veterinarians specializing in aquaculture, it is likely that a VFP will refer the therapist to a local store specializing in freshwater or tropical fish for supplies and information. Although reptiles may be interesting to certain patients, in general they are noninteractive, are the object of some phobias, and may carry a high risk of zoonotic disease (see later). Reptiles are usually not recommended as therapeutic animals (Hess *et al.*, 2005). However, when reptiles may be utilized, precautions need to be put into place. Fine (2005) noted that antiseptic hand wash needs to be available at all times, especially after the client handles the animal. There are several gentle species of reptiles that may be appropriate to incorporate. Bearded dragons tend to be gentle animals and are very comfortable being handled. Therapists who consider utilizing reptiles need to be in contact with a specialist who can explain the physical needs of the animal.

It is becoming more common for birds of various species to be used as therapeutic assistants. With the exception of cockatiels, love birds, and budgerigars, most of the parrot species should be considered wild animals in the process of becoming domesticated. Certain individual birds of other species may be appropriate for patients who benefit from interaction and visual stimuli. However, it is important that these birds be evaluated carefully to ensure that they are tame, handled easily by a variety of people, and predictable. Risks to the patient include unintentional scratches or intentional bites associated with inexperience in handling pet birds. Despite the increasing popularity of birds as pets and the rapidly growing veterinary specialty of avian medicine and surgery, our knowledge about the behavior and the emotional and physical well-being of these creatures is still limited. Fine (2003) noted the strong commitment therapists must consider when they utilize larger birds. Clinicians need to be aware of the life span of these animals as well as their needs for special care. Unfortunately, many people do not realize that the attention that one gives a bird early in its life is the same amount required when it ages. Therefore, careful planning needs to be instituted so that one will be able to live harmoniously with a bird over time. It is highly recommended if birds are to be considered that appropriate training be well thought out and utilized.

Rabbits and "pocket pets" such as small mammals (e.g., guinea pigs, hamsters, mice, and rats) offer a visual and tactile experience that may have therapeutic benefit. However, they also have an element of unpredictability and are somewhat fragile because of their size.

Cats are a popular therapeutic animal because their soft fur and audible purr in response to petting can have a very positive effect on patients. Care must be taken, however, to choose animals that have a docile disposition and manage their claws in order to prevent accidental or intentional scratches. The claws can be clipped short on a regular basis or protected with a covering such as Soft Paws.

Dogs are certainly the most common therapeutic animals and the subject of the majority of research on the subject. This is undoubtedly a result of their trainability, sociability, and predictability. The latter is a result of years of breeding for specific traits, which allows the VFP to make recommendations depending on which personality characteristics will help achieve therapeutic objectives.

It is important to remember that selection of a particular species is just the first step. If a dog, cat, or even guinea pig or rabbit is chosen, an appropriate breed should be identified. Years of selective breeding offer some consistency in physical characteristics, personality, and behavioral tendencies within breeds. This does not, however, guarantee identical performance by individual members of a given breed. Mixed breed dogs (and cats) may also be considered. In this case, determining the breed influence and applying a temperament test (slightly better than guessing, depending on the evaluator) might help suggest whether an individual animal might have the desired traits.

B. Developing a Health Maintenance Plan

Following the selection of an appropriate therapeutic animal, the VFP can develop a life stage health maintenance plan for the animal. In order to function effectively in AAT, the animal must maintain optimal physiological and psychological health. The plan must be based on a thorough risk assessment that takes into account genetic and environmental factors, zoonotic potential, behavior requirements, nutritional needs, and special demands of the therapeutic job the animal is to perform. It also must take into account the personality of the animal.

1. Genetics

Certain breeds of dogs and cats have a greater risk of suffering from a genetic disease. Persian cats, for example, are at risk for polycystic kidney disease, which can lead to kidney failure. Doberman pinschers and papillons may be afflicted with von Willebrand's disease, which prolongs bleeding time.

Labrador retrievers and miniature poodles may suffer from progressive retinal atrophy, which can result in vision deficits. There are tests for these and many other genetic diseases affecting a wide range of breeds. Mixed breed animals whose ancestry includes one or more of these breeds may also be at risk. The VFP can recommend appropriate tests for the individual animal and propose actions based on the results of those tests. Certain diseases may result in a shortened life span or disability that may interfere with the desired AAT function. Affected animals would not qualify for AAT. Other diseases may require careful monitoring but may not interfere with the AAT function. The VFP and the therapist together can determine if the benefit of using a specific individual in an AAT program outweighs the risk of the disease.

Some diseases, such as hip dysplasia, have both a genetic and a nongenetic component. A long-term study demonstrated that Labrador retrievers whose daily calorie consumption from the age of eight weeks to eight years was restricted to 75% of that of paired littermates suffered from a significantly lower incidence of hip dysplasia and other types of arthritis (Kealy *et al.*, 2002).

In this case, nutrition apparently affects the expression of the genes for hip dysplasia. There is very little known about genetic diseases in other species (in addition to the mouse) that may be considered for AAT.

2. Environmental Exposures

Control of infectious disease in small mammals is usually managed by maintaining high standards of husbandry, including cleanliness and strict regulation of the environment. Usually these animals are restricted to cages or other small areas and are not exposed to unknown animals or environments, reducing the possibility of encountering an infectious disease. The VFP can advise the therapist on the appropriate husbandry to minimize disease potential, while promoting quality of life.

Birds are generally confined, and exposure to unfamiliar animals is restricted. Although there have been vaccines developed to protect birds from certain diseases, their risks and effectiveness have been controversial and their use is generally not recommended for pet birds who are the only birds in the household or who share it with a small number of other birds. Cleanliness, good nutrition, attention to social and environmental needs, and regular health examinations comprise a major part of disease prevention for pet birds.

For many years, annual vaccinations have been the cornerstone of disease prevention in dogs and cats. However, the discovery of a cancer that seemed to be associated with one or more feline vaccines caused the veterinary profession to rethink its recommended vaccine protocols. It was discovered that the immunity conferred by some vaccines was longer than one year, and the wisdom of vaccinating all dogs or all cats according to the same "one size fits all" protocol has been questioned. Does an urban dog with no exposure to ponds or wetlands where *Leptospira* thrives really need to be vaccinated against that organism? Does that same dog who does not run through woods inhabited by ticks need a vaccine against Lyme disease? Do indoor adult cats with no exposure to other cats need to be vaccinated against feline leukemia? It has become apparent that vaccine protocols must be customized for each individual animal based on a careful risk assessment. The VFP can work with the therapist to determine the appropriate vaccines and vaccination schedule for the therapy dog or cat based on the animal's likelihood of exposure.

3. Zoonoses

Zoonoses (discussed in Chapter 15) are diseases that can be transmitted from animals to humans. The VFP can develop a program of diagnostic tests and therapies to minimize or eliminate the potential of disease that might spread to humans involved with the AAT. The program should take into account the species, age, and origin of the animal; the environmental exposures of the animal; the degree of interactivity with the patient/client; and the age and health of the patient/client. The program should become part of the health maintenance plan for the animal.

4. Behavior

Therapists must understand what constitutes normal behavior for the species considered for involvement in the AAT. The VFP can help the therapist identify which behaviors will support and which will interfere with therapeutic objectives. Then a behavioral protocol can be designed that will promote appropriate behaviors and discourage those that are inappropriate. Many animals, for example, can be taught through positive reinforcement to sit quietly and to tolerate handling by strangers. Some species of birds can be taught to "step up" onto a proffered finger or arm and to speak various phrases. Of all the potential AAT partners, dogs are probably the most trainable.

All dogs should undergo basic obedience training, and the VFP can recommend an appropriate local training facility. It is important for the VFP and the therapist to discuss in detail the concept of "behavioral wellness" (Hetts, 2004), which is a proactive approach ensuring that the pet is well adapted to its role in the family, in the AAT program, and in society. At a minimum, AAT dogs should receive Canine Good Citizen certification through the American Kennel Club or be certified through Delta Society's Pet Partners (Fine and Stein, 2003). Dogs may then be taught additional behaviors that may be helpful to the therapy. The training can be arranged either through the veterinary family practice or through a recommended trainer or veterinary behaviorist.

Occasionally, a dog develops some unacceptable behaviors that may threaten the success of the therapy. It is essential to differentiate signs of stress or discomfort from aberrant behavior. (See the discussion of stress in Section II.B.6.) If the VFP and the therapist agree that it is not an indication of stress or an indication of a health problem, it may be appropriate to consult with a behaviorist in order to determine the cause of the problem and to create a program that will eliminate the problem behavior. If, however, a health problem is causing the undesired behavior, it should be addressed immediately. If the animal is showing signs of stress, the cause must be identified and eliminated or the animal must be given appropriate training to deal with it. If the therapy work itself proves to be too stressful for the animal, it must be removed from the program.

5. Nutrition

An important part of the health maintenance plan is nutritional management. Nutritional needs of the therapy animal will change according to life stage, state of health, and types and degrees of activity. Young animals require more calories per body weight than older animals. Animals in active training also require more calories than those that are not. Food intolerance is not uncommon in dogs and cats. It may require testing to identify the offending food and research to find an acceptable food. Large and giant breed dogs require fewer calories and a more calcium-restricted diet than medium and small dogs. Older animals may benefit from increased antioxidants. Prevention of obesity is extremely important. The VFP will help identify the specific nutritional needs of each AAT animal and work with the therapist to develop a nutritional program to meet those needs. Attention needs to be given to the treats animals may receive during a therapy day. Clinicians should consider allocating a portion of the animal's food each day that may be given as treats. This will reduce the chances of obesity.

6. Quality of Life (QOL)

Maintaining or enhancing the quality of life of the therapy animal is a shared goal of the VFP and the therapist. Many medical judgments are made based on how the result will affect the patient's QOL. Exactly what is meant by "quality of life" is often very subjective and personal. When veterinarians think of QOL, they generally associate it with freedom from disease, hunger, thirst, and pain, especially the latter. Pet owners may consider other behaviors or attitudes of the animal as indicators that may suggest the QOL of their pet. Shalock (1996) pointed out that there are two approaches to measure QOL. The objective approach assesses external, objective, and social indicators such as health and safety. The subjective represents a perception of life experiences that include areas such as physical well-being. When evaluating an animal's QOL, the primary areas include health and wellness, safety, and nurturance and care the animal receives. However, there is often a risk that anthropomorphism will invalidate their assessment (Wojciechowska and Hewson, 2005). MacMillan (2000) pointed out that although QOL is often an important factor when evaluating outcomes of therapeutic interventions or when making decisions about therapy or euthanasia, there is no accepted definition of QOL and no validated criteria to measure it.

MacMillan (2000) proposed that affect (subjective feelings) about a physical or emotional state defines the QOL in animals. The challenge is to identify those feelings. He also suggested that QOL is a "continuum of feeling, ranging from comfort to extreme discomfort." Instruments have been developed attempting to define QOL in dogs. Wiseman-Orr *et al.* (2004) described an instrument in the form of a questionnaire designed to measure QOL in dogs afflicted with chronic pain due to osteoarthritis. By identifying behavioral domains and verbal descriptors (terms used by owners to describe aspects of behavior), the authors were able to construct a questionnaire that may be appropriate for a proxy measurement of chronic pain and quality of life. Clinical application of this questionnaire has not been reported. Wojciechowska *et al.* (2005) evaluated a different questionnaire for pet owners that was designed to demonstrate a difference in QOL between sick and healthy dogs visiting a veterinary teaching hospital. The QOL questionnaire did not differentiate sick from healthy dogs. Inherent methodological factors may have been responsible for the failure of the questionnaire, but the study confirmed the difficulty of trying to objectify QOL.

These studies attempted to define the QOL of one individual in comparison with the QOL of a larger population. MacMillan (2000) noted that "Quality of life is a uniquely individual experience and should be measured from the perspective of the individual." Perhaps a better approach would be to construct an instrument that would essentially involve a longitudinal study of an individual that monitors an animal's affect under varying environmental and physiological conditions.

Until such an instrument is developed, the VFP and the therapist must determine jointly what characterizes an excellent quality of life for the therapy animal. Specifically, what behaviors can be identified that confirm that the animal is comfortable, and what appears to increase the animal's pleasure? Conversely, what behaviors communicate discomfort, and what does the animal perceive as unpleasant? The answers to these questions will serve as

TABLE III Veterinary Associations with Interests in Selected Species or Practice Areas

American Association of Feline Practitioners (www.aafponline.org)
American Board of Veterinary Practitioners (www.abvp.org)
Association of Avian Veterinarians (www.aav.org)
Association of Human–Animal Bond Veterinarians (www.aahabv.org)
Association of Reptilian and Amphibian Veterinarians (www.arav.org)
Association of Veterinary Family Practitioners (www.veterinaryfamilypractice.org)

guidelines to evaluating the therapy animal's QOL. These factors will change as the animal ages and has more varied experiences.

As a part of this exercise, the therapist must learn to identify signs of stress in his or her therapy animal. Signs of stress vary across species and among individuals. Although stress assessment tools have been developed, they have been shown to have weaknesses and are not entirely reliable (McCobb *et al.*, 2005). Together, the VFP and the therapist can ascertain what signs will indicate that the therapy animal is suffering from stress and therefore discomfort.

III. SELECTION OF AN APPROPRIATE VETERINARY FAMILY PRACTITIONER

Selection of an appropriate veterinarian is of paramount importance to anyone who has a therapy animal in their household. Although veterinarians are becoming more aware of the increasing use of animals in therapy and other types of service, they may or may not have any experience with the various types of therapy work. What is most important is that the veterinarian has an interest in and experience with the species and be knowledgeable about that species' behavior and physical needs. Table III lists veterinary associations or boards, a membership in which indicates a strong interest or specialty training in designated areas. Although membership in one of these associations does not guarantee expertise, it suggests that the veterinarian has a strong interest in the area and that there is likelihood that he or she has sought additional relevant training.

The veterinarian and hospital staff must be willing to work closely with the therapist to accomplish all of the work described in previous paragraphs. It would be of value for the therapist to schedule a preliminary appointment with the veterinarian to see if the veterinarian and hospital appear to be a good fit. A tour of the hospital should be arranged to observe the staff, watching for signals that they are friendly and happy to be there. Some questions that could be asked of the veterinarian are listed in Table IV.

TABLE IV Questions an Owner of a Therapy Animal May Ask during an Interview with a Veterinarian

- What is your experience with AAT/AAA? (Answer should describe specific type.)
- What suggestions and guidance can you provide on best practices for the care of therapy animals?
- What is your experience with the particular species (if other than dog or cat)?
- Do you have a special interest in a particular area of veterinary practice?
- Are you a member of any veterinary associations? (See list in Table III.)
- Are you a member of any other human–animal bond organizations (e.g., Delta Society, local humane society)?
- What courses do you attend for continuing education? (Ideally, courses should relate to the species of interest, including behavior, nutrition, and genetics, in addition to general medicine, surgery, and dentistry.)
- What do you recommend for vaccinations? (Answer should be that it varies depending on the animal's exposure, age, function, etc.)
- Are behavior training services offered by the hospital, or can you recommend a reputable local trainer?
- Do you refer to veterinary specialists? Which ones?
- Do you offer emergency services or refer to an emergency hospital?
- What are the key factors you consider when developing a life maintenance plan for an animal? (The answer should include the role of the animal in the family, any functional demands on the animal, the environment, species, age, sex, breed, etc.)
- What suggestions can you provide to enhance the QOL of the therapy animal?
- Can you provide sound medical guidelines that should be considered for the daily routine of specific therapy animals?
- What guidelines would you suggest that the therapists should consider in visits to the office? How often and what should checkups consist of?

IV. CONCLUSION

In order for the therapy animal to perform optimally, it must be in good health, behave appropriately, and receive pleasure from the work. These conditions can best be achieved by choosing an appropriate animal for the AAT and developing a plan for lifelong health maintenance. This plan can be achieved by developing a strong partnership with the AAT clinical team, the veterinarian staff, and the primary caretaker of the therapy animal. Establishing a lifelong plan will offer an animal the best opportunity to achieve healthy QOL while providing support to humans who are in need.

REFERENCES

American Veterinary Medical Association (2001). Wellness guidelines for animals used in animal-assisted activity, animal-assisted therapy, and resident animal programs. Available at http://www.avma.org/noah/members/policy/wellness_guidelines.asp. Accessed 8/22/05.

Brown, J., and Silverman, J. (1999). The current and future market for veterinarians and veterinary medical services in the United States. *J. Am. Vet. Med. Assoc.* **215**, 161–183.

Fiala, J. (2004). CVMA covets heightened legal status for pets. *DVMNewsmagazine* **35**, 36–39.

Fiala, J. (2005). CVMA sues city over declaw ban. *DVMNewsmagazine*. Available at http://dvmnewsmagazine.com/dvm/article/articleDetail.jsp?d=155735. Accessed 08/20/05.

Fine, A. H. (2003). Animal assisted therapy and clinical practice. Psycho-Legal Associates CEU meeting, Nov. 1, Seattle, WA.

Fine, A. H. (2005). Animal assisted therapy and clinical practice. Psycho-Legal Associates CEU meeting, May 2, San Francisco, CA.

Fine, A.H., and Stein, L. (2003). Animal assisted therapy and clinical practice Psycho-Legal Associates CEU meeting, Oct. 25, Pasadena, CA.

Grieve, G., Neuhoff, K., Thomas, R., Welborn, L., Albers, J., and Parone, J. (2003). "The Path to High-Quality Care: Practical Tips for Improving Compliance." American Animal Hospital Association, Lakewood, CO.

Hess, L., Crimi, M., New, J., Orosz, S., and Pitts, J. (2005). The veterinarian's role in preventing and controlling disease in exotic animals in assisted-care facilities. *J. Avian Med. Surg.* **19**, 46–55.

Hetts, S., Heinke, M., and Estep, D. (2004). Behavioral wellness concepts for general veterinary practice. *J. Am. Vet. Med. Assoc.* **225**, 506–513.

Johnson, R., and Meadows, R. (2000). Promoting wellness through nurse-veterinary collaboration. *West. J. Nurs. Res.* **22**, 773–775.

Kealy, R., Lawler, D., Ballam, J., Lust, G., Biery, D., Smith, D., and Mantz, S. (2002). Evaluation of the effect of limited food consumption on radiographic evidence of osteoarthritis in dogs. *J. Am. Vet. Med. Assoc.* **217**, 1678–1680.

Lofflin, J. (2004). The changing status of pets. *Vet. Econ.* **45**, 33–38.

McCobb, E., Patronek, G., Marder, A., Dinnage, J., and Stone, M. (2005). Assessment of stress levels in cats in four animal shelters. *J. Am. Vet. Med. Assoc.* **226**, 548–555.

McMillan, F. (2000). Quality of life in animals. *J. Am. Vet. Med. Assoc.* **216**, 1904–1910.

Sapperfield, M. (2002). In San Francisco, pet owners recast as "guardians." *The Christian Science Monitor.* Available at http://www.csmonitor.com/2002/1220/p01s02-usgn.html. Accessed 08/20/05.

Schalock, R. (1996). The quality of children's lives. *In* "Therapeutic Recreation for Exceptional Children" (A. Fine and N. Fine, eds.). Charles C. Thomas, Springfield, IL.

Wisemann-Orr, M., Nolan, A., Reid, J., and Scott, E. (2004). Development of a questionnaire to measure the effects of chronic pain on health-related quality of life in dogs. *Am. J. Vet. Res.* **65**, 1077–1084.

Wojciechowska, J., and Hewson, C. (2005). Quality of life assessment in pet dogs. *J. Am. Vet. Med. Assoc.* **226**, 722–728.

Wojciechowska, J., Hewson, C., Stryhn, H., Guy, N., Patronek, G., and Timmons, V. (2005). Evaluation of a questionnaire regarding nonphysical aspects of quality of life in sick and healthy dogs. *Am. J. Vet. Res.* **66**, 1453–1460.

CHAPTER 22

The Future of Research, Education, and Clinical Practice in the Animal–Human Bond and Animal-Assisted Therapy

Part A: The Role of Ethology in the Field of Human–Animal Relations and Animal-Assisted Therapy

DENNIS C. TURNER
Institute for Applied Ethology and Animal Psychology, CH-8816 Hirzel, and University of Zurich, Switzerland

I. INTRODUCTION

As pointed out over two decades ago (Turner, 1984), the multidisciplinary fields of human–animal relations[1] and animal-assisted therapy (AAT) lacked quantitative, controlled observations on behavior and interactions between owners and their pets and between patients and therapy animals. Without intending to belittle the importance of other disciplines involved or interested in this field, the role that ethology has, and could continue to play, in research and education on the human–animal relationship and AAT should not be underestimated.

Ethology can be defined as the observational, often comparative study of animal and/or human behavior. While in the long run, ethologists are mostly concerned with the biological basis of behavior, their methods and results are not without consequences for the applied fields of human–animal interaction

[1]Most recently called "anthrozoology," defined as "the study of the relationships between humans and domesticated and/or feral animals" (Cambridge Dictionary of Human Biology and Evolution, 2005).

Handbook on Animal-Assisted Therapy: Theoretical Foundations and Guidelines for Practice, 2e

and AAT. As a significant example, one may consider the early studies on dog and cat socialization toward conspecifics and humans (for an excellent summary, see McCune *et al.*, 1995): Both species exhibit a sensitive phase of socialization early in life, during which contacts with members of their own species and/or other species (including humans) influence the social inclinations of individuals for the rest of their lives. In dogs, this sensitive phase occurs from 4 to 10 or 12 weeks of age depending on the author (see Serpell and Jagoe, 1995); in cats, from 2 to 8 (toward humans) or 10 weeks of age (toward conspecifics) (Karsh and Turner, 1988; Schaer, 1989; Turner, 2000a). Certainly in cats (Hediger, 1988), probably also in dogs (Reichlin, 1994), socialization can take place simultaneously and independently toward members of the same species and toward humans. That dogs and cats involved in visitation and residential therapy programs are socialized toward both is of crucial importance for both risk management and outcomes, not to mention the welfare of the animals themselves (Hubrecht and Turner, 1998; Turner, 2005a).

Animal welfare laws in many countries require that animals be housed and treated in such a way that all of their species-specific needs can be satisfied and that they are not subjected to stress or pain. Therapy animals are no exception. Regarding behavioral and psychosocial needs, ethological studies provide the necessary background information (Rochlitz, 2005a; Turner, 1995a, 2005b); regarding stress and pain avoidance, studies from both ethology and veterinary medicine (e.g., Broom and Johnson, 1993; Casey and Bradshaw, 2005) are usually the sources of factual information. Hubrecht and Turner (1998), for dogs and cats, and Rochlitz (2005b), for cats, have provided the most recent reviews on companion animal welfare in private and institutional settings, but more work is needed in this area. The International Association of Human–Animal Interaction Organizations (IAHAIO) has emphasized the importance of the welfare of therapy animals in its "IAHAIO Prague Guidelines on Animal-Assisted Activities and Animal-Assisted Therapy."[2]

There have been relatively few ethological studies of the interactions between pets and people, with most of these on cats and many from the research team surrounding the author (Bradshaw and Cameron-Beaumont, 2000; Cook and Bradshaw, 1996; Goodwin and Bradshaw, 1996, 1997, 1998; McCune, 1995; Meier and Turner, 1985; Mertens, 1991; Mertens and Turner, 1988; Rieger and Turner, 1999; Turner, 1991, 1995b, 2000b; Turner and Rieger, 2001; Turner *et al.*, 1986). These have provided information on the "mechanics" of human–cat interactions; differences between interactions involving men, women, boys, and girls and involving elderly persons *vs* younger adults; differences in interactions between several breeds of cats; and the influence of

[2]See www.iahaio.org for the full text.

housing conditions on such interactions. Many of these results (should) have consequences for animal visitation and (especially psycho-) therapy programs.

As appropriate in any interdisciplinary field, advances in our knowledge about the human–animal relationship and its therapeutic value can also be secured by combining the methods and results of other disciplines with those of ethology. Serpell (1983) was the first researcher to consider aspects of a companion animal's behavior in the interpretation results from a nonethological study of the human–dog relationship. He found associations between owner affection toward the dog and such dog behavior and character traits as welcoming behavior, attentiveness, expressiveness, and sensitivity. Over the years, Turner and his research team have borrowed and expanded upon the methodology of Serpell's first study to examine the ethology *and* psychology of human–cat relationships (Kannchen and Turner, 1998; Rieger and Turner, 1999; Stammbach and Turner, 1999; Turner, 1991, 1995b, 2000b, 2002; Turner and Rieger, 2001; Turner and Stammbach-Geering, 1990; Turner *et al.*, 2003).

What have ethological studies of human–animal interactions and relationships provided us so far? A few examples, based on the literature cited earlier, are called for. From the cat research group of Turner, we now know that domestic cats show no spontaneous preference for a particular age/sex class of potential human partners but indeed *react* to differences in human behavior toward the cats between the different age/sex classes and, therefore, show behavior that would lead us to believe they have preferences. Women and girls tend to interact with cats on the floor while men often do this from a seated position. Children, especially boys, tend to approach a cat quickly and directly and are often first rejected by the animal for this. Adults usually call the cat first and allow the cat to do the approaching. Women speak with their cats more often than men, and the cats also vocalize more often with them than with men. Women are also approached more frequently by cats, and the animals are generally more willing to cooperate with them than with men. Retired persons show more tolerance or acceptance of the cats' natural behavior and desire less conformity by the cats to their own lifestyles than younger adults. When they interact with their cats, elderly persons do so for longer periods of time, often in closer physical contact with the animals, than younger adults, who nevertheless speak more often with/to their cats from a distance.

Differences in cat behavior related to the animals' sex have been sought but not (yet) found, although most studies (as well as most cats kept by private persons) were of neutered or spayed animals in past studies. Individual differences in behavior between cats are always statistically significant, and these have had to be accounted for in any analysis of other parameters postulated to affect their behavior. Nevertheless, various personality types (e.g., cats that prefer playing while others prefer the physical contact of stroking) have been discovered (also statistically) among domestic nonpurebred animals. Astonishingly, only one observational study has been published comparing the behavior of just two breeds (Siamese and Persian/longhair) and nonpurebred cats in their interactions with humans (Turner, 1995b, 2000b). Differences relevant to potential therapy work with cats were found. Nonobservational studies comparing the character traits of many different dog breeds have been conducted with highly significant results for AAA/AAT work (Hart, 1995; Hart and Hart, 1985, 1988). However, ethological studies along the same lines are lacking, with the possible exception of Schalke and colleagues (2005).

What have studies that combine observational data with indirect subjective assessments of cat traits and relationship quality by their owners provided? Turner and Stammbach-Geering (1990) and Turner (1991) found correlations that help explain the widespread popularity of cats, as well as one key to a harmonious relationship between a person and his or her cat: Cats are considered by their owners either to be very independent and unlike humans (who consider themselves, in this case, "dependent") or to be dependent and human-like. Some people appreciate the independent nature of the cat, whereas others appreciate their presumed "dependency" on human care. The authors also discovered that the more willing the owner is to fulfill the cat's interactional wishes, then the more willing the cat is to reciprocate at other times. However, the cat also accepts a lower willingness on the part of the owner and adapts its own willingness to interact to that. This "meshing" of interactional goals is one indication of relationship quality.

Stammbach and Turner (1999) and Kannchen and Turner (1998; see also Turner 2002) combined psychological assessment tools measuring human social support levels, self-perceived emotional support from the cat, and attachment to the cat with direct observations of interactions between women and their cats. Emotional attachment to the cat was correlated negatively with the amount of human social support the owner could count on and correlated positively with the self-estimated amount of emotional support provided by the cat. Attachment to the cat was found to be the more predominant factor governing interactional behavior rather than the amount of human support available to the owner.

Rieger and Turner (1999), Turner and Rieger (2001), and Turner and colleagues (2003) used psychological tools and ethological observations to assess how momentary moods, particularly depressiveness, affect the behavior of singly living persons, respectively, persons with a sponse, toward their cats. They emphasized that these persons, who had volunteered for the studies, were not necessarily clinically depressive. They discovered that the more a person was depressed, the fewer "intentions" to interact were shown. However, the more a person was depressed, the more he or she directly started an interaction. This means that depressed persons had an initial inhibition to initiate that was compensated by the presence of the cat. People who became less depressed after two hours owned cats that were more willing to comply with the humans' intents than those of people whose "depressiveness" had not changed or became worse. When not interacting, the cat reacted the same way to all moods of the humans. This neutral attitude possibly makes the cat an attractive pacemaker against an inhibition to initiate. Within an interaction the cats were indeed affected by the mood: they showed more head and flank rubbing toward depressive persons. However, apparently only the willingness of the cat to comply was responsible for reducing depressiveness. The authors interpreted their results after a model of intraspecific communication between human couples in which one partner is clinically depressed (Hell, 1994) and found striking similarities. The potential of these findings for AAT sessions involving cats is obvious.

While Rieger and Turner (1999) and Turner and Rieger (2001) found that cats were successful in improving "negative" moods, but not increasing already "good moods" among single persons, Turner and colleagues (2003) found that a spouse was indeed capable of the latter. Nevertheless, they also found that a companion cat was about as successful as a spouse at improving negative moods.

II. UNANSWERED RESEARCH QUESTIONS

Despite the aforementioned relevant results from ethological studies and those from investigations combining the methods and interpretations of other disciplines with those from direct observations, we have only begun to "scratch the surface" in the ethological analysis of human–pet relationships. This is true for human–cat, but especially so for human–dog, relationships. Given the heavy involvement of dogs in AAA/AAT programs, it would be prudent to encourage similar studies of dog behavior and human–dog interactions. In particular, the breed differences in behavior and character traits reported in studies using only indirect methods (Hart and Hart, 1985, 1988) are extremely relevant to therapy work and should be substantiated by independent analysis of observational data. Further work on behavioral differences between cat breeds, in addition to those found between the two character extremes represented by Siamese and Persian cats, is also called for.

Another reason to promote comparative ethological studies of dog–human interactions is the reported difference in general *Gestalt* of the human–dog *vs* the human–cat relationship (Turner, 1985, 1988): a dog's social life is organized around dominance–subordinance relationships, whereas cat sociality (assuming socialization toward humans in the first place) is based on "give and take," mutuality/reciprocity, and respect of their independent nature (Turner, 1995c). This basic difference must be considered, especially in psychosocial therapy. Sex differences in dog behavior toward humans have been found (Hart and Hart, 1985, 1988; Sonderegger and Turner, 1996), but these still need to be examined in intact (nonspayed and nonneutered) cats. More detailed work on the communication signals used by dogs and cats in intra- and interspecific interactions is also required, particularly comparative studies to assess whether the same signals have the same meaning when directed to another species and how other species interpret them. Mertens and Turner (1988), Goodwin and Bradshaw (1996, 1997, 1998), and Bradshaw and Cameron-Beaumont (2000) have made a start, but we have much more to discover in this area.

The study of Rieger and Turner (1999; see also Turner and Rieger, 2001; Turner *et al.*, 2003) showed for the first time that moods of cat owners affect their interactional behavior and that the cats can indeed help persons out of a momentary depressive mood. The mechanism through which this probably occurs was postulated but still needs to be tested; trials with clinically depressed persons must be conducted. This study also produced the rather surprising (and difficult to defend in front of cat enthusiasts!) result that the cats did not react measurably to the different moods of their owners from the outset, only within an ongoing interaction. However, it is probable that humans (and cats) send out very fine signals (e.g., gaze; see Goodwin and Bradshaw, 1998) not picked up by the ethogram used in this first study. Again, a finer analysis of communication between cats and their owners using video to record facial mimicry and so on would be helpful.

Other species than dogs and cats are involved in some AAA/AAT programs, reportedly with positive outcomes. The effect of watching caged birds or aquarium fish in lowering blood pressure and pulse rate is well documented (Katcher *et al.*, 1983) and their presence can significantly improve the quality of life of residents in institutions (Olbrich, 1995). Nature programs (also involving animals) have reported good results in the treatment of ADHD and CD children (Katcher and Wilkins, 2000). Rabbits, guinea pigs, and hamsters are involved in some programs but are also occasionally housed and/or handled improperly. More ethological studies on proper housing of these species and *better education* of the AAA/AAT specialists using them are urgently needed (see later). Again comparative ethological studies of human interactions with these species would be useful: Turner (1996, 2005c) has postulated differences in the benefits accrued depending on whether the therapy animal species is interactive and initiative (i.e., establishes contact with the patient of its own volition, such as dogs and many cats do) or simply present during the therapy session as an "icebreaker" (bridge to the therapist) or topic for therapeutic discussion. Presumably many rodent species, caged birds, and fish serve this function.

To summarize, it is clear from the aforementioned studies that ethology and ethological methods have much to offer the field of human–companion animal relations and, potentially, animal-assisted therapy but that much remains to be done. We have, or can expect, information on how to ensure socialization of the animals involved in therapy programs or to assess the degree of socialization in animals up for selection; on how to house, handle, and care properly for the animals involved to minimize stress and ensure their health and welfare, thus maximizing potential benefits to the recipients of therapy; regarding differences in interactive behavior among healthy women, men, girls, and boys and between different species and breeds of intact, neutered, or spayed male and female therapy animals, which provide baseline information for therapeutic work with less fortunate human beings; regarding matching the animal and recipient of the therapeutic activities; assessing changes and improvement in interspecific (human–animal) relationship quality, which could (should) parallel changes in interpersonal relationship establishment and quality; and regarding the mechanisms explaining why animals work as (co)therapeutic agents.

It is equally clear that the combination of theories, methods, and interpretations from different disciplines can lead to major advances in our understanding of those relations. Therefore, any educational program on human–animal relationships and animal-assisted therapy must, of necessity, be interdisciplinary.

III. A MODEL CURRICULUM FOR CONTINUING EDUCATION IN ANIMAL-ASSISTED THERAPY AND ANIMAL-ASSISTED ACTIVITIES

A number of universities, many in North America, now have faculty positions and/or offer courses in human–animal relations (e.g., University of Pennsylvania, Philadelphia; Tufts University, North Grafton; University of California at Davis; Purdue University, West Lafayette; Bristol University, UK; University of Cambridge, UK; Virginia Commonwealth University, Richmond; Virginia Polytechnic Institute and State University, Blacksburg; University of Zurich, Switzerland Medical Biology program), and more will certainly be added to the list as this field expands. IAHAIO has attempted to encourage this with Resolution 5 of its Geneva Declaration (1995) and Resolution 4 of the IAHAIO Prague Guidelines on Animal-Assisted Activities and Animal-Assisted Therapy[3]

[3] See www.iahaio.org for the full text.

(1998). However, as of 1998, no complete continuing education curriculum aimed at training professionals and/or paraprofessionals in the proper involvement of animals was operative.

With this in mind, a model two-year curriculum was developed by an interdisciplinary team representing the fields of ethology, human–animal interactions, animal welfare, psychology, psychiatry, psychotherapy, and social work (Turner *et al.*, 1998). This was offered for the first time in Europe (Zurich, Switzerland) in April 1999 and has been repeated biannually ever since. During development of the curriculum, emphasis was placed on the following general points considered to be essential to the outcome: Course work and activities should be scheduled (mostly) evenings and on weekends to allow participation by persons (self-)employed elsewhere. A two-tiered level, one for professional counselors/therapists and one for persons active in social institutions,[4] should be offered; some courses would be attended by persons studying at both levels, and other activities would be offered separately for each level. Admission criteria for both levels must be defined clearly. Lecturers and supervisors must be qualified and experienced in the subjects they teach or supervise. Theoretical background information, as well as practical examples, should be covered. Participants at both levels should be given the opportunity to experience animal-assisted activities in action during supervised "field trips." For professional counselors, confidential "suitability evaluations" should take place during the program and the "supervision group" modus must be followed during advanced work. Participants at both levels should complete mandatory literature reviews, and a supervised, written final "project report" should be required (to be judged and approved by a joint commission of professionals in the field). Finally, an official certificate, specific for each level, should be awarded upon successful completion of all course requirements.

Topics covered in this two-year curriculum include introduction to the study of human–animal relationships and theories explaining them; review of psychology theory, especially developmental psychology; review of symptoms of frequent psychological disorders; neuroses and psychopathology; ethology of human–animal interactions; animals as sources of social support; animal welfare; ethical considerations; risk management (safety, zoonoses, animal selection); communication training; organization of AAAs in institutions; therapeutic riding/hippotherapy; work therapy with farm animals; and special needs and problems of the elderly, children, and juveniles, the mentally and

[4]This takes into account the facts that (1) use of the title "therapist" is legally regulated in most countries, (2) animal-assisted therapy is a goal-directed intervention under either medical or therapeutic services supervision, and (3) AAA specialists also need quality training and certification.

physically challenged, persons with severe psychological disturbances, and persons in correctional institutions. Visits to institutions offering AAT/AAAs and those providing animals for such are to be included.

This curriculum is offered by the Swiss government (eduQua-)certified I.E.A.P. continuing education institute and in Japan, together with Azabu University Graduate School (Fuchinobe/Tokyo), as the first such postgraduate program in the world. Most recently, I.E.A.P. offers all of its curricula "in association with the Zoology Institute, University of Zurich."

The same year the I.E.A.P. program began, the Institute for Social Learning with Animals in Wedemark, Germany (Ingrid Stephan, director), in cooperation with the University of Wurzburg, instigated an excellent continuing education program in animal-assisted pedagogy, and the two institutes are currently forging closer ties, exchanging guest professors and lecturers. Then in 2004 the University of Veterinary Medicine, Vienna, in Austria, started up its university-based program in this field. In the same year these three institutions founded the European Society for Animal-Assisted Therapy (ESAAT) to work toward official European-wide recognition of the professions/vocations "animal-assisted therapist," "animal-assisted pedagogue," and "animal-assisted activity specialist" and to ensure minimum standards for the curricula in AAT, AAP, and AAA for persons who already have professional/vocational training, requiring at least 225 hours of interdisciplinary teaching and practical work (Leibetseder *et al.*, 2004). Training in all three areas must include the following topics.

1. Human–animal communication; theories to explain the healing and helping effects on animals and humans; knowledge about somatic, social, and psychological effects of animals on humans
2. Methods for pedagogic and therapeutic work with animals in different areas of application; methods of evaluation
3. Ethical questions and animal welfare; species-appropriate housing, care, and handling; normal behavior and behavioral development of animals; introduction to behavioral problems and illnesses; training methods for animals
4. Hygienic requirements for the pedagogic and therapeutic involvement of animals; hygiene plans; risk management
5. Tutored practical experience
6. Organization of professional activities with animals; practical, economical, and administrative requirements

Obviously, the curriculum must be offered by an interdisciplinary team of experts but also be "interdisciplinary" in another respect, namely combining theory and practice and offering sound information based on research results of academicians, as well as on the experience of practitioners in the field.

Most recently (2006), the International Society for Animal-Assisted Therapy (ISAAT) was founded to gather and accredit institutions of higher education offering such curricula throughout the world.

REFERENCES

Bradshaw, J., and Cameron-Beaumont, C. (2000). The signaling repertoire of the domestic cat and its undomesticated relatives. *In* "The Domestic Cat: The Biology of Its Behaviour" (D. C. Turner and P. Bateson, eds.), 2nd Ed. Cambridge University Press, Cambridge, MA.

Broom, D. M., and Johnson, K. G. (1993). "Stress and Animal Welfare." Capman and Hall, London.

"Cambridge Dictionary of Human Biology and Evolution" (2005). Cambridge University Press, Cambridge, MA.

Casey, R., and Bradshaw, J. (2005). The assessment of welfare. *In* "The Welfare of Cats" (I. Rochlitz, ed.). Springer, Dordrecht, The Netherlands.

Cook, S. E., and Bradshaw, J. W. S. (1996). Reliability and validity of a holding test to measure "friendliness" in cats. ISAZ Conference, July 1996, Downing College, Cambridge. [Abstract]

Goodwin, D., and Bradshaw, J. W. S. (1996). The relationship between dog/dog and dog/human dominance interactions. ISAZ Conference, July 1996, Downing College, Cambridge. [Abstract]

Goodwin, D., and Bradshaw, J. W. S. (1997). Gaze and mutual gaze: Its importance in cat/human and cat/cat interactions. ISAZ Conference, July 1997, Tufts University School of Veterinary Medicince, North Grafton. [Abstract]

Goodwin, D., and Bradshaw, J. W. S. (1998). Regulation of interactions between cats and humans by gaze and mutal gaze. ISAZ Conference, September 1998, Prague, CZ. [Abstract]

Hart, B. L. (1995). Analysing breed and gender differences in behaviour. *In* "The Domestic Dog: Its Evolution, Behaviour and Interactions with People" (J. A. Serpell, ed.). Cambridge University Press, Cambridge, MA.

Hart, B. L., and Hart, L. A. (1985). "Canine and Feline Behavioral Therapy." Lea and Febiger, Philadelphia, PA.

Hart, B. L., and Hart. L. A. (1988). "The Perfect Puppy: How to Choose Your Dog by Its Behavior." Freeman, New York.

Hediger, A. (1988). "Die Freundlichkeit der Katze zum Menschen im Vergleich zur Freundlichkeit der Katze zur Katze." M.Sc. thesis, Zoology Institute, University of Zurich.

Hell, D. (1994). "Welchen Sinn macht Depression? Ein integrativer Ansatz." Rohwolt, Reinbeck bei Hamburg.

Hubrecht, R., and Turner, D. C. (1998). Companion animal welfare in private and institutional settings. *In* "Companion Animals in Human Health" (C. C. Wilson and D. C. Turner, eds.). Sage, Thousand Oaks, CA.

Kannchen, S., and Turner, D. C. (1998). The influence of human social support levels and degree of attachment to the animal on behavioural interactions between owners and cats. Abstract Book, 8th International Conference on Human-Animal Interactions, Prague: The Changing Roles of Animals in Society. Afirac, Paris.

Karsh, E. B., and Turner, D. C. (1988). The human–cat relationship. *In* "The Domestic Cat: The Biology of Its Behaviour" (D. C. Turner and P. Bateson, eds.). University of Cambridge Press, Cambridge, MA.

Katcher, A. H., Friedmann, E., Beck, A. M., and Lynch, J. (1983). Looking, talking, and blood pressure: the physiological consequences of interacting with the living environment. *In* "New Perspectives on Our Lives with Companion Animals" (A. H. Katcher and A. M. Beck, eds.). University of Pennsylvania Press, Philadelphia, PA.

Katcher, A. H., and Wilkins, G. G. (2000). The centaur's lessons: Therapeutic education through the care of animals and nature study. *In* "Handbook on Animal-Assisted Therapy: Theoretical Foundations and Guidelines"(A. Fine, ed). Academic Press, San Diego, CA.

Leibetseder, J., Olbrich, E., Stephan, I., Tanner-Frick, R., and Turner, D. C. (2004). Standards for education and training in animal-assisted therapy, animal-assisted pedagogy and animal-assisted activities. *In* "People and Animals: A Timeless Relationship" (A. Dochterty, A. Podberscek, and M. Whyham, eds.). Society for Companion Animal Studies, Burford, Oxon, UK.

McCune, S. (1995). The impact of paternity and early socialisation on the development of cats' behaviour to people and novel objects. *Appl. Anim. Behav. Sci.* 45(1–2), 111–126.

McCune, S., McPherson, J. A., and Bradshaw, J. W. S. (1995). Avoiding problems: The importance of socialisation. *In* "The Waltham Book of Human-Animal Interaction: Benefits and Responsibilities of Pet Ownership" (I. Robinson, ed.). Pergamon Press, Oxford, UK.

Meier, M., and Turner, D. C. (1985). Reactions of house cats during encounters with a strange person: Evidence for two personality types. *J. Delta Soc.* (later *Anthrozoös*) 2(1), 45–53.

Mertens, C. (1991). Human–cat interactions in the home setting. *Anthrozoös* 4(4), 214–231.

Mertens, C., and Turner, D. C. (1988). Experimental analysis of human–cat interactions during first encounters. *Anthrozoös* 2(2), 83–97.

Olbrich, E. (1995). Budgerigars in old people's homes: Influence on behaviour and quality of life. Abstract Book, 7th International Conference on Human-Animal Interactions, Geneva: Animals, Health and Quality of Life. Afirac, Paris.

Reichlin, B. (1994). "Begrüssungsverhalten vor dem Hundeferienheim in Abhängigkeit von früheren Erfahrungen." Abschlussarbeit, I.E.T. I.E.T./I.E.A. P., Hirzel, Schweiz.

Rieger, G., and Turner, D. C. (1999). How depressive moods affect the behavior of singly living persons toward their cats. *Anthrozoös* 12(4), 224–233.

Rochlitz, I. (2005a). Housing and welfare. *In* "The Welfare of Cats" (I. Rochlitz, ed.). Springer Press, Dordrecht, The Netherlands.

Rochlitz, I. (2005b). "The Welfare of Cats." Springer Press, Dordrecht, The Netherlands.

Schaer, R. (1989). "Die Hauskatze." Verlag Eugen Ulmer, Stuttgart.

Schalke, E., Mittmann, A., and Bruns, S. (2005). Assessment of behaviour of dogs of the pitbull-type and five other breeds by temperament testing according to the guidelines of the Dangerous Animals Act of Niedersachsen, Germany, of July 5th, 2000 (in German). *In* "Aktuelle Arbeiten zur artgemässen Tierhaltung, KTBL-Schrift 437." Deutsche Veterinärmedizinische Gesellschaft e. V., Giessen.

Serpell, J. A. (1983). The personality of the dog and its influence on the pet-owner bond. *In* "New Perspectives on Our Lives with Companion Animals" (A. H. Katcher and A. M. Beck, eds.). University of Pennsylvania Press, Philadelphia, PA.

Serpell, J., and Jagoe, J. A. (1995). Early experience and the development of behaviour. *In* "The Domestic Dog: Its Evolution, Behaviour and Interactions with People." Cambridge University Press, Cambridge, MA.

Sonderegger, S. M., and Turner, D. C. (1996). Introducing dogs into kennels: Prediction of social tendencies to facilitate integration. *Anim. Welf.* 5(4), 391–404.

Stammbach, K. B., and Turner, D. C. (1999). Understanding the human-cat relationship: Human social support or attachment. *Anthrozoös* 12(3), 162–168.

Turner, D. C. (1984). Overview of research on human-animal interaction in Switzerland. *J. Delta Soc.* (later *Anthrozoös*) 1(1), 38–39.

Turner, D. C. (1985). The human–cat relationship: Methods of analysis. *In* "The Human-Pet Relationship, International Symposium on the Occasion of the 80th Birthday of Nobel Prize Winner Prof. Dr. Konrad Lorenz, October 1983." IEMT and Austrian Academy of Sciences, Vienna, Austria.

Turner, D. C. (1988). Cat behaviour and the human–cat relationship. *Animal. Famil.* **3**(2), 16–21.

Turner, D. C. (1991). The ethology of the human–cat relationship. *Swiss Arch. Vet. Med.* (SAT, in German) **133**(2), 63–70.

Turner, D. C. (1995a). Ethology and companion animal welfare. *Swiss Arch. Vet. Med.* (SAT, in German) **137**, 45–49.

Turner, D. C. (1995b). "Die Mensch–Katze–Beziehung. Ethologische und psychologische Aspekte." Gustav Fischer Verlag (later, Enke Verlag), Stuttgart, Germany.

Turner, D. C. (1995c). The human-cat relationship. *In* "The Waltham Book of Human-Animal Interaction" (I. Robinson, ed.). Pergamon Press, Oxford, UK.

Turner, D. C. (1996). Ethological aspects of the human-animal relationship: Differences between animal species. Continuing Education Course on Pet Therapy, World Health Organization, WHO Research and Training Centre, Teramo, Italy, June 10/11, 1996.

Turner, D. C. (2000a). The human-cat relationship. *In* "The Domestic Cat: The Biology of Its Behaviour" (D. C. Turner and P. Bateson, eds.), 2nd Ed. Cambridge University Press, Cambridge, MA.

Turner, D. C. (2000b). Human–cat interactions: Relationships with, and breed differences between, non-pedigree, Persian and Siamese cats. *In* "Companion Animals and Us: Exploring the Relationships between People and Pets" (A. L. Podberscek, E. Paul, and J. A. Serpell, eds.). Cambridge University Press, Cambridge, MA.

Turner, D. C. (2002). The behaviour of dogs and cats. Points of contact between man and animal (in German). *Vierteljahrsschrift der Naturforschenden Gesellschaft Zürich* **147**(2), 51–61.

Turner, D. C. (2005a). Die beliebte Hauskatze—ein echtes "Heimtier." *In* "Mit Tiere leben im Alter" (M. Gäng and D. C. Turner, eds.). Ernst Reihnardt Verlag, München.

Turner, D. C. (2005b). Human-companion animal relationships, housing and behavioural problems from an ethologist's view (in German). *In* "Aktuelle Arbeiten zur artgemässen Tierhaltung, KTBL-Schrift 437." Deutsche Veterinärmedizinische Gesellschaft e. V., Giessen.

Turner, D. C. (2005c). A word about other species (in German). *In* "Mit Tiere leben im Alter" (M. Gäng and D. C. Turner, eds.). Ernst Reihnardt Verlag, München.

Turner, D. C., Feaver, J., Mendl, M., and Bateson, P. (1986). Variations in domestic cat behaviour towards humans: A paternal effect. *Anim. Behav.* **34**, 1890–1892.

Turner, D. C., Frick Tanner, E., Tanner-Frick, R., and Kaeser, I. (1998). A curriculum for continuing education in animal-assisted counselling/therapy and animal-assisted activities. Abstract Book, 8th International Conference on Human-Animal Interactions, Prague: The Changing Roles of Animals in Society. Afirac, Paris.

Turner, D. C., and Rieger, G. (2001). Singly living people and their cats: A study of human mood and subsequent behavior. *Anthrozoös* **14**(1), 38–46.

Turner, D. C., Rieger, G., and Gygax, L. (2003). Spouses and cats and their effects on human mood. *Anthrozoös* **16**(3), 213–228.

Turner, D. C., and Stammbach-Geering, K. (1990). Owner assessment and the ethology of human–cat relationships. *In* "Pets, Benefits and Practice" (I. Burger, ed.). British Veterinary Association, London.

CHAPTER 22

The Future of Research, Education, and Clinical Practice in the Animal–Human Bond and Animal-Assisted Therapy

Part B: Human–Animal Interactions and Health: Best Evidence and Where We Go from Here

CINDY C. WILSON
Department of Family Medicine, Uniformed Services University of the Health Sciences, Kensington, Maryland 20895

I. INTRODUCTION

The original title of this chapter was "Human–Animal Interactions and Health: Best Evidence. However, as the chapter developed, I felt that it was necessary to extend that title to add "where we go from here." Like Alice in Wonderland, I would like to take a look through the looking glass at human–animal interactions and health. My intent is to give an overview of how human–animal interactions and health may fit into the expectations of an evidence-based clinical model; why human–animal interactions and health may *not* fit that model; and where we should go from here as colleagues intent upon improving the health of others through human–animal interactions.

I was fortunate to have entered the field of human–animal interactions (HAIs) at an early stage of its development. There was almost a limitless amount to discover and study. However, it was a time when the topic of HAIs and health was not perceived as "mainstream" research. Senior colleagues often looked askance at me not only because of my interest in the topic but also because of my willingness to apply for a new faculty grant on this topic as a beginning assistant

Handbook on Animal-Assisted Therapy: Theoretical Foundations and Guidelines for Practice, 2e

professor at a major university. There was the expectation that I would be required to pursue research data, publication, and, ultimately, tenure with this area of research on my curriculum vita. It is hard enough to teach, do research, and publish in "A" level journals without trying to do so on a topic that was less than "traditional" as well as complex and difficult to tease out its actual outcome (i.e., health) effects. I saw it as a challenge, an opportunity to take an element from the natural living environment and measure its effect on humans. It was this challenge that I would like to extend to my colleagues in the field today.

Clearly, I was not alone in this desire, for professionals from many disciplines have examined the health benefit(s) a companion animal can have for persons with special needs and or specific health problems. So, if you will, join me for a short time as we "take a look through the looking glass" at the evidence that we have to date (Carroll, 2000).

Pets can lower blood pressures (Anderson *et al.*, 1992; Baun *et al.*, 1984; Friedman, 1983; Friedmann *et al.*, 2000; Grossberg, 1988; Wilson, 1987), heart rates (DeShriver and Riddick, 1990; Wilson, 1987), and anxiety (Wilson, 1991); enhance social environments (Brickel and Brickel, 1980/81; Mugford and McComisky, 1975; Wells, 2004); decrease depression (Bolin, 1987); and increase exercise (Serpell, 1991), cardiovascular fitness (Anderson *et al.*, 1992; Friedmann and Thomas, 1995; Friedmann et. al, 1980), and survival postmyocardial infarction (Friedmann, 1980, 1995). More recently, the therapeutic use of companion animals in nursing health care (Jorgenson, 1997), as well as the psychosocial impact of pets (Bryant, 1990) on children as well as on caregivers (Wilson, 2001) and the role of the pet as a preventive health intervention (Wilson, 2001) has been evaluated. Barak *et al.* (2001) described the usefulness of animal-assisted therapy for elderly schizophrenic patients in a one-year controlled trial. On a larger scale, Siegel (1990) focused on the role of pets and stress and health. More specifically she evaluated the intervening factors that might exacerbate the impact of stress on health and those variables that might mitigate the deleterious effect of stress, including pet ownership. She found that elderly pet owners use health services less than nonpet owners and that this difference is magnified among persons with a high level of life stress. Furthermore, her research with HIV-infected men suggests that pet ownership moderates the relationship between symptoms of HIV disease and psychological depression (Siegel, 1990).

II. REVIEWS

It was concluded in a state-of-the-art review of HAI studies related to older persons that the critical issue for all planned animal interventions, regardless of context, is a scientifically accumulated body of evidence that documents the effectiveness and limitations of the particular technique, approach, or program used. This early call for evidence-based interventions has largely gone unheeded in HAI research.

A later review, focusing on animal-assisted therapy studies, went one step further and divided the existing literature by the types of research design used (i.e., descriptive or hypothesis-generating studies and hypothesis-testing studies). The majority of studies on animal-assisted therapy fell into the category of hypothesis-generating studies. Few hypothesis-testing studies existed at that time and those that existed were largely studies of the health effects of animals. Both reviews (Beck and Katcher, 1984; Wilson and Netting, 1983) found little research focused on evaluations of the therapeutic effectiveness of formal animal-assisted therapy programs. However, these reviews did begin to build the "evidence."

The Working Group Summary from the National Institutes of Health Technology Assessment Conference on the Health Benefits of Pets concluded that although future research could begin without explicit hypotheses, investigations must proceed from descriptive studies (i.e., observational) of representative random samples to cross-sectional and retrospective studies and finally to prospective longitudinal studies (National Institutes of Health, 1988). Further, the working group noted that sample sizes were often too small to support the conclusions drawn and methodology was often flawed. The group concluded that there was inadequate evidence to support definitive conclusions regarding the health benefits of interacting with pets but pointed out many promising areas of research. Highlighting the large number of households with pets, the report contends that even a small positive impact might benefit thousands of people. However, based on the design of studies to date, such conclusions cannot be made.

More recently, Barba (1995) reviewed 52 research papers from the period of 1988 to 1993 using a shortened version of the Selby Research Assessment Form II (RAF). The research was evaluated on the basis of "general characteristics of published research articles, educational preparation of authors, journals, grant funding, etc; purposes, quality of literature reviews, and conceptual frameworks of the research; types of settings and sampling techniques used; common problems in the methodology, sampling, and analysis; and stated implications for future research" (Barba, 1995). Barba concluded that gains were made in knowledge of the impact of HAI even though most studies were nonexperimental. Although samples were large enough, most were nonprobability, nongeneralizable samples. The limitation of the research was not the nonprobability samples per se but rather the inappropriate generalizations of results.

Garrity and Stallones (1998) identified 25 empirical HAI studies from scientific literature between 1990 and 1995. Four of the 25 studies were descriptive and exploratory (Blenner, 1991; Carmack, 1991; Loughlin and Dowrick, 1993; Peretti, 1990). Sixteen of the 25 studies were correlational research and generally cross-sectional in nature (Anderson *et al.*, 1992; Cox, 1993; Fritz *et al.*, 1995; Hirsch and Whitman, 1994; Kidd and Kidd, 1994; Loyer-Carlson, 1992; Miller *et al.*, 1992; Rogers *et al.*, 1993; Stallones *et al.*, 1990; Straede and Gates, 1993; St Yves *et al.*, 1990; Watson and Weinstein, 1993; Zasloff and Kidd, 1994). Three of these correlational studies were longitudinal in nature (Serpell, 1991; Siegel, 1990; Tucker *et al.*, 1995). The concern about these correlational types of studies is the tendency to ascribe causality to relationships between variables. Five of the 25 studies were experimental in nature, with appropriate designs to address causation (Allen *et al.*, 1991; Deshriver and Riddick, 1990; Friedmann *et al.*, 1993; Nielson and Delude, 1994; Wilson, 1991). In these studies, there was an introduction of an experimental intervention, such as a pet dog, into a natural (e.g., home) setting in which some potential confounding factors were controlled.

Friedman *et al.* (2000) provided a succinct review of health and wellness and the relationship animals play in these dynamic processes. As part of her review, Friedman addressed the evidence for long-term health benefits of human–animal interactions on the cardiovascular system (Anderson *et al.*, 1992; Friedmann *et al.*, 1980; Friedmann and Thomas, 1995). While one-year survival rates were significantly higher for pet owners in these studies, researchers were unable to explain this association. Various types of pets (dogs versus cats) impacted health in different ways. Increased survival rates were not observed for cat owners (Friedmann and Thomas, 1995). Cat owners were more likely to be readmitted to a hospital for further cardiac problems (Rajack, 1997). Unfortunately, these studies cannot be compared easily, as their designs differed (case control and cross-sectional epidemiologic studies). Friedman (2000) suggested that future studies should address potential interactive factors such as gender and other demographic variables in determining the health effects of human–animal interactions.

Each of the reviews focused on slightly different perspectives; however, the call for well-designed research resonates throughout, as does the message from the Cheshire Cat to Alice. If the researcher knows where they want to go, then the research design *does* matter, as does the manner in which we *build the evidence* for health benefits of HAIs.

Researchers have postulated that one way to move the field forward is by the use of conceptual frameworks already accepted in the domains of health. Models that have been proposed by HAI researchers include, but are not limited to, Erickson's life cycle stage theory (Melson, 1998), the life course development or continuity model (Wilson, 1987), Lewin's health belief model (Wilson, 1991), Cobb's social support theory (Wilson *et al.*, 1998), and family cohesion theory (Triebenbacher, 1998). However, with all of the critical reviews and suggested frameworks for studying HAIs, criticisms of studies remain the same and the field appears to be stagnant. Today, I am suggesting that HAIs and health would fit well into an evidence-based medicine model. I would like to explore the possibilities with you.

More than 100 years ago, esteemed physician William Osler stated that "In seeking absolute truth, we aim at the unattainable and must be content with finding broken portions" (Osler, 1985). Most researchers and animal-assisted therapists know the literature on health benefits of animals. However, have we used it effectively to build the evidence and establish credibility as a field within the helping professions? Today, these so-called broken portions are becoming increasingly more numerous, varied in source and type, and difficult to incorporate into the complexities of modern clinical models of practice. Evidence-based medicine/research is neither a burgeoning new specialty nor a radically different approach to assembling these broken portions of information (Evidence-Based Medicine Working Group, 1992; Rao *et al.*, 1998). Rather, it is a logical and systematic approach to assembling these broken portions of data to provide answers. Let us review the rules of evidence-based health care and how it can be used for effective practice. Then we will address ways that senior program directors and researchers should be fostering a more proactive approach to building the knowledge base and hence the ability to focus our research and program evaluations to gain additional professional acceptance and acknowledgment of the timeless value of human–animal interactions.

III. BUILDING THE EVIDENCE

William James once paraphrased Kierkegaard saying that "we live forwards, but we understand backwards" (James, 1912). Metaphorically, this is another view through the looking glass. Using his philosophy, I suggest that we draw from the clinical literature and evidence-based medicine as a means of looking backwards—seeing what we could "see" if certain steps are taken now that will push the field to the next level.

A. Defining Relevant Terms

I have always believed that the use of the term "human–animal interactions" is the best index term for all of the research that is done in this area. Within that label would be terms familiar to us all (e.g., animal-assisted therapy, animal-assisted activities, human–animal bond). All therapies, interventions, and assistance involve "interactions." Unfortunately, in the databases of "evidence" (e.g., Cochrane, PubMed), that term does not occur. In fact, the most commonly used database in the United States for health-related topics is MEDLINE, and there is no Mesh heading for human–animal interactions. The closest approximation to access journals is "bonding-human-pet" (L. M. Spitzer, personal communication, 2005). In Europe, in addition to Medline, another commonly used database for health-related inquiries is Embase. As in MEDLINE, there is no key search term for human–animal interactions.

B. Defining the Evidence Hierarchy

In order to take its place as "best evidence," human–animal interaction research must advance in the hierarchy. As shown in Figure 1, the "evidence" goes from less causal research methods (case reports/studies, case series, surveys, qualitative research, and anecdotes) to increasingly more sophisticated research methods (nonrandomized trials and observational studies) to what has been the "gold standard" (randomized controlled trials [RCTS]) (Summerskill, 2001). At the top of this pyramid is the penultimate of causal research methods, the systematic review of randomized, controlled trials, more commonly know as "meta-analysis."

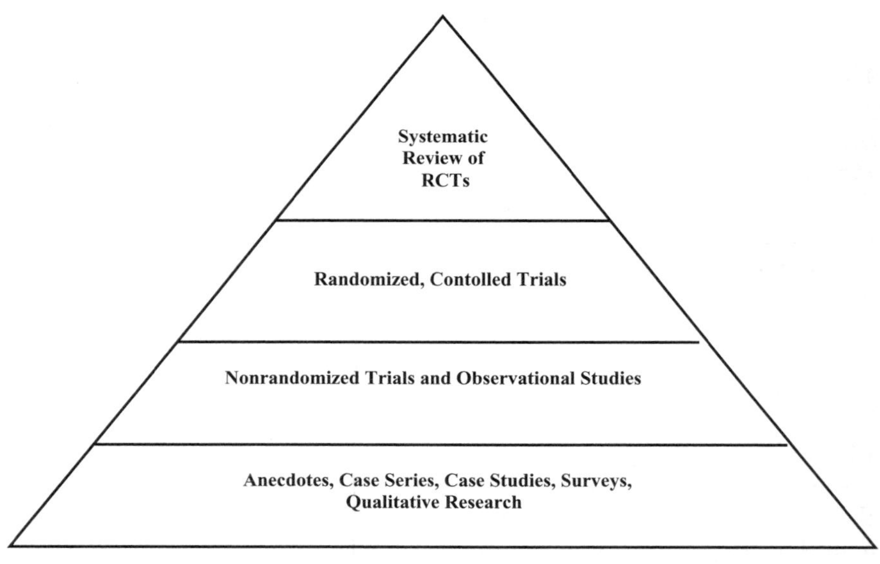

FIGURE 1 The hierarchy of evidence. Adapted from Summerskill (2001).

IV. ESTABLISHING THE CHALLENGES TO HUMAN–ANIMAL INTERACTION RESEARCH

There are five challenges to HAI research and to building the evidence base. I would like to address these five areas briefly.

A. Establishing and Applying High-Quality Standards of Research

Research has been ongoing in this area for years. Certainly there are many nonrandomized trials and observational studies (i.e., the third level of evidence); in fact, there are several randomized, controlled trials. It is, however, at this level where the hierarchy stalls. Research in this area has not developed with the same sophistication as other health-related topics. So how do we do this? We begin by using common definitions and guidelines for trials. We quit saying that we are "different" and utilize our research and program assessment skill with competence. We replicate and extend studies with larger sample sizes and appropriate controls. We measure cause and effect rather than association(s). We conduct basic research to determine the underlying causes of the biochemical impact, if any, the HAI has on humans as well as the animal. And we balance research designs. Recall from the review by Garrity and Stallones (1998) that only 25% of the research studies reviewed were experimental. This is not the balance that we need to have high-quality standards of HAI research.

B. Adapting to the Evolving Nature of Science in Human–Animal Interaction Research

As time progresses, and the sophistication of the studies of health benefits of HAIs increases, the evidence will evolve. This has certainly been true in clinical medicine where treatments and interventions have improved as scientific evidence supported change. In fact, medicine has adapted to the concept of "the evidence base" in medical practice.

Taking this approach, from the studies I reviewed briefly in the beginning of my discussion, there would be "evidence" of positive effects of human–animal interventions ~22.5% of the time, insufficient evidence of effects ~21.3% of the time, no effect ~20% of the time, and actual harmful effects (e.g., allergies, scratches, negative responses to animals) ~6.9% of the time. Unfortunately, it was really impossible to conduct a systematic review as expected in both the Ovid and the Cochrane databases. Current change in patient care is based on the type of "evidence" that is available. It is hoped that future physicians and scientists can turn to the Ovid and the Cochrane databases to determine what the evidence says about the effects of human–animal interventions based on the causal hierarchy of studies. Unfortunately, the only systematic review currently found is the study by Forbes reviewing strategies for managing behavioral symptomatology with Alzheimer's dementia (Forbes, 1998).

As new concepts emerge, there will be more opportunities to assess the effectiveness of HAIs. I caution those who would conceptualize an animal intervention as an alternative therapy. Alternative medicine as a field has had many of the same criticisms as ours and is currently being encouraged to adopt the evidence-based medicine model in order to attain credibility.

One of the common techniques in basic science is to determine an assay sensitivity. One of the issues that we have yet to address, as seen by the number of "little to no effect" outcome studies, is how we measure the impact of HAI on health; it may not be sensitive enough to detect the effect.

C. Accommodating the Diverse Nature of Human–Animal Interaction Models

Many of the prior studies that had insufficient or no effects are categorized as such on the basis of statistical significance. However, these studies may well have produced clinically valuable evidence. We need to conceptualize a framework in which these data may be useful to programs and individuals. An analogy from medicine would be studies whereby "me-too" drugs for hypertension do not have statistically significant effects on a patient sample. However, they lower blood pressure and heart rate in a clinically significant amount and without the side effects of the original drug. Should we discard these drugs as unimportant? Ignore their potential as therapeutic agents? I think not.

As we look again at the hierarchy of evidence, there is another overlay that we need to consider. It is the overlay of "users" of the evidence. For example, if we are to look at the effect(s) of an intervention, Figure 2 shows we would have basic scientists, clinical researchers, and regulators of the use of animal interventions. In fact, we already have these user groups in place, and it is the area in which many of us are most comfortable. However, there is also the area of "use" (or usefulness) testing whereby the outcome is the actual use of the intervention in the context of the public's health and its use to practitioners and to patients/clients. Figure 2 shows how this again builds the evidence (Summerskill, 2001). An example of this type of study would be the Maxicare study (Siegel, 1990) or the Australian Heart Study (Anderson *et al.*, 1992).

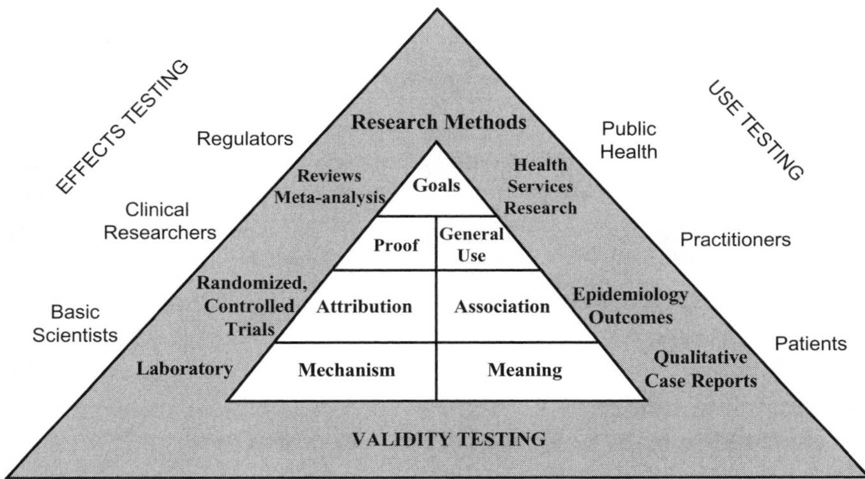

FIGURE 2 The evidence hierarchy and its users. Adapted from Summerskill (2001).

We cannot ignore the ethical issues of how the "evidence" is collected. Again, it matters which way we are going, so we must have a plan of how to get there. It is a time of controversy with respect to institutional review boards. Decisions made about how to conduct the research really do matter to the participants and should matter to us all.

Once we have the evidence, there is the expectation that the research quality must be measured. How likely is it that the effects reported are due to the independent variable (the animal/pet/companion), that is, what is the internal validity of the study? We can ensure the internal validity of the study through randomization (subject assignment to groups in a random manner), baseline comparability (balanced demographics and prognostic factors), change of intervention (loss to follow-up, contamination, poor compliance), blinding (Did patients/clients and investigators know who got the treatment?), and outcome analysis (Was the objectivity, sensitivity, and reliability assessed? Was the number treated large? Were *p* values significant? Were there multiple outcomes and were all measured?). At the same time, the questions regarding how likely it is that the observed effects would occur outside the study and in different settings and the external validity of the study must be considered.

Not only must internal and external validity of the study be measured, but also the generalizability of data (Is there a wide enough range of patients/clients/subjects to represent the field of actual practice use of the outcome?) must be assessed. Is this study reproducible? Is what was done clear? Is the treatment intervention transferable? Was the outcome clinically significant? Was adherence good? Was there feedback for the participants, and is the intervention practical in your practice setting? Were the outcomes of the study clinically relevant as well as important to the patients for which it is intended?

Last in the list of accommodations is the evaluation of model validity. Within that evaluation, was thought given to using a model that was *representative* of the concept? Was the use of the animal intervention strategy adequate? Was the intervention clearly described? Did the researchers classify participants, determine the intervention, and assess the outcomes according to the system (i.e., model) being assessed? Moreover, were participants believers in the intervention? Was the intervention adapted to the culture of the participants, and what was the impact of informed consent?

D. Addressing the Underlying Assumptions of Human–Animal Interaction

Time for reflection on the underlying assumptions about this area of inquiry is past due. Are we making too much of a natural phenomenon? Are the potential benefits of human–animal interactions found only in Western science? Are there alternative outcomes of benefit that we should be considering? Are there limits to the scientific level of inquiry in the field?

"So many questions—so little time." As the rabbit said to Alice in Wonderland, "I'm late, I'm late!" (Carroll, 2000)—24 years late . . . in realizing that I am responsible for *not* moving this field along as well as I could have.

How *do* we progress in a meaningful manner as a field of scientific inquiry? I have just outlined a rigorous approach to sound studies in the field. However, this is not new nor is it revolutionary. What I would like to propose as a possible solution is a change in professional roles and behaviors—changes that I as well as many of my colleagues need to make.

E. Providing Quality Training/Mentoring for Investigators and Program Developers

One of the first steps we need to take is the development of an international working group to educate and support national organizations, directors of major programs, and key researchers on the educational strategies most productive to building the hierarchy of evidence. Principles of evidence-based HAIs are equally applicable to allied health care providers/workers (e.g., physicians, nurses, physical therapists, occupational therapists, clinical psychologists, social workers, health and social service program directors, animal-assisted therapy program directors, behavioralists, and public health workers, to name a few). This would also help build alliances between disciplines, minimize the "turf" wars, and improve collaborative efforts.

Second, this working group could lobby the appropriate database professionals to include human–animal interactions as key search terms. This would address the issues of common definitions and terms. For the PubMed/MEDLINE database, that could be accomplished through negotiations with the staff at the National Library of Medicine (http://www.nlm.nih.gov/mesh/staff). For the European sector, lobbying for a change in Embase terms would also be appropriate, as there is even less specificity in search terms than in MEDLINE with "pet therapy" used only as a text word but not as a descriptor per se (Spitzer, 2005). The closest term to human–animal interactions found by a reference librarian was "animal use."

Third, practitioners (and I use that term to cover individuals involved in program development and evaluation and/or research) must recognize that the evidence comes from a broader perspective than their own discipline. Indeed the interdisciplinary nature of the HAI field is actually a benefit in this era of funding. Translational research is the name of the game: from basic science to the patient . . . from applied science to the recipient. We need to build these relationships across disciplines and then incorporate or blend our research questions into larger studies. This will address many of the validity issues that I posed while providing investigators with a greater potential for extramural funding.

Fourth, senior-level practitioners have failed the field. We have not mentored younger practitioners adequately to build the hierarchy of evidence in our own discipline, much less across disciplines. We must integrate not only our graduate students and our junior colleagues into our research and evaluation teams, but we must also work with senior colleagues from other allied health and social service fields to incorporate our research and programmatic questions into larger studies. We must be willing to position junior colleagues as principal investigators in order to help them remain active in the research arena while progressing through the academic requirements for promotion. Thus, we would be building the evidence and advancing their careers as well.

Fifth, we must reevaluate our existing studies and program evaluations in light of validity and also extrapolation issues. We must integrate our research questions into large population studies to gain the same credibility as studies such as Framingham, the Australian Heart Study, the women's initiative, and others. However, we must also keep in mind that the largest sample size in the world does not help us if there is little or no comparability to the patients/participants that we need to serve.

In summary, every practitioner/researcher in the field of HAIs should know how to search out the evidence but also how to build systematic evidence in the literature. We should be able to differentiate between good evidence and limited evidence and have the ability to evaluate the clinical applicability and relevance. Everything that is measurable is not necessarily important and everything that is not measurable should not be dismissed. As evaluators of the evidence as well as advocates for the timeless health benefits of companion animals, we must know how to build the evidence for that which is measurable and be able to differentiate the value of that which is not.

Our role as leaders in the field must be to help build the evidence and guide the development of the hierarchy, as well as obtain the funding to support these endeavors. We must take what is "known," fix the weaknesses we have identified, and develop an ongoing strategy to communicate the timeless impact of human–animal interactions. We cannot continue to critique the field of efforts without undertaking to help make the changes needed.

ACKNOWLEDGMENTS

This chapter was presented, in part, at the 10th International Conference on Human–Animal Interactions, October 2004, Glasgow, Scotland. The views contained herein are those of the author and do not represent the Uniformed Services University of the Health Science or the Department of Defense.

REFERENCES

Allen, K. M., Blascovich, J., Tomaka, J., and Kelsey, R. M. (1991). Presence of human friends and pet dogs as moderators of autonomic responses to stress in women. *J. Personal. Soc. Psychol.* **61**, 582–589.

Anderson, W. P., Reid, C. M., and Jennings, G. L. (1992). Pet ownership and risk factors for cardiovascular disease. *Med. J. Austr.* **157**, 298–301.

Barak, Y., Savorai, O., Mavashev, S., and Beni, A. (2001). Animal-assisted therapy for elderly schizophrenic patients: A one-year controlled trial. *American Journal of Geriatric Psychiatry*, **9**(4), 439–442.

Barba, B. E. (1995). A critical review of the research on the human/companion animal relationship; 1988–1993. *Anthrozoös* **VIII**(1), 9–14.

Baun, M., Bergstrom, N., Langston, N., and Thoma, L. (1984). Physiological effects of human/companion animal bonding. *Nursing Research*, **33**, 126–129.

Beck, A. M., and Katcher, A. H. (1984). A new look at pet-facilitated therapy. *Journal of the American Veterinary Medicine Association*, **184**(4), 414–421.

Blenner, J. L. (1991). The therapeutic functions of animals in infertility. *Holist. Nurs. Pract.* **5**, 6–10.

Bolin, S. E. (1987). The effects of companion animals during conjugal bereavement. *Anthrozoös*, **1**, 26–35.

Brickel, C. M., and Brickel, G. K. (1980/81). A review of the role of pet animals on psychotherapy with the elderly. *International Journal on Aging and Human Development*, **12**, 119–128.

Bryant, B. (1990). The richness of the child-pet relationship: A consideration of both benefits and costs of pets to children. *Anthrozoös*, **3**(253–261).

Carmack, B. J. (1991). The role of companion animals with persons with AIDS/HIV. *Holist. Nurs. Pract.* **5**, 24–31.

Carroll, L. (2000). "Alice's Adventures in Wonderland and through the Looking Glass." Signet Classic.

Cox, R. P. (1993). The human/animal bond as a correlate of family functioning. *Clin. Nurs. Res.* **2**, 222–231.

Deshriver, M. M., and Riddick, C. C. (1990). Effects of watching aquariums on elders' stress. *Anthrozoös* **4**, 44–48.

Evidence-Based Medicine Working Group (1992). Evidence-based medicine: A new approach to teaching and the practice of medicine. *JAMA* **268**, 2420–2425.

Forbes, D. A. (1998). Strategies for managing behavioural symptomatology associated with dementia of the Alzheimer type: A systematic overview. *Can. J. Nurs. Res.* **30**(2), 67–86.

Friedmann, E., Katcher, A. H., Lynch, J. J., and Thomas, S. A. (1980). Animal companions and one-year survival of patients after discharge from a coronary unit. *Public Health Rep.* **95**, 307–312.

Friedmann, E., Katcher, A. H., Thomas, S. A., Lynch, J. J., and Messent, P. R. (1983). Social interaction and blood pressure: The influence of animal companions. *Journal of Nervous and Mental Disease*, **171**, 461–465.

Friedmann, E., Locker, B. Z., and Lockwood, R. (1993). Perception of animals and cardiovascular responses during verbalization with an animal present. *Anthrozoös* **6**, 115–134.

Friedmann, E., and Thomas, S. A. (1995). Pet ownership, social support, and one-year survival after acute myocardial infarction in the cardiac arrhythmia suppression trial (CAAST). *Am. J. Cardiol.* **76**, 1213–1217.

Friedmann, E., Thomas, S. A., and Eddy, T. J. (2000). Companion animals and human health: Physical and cardiovascular influences. *In* "Companion Animals and Us: Exploring the Relationship between People and Pets" (A. L. Podberscek, E. S. Paul, and J. A. Serpell, eds.), pp. 125–142. Cambridge University Press, Cambridge, MA.

Fritz, C. L., Farver, T. B., Kass, P. H., and Hart, L. A. (1995). Association with companion animals and the expression of noncognitive symptoms in Alzheimer's patients. *J. Nerv. Ment. Dis.* **183**(7), 459–463.

Garrity, T. F., and Stallones, L. (1998). Effects of pet contact. *In* "Companion Animals in Human Health" (C. C. Wilson and D. C. Turner, eds.), pp. 3–22. Sage, Thousand Oaks, CA.

Grossberg, J. M., Alf, E. F., and Vormbrock, J. K. (1988). Does pet dog presence reduce human cardiovascular responses to stress? *Anthrozoös*, **2**, 38–44.

Hirsch, A. R., and Whitman, B. W. (1994). Pet ownership and prophylaxis of headache and chronic pain. *Headache* **34**, 542–543.

James, W. (1912). Is radical empiricism solopsistic? *In* "Essays in Radical Empiricism," pp. 234–240. Longman Green and Co., New York.

Jorgenson, J. (1997). Therapeutic use of companion animals in health care. *Image: Journal of Nursing Scholarship*, **29**(3), 249–254.

Kidd, A. H., and Kidd, R. M. (1994). Benefits and liabilities of pets for the homeless. *Psychol. Rep.* **74**, 715–722.

Loughlin, C. A., and Dowrick, D. W. (1993). Psychological needs filled by avian companions. *Anthrozoös* **6**, 166–172.

Loyer-Carlson, V. (1992). Pets and perceived family life quality. *Psychol. Rep.* **70**, 947–952.

Melson, G. F. (1998). The role of companion animals in human development. *In* "Companion Animals in Human Health" (C. C. Wilson and D. C. Turner, eds.), pp. 219–236. Sage, Thousand Oaks, CA.

Miller, D., Staats, S., and Partlo, C. (1992). Discriminating positive and negative aspects of pet interaction: Sex differences in the older population. *Soc. Indicat. Res.* **27**, 363–374.

Mugford, R. A., and M'Comisky, J. C. (1975). Some recent work on psychotherapeutic value of age birds with old people. Baltimore: Wilkins and Wilkins.

National Institutes of Health (1988). Summary of working group: Health benefits of pets (No. DHHS Publication 1988-216-107). U.S. Government Printing Office, Washington, DC.

Nielson, J. A., and Delude, L. A. (1994). Pets as adjunct therapists in a residence for former psychiatric patients. *Anthrozoös* 7, 166–171.

Osler, W. (1985). Aequaminitas. *In* "The Collected Essays of Sir William Osler" (J. P. McGovern and C. G. Roland, eds.), Vol. I, pp. 7–15. Classic of Medicine Library, A division of Gryphon Eds., Ltd., Birmingham, AL.

Peretti, P. O. (1990). Elderly-animal friendship bonds. *Soc. Behav. Personal.* **18**, 151–156.

Rajack, L. S. (1997). "Pets and Human Health: The Influences of Pets on Cardiovascular and Other Aspects of Owner's Health." University of Cambridge, Cambridge, UK.

Rao, G., Robbins, C. W., and Roberts, R. G. (1998). Evidence based medicine. *In* "Home Study Self-Assessment Program," Monograph 225, p. 48. American Academy of Family Physicians, Kansas City, MO.

Rogers, J., Hart, L. A., and Bolt, R. P. (1993). The role of pet dogs in casual conversations of elderly adults. *J. Soc. Psychol.* **133**, 265–277.

Serpell, J. (1991). Beneficial effects of pet ownership on some aspects of human health and behavior. *J. R. Med. Soc.* **84**, 717–720.

Siegel, J. M. (1990). Stressful life events and use of physician services among the elderly: The moderating role of pet ownership. *J. Personal. Soc. Psychol.* **58**(6), 1081–1086.

Stallones, L., Marx, M., Garrity, T. F., and Johnson, T. P. (1990). Pet ownership and attachment in relation to the health of U.S. adults, 21 to 64 years of age. *Anthrozoös* **4**, 100–112.

Straede, C. M., and Gates, G. R. (1993). Psychological health in a population of Australian cat owners. *Anthrozoös* **6**, 30–42.

St Yves, A., Freeston, M. H., Jacques, C., and Robitaille, C. (1990). Love of animals and interpersonal affectionate behavior. *Psychol. Rep.* **67**, 1067–1075.

Summerskill, W. S. M. (2001). Hierarchy of evidence. *In* "Key Topics in Evidence-Based Medicine" (D. McGovern, R. M. Valori, W. S. M. Summerskill, and M. Levi, eds.), p. 15. BIOS Scientific Publishers, Ltd., Oxford, UK.

Triebenbacher, S. L. (1998). The relationship between attachment to companion animals and self-esteem: A developmental perspective. *In* "Companion animals in human health" (C. C. Wilson and D. C. Turner eds.), pp. 135–148. Thousand Oaks: Sage.

Tucker, J. S., Friedman, H. S., Tsai, C. M., and Martin, L. R. (1995). Playing with pets and longevity among older people. *Psychol. Aging* **10**, 3–7.

Watson, N. L., and Weinstein, M. (1993). Pet ownership in relation to depression, anxiety, and anger in working women. *Anthrozoös* **6**, 135–138.

Wells, D. (2004). The facilitation of social interactions by domestic dogs. *Anthrozoös*, **17**(4), 340–352.

Wilson, C. C. (1987). Physiological responses of college students to a pet. *J. Nerv. Ment. Dis.* **175**(10), 606–612.

Wilson, C. C. (1991). The pet as an anxiolytic intervention. *J. Nerv. Ment. Dis.* **179**(8), 482–489.

Wilson, C. C., Fuller, G. F., and Triebenbacher, S. L. (1998). "Human-Animal Interactions, Social Exchange Theory, and Caregivers: A Different Approach." Paper presented at the 8th International Conference on Human-Animal Interactions, Prague, Czech Republic.

Wilson, C. C., Fuller, G. F., and Cruess, D. F. (2001a). The emotional attachment of caregivers to companion animals. Paper presented at the 9th International Conference on Human-Animal Interactions, Rio de Janeiro, Brazil.

Wilson, C. C., and Netting, F. E. (1983). Companion animals and the elderly: A state-of-the-art summary. *Journal of the American Veterinary Medicine Association*, **183**(12), 1425–1429.

Zasloff, R. L., and Kidd, A. H. (1994). Loneliness and pet ownership among single women. *Psychol. Rep.* **75**, 747–752.

CHAPTER 22

The Future of Research, Education, and Clinical Practice in the Animal–Human Bond and Animal-Assisted Therapy

Part C: The Role of Animal-Assisted Therapy in Clinical Practice: The Importance of Demonstrating Empirically Oriented Psychotherapies

AUBREY H. FINE
College of Education and Integrative Studies, California State Polytechnic University, Pomona, California 91768

JEFFERY S. MIO
Psychology and Sociology Department, California State Polytechnic University, Pomona, California 91768

We are both frequently asked whenever we give presentations for clinicians, questions that require simple solutions for therapy cases which by their nature are complex. For example, when Dr. Mio makes a presentation on the use of metaphors in politics, he often gets a question from a therapist asking something like, "What kind of metaphor works with someone who is depressed?" Similarly, Dr. Fine is commonly asked what kinds of dogs work best with specific kinds of illnesses, or perhaps what is the best approach to utilize the animals with specific groups of people? These kinds of questions imply that the questioner is looking for the "magic bullet"—a phrase, a statement, or an animal that would instantly lead to therapeutic cure of a disorder.

Handbook on Animal-Assisted Therapy: Theoretical Foundations and Guidelines for Practice, 2e

I. SKILL OF THE THERAPIST

While these kinds of questions might seem naive to the outside observer, we have found that when talking about animal-asisted therapy (AAT), quite often inexperienced therapists—or for that matter, some patients—have unreasonable expectations for the modality. They do not seem to appreciate the complexity of delivering such a therapeutic intervention. Writers have argued for decades that special attention needs to be given to the skills of the therapist in implementing such therapies. Draper *et al.* (1990) stressed that the therapist "must possess appropriate competence in a definable therapy in absence of the animal" (p. 172). They believe that a therapist's competence and knowledge are the most important aspects of the therapeutic team. Others have investigated exactly what these therapist values are. For years, Strupp (1960, 1973, 1986) has examined factors that therapists bring into therapy. He has concluded that the two major components of psychotherapy are (1) psychotherapy occurs within an interpersonal context (the therapeutic context or a therapeutic alliance), and (2) psychotherapy involves learning, be it learning new skills or unlearning unsuccessful patterns of behaviors. In order for therapists to create a therapeutic context, therapists need to be theoretically grounded and be competent or skillful in the therapeutic process. "As we have seen, the therapist's skill is significantly manifested by an ability to create a particular interpersonal context and, within that context, to foster certain kinds of learning" (Strupp, 1986, p. 126).

Stiles and colleagues (1986) would agree with Strupp's analysis. They contend, "Most of the proposed general therapist factors [of good psychotherapy] fall into two broad groups: (a) warm involvement with the client and (b) communication of a new perspective on the client's person and situation" (p. 172). Applying this to AAT, one might see that a gentle, loving animal, such as a golden retriever, may enhance a warm therapeutic environment, whereas an enigmatic animal, such as a bird, may help stimulate a discussion in a new and interesting direction. However, the animal itself cannot "cause" therapeutic change; it can only assist in this change. Again, therapists need to be *skilled* therapists in order to providently use animals in treatment.

For example, skilled therapists might use AAT as one of the tools they have at their disposal, and with the sensitive use of animals, they may very well achieve a therapeutic breakthrough. There are times that the animal makes breakthroughs that may be very difficult for the therapist to immediately achieve. Draper *et al.* (1990) suggested that the animal contributes by acting as a "prosthesis" to help establish and sustain the therapeutic relationship by the therapist. Pomp (1998) pointed out that the animal's presence encourages clients to readjust their boundaries of social comfort. Most clients appear more willing to disclose and to open up as a consequence of being surrounded by animals. Others point out that the presence of the animals enables the patient to begin feeling more comfortable and safer, thus leading to a stronger therapeutic alliance. However, Bowers and MacDonald (2001) stressed that a skilled therapist needs to be in charge of the therapy to interpret the interactions in order to go beyond and to establish therapeutic gain. It is not necessarily the fact of using animals in therapy that leads to the breakthrough but the understanding of *how* an animal may lead to a positive result.

It has been reported that since the 1960s, the number of psychotherapy approaches and theories have increased approximately 600% (Miller *et al.*, 1996). Garfield and Begin (1994) suggested that there are an estimated 200 therapy models today, including strategies such as AAT. Although some may believe that this expansion of theories has merit, others fiercely disagree. The opponents seem to be concerned with the dilution of what is considered effective therapy rather than just "pop" therapy. We believe that pop therapies negatively bias the public about the merits of psychotherapy.

II. WHAT CONSTITUTES GOOD THERAPY?

Hubble *et al.* (1999) edited a provocative book on what contributes to the therapeutic process. Many of the contributors reviewed what they saw as common positive factors in therapy. Assay and Lambert (1999) synthesized the research findings and determined that "regardless of a therapist's theoretical orientation and techniques" (e.g., biofeedback, systematic desensitization) (p. 31), all forms of therapy seem to have common therapeutic factors that enhance their success. These factors can be divided into four broad areas, including extra therapeutic changes, therapeutic relationships, techniques, and expectancy effects. Assay and Lambert referred to a paper by Lambert (1992) that highlighted the effects of each of these categories. According to Lambert (1992), as much as 40% of the improvement gained in psychotherapy is due directly to client variables (extra therapeutic changes), such as the severity of the disturbance, motivation for change, psychological health, and the ability to identify the problem. However, research has consistently highlighted the importance of expectancy and placebo effects. Lambert sees this dimension contributing to 15% of the variance of change. Thus, expectancy for change and the hope demonstrated by the client that therapy will make a marked difference contribute 55% of the therapeutic change. Ironically, only about 15% of the variance of therapeutic change is attributed to the superiority of one approach over another.

The last major component Lambert (1992) addressed is the relationship factors that support therapeutic alliance. Factors such as warmth, affirmation, and kindness are the backbone of this component. Researchers such as Najavitis and Strupp (1994) and Gatson (1990), as well as Lambert (1992), suggest that about 30% of the variance in the therapeutic outcome is directly impacted by therapeutic relationships. In a paper prepared by Bower (2005), a question is posed inquiring whether the actual psychotherapy treatments cure disorders or if the established relationships have more healing powers. This inference could lead to an important question in the needed research agenda for AAT: Does having a trained therapy animal enhance the therapeutic alliance and relationship?

Although this initial information is relevant, the answer to the debate on what actually constitutes best practice in therapy continues to elude many professions, including psychology (Bower, 2005). A major thrust over the past decade in many health care environments, including medicine, has been the quest to secure and develop evidence-based practices (as discussed previously in Chapter 3). In an article in the *New York Times Magazine*, Hitt (2001) pointed out that evidence-based medicine is one of the breakthrough ideas of 2001. Although the field of medicine has portrayed itself as the discipline that is led by science, surprisingly there are not as many best-practice treatments in medicine as the consumer is led to believe.

According to the Institute of Medicine's (2001) definition of quality health care for the 21st century, "evidence-based practice" is the integration of best research practice with clinical expertise and patient values. The impetus of evidence-based practices in mental health has become a highly discussed topic since the early 1990s. In 1993, the American Psychological Association (APA) Division 12 (Society of Clinical Psychology) began developing and elaborating on a "list of empirically supported, manualized psychological interventions" for specific disorders. The list was developed on the basis of "randomized and controlled studies" (Norcross *et al.*, 2006, p. 5). Since Division 12's benchmark efforts, several other divisions in APA have also issued their own preliminary guidelines for empirically supported interventions. The challenge that many of these divisions and organizations are now wrestling with is how one accurately measures and determines treatment efficacy and what constitutes evidence (Goodheart, 2004). Norcross *et al.* (2006) have edited what appears to be a seminal book that addresses the numerous variables that should be considered in conceptualizing evidence-based research as a whole. We will synthesize and report on some of their findings and use them as a springboard for our discussions. They suggest the following.

A. Clinical expertise, patient values, and the need for scientific research on techniques are the areas where evidence is definitely needed.
B. Scientific research is the benchmark for evidence-based treatment. Research consists of a variety of methodologies and designs. Random

clinical designs seem to have the most merit and are considered the gold standard for all disciplines (Bower, 2005). However, qualitative research methods (including ethnography, phenomenology, family analysis, ethnomethodology, case studies, single-participant designs) are all appropriate to also assess and gather evidence. Qualitative research could be valuable for taking insights and comments made by patients or clinicians and studying them in a more systematic manner.

C. The treatment method, the impact of the individual therapist, the therapeutic relationship, and the role of the patient are vital dimensions worthy of more clarity and investigation.

D. The available research needs to demonstrate that psychological treatments that eventually have empirical support are superior to no treatment or placebo treatment.

III. HOW BEST TO STUDY ANIMAL-ASSISTED THERAPY?

Using Norcross *et al.* (2006) as our catalyst for how to best research AAT, clinical research with small sets of individuals has been the accepted practice for social sciences for several years (Chambless, 2005; Chambless and Ollendick, 2001; Roth and Fonagy, 1996). Those interested in advancing AAT into a more accepted evidence-based intervention must consider the steps that need to be taken to document its efficacy (see Chapters 3 and 22B). According to the APA, there are criteria used to judge evidence-based interventions. The following are some of the variables reviewed: (1) between-group designs demonstrating superiority to wait-list controls; (2) between-group designs demonstrating superiority to psychotherapy placebo; (3) between-group designs demonstrating superiority to some other forms of psychotherapy; (4) a large series of single-case designs demonstrating therapeutic efficacy; and (5) findings from at least two different investigators. These were general criteria used by a major task force examining empirically supported treatments commissioned by Division 12 (Chambless and Ollendick, 2001).

Clearly, the gold standard for research of this type is to have a random assignment to an AAT format and a traditional therapy format and then to determine which format led to a better therapeutic outcome. Another variation on this is to have three groups, with the third group using an animal surrogate, such as a stuffed animal or a large pillow. While this methodology may be a theoretical gold standard, one must also carefully choose what one's measure of therapeutic success is. For example, measures for anxiety or depression [e.g., Beck Depression Inventory (Beck, 1967); Brief Depression Rating Scale (Kellner, 1986); Costello–Comrey Depression and Anxiety Scales (Costello and Comrey, 1967); Zung Self-Rating Anxiety Scale (Zung, 1971);

and Zung Self-Rating Depression Scale (Zung, 1965)] tend to be global measures that are insensitive to subtle changes. Thus, if AAT is only subtly effective, then it will not yield statistically significant results on these global measures.

Another issue to consider is that of proof. Even if AAT proves to be statistically significantly different from normal therapy, it could be that there are consistently small differences that are not clinically significant. Alternatively, there could be those who clearly benefit from AAT, but these individuals can be counterbalanced by others who may do worse with AAT, especially those clients who have aversive reactions to or fears about animals, or AAT practices that are not clinically sound. Unfortunately, as many realize, a majority of published studies only highlight behavioral changes in one direction or another. Those studies that do not demonstrate any differences or therapeutic impact tend not to be published. Denmark and colleagues (1988) highlighted this position and suggested that studies not finding any convincing outcomes are rarely published. They suggested that we may very well believe there to be greater differences between genders because studies that found no differences are not published, so *only* those studies that found gender differences were published. Applied to research on AAT, the void in publications does not allow for a clearer understanding of the potential uses and misuses of AAT.

IV. ESTABLISHING LEVELS OF PROOF: THE DIFFERENCE BETWEEN EPISTEMOLOGICAL AND METAPHYSICAL EVIDENCE

To secure respectability as an effective evidence-based intervention, a methodology needs to establish a track level of acceptable proof that supports its position. Thus, the most logical question that follows is what level of proof is needed in order to be satisfied that there is a true benefit from AAT. This is akin to the difference between metaphysical and epistemological proof that is discussed in philosophy (Smith and Medin, 1981). From an epistemological perspective, we require empirical proof. From a metaphysical perspective, we may "know" that something exists. For example, years ago I (JSM) *know* that I made a difference in a particular client whom I took over from a therapist completing his fellowship. This 70+-year-old client did not drive and would not take public transportation, so his 60+-year-old brother had to drive him to therapy at our clinic. As time went on, this client eventually decided to take public transportation to our clinic and took a leadership role in getting people at his board-and-care facility to participate in various activities. Why did I succeed where my predecessor did not? Again, at a metaphysical level, I know that I made a difference. However, as a researcher, I know that I would never have been able to design a research study a priori that would have measured what I did differently. My determination of the reason for the success of this case came postdictively. When the client felt better and was able to overcome his negativity, he told me that the previous therapist was a smoker and smoked constantly throughout the session. Thus, they were never able to develop a therapeutic alliance. Because I was a much calmer therapist who did not smoke or have any nervous twitches, he was able to make a connection with me. If one were to evaluate the general theoretical approaches to therapy that my predecessor and I had, one would categorize us in the same category. However, my personal characteristics made me a better therapist for this particular client.

The same holds true in my (AHF) work with my patients. Over the years, I have witnessed so many remarkable changes as a result of the animals that support my work. Trying not to anthropomorphize my impressions, there are many case examples that I could consider to highlight how AAT made a significant difference. In "Afternoons with Puppy" (Fine and Eisen, in press), several case studies are reported, which are viewed metaphysically to illustrate the phenomena of change. The case study about Seth will now be discussed.

Initially, when I was contacted by Seth's family, his mother was very concerned about his language development and his inability to relate with his peers, and adults. He struggled significantly with his peers, and his behavior, according to his mother, was quite "odd." Furthermore, the mother reported that he was constantly having tantrums and was obsessed with storms and the sounds of raindrops. Early on, his curiosity with rain concerned her, but as he aged, Seth became so obsessed with the rain that he did not want to do anything else except to listen to the water fall. Over the years, his obsession with the weather became even more visibly intense. He could be seen standing in his room motionless for long periods of time, aimlessly looking out the window.

Seth was also having a hard time fitting into school and was eventually enrolled in special education, initially in a language-delayed class and eventually into a special day class program. Within school he was very isolated and had tremendous challenges relating to any of his peers.

> After working with Seth and conducting a thorough evaluation, I eventually diagnosed him with Asperger's syndrome, along with an obsessive-compulsive disorder because of his visible interest in the weather. As with other children with Asperger's, Seth had trouble keeping up with his studies at school and making friends. He was placed in a special day class for several years until his family urged that he become more integrated. With the support of tutors, Seth received a more minimal intervention, and over the course of years he was integrated into regular education, with monitoring and support.
>
> In overall good physical health, Seth was a little large for his age and would eventually grow up to be a tall, muscular high school graduate. But when we first

> met, he was quiet, locked into loneliness, and had frequent bouts of anger. This changed over the period of years when he began to integrate with my various therapy animals, including a young dusky conjure named Boomer. Although Seth eventually connected with most of the animals in my office, it was this small brilliant green–feathered bird that captured his attention and seemed to make a difference. The animals seemed to help Seth relax, and over the course of months, he seemed more open to talk when surrounded by their company. Although I had several birds, Boomer's playful personality and her willingness to be held by Seth cemented their bond instantly. Observing the two together, I began to consider how I could integrate Boomer more intimately into Seth's treatment. I also began to notice that Boomer's presence seemed to decrease the agitation and anxiety that Seth would traditionally display. He noted early in therapy, "I cannot get mad when I hold her. She trusts me and I would never hurt her." That statement seemed to be the catalyst for our future efforts.

My impressions from this intervention led me to believe, at least metaphysically, that the intervention that included Boomer made a significant impact. Empirically, self-reports and reports from others would also concur. Nevertheless, the degree of "proof" that was established still leaves many other unanswered questions and too many skeptics with a rationale for their apprehensions.

It might be difficult to construct empirical studies that will yield epistemological proof. Animals can be unpredictable. This unpredictability can be used to therapeutic advantage or can be an impediment to therapy. For example, a dog may shy away from a client, thus unintentionally reinforcing the client's self-image that she is unlovable. Alternatively, if this dog were to warm up to the client, she may discover that she has the capacity to be loved. In another example, I recall hearing about an inexperienced therapist attempting to apply AAT in her practice. She loved bringing her dog to the therapy sessions but recognized that the dog would constantly growl at her male clients. She was embarrassed about these actions and would reassure all her male clients to not take the growls personally. She also would let them know that the growls would eventually stop once the dog got used to them. Although her perceptions were accurate, was the dog's presence more of a detractor than a help? These two examples vividly highlight how the animal's unpredictable behavior could actually be an impediment to therapy. Thus, the general notion of the effectiveness of AAT may not necessarily be dependent on the paradigm of AAT but on the spontaneous reactions of the animal–client interactions.

V. GAINING RESPECTABILITY FOR ANIMAL-ASSISTED THERAPY

Over the course of close to three decades, I (AHF) have incorporated animals as adjuncts to the therapy. I have observed firsthand many of the benefits discussed throughout the book. Nevertheless, I have become cautious and skeptical of those who make unreasonable comments about the power of this medium. Therapists incorporating AAT may have to reconsider their therapeutic approach so that they more naturally integrate the animal into the process. More importantly, it behooves leading researchers and clinicians to come together to generate more rigid guidelines for the utilization of animal-assisted interventions to develop clearer expectations and protocols. For AAT to eventually gain respectability in the mental health arena, there is a strong need for evidence-based research to document the interventions. The question that we must now ask is how can we move this type of intervention closer to more respectability?

Many ideas come to mind. For example, in the spring of 2004, several leading authorities in the human–animal bond movement, specifically AAT, congregated at the University of Pennsylvania to discuss suggested research agendas for applying AAT with specific psychiatric populations. Although the meeting was brief, it provided a forum for leading scholars and clinicians in mental health to meet with their counterparts applying and studying AAT. We believe that this type of venue is a good place to begin wrestling with agendas for research and methods to implement the process. It is suggested that a possible mission of some of the university centers studying the human–animal bond (throughout the globe) could be to act as a clearinghouse of efficacy-based studies. If funding could be secured, scholars at various institutions could spearhead various evidence-based studies. It seems that a major area for evidence-based research could be how AAT enhances therapeutic alliance. Numerous studies could be established with clinicians providing guidance for the research team. With appropriate coordination, studies could be initiated that measured many of the dimensions that advocates claim AAT/AAI impacts. If an appropriate timeline could be established, within several years, there could be more respectable evidence-based studies generated on the area. Furthermore, the organizations involved in promoting all animal-assisted interventions need to clarify the terms used to describe various interventions. We strongly urge that these organizations raise the public's awareness by delineating what should be classified as therapy and by whom these services should be rendered. It is imperative for the general community to recognize that there is a difference in services rendered in animal-assisted activities in comparison to animal-assisted therapy. When these treatments are defined more clearly, it may make it easier for mental health practitioners and those not familiar with AAT to understand the spectrum of interventions made available.

VI. EPILOGUE

What needs clarification is how front-line clinicians can support researchers in documenting therapeutic gains using AAT. There are daily procedures that therapists utilize (e.g., clinical notes) that, if put to use, could be applied to document changes. This documentation may also include self-reports, surveys, and questionnaires completed by the client and significant others. Utilizing some of these alternatives for documenting change could also be quite revealing.

As most researchers know, one cannot make statistical inferences from single-case studies. However, a group of single-case studies can point toward a trend and help researchers generate hypotheses to examine. Moreover, a collection of single-case observations can help investigators determine the answers to various issues, including (a) if there are protocols in using animals that work better with specific disorders; (b) if there are contraindications for AAT with specific disorders; and (c) if animals should be involved with every session.

For years, there has been an uneasy relation between researcher and clinician. The collaboration we suggest between these two groups of psychologists has the potential of contributing much to the field and may even become a desired pet project. If the clinical community wants to increase the stature of AAT to a more critically accepted evidence-based approach, more scientific evidence is needed to make the skeptics more convinced that this is "more than just puppy love."

REFERENCES

Assay, T., and Lambert, L. (1999). The empirical case for the common factors in therapy. *In* "The Heart and Soul of Change" (M. A. Hubble, B. Duncan, and S. Miller, eds.), pp. 20–34. American Psychological Association, Washington, DC.

Beck, A. T. (1967). "Depression: Clinical, Experimental, and Theoretical Aspects." Harper and Row, New York.

Bower, B. (2005). Questions on the couch: Researchers spar over how to best evaluate psychotherapy. *Science* **168**(19), 299–301.

Bowers, M. J., and MacDonald, P. M. (2001). The effectiveness of equine-facilitated psychotherapy with at-risk adolescents. *J. Psychol. Behav. Sci.* **15**, 62–76.

Chambless, D. L. (2005). Compendium of empirically supported therapies. *In* "Psychologists' Desk Reference" (G. P. Koocher, J. C. Norcross, and S. S. Hill III, eds.), 2nd Ed., pp. 183–192. Oxford University Press, New York.

Chambless, D. L., and Ollendick, T. H. (2001). Empirically supported psychological interventions: Controversies and evidence. *Annu. Rev. Psychol.* **52**, 685–716.

Costello, C. G., and Comrey, A. L. (1967). Scales for measuring depression and anxiety. *J. Psychol.* **66**, 303–313.

Denmark, F., Russo, N. F., Frieze, I. H., and Sechzer, J. A. (1988). Guidelines for avoiding sexism in psychological research: A report of an ad hoc committee on nonsexist research. *Am. Psychol.* **43**, 582–585.

Draper, R. J., Gerber, G. J., and Layng, E. M. (1990). Defining the role of pet animals in psychotherapy. *Psychiatr. J. Univ. Ottawa* **15**, 169–172.

Fine, A., and Eisen, C. (In press). Afternoons with Puppy: Lessons for Life from a Therapist and His Animals. Purdue University Press, West Lafayette, IN.

Garfield, S., and Bergin, A. (1994). Introduction and historical overview. *In* "Handbook of Psychotherapy and Behavior Change" (A. E. Bergin and S. L. Garfield, eds.), 4th Ed., pp. 13–18. Wiley, New York.

Gatson, L. (1990). The concept of the alliance and its role in psychotherapy: Theoretical and empirical consideration. *Psychotherapy* 27, 143–153.

Goodheart, C. D. (2004). Multiple streams of evidence for psychotherapy practice. *In* "Best Psychotherapy Based on the Integration of Research Evidence, Clinical Judgment and Patient Values." Symposium presented at the 112th Annual Convention of the American Psychological Association, Honolulu, HI.

Hitt, J. (2001, December 9). Evidence-based medicine. *New York Times Magazine*, p. 68.

Hubble M., Duncan, B., and Miller, S. (eds.) (1999). "The Heart and Soul of Change." American Psychological Association, Washington, DC.

Institute of Medicine (2001). "Crossing the Quality Chasm: A New Health System for the 21st Century." National Academy Press, Washington, DC.

Kellner, R. (1986). The Brief Depression Rating Scale. *In* "Assessment of Depression" (N. Sartorius and T. A. Ban, eds.), pp. 179–183. Springer-Verlag, New York.

Lambert, M. J. (1992). Implications of outcome research for psychotherapy integration. *In* "Handbook of Psychotherapy Integration" (J. C. Norcross and M. R. Goldstein, eds.), pp. 94–129. Basic Books, New York.

Miller, S. D., Hubble, M., and Duncan, B. (1996). Psychotherapy Is Dead, Long Live Psychotherapy. Workshop presented at the 19th Annual Family Therapy Network Symposium, Washington, DC.

Najavitis, L. M., and Strupp, H. H. (1994). Differences in effectiveness of psychodynamic therapists: A process-outcome study. *Psychotherapy* **31**, 187–197.

Norcross, J., Beutler, L., and Levant, R. (2006). "Evidence-Based Practices in Mental Health." American Psychological Association, Washington, DC.

Pomp, K. (1998). "Attachment Functions of Animal-Facilitated Child Psychotherapy." Unpublished manuscript. Karl Menninger School of Psychiatry and Mental Health Sciences, Topeka, KS.

Roth, A. D., and Fogarty, P. (1996). "What Works for Whom? A Critical Review of Psychotherapy Research." Guilford Press, New York.

Smith, E. E., and Medin, D. L. (1981). "Categories and Concepts." Harvard University Press, Cambridge, MA.

Stiles, W. B., Shapiro, D. A., and Elliott, R. (1986). Are all psychotherapies equivalent? *Am. Psychol.* **41**, 165–180.

Strupp, H. H. (1960). Nature of psychotherapist's contribution to treatment process: Some research results and speculations. *Arch. Gen. Psychiatr.* **23**, 393–401.

Strupp, H. H. (1973). On the basic ingredients of psychotherapy. *J. Consult. Clin. Psychol.* **41**, 1–8.

Strupp, H. H. (1986). Psychotherapy: Research, practice, and public policy (how to avoid dead ends). *Am. Psychol.* **41**, 120–130.

Zung, W. K. (1965). A self-rating depression scale. *Arch. Gen. Psychiatr.* **12**, 63–70.

Zung, W. K. (1971). A rating instrument for anxiety disorders. *Psychosomatics* **12**, 371–379.

INDEX

Page numbers with "t" denote tables; those with "f" denote figures

A

B

C

D

H

I